Resilience and Vulnerability

Adaptation in the Context of Childhood Adversities

Childhood resilience is the phenomenon of positive adaptation despite significant life adversities. While interest in resilience has burgeoned in recent years, there remains considerable uncertainty about what exactly research has taught us about this phenomenon. Integrated in this book are contributions from leading scientists who have each studied children's adjustment across risks common in contemporary society. Chapters in the first half of the book focus on risks emanating from the family; chapters in the second half focus on risks stemming from the wider community. All contributors have explicitly addressed a common set of core themes, including the criteria they used to judge resilience within particular risk settings, the major factors that predict resilience in these settings, the limits to resilience (vulnerabilities coexisting with manifest success), and directions for interventions. In the concluding chapter, the editor integrates evidence presented throughout all preceding chapters to distill (a) substantive considerations for future research and (b) salient directions for interventions and social policies based on accumulated research knowledge.

Suniya S. Luthar is Professor of Psychology and Education at Teachers College, Columbia University. She is the author of *Children in Poverty: Risk and Protective Forces in Adjustment* (1999) and the coeditor of *Developmental Psychopathology: Perspectives on Adjustment, Risk, and Disorder* (1997). Dr. Luthar is Associate Editor of the journal *Development and Psychopathology* and has been a member of the editorial boards of both *Child Development* and *Developmental Psychology*. Professional awards include a Dissertation Award from APA's Division 37 (Child, Youth, & Family Services; 1990), a K–21 Research Scientist Development Award from the National Institute on Drug Abuse (1993–1998), an American Mensa Education and Research Foundation Award for Excellence in Research on Intelligence (1995), and a Boyd McCandless Young Scientist Award from APA's Division 7 (Developmental Psychology, 1998).

Resilience and Vulnerability

Adaptation in the Context of Childhood Adversities

Edited by

SUNIYA S. LUTHAR

Teachers College, Columbia University

CAMBRIDGE
UNIVERSITY PRESS

PUBLISHED BY THE PRESS SYNDICATE OF THE UNIVERSITY OF CAMBRIDGE
The Pitt Building, Trumpington Street, Cambridge, United Kingdom

CAMBRIDGE UNIVERSITY PRESS
The Edinburgh Building, Cambridge CB2 2RU, UK
40 West 20th Street, New York, NY 10011-4211, USA
477 Williamstown Road, Port Melbourne, VIC 3207, Australia
Ruiz de Alarcón 13, 28014 Madrid, Spain
Dock House, The Waterfront, Cape Town 8001, South Africa

http://www.cambridge.org

First published 2003

Printed in the United States of America

Typeface ITC New Baskerville 10/13 pt.   *System* LATEX 2_ε [TB]

A catalog record for this book is available from the British Library.

Library of Congress Cataloging in Publication Data

Resilience and vulnerability : adaptation in the context of childhood adversities /
edited by Suniya S. Luthar.
p. cm.
Includes bibliographical references and index.
ISBN 0-521-80701-8 (hb) – ISBN 0-521-00161-7 (pbk.)
1. Resilience (Personality trait) in children.   2. Adaptability (Psychology) in children.
I. Luthar, Suniya S.
BF723.R46 R47   2003
155.4′1824 – dc21   2002073614

ISBN 0 521 80701 8 hardback
ISBN 0 521 00161 7 paperback

For my children,
Nik and Nina

Contents

Contributors

Odette Alarcón
Center for Research on Women
Wellesley College
Wellesley, MA

Tim Ayers
Prevention Research Center
Arizona State University
Phoenix, AZ

Kerry E. Bolger
Department of Human Development and Family Studies
University of Wisconsin
Madison, WI

Ana Mari Cauce
Department of Psychology
University of Washington
Seattle, WA

Ineke Ceder
Center for Research on Women
Wellesley College
Wellesley, MA

Dante Cicchetti
Mt. Hope Family Center
University of Rochester
Rochester, NY

Bryan Cochran
Department of Psychology
University of Washington
Seattle, WA

W. John Curtis
Mt. Hope Family Center
University of Rochester
Rochester, NY

Karen D'Avanzo
School of Medicine
Yale University
New Haven, CT

Caroline Davis
Prevention Research Center
Arizona State University
Phoenix, AZ

Byron Egeland
Institute of Child Development
University of Minnesota
Minneapolis, MN

Anne Mitchell Elmore
Westat Inc.
Rockville, MD

Sumru Erkut
Center for Research on Women
Wellesley College
Wellesley, MA

David M. Fergusson
Department of Psychological Medicine
Christchurch School of Medicine
Christchurch, New Zealand

Jacqueline P. Fields
Center for Research on Women
Wellesley College
Wellesley, MA

Hiram E. Fitzgerald
Department of Psychology
Michigan State University
East Lansing, MI

Cynthia García Coll
Center for the Study of Human Development
Brown University
Providence, RI

Joshua Ginzler
Department of Psychology
University of Washington
Seattle, WA

Deborah Gorman-Smith
Institute for Juvenile Research
Department of Psychiatry
University of Illinois at Chicago
Chicago, IL

Leslie Morrison Gutman
Center for Human Growth and Development
University of Michigan
Ann Arbor, MI

Rachel Haine
Prevention Research Center
Arizona State University
Phoenix, AZ

Constance Hammen
Department of Psychology
University of California
Los Angeles, CA

E. Mavis Hetherington
Department of Psychology
University of Virginia
Charlottesville, VA

Sarah Hites
Department of Psychology
University of Vermont
Burlington, VT

L. John Horwood
Department of Psychological Medicine
Christchurch School of Medicine
Christchurch, New Zealand

Suniya S. Luthar
Department of Human Development
Teachers College, Columbia University
New York, NY

Ann S. Masten
Institute of Child Development
University of Minnesota
Minneapolis, MN

Charles A. Nelson
Institute of Child Development
University of Minnesota
Minneapolis, MN

Suh-Ruu Ou
School of Social Work
University of Wisconsin
Madison, WI

Elizabeth B. Owens
Institute of Human Development
University of California
Berkeley, CA

Charlotte J. Patterson
Department of Psychology
University of Virginia
Charlottesville, VA

Stephen C. Peck
Institute for Research on Women and Gender
University of Michigan
Ann Arbor, MI

Sara Pedersen
Psychology Department
New York University
New York, NY

Jenifer L. Powell
Institute of Child Development
University of Minnesota
Minneapolis, MN

Leon I. Puttler
Department of Psychiatry
University of Michigan
Ann Arbor, MI

Arthur J. Reynolds
School of Social Work
University of Wisconsin
Madison, WI

Melanie Domenech Rodriguez
Department of Psychology
University of Washington
Seattle, WA

Michael Rutter
Social, Genetic and Developmental Psychiatry Research Centre
Institute of Psychiatry
London, UK

Arnold Sameroff
Center for Human Growth and Development
University of Michigan
Ann Arbor, MI

Irwin Sandler
Prevention Research Center
Arizona State University
Phoenix, AZ

Edward Seidman
Psychology Department
New York University
New York, NY

Ronald Seifer
E. P. Bradley Hospital
Brown University
Providence, RI

Daniel S. Shaw
Department of Psychology
University of Pittsburgh
Pittsburgh, PA

L. Alan Sroufe
Institute of Child Development
University of Minnesota
Minneapolis, MN

Angela Stewart
Department of Psychology
University of Washington
Seattle, WA

Laura A. Szalacha
Center for the Study of Human Development
Brown University
Providence, RI

Patrick H. Tolan
Institute for Juvenile Research
Department of Psychiatry
University of Illinois at Chicago
Chicago, IL

Sharlene Wolchik
Prevention Research Center
Arizona State University
Phoenix, AZ

Maria M. Wong
Department of Psychiatry
University of Michigan
Ann Arbor, MI

Peter A. Wyman
Department of Psychiatry and of Clinical and
    Social Sciences in Psychology
University of Rochester
Rochester, NY

Tuppett M. Yates
Institute of Child Development
University of Minnesota
Minneapolis, MN

Laurel Bidwell Zelazo
Department of Human Development
Teachers College, Columbia University
New York, NY

Robert A. Zucker
Department of Psychiatry
University of Michigan
Ann Arbor, MI

Foreword

Dante Cicchetti

For more than three decades, researchers interested in children who develop well in the context of significant adversity have endeavored to enhance understanding of the pathways to psychopathology, to elucidate the processes that eventuate in normal development, and to inform preventive interventions and social policies that could improve the lives of vulnerable children and families (see, e.g., Cicchetti & Garmezy, 1993; Garmezy, 1971; Luthar & Cicchetti, 2000; Luthar, Cicchetti, & Becker, 2000; Masten, 2001; Masten, Best, & Garmezy 1990; Werner & Smith, 1982, 1992). Investigations in the area of risk and resilience have caused scientists to rethink their prior assumptions about the causes and course of psychopathology and have resulted in a reformulation of the deficit models that characterized earlier viewpoints about the development of children who have experienced disadvantage and great adversity (Garmezy & Streitman, 1974; Luthar & Zigler, 1991; Masten & Garmezy, 1985; Rutter, 1985).

Studies conducted on high-risk and mentally disordered populations across the life span frequently portrayed the developmental course as deterministic, inevitably resulting in maladaptive and pathological outcomes. Investigations ranging from genetic and biological predispositions, to psychopathology, to assaults on development associated with inadequate caregiving, traumatic occurrences within the home, and exposure to community violence graphically convey the multiplicity of risks that can eventuate in disordered outcomes.

Before investigations on resilience could occur, a significant and illustrative history of research detailing the precursors to, as well as the contemporary patterns of, stress resistance had to take place (see, e.g.,

Garmezy & Rutter, 1983; Luthar & Zigler, 1991). In many of these early studies, researchers had discovered evidence of adaptive behavior; however, the nomenclature for labeling these results as indicative of resilience had not yet emerged. Despite this state of affairs, the historical roots of resilience can be traced to early programs of research on individuals with schizophrenia and on persons exposed to extreme stress and poverty, as well as on the functioning of individuals who experienced traumatic occurrences earlier in their lives (Cicchetti & Garmezy, 1993; Luthar et al., 2000; Pavenstedt, 1965). The seminal work of Garmezy and his colleagues (Garmezy, 1971, 1974; Garmezy, Masten, & Tellegen, 1984; Garmezy & Streitman, 1974) is among the earliest examples of efforts to emphasize the importance of examining protective factors in high-risk populations. This research laid the groundwork for contemporary investigations in the area of resilience (Masten & Curtis, 2000).

Following publication of the early research on resilience, scholarly interest in this topic has burgeoned. In two recent reviews of the scientific literature on resilience, it was concluded that continued examinations of the construct of resilience had the potential to affirm, challenge, and expand extant developmental theory, to suggest useful avenues for preventive interventions to promote competent functioning and resilient adaptation, and to foster the implementation of social policies that could decrease the vast erosion of human potential that mental disorder, maladaptive functioning, and economic misery engender (Luthar & Cicchetti, 2000; Luthar et al., 2000). However, an important conclusion that emanated from the aforementioned reviews was that it was essential for resilience researchers to enhance the scientific rigor of their investigations. Luthar and her colleagues (2000) reasoned that because studies in the area of resilience bear directly on matters of social policy import, researchers must have high standards of evidence and engage in self-scrutiny in their work.

In this timely and important volume, edited by Suniya Luthar, one of the world's premier theorists and researchers on the topic, contributors were given the charge of critically examining resilience, the more optimistic component of the psychopathology–risk equation. Resilience is operationally defined in this volume as a dynamic developmental process reflecting evidence of positive adaptation despite significant life adversity (cf. Egeland, Carlson, & Sroufe, 1993; Luthar et al., 2000; Masten, 2001). Resilience is not believed to be an individual child attribute operating in isolation; rather, it is viewed as a phenomenon, a hypothetical construct, that must be inferred from an individual's manifesting competent functioning despite experiencing significant adversity (Luthar et al., 2000; Masten & Coatsworth, 1995). In keeping with the myriad familial and exosystemic influences that have been demonstrated to be protective factors or mechanisms in the development of resilience, the majority of the chapters in this volume address these risks through the contributors' coverage of an array of mental disorders and adverse conditions that have been the subject of substantial scientific investigation.

Contributors to this volume were asked to address four themes of significance to resilience research: (1) providing operational definitions of the chosen risk condition and of the methods utilized in its investigation; (2) elucidating salient vulnerability and protective mechanisms; (3) articulating limits to resilient adaptation; and (4) addressing the implications of findings on resilience for intervention and policy formulation. These issues are consistent with a developmental psychopathology perspective, and attention to them will be critical for making the construct of resilience relevant to researchers, social policy formulators, and intervenors.

The authors of the chapters in this volume have done an admirable job of providing accessible, thoughtful, and scholarly discussions of the state of resilience research in their respective areas of expertise. It is apparent that in spite of the challenges linked with examining this dynamic construct, research on resilience has become more sophisticated over the decades since its inception. Moreover, it is clear that the ongoing investigation of resilient trajectories proffers considerable potential for refining the understanding of the processes that contribute to normal and pathological development.

Despite the contributions it has made to date, the field of resilience currently possesses at least two major limitations. First, there has been a paucity of investigations that have included biological and genetic variables as potential protective factors or mechanisms in the development of resilience. Second, and a corollary of the first limitation, few investigators on resilience have conducted their studies at multiple levels of analysis. The editor of the present volume clearly possessed insight into these shortcomings of the extant resilience literature. Luthar had the prescience to solicit chapters from experts in the fields of neuroscience and genetics. With the goal of transcending the current focus on psychosocial indices of resilience, the authors of these chapters were asked to discuss the implications that research conducted in the neurosciences and genetics can have for elucidating the pathways to resilience and for suggesting means of promoting competent functioning in individuals experiencing substantial adversity.

It is unfortunate that we possess such limited information on these aspects of resilience. Indeed, one of the basic mechanisms of resilience, that of self-righting, has its roots in embryology and genetics (Waddington, 1957). Moreover, much of the research in the area of resilience is found in the interdisciplinary science of developmental psychopathology, a field that advocates the integration of multiple levels of analysis in the study of risk and resilience within individuals over time (Cicchetti, 1993; Cicchetti & Cannon, 1999; Cicchetti & Dawson, 2002; Cicchetti & Sroufe, 2000).

There are historical parallels in other areas that attest to the advances in understanding a phenomenon that can be obtained by integrating efforts that had been previously separate and distinct. Cowan, Harter, and Kandel (2000) and Kandel and Squire (2000) have described the unprecedented growth and achievements in the fields of neuroanatomy, neurophysiology, and neurochemistry that have occurred during the past several decades. Despite the successes of research in these isolated areas, the current excitement engendered by neurobiological research stems from the integration of several previously independent disciplines into the interdisciplinary framework known as *neuroscience* (Cowan et al., 2000; Kandel & Squire, 2000). Although a number of landmark discoveries took place during the latter part of the 19th century and the first half of the 20th, none of these findings transcended traditional disciplinary boundaries, the defining feature of the contemporary field of neuroscience.

Similarly, although 20th-century biology triumphed because of its focus on the intensive analysis of the individual components of complex biological systems, Lander and Weinberg (2000) have asserted that in the 21st century, the discipline will need to focus increasingly on the examination of entire biological systems. By endeavoring to comprehend how component parts work together to create a whole, scientists will move beyond reductionist approaches to collaborative multidisciplinary investigations that seek to gain a holistic view of cells, tissues, and complex neural systems.

Research in the area of resilience must follow these interdisciplinary, multiple levels of analysis perspectives. There are a number of ways that the incorporation of biological and molecular genetic techniques and the utilization of multiple levels of analysis approach could augment knowledge on pathways to resilient adaptation. For example, we know that experience and neurobiological development are mutually influencing. It has been demonstrated that experience exerts actions on the brain by feeding back upon it to modify gene expression and brain structure, function, and organization (Kandel, 1998). Furthermore, it has been discovered that alterations in gene expression induced by learning and by social and psychological experiences produce changes in patterns of neuronal and synaptic connections and thus in the function of nerve cells (Kandel, 1998). These modifications not only play a prominent role in initiating and maintaining the behavioral anomalies provoked by social and psychological experiences, they also can contribute to the biological bases of individuality as well as to individuals' being differentially affected by similar experiences.

Thus, although brain development is guided and controlled to some extent by genetic information, a significant portion of brain structuration and neural patterning is thought to occur through interactions of the individual with the environment. Changes in the internal and external environments may lead to improvements in the ability of the individual to grapple with developmental challenges, including the experience of significant adversity. Consequently, although historical factors canalize and constrain the adaptive process to some degree, plasticity is possible as a result of adaptive neural and psychological self-organization (Cicchetti & Tucker, 1994). Moreover, because the mechanisms of plasticity cause the brain's anatomical differentiation to be dependent upon stimulation from the environment, it is now clear that the cytoarchitecture of the cerebral cortex is shaped by input from the social environment. Because the human cortex is only diffusely structured by the genetic plan, and because its eventual differentiation is highly reactive to the individual's active coping in a particular environment, we may expect that both abnormal and resilient outcomes following the experience of significant adversity would encompass a diverse range of cortical network anatomies and personalities.

Future research on the determinants of resilient adaptation in individuals subjected to acute and chronic adversity should examine the biological stress responses of such individuals to ascertain whether their patterns of neuroendocrine regulation differ from those of nonresilient, stress-affected individuals. Persistent overactivation of the stress system (i.e., the limbic-hypothalamic-pituitary-adrenal [LHPA] axis) affects the morphology of the hippocampus and subsequent stress sensitivity (Cicchetti & Walker, 2001a). Likewise, because activation of the stress system impacts

other physiological systems, investigations of systemic immune functioning may yield insights into resilience. Moreover, investigators should
utilize structural and functional neuroimaging techniques (e.g., magnetic resonance imaging, functional magnetic resonance imaging, spectroscopy), brain event–related potentials, and indices of autonomic nervous system functioning to ascertain whether individuals designated as
resilient by psychological assessments manifest different biological profiles than do their nonresilient counterparts. Sophisticated longitudinal
research designs will be needed to answer these complex questions, as
resilience is not a static construct. Rather, as discussed by a number of
contributors to this volume, an individual may be more or less resilient
during various periods of development.

Changes in the LHPA axis mediate the longer-term structural and
functional changes in the brain that may arise due to stressful experiences. The impact of hormones on behavior is partially a consequence of
their effects on gene expression (McEwen, 1994; Watson & Gametcheu,
1999). It is the glucocorticoid receptors in the cell's nucleus that are
responsible for the influence of stress hormones on the expression of
genes (Cicchetti & Walker, 2001b). Because stress hormones can exert
such direct effects on the genes that control brain structure and function, research that strives to identify stress-sensitive neural processes in
developing individuals is important.

Recently, there has been great progress in the understanding of how
to study gene expression. These advances offer exciting new opportunities for enhancing knowledge not only of the genesis and epigenesis of
psychopathology, but also of resilience. Molecular genetic methods now
exist that enable researchers to investigate the expression of particular
genes or of large numbers of genes simultaneously (*gene profiles*). Through
the utilization of DNA microarrays, researchers can determine the type
and quantity of messenger RNA (mRNA) being produced by a given cell,
thereby indicating which genes are *turned on* (i.e., activated) (Hacia &
Collins, 1999; Mirnics, Middleton, Lewis, & Levitt, 2001; Raychaudhuri,
Sutphin, Chang, & Altman, 2001). DNA microarrays can be used to index
changes in the expression of genes that are essential for brain function
(Greenberg, 2001; Walker & Walder, in press). By examining concurrent
environmental, behavioral, psychological, hormonal, gene expression,
and neurobiological changes longitudinally in individuals who have experienced great adversity, researchers may be in a stronger position to
elucidate the development of resilient adaptation. For example, such

multilevel investigations may reveal the mechanisms responsible for inhibiting the expression of genes that are probabilistically associated with maladaptive developmental outcomes and psychopathology. Likewise, these interdisciplinary approaches may proffer insights into the mechanisms that turn on genes that may serve a protective function for individuals experiencing adversity. Furthermore, a particular condition may not pose risk in the context of another *protective* condition. As Suomi (2001) has discovered, a defect in the serotonin transporter gene conveys no detectable liability (e.g., impulsiveness, distractibility) for rhesus monkeys reared by nurturant foster mothers. In fact, such monkeys become leaders of their peer group.

As evidenced in this volume, the examination of resilience also possesses vast potential for contributing to the development of interventions. For example, Cicchetti and Rogosch (1997) found different predictors of adaptive outcome in maltreated versus nonmaltreated school-age children. Whereas relationship features and ego resilience contributed to positive outcomes in nonmaltreated youngsters, self-system processes, ego resilience, and ego overcontrol were predictive of resilient functioning in maltreated children. Thus, interventions designed to foster self-determination in children who have experienced maltreatment emerge as an exciting research-informed intervention strategy.

In closing, it is gratifying to see this eminent group of scholars striving to utilize rigorous scientific theories and methods in order to ensure that the construct of resilience is empirically grounded. This is critical if work in the area of resilience is to be appropriately applied to intervention and policy arenas. The present volume serves as the bastion of resilience research, elucidating progress and promise, as well as continued challenges facing investigators in this area.

References

Cicchetti, D. (1993). Developmental psychopathology: Reactions, reflections, projections. *Developmental Review, 13,* 471–502.

Cicchetti, D., & Cannon, T. D. (1999). Neurodevelopmental processes in the ontogenesis and epigenesis of psychopathology. *Development and Psychopathology, 11,* 375–393.

Cicchetti, D., & Dawson, G. (2002). Multiple levels of analysis. *Development and Psychopathology, 14,* 417–420.

Cicchetti, D., & Garmezy, N. (1993). Prospects and promises in the study of resilience. *Development and Psychopathology, 5,* 497–502.

Cicchetti, D., & Rogosch, F. A. (1997). The role of self-organization in the promotion of resilience in maltreated children. *Development and Psychopathology, 9,* 799–817.

Cicchetti, D., & Sroufe, L. A. (2000). Editorial: The past as prologue to the future: The times, they've been a changin'. *Development and Psychopathology, 12,* 255–264.

Cicchetti, D., & Tucker, D. (1994). Development and self-regulatory structures of the mind. *Development and Psychopathology, 6,* 533–549.

Cicchetti, D., & Walker, E. F. (Eds.). (2001a). Stress and development: Biological and psychological consequences. Special Issue. *Development and Psychopathology, 13,* 413–753.

Cicchetti, D., & Walker, E. F. (2001b). Stress and development: Biological and psychological consequences. *Development and Psychopathology, 13,* 413–418.

Cowan, W. M., Harter, D. H., & Kandel, E. R. (2000). The emergence of modern neuroscience: Some implications for neurology and psychiatry. *Annual Review of Neuroscience, 23,* 323–391.

Egeland, B., Carlson, E., & Sroufe, L. A. (1993). Resilience as process. *Development and Psychopathology, 5,* 517–528.

Garmezy, N. (1971). Vulnerability research and the issue of primary prevention. *American Journal of Orthopsychiatry, 41,* 101–116.

Garmezy, N. (1974). Children at risk: The search for the antecedents of schizophrenia. *Schizophrenia Bulletin, 8,* 14–90.

Garmezy, N., Masten, A. S., & Tellegen, A. (1984). The study of stress and competence in children: A building block for developmental psychopathology. *Child Development, 55,* 97–111.

Garmezy, N., & Rutter, M. (Eds.). (1983). *Stress, coping and development in children.* New York: McGraw-Hill.

Garmezy, N., & Streitman, S. (1974). Children at risk: Conceptual models and research methods. *Schizophrenia Bulletin, 9,* 55–125.

Greenberg, S. A. (2001). DNA microarray gene expression analysis technology and its application to neurological disorders. *Neurology, 57,* 755–761.

Hacia, J. G., & Collins, F. S. (1999). Mutational analysis using oligonucleotide micorarrays. *Journal of Medical Genetics, 36,* 730–736.

Kandel, E. R. (1998). A new intellectual framework for psychiatry. *American Journal of Psychiatry, 155,* 475–489.

Kandel, E. R., & Squire, L. (2000). Neuroscience: Breaking down scientific barriers to the study of brain and mind. *Science, 90,* 1113–1120.

Lander, E. S., & Weinberg, R. A. (2000). Genomics: Journey to the center of biology. *Science, 287,* 1777–1782.

Luthar, S. S., & Cicchetti, D. (2000). The construct of resilience: Implications for intervention and social policy. *Development and Psychopathology, 12,* 555–598.

Luthar, S. S., Cicchetti, D., & Becker, B. (2000). The construct of resilience: A critical evaluation and guidelines for future work. *Child Development, 71,* 543–562.

Luthar, S., S & Zigler, E. (1991). Vulnerability and competence: A review of research on resilience in childhood. *American Journal of Orthopsychiatry, 61,* 6–22.

Masten, A. S. (2001). Ordinary magic: Resilience processes in development. *American Psychologist, 56,* 227–238.

Masten, A., Best, K., & Garmezy, N. (1990). Resilience and development: Contributions from the study of children who overcome adversity. *Development and Psychopathology, 2,* 425–444.

Masten, A., & Coatsworth, D. J. (1995). Competence, resilience, and psychopathology. In D. Cicchetti & D. Cohen (Eds.), *Developmental psychopathology, Vol. 2: Risk disorder and adaptation* (pp. 715–752). New York: Wiley.

Masten, A. M., & Curtis, W. J. (2000). Integrating competence and psychopathology: Pathways toward a comprehensive science of adaptation in development. *Development and Psychopathology, 12,* 529–550.

Masten, A., & Garmezy, N. (1985). Risk, vulnerability, and protective factors in developmental psychopathology. In B. Lahey & A. Kazdin (Eds.), *Advances in clinical child psychology* (Vol. 8, pp. 1–52). New York: Plenum Press.

McEwen, B. S. (1994). Steroid hormone actions on the brain: When is the genome involved? *Hormones and Behavior, 28,* 396–405.

Mirnics, K., Middleton, F. A., Lewis, D. A., & Levitt, P. (2001). Analysis of complex brain disorders with gene expression microarrays: Schizophrenia as a disease of the synapse. *Trends in Neurosciences, 24,* 479–486.

Pavenstedt, E. (1965). A comparison of the child-rearing environment of upper-lower and very low-lower class families. *American Journal of Orthopsychiatry, 35,* 89–98.

Raychaudhuri, S., Sutphin, P. D., Chang, J. T., & Altman, R. B. (2001). Basic microarray analysis: Grouping and feature reduction. *Trends in Biotechnology, 19,* 189–193.

Rutter, M. (1985). Resilience in the face of adversity: Protective factors and resistance to psychiatric disorder. *British Journal of Psychiatry, 128,* 493–509.

Suomi, S. (2001). Parents, peers, and the process of socialization in primates. In J. Borkowski, S. Ramey, & M. Bristol-Power (Eds.), *Parenting and the child's world.* Mahwah: NJ: Erlbaum.

Wadddington, C. H. (1957). *The strategy of genes.* London: Allen and Unwin.

Walker, E. F., & Walder, D. (in press). Neurohormonal aspects of the development of psychotic disorders. In D. Cicchetti & E. F. Walker (Eds.), *Neurodevelopmental mechanisms in psychopathology.* New York: Cambridge University Press.

Watson, C., & Gametchu, B. (1999). Membrane-initiated steroid actions and the proteins that mediate them. *Proceedings of the Society for Experimental Biology and Medicine, 220,* 9–19.

Werner, E., & Smith, R. (1982). *Vulnerable but invincible: A study of resilient children.* New York: McGraw-Hill.

Werner, E., & Smith, R. (1992). *Overcoming the odds: High-risk children from birth to adulthood.* Ithaca, NY: Cornell University Press.

Preface

This book contains an integrative review of major research findings on resilient adaptation during childhood. As used here, the term *resilience* represents *the manifestation of positive adaptation despite significant life adversity*. Resilience is not a child attribute that can be directly measured; rather, it is a process or phenomenon that is inferred from the dual coexisting conditions of high adversity and relatively positive adaptation in spite of this.

The impetus for this volume stemmed from the widespread and growing appeal of the construct of resilience for scientific researchers, practitioners, and lay people, along with continuing uncertainty about the substantive lessons that derive from research on this construct. Although many believe that research on risk and resilience can yield substantial gains, there have not been concerted efforts to distill salient take-home messages emanating from diverse research programs. It is in an effort at such knowledge integration that this book was compiled. Included here are contributions from several leading scientists, all of whom have studied childhood adaptation across some type of life adversity. The authors are *not* necessarily proponents of the construct of resilience; the central purpose of this book is to integrate findings on children's adjustment in the face of risk rather than to advocate for resilience as a superlative or flawless scientific construct.

CONTENTS AND ORGANIZATION

Compilation of any book of this type inevitably presents difficult choices with regard to breadth versus depth of information, and in this volume the bias is more toward the latter. Rather than touching briefly upon several disparate risk indices on which relatively little empirical evidence has been obtained so far (e.g., exposure to natural disasters), an effort has been made to integrate existing knowledge on adversity conditions (a) that are relatively common in contemporary society and (b) that have been examined by different research groups via rigorous quantitative research. Thus, there are multiple chapters on each of several discrete themes, such as mental illness in parents and exposure to poverty during childhood. A major goal is to ascertain the degree to which findings on each of these risks are mutually coherent across different studies, as opposed to being largely idiosyncratic, limited to particular investigations or research groups. Such integration of knowledge is critical to allow for meaningful derivation of intervention directions to address problems that commonly affect young people today.

The introductory chapter of this volume presents a brief review of the history of the field of resilience and a description of the pioneering Project Competence initiated by Norman Garmezy, Ann Masten, and their research collaborators. Embedding their own findings within the broader scientific literature, Masten and Powell also present a resilience framework relevant to current efforts in research, practice, and social policy. Following this introductory chapter are the two major parts of this volume, each encompassing a group of environmental risks commonly studied by resilience researchers: those emanating from the *family* and from the wider *community*. In both parts, the chapters contain overviews of available scientific evidence rather than results of single studies. Themes common to all chapters include (a) descriptions of the major risks considered and criteria used to judge successful adaptation in the face of these risks, (b) findings on protective and vulnerability processes, (c) limits to resilience, or the degree to which success in one domain coexists with problems in others, and (d) directions for future research and implications for interventions. The concluding chapters of both parts present research at the interface of science and interventions, elucidating the reciprocal nature of the benefits: Pure science illuminates the nature of protective processes, and intervention research, by changing these, provides a stringent test of whether they are in fact health-promoting.

Following these two major parts are commentaries based on biological and genetics research, areas neglected in existing studies of resilience. John Curtis and Charles Nelson present evidence on brain plasticity, exploring parallels in findings on environmental enrichment among animals as opposed to humans. Drawing upon genetics research,

Sir Michael Rutter – whose writings have enormously shaped the field of resilience since its very inception – delineates issues that need careful attention in future studies in this area. The concluding chapter contains a distillation of salient themes that recur across all chapters in the book, with separate summaries of implications for future research, and for interventions and policies based on the notion of resilience.

The contributors to this volume include some of the most distinguished leaders in developmental science. I am honored to have had this opportunity to work with them, and I am grateful for their forbearance in collaboratively finessing chapters toward a unifying set of themes. For various forms of support over time, I am indebted to my family and several colleagues and students, most especially, P. E. Mow. Deepest appreciation, finally, to the parents and children who, in sharing their lives as participants in our studies, have contributed immeasurably to our understanding of adjustment in the face of adversity. In the years ahead, I hope that the accumulated knowledge within this volume will not only stimulate continued resilience research of the highest caliber but, equally, will be channeled into efforts to improve the life circumstances of vulnerable children and families. Concerted movement in this direction is something that we, in applied developmental science, must treat as our responsibility to them.

Suniya S. Luthar

1

A Resilience Framework for Research, Policy, and Practice

Ann S. Masten and Jenifer L. Powell

It was a search for understanding the nature and origins of schizophrenia that brought Norman Garmezy to the study of children at risk for psychopathology, a pursuit that eventually led to the Project Competence studies of competence, adversity, and resilience (Garmezy, 1973). During the 1940s and 1950s, Garmezy developed an interest in the significance of competence in the history and prognosis of patients with serious mental disorders, with a particular focus on premorbid functioning in patients with schizophrenia (Garmezy & Rodnick, 1959). Eventually, the search for antecedents of psychopathology led Garmezy and others to study children of mentally ill parents because of their elevated risk of developing disorders. After his move to the University of Minnesota in 1961, Garmezy began to focus his work on children, and subsequently played a leading

The program of research known as Project Competence was founded by Norman Garmezy, Professor Emeritus of Psychology at the University of Minnesota, who has been a great mentor and colleague to many investigators in the study of resilience over many years, including the first author. Auke Tellegen, also Professor Emeritus of Psychology, joined Garmezy as Co-Principal Investigator on the longitudinal study and continues to contribute his remarkable methodological talents and wisdom to the project. The William T. Grant Foundation has supported the longitudinal study from the outset; we are deeply grateful for their abiding support for Project Competence. The National Institute of Mental Health supported this project in multiple ways, through grants for the first 10 years of assessments in the longitudinal study and also through a lifetime career development award to Professor Garmezy and training grants that supported students. The National Science Foundation (NSF/SBR-9729111), along with the Grant Foundation (97-1845–97), has supported the current 20-year follow-up of the longitudinal cohort through grants to Masten and Tellegen. The authors also want to express their gratitude to the many participants who have shared their lives so that others could learn and also to the many colleagues and fellow students who have made our journey so interesting.

role in an international consortium of investigators who adopted the *risk strategy* for uncovering clues to the etiology and possible prevention or treatment of serious mental disorders (Watt, Anthony, Wynne, & Rolf, 1984).

It was not long before Garmezy's interest in competence resurfaced. He became intrigued with observations that many children at risk for psychopathology were developing surprisingly well. By the early 1970s, he and his students turned their attention to the study of competence in children at risk due to parental mental illness and other risk factors, including poverty and stressful life experiences. At this time, Garmezy named his research program Project Competence.

The search for understanding how problems develop during childhood and how they might be prevented required collaboration across disciplines that were well represented at the University of Minnesota, including clinical psychology, developmental psychology, behavior genetics, and psychiatry. The work of Garmezy and his students was influenced by outstanding scientists and colleagues from multiple disciplines at Minnesota, as well as by Garmezy's connections to the international consortium of risk investigators. This rich scientific climate not only gave rise to Project Competence, but also played a major role in the emergence of developmental psychopathology, the study of mental health problems in the full context of human development (Cicchetti, 1984, 1990; Masten & Braswell, 1991).

An influential group of investigators, including Norman Garmezy, E. James Anthony, Lois Murphy, Michael Rutter, and Emmy Werner, began to speak and write about the significance of children developing well despite their risk status or exposure to adversity (Masten, 1999, 2001). The insight of these pioneers extended beyond the observation of good adaptation or development when one might expect problems or disorder. Their achievement was in realizing, and then convincing others, that understanding what would come to be called *resilience* in individual development had the potential to inform policy, prevention programs, and interventions. Their work and ideas inspired others to undertake studies of competence and mental health in the lives of children threatened by significant risk or adversity, with the ultimate goal of improving the chances and development of future generations of children faced with such risks.

In this chapter, we describe a resilience framework for research, policy, and practice that evolved in the Project Competence studies during the first generation of research on resilience. First, we discuss the conceptual framework for Project Competence, highlighting findings from the core longitudinal study that began in the late 1970s. Second, we embed these findings in the broader resilience literature to discuss their meaning in terms of adaptive processes for human development. Finally, we discuss a resilience framework for policy and practice emerging from research on resilience, including implications for conceptualizing the missions, models, measures, and methods of intervention.

PROJECT COMPETENCE

As captured by the name, concepts of competence have been central to the Project Competence studies at the University of Minnesota from their inception. This emphasis was unusual in the 1970s because medical models that focused on symptoms and negative outcomes dominated the study of psychopathology and risk at the time. Competence was a coherent theme of Garmezy's work, extending back to his early experiences with Phillips and Rodnick in the 1940s and 1950s. Phillips, in his classic 1968 book *Human Adaptation and Its Failures*, wrote, "The key to the prediction of future effectiveness in society lies in asking: 'How well has this person met, and how well does he now meet, the expectations implicitly set by society for individuals of his age and sex group?'" (p. 3). This perspective on competence was closely related to the concept of *developmental tasks* that would later become a central theme of both Project Competence and developmental psychopathology.

Early work on the measurement of competence in school children by Garmezy and his students set the stage for a study planned in 1976–1977, the year Ann Masten joined Project Competence as a graduate student. When it was implemented in 1977 and 1978, this study was directed at understanding the linkages between competence, adversity, internal functioning, and a host of individual and family attributes in a normative school cohort of 205 children (29% of ethnic/racial minority heritage). These children were attending third to sixth grades in two urban Minneapolis elementary schools, chosen in collaboration with the school superintendent and principals because they were representative of the public school population of the district at the time, which was diverse in socioeconomic status (SES) and approximately 27% minority. The study began as a cross-sectional investigation, but it soon became clear that following the children over time would provide better data on competence and resilience. Follow-up studies were undertaken after 7, 10, and 20 years, with excellent retention of the original cohort.

The core longitudinal study did not involve a high-risk sample. Instead, it was designed to examine competence among a normative school cohort of children who had experienced many kinds and levels of adversity. Other Project Competence studies initiated at around the same time focused on risk samples (Garmezy & Tellegen, 1984). These included a cohort of children born with congenital heart defects and another cohort with physical handicaps. More recent studies in Project Competence have focused on high-risk samples of children living in homeless shelters and young war refugees. Although diverse in many ways, these studies have all focused on competence, risk, and resilience. A general framework for conceptualizing and operationalizing the study of resilience evolved from this body of work, along with conclusions about the key question of "What makes a difference?" in the lives of children threatened by adversity or burdened by risk.

The Two Fundamental Judgments Required for Defining Resilience

Resilience refers to patterns of positive adaptation in the context of significant risk or adversity. Resilience is an inference about a person's life that requires *two fundamental judgments*: (1) that a person is "doing okay" and (2) that there is now or has been significant risk or adversity to overcome (Masten & Coatsworth, 1998). When a person is called resilient, whether in casual conversation or systematic research, a diagnosis in effect has been made, involving explicit or implicit criteria and a judgment call about a person matching characteristic features of resilience. Technically, to call a person resilient would be improper in diagnostic terminology because resilience is a description of a general pattern, whereas diagnosis occurs when the individual is matched to the pattern. It might be more appropriate to say that "This person has a resilient pattern" or "This person shows the features of resilience." It is also important to keep in mind that identifying resilience from explicit or implicit diagnostic criteria is not assumed to describe people in totality or to define their lives at all times. Hence, one would expect individuals who meet the criteria for resilience to differ in many other ways, and one would not expect a resilient person, however defined at one point in time, to be doing well every minute of the day, under all imaginable circumstances, or in perpetuity. Resilience is not a trait of an individual, though individuals manifest resilience in their behavior and life patterns.

Competence in Developmental Perspective

In Project Competence, the criteria for the first fundamental judgment – "doing okay" – have centered on the concept of *psychosocial competence* (Masten & Coatsworth, 1998). We have defined competence in terms of a track record of effective performance in developmental tasks that are salient for people of a given age, society or context, and historical time (Masten et al., 1995, 1999). For example, in American society, it is widely expected that school-age children will achieve in school (academic competence), get along with other children and make friends (social competence), and follow rules of conduct in the home, school, and community (conduct). These three broad developmental tasks are important throughout middle childhood and adolescence, but the actual expectations for behavior change with age and development. For example, adolescents would be expected to have more intimate friendships and more advanced academic performance than younger children. Moreover, as individuals grow older, new domains of competence become salient. Assessment of both current and emerging domains is important in a longitudinal study of adaptation over time. Thus, for adolescence, our assessments included indicators of romantic and work competence, which are key criteria of adult competence but are just starting to become important domains of functioning during adolescence. There also are domains of competence that become *less* salient as development unfolds. For example, at the 20-year follow-up, at around age 30, school performance was less salient than it was during the school years, though the repercussions of earlier low or high academic attainment were still evident for many members of the cohort.

In the longitudinal study, it was necessary to develop and refine ideas and methods for assessing competence, because so little attention had been given to positive aspects of adaptation prior to the 1970s, particularly for children. At the outset and for each subsequent follow-up, we aimed to assess multiple developmentally appropriate domains of competence with two or more informants and multiple methods. In the first assessment period, informants included parents, the child, teachers, peers, and multiple test administrators (Garmezy, Masten, & Tellegen, 1984; Garmezy & Tellegen, 1984; Masten et al., 1988, 1995, 1999). Methods included interviews, questionnaires, peer nominations, the gleaning of grades and test scores from records, and the administration of a variety of standardized tests and newly created instruments. Our assessments have utilized standardized tests scored with national age or grade norms, measures scored in comparison to a natural peer group (e.g., scores standardized within the classroom for peer reputation), and measures with scores standardized within the study sample. In our definitions of competence, "doing okay" does not require outstanding achievements, but instead refers to behavior within or above the expected average range for a normative cohort.

Competence assessments during the elementary school years focused on academic achievement, peer relations, and socialized conduct (compliance and rule-abiding behavior versus antisocial or rule-breaking behavior in different contexts), though we also collected information about many other aspects of positive adaptation, such as participation in sports and other activities. Data were also collected on internal adaptation, including well-being and symptoms of distress. Although our definition of competence focused on an observable track record of effective adaptation in the child's world of home, school, and neighborhood, we have had a keen interest in understanding how positive or negative aspects of internal functioning and traditional measures of behavioral and emotional symptoms are related to competence in age-salient developmental tasks.

Our findings in Project Competence have corroborated the multidimensionality of competence in childhood and adolescence, demonstrated the robust nature of these dimensions over time, and yielded extensive data on the correlates and consequences of competence in different domains for other aspects of behavior, ranging from personality to psychopathology (e.g., Gest, 1997; Masten, 1986; Masten et al., 1995, 1999; Morison & Masten, 1991; Neemann, Hubbard, & Masten, 1995; Pellegrini, Masten, Garmezy, & Ferrarese, 1987; Shiner, 2000). Just to highlight a few of these findings, competence in major developmental tasks has shown a strong pattern of association with past and future competence and also with adaptive resources, such as intellectual skills, effective parents, and socioeconomic advantages. The personality trait of negative emotionality, which appears to have early roots and shows considerable continuity across 10 years or more from late adolescence to young adulthood, has strong ties to competence problems in our study. Conduct is highly stable over time, from childhood to early adulthood, and becomes strongly linked with academic performance and attainment over time. In childhood, antisocial behavior appears to undermine academic achievement, which, in turn, appears to contribute to later problems in multiple competence domains and internal well-being – an apparent *cascade effect*. However, children who leave their conduct problems behind in elementary school do not appear to have residual problems later in development, an encouraging observation for those engaged in efforts to intervene early with conduct problems.

The criteria by which "doing okay" is determined in studies of resilience have varied considerably. Definitions have ranged from simply an absence of disorder or mental health problems, to a focus on competence in developmental tasks (as with the Project Competence studies), to the inclusion of both competence criteria and an absence of symptoms (Masten, 2001). There is considerable debate about the best criteria for good adaptation or adjustment, particularly in regard to defining good adaptation in different cultural contexts, determining who should define these criteria, and deciding how to aggregate findings when different criteria were used (Luthar, 1999; Luthar, Cicchetti, & Becker, 2000; Masten 1999, 2001; Masten & Coatsworth, 1998; Rutter, 2000). Nonetheless, we would argue that an important contribution of the resilience framework is the attention it brings to positive outcomes, resulting in a more comprehensive approach to assessment and intervention.

Threats to the Development of Competence: Risk and Adversity

Premature birth, poverty, mental illness in a parent, divorce, war, maltreatment – many kinds of adversity experienced by children have been studied by investigators of risk and resilience (Garmezy & Rutter, 1983; Haggerty, Sherrod, Garmezy, & Rutter, 1994; Luthar, Burack, Cicchetti, & Weisz, 1997; Rolf, Masten, Cicchetti, Nuechterlein, & Weintraub, 1990). Such experiences are established risk factors for development in that there is good evidence that these conditions predict higher rates of negative or undesirable outcomes. Early studies of risk often focused attention on one risk factor. However, it was soon apparent that risk factors more typically co-occur with other risk factors, usually encompass a sequence of stressful experiences rather than a single event, and often pile up in the lives of children over time (Garmezy & Masten, 1994; Rolf et al, 1990; Rutter, 1979; Sameroff & Chandler, 1975; Sameroff & Seifer, 1983). As a result, many investigators shifted their attention to *cumulative risk*, studied either by aggregating information about stressful life experiences or by aggregating risk indicators.

In Project Competence, cumulative risk or adversity has been examined in a number of different ways. In the core study, for example, we have developed both life event questionnaires that tally negative experiences over the previous year and interview methods that assess the

nature of potentially stressful events in more detail over longer periods of time. Our most comprehensive strategy involved compiling all of
the information from the longitudinal assessments into a computerized
life history data base, creating life charts that could be judged by clinicians on severity rating scales with excellent reliability (Gest, Reed, &
Masten, 1999).

In all our assessments of adversity, we have been careful to distinguish *nonindependent* events (events related to a person's own behavior,
such as breaking up with a boyfriend or being expelled from school)
from *independent* events (e.g., death of a parent) (Masten, Neemann, &
Andenas, 1994). For most participants in the core study, the rates of
nonindependent events increased as they grew older (Gest et al., 1999).
This general developmental trend is not surprising, because adolescents
make many more choices about activities, friends, and time use that can
result in stressful life experiences. However, maladaptive youth displayed
a larger increase in nonindependent events over time, suggesting that
they were contributing to their own adversity at considerably higher rates
than their competent peers (Gest et al., 1999).

Other Project Competence studies have focused on cumulative risk
as indexed by tallies of known risk factors, such as low parental education, single-parent household, foster placement, or maltreatment. If
behavior problems, academic achievement, or health outcomes are plotted as a function of risk tallies, striking risk gradients can be observed.
Even among homeless families, in which all children are experiencing
the major stressor of homelessness, risk gradients are evident: On average, the higher the number of risk factors, the more problems observed (Masten, Miliotis, Graham-Bermann, Ramirez, & Neemann, 1993;
Masten & Sesma, 1999). On the other hand, homeless children with few
or no risk factors often are much better behaved than their high-risk
peers in school and at home, leading one to consider what *low risk* means
on a risk gradient. In many cases, it means that a child has more assets and
resources, because so many risk factors are actually bipolar indicators of
high and low risks and advantages. Low risk often indicates better SES or
parenting, for example, as well as fewer stressful life experiences. One of
the drawbacks to the more comprehensive cumulative risk approaches to
understanding risk and resilience is that aggregation, although resulting
in a better overall prediction of outcome, obscures what may be important distinctions in the nature of the resources and threats children have
faced and is not conducive to a search for specific processes of stress or
adaptation (Masten, 1999; Windle, 1999).

Resilience studies have also considered extreme trauma in the form of war, extreme privation, and natural disasters. In Project Competence, we have studied Cambodian youth who survived the massive trauma of war perpetrated by the Khmer Rouge in the 1970s and who later immigrated to Minnesota (Hubbard, Realmuto, Northwood, & Masten, 1995; Wright, Masten, Northwood, & Hubbard, 1997). In massive trauma, adversity is experienced on an extreme and devastating scale. Children in war commonly experience loss and witness atrocities outside the realm of normal human experience. Thus, we were not surprised to find that many of the Cambodian youth suffered long-term symptoms of trauma associated with posttraumatic stress disorder. Yet, these youth were all resilient compared to their peers who did not survive. Many were getting on with their lives as adolescents in a new country with impressive competence: going to school, making friends, and well on their way to becoming productive adult citizens of the United States.

In the Project Competence studies, we have observed many individuals who are growing up competent. Some of these adaptive young people have encountered very little in the way of risk, either in the form of disadvantages or stressful life experiences. Others come from a childhood characterized by great risk and adversity. The conceptual framework for understanding resilience must account for great differences in outcome among children who share high levels of risk or adversity and also must consider whether children who succeed in the context of high risk differ from children who succeed in a low-risk context.

Competence in the Presence of Risk: Protective Processes

Accounting for resilience in the lives of children entails a search for the processes that protect development from the ravages of hazardous growing conditions. Studies of resilience have taken a variety of approaches to try to identify the factors associated with better adaptation among children at risk, and then to understand whatever processes may underlie those correlates or predictors of good adaptation. Two major approaches have characterized the research on resilience: the variable-focused approach and the person-focused approach (Masten, 2001; Masten & Coatsworth, 1998). In Project Competence, we have taken both approaches in an effort to understand resilience from multiple perspectives.

Variable-focused approaches examine the links among competence, adversity, and a host of potential protective factors indexed by variables that describe differences among individual children and the nature of their relationships and interactions with the world in which they live. Multivariate statistics are used to test models of resilience that hypothesize additive, mediating, and moderating effects of contributing variables. Over the years, we have presented and tested a series of such variable-based models of resilience (e.g., Garmezy et al., 1984; Masten et al., 1988, 1999). These models are important, not only to test hypothesized protective factors, but also because they can serve as models of intervention. For example, additive or compensatory models suggest that more resources, such as better parenting, intellectual skills, or social support, can offset the negative effects of risks or adversity so that children have better outcomes. Thus, increasing the key assets in quality or number could theoretically improve the competence of children at risk. Moderating models, on the other hand, test for interaction effects in which a variable functions to alter the impact of risk or adversity on the outcome, increasing or decreasing individual susceptibility to the harmfulness of the stressor or protecting the child in some way from the full effects of the threat. Some moderators are risk-activated, analogous to an airbag buffering the impact of an automobile accident or antibodies responding to infection. Examples would be emergency services or a parent spurred into action by a threatening event. Other moderators are always active in a child's life, such as personality or cognitive differences, but they alter the impact of adversities when they occur. Some children are more upset than other children by the same event because of such differences.

Our variable-focused analyses in the core study, both in cross-sectional and longitudinal analyses, have focused on the role in competence and resilience of parenting quality, intellectual functioning, and family socioeconomic resources. Regardless of adversity levels, these key resources have been consistently associated with competence, with some resources identified as more important for specific aspects of competence. For example, good intellectual skills are better predictors of academic achievement than social success.

Moderating effects were also tested. One of the most persistent findings in the literature on IQ scores was also corroborated in our study: Intellectual functioning moderated the association between adversity and conduct, both cross-sectionally and over time (Masten et al., 1999). At very high lifetime adversity levels, IQ scores became a strong predictor of conduct, suggesting that children with poor cognitive skills who experience adversity are at particularly high risk for developing antisocial behavior problems. Our results are also consistent with a moderating role of parenting for conduct. If adversity is high and parenting quality is low, the risk for antisocial behavior is greater. Such analyses do not reveal processes, but our findings are consistent with the idea that reasonably good cognitive development and parenting protect the development of competence. Parenting quality may also reduce adversity exposure; we found that negative life events are more common in the families of less effective parents (Gest, Neemann, Hubbard, Masten, & Tellegen, 1993).

SES advantages overlapped with parenting and cognitive skills as a predictor of multiple domains of competence. In most cases, SES effects could be attributed to these more proximal attributes. However, SES had a partially unique relation to academic attainment, beyond the effects of parenting or cognitive functioning, suggesting that it may be a marker of advantages accruing from the educational background of parents, their connections, and the education-enhancing opportunities afforded by such advantages (Masten et al., 1999).

In contrast to variable-focused approaches, person-focused strategies focus on identifying people who meet definitional criteria for resilience, whose lives and attributes are then studied by investigators, particularly in comparison to maladaptive individuals who have similar levels of risk or adversity but who display markedly different outcomes. This approach is less sensitive than variable-focused strategies for identifying processes related to specific domains of competence, but it may better reflect the actual patterns of resilience occurring naturally (Masten, 2001, Masten & Coatsworth, 1998; Masten et al., 1999). Case studies, for example, can offer inspiring clues about resilience, though their generalizability is problematic (Masten & O'Connor, 1989). Like other longitudinal investigators, we have observed striking case examples of resilience in the core study. Some illustrate in human form the meaning of the numbers in our analyses, whereas others offer tantalizing clues for further study. Our current conversations with members of the longitudinal cohort around age 30 have revealed some striking "turnaround" cases consistent with anecdotal reports of other resilience investigators. These cases suggest that there may be an important window of opportunity in the transition to adulthood for some youth, allowing them to restructure their environments in ways that favor competence. Moving, joining the military, and making a wise marriage appear to have life-altering potential for some youth (Rutter, 1990; Werner & Smith, 1992).

The limitations of unique cases have led us and others to aggregate case data in a number of ways. In the core study, for example, we have compared diagnostic groups of *resilient, maladaptive,* and *competent*

(but low-adversity) youth, defined by strict diagnostic criteria for placement in a category. Additionally, we have identified similar groups
through empirical cluster analysis and also through clinical nominations
by skilled interviewers (Masten et al., 1999). All of these strategies converge on the same conclusions. First, resilience is a readily observable
pattern in the lives of a normative sample of youth. Such youth can be
identified reliably by different methods. Second, resilient children and
youth have much in common with competent peers who have overcome
far less adversity to succeed, and they differ in many ways from maladaptive peers with similar levels of adversity. Competent and resilient young
people have more resources at hand, including effective adults in their
lives in a parenting role, average or better cognitive development, and
positive self-regard. Maladaptive young people, on the other hand, have
few internal, family, or other resources. They are more inclined to experience negative emotions and appear to be stress-prone, both in the sense
of getting into stressful situations of their own making and in the sense of
stress-reactivity, responding poorly to challenges. Not surprisingly, their
self-worth is lower, both in adolescence and even now, many years later.
Lastly, competence appears to have staying power. In terms of both the
tasks of adult life and happiness, competent and resilient youth continue
to do well in their early adult years.

Results from other Project Competence studies also underscore the
importance of parenting quality and intellectual skills for competence
and resilience. As in more normative populations, the academic achievement and school success of homeless children are associated with effective parents and higher verbal IQ scores (Masten et al., 1997; Miliotis,
Sesma, & Masten, 1999). Across a wide variety of samples, methods, and
approaches, there appears to be a core of individual and family attributes
persistently related to competence in the context of risk and adversity.
At the same time, there are certainly unique qualities associated with resilience under particular circumstances. For example, it was clearly an
advantage for Cambodian war refugees if they were able to learn English
more readily (Hubbard, 1997). Nonetheless, the frequency with which
the same predictors of resilience emerge from very diverse studies conveys
a powerful message.

Human Adaptational Systems as Protective Factors: Ordinary Magic

Beginning with the earliest reviews of research on resilience in childhood and adolescence, a common set of findings has emerged and has

TABLE 1.1. *Examples of Attributes of Individuals and Their Contexts Often Associated with Resilience*

Individual Differences
Cognitive abilities (IQ scores, attentional skills, executive functioning skills)
Self-perceptions of competence, worth, confidence (self-efficacy, self-esteem)
Temperament and personality (adaptability, sociability)
Self-regulation skills (impulse control, affect and arousal regulation)
Positive outlook on life (hopefulness, belief that life has meaning, faith)

Relationships
Parenting quality (including warmth, structure and monitoring, expectations)
Close relationships with competent adults (parents, relatives, mentors)
Connections to prosocial and rule-abiding peers (among older children)

Community Resources and Opportunities
Good schools
Connections to prosocial organizations (such as clubs or religious groups)
Neighborhood quality (public safety, collective supervision, libraries, recreation centers)
Quality of social services and health care

---

been reconfirmed time and again (Masten, 1999, 2001). Garmezy (1985) described three major categories of protective factors on the basis of his early reviews of the literature: *individual attributes*, such as good intellectual skills, positive temperament, and positive views of the self; *family qualities*, such as high warmth, cohesion, expectations, and involvement; and *supportive systems outside the family*, such as strong social networks or good schools. Evidence has continued to accumulate for the association of such child, family, and community resources with better outcomes among children who have faced major adversity (Luthar et al., 2000; Masten, 2001; Masten & Coatsworth, 1998; Rutter, 2000; Werner, 2000). Examples of such resources are listed in Table 1.1.

In many cases, studies that link these attributes of children or their resources to better child outcomes have established only a simple association of these factors with good versus poor outcomes in the context of risk or adversity. Clearly, these are correlates of better competence under adverse conditions, and in this general sense can be viewed as *protective factors*. However, it is also the case that most of these are well-established correlates of doing well in general, under low-adversity conditions as well as high-risk conditions. Thus, these qualities could represent resources that have the potential to counterbalance adversity in an *additive* model of resilience in which assets outweigh risks (see Masten, 1999, 2001; Luthar et al., 2000, for recent discussions of resilience models).

There is less evidence implicating these factors as vulnerability or protective influences that *moderate* the impact of adversity on development or show a uniquely important role under hazardous conditions. The best evidence for moderating effects has accrued for general intellectual functioning, typically measured by IQ tests, and for parenting quality, particularly with respect to the presence or absence of parenting characterized by age-appropriate monitoring, closeness, and high expectations instead of neglect, rejection, or harshness (Masten, 2001). Although cognitive abilities and effective parenting have broad implications for child health, competence, and well-being in general, these qualities appear to have particular importance when adversity levels are high.

What might these convergent findings mean for resilience? Our work in Project Competence, together with the growing literature on resilience from diverse corners of the world, has convinced us that the "short list" of protective factors (shown in Table 1.1) signifies the importance of fundamental human adaptational systems for the development of competence under both favorable and unfavorable conditions (Masten, 2001; Masten & Coatsworth, 1998; Masten & Reed, 2002). Human adaptation and development are enormously complex, of course. However, the salience of some protective factors within the resilience literature strongly suggests that we should focus on the significance of some basic protective systems for human development if we intend to foster better outcomes among children at risk due to hazardous rearing conditions or experiences. These would include attachment (systems underlying close relationships in development), mastery motivation (pleasure from mastering developmental tasks; self-efficacy system), self-regulation (emotional and behavioral regulation; impulse control), and cognitive development and learning (neurobehavioral systems; information systems), as well as more macrolevel systems of human organization. Cultural evolution has provided children and adults with extended families, religious systems, and other social systems of ethnic groups and societies that offer adaptive advantages.

Human adaptational systems have been the focus of intense study by many disciplines, and further examination of their nature and role in individual adaptation is beyond the scope of this discussion. However, several conclusions follow from the speculation that much of the resilience observed and described in the literature emerges from the operation of such systems. First, resilience typically arises from the operation of common human adaptational systems rather than from rare or extraordinary processes. Second, these systems stem from a long history of biological and cultural evolution that has equipped humans with powerful tools for adaptive functioning. Third, these systems *develop* and, therefore, adversity may wreak its greatest damage through harm to the development of key adaptive systems (e.g., brain damage or the deprivation of parenting). It follows that sustaining or restoring conditions essential to cognitive and social development is a high priority for protecting child development and for promoting resilience among children in risky rearing situations. Fourth, renewed attention to the adaptive systems that promote healthy development, broadly conceived, has the potential to guide policy and practice; if the greatest threats to children are those adversities that undermine the development and operation of primary human adaptational systems, then efforts to promote competence and resilience in children at risk may do well to focus attention on protecting, restoring, and facilitating these powerful tools of human adaptation.

The conclusion that resilience arises from *ordinary magic* (Masten, 2001) refers to the idea that human individuals are capable of astonishing resistance, coping, recovery, and success in the face of adversity, equipped only with the usual human adaptational capabilities and resources, functioning normally. Certainly, there are individual cases and situations in which a special, rare, or extraordinary asset or process makes the difference. However, the literature on resilience suggests that there are some fundamental systems characteristic of human functioning that have great adaptational significance across diverse stressors and threatening situations. These systems are versatile and responsive to a wide variety of challenges, both normative and nonnormative; their manifestations take many forms, influenced by the nature and development of the child at the time, as well as by the nature of the situation or context. Thus, effective parents alter their actions on behalf of their child, depending on the nature of the threat, their knowledge of the child, and their judgments about what needs to be done given the situation at hand to achieve a desired outcome. A parent might intervene in different ways to promote resilience in a sibling, or for the same child in a different situation, or for the same child at a different age. Similarly, the actions of an intelligent child to deal with a life-threatening experience would be expected to differ, depending on other qualities of the child (e.g., cautious or bold in general; current level of fear or arousal), the nature of the threatening situation, that child's appraisal of the situation and available resources, and when in this child's development the experience occurs. The operational quality of these systems is often judged by a track record of effectiveness across situations and time, or it is assessed through methods that have shown predictive validity for behaviors that are adaptive from the point of view of a given culture and historical context. Thus, IQ tests predict academic achievement, a valued aspect of competence in modern societies. *Authoritative parenting* measures have shown validity as predictors of multiple aspects of valued achievement and conduct in children in contemporary American society (Steinberg, Mounts, Lamborn, & Dornbusch, 1991).

The conclusion that resilience usually arises from the operation of ordinary adaptive processes, rather than rare or extraordinary ones, provides an optimistic outlook for intervention. Resilience research also suggests a framework for conceptualizing, implementing, and learning from interventions and policy based on such a framework.

A RESILIENCE FRAMEWORK FOR POLICY AND PRACTICE

The search for understanding resilience gave rise to a new framework for research and a body of knowledge about risk and protective factors with implications for policy and practice. There has been a "sea change" in the way we think about helping children at risk that reflects the influence of many scholars in developmental and prevention sciences, including resilience investigators, prevention investigators, and developmental psychopathologists (Cicchetti, Rappaport, Sandler, & Weissberg, 2000; Cowen, 2000; Luthar & Cicchetti, 2000; Masten, 2001; Masten & Coatsworth, 1998). The actions of intervention programs now are much more likely to be described in terms of redirecting development or promoting competence and wellness. Wyman et al. (2000) argue for a conceptualization of intervention based on resilience as *cumulative competence promotion and stress protection*. Investigators are more likely to attribute the success of their interventions to a focus on competence enhancement or the strengthening of cumulative protections in a child's life (e.g., Hawkins, Catalano, Kosterman, Abbot, and Hill, 1999).

Reformulating Intervention

A resilience framework has implications for the conceptualization of interventions, mission statements, and models guiding programs. It also

TABLE 1.2. *A Resilience Framework for Policy and Practice*

Mission: Frame goals in positive terms
Promote competence
Shift developmental course in more positive directions

Models: Include positive predictors and outcomes in models of change
Competence or health as well as problems or psychopathology
Developmental tasks
Assets as well as risk factors
Protective factors as well as vulnerabilities

Measures: Assess the positive as well as the negative
Assess strengths in the child, family, relationships, school, community
Evaluate change on positive as well as negative indicators

Methods: Consider multiple strategies based on resilience models
Risk-focused: Reduce risk exposure, prevent adversity
Asset-focused: Boost child's resources or enhance key assets in child's life
Process-focused: Mobilize the power of human adaptational systems

---

has implications for what is measured and the strategies to consider (see Table 1.2).

Mission

A resilience approach brings far greater attention to positive objectives and developmental criteria. The conclusions we have outlined also have strong implications in regard to priorities for policy and intervention, because it is clearly important to nurture and protect the fundamental adaptive systems for human development before moving on to foster the many other tools that benefit the lives of children.

Within a resilience framework, it is recognized that promoting competence is one of the best ways to prevent problems and is also a far more appealing way to frame goals for stakeholders, who are essential to the successful implementation of any program. Parents and teachers are often more enthusiastic, for example, about plans to foster success in their children and students than about plans to prevent teenage pregnancy, delinquency, and school dropout. Moreover, comprehensive interventions for children at risk appear to *work better* with respect to both positive and negative outcomes when goals include the promotion of competence and positive achievements, in addition to the prevention or treatment of symptoms and negative behaviors (Cicchetti et al., 2000; Masten, 2001).

Models

A resilience framework has implications for the detailed models of change that implicitly or explicitly guide policy and intervention, as well as for the overarching conceptualization of these endeavors. Models include assets and strengths as well as negative indicators of starting points and outcomes of interventions. Competence and health status are emphasized instead of, or along with, symptoms and disorder. Processes of interest include protective and buffering effects, along with vulnerability and exacerbating effects. The function of the new policy or intervention plan is conceived in these models in terms of redirecting development in more positive directions, improving the odds of a good outcome, facilitating protection, enhancing or protecting assets, reducing vulnerability, preventing or reducing risk, and so forth. Goals and processes can also be framed in parallel economic terms: building human capital through the investment of social and financial capital (Coleman, 1988; Furstenberg & Hughes, 1995).

At its best, resilience research integrates developmental theory and knowledge into theory and research designs concerned with the etiology and prevention of psychopathology, as well as with the promotion of competence. Similarly, good models of how to improve children's lives must be developmental to the core and, ideally, should be fully informed by current developmental theory and knowledge pertinent to the goals of the program. Models influenced by developmental theory and research may reflect attention to developmental tasks salient for particular ages, target multiple domains of functioning, and conceptualize interventions in terms of affecting ongoing processes that may benefit maximally from assistance at several different points in development as new challenges arise and new tasks emerge.

Theoretical and empirical models of how good developmental outcomes and adjustment happen, particularly in the context of risk, inherently represent models of intervention. These models and their implications have been elucidated by Project Competence investigators (Garmezy et al., 1984; Masten, 1999, 2001; Masten & Coatsworth, 1998) and also by many other resilience and prevention scholars (e.g., Cowen, 2000; Egeland, Carlson, & Sroufe, 1993; Luthar et al., 2000; Luthar & Cicchetti, 2000; Weissberg, Caplan, & Harwood, 1991; Weissberg & Greenberg, 1998; Wyman, Sandler, Wolchik, & Nelson, 2000). Some of the models framed from a resilience perspective are very broad (including most of the models cited previously), but others are more specifically focused on policies or programs to intervene around specific threats, such as divorce, or specific outcomes, such as school achievement or delinquency prevention. Recent examples include the successful interventions designed by Forgatch and DeGarmo (1999) to help children through divorce by protecting parenting and by Hawkins, Catalano, and their colleagues (1999) to prevent risky behaviors in adolescence by increasing school bonding and achievement.

Measures

It follows from the focus on assets, competence, and protective processes that tools for assessing status and evaluating change need to include these elements of behavior, context, and process, along with more traditional measures of risk factors, symptoms, problems, and risky or pathological processes. Although the importance of assessing competence in terms of developmental tasks was recognized long ago in research and clinical work on mental illness and mental retardation, the popularity of the medical model, emphasizing symptoms, disease, and treatment, impeded the development of good measures of positive aspects of behavior, relationships, and communities (Masten & Curtis, 2000). Often the importance of success in developmental tasks was captured only by diagnostic criteria and evaluations related to impairment in adaptive functioning. Resilience research has highlighted the importance of tracking the effectiveness of functioning in major developmental tasks and also of the assessment of qualities in relationships, schools, and communities that appear to make a difference. This framework spurred the development of more and better tools for measuring assets, competence, and protective processes, along with risks, deficits, pathology, and problems. However, there is certainly work to be done in making these tools more field-friendly; research-based tools are often impractical for widespread use in the community because they are too labor-intensive or expensive in other ways.

Methods

A resilience framework suggests several major strategies of intervention for policy and program designers to consider. *Risk-focused* designs attempt to eliminate or reduce the level of risk exposure in development. Examples include prenatal care to prevent low birth weight, home visiting programs to lower the risk of maltreatment, safety education or policies to prevent injuries to farm children, anti-bullying campaigns to reduce peer victimization, vaccination to prevent illness, and cleaning up environmental lead or land mines to reduce child illness or injury. *Asset-focused* designs include attempts to directly provide more or better assets in the lives of children. Alternatively, they attempt to increase the presence or power of the people who are themselves assets to children, such as parents and teachers. Examples include tutoring or teacher training to enhance learning in children, job training for parents, building new schools, recreation centers, or libraries, and restoring community services in a disaster area. *Process-oriented* programs attempt to mobilize or improve the most powerful adaptational systems for children, including key relationships, human intellectual functioning, self-regulation systems, and the mastery-motivation system. Such programs might aim to enhance attachment relationships with primary caregivers, establish mentoring relationships with competent and caring adults, or provide opportunities to develop talents, learn new skills, or develop cultural traditions. They can also focus on training children in self-monitoring, meditation, anger management, or other self-regulation skills. Process-oriented efforts can target different system levels (e.g., individual, family, school, neighborhood, culture) or their interaction (e.g., family–school connections, self-regulation in the peer context).

Some strategies fit more than one category, either because they have dual effects or because they are multifaceted programs. For example, good prenatal care and home visiting programs may effectively reduce the risk of premature birth or maltreatment (well-established risk factors for later developmental problems) at the same time that they promote healthy brain development (protecting one of nature's most powerful adaptive systems, human cognition). Early intervention programs targeting children at risk due to poverty or disadvantage have successfully included many of these strategies simultaneously, utilizing a comprehensive approach (Ramey & Ramey, 1998).

Ultimately, intervention and prevention programs that are carefully designed to evaluate and test contrasting or competing models of resilience will offer the most compelling evidence for or against hypothesized protective effects (Luthar & Cicchetti, 2000; Masten, 1999; Masten & Coatsworth, 1998; Werner, 2000). Children cannot be randomly assigned to adversity or parents or personal resources. Instead, the dynamic power of protective processes can best be demonstrated through efforts to change the existing odds in favor of good development. The careful study of change, both in these intervention programs and in basic longitudinal studies, should lead in turn to reformulation and refinement of theories about risk and protection. Ideally, such research will form a bridge with two-way traffic between science and practice, each informing the other.

Closing Thoughts

The Project Competence studies of competence, risk, and resilience reflect in small part the large transformation that occurred in the last quarter of the twentieth century in the ways that child and adolescent problems were conceptualized. The study of resilience was part of a *Zeitgeist* that gave rise to developmental psychopathology and a more integrated science of human development and its variations. Research on resilience underscored the importance of understanding good as well as poor adaptation, competence as well as symptoms, and protective processes as well as risk processes.

The first generation of research on resilience phenomena, including the Project Competence studies over the past 30 years, has provided concepts, models, measures, and general findings, as well as provocative questions and controversies that provide direction for the future. Even this early work yielded useful insights for policy and intervention. But a deeper understanding is needed of the processes that produce resilience under different conditions for different children in order to guide the efficacy and efficiency of policies and programs designed to shift the odds for good developmental outcomes in more favorable directions. Careful study of "what works" in interventions and programs based on risk/resilience frameworks will play an important role in refining theory and models of competence and psychopathology in development.

References

Cicchetti, D. (1984). The emergence of developmental psychopathology. *Child Development, 55,* 1–7.

Cicchetti, D. (1990). A historical perspective on the discipline of developmental psychopathology. In J. Rolf, A. S. Masten, D. Cicchetti, K. H. Nuechterlein, & S. Weintraub (Eds.), *Risk and protective factors in the development of psychopathology* (pp. 2–28). New York: Cambridge University Press.

Cicchetti, D., Rappaport, J., Sandler, I., & Weissberg, R. P. (Eds.). (2000). *The promotion of wellness in children and adolescents.* Washington, DC: Child Welfare League of America Press.

Coleman, J. S. (1988). Social capital in the creation of human capital. *American Journal of Sociology, 94*(Suppl.), S95–S120.

Cowen, E. L. (2000). Psychological wellness: Some hopes for the future. In D. Cicchetti, J. Rappaport, I. Sandler, & R. P. Weissberg (Eds.), *The promotion of wellness in children and adolescents* (pp. 477–503). Washington, DC: Child Welfare League of America Press.

Egeland, B., Carlson, E., & Sroufe, L. A. (1993). Resilience as process. *Development and Psychopathology, 5,* 517–528.

Forgatch, M. S., & DeGarmo, D. S. (1999). Parenting through change: An effective prevention program for single mothers. *Journal of Consulting and Clinical Psychology, 67,* 711–724.

Furstenberg, F. F., & Hughes, M. E. (1995). Social capital and successful development among at-risk youth. *Journal of Marriage and the Family, 57,* 580–592.

Garmezy, N. (1973). Competence and adaptation in adult schizophrenic patients and children at risk. In S. R. Dean (Ed.), *Schizophrenia: The first ten Dean Award lectures* (pp. 163–204). New York: MSS Information.

Garmezy, N. (1985). Stress-resistant children: The search for protective factors. In J. E. Stevenson (Ed.), *Recent research in developmental pathopathology: Journal of Child Psychology and Psychiatry Book Supplement #4* (pp. 213–233). Oxford: Pergamon Press.

Garmezy, N., & Masten, A. S. (1994). Chronic adversities. In M. Rutter, L Herzov, & E. Taylor (Eds.), *Child and adolescent psychiatry* (pp. 191–208). Oxford: Blackwell Scientific.

Garmezy, N., Masten, A. S., & Tellegen, A. (1984). The study of stress and competence in children: A building block for developmental psychopathology. *Child Development, 55,* 97–111.

Garmezy, N., & Rodnick, E. (1959). Premorbid adjustment and performance in schizophrenia: Implications for interpreting heterogeneity in schizophrenia. *Journal of Nervous and Mental Disease, 129,* 450–466.

Garmezy, N., & Rutter, M. (1983) (Eds.). *Stress, coping, and development in children.* New York: McGraw-Hill.

Garmezy, N., & Tellegen, A. (1984). Studies of stress-resistant children: Methods, variables, and preliminary findings. In F. Morrison, C. Lord, & D. Keating (Eds.), *Advances in applied developmental psychology,* (Vol. 1, pp. 231–287). New York: Academic Press.

Gest, S. D. (1997). Behavioral inhibition: Stability and associations with adaptation from childhood to adolescence. *Journal of Personality and Social Psychology, 72,* 467–475.

Gest, S. D., Neemann, J., Hubbard, J. J., Masten, A. S., & Tellegen, A. (1993). Parenting quality, adversity, and conduct problems in adolescence: Testing process-oriented models of resilience. *Development and Psychopathology, 5,* 663–682.

Gest, S. D., Reed, M.-G., J., & Masten, A. S. (1999). Measuring developmental changes in exposure to adversity: A life chart and rating scale approach. *Development and Psychopathology, 11,* 171–192.

Haggerty, R. J., Sherrod, L. R., Garmezy, N., & Rutter, M. (1994). *Stress, risk, and resilience in children and adolescents.* New York: Cambridge University Press.

Hawkins, J. D., Catalano, R. F., Kosterman, R., Abbott, R., & Hill, K. G. (1999). Preventing adolescent health-risk behavior by strengthening protection during childhood. *Archives of Pediatrics and Adolescent Medicine, 153,* 226–234.

Hubbard, J. J. (1997). *Adaptive functioning and post-trauma symptoms in adolescent survivors of massive childhood trauma.* Doctoral dissertation, University of Minnesota, Twin Cities.

Hubbard, J. J., Realmuto, G. M., Northwood, A. K., & Masten, A. S. (1995). Comorbidity of psychiatric diagnoses with post-traumatic stress disorder in survivors of childhood trauma. *Journal of the American Academy of Child and Adolescent Psychiatry, 34,* 1167–1173.

Luthar, S. S. (1999). Measurement issues in the empirical study of resilience: An overview. In M. Glanz & J. L. Johnson (Eds.), *Resilience and development: Positive life adaptations* (pp. 129–160). New York: Plenum.

Luthar, S. S., & Cicchetti, D. (2000). The construct of resilience: Implications for interventions and social policies. *Development and Psychopathology, 12,* 857–885.

Luthar, S. S., Burack, J. A., Cicchetti, D., & Weisz, J. R. (Eds.). (1997). *Developmental psychopathology: Pespectives on adjustment, risk, and disorder.* New York: Cambridge University Press.

Luthar, S. S., Cicchetti, D., & Becker, B. (2000). The construct of resilience: A critical evaluation and guidelines for future work. *Child Development, 71,* 543–562.

Masten, A. S. (1986). Humor and competence in school-aged children. *Child Development, 57,* 461–473.

Masten, A. S. (1999). Resilience comes of age: Reflections on the past and outlook for the next generation of research. In M. D. Glantz & J. Johnson (Eds.), *Resilience and development: Positive life adaptations* (pp. 281–296). New York: Plenum.

Masten, A. S. (2001). Ordinary magic: Resilience processes in development. *American Psychologist, 56,* 227–238.

Masten, A. S., & Braswell, L. (1991). Developmental psychopathology: An integrative framework. In P. R. Martin (Ed.), *Handbook of behavior therapy and psychological science: An integrative approach* (pp. 35–56). New York: Pergamon Press.

Masten, A. S., & Coatsworth, J. D. (1998). The development of competence in favorable and unfavorable environments: Lessons from successful children. *American Psychologist, 53,* 205–220.

Masten, A. S., Coatsworth, J. D., Neemann, J., Gest, S. D., Tellegen, A., & Garmezy, N. (1995). The structure and coherence of competence from childhood through adolescence. *Child Development, 66,* 1635–1659.

Masten, A. S., & Curtis, W. J. (2000). Integrating competence and psychopathology: Pathways toward a comprehensive science of adaptation in development. *Development and Psychopathology, 12,* 529–550.

Masten, A. S., Garmezy, N., Tellegen, A., Pellegrini, D. S., Larkin, K., & Larsen, A. (1988). Competence and stress in school children: The moderating effects of individual and family qualities. *Journal of Child Psychology and Psychiatry, 29,* 745–764.

Masten, A. S., Hubbard, J. J., Gest, S. D., Tellegen, A., Garmezy, N., & Ramirez, M. (1999). Competence in the context of adversity: Pathways to resilience and maladaptation from childhood to late adolescence. *Development and Psychopathology, 11,* 143–169.

Masten, A. S., Miliotis, D., Graham-Bermann, S., Ramirez, M., & Neemann, J. (1993). Children in homeless families: Risks to mental health and development. *Journal of Consulting and Clinical Psychology, 61,* 335–343.

Masten, A. S., Neemann, J., & Andenas, S. (1994). Life events and adjustments in adolescents: The significance of event independence, desirability, and chronicity. *Journal of Research on Adolescence, 4,* 71–97.

Masten, A. S., & O'Connor, M. J. (1989). Vulnerability, stress, and resilience in the early development of a high risk child. *Journal of the American Academy of Child and Adolescent Psychiatry, 28*, 274–278.

Masten, A. S., & Reed, M.-G. (2002). Resilience in development. In C. R. Snyder & S. J. Lopez (Eds.), *The handbook of positive psychology* (pp. 74–88). New York: Oxford University Press.

Masten, A. S., & Sesma, A. (1999). Risk and resilience among children homeless in Minneapolis. *CURA Reporter, 29*(1), 1–6.

Masten, A. S., Sesma, A., Fraser, S. M., Lawrence, C., Miliotis, D., & Dionne, J. A. (1997). Educational risks for children experiencing homelessness. *Journal of School Psychology, 35*, 27–46.

Miliotis, D., Sesma, A., & Masten, A. S. (1999). Parenting as a protective process for school success in children from homeless families. *Early Education and Development, 10*, 111–133.

Morison, P., & Masten, A. S. (1991). Peer reputation in middle childhood as a predictor of adaptation in adolescence: A 7-year follow-up. *Child Development, 62*, 991–1007.

Neemann, J., Hubbard, J., & Masten, A. S. (1995). The changing importance of romantic relationship involvement to competence from late childhood to late adolescence. *Development and Psychopathology, 7*, 727–750.

Pellegrini, D. S., Masten, A. S., Garmezy, N., & Ferrarese, M. J. (1987). Correlates of social and academic competence in middle childhood. *Journal of Child Psychology and Psychiatry, 28*, 699–714.

Phillips, L. (1968). *Human adaptation and its failures.* New York: Academic Press.

Ramey, C. T., & Ramey, S. L. (1998). Early intervention and early experience. *American Psychologist, 53*, 109–120.

Rolf, J., Masten, A. S., Cicchetti, D., Nuechterlein, K., & Weintraub, S., (Eds.). (1990). *Risk and protective factors in the development of psychopathology.* New York: Cambridge University Press.

Rutter, M. (1979). Protective factors in children's responses to stress and disadvantage. In M. W. Kent & J. E. Rolf (Eds.), *Primary prevention of psychopathology, Vol. 3: Social competence in children* (pp. 49–74). Hanover, NH: University Press of New England.

Rutter, M. (1990). Psychosocial resilience and protective mechanisms. In J. Rolf, A. S. Masten, D. Cicchetti, K. H. Nuechterlein, & S. Weintraub (Eds.), *Risk and protective factors in the development of psychopathology* (pp. 181–214). New York: Cambridge University Press.

Rutter, M. (2000). Resilience reconsidered: Conceptual considerations, empirical findings, and policy implications. In J. P. Shonkoff & S. J. Meisels (Eds.), *Handbook of early intervention* (2nd ed., pp. 651–681). New York: Cambridge University Press.

Sameroff, A. J., & Chandler, M. J. (1975). Reproductive risk and the continuum of caretaking casualty. In F. D. Horowitz (Ed.), *Review of child development research* (Vol. 4, pp. 187–224). Chicago: University of Chicago Press.

Sameroff, A. J., & Seifer, R. (1983). Familial risk and child competence. *Child Development, 54*, 1254–1268.

Shiner, R. L. (2000). Linking childhood personality with adaptation: Evidence for continuity and change across time into late adolescence. *Journal of Personality and Social Psychology, 78,* 310–325.

Steinberg, L., Mounts, N. S., Lamborn, S. D., & Dornbusch, S. M. (1991). Authoritative parenting and adolescent adjustment across varied ecological niches. *Journal of Research on Adolescence, 1,* 19–36.

Watt, N. F., Anthony, E. J., Wynne, L. C., & Rolf, J. E. (1984). *Children at risk for schizophrenia: A longitudinal perspective.* New York: Cambridge University Press.

Weissberg, R. P., Caplan, M. Z., & Harwood, R. L. (1991). Promoting competence enhancing environments: A systems-based perspective on primary prevention. *Journal of Consulting and Clinical Psychology, 59,* 830–841.

Weissberg, R. P., & Greenberg, M. T. (1998). School and community competence-enhancement and prevention programs. In I. E. Siegel & K. A. Renninger (Eds.), *Handbook of child psychology: Vol. 4. Child psychology in practice* (pp. 877–954). New York: Wiley.

Werner, E. (2000). Protective factors and individual resilience. In J. P. Shonkoff & S. J. Meisels (Eds.), *Handbook of early intervention* (2nd ed., pp. 115–132). New York: Cambridge University Press.

Werner, E. E., & Smith, R. S. (1982). *Vulnerable but invincible: A study of resilient children.* New York: McGraw-Hill.

Werner, E. E., & Smith, R. S. (1992). *Overcoming the odds: High risk children from birth to adulthood.* Ithaca, NY: Cornell University Press.

Windle, M. (1999). Critical conceptual and measurement issues in the study of resilience. In M. D. Glantz & J. L. Johnson (Eds.), *Resilience and development: Positive life adaptations* (pp. 161–176). New York: Kluwer Academic/Plenum.

Wright, M. O'D., Masten, A. S., Northwood, A., & Hubbard, J. (1997). Long-term effects of massive trauma: Developmental and psychobiological perspectives. In D. Cicchetti & S. L. Toth (Eds.), *Rochester symposium on developmental psychopathology, Vol. 8., The effects of trauma on the developmental process* (pp. 181–225). Rochester, NY: University of Rochester Press.

Wyman, P. A., Sandler, I., Wolchik, S., & Nelson, K. (2000). Resilience as cumulative competence promotion and stress protection: Theory and intervention. In D. Cicchetti, J. Rapport, I. Sandler, & R. P. Weissberg (Eds.), *The promotion of wellness in children and adolescents* (pp. 133–184). Washington, DC: Child Welfare League of America Press.

PART I

FAMILIAL ADVERSITIES

Parental Psychopathology and Family Processes

2

Young Children with Mentally Ill Parents

Resilient Developmental Systems

Ronald Seifer

Mental illness is a family matter. When one member has mental illness, it affects all others in the family. In their simplest forms, the distress and functional impairment of the ill family member are felt on a daily basis by others in the household – in ways that range from empathizing with the distress, to disruption of interpersonal relationships within the family, to compromised family functioning in which tasks of daily life are not accomplished. At a more complex level, when the mentally ill family member is a parent, there are well-established risks for the children in that family. Rates of mental illness are higher throughout the children's lifespan (particularly during the typical risk periods for mental illnesses), difficulties in school are more frequent, and problems in general social adjustment (such as delinquent behavior) are manifest. Still, the mechanisms by which this risk is manifest remain obscure.

In this chapter, I describe the current state of our knowledge regarding resilience in infants and young children who have a parent with mental illness. I begin by addressing some basic issues regarding how general models of resilience may be adapted to the particular circumstances of infants and toddlers. Following this, I summarize relevant research that may be interpreted in a resilience framework. I conclude with a summary model of processes identified to date in this population, along with some commentary on how well the resilience model will ultimately serve to aid understanding in this field.

This work was supported by grants from the National Institute of Mental Health. Correspondence to Brown University, E. P. Bradley Hospital, 1011 Veterans Memorial Parkway, East Providence, RI 02915. E-mail to ronald_seifer@brown.edu.

RESILIENCE MODELS: APPLICATION TO THE FIRST YEARS
OF LIFE

Differences in the lives of children whose parent has mental illness are evident from the first weeks of life (see Seifer & Dickstein, 2000, for a summary of this work). These differences are most obvious in the social-emotional domain of functioning. Relationship processes, as indexed by variables such as attachment status, reveal small but consistent trends toward insecurity and perhaps disorganization. Affective responsiveness is less well organized. This may be seen, for example, in en face inter-actions (close interactions in which parents and infants are facing one another) in procedures like the still face. Cognitive and motor develop-ment, in contrast, rarely is different in children of mentally ill parents (a notable exception is delay in motor accomplishments in children of schizophrenic mothers). These differences in the children are observed in the context of distinct patterns of behavior in the parents, including affective dysregulation, distorted cognitions (with particular interest in cognitions about the child), and less involved and supportive interaction patterns. Note that almost all of the studies in this field focus on moth-ers, as is the case in most human development research in which parental influences are a focus.

Infants and young children present some unique challenges when considering how to identify resilience processes. In the context of early childhood adaptation to parental mental illness, it is simple to identify a straightforward resilience formulation. The identified risk in such studies is the parental illness. It is also simple to identify many potential protec-tive factors, including variables such as child temperament, parenting behavior, family functioning, marital functioning, and parental course of illness. Within this formulation, resilience would be evident by a partic-ular type of statistical interaction (minimal differences within the non-ill group, substantial improvement within the ill group) or by multiple pre-diction of child outcome by risk and protective variables. Unfortunately, operationalizing such models is not straightforward.

Children in the first years of life have not yet established a develop-mental pathway that is substantially independent of caregivers. There is widespread appreciation that when studying behavioral processes in infants and preschool children (whether normative or deviant), it is imperative that the caregiving system be an integral part of the assess-ment of behavioral adjustment (Sameroff & Emde, 1989; Zero to Three, 1995). This feature places an additional burden on the already complex research agenda of identifying resilience. What is the focus of the developmental outcome? Is it the child, the caregiver, of the child-caregiver system?

Young age brings with it another inherent complication when examining resilience. These young children have simply not had a long enough life to play out the contingent processes basic to some manifestations of resilience. Many of the processes identified in resilient youth do not appear fully formed, but take place over extended development periods. For example, establishing a relationship with a trusted adult (who may compensate for the deficiencies of an ill parent) may take years. Furthermore, the opportunities for such experiences may be linked to the developmental stage of the child. Infants and young children spend the vast majority of their time in a limited variety of social contexts, such as home, child care, or preschool. The increasingly independent access to larger and more varied social communities characteristic of older youth is not available in the first years of life.

Developmental considerations affect analysis of resilience in other ways. Young children have not yet developed many skills and functions that underlie potential resilience processes. Verbal skills are minimal; social relationships are just emerging from the caregiving context; emotion-processing abilities are limited; many cognitive developments have yet to emerge. This complex of developmental immaturity provides children with few resources to overcome adversity.

How do we search for resilience under these conditions? As I alluded to earlier, the classic definition of resilience may require some modification when addressing the development of infants and preschoolers. The most restrictive version of the classic model would consider the risk condition of parental psychopathology as conferring a developmental hazard on the child. When resilience processes are at work, however, the result is a positive child outcome. The restrictive aspect of this model is that an interaction effect is required. The resilience process is operative only when the risk condition is present; otherwise, it has no effect on the child's outcome (Rutter, 1987).

A variant of the classic model, which is generally well accepted, contains the same basic elements. The major difference in this less restrictive model is that there need not be an interaction effect. Instead, any characteristic demonstrated to result in a positive child outcome in the presence of risk is deemed indicative of a resilience process (Luthar, Cicchetti, & Becker, 2000). Such effects may be in the form of multiple prediction or include a mediated set of relations.

When searching for resilience in infants and young children, either variant of the classic model requires further revision to be a useful aid in understanding the core phenomena. Because of the undifferentiated nature of the caregiver–child relationship, along with the developmental immaturity and short life experience of the child, the focus of attention needs to be broadened. On the one hand, the locus of the resilience process is not simply the child, but rather the parent–child system. On the other, the positive outcome may also be viewed as inhering in the parent–child system rather than in the child alone. Elaborating on this last point, when examining risk and resilience processes in children so young, it is difficult to identify developmental outcomes that can be considered to be organized adverse responses to the risk that have functional significance for the child. What is more amenable to identification at this point in development is a set of interim outcomes that would not be considered to be fully formed adverse consequences of the risk. Instead, such interim outcomes might be viewed as perturbations to caregiving systems that if not resolved will continue to increase the risk for poor child outcomes (Sameroff & Emde, 1989). As with the resilience processes, the locus of the interim outcomes is best understood as being part of the caregiving system as opposed to the child alone.

This alternative model sets up a somewhat different agenda for describing resilience in the infants and toddlers under discussion. The interim outcomes described previously have two qualities different from those of most other analyses of resilience. First, they may not superficially appear to be the positive or negative indicators of development ordinarily discussed in the context of resilience. For example, typical outcome indicators might be academic success, occupational status, diagnosed mental illness, significant social isolation, or criminal behavior. The indicators in early childhood are more subtle – for example, the quality of relationships or the management of emotions. Second, they do not necessarily pertain to the child, but instead to the parent–child system – for example, the parent's cognitions about the child. These differences stem from a fundamental view of resilience that defines it as forces that pressure development in a positive direction.

As I will detail in the sections to follow, many of the resilience factors that can be identified from existing research on infants and toddlers are best characterized as processes affecting developments that may subsequently have long-lasting consequences for the children. For the most part, these are research findings that are tantalizing regarding whether there is a demonstration of resilience. As noted previously, in most cases it is difficult to establish a definitive adverse outcome in children that is ameliorated by the resilience process in question.

RESEARCH FINDINGS

Few studies that examine infants and toddlers with mentally ill parents have been explicitly designed to examine resilience processes. Instead, most have been set up to elucidate how children's early development proceeds in the context of this demonstrated risk factor. This treatment of resilience will thus focus on inferences that can be made about the developmental pathways that appear to be initiated early in the lives of the children of mentally ill parents. In summarizing this research, I will categorize the findings in terms of children's emotion processing, parents' emotion processing, parents' interactive behavior, and parents' cognitions about their children. Because few of these studies have been cast as examining resilience processes, I will present the findings as the authors originally stated them (typically in terms of negative consequences of parental illness). I will add integrative material that interprets findings in terms of resilience. In almost all of the studies described, depression is the mental illness in question. There are few studies in which other mental illness have been the focus early in life, and these have tended not to be informative regarding resilience processes.

Child Emotion Processing

Attachment
Much of the research that examines children's emotion processing involves the organized behavior system reflected in attachment status. This is understandable on two counts: Attachment is one of the few developmental outcomes that is well established and measurable in the first years of life, and there is evidence that attachment has some level of enduring consequences in the years to follow. These studies have focused on both *insecure* attachment (organized strategies of children resulting in less than optimal resolution of relationship perturbation) and *disorganized* attachment (lack of an organized response to such perturbation). The latter (disorganized attachment) is viewed as indicative of more serious compromise of the caregiving relationship.

Most of the studies have focused on attachment as an important interim parent–child relationship outcome, with designs that examine how depression in combination with other factors predicts attachment status. The normative literature on attachment emphasizes the importance of parenting sensitivity (contingent, appropriate responsiveness to the child's signals) as a mechanism for promoting secure attachment in infants. Surprisingly, this set of associations has not been a major focus in work with ill parents and their infants. One study that addressed these issues in the same sample found that maternal depression was indeed associated with lower maternal sensitivity and more insecure infant attachment (Hipwell, Goosens, Melhuish, & Kumar, 2000). Still, this report is vague as to whether maternal sensitivity mediated the association of depression and attachment (or even predicted attachment status) while emphasizing the importance of severity of maternal illness. Somewhat related to the issue of sensitivity is that children are more likely to have insecure attachment when mothers have high illusory control – the belief of control over behavior when their input had no effect during a laboratory procedure (Donovan & Leavitt, 1989). Maternal depression is only weakly associated with the insecure attachment outcomes, and thus the interpretation of illusory control as a mediator is suspect.

Maternal depression in the presence of high social-contextual risk is associated with insecure attachment in 2-year-olds (Cicchetti, Rogosch, & Toth, 1998). These children also are more likely to exhibit behavior problems – an instance in which attachment itself functions as a mediator. Chronic family adversity – the presence of multiple social-contextual risks, including maternal depression – is related to children's insecure attachment in another study of risks for early conduct problems (Shaw & Vondra, 1993). Stability of attachment patterns appears related to depression: Children are more likely to shift from secure to insecure (during adolescence) in the context of poverty, maltreatment, and maternal depression (Weinfield, Sroufe, & Egeland, 2000).

Disorganized attachment is associated with the stable presence of mothers' depressive symptoms (Teti, Gelfand, Messinger, & Isabella, 1995). Additional factors of parenting stress and parenting behavior also add to the prediction of disorganization. In a similar vein, highly stressed depressed mothers participating in a home-visiting intervention are less likely to have children with disorganized attachment or with insecure attachment (Lyons-Ruth, Connell, Grunebaum, & Botein, 1990). This intervention was designed to provide emotional and tangible support to the mothers in an effort to ameliorate the parenting stresses of the type identified in Teti et al.'s (1995) work. A counterintuitive finding in the intervention study is that mothers' parenting sensitivity is unrelated to intervention participation. This indicator of parenting behavior is presumed by many to be the strongest predictor of attachment status.

In terms of resilience, these studies of attachment outcomes indicate that in the presence of maternal depression, the absence of other social-contextual risks will protect children from the individual risk of parental illness. Similarly, the resolution of mothers' depressive symptoms will more often result in adaptive relationship functioning of children. Depressed mothers' sensitivity to their infants' interactive behavior may serve as a mechanism that promotes more secure relationship functioning. Lyons-Ruth et al.'s (1990) intervention study provides the strongest evidence of a resilience process in which continuity of a supportive relationship reduces the risk associated with the mothers' psychopathology (akin to the effect on parenting stress in the Teti et al. 1995 study). All of these resilience processes are best viewed as processes in the caregiving system rather than as individual child processes.

It is theoretically attractive to think that the quality of attachment relationships would also serve as protection against risks conferred by parental mental illness. Surprisingly little data exist concerning this proposition. The Ciccetti et al. (1998) and Shaw and Vondra (1995) studies (the latter is described later) are notable exceptions. This state of affairs suggests the possibility that researchers have investigated this point but to date have not found evidence supportive of a resilience process involving attachment security, hence the lack of published material.

Infant Negativity
In contrast to the more organized attachment behaviors, the simple expression of negativity by infants and toddlers is also implicated in risk and resilience processes. Child negativity may be indicative of a constitutional difference in a subset of at-risk children, perhaps identifying the most vulnerable. Negativity may also be significant because of its fundamental importance in the course of everyday parent–child interactions. Interacting with a difficult relationship partner may be the most challenging situation for a young parent. Furthermore, this challenge may be heightened for a parent working with the more limited resources associated with mental illness.

Examination of en-face interactions has been widely used to study interactive processes in the first year of life. This method provides the opportunity to examine the social behavior of infants when the social demands are well identified, as when the procedure includes a period when mothers are instructed to maintain a still face. Furthermore, the procedure lends itself to microanalytic processing, facilitating identification of infants' behavioral and emotional signals to their social partners. The expression of emotion by infants during the still-face procedure is viewed as indicative of adaptive social signaling to an (inappropriately) unresponsive caregiver.

Infants of depressed and well mothers who show little smiling during the still-face procedure have higher rates of externalizing problem behaviors at 18 months of age. Less crying during this procedure is also associated with lower rates of internalizing problem behavior at 18 months. This may indicate that children who continue to signal mothers to engage in normative social discourse, rather than becoming affectively dysregulated, ultimately develop fewer symptoms. These findings were only loosely related to whether or not mothers were depressed, calling into question a strong mediation or multiple predictor interpretation (Moore, Cohn, & Campbell, 2001).

Infant negativity expressed more generally, indexed by measures of temperament, interacts with maternal depression to predict sensitive parenting (Pauli-Pott, Mertesacker, Bade, Bauer, & Beckmann, 2000). Unlike most studies of infant temperament, both mothers and observers provided information about the children, eliminating an important method confound; both measures revealed the same interaction effect. Work in my own laboratory reveals a similar finding in preliminary analyses (unpublished). Associations between maternal depression and parenting sensitivity are moderated by infant negativity; the association is stronger when infants express higher negativity.

In the study by Shaw and Vondra (described previously), girls have more behavior problems at 3 years of age when mothers are depressed and the child had a difficult temperament in infancy. For boys, more behavior problems are associated with the combination of maternal depression and low maternal involvement. Furthermore, insecure attachment is in general associated with later behavior problems (Shaw & Vondra, 1995). Thus, negative emotionality and attachment insecurity both appear to behave as predictors of behavior problems in the context of risk due to maternal depression.

A different approach to negative affect is to examine physiologic correlates in the infants. A pattern of asymmetrical electroencephalographic (EEG) activation has been well established to be related to negative affectivity (Davidson, Schaffer, & Sron, 1985; Fox & Davidson, 1988). Dawson and colleagues found that children of nondepressed mothers show the typical pattern of EEG asymmetry during play, whereas children of depressed mothers do not. During separations from their mother, children of depressed mothers show heightened asymmetric activation. Their behavioral responses are also different: The children of depressed mothers show lower peak distress and longer latency to distress (Dawson, Klinger, Panagiotides, Hill, & Spieker, 1992; see also Dawson, Hessl, & Frey, 1994).

The evidence for resilience in these studies of emotion expression implies that children of depressed mothers who maintain positive emotional states will be more likely to have more positive social and behavioral adjustment. Also, those infants who respond more normatively to the day-to-day perturbations in the flow of parent–child interactions may be less liable to develop behavior problems (although the link to the risk of parental illness is tenuous). Finally, those infants whose EEG activation is consistent with normative patterns may be more likely to exhibit typical behavioral expression of emotion, perhaps reflecting a constitutional bias toward adaptive functioning.

Parenting Behavior

Parenting Sensitivity

Several studies have examined parenting behaviors as predicted by parental mental illness and other factors. When viewed from the perspective of resilience, these studies reflect the type of extension of the classic resilience model I discussed earlier – viewing the outcome as a property of the caregiving system rather than of the child at risk. Many of the studies that lend themselves to a resilience interpretation focus on the construct of parenting sensitivity, which I noted earlier has been viewed as an important predictor of child attachment security.

Findings from the National Institute of Child Health and Human Development (NICHD) study of child care provide evidence regarding maternal depression and parenting sensitivity. Multiple prediction of sensitivity by depression, demographic factors, and infant negativity was identified. Still, there remained independent prediction of sensitivity by depression (NICHD, 1999a). These differences in maternal sensitivity are, in turn, associated with several child outcomes in the preschool period. These outcomes include school readiness, expressive language, verbal comprehension, competent social behavior, and behavior problems. Parenting sensitivity mediates the association between depression and these outcomes; some interactions of small magnitude are found as well (NICHD, 1999b).

Fathers who are alcoholic and depressed are likely to engage in insensitive parenting (Das Eiden, Cavez, & Leonard, 1999). Similar effects have been found for mothers, but there was a smaller number of alcoholic mothers in the study. Taking a slightly different tack, Donovan, Leavitt, & Walsh, (1998) find that sensitivity – defined as the ability to detect infant crying in a signal detection paradigm – is associated with maternal depression, conflict over work and parenting roles, and marital happiness.

There are many studies in which parenting sensitivity functions more as the protective process than as the indicator of developmental outcome. Many of these were reviewed earlier in the discussion of child emotion processing, in which the combination of parental illness and insensitive parenting is associated with poorer child functioning (Hipwell et al., 2000; Pauli-Pott et al., 2000; Teti et al., 1995). With respect to a different child outcome, the combination of maternal depression and insensitive parenting is associated with poorer child cognitive functioning at 18 months and 5 years of age (Murray, Fioru-Cowley, Hooper, & Cooper, 1996a; Murray, Hipwell, Hooper, & Stein, 1996b).

Resilience may be discerned in these studies in that sensitive parenting is less likely to be manifest when depression occurs in isolation. When depression co-occurs with other factors, such as alcoholism, infant negativity, marital distress, or internal conflicts, insensitive parenting is more likely to occur. Parenting sensitivity, in turn, may be viewed as integral to resilience processes when other outcomes are considered (see the preceding discussion regarding the child's emotion processing). Taken together, research on parenting sensitivity points to complex developmental pathways from parental mental illness to positive or negative child outcomes.

Other Parenting Behavior
The language environment parents provide for children affects their cognitive and emotional growth. Although this has not been a major focus in studies of parental illness, two studies are relevant for the present agenda. The content of mothers' speech relevant to their infants in combination with mothers' depression predicts cognitive development in the second year of life (Murray, Kempton, Woolgar, & Hooper, 1993). There is also evidence that depressed mothers do not adjust their speech to their infants, as is typical of most adults, that is, the use of "motherese" or characteristic pacing and intonation of speech (Bettes, 1988). Still another aspect of parent–child interaction is the presence of overt conflict during

social discourse. When such conflict occurs in the context of mothers' depression, there is a higher incidence of behavior problems (Leadbeater, Bishop, & Raver, 1996). The conclusion regarding resilience processes that can be inferred from this work is that parental adjustment to the language contexts of infants and the absence of overt conflict may contribute to positive adjustment in children of ill parents.

Parent Emotion Processing

The vast majority of studies relevant to resilience in young children born to mentally ill parents involve depression. Surprisingly, most of these studies do not address emotion processing in these parents with affective disorders. Still, a few studies do speak to this issue by addressing affective symptoms and family conflict.

One component of emotion processing is the maintenance of affective symptoms associated with the disorder itself. Hostile behavior in school and at home is more frequent in children whose mothers have consistent depression in the first years versus those whose symptoms resolved (Alpern & Lyons-Ruth, 1993). Campbell, Cohn, & Myers (1995) find depression chronicity in the first year of life to be associated with poorer-quality mother–infant interaction. In our own research, we have found that nonspecific aspects of mental illness are associated with child social-emotional and cognitive outcomes (Sameroff, Seifer, & Zax, 1982), with chronicity of illness the most relevant characteristic for the present discussion. In a different study where we examine the issue of symptom maintenance more precisely, mothers' depressive symptoms in the second and third years of life are associated with family functioning as well as child behavior problems (Seifer, Dickstein, Sameroff, Magee, & Hayden, 2001). In both of these studies we find that the nondiagnostic illness parameters predict child behavior after controlling for the presence of a lifetime diagnosis of depression.

When overt conflict in families is examined, the association of depression and intrusive parenting is mediated by this conflict (McElwain & Volling, 1999). This is similar to the finding discussed earlier regarding overt parent–child conflict (Leadbeater et al., 1996). Other studies have examined emotion not in the behavior of ill parents, but in their verbalizations. Expressed emotion (which in prior work has been associated with relapse in ill adults) in combination with maternal depression is associated with intrusive, hostile parenting (Jacobsen, Hibbs, & Ziegenhain, 2000).

Resilience in these studies may again be interpreted as the absence of additional negative features beyond the risk of parental illness. Absence of continuing symptoms, overtly hostile behavior, or verbally expressed hostility may portend more positive development in the children and in the caregiving system.

Parent Cognitions about the Self and the Child

When considering parents' contributions to resilience processes, the focus so far has been on behavior. Another set of findings concerns cognitions that parents have about their child. These cognitions take many forms, ranging from positive or negative feelings about the child, attributions about the child's abilities, and attributions about the parents themselves.

Attributions about the Child

Parents hold strong opinions about the characteristics of their children, and these opinions likely affect the caregiving environment provided for these children. Furthermore, cognitive distortions are often a component of psychopathology. Depressed mothers who perceive their children to be vulnerable have children who are less exploratory and perform worse on standardized developmental tests at 1 year of age (Field et al., 1996). Anxious and depressed mothers perceive their infants to be fussy, hungry, and demanding. These mothers, in turn, have more feeding difficulties and stop breast-feeding earlier than those without negative perceptions (Hellin & Waller, 1992). In a slightly different vein, anxious mothers who perceive their infants as having low intentionality in their behavior themselves evidence less sensitive parenting behavior (Feldman & Reznick, 1996).

Feelings about the Child

The studies described previously focus on parents' understanding of their children's developmental competence. A few studies focus on parents' more immediate emotional responses to their children, perhaps indexing more strongly arousing (and less socially desirable) thoughts and feelings about their children. Unfortunately, the studies only reveal tantalizing clues about whether these are important processes to consider. Parents who are alcoholic and have psychopathology are more often aggravated with their children (Das Eiden & Leonard, 2000). Depressed parents with low social support and poor marital quality may be more susceptible to having less investment in their children (Bradley, Whiteside-Mansell, Brisby, & Caldwell, 1997). Still, these studies reveal little about the consequences of these attributions for child or caregiving system adaptation.

Attributions about the Self

Parents not only have thoughts and feeling about their children, but also a parallel set of cognitions about themselves. Depressed mothers have lower perceived self-efficacy, which in turn is associated with lower behavioral competence with their children (Teti & Gelfand, 1991). Depressed mothers with a low internal locus of control (a component of dysfunctional attributional styles associated with depression) behave in a more controlling style when interacting with their children (Houck, Booth, & Barnard, 1991). A slightly different approach examined mothers who stayed at home with their children but who had a stated preference for being in the work force. Mothers with this attribution about their own roles have higher levels of depression (Hock & DeMeis, 1990). Still another way of viewing parents' attributions is by using the illusory control paradigm described earlier. Depressed parents with higher illusory control have more insecurely attached infants (Donovan & Leavitt, 1989).

In our own work, we have examined an aspect of parents' attributions about the caregiving system based on the construct of goodness of fit. In essence, this attribution concerns the degree to which parents perceive the characteristics of their child (e.g., negative mood, activity level, sleep habits) as being a good or poor fit with their own or their family's expectations for the child. This approach also includes parents' emotional response to these perceived mismatches and the adequacy of their coping strategies. Preliminary analyses of these unpublished data indicate that goodness of fit mediates associations between depression and parenting sensitivity and between depression and child social-emotional competence.

Resilience processes may be inferred from these findings in many ways. In the context of depression, the presence of positive parental cognitions about children portends well for more positive parenting behaviors in the caregiving system, with some evidence of more positive developments in children's social and cognitive development.

SUMMARY AND INTEGRATION

The intergenerational transmission of psychopathology has been a focus of research for over a century. The risk to children when parents have mental illness has been well established. Beyond this simple risk, the degree of consensus in the field begins to decline. Some assert strong specificity in transmission, whereby children are at risk for the specific condition of their parents, often attributed to genetic factors. Others view the evidence as supporting a more varied picture, in which the risks conferred on children are far less specific and not restricted to the realm of mental illness. Instead, a more diverse set of developmental pathways is required to appreciate the manner in which children adapt to their circumstance of having a mentally ill parent (Seifer, 1995).

Developmental Models

When examining familial patterns of mental illness, an increase in the children's incidence of the specific disorder is typically identified in the parent. Still, the children are at risk for many things aside from attaining the same diagnosis as their parent – other mental health problems, school failure, low occupational status, substance abuse, health risk behavior, antisocial behavior, and poor social relationships. Conversely, diverse risks in the parental generation may converge on the same developmental outcome (such as a specific psychopathology diagnosis). From a more quantitative perspective, the findings from many studies of multiple risk factors point to the conclusion that a greater number of risks, regardless of what those risks may be, predicts a wide variety of adverse child outcomes (Burchinal, Roberts, Hooper, & Zeisel, 2000; Sameroff, Seifer, Baldwin, & Baldwin, 1993).

With this backdrop, the examination of infants and preschool children has proceeded within the more inclusive examination of multiple outcomes and processes, if only for the simple reason that diagnosing the syndromes of adult psychopathology makes little sense in children this young. What is also apparent is that many young children with mentally ill parents show no indication of an adverse outcome. As in other areas of research, this has spurred a search for resilience processes to aid understanding of why some children succumb to the risk, whereas others do not (Garmezy, 1985).

In this chapter I have reviewed many studies that may shed light on these issues. How can this set of research findings best be summarized? Several general points can be made. First, few existing studies have been explicitly designed to identify protective processes. Thus, as I have emphasized throughout, there is some degree of inference (beyond that

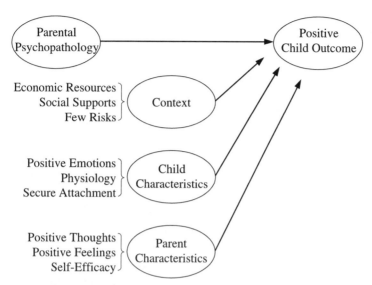

FIGURE 2.1 Resilience processes in young children of mentally ill parents.

normally found in resilience research) when interpreting the studies. Second, the research methods are very diverse. Although not enumerated in the discussion of specific findings, the definition of the initial risk was quite varied, ranging from psychopathology diagnosed by clinicians to self-reported subclinical symptom expression. This may result in some interpretation errors because the different studies reference different populations. Third, many components of the caregiving system may reveal evidence of resilience processes. These range from child attachment, to parenting sensitivity, to attributions parents hold about their children.

From the perspective of identifying specific developmental processes, the pathways to child competence are typically viewed as having many predictors, mediators, and moderators. This is in contrast to the relatively streamlined resilience models, where single protective processes buffer the effects of single risks. Given the multiplicity of research findings I have described in this chapter, it is likely that single-factor models will prove to be insufficient for elucidating resilience in this population of children; this array of forces is depicted in Figure 2.1. The arguments supportive of examining many factors simultaneously in multiple risk models – lack of specificity, accumulation of adversity, and increased predictive power – will likely apply to resilience models as well (Sameroff et al., 1993; Seifer, 1995).

Inferences Regarding Prevention

The relatively abstract presentation of research findings begs the question of what can and should be done to aid the young children known to be at risk because of their parents' psychopathology. Obviously, the best way to answer this question would be in the context of evaluating clinical trials of different prevention approaches designed to reduce the morbidity in this group of children. Unfortunately, little such evidence exists (e.g., Cicchetti, Toth, & Rogosch, 1999). We are thus left with making reasonable inferences from existing research to guide such prevention efforts. Several tentative conclusions can be drawn.

First, it is unlikely that a narrowly focused approach will be successful. Most of the effects noted early in life are small in magnitude and cover a diverse range of functions. Second, short-term approaches will also likely be ineffective. The little available work with mentally ill mothers, as well as other work with high-risk families early in life, suggests that intensive approaches over months or years are required to produce meaningful effects (Cicchetti et al., 1999; Olds et al., 1997). Third, intervention will need to focus on parent–child and family systems. At young ages, children's outcomes are intimately tied to the functioning of their caregivers. As I noted in the review of existing literature, differentiating purely child-focused outcomes does not tell the whole story; focusing on the caregiving system provides more insight into resilience processes. Finally, processes that are promising targets of preventive efforts include affective symptoms of the parent's illness, comorbid problems such as substance abuse, parenting behavior, parents' appraisals of their children, parent and family emotion management, family responses to difficult child behavior, and relationship formation. Also, even though it is not a major focus of many studies, poverty most likely exacerbates all of the difficulties families face in this realm, ranging from increased rates of psychopathology, to more coexisting risk factors, to fewer resources to counteract these multiple risks.

Developing effective preventions is not an easy task, and features peculiar to mentally ill mothers of young children present some unique difficulties. Psychopathology in young mothers is widely recognized as a problem, but important barriers to identifying families in need of assistance remain. Social stigma regarding mental illness continues to exist and may be particularly strong in new mothers, who are generally perceived to have entered a uniquely rewarding phase of their lives. The natural course of affective symptoms in the first year of the child's life also presents barriers. Many (perhaps most) new mothers have an increase in depressive symptoms that typically pass with time. Still, many of these women do in fact experience significant psychopathology, and our current health care system is not designed to have regular contact with new mothers provided by individuals who are well trained to distinguish mental illness from the normative dysphoria associated with childbirth. A related issue is that our health care and social service systems tend to be fragmented, with different components addressing a narrow range of focused problems. An important consequence is that the presence of multiple risk conditions often goes undetected, leaving the most vulnerable families without much-needed assistance. Thus, in addition to developing approaches that are effective in preventing developmental problems in children, we need to become much more sophisticated at identifying mothers who might benefit from such prevention efforts before their children become too old to reap those benefits.

Early Development and Resilience Models

In the end, it is important to consider the question of how well resilience models fit the phenomena under study, ultimately providing guidance about how to assist children at risk. One answer to this question is that the models clearly reveal an important fact – that some children do well despite the adversities that accompany their early development. Another answer is that the models are probably interim aids to our understanding that will eventually need significant updating. The two areas where this is most apparent are (1) the simultaneous handling of multiple influences and (2) the variable-centeredness of the models. Both of these points emphasize the individual pathways that children take through their development. Adequately describing such pathways will ultimately require models more complex than those containing a few variables having more or less the same influences across diverse populations of children.

In summarizing the empirical work, I drew mainly from studies designed from a risk perspective, resulting in findings about negative child/caregiving system outcomes and processes. When making interpretations about resilience, I simply inferred that absence of the negative influences (or presence of the same influences in a positive direction) would result in positive child outcomes. Two potential problems are that this inference might simply be incorrect (since full evidence was not contained in these studies) and that an interpretation of resilience may be suspect if it is based simply on the absence of multiple risks. This issue of multiple factors highlights the point that individual development is a product of the interplay of individual and contextual factors. In fact, one of the difficulties in organizing the research on these young children was differentiating the outcome factors from the protective factors; they were often interchangeable across studies.

A final point to consider is that resilience models are often portrayed as depictions of individuals overcoming externally imposed adversities. The danger in using such an emphasis is to make overly negative attributions about those individuals who do not evidence such success. They may not be the victims of their own weaknesses as much as they are the victims of their multiply risky contexts. Particularly with young children, in whom the distinction between individual characteristics and caregiving-system influences is blurred, inferring internal versus external sources of developmental outcomes can be fraught with error.

Despite some potential shortcomings of the general approach, resilience models continue to provide an important reminder to emphasize positive aspects of individual development that are often neglected in a discipline driven by understanding negative life outcomes (Masten, 2001; Seligman & Czikszentmihalyi, 2000). This positive focus may be particularly important when examining the development of infants and young children, who may be the best candidates for interventions that result from increased understanding of the processes that yield positive outcomes under conditions of risk. The existing data suggest there are many processes amenable to such interventions. But the small effect sizes typical in these studies also suggest that addressing any single process will likely have only a small impact on children's developmental outcomes. Instead, improving the course of children's lives when faced with familial mental illness will likely require multifaceted approaches that address the range of functions examined earlier – relationship quality, emotion regulation (of parents and children), parenting behavior, and parents' attributions about themselves and their children.

References

Alpern, L., & Lyons-Ruth, K. (1993). Preschool children at social risk: Chronicity and timing of maternal depressive symptoms and child behavior problems at school and at home. *Development and Psychopathology, 5,* 371–387.
Bettes, B. A. (1988). Maternal depression and motherese: Temporal and intonational features. *Child Development, 59,* 1089–1096.
Bradley, R. H., Whiteside-Mansell, L., Brisby, J. A., & Caldwell, B. M. (1997). Parents' socioemotional investment in children. *Journal of Marriage and the Family, 59,* 77–90.

Burchinal, M. R., Roberts, J. E., Hooper, S., & Zeisel, S. A. (2000). Cumulative risk and early cognitive development: A comparison of statistical risk models. *Developmental Psychology, 36*, 793–807.

Campbell, S. D., Cohn, J. F., & Meyers, T. (1995). Depression in first-time mothers: Mother–infant interaction and depression chronicity. *Developmental Psychology, 31*, 349–357.

Cicchetti, D., Rogosch, F. A., & Toth, S. L. (1998). Maternal depressive disorder and contextual risk: Contributions to the development of attachment insecurity and behavior problems in toddlerhood. *Development and Psychopathology, 10*, 283–300.

Cicchetti, D., Toth, S. L., & Rogosch, F. A. (1999). The effectiveness of toddler–parent pschotherapy to increase attachment security in offspring of depressed mothers. *Attachment and Human Development, 1*, 34–66.

Das Eiden, R., Cavez, F., & Leonard, K. E. (1999). Parent–infant interactions among families with alcoholic fathers. *Development and Psychopathology, 11*, 745–762.

Das Eiden, R., & Leonard, K. E. (2000). Paternal alcoholism, parental psychopathology, and aggravation with infants. *Journal of Substance Abuse, 11*, 17–29.

Davidson, R. J., Schaffer, C. E., & Sron, C. (1985). Effects of lateralized presentation of faces on self-reports of emotion and EEG asymmetry in depressed and non-depressed subjects. *Psychophysiology, 22*, 353–364.

Dawson, G., Hessl, D., & Frey, K. (1994). Social influences on early developing biological and behavioral systems related to risk for affective disorder. *Development and Psychopathology, 6*, 759–779.

Dawson, G., Klinger, L. G., Panagiotides, H., Hill, D., & Spieker, S. (1992). Frontal lobe activity and affective behavior of infants of mothers with depressive symptoms. *Child Development, 63*, 725–737.

Donovan, W. L., & Leavitt, L. A. (1989). Maternal self-efficacy and infant attachment: Integrating physiology, perceptions, and behavior. *Child Development, 60*, 460–472.

Donovan, W. L., Leavitt, L. A., & Walsh, R. O. (1998). Conflict and depression predict maternal sensitivity to infant cries. *Infant Behavior and Development, 21*, 505–517.

Feldman, R., & Reznick, J. S. (1996). Maternal perception of infant intentionality at 4 and 8 motnhs. *Infant Behavior and Development, 19*, 483–496.

Field, T., Estroff, D. B., Yando, R., del Valle, C., Malphurs, J., & Hart, S. (1996). Depressed mothers' perceptions of infant vulnerability are related to later development. *Child Psychiatry and Human Development, 27*, 43–53.

Fox, N. A., & Davidson, R. J. (1988). Patterns of brain electrical activity during facial sign of emotion in 10-month-old infants. *Developmental Psychology, 24*, 230–236.

Garmezy, N. (1985). Stress-resistant children: The search for protective factors. In J. E. Stevenson (Ed.), *Recent research in developmental psychopathology* (pp. 213–233). Oxford: Pergamon Press.

Hellin, K., & Waller, G. (1992). Mothers' mood and infant feeding: Prediction of problems and practices. *Journal of Reproductive and Infant Psychology, 10*, 39–51.

Hipwell, A. E., Goosens, E. C., Melhuish, E. C., & Kumar, R. (2000). Severe maternal psychopathology and infant–mother attachment. *Development and Psychopathology, 12,* 157–175.

Hock, E., & DeMeis, D. K. (1990). Depression in mothers of infants: The role of maternal employment. *Developmental Psychology, 26,* 285–291.

Houck, G. M., Booth, C. L., & Barnard, K. E. (1991). Maternal depression and locus of control orientation as predictors of dyadic play behavior. *Infant Mental Health Journal, 12,* 347–360.

Jacobsen, T., Hibbs, E., & Ziegenhain, U. (2000). Expressed emotion related to attachment disorganization in early childhood: A preliminary report. *Journal of Child Psychology and Psychiatry and Allied Disciplines, 41,* 899–906.

Leadbeater, B. J., Bishop, S. J., & Raver, C. C. (1996). Quality of mother–toddler interactions, maternal depressive symptoms, and behavior problems in preschoolers of adolescent mothers. *Developmental Psychology, 32,* 280–288.

Luthar, S. S., Cicchetti, D., & Becker, B. (2000). The construct of resilience: A critical evaluation and guidelines for future work. *Child Development, 71,* 543–562.

Lyons-Ruth, K., Connell, D. B., Grunebaum, H. U., & Botein. (1990). Infants at social risk: Maternal depression and family support services as mediators of infant developments and security of attachment. *Child Development, 61,* 85–98.

Masten, A. (2001). Ordinary magic: Resilience processes in development. *American Psychologist, 56,* 227–238.

McElwain, N. L., & Volling, B. L. (1999). Depressed mood and marital conflict: Relations to maternal and paternal intrusiveness with one-year-old infants. *Journal of Applied Developmental Psychology, 20,* 63–83.

Moore, G. A., Cohn, J. F., & Campbell, S. B. (2001). Infant affective responses to mother's still face at 6 months differentially predict externalizing and internalizing behaviors at 18 months. *Developmental Psychology, 37,* 706–714.

Murray, L., Fioru-Cowley, A., Hooper, R., & Cooper, P. (1996a). The impact of postnatal depression and associated adversity on early mother–infant interactions and later outcomes. *Child Development, 67,* 2512–2526.

Murray, L., Hipwell, A., Hooper, R., & Stein, A. (1996b). The cognitive development of 5-year-old children of postnatally depressed mothers. *Journal of Child Psyhology and Psychiatry and Allied Disciplines, 37,* 927–935.

Murray, L., Kempton, C., Woolgar, M., & Hooper, R. (1993). Depressed mothers' speech to their infants and its relation to infant gender and cognitive development. *Journal of Child Psychology and Psychiatry and Allied Disciplines, 34,* 1083–1101.

NICHD Early Child Care Research Network. (1999a). Child care and mother–child interaction in the first 3 years of life. *Developmental Psychology, 35,* 1399–1413.

NICHD Early Child Care Research Network. (1999b). Chronicity of maternal depressive symptoms, maternal sensitivity, and child functioning at 36 months. *Developmental Psychology, 35,* 1297–1310.

Olds, D. L., Eckenrode, J., Henderson, C. R., Jr., Kitzman, H., Powers, J., Cole, R., Sidora, K., Morris, P., Pettitt, L. M., & Luckey, D. (1997). Long-term effects of home visitation on maternal life course and child abuse and neglect: Fifteen-year follow-up of a randomized trial. *Journal of the American Medical Association, 278*(8), 637–743.

Pauli-Pott, U., Mertesacker, B., Bade, U., Bauer, C., & Beckmann, D. (2000). Contexts of relations of infant negative emotionality and caregiver's reactivity/ sensitivity. *Infant Behavior and Development, 23,* 23–39.

Rutter, M. (1987). Psychosocial resilience and protective mechanisms. *American Journal of Orthopsychiatry, 57,* 316–331.

Sameroff, A. J., & Emde, R. N. (1989). *Relationship disturbances in early childhood: A developmental approach.* New York: Basic Books.

Sameroff, A. J., Seifer, R., Baldwin, A., & Baldwin, C. P. (1993). Stability of intelligence from preschool to adolescence: The influence of social and family risk factors. *Child Development, 64,* 80–97.

Sameroff, A. J., Seifer, R., & Zax, M. (1982). Early development of children at risk for emotional disorder. *Monographs of the Society for Research in Child Development, 47* (serial no. 199).

Seifer, R. (1995). Perils and pitfalls of high risk research. *Developmental Psychology, 31,* 420–424.

Seifer, R., & Dickstein, S. (2000). Parental mental illness and infant development. In C. Zeanah (Ed.), *Handbook of infant mental health* (2nd ed., pp. 145–160). New York: Guilford Press.

Seifer, R., Dickstein, S., Sameroff, A. J., Magee, K. D., & Hayden, L. C. (2001). Infant mental health and variability of parental depressive symptoms. *Journal of the American Academy of Child and Adolescent Psychiatry, 40,* 1375–1382.

Seligman, M. E. P., & Czikszentmihalyi, M. (2000). Positive psychology: An introduction. *American Psychologist, 55,* 5–14.

Shaw, D. S., & Vondra, J. I. (1993). Chronic family adversity and infant attachment security. *Journal of Child Psychology and Psychiatry, 34,* 1205–1215.

Shaw, D. S., & Vondra, J. I. (1995). Infant attachment security and maternal predictors of early behavior problems: A longitudinal study of low-income families. *Journal of Abnormal Child Psychology, 23*(3), 335–357.

Teti, D. M., & Gelfand, D. M. (1991). Behavioral competence among mothers of infants in the first year: The mediational role of maternal self-efficacy. *Child Development, 62,* 918–929.

Teti, D. M., Gelfand, D. M., Messinger, D. S., & Isabella, R. (1995). Maternal depression and the quality of early attachment: An examination of infants, preschoolers, and their mothers. *Developmental Psychology, 31,* 364–376.

Weinfield, N. S., Sroufe, L. A., & Egeland, B. (2000). Attachment from infancy to early adulthood in a high-risk sample: Continuity, discontinuity, and their correlates. *Child Development, 71,* 695–702.

Zero to Three/National Center for Clinical Infant Programs. (1995). *Diagnostic Classification: 0–3.* Arlington, VA: Zero To Three/National Center for Clinical Infant Programs.

3

Risk and Protective Factors for Children of Depressed Parents

Constance Hammen

It is now well established that depression runs in families and that maternal depression may be associated with a variety of maladaptive outcomes in children. Because of the high frequency of depression worldwide – especially among women of child-bearing age (e.g., Weissman & Olfson, 1995), this is a high-risk problem of considerable magnitude, and one with the potential for transmission through multiple generations. The topic of resilience, however, has been relatively neglected despite the fact that many, if not most, offspring of depressed parents do not apparently suffer major negative consequences – and despite the potential yield of preventive interventions for children at risk. This chapter will explore the contribution of the mood disorders field to resilience research, following a brief analysis of the depression high-risk research and a discussion of risk and protective factors and mechanisms. Finally, implications and directions for future research and intervention will be presented.

NEGATIVE OUTCOMES OF CHILDREN OF DEPRESSED PARENTS

There has been considerable research in the past 15–20 years that demonstrates the negative consequences of parental depression for children.[1] Despite the solid empirical base establishing risk to children, remarkably little research has answered, or even explored, many key questions concerning the phenomena and the mechanisms, much less issues concerning resilience. Heterogeneity in many of the key constructs is one important source of the limited conclusions to date, and therefore several definitional problems are noted prior to a summary of the research on children's outcomes. Suggestions for further research to address these gaps are presented near the end of the chapter.

Defining Constructs in Studies of Children of Depressed Parents

In the vast majority of studies, the focus has been on *maternal* depression, not only because depressed women are more numerous in both clinical and community studies, but also because they are more likely to serve as the primary caretaker and may also be more accessible for research participation. Fathers' depression status appears to confer similar risks (e.g., Weissman, Fendrich, Warner, & Wickramaratne, 1992) but has been less frequently investigated.

The construct of depression is complex, and studies have varied considerably in defining maternal depression by diagnostic criteria (e.g., major depression) or by self-reported symptoms that may or may not be persistent, impairing, or specific to depressive disorders. Typically, little information is provided about the features of depression however defined, such as whether it is recurrent, its age of onset, and its severity. Moreover, studies have differed in the kinds of populations studied, with many employing clinical treatment-seeking samples and others based on community samples or specific subsamples varying by socioeconomic status. The heterogeneity of the definitions of depression occurring in the context of different samples introduces considerable noise into the attempts to refine models of mechanisms of risk. Nonetheless, the relatively consistent findings of negative impact on children despite variously defined maternal depression is noteworthy.

Children's outcomes in high-risk studies have been defined to some extent by children's age. Research on infants and young children, accordingly, has included diverse cognitive and social-emotional indices of development and functioning. Older children have been more likely to be characterized by the presence or absence of diagnoses of depressive or other disorders. Unfortunately, such a focus has restricted the range of children's characteristics and functioning that would permit fuller exploration of constructs of resilience and adaptation.

Outcomes of Children of Depressed Parents

As noted, depression high-risk research has variously referred to self-reported symptoms or to depression syndromes in community samples or in treatment-seeking populations. To some extent, these populations also tend to differ in the ages of children studied. The following sections are organized by child age. They represent a *selective* review, with a particular focus on major and more recent studies.

Studies of Infants and Young Children

Studies of infants and young children who are offspring of depressed parents have yielded complex results, in part because the methods of assessing outcomes are heterogeneous, as noted previously, lacking a universal standard for comparison such as the diagnostic criteria of the DSM. Also, the samples have varied greatly in the operational definitions of maternal depression, as noted previously. In lieu of a detailed analysis of such diverse studies, therefore, several general observations may be made (and see Cummings & Davies, 1994; Downey & Coyne, 1990; Gelfand & Teti, 1990, for more detailed reviews). First, there appears to be evidence of relative deficits in cognitive performance in infants and young children of depressed mothers (e.g., Brennan, Hammen, Andersen, Bor, Najman, & Williams, 2000; NICHD Early Child Care Research Network, 1999). Second, various studies indicate an array of dysfunctions in socioemotional and behavioral regulation in infants and toddlers (e.g., Brennan et al., 2001; Cohn, Matias, Tronick, Lyons-Ruth, & Connell, 1986; Cox, Puckering, Pound, & Mills, 1987; NICHD Early Child Care Research Network, 1999; Zahn-Waxler, McKnew, Cummings, Davenport, & Radke-Yarrow, 1984). Such impairments may also take the form of insecure or disordered attachment (e.g., Lyons-Ruth, Zoll, Connell, & Gruenbaum, 1986; Teti, Gelfand, Messinger, & Isabella, 1995). Third, some infants and toddlers with depressed mothers appear to exhibit potential neuroregulatory patterns that might reflect dysfunctions in stress responsivity and approach-related behaviors (e.g., Dawson, Hessl, & Frey, 1994; Field, Fox, Pickens, & Nawrocki, 1995).

Studies of School-Age Children and Adolescents

The benchmark studies of offspring of depressed parents have emphasized the diagnostic status of children of at least school age, based on both direct clinical interviews of the child and parent, using case-control designs. Much of this research has been reviewed elsewhere (e.g., Beardslee, Versage, & Gladstone, 1998; Downey & Coyne, 1990; Hammen, 1999). The studies consistently indicate high rates of major depressive disorder in offspring of *treatment-seeking* parents, ranging from 45% in 8- to 16-year-olds in Hammen, Burge, Burney, and Adrian (1990), to 38% among 6- to 23-year-olds in Weissman et al. (1987), to 20–24% in other samples studied (e.g., Beardslee et al., 1998; Goodman, Adamson, Riniti, & Cole, 1994). In contrast, children of comparison families reported depression rates of 4–24%, depending on the sample ages. Wickramaratne and Weissman (1998) noted that parental depression is associated with an eight-fold increase in childhood onset of depression and a five-fold increase in early adult onset of depression compared to a control group of nondepressed families. Rates of other disorders are also significantly elevated compared to those of control groups and include anxiety disorders, disruptive behavioral disorders, and substance use disorders. For instance, rates of *any diagnosis* ranged from 65% to 82% across the studies noted. Two studies that followed the offspring longitudinally also found that depressive disorders were likely to recur, and that the offspring continued to be impaired in social and other role functioning (e.g., Hammen et al., 1990; Weissman, Warner, Wickramaratne, Moreau, & Olfson, 1997).

Studies based on community or nonreferred populations are rare but informative, because they presumably reflect the much more prevalent forms and impact of parental depressive disorders. Beardslee et al. (1993) reported a rate of 26% of major depressive disorder in the children of depressed parents seen in a health maintenance (medical) organization compared with 10% in children of well parents (average age, 18). Similarly, Hammen and Brennan (2001) found a rate of 20% of major depressive disorder in 15-year-old offspring of untreated depressed mothers in an Australian community compared to 10% among control families. Additionally, both samples found significantly higher rates of nonaffective disorders in the children of depressed parents.

Overall, therefore, the risk of major depression is more than twice as high in children of depressed parents, and may be even higher among parents with more severe disorders who seek treatment. Nonaffective disorders and functional impairments are also noted, and limited follow-up data suggest continued dysfunction over time.

VULNERABILITY AND PROTECTIVE FACTORS FOR CHILDREN AT RISK FOR DEPRESSION

Mediators of Risk

The major domains of investigation of risk factors have included genetic/biological variables, family environment factors including both quality of parental relationships and relationships between the depressed

parent and the child, and external environment factors including socioeconomic conditions and stressful life events.

Genetic and Biological Risk Factors

Most of the initial case-control studies of children of depressed parents
were implicitly based on a model of genetic vulnerability, and indeed,
there continues to be a strong presumption of a heritable component.
Depression undeniably runs in families. Many studies of the first-degree
relatives of depressed patients have reported rates of depression ranging between 7% and 30% across studies – considerably in excess of the
rates in the general population (Gershon, 1990; Winokur, Coryell, Keller,
Endicott, & Leon, 1995). Genetic strategies that are less confounded with
environmental factors than are family studies are also suggestive. Twin
studies using biometric model-testing analyses are consistent with moderate heritability in both community and clinical samples (e.g., Kendler,
Neale, Kessler, Heath, & Eaves, 1992; Kendler & Prescott, 1999; McGuffin,
Katz, Watkins, & Rutherford, 1996). To date, there is no consensus on
whether more severe forms of depression are especially likely to be
genetically related (e.g., Kendler, Gardner, & Prescott, 1999; Lyons et al.,
1998; McGuffin, Katz, Watkins, & Rutherford, 1996). Overall, the genetic
effects appear to be significant but account for less variance than nongenetic factors, and there is no evidence of a single depressive gene or
defect – and likely never will be, given the apparent heterogeneity of depression and the multiple causal pathways. Also, it is not at all clear what
it is that may be transmitted – abnormal biological stress responses, negative affectivity, deficits in emotion regulation, or others. As Goodman
and Gotlib (1999) point out, environmental variables such as parenting
quality, life stress, and marital conflict that increase children's risk of depression may themselves be heritable (e.g., Plomin, Reiss, Hetherington,
& Howe, 1994).

Numerous biological processes such as abnormalities in brain structure and function, neurotransmitter processes, and neurohormonal processes have been studied as possible mechanisms of depression vulnerability; a full review is beyond the scope of this chapter. It has been speculated
that infants of depressed mothers may be born with – or acquire through
maladaptive parenting and stress exposure – dysfunctional neuroregulatory processes essential to emotion regulation (e.g., Goodman & Gotlib,
1999). A particularly active and promising line of research links preclin-
ical and developmental studies in a focus on the role of stress (or inherited stress reactivity) on the developing brain. Abnormal processes of

cortisol and other neurohormones of the hypothalamic-pituitary-adrenal axis may serve as risk markers for dysfunctions in stress reactivity. The impact on the developing brain during prenatal and early life of severely stressful events may sensitize the individual biologically in ways that lead to depressive reactions even when stress precipitants are relatively mild (e.g., see Ladd et al., 2000; Plotsky, Owens, & Nemeroff, 1998; Post, 1992). If genetic and neurohormonal studies proceed to the point of identifying markers of vulnerability, the opportunity for more fully elaborating precise psychosocial mechanisms of risk and resilience will be greatly improved.

Quality of the Parent–Child Relationship
Apart from genetic mechanisms of risk, parenting behaviors have provided the most obvious focus of study of the impact of parental depression on children. The nature and quality of parenting behaviors have been studied extensively in samples of varying ages using diverse observational methods. According to a review by Lovejoy, Graczyk, O'Hare, and Neuman (2000), three variables have been identified that represent the focus of most studies: negative/hostile interactions (negative affect, criticism, negative facial expression), positive behaviors (pleasant affect, praise, affectionate contact), and disengagement (ignoring, withdrawal, silence, gaze aversion). A meta-analysis of 46 somewhat overlapping studies found several significant patterns (Lovejoy et al., 2000). Overall, depressed mothers differed from nondepressed mothers, displaying more negative and disengaged behaviors, associated with moderate effect sizes; depressed mothers were less positive, described by small effect sizes. These patterns were further explored in tests of the effects of variables that moderated effects of mothers' depression on their parenting behaviors, including timing of depression (current or lifetime), socioeconomic status, nature of the depression assessed, child age, and type of observation. Negative interactions were more pronounced among currently depressed women compared to those with lifetime diagnoses, but no other moderators were significant in relation to negative behaviors. Disengagement behaviors were not moderated by any of the key variables, and positive behaviors were most notably moderated by socioeconomic status and age of the child. Among disadvantaged women, the association between maternal depression and (low) positive interaction was moderate, but there was no association among nondisadvantaged women. The association of maternal depression and low positive interaction was moderate for mothers of infants and small for mothers of

toddlers and preschoolers. It should be noted that the analyses did not contain enough samples of children 6 years of age and older to include in the comparison (Lovejoy et al., 2000).

Overall, these analyses indicate a consistent pattern linking maternal depression to maladaptive parenting behaviors, confirming prior reviews (e.g., Cummings & Davies, 1994). However, relatively few studies have gone beyond this observation to establish parenting behaviors as the mechanism linking parental depression and children's disorders or to clarify the processes by which they affect children's outcomes. It is speculated that there are multiple developmentally specific consequences of dysfunctional parenting that contribute to maladjustment in youngsters. In the case of maternal depression, it might be that the negative consequences are especially pronounced because of the unique ways in which depression disrupts effective parenting. For example, Goodman and Gotlib (1999) have suggested several potential consequences of depression-related maladaptive parenting: negative or unresponsive behaviors leading to insecure attachment or poor emotional self-regulation, as well as less stimulation and contingent responding that result in suboptimal cognitive development. Negative or disengaged interactions may also discourage the acquisition of important interpersonal skills and problem-solving abilities that may leave children with poor coping skills and dysfunctional cognitions about themselves and others, eventually leading to depressive reactions or impaired social functioning.

There is some evidence from observational studies that dysfunctional styles of parent–infant or parent–child interaction are, indeed, associated with maladaptive social skills, attachment, cognitions about the self, and other indicators of impairment that might eventuate in depression (e.g., Goodman, Brogan, Lynch, & Fielding, 1993; Jaenicke et al., 1987; NICHD Early Child Care Research Network, 1999; Teti et al., 1995). In addition to cross-sectional studies, a few longitudinal analyses indicate that poor quality of parent–child interactions predicted disorders and dysfunction over time (e.g., Hammen, Burge, & Stansbury, 1990; NICHD Early Child Care Research Network, 1999).

Overall, therefore, the evidence is relatively strong regarding the links between maternal depression and parent–child interaction difficulties, on the one hand, and between the latter and impairment in various aspects of children's behaviors, on the other hand. However, more work is needed to clarify the processes and mechanisms – as well as the question of their specificity to parental depression or depressive outcomes in offspring.

Marital Factors and Children's Risk

Three interrelated aspects of family structure are presumed to be associated with children's risk in families with a depressed parent: marital conflict, divorce, and psychiatric disorder in the nondepressed parent. Ample evidence attests to the nonspecific negative effects of marital conflict on children (see the chapters by Hetherington and Elmore and by Sandler et al. in this volume). Divorce and marital discord are frequently observed among depressed individuals (e.g., Bruce & Kim, 1992; Gotlib & Lee, 1990). As Goodman and Gotlib (1999) have pointed out, marital hostility may mediate the association between parental illness and children's maladjustment (see also Downey & Coyne, 1990). Recently, evidence has accumulated to support Merikangas's (1984) original observation of *assortative mating* among depressed patients. Several studies have shown that depressed women commonly have children with men whose own psychiatric histories show elevated rates of disorder (Brennan, Hammen, Katz, & LeBrocque, in press; Goodman et al., 1993; Hammen, 1991a). Although it is conceivable that fathers' disorders are a direct cause of dysfunction in the children of depressed women (e.g., via genetic mechanisms), it is even more likely that paternal psychopathology increases marital discord, family stress, and disruption that affect children's outcomes.

Although the three overlapping factors of marital distress, divorce, and partner disorder may exert important influences on the outcomes of children in families with a depressed parent, the mechanisms of action remain to be clarified. Each of these variables may affect the extent to which the coparent is available both physically and emotionally; single- or dual-parent families might differentially expose the children to adverse economic conditions and other sources of stress. Certainly, marital discord exposes children to stressful conditions that affect their own sense of worth and efficacy, but it may also teach maladaptive methods of resolving interpersonal conflict. Thus, a cascade of environmental challenges, maladaptive learning experiences, and emotionally wrenching occurrences may also affect the children's likelihood of developing disorders and impaired functioning.

To date, only a few studies have specifically examined the role of marital discord as a possible factor in the association between parental depression and children's negative outcomes. Fendrich, Warner, and Weissman (1990) and Goodman et al. (1993) found that marital conflict appeared to exacerbate the effects of parental depression on children's outcomes. Davies, Dumenci, and Windle (1999) found that maternal depressive

symptoms served as a mediator of the effects of marital distress on adolescent depressive symptoms, whereas marital distress was the mediator
of the effects of maternal depression on youth externalizing symptoms.
Fendrich et al. (1990) also reported different effects of parental variables on children's depressive versus conduct disorders, reminding us
that different predictors may be associated with different youth outcome
variables.

Stressful Life Events and Conditions
Marital conflict and divorce are prime examples of stressful circumstances
that help to account for children's risk as a function of parental depression. Additional stressors may be highly elevated in families of depressed
parents, conferring risk to children who may already have dysfunctional
coping skills. Even appropriate coping skills might prove to be inadequate to contend with the chronic and episodic stressors of depressed
families (e.g., Hammen, Burge, & Adrian, 1991). The depression itself
is commonly accompanied by financial, health, marital, and general interpersonal difficulties, due both to the consequences of depression and
to stable conditions that might have given rise to the parent's depression. Hammen et al. (1987) found that chronic stress in the family was a
unique predictor of children's adjustment and symptoms, even beyond
the effects of the mother's symptoms and history of mood disorder. In addition, it appears that depressed adults – and their offspring – "generate"
stressful life events in the sense of experiencing elevated rates of stressors
to which they have at least partly contributed (e.g., Adrian & Hammen,
1993; Hammen, 1991b). Stressors and stressful conditions are, of course,
among the most reliable precipitants of depressive reactions in adults
and presumably also in children (e.g., Brown & Harris, 1989). Thus, the
occurrence of stressors – especially as moderated by coping capabilities –
may play an important role in the outcomes of children of depressed
parents.

Methodologically, many studies have tended to emphasize single or a
few predictive variables. However, several investigations have evaluated
multiple risk factors and the role of parental depression. Many of these
models are based on the assumption that it is not parental depression as
such, but rather depression in the context of correlated risk factors, that
accounts for children's maladaptive outcomes. The findings of such studies are of great interest but yield a somewhat confusing picture of the role
of depression as such, based on different methods, samples, and conclusions. For example, Canino, Bird, Rudio-Stipec, Bravo, & Alegria (1990)

concluded that parental psychopathology contributed to children's dysfunction beyond that associated with stress and marital conflict (and argued that the latter risk factors "mediated" the effect of parental pathology, although they did not actually test for mediation in a statistical sense). Harnish, Dodge, and Valente (1995) found that observed parent–child interactions partially mediated the effects of maternal depression on children's behavior problems, taking into account the effects of socioeconomic status. In different clinical samples, Weissman and her colleagues (Fendrich et al., 1990; Warner, Mufson, & Weissman, 1995) generally found limited effects of family risk factors (such as marital discord or "chaotic family environment") compared to parental major depression contributing to offspring major depression – though their statistical analyses do not provide straightforward comparative tests. Goodman et al. (1993) generally found that children's poor social and emotional competence was related to fathers' psychiatric status and parents' marital status; maternal depression alone in the absence of other such risk factors was minimally related to children's outcomes. Seifer et al. (1996) found that maternal depressed mood and adaptive functioning (though not diagnosis) predicted infant social competence beyond that contributed by an aggregate measure of contextual risks (e.g., life events, socioeconomic adversity, father absence, and others). Recently, Brennan et al. (2001) found that the combination of mother depression and father substance abuse was especially predictive of depression in the adolescent offspring, mediated by family stress and negative father–child relations.

Taken together, these studies provide generally positive support for a multiple risk factor approach to children's outcomes, but they are mixed with respect to the contributions of parental depression. Moreover, all of the studies are cross-sectional, leaving the question of direction of effects unresolved. Only a small number of longitudinal studies have addressed the role of parental depression in a multiple risk factor model. Fergusson, Horwood, and Lynskey (1995) studied adolescents' depressive symptoms as a function of maternal factors examined over a 13-year period. They concluded that although maternal depression was related to daughters' (but not sons') depression, the effect was explained by the association of depression and social context factors. Thus, maternal depression did not contribute to girls' depression beyond effects due to adversity. Billings and Moos (1985), using one of the very first multiple risk factor models, addressed the issue indirectly, concluding that social and family risk factors were associated with maladaptive outcomes in offspring of depressed parents even when the parents were no longer depressed. Finally,

Hammen (1991a) found support for a general model of offspring outcomes over time as a function of parental disorder, adversity, and quality of parent–child relationships.

Vulnerability and Protective Factors

Although it is apparent that many offspring of depressed parents do not suffer ill effects, characterizing the complexity previously described in efforts to understand negative outcomes has taken precedence over studies of why and under what conditions some children are healthy and well adjusted. Nevertheless, despite limited research, there are several potentially fruitful lines of investigation that merit pursuit.

Protective/Risk Factors in Main Effects Analyses

Complexities in the definitions of key terms have often been noted in the resilience literature. Is the absence or low level of a risk factor a protective factor? Is the absence of a protective factor a risk factor? A related conceptual issue is the blurring of the distinction between dependent and independent variables. Thus, for example, the construct of social competence may be viewed as a protective factor, but it could also be an outcome, depending on the research questions and context. Investigators have sometimes made distinctions between *main effects* and interaction models of resilience. The field of depression high-risk research has not particularly weighed in on the definitional matters in general or approached the empirical questions frequently. Nevertheless, the existing research provides potentially important clues about the conditions under which children appear to be protected (or at greater risk) if exposed to parental depression.

Although most of the multiple risk factor studies reviewed earlier have been oriented toward predicting children's adverse outcomes, it could be inferred that low levels of key negative variables are associated with better child outcomes. That is, low levels of the risk factors even in the presence of maternal depression might be associated with a reduced likelihood that the children will have maladaptive outcomes. Thus, one version of a main effects or risk-variable counting approach suggests that less negative or more positive mother–child interactions, less marital discord, intact family, and less family chronic and episodic stress predict better (less negative) outcomes for children. As noted previously, for example, children's outcomes have been shown to be affected by the quality of the parenting relationship (e.g., Lovejoy et al., 2000), by stressors such as divorce and marital conflict, and by chronic economic, health, and relationships adversity (e.g., Fergusson et al., 1995; Hammen et al., 1987; Seifer et al., 1996).

A related but slightly different strategy has been to identify characteristics of the child or the family environment that are not simply an absence of risk factors, but are thought to contribute directly to healthy and adaptive functioning. Based on general theories of youth resilience or specifically on models of depression, such approaches have speculated that intelligence, a positive self-concept, cognitive and behavioral coping skills, good school functioning, positive social relationships or friendships, or supportive adult relationships, for example, may protect the child (e.g., reviewed in Conrad & Hammen, 1993).

There has been relatively limited study of such personal protective factors in depressed families. Early work by Beardslee and Podorefsky (1988) on a small sample of resilient offspring of depressed parents found that they were characterized by "high self-understanding," which included awareness of the parent's depressive illness and the ability to remain psychologically separated from it, as well as deep involvement in school and extracurricular activities. Radke-Yarrow and Sherman (1990) evaluated the effects of three hypothesized protective factors: high intelligence, social charm, and what they termed a *match* between a child characteristic and a parental need (e.g., being a boy if that was what the parent really valued). Exploratory analyses in a small sample tended to support their hypotheses, suggesting ideas for further, more systematic study.

Hammen (1991a) defined seven variables as potentially protective for children at risk for mood disorders: positive self-concept, social competence, good academic performance, low current maternal depression, low chronic stress in the family, absence of paternal diagnosis, and father present in the home. Results indicated a significant linear association between number of protective factors and less severe (or absence of) diagnosable depression (as well as fewer of any diagnosable conditions).

Interaction Models to Predict Resilience in High-Risk Children
Another approach to resilience in the face of adversity has been to demonstrate that the protective factor interacts with the risk factor such that it has an effect on those at high risk but no or little effect on those at low risk (e.g., Garmezy, Masten, & Tellegen, 1984; Rutter, 1990). Conrad and Hammen (1993) argued that if the factor has positive effects on both groups, it might be better termed a *resource* factor rather than a *protective* factor. This approach rarely has been employed to date in depression

high-risk research. Conrad and Hammen (1993) adopted this approach in analyses with a small sample of women with recurrent unipolar depression, non-ill women, and their 8- to 16-year-old children. Nine variables were studied that were available in the overall project and that had been identified in previous studies of resilience in children exposed to adversity, and they were entered in separate regression analyses, with the interaction term, to predict children's diagnostic status. Only one variable was considered to be a protective factor, evidenced by a significant interaction with maternal depression status; children's higher social competence was more closely associated with better diagnostic outcomes for the high-risk children compared with those at low risk. Additionally, several variables were deemed resource factors – main effects predictors of outcome: self-concept, academic performance, positive perceptions of the mother's parenting behaviors, maternal social competence, the mother currently married to a non-ill father, and the child's having contact with adult friends (children's friendships were marginally significantly predictive).

A conceptually similar design to identify possible protective factors for children of depressed mothers was employed by Garber and Little (1999). These investigators identified a subsample of "competent" adolescent offspring, defined as having no current or lifetime history of disorder and parent, teacher, and child symptom and behavioral ratings in the normal range and with normal global functioning scores. Fifty-one of 185 offspring of depressed women were so defined. Over a 2-year period during the transition to junior high school, 18 of these children developed diagnosable disorders and 33 remained well. Analyses compared these two competence groups. The main findings were that the youth who remained competent compared with those who developed difficulties were initially more committed to academic achievement, had more positive coping skills, reported more family cohesion and less conflict, rated their mothers as more accepting, and reported more support from parents, relatives, and friends. Notably also, the stably competent offspring did *not* differ in IQ, academic ability, positive self-concept, attribution style, or actual social competence. Specifically attempting to account for processes of resilience in the face of adversity among the high-competence children, Garber and Little (1999) also examined moderators of school stress, which is generally elevated in the transition to junior high school. They found a significant interaction such that high-competence youth experiencing high levels of stress were significantly more committed to achievement and reported a more positive family environment. Coping style and reported social support, on the other hand, did not moderate the association between school problems and competence.

The National Institute of Child Health and Human Development (NICHD) study is an elegant example of attempts to clarify processes linking maternal depression and children's outcomes over a longitudinal course, evaluating the quality of mother–child interaction as a moderator. This study found that observed sensitivity of depressed women to their infants moderated the effects of the depression in that relatively more sensitive and responsive women who presumably had better-quality relations with their children and talked more with them had children with better language development and fewer behavioral problems at 36 months (NICHD Early Child Care Research Network, 1999).

LIMITS OF RESILIENT ADAPTATION

Among offspring at risk due to parental depression, the risk period for developing depressive disorders may span many years. Therefore, a child who has not shown evidence of depression by early adolescence may nonetheless continue to be at risk for depression through early adulthood – and, theoretically, even longer. Moreover, because depression occurs with considerable frequency in the general population, a resilient outcome might consist of less severe or less frequent recurrence of depression. Thus, decisions about who is resilient or not may be quite complex, varying with time, development, and circumstances (e.g., see Garber & Little, 1999). Moreover, the relatively high rate of nonmood disorders among offspring suggests that resilience should be defined as absence of any psychopathology, and as with mood disorders, the age of risk for development of certain disorders such as anxiety and substance use disorders may persist into adulthood. To date, the paucity of longitudinal studies of offspring of depressed parents makes it impossible to truly define resilience as a stable, reliable outcome.

A further limitation imposed by the absence of universal criteria for defining negative and positive outcomes concerns the possibility that even offspring who do not have psychopathology may nonetheless transmit depression or other disorders to their own children through maladaptive marital and parenting skills. It remains to be seen – although a focus of some of the author's current work – whether youth of depressed parents who themselves may not display depressive or other disorder negotiate the worlds of work and family adaptively. A specific issue is whether exposure to difficult family environments that include parental depression might impair the youth's own adult functioning, especially in intimate family roles.

Some investigators of children of depressed mothers have also noted that one deceptively dysfunctional adaptation may be adoption of the caretaker role by the child, a kind of false maturity or even enmeshment that could portend later relationship or personal dysfunction (e.g., Radke-Yarrow, Zahn-Waxler, Richardson, & Susman, 1994). Such potentially subtle outcomes may initially appear to be healthy but are likely to have negative consequences. Given the small number of longitudinal studies of children of depressed parents, the issue of stability of apparent adjustment and the ability to function well in important roles are questions of high priority in the goal of understanding resilience.

CURRENT LIMITATIONS AND DIRECTIONS FOR FUTURE RESEARCH

Some of the critical requirements in the high-risk depression field include the need for more precision in operationalizing the key risk and outcome constructs and the more rigorous exploration of the mechanisms by which depression exerts its toll – including additional focus on vulnerability and protective factors and processes.

Defining Depression

There are a number of limitations in the use of key constructs in the depression high-risk field, and greater precision and elaboration will greatly benefit our understanding of risk mechanisms and protective processes. *Parental depression,* for instance, has largely excluded fathers, and their role both as depressed parents and as possible resources for children of depressed mothers needs to be explored. It is increasingly apparent that depressed women are married to (or have children with) men who themselves may have diagnosable conditions at rates beyond population norms. Thus, results attributed to maternal depression in the family may, in fact, involve more complex patterns of family psychopathology.

Moreover, depression itself is more likely to co-occur with other forms of disorder (e.g., Blazer, Kessler, McGonagle, & Swartz, 1994), but comorbidity is rarely taken into account in analyses of children's outcomes or the mechanisms of risk. It is well known that depression often co-occurs with or follows anxiety disorders, and is frequently observed in individuals who have substance abuse disorders, eating disorders, attention deficit disorder, schizophrenia, and many other Axis I disorders. Depression is also commonly accompanied by Axis II psychopathology, which may greatly complicate the course of depression, adjustment in primary roles, and treatment outcomes (e.g., Shea et al., 1990).

With even greater potential for confusion than patterns of parental depression is the construct of depression itself. As represented in research, depression has referred variously to those who show a potentially transitory elevation of self-reported symptoms, to those exhibiting a single episode of diagnosed major depressive disorder, and to those with recurrent, severe, and highly impairing depressions. Whether symptoms are brief, intermittent, or prolonged and whether their severity is mild, moderate, or marked are all dimensions that might greatly affect the extent of children's dysfunctional outcomes, but that also might mean that different risk and resilience mechanisms are operative. Relatedly, research based on clinical populations of treatment-seeking individuals is likely to yield different results than studies based on untreated community samples – even when the phenomena of depression might be relatively similar. Those who seek help may be more likely to have severe, complex, and co-occurring disorders, as well as to live in circumstances deficient in resources for coping with the disorders. Numerous other characteristics of depression, such as age of onset, family history of mood disorders, and timing in relation to children's exposure, as well as the symptom profiles themselves (e.g., withdrawn, irritable), may greatly affect the nature and mechanisms of risk and resilience. Even fairly fundamental issues such as the mother's mood state at the time of the study in relation to her typical state are rarely controlled for or addressed in most offspring research on mood disorders. Taken together, these considerations about depression pose a considerable challenge for research designs, generalizability, and accumulation of a consistent and informative base of data on which to build interventions. Research that clarifies and refines the conditions under which depression is relatively more or less likely to affect children is urgently needed.

Children's Outcomes

Studies of children's risk due to parental depression have understandably tended to operationalize outcomes based on the goals and orientations of the investigators. Thus, much of the initial research was conducted in psychiatric settings within a largely medical (genetic) model evaluating evidence of *diagnostic conditions* in the children, with particular emphasis on mood disorders. In contrast, much of the more recent research on mechanisms of risk has been conducted by developmental psychopathologists evaluating behavioral and cognitive outcomes. Furthermore, the two streams of research have tended to study children of different ages, requiring developmentally appropriate assessments but rendering comparisons and generalizations across different age samples difficult. It would be highly desirable for psychiatry-based investigations to include more indicators of functional outcomes in relevant roles for children (e.g., social and academic performance and competencies), whereas assessment methods for children's adaptive behaviors, with standardized procedures for developmental norms, would be of great use especially for younger children. It should also be noted that most depression offspring studies generally have not predicted, or examined, possible gender-specific outcomes.

There are also important unresolved issues concerning the stability of outcomes, especially in infants and young children. Much of the research on infant variables in families with maternal depression has been limited to cross-sectional designs with samples varying widely in maternal depression characteristics and environmental features. Accordingly, although such studies may be useful to illuminate potential mechanisms (e.g., parenting behavior), they leave open the question of long-term features of the children's adaptation and functioning. Moreover, little research has addressed the issue of how competent or impaired functioning in one period is related to subsequent functioning. Thus, study of the processes and predictors of competence and resilience would benefit from investigation of their components and continuities so that researchers would have a better sense of the appropriate targets to examine.

As noted, there is a relative dearth of research on children's positive or adaptive outcomes in the face of parental depressive disorder. Defining and measuring such outcomes is an important priority. Relatedly, in order to supplement the focus on individual and family factors as outcomes and predictors, it is important to extend assessments to include key community-level variables, such as social supports, quality of the neighborhood, schools, religious beliefs and activities, and the like.

Conceptual and Empirical Challenges

In addition to notable limitations in the domains that have been used to describe children's outcomes as offspring of depressed parents, conceptual gaps have limited our understanding of the best markers or mechanisms to identify in order to help clarify processes of transmission of risk to children – or of resilient outcomes. It is increasingly recognized that it is desirable for the field to proceed now from verifying negative outcomes and identifying risk factors to developing research strategies that illuminate the mechanisms by which vulnerability to adverse outcomes occurs. For instance, Goodman and Gotlib (1999) proposed a research agenda for a developmentally sensitive, integrative (and complex) approach to clarifying risk mechanisms. However valid, such a model may be prohibitively difficult to test, involving not only multiple variables at the biological, interpersonal, and environmental levels, but also their dynamic and reciprocal effects.

Specifically, there are several key obstacles associated with identification of the vulnerability (and protective) factors related to the impact of maternal depression on children's outcomes. One is that maternal depression commonly co-occurs with several personal and environmental variables that themselves might be mediators or moderators of the impact of depression, or indeed, might themselves be the causal factors in children's diagnoses and maladjustment. These include, for example, clinical history and comorbid conditions, marital difficulties or divorce, adverse economic conditions and other chronic stressors such as family and health problems, and relatively poor quality of the parent–child relationship. The second obstacle is that such circumstances and the relationships among them have not, for the most part, been fully evaluated and their relative contributions clarified. Although several multifactorial models have been proposed, few studies have been large enough and endowed with sufficient numbers of relevant variables to clarify their empirical contributions. Indeed, the associations among variables may be so complex and dynamic that they may never be fully tested. A third and related obstacle is that even when risk factors have been shown to be empirically associated with outcomes in the children of depressed parents, the mechanisms by which such factors operate remain largely obscure. It will be a challenge for future waves of high-risk research to grapple with these complexities. Even though daunting, the extensive interest in offspring of depressed parents, and the diverse research approaches to the issue, promise exciting future developments.

IMPLICATIONS FOR INTERVENTIONS AND SOCIAL POLICIES

Despite the myriad unresolved issues concerning the features of parental depression and the mechanisms that predict depression or resilience in children, there are several indisputable implications for interventions. Foremost is the need for treatment of depressed parents. Although this is obvious, many (perhaps the majority of) depressed individuals do not seek treatment for their depression due to misattributions of its meaning and impact or due to the belief that it is a weakness of character requiring mind over matter. Moreover, it is poorly understood that depression takes a toll on the entire family and the marital relationship, as well as having an impact on children. It is also likely that the depressed adult *remains* at risk for depression because of the highly stressful impact of enduring marital difficulties or parent–child relationship problems. Thus, treatment of the depressed individual is really about treatment of the entire family, and the mutual effects of spouses and children on each other may warrant specific direct treatment. All too often, disorders such as depression are presented as if they are entirely intraindividual problems, and their treatments typically reflect this bias. Policies that promote understanding of the more general implications of depression – and that encourage treatment rather than forbearance or denial – are important.

A related obvious implication is that treatment of depressed parents to alleviate their depression may help to prevent negative outcomes in the children, to the extent that those outcomes are associated with the family milieu or the interaction of genetic vulnerability and environmental conditions. Similarly, treatments that target potentially critical mediators of adverse outcomes in high-risk families – such as treatments for marital discord or maladaptive parenting – could also be developed as important interventions to prevent depression in the offspring. It would be useful to evaluate outcomes of treatments for adult depression not only in terms of individual reduction of symptoms, but also in terms of the impact of the intervention on the outcomes of the children. It is possible that some forms of treatment, such as interpersonal psychotherapy or behavioral marital therapy, for instance, might be especially effective in reducing the risk of children's depression.

Surprisingly few research programs have been designed to assess the impact of parental treatment on children or to focus on depressed families as a high-risk target of preventive intervention (e.g., Beardslee, Wright, Salt, & Drezner, 1997). Beardslee's work, for example, is unique in aiming at preventive intervention for high-risk families. His findings suggests that an intervention based mainly on informing parents and children about depression and its effects on the family may have positive and enduring effects on the children's adjustment. It may be that relatively simple psychoeducational interventions that teach family members about the realities of depression – and that attempt to teach parents and children to make appropriate attributions about each other's behaviors – could help reduce some of the toll of depression. It is notable, for instance, that some children of mentally ill parents, such as those with schizophrenia or bipolar disorder, have been found to have better adjustment in some cases than those with depressed parents (e.g., Hammen, 1991a). It may be speculated that children who see their parent as ill may be less affected by maladaptive parenting because they are able to see it as due to the illness rather than to something bad about themselves or the parent.

A further obvious implication is that many children who are themselves in treatment for depression or have other disorders may, in fact, have depressed parents whose behaviors and family-environment circumstances contribute to the children's disturbance and dysfunction. It is relatively rare for empirically tested treatments for children's depression to include components that deal with parental disorder – or even family functioning (e.g., Hammen, Rudolph, Weisz, Rao, & Burge, 1999). Thus, inclusion of assessment and treatment of *parental* depression would be an important first step in improving treatments of depression for children and adolescents.

Despite the remaining empirical gaps in understanding risk processes, it does seem highly likely that a key element of the transmission of the depression risk is the quality of the parent–child relationship, with its many implications for attachment representations and interpersonal skills. Therefore, it makes sense that preventive interventions should focus preferentially on changes and improvements in the parenting interaction patterns or on helping children to cope more effectively with parental behaviors. Coping could also include promoting compensatory relationships with other adults and supportive friends.

Beyond these limited speculations, however, it might be concluded that one of the primary goals of preventive interventions in high-risk families might be to serve as experimental studies aimed at shedding further light on risk factors and vulnerability mechanisms. There is much to be learned – and much at stake – prompting the call for increased efforts to outline more precisely how depression affects families and the long-term adjustment of children.

SUMMARY AND CONCLUSIONS

Children of depressed mothers are at high risk for maladjustment, with 65–80% of those in clinical samples of mothers developing at least one psychiatric disorder by the age of 18 years. Mechanisms potentially involved in risk transmission (mediators) include hereditary and biological factors, disturbances in dimensions of parenting, martial conflict, and other stressful family life events.

Vulnerability associated with parental depression is substantially enhanced in the presence of factors that tend to co-occur with depression, including chronic stress, low cohesion in the family, psychiatric disorder in the other parent, and marital discord. Despite ample research on risk factors, there is considerable lack of precision in our understanding of risk mechanisms. Conversely, although based on sparse research, relatively *low* maladjustment among children is associated with high sensitivity and responsiveness in depressed mothers' parenting behaviors and the availability of adult social supports. Among child attributes, protective effects have been suggested for high intelligence, strong commitment to academics, good coping skills, a positive self-concept, and high self-understanding, as well as high social competence. In general, findings concerning these various risk modifiers have involved main effect associations rather than interaction effects.

In future studies of children of depressed parents, there is a need for greater precision and comprehensiveness in defining central constructs, more attention to depression among fathers, increased use of longitudinal designs, and enhanced attention to underlying mechanisms. At the same time, empirical evidence that does exist clearly converges in underscoring the critical roles of parent–child interactions and stressful contextual factors in relation to children's competence and maladjustment. Concerted attention to these dimensions is vital in future interventions and policies for families affected by parental depression.

Note

1. For simplicity, the term *children* will refer collectively to children and adolescents.

References

Adrian, C., & Hammen, C. (1993). Stress exposure and stress generation in children of depressed mothers. *Journal of Consulting and Clinical Psychology, 61*, 354–359.

Beardslee, W., Keller, M., Lavori, P., Klerman, G., Dorer, D., & Samuelson, H. (1988). Psychiatric disorder in adolescent offspring of parents with affective disorder in a nonreferred sample. *Journal of Affective Disorders, 15*, 313–322.

Beardslee, W. R., & Podorefsky, D. (1988). Resilient adolescents whose parents have serious affective and other psychiatric disorders: Importance of self-understanding and relationships. *American Journal of Psychiatry, 145*(1), 63–69.

Beardslee, W. R., Salt, P., Porterfield, K., Rothberg, P. C., wan de Velde, P., Swatling, S., Hoke, L., Moilanen, D. L., & Wheelock, I. (1993). Comparison of preventive interventions for families with parental affective disorder. *Journal of the American Academy of Child and Adolescent Psychiatry, 32*, 254–263.

Beardslee, W. R., Versage, E. M., & Gladstone, T. R. (1998). Children of affectively ill parents: A review of the past 10 years. *Journal of the American Academy of Child and Adolescent Psychiatry, 37*, 1134–1141.

Beardslee, W. R., Wright, E. J., Salt, P., & Drezner, K. (1997). Examination of children's responses to two preventive intervention strategies over time. *Journal of the American Academy of Child and Adolescent Psychiatry, 36*, 196–204.

Billings, A. G., & Moos, R. H. (1985). Children of parents with unipolar depression: A controlled 1-year follow-up. *Journal of Abnormal Child Psychology, 14*, 149–166.

Blazer, D. G., Kessler, R. C., McGonagle, K. A., & Swartz, M. S. (1994). The prevalence and distribution of major depression in a national community sample: The national comorbidity survey. *American Journal of Psychiatry, 151*, 979–986.

Brennan, P., Hammen, C., Andersen, M., Bor, W., Najman, J., & Williams, G. (2000). Chronicity, severity, and timing of maternal depressive symptoms: Relationships with child outcomes at age five. *Developmental Psychology, 36*, 759–766.

Brennan, P., Hammen, C., Katz, A., & LeBrocque, R. (in press). Maternal depression, paternal psychopathology, and adolescent diagnostic outcomes. *Journal of Consulting and Clinical Psychology.*

Brown, G. W., & Harris, T. O. (1989). Depression. In G. W. Harris & T. O. Harris (Eds.), *Life events and illness* (pp. 49–93). New York: Guilford Press.

Bruce, M. L., & Kim, K. M. (1992). Differences in the effects of divorce on major depression in men and women. *American Journal of Psychiatry, 149*, 914–917.

Canino, G., Bird, H., Rudio-Stipec, M., Bravo, M., & Alegria, M. (1990). Children of parents with psychiatric disorder in the community. *Journal of the American Academy of Child and Adolescent Psychiatry, 29*, 398–406.

Cohn, J. F., Matias, R., Tronick, E. Z., Lyons-Ruth, K., & Connell, D. (1986). Face-to-face interactions, spontaneous and structured, of mothers with depressive symptoms. *New Directions for Child Development, 34*, 31–46.

Conrad, M., & Hammen, C. (1993). Protective and resilience factors in high and low risk children: A comparison of children of unipolar, bipolar, medically ill and normal mothers. *Development and Psychopathology, 5*, 593–607.

Cox, A. D., Puckering, C., Pound, A., & Mills, M. (1987). The impact of maternal depression in young children. *Journal of Child Psychology and Psychiatry and Allied Disciplines, 28*, 917–928.

Cummings, E. M., & Davies, P. T. (1994). Maternal depression and child development. *Journal of Child Psychology and Psychiatry, 35*, 73–112.

Davies, P. T., Dumenci, L., & Windle, M. (1999). The interplay between maternal depressive symptoms and marital distress in the prediction of adolescent adjustment. *Journal of Marriage and the Family, 61*, 238–254.

Dawson, G., Hessl, D., & Frey, K. (1994). Social influences on early developing biological and behavioral systems related to risk for affective disorder. *Development and Psychopathology, 6,* 759–779.

Downey, G., & Coyne, J. C. (1990). Children of depressed parents: An integrative review. *Psychological Bulletin, 108,* 50–76.

Fendrich, M., Warner, V., & Weissman, M. M. (1990). Family risk factors, parental depression, and psychopathology in offspring. *Developmental Psychology, 26,* 40–50.

Ferguson, D., Horwood, L. J., & Lynskey, M. (1995). Maternal depressive symptoms and depressive symptoms in adolescents. *Journal of Child Psychology and Psychiatry, 36,* 1161–1178.

Field, T., Fox, N. A., Pickens, J., & Nawrocki, T. (1995). Relative right frontal EEG activation in 3- to 6-month-old infants of "depressed" mothers. *Developmental Psychology, 31,* 358–363.

Garber, J., & Little, S. (1999). Predictors of competence among offspring of depressed mothers. *Journal of Adolescent Research, 14,* 44–71.

Garmezy, N., Masten, A. S., & Tellegen, A. (1984). A study of stress and competence in children: A building block for developmental psychopathology. *Child Development, 55,* 97–111.

Gelfand, D. M., & Teti, D. M. (1990). The effects of maternal depression on children. *Clinical Psychology Review, 10,* 320–354.

Gershon, E. S. (1990). Genetics. In F. K. Goodwin & K. R. Jamison (Eds.), *Manic depressive illness* (pp. 373–401). New York: Oxford University Press.

Goodman, S. H., Adamson, L. B., Riniti, J., & Cole, S. (1994). Mothers' expressed attitudes: Associations with maternal depression and children's self-esteem and psychopathology. *Journal of the American Academy of Child and Adolescent Psychiatry, 33,* 1265–1274.

Goodman, S. H., Brogan, D., Lynch, M. E., & Fielding B. (1993). Social and emotional competence in children of depressed mothers. *Child Development, 64,* 516–531.

Goodman, S. H., & Gotlib, I. (1999). Risk for psychopathology in the children of depressed mothers: A developmental model for understanding mechanisms of transmission. *Psychological Review, 106,* 458–490.

Gotlib, I. H., & Lee, C. M. (1990). Children of depressed mothers: A review and directions for future research. In C. D. McCann & N. S. Endler (Eds.), *Depression: New directions in theory, research, and practice* (pp. 187–208). Toronto, Canada: Wall & Thompson.

Hammen, C. (1991a). *Depression runs in families: The social context of risk and resilience in children of depressed mothers.* New York: Springer-Verlag.

Hammen, C. (1991b). The generation of stress in the course of unipolar depression. *Journal of Abnormal Psychology, 100,* 555–561.

Hammen, C. (1999). Children of affectively ill parents. In H.-C. Steinhausen & F. Verhulst (Eds.), *Risks and outcomes in developmental psychopathology* (pp. 38–53). Oxford: Oxford University Press.

Hammen, C., Adrian, C., Gordon, D., Burge, D., Jaenicke, C., & Hiroto, D. (1987). Children of depressed mothers: Maternal strain and symptom predictors of dysfunction. *Journal of Abnormal Psychology, 96,* 190–198.

Hammen, C., & Brennan, P. (2001). Depressed adolescents of depressed and non-depressed mothers: Tests of an interpersonal impairment hypothesis. *Journal of Consulting and Clinical Psychology, 69,* 284–294.

Hammen, C., Burge, D., & Adrian, C. (1991). Timing of mother and child depression in a longitudinal study of children at risk. *Journal of Consulting and Clinical Psychology, 59,* 341–345.

Hammen, C., Burge, D., Burney, E., & Adrian, C. (1990). Longitudinal study of diagnoses in children of women with unipolar and bipolar affective disorder. *Archives of General Psychiatry, 47,* 1112–1117.

Hammen, C., Burge, D., & Stansbury, K. (1990). Relationship of mother and child variables to child outcomes in a high risk sample: A causal modeling analysis. *Developmental Psychology, 26,* 24–30.

Hammen, C., Rudolph, K., Weisz, J., Rao, U., & Burge, D. (1999). The context of depression in clinic-referred youth: Neglected areas in treatment. *Journal of the American Academy of Child and Adolescent Psychiatry, 38,* 64–71.

Harnish, J., Dodge, K., & Valente, E. (1995). Mother–child interaction quality as a partial mediator of the roles of maternal depressive symptomatology and socioeconomic status in the development of child behavior problems. *Child Development, 66,* 739–753.

Jaenicke, C., Hammen, C., Zupan, B., Hiroto, D., Gordon, D., Adrian, C., & Burge, D. (1987). Cognitive vulnerability in children at risk for depression. *Journal of Abnormal Child Psychology, 15,* 559–572.

Kendler, K. S., Neale, M. C., Kessler, R. C., Heath, A. C., & Eaves, L. J. (1992). A population-based twin study of major depression in women. *Archives of General Psychiatry, 49,* 257–266.

Kendler, K. S., & Prescott, C. A. (1999). A population-based twin study of lifetime major depression in men and women. *Archives of General Psychiatry, 56,* 39–44.

Ladd, C., Huot, R., Thrivikraman, K. V., Nemeroff, C. B., Meaney, M., & Plotsky, P. (2000). Long-term behavioral and neuroendocrine adaptations to adverse early experience. In E. A. Mayer & C. B. Saper (Eds.), *Progress in brain research* (Vol. 122, pp. 81–103). New York: Elsevier Science.

Lovejoy, M. C., Graczyk, P. A., O'Hare, E., & Neuman, G. (2000). Maternal depression and parenting behavior: A meta-analytic review. *Clinical Psychology Review, 20,* 561–592.

Lyons, M. J., Eisen, S. A., Goldberg, J., True, W., Lin, N., Meyer, J. M., Toomey, R., Faraone, S. V., Merla-Ramos, M., & Tsuang, M. T . (1998). A registry-based twin study of depression in men. *Archives of General Psychiatry, 55,* 468–472.

Lyons-Ruth, K., Zoll, D., Connell, D., & Grunebaum, H. U. (1986). The depressed mother and her one-year-old infant: Environment, interaction, attachment, and infant development. In E. Tronick & T. Field (Eds.), *Maternal depression and infant disturbance* (New Directions for Child Development, No. 34, pp. 31–46). San Francisco: Jossey-Bass.

McGuffin, P., Katz, R., Watkins, S., & Rutherford, J. (1996). A hospital-based twin register of the heritability of DSM-IV unipolar depression. *Archives of General Psychiatry, 53,* 129–136.

Merikangas, K. R. (1984). Divorce and assortative mating among depressed patients. *American Journal of Psychiatry, 141,* 74–76.

NICHD Early Child Care Research Network. (1999). Chronicity of maternal depressive symptoms, maternal sensitivity, and child functioning at 36 months. *Developmental Psychology, 35,* 1297–1310.

Plomin, R., Reiss, D., Hetherington, E. M., & Howe, G. (1994). Nature and nurture: Genetic contributions to measures of the family environment. *Developmental Psychology, 30,* 32–43.

Plotsky, P. M., Owens, M. J., & Nemeroff, C. B. (1998). Psychoneuroendocrinology of depression. *Psychoneuroendocrinology, 21,* 293–307.

Post, R. M. (1992). Transduction of psychosocial stress into the neurobiology of recurrent affective disorder. *American Journal of Psychiatry, 149,* 999–1010.

Radke-Yarrow, M., & Sherman, T. (1990). Hard growing: Children who survive. In J. Rolf, A. Masten, D. Cicchetti, K. Nuechterlein, & S. Weintraub (Eds.), *Risk and protective factors in the development of psychopathology* (pp. 97–119). Cambridge: Cambridge University Press.

Radke-Yarrow, M., Zahn-Waxler, M., Richardson, D., & Susman, A. (1994). Caring behavior in children of clinically depressed and well mothers. *Child Development, 65,* 1405–1414.

Rutter, M. (1990). Psychosocial resilience and protective mechanisms. In J. Rolf, A. S. Masten, D. Cicchetti, K. H. Nuechterlein, & S. Weintraub (Eds.), *Risk and protective factors in the development of psychopathology* (pp. 181–214). New York: Cambridge University Press.

Seifer, R., Sameroff, A., Dickstein, S., Keitner, G., Miller, I., Rasmussen, S., & Hayden, L. (1996). Parental psychopathology, multiple contextual risks, and one-year outcomes in children. *Journal of Clinical Child Psychology, 25,* 423–435.

Shea, M. T., Pilkonis, P. A., Beckham, E., Collins, J. F., Elkin, I., Sotsky, S. M., & Docherty, J. P. (1990). Personality disorders and treatment outcome in the NIMH Treatment of Depression Collaborative Research Program. *American Journal of Psychiatry, 98,* 468–477.

Teti, D. M., Gelfand, D. M., Messinger, D. S., & Isabella, R. (1995). Maternal depression and the quality of early attachment: An examination of infants, preschoolers, and their mothers. *Developmental Psychology, 31,* 364–376.

Warner, V., Mufson, L., & Weissman, M. M. (1995). Offspring at high and low risk for depression and anxiety: Mechanisms of psychiatric disorder. *Journal of the American Academy of Child and Adolescent Psychiatry, 34,* 786–797.

Weissman, M. M., Gammon, G., John, K., Merikangas, K., Warner, V., Prusoff, B., & Sholomskas, D. (1987). Children of depressed parents: Increased psychopathology and early onset of major depression. *Archives of General Psychiatry, 44,* 847–853.

Weissman, M. M., Fendrich, M., Warner, V., & Wickramaratne, P. J. (1992). Incidence of psychiatric disorder in offspring at high and low risk for depression. *Journal of the Academy of Child and Adolescent Psychiatry, 31,* 640–648.

Weissman, M. M., & Olfson, M. (1995). Depression in women: Implications for health care research. *Science, 269,* 799–801.

Weissman, M. M., Warner, V., Wickramaratne, P., Moreau, D., & Olfson, M. (1997). Offspring of depressed parents: 10 years later. *Archives of General Psychiatry, 54,* 932–940.

Wickramaratne, P. J., & Weissman, M. M. (1998). Onset of psychopathology in offspring by developmental phase and parental depression. *Journal of the American Academy of Child and Adolescent Psychiatry, 37,* 933–942.

Winokur, G., Coryell, W., Keller, M., Endicott, J., & Leon, A. (1995). A family study of manic-depressive (bipolar I) disease: Is it a distinct illness separable from primary unipolar depression? *Archives of General Psychiatry, 52,* 367–373.

Zahn-Waxler, C., McKnew, D. H., Cummings, E. M., Davenport, Y., & Radke-Yarrow, M. (1984). Problem behaviors and peer interactions of young children with a manic-depressive parent. *American Journal of Psychiatry, 141,* 236–240.

4

Resilience and Vulnerability among Sons of Alcoholics

Relationship to Developmental Outcomes between Early Childhood and Adolescence

Robert A. Zucker, Maria M. Wong, Leon I. Puttler, and Hiram E. Fitzgerald

INTRODUCTION

Children of alcoholics (COAs) are at substantially elevated risk for alcoholism in adulthood (Goodwin, 1979; Russell, 1990). Behavioral and cognitive deficits have also been identified as more common in this population (Fitzgerald et al., 1993; Sher, 1991; West & Prinz, 1987) and are of interest as possible mediators of later alcohol abuse and alcoholism. However, simply contrasting COAs and non-COAs does not enhance our understanding of the developmental course leading to such psychosocial outcomes. Although numerous studies have provided evidence for increased rates of alcohol-related difficulties among COAs, some have not observed differences in either drinking behavior or behavioral impairment (Alterman, Searles, & Hall, 1989; Bates & Pandina, 1992; Gillen & Hesselbrock, 1992; Pandina & Johnson, 1989). These discrepancies are likely due to the variable backgrounds of alcoholic parents, the multiple risks they transmit to their offspring, and the individual characteristics of the children. In fact, such discrepancies have increasingly led to the position that the COA population varies on a number of dimensions of vulnerability, and the manner in which the dimensions cluster produces considerable heterogeneity in the population.

In this vein, a number of parental alcoholism characteristics have been linked to adverse behavioral and cognitive child outcomes. Zucker and

This work was supported in part by a National Institute on Alcohol Abuse and Alcoholism grant to Robert A. Zucker and Hiram E. Fitzgerald (5R01 AA07065). The authors wish to express their gratitude to the editor for her thoughtful comments and focused questions, which have contributed significantly to the quality of this chapter. Correspondence may be addressed to zuckerra@umich.edu colleagues (Zucker, Ellis, Bingham, & Fitzgerald, 1996a) have observed that psychosocial outcomes among COAs varied as a function of the presence or absence of paternal comorbid antisocial behavior, with poorer outcomes uniformly present among children whose parent(s) were antisocial as well as alcoholic. In contrast, COAs whose parents lacked this comorbidity sometimes performed less well than controls but in other instances were indistinguishable from them. Domains where differences were found included externalizing and internalizing behavior problems, impaired intellectual and academic functioning, and poorer neurocognitive functioning (Mun, Fitzgerald, Puttler, Zucker, & von Eye, 2000; Poon, Ellis, Fitzgerald, & Zucker, 2000; Puttler, Zucker, Fitzgerald, & Bingham, 1998; Zucker, Ellis, Fitzgerald, Bingham, & Sanford, 1996b). Chassin, Rogosch, and Barrera (1991) and Finn et al. (1997) also found that the externalizing symptomatology among COAs was related to parental alcoholism as well as comorbid psychopathology, including both depression and antisocial personality disorder diagnoses. In other work, Jacob and Leonard (1986) showed that paternal depression comorbid with the alcoholism was associated with elevated levels of both internalizing and externalizing behavior problems.

A number of other child characteristics have also been associated with an increased risk for alcoholism. These include differences in risky temperament involving hyperactivity, emotionality, impulsivity, and low attention span, as well as biological irregularity (Jansen, Fitzgerald, & Zucker, 1995; Lerner, 1984; Tarter, 1988; Windle, 1991; Wong, Zucker, Puttler, & Fitzgerald, 1999), conduct problems (Henry et al., 1993), and a combination of negative mood and behavioral undercontrol (Chassin, 1994; Hussong & Chassin, 1994).

In contrast, the field has paid almost no attention to the characteristics that may be protective in the development of alcoholism and its intermediate adverse outcomes. There are two notable exceptions. One is a paper by Emmy Werner (1986) reporting data from the Kauai Longitudinal Study. She found that despite impoverished circumstances, an affectionate and nurturing relationship in early life, lower early life stress, an affectionate temperament, and an internal locus of control were all protective against an alcohol problem outcome at age 18. The Werner study is suggestive rather than definitive because it lacked a control group, thus leaving open the possibility that early differences in both the child and the environment were correlated selective factors that predetermined the later outcome. The second study, by Joan McCord (1988), did have a control group and used the Cambridge–Somerville study database to explore the protection issue. McCord's findings showed the critical role of the nonalcoholic spouse as a supporter of the father's alcoholism, on the one hand, or as someone who could help the child to differentiate from it, on the other. When the mother was supportive of the father and his drinking, alcoholism was more likely among offspring. When the nonalcoholic mother was higher in control/supervision of her son, alcoholism was less likely. Berlin and Davis (1989) also observed the critical nature of the mother's support and nurturance as a factor leading to a nonalcoholic outcome in adulthood.

Given the importance of preventing this major disorder, it is perhaps surprising that more work has not been done to understand these mechanisms. In this chapter, we examine the behavioral correlates of resilience and vulnerability among initially preschool-age COAs, as a way of identifying those differentiating factors that relate to later positive outcomes. We use a person-centered (Magnusson, 1988) rather than a variable-centered approach in defining who are and who are not "resilient children." We then track whether these early childhood characteristics remain in place over time, and we examine their developmental correlates during middle childhood and adolescence. In contrast to the earlier work in this area, which has looked primarily at relational factors, we have focused heavily on characterization of the early quality of the child's adaptation intellectually, temperamentally, and symptomatically. We then ask: To what extent are the early adaptation differences still detectable at later points in childhood? To the extent that they are detectable, do they present differently at later ages? To the extent that they are not, is there evidence that the initial resilient adaptation makes a difference, even in interaction with an adverse environment? And last, what factors, both early on as well as later in development, mediate the later outcomes?

ADAPTATION IN THE FACE OF DIFFERING LEVELS OF ADVERSITY: A 2 × 2 MATRIX

The work we report is part of an ongoing prospective family study begun in the mid 1980s, that utilizes a high-risk design for adult alcoholism and other eventual substance-abusing outcomes among the offspring (Zucker & Fitzgerald, 1991). Following the work of Rutter (1987), we define resilience as "a successful adaptation despite adversity." The adversity index we use is one that assesses exposure to a highly pathological family environment. We created a summative parental psychopathology measure that evaluates both the currency and the severity of alcohol use disorder,

Child Psychopathology

		In Normal Range	High
	Low	Nonchallenged (*N*=175)	Troubled (*N*=28)
Family Adversity			
	High	Resilient (*N*=66)	Vulnerable (*N*=34)

FIGURE 4.1 Defining the different adaptation groups during the preschool years.

as well as the presence/absence of antisocial behavior in both parents. We characterized the child's adaptation with a global sociobehavioral psychopathology measure. Successful adaptation was defined as being within normal limits on this global index (A later section of the chapter provides more detail on both these indices.)

The 2×2 grid created by these dimensions is shown in Figure 4.1, with *Resilient* children defined as those with"high adaptation in the context of high adversity." A brief review of the labels for the other three cells is instructive. We call the "normal adaptation under conditions of low adversity" group *Nonchallenged* to emphasize that their behavior is unremarkable within a family context involving low parent psychopathology that exerts no pressure for deviance and that is more likely to be nurturant and encouraging. The "low adaptation (high psychopathology) under conditions of high family adversity" group is labeled *Vulnerable* in order to emphasize the continuing exposure to family trouble that takes place here. Other evidence from our group shows that these children have been negatively impacted by this exposure (cf. Wong et al., 1999). Finally, those children with "high psychopathology under conditions of low adversity" are characterized as *Troubled* to emphasize that, even without the familial adversity, they still show poor behavioral adaptation. In other words, they appear to be carrying their trouble along with them, regardless of the lack of environmental press.

In the remainder of the chapter, we describe the characteristics of these children, focusing on baseline characteristics during the preschool years. Then we describe developmental outcomes in middle childhood

(6–8 years old), late childhood (9–11 years old), and early adolescence (12–14 years old). The two contrasts of greatest interest are those between resilient and vulnerable children, on the one hand, and resilient and nonchallenged children, on the other. These contrasts address two questions: (1) Both initially and over time, to what degree are resilient children distinguishable from their less well functioning peers who are growing up in similarly hampering circumstances? (2) Both initially and over time, how, if at all, are resilient youngsters from high-adversity environments distinguishable from their nonchallenged peers? Both groups of children at least superficially start with approximately the same level of adaptation, but one group has substantially more difficulty to negotiate than the other.

In addressing these questions, we looked for early differences in temperament and intelligence, characteristics that may be indicative of early behavioral competence. We tracked these characteristics into later childhood, and also examined variations in self-esteem, intellectual achievement, and behavior, for information about the developmental course of these early differences in adaptation to risk. In later analyses, we moved from a person-based characterization of risk to a dimensional one, and examined what factors predict the adverse outcomes of behavioral difficulty in adolescence and what factors are protective. We also examined whether different factors are protective in COAs compared to non-COAs. The chapter ends with some discussion of the implications of these findings for intervention and prevention for this very high risk population (Grant, 2000; Zucker et al., 2000).

TRACKING VULNERABILITY AND RESILIENCE IN A
PROSPECTIVE LONGITUDINAL STUDY

Our data come from the ongoing Michigan–Michigan State University Longitudinal Study (Zucker et al., 2000; Zucker & Fitzgerald, 1991). The subsample for this report involves boys and their biological parents. The children at Waves 1, 2, 3, and 4 were 3 to 5, 6 to 8, 9 to 11, and 12 to 14 years old, respectively. The study involves a population-based sample of alcoholic men, their wives (whose substance abuse status was irrelevant for inclusion in the study), and their initially 3- to 5-year-old sons. Another recruitment effort brought daughters into the project, but their data are not yet ready to report.[1] Both biological parents were required to be coupled and living with the child at the time of recruitment. Study exclusionary criteria ruled out fetal alcohol syndrome (Fitzgerald et al., 1993).

A contrast/control group of families who resided in the same neighborhoods as the alcoholic families was also recruited. Parents in the contrast group had no adult lifetime history of substance abuse/dependence, and their offspring were age-matched to the male child in the alcoholic family residing in the same neighborhood (for a detailed description of the study design, recruitment strategies, and eligibility criteria, see Zucker et al., 1996b, 2000).

All families were Caucasian Americans since the study locale contained less than 4% of non-Caucasian families who met the inclusion criteria. Given the extensive literature showing a relationship between substance abuse and ethnic/racial status, including such variation in the study without being able to model its effects statistically would only contribute to error. Therefore, the project originally opted to exclude this variation. The ongoing study is currently recruiting an additional sample of both African American and Hispanic families; these data are not yet available for analysis.

ASSESSING ADAPTATION AND ADVERSITY

Adaptation

We used information from the Child Behavior Checklist (CBCL) (Achenbach, 1991) for the indicator of child risk/adaptation and a family index at Wave 1 (when children were 3–5 years old) for the environmental adversity measure. Successful adaptation was defined as the absence of significant symptoms on the CBCL. The cutoff for this was set to be at or below the 80th percentile on the CBCL Total Behavior Problems broadband measure. The norm group we used was the entire Longitudinal Study sample. The 80th percentile cutoff involves behavioral deviation that is somewhat less than one standard deviation (SD) above the norm (the precise value is 0.84 SD), which seemed like a reasonable, albeit arbitrary, cut point differentiating symptomatic from "within normal range" behavior.

Family Adversity Indicators I

Parent alcoholism (abuse/dependence) (ALC) was screened first by the Short Michigan Alcohol Screening Test (Selzer, Vinokur, & van Rooijen, 1975) and followed up with a more intensive assessment involving the Diagnostic Interview Schedule Version III (DIS) (Robins, Helzer,

Croughan, & Ratcliff, 1980) and the Drinking and Drug History questionnaire (Zucker, Fitzgerald, & Noll, 1990). On the basis of information collected by all three instruments, a diagnosis of alcohol abuse/dependence
(lifetime as well as past 3 years) was made by a trained clinician using
DSM IV criteria. To compute the family adversity measure, we required a
dimensional indicator of the presence/severity of an ALC diagnosis. To
produce this, diagnoses were scored as follows: $0 =$ no lifetime diagnosis,
$1 =$ alcohol abuse/dependence diagnosis prior to the past 3 years, and
$2 =$ alcohol abuse/dependence diagnosis in the past 3 years.

Family Adversity Indicators II

Parent antisocial personality disorder (ASPD) is the second component in
the adversity measure. ASPD was assessed by the DIS and the Antisocial
Behavior Inventory (Zucker et al., 1996b; Zucker, Noll, Ham, Fitzgerald,
& Sullivan, 1994). Information on the Antisocial Behavior Inventory was
used to supplement DIS data in establishing a diagnosis. For the risk
index, ASPD was scored as follows: $0 =$ no diagnosis, $2 =$ presence of
diagnosis. Only a lifetime indicator was used here because this is a personality disorder (DSM IV Axis II) diagnosis that requires a long course
over childhood and adulthood in order to be established.

Family Adversity Index

The adversity index was a composite measure used to evaluate the joint
contribution of parental alcoholism and comorbid antisociality. The index summed the individual ALC and ASPD scores of each parent at
Wave 1 and then was summed across them both. Thus, a composite
parental psychopathology indicator was generated that involved currency
of the parental alcoholism, the presence of the antisocial comorbidity,
and the degree of penetration in the family of both of these attributes as
a function of being shared or not shared by both the father and mother.
The adversity score had a range of 0–8. A score of 0–3 was classified as
"low family adversity"; a score of 4–8 was considered "high family adversity." This cutoff ensured that families in the high-adversity group would
either receive an antisocial alcoholic diagnosis (64%), or involve both
parents with currently active alcoholism (52%) or both (13%).

   The adversity index assesses exposure to a highly pathological family
environment. The index has already been used successfully in other work
to dimensionalize level of family strain (Wong et al., 1999). It is important

to emphasize that the measure, although established by way of parental psychopathology, is an effective proxy for a number of other pertinent indicators of family adversity, including conflict, violence, economic difficulty, family crises, other psychiatric comorbidity, and trouble with the law (Zucker et al., 1996a, 1996b). Finally, on the basis of national Epidemiologic Catchment Area Study alcoholism comorbidity rates (Helzer et al., 1991) and national familial alcoholism figures (Grant, 2000; Huang, Cerbone, & Gfroerer, 1998), these criteria would yield a population encompassing slightly less than 1% of U.S. households and approximately 20% of alcoholic families. (This calculates out to a population N of approximately 1.3 million children under the age of 18.) We think this is a reasonable cutoff for a label of *significant adversity*; it marks a relatively uncommon level of difficulty, but one that is not so rare as to be minuscule.

Using the specified cut points for the two indices, the children were classified into the four adaptation groups. Among the low-adversity families, children who scored at or above the 80th percentile were called the *troubled group*, and children who scored below the 80th percentile were called the *nonchallenged group*. Among the high-adversity families, children who scored at or above the 80th percentile were called the *vulnerable group* and children who scored below the 80th percentile were called the *resilient group* (see Figure 4.1).

Behavioral Problems

In addition to using the CBCL to establish the different adaptation groups at Wave 1, we used this measure at later waves to assess the children's behavioral problems. The CBCL is the most widely used instrument in clinical settings for measuring children's social and emotional functioning. The two broad band subscales (Externalizing and Internalizing Problems) and the Total Behavior Problems score are used here, and ratings were based on an average of both mother and father ratings of their child's behavior over the past 6 months. The instrument uses a 3-point rating scale ($0 =$ not true, $1 =$ somewhat or sometimes true, and $2 =$ very true or often true).

Temperament

Child temperament was measured by the Dimensions of Temperament Survey (DOTS) (Lerner, Palermo, Spiro, & Nesselroade, 1982) at Waves 1 and 2. The DOTS measures five dimensions of temperament: activity level, attention span/distractibility, adaptability/approach-withdrawal, rhythmicity, and reactivity. Both biological parents completed the temperament measure, and their scores were averaged to obtain a single rating.

Intellectual Functioning

Children's intellectual functioning was measured by standardized intellectual assessments involving the Third Revision (Form L-M) of the Stanford–Binet Intelligence Scale (Terman & Merrill, 1973) when children were 3 to 5 and the Wechsler Intelligence Scale for Children-Revised (WISC-R) (Wechsler, 1974) when they were 6 to 8.

Academic Achievement

All children at Waves 2, 3, and 4 completed the Wide Range Achievement Test-Revised Academic Assessment (WRAT-R) (Jastak & Wilkinson, 1984). The WRAT-R allows for the brief individual assessment of reading, written spelling, and arithmetic computation. It provides a metric that allows comparisons of achievement across schools. Percentile scores were used to indicate children's achievement relative to that of their peers of similar grade levels.

Self-Esteem

Self-esteem was measured by the Harter Perceived Competence Scale for Children (PCSC) (Harter, 1979) at Wave 3. This instrument was designed to measure children's sense of their own abilities and stature vis-à-vis other children in terms of school-related matters, peer relationships, athletic activities, and general feeling of self-worth. Although this content is sometimes regarded as a characteristic intrinsic to the child, we treat it here as a dependent variable, that is, as an outgrowth of the child's experiences.

CHARACTERISTICS OF THE CHILDREN IN THE PRESCHOOL YEARS

Our expectation that more children from the high- than the low-adversity families would be high in total behavior problems proved to be the case. Among the high-adversity families, the percentage of families with high and low levels of problems were 66.0% and 34.0%, respectively. Among the low-adversity families, the percentage of families with low and high levels of problems were 86.2% and 13.8%, respectively ($\chi^2(1) =$ 16.81, $p < .001$).

The four groups of children also showed differences in intellectual functioning at Wave 1. There was an overall group difference in their performance on the Stanford Binet: $F(3,287) = 5.17$, $p < .01$. The nonchallenged group had the highest IQ ($M = 105.99$, $SD = 14.29$), followed by the resilient group ($M = 103.47$, $SD = 12.63$), the troubled group ($M = 97.85$, $SD = 14.41$), and the vulnerable group ($M = 97.79$, $SD = 13.77$). The higher IQ of the nonchallenged group was also significantly different from that of both the troubled and the vulnerable groups (post hoc Tukey test).

Temperamentally, the four groups of children also were different. Of the five dimensions measured on the DOTS, there were significant group differences on four: activity level: $F(3,286) = 4.63$, $p <$ .01, attention span: $F(3,287) = 4.85$, $p < .01$, rhythmicity: $F(3,287) =$ 2, 82, $p < .05$, and emotion reactivity: $F(3,287) = 10.07$, $p < .001$. No differences were found on approach/withdrawal: $F(3,287) = 1.05$, n.s. Post hoc Tukey tests showed that the resilient group was significantly lower in emotional reactivity than the vulnerable and troubled groups. Compared to the nonchallenged group, the vulnerable group had a significantly higher activity level, a lower attention span, and higher emotional reactivity. The troubled group was significantly higher on emotional reactivity than the nonchallenged group.

DEVELOPMENTAL OUTCOMES FROM CHILDHOOD TO EARLY ADOLESCENCE: DIFFERING TRAJECTORIES

Outcomes in middle childhood, late childhood, and early adolescence as a function of membership in the different preschool child adaptation groups are shown in Table 4.1.

Behavioral Problems

Figure 4.2 shows the trajectory of externalizing problems for each of the groups, and Figure 4.3 shows the trajectory of internalizing problems. As Table 4.1 shows, at all ages significant overall group differences were found on both externalizing and internalizing problems. Figure 4.2 shows that the nonchallenged group had the lowest level of externalizing problems, followed by the resilient group, the troubled group, and

TABLE 4.1. *Comparisons of Adaptational Characteristics at Baseline and Developmental Outcomes among the Four Adaptation Groups between Early and Middle Childhood and Early Adolescence*

	1. Troubled LO ADV LO COMP	2. Nonchallenged LO ADV HI COMP	3. Vulnerable HI ADV LOW COMP	4. Resilient HI ADV HI COMP	Overall Group Differences	Posthoc Tukey HSD tests ($p < .05$)
Adaptation Characteristics at Baseline						
Ages 3–5						
Total problems	46.23 ($\pm$5.95)	23.74 ($\pm$8.22)	52.24 ($\pm$14.99)	26.43 ($\pm$8.34)	$F(3,299) = 128.65^{***}$	1&2, 1&3, 1&4, 2&3, 3&4
Internalizing problems	8.59 ($\pm$2.77)	4.30 ($\pm$2.57)	9.19 ($\pm$5.35)	4.55 ($\pm$2.85)	$F(3,288) = 35.43^{***}$	1&2, 1&4, 2&3, 3&4
Externalizing problems	11.61 ($\pm$1.85)	6.16 ($\pm$2.47)	14.02 ($\pm$3.44)	6.94 ($\pm$2.51)	$F(3,288) = 112.84^{***}$	1&2, 1&3, 1&4, 2&3, 3&4
Adaptation Indicators over Time						
Ages 6–8						
Internalizing problems	9.46 ($\pm$3.80)	5.81 ($\pm$3.97)	8.77 ($\pm$3.28)	5.73 ($\pm$3.67)	$F(3,210) = 7.18^{***}$	1&2, 1&4, 2&3, 3&4
Externalizing problems	9.09 ($\pm$3.89)	5.63 ($\pm$3.03)	10.43 ($\pm$4.28)	7.16 ($\pm$3.23)	$F(3,210) = 15.69^{***}$	1&2, 2&3, 2&4, 3&4
Ages 9–11						
Internalizing problems	8.31 ($\pm$4.72)	5.46 ($\pm$4.06)	8.3 ($\pm$6.03)	6.09 ($\pm$4.23)	$F(3,210) = 4.22^{**}$	1&2, 2&3
Externalizing problems	7.52 ($\pm$4.55)	5.33 ($\pm$3.46)	8.52 ($\pm$5.24)	6.55 ($\pm$4.07)	$F(3,210) = 5.35^{***}$	2&3
Self-esteem	20.7 ($\pm$2.05)	21.06 ($\pm$2.82)	19 ($\pm$3.79)	19.82 ($\pm$3.53)	$F(3,220) = 3.91^{**}$	2&3
Ages 12–14						
Internalizing problems	8.15 ($\pm$4.55)	5.07 ($\pm$3.85)	7.70 ($\pm$5.00)	7.16 ($\pm$4.50)	$F(3,208) = 6.21^{***}$	1&2, 2&3, 2&4
Externalizing problems	13.09 ($\pm$6.31)	7.77 ($\pm$5.04)	15.90 ($\pm$9.05)	10.73 ($\pm$7.47)	$F(3,208) = 14.35^{***}$	1&2, 2&3, 2&4, 3&4
Protective Factors						
Intellectual functioning Ages 6–8						
Verbal IQ	105.05 ($\pm$16.50)	108.43 ($\pm$13.28)	98.65 ($\pm$11.32)	104.2 ($\pm$11.31)	$F(3,208) = 3.50^{*}$	2&3
Performance IQ	107.89 ($\pm$16.86)	108.46 ($\pm$15.80)	106.47 ($\pm$16.61)	101.83 ($\pm$10.66)	$F(3,208) = 2.01$	
Full scale IQ	106.79 ($\pm$16.92)	109.32 ($\pm$14.21)	102.12 ($\pm$13.22)	103.15 ($\pm$10.33)	$F(3,208) = 3.00^{*}$	

Intellectual functioning Ages 12–14					
Verbal IQ	103.85 (±13.28)	106.06 (±13.49)	99.13 (±11.31)	103.73 (±11.65)	$F(3,191) = 2.01$	
Performance IQ	105.65 (±15.50)	108.45 (±16.86)	104.92 (±11.20)	102.33 (±11.08)	$F(3,191) = 1.75$	
Full scale IQ	105.05 (±14.31)	107.95 (±15.15)	102.04 (±10.62)	103.05 (±10.26)	$F(3,191) = 2.07$	
Academic achievement Ages 6–8					
Reading	41.16 (±30.67)	45.81 (±28.37)	37.31 (±23.31)	41.08 (±30.27)	$F(3,206) = .67$	
Spelling	32.74 (±28.22)	39.19 (±27.24)	34.67 (±24.18)	36.5 (±27.51)	$F(3,206) = .43$	
Arithmetic	40.47 (±27.79)	48.11 (±27.90)	32.56 (±22.93)	37.13 (±26.85)	$F(3,206) = 2.89^*$	
Academic achievement Ages 9–11					
Reading	51 (±27.13)	56.04 (±27.17)	37.25 (±23.82)	50.49 (±29.13)	$F(3,216) = 2.95^*$	2&3
Spelling	48.95 (±30.32)	46.34 (±28.30)	28.65 (±19.88)	43.05 (±31.88)	$F(3,216) = 2.43$	2&3
Arithmetic	46.11 (±26.93)	48.88 (±30.65)	37.1 (±24.39)	40.02 (±27.17)	$F(3,216) = 1.67$	
Academic achievement Ages 12–14					
Reading	52.86 (±29.11)	57.67 (±23.27)	36.88 (±22.86)	57.95 (±28.29)	$F(3,194) = 4.89^{**}$	2&3, 3&4
Spelling	47.1 (±30.10)	53.81 (±26.77)	33.75 (±23.95)	53.45 (±30.31)	$F(3,192) = 3.76^*$	2&3, 3&4
Arithmetic	46.62 (±25.53)	55.11 (±28.37)	36.75 (±27.5)	43.26 (±27.47)	$F(3,194) = 3.95^{**}$	2&3
Temperament Age 6–8					
Activity	1.5 (±.98)	1.12 (±1.07)	1.12 (±1.26)	1.52 (±1.17)	$F(3,206) = 1.82$	
Attention	5.98 (±2.44)	6.56 (±2.51)	3.88 (±2.15)	5.6 (±2.46)	$F(3,207) = 6.72^{***}$	2&3
Approach	3.48 (±1.81)	3.8 (±1.77)	3.65 (±1.27)	4.13 (±1.56)	$F(3,207) = 0.74$	
Rhythmicity	6.03 (±1.30)	6.65 (±1.37)	6.50 (±1.35)	6.38 (±1.29)	$F(3,207) = 1.25$	
Reactivity	3.64 (±1.1)	2.53 (±1.24)	3.82 (±1.1)	3.07 (±1.4)	$F(3,207) = 8.99^{***}$	1&2, 2&3

$^* p < .05$, $^{**} p < .01$, $^{***} p < .001$; cell entries are means (± standard deviations).
ADV, Adversity; COMP, competence.

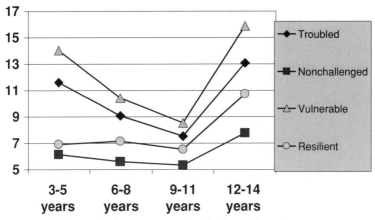

FIGURE 4.2 Externalizing symptoms in the four adaptation groups.

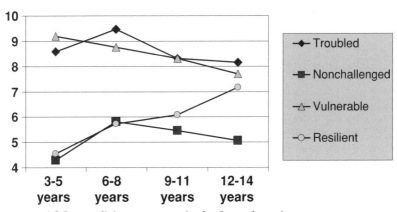

FIGURE 4.3 Internalizing symptoms in the four adaptation groups.

the vulnerable group. At all ages, the vulnerable group had the highest level of externalizing problems, and the posthoc test of group differences shows reliable differences between the most challenged group (the vulnerable children) and the least challenged one at all ages. Figure 4.2 also shows a consistent pattern of decline in externalizing behavior over childhood, a pattern that is normative for this age range (Achenbach, 1991). In addition, there is increasing convergence in level of externalizing difficulties. At the transition to adolescence we again see the normative pattern of a developmental shift involving increasing externalizing (aggressive/delinquent/impulsive) behavior (cf. Jessor & Jessor, 1977). The individual difference data are also of considerable interest. Whereas the resilient children are not distinguishable from their nonchallenged peers as preschoolers, they show a small but reliably higher level as they grow older. At the same time, they still occupy an intermediary place, having a lower level of externalizing problems than their vulnerable peers. In addition, the divergence of slopes between ages 9 to 11 and 12 to 14 shows an interaction between group membership individual differences and increasing levels of environmental adversity. Repeated measures analysis of variance showed that both the main effect of time (Wilks' Lambda $F(3,141) = 29.83$, $p < .001$) and the interaction effect between time and adaptation groups (Wilks' Lambda $F(9,343.31) = 3.06$, $p < .01$) were significant, indicating that level of externalizing problems across time was different for the four adaptation groups. This interactional relationship has already been observed cross-sectionally among these children as preschoolers (Wong et al., 1999). The present data show parallels developmentally.

Figure 4.3 presents the trajectories for internalizing problems; here also the nonchallenged group had the lowest level of problems, followed by the resilient group. The troubled group was similar to the vulnerable group. An important pattern exists here that is revealed both by the figure and by the posthoc tests of individual group differences (see Table 4.1). At ages 3–5 and 6–8 an identical individual difference pattern exists. Nonchallenged and resilient children are significantly lower in internalizing symptoms than both vulnerable and troubled children, and there are no differences between the resilient and nonchallenged children. As Figure 4.3 also shows, this pattern begins to diverge following Wave 2, and by early adolescence the nonchallenged group is significantly lower than all the others, and no differences exist between any of the other three groups. In other words, at this juncture the resilient children have developed a level of internalizing symptoms similar to that of both the vulnerable and the troubled children. Here also we tested this group by time interaction with a repeated measures analysis of variance. It showed a significant effect of time (Wilks' Lambda $F(3,141) = 29.83$, $p < .05$). The interaction effect between time and adaptation groups (Wilks' Lambda $F(9,343.31) = 1.35$, n.s.; Roy's Largest Root $F(3,143) = 3.53$, $p < .05$) was small but also significant, indicating that the developmental trajectories of internalizing problems were different for the four adaptation groups.

The significance of these behavioral problem findings needs to be underscored. With the overall focus of this chapter on resilience and vulnerability among children at long-term risk for the development of alcohol and other drug problems, the primary outcome of interest is the emergence of such substance abuse. The age of the sample currently precludes evaluation of the differential emergence of this substance abuse endpoint. Nonetheless, from the perspective of risk development for this endpoint, our findings present a very clear picture. Externalizing behavior is known to be an excellent proxy indicator for early substance use as well as precocious abuse (Zucker, 2000; Zucker, Chermack, & Curran, 2000a). So is a high level of internalizing behavior (Caspi, Moffitt, Newman, & Silva, 1996). On both of these grounds, the results indicate that the children identified as vulnerable are at highest risk, the nonchallenged group is at lowest risk, and the resilient group is at intermediary risk, in particular because of the increasing experience of internalizing problems as they move into adolescence. Moreover, the middle childhood way point would appear to be a significant nodal point for intervention activity. We address this issue at the end of the chapter.

Intellectual Functioning

Generally speaking, there were few differences between the four groups in intellectual functioning in middle childhood (Wave 2) and early adolescence (Wave 4) (these data were not collected at Wave 3). At Wave 2, there were overall group differences in verbal IQ, with the vulnerable group having the lowest IQ (Table 4.1) and also being significantly lower than the nonchallenged group. No reliable differences were present for performance IQ, although here too, the nonchallenged group showed the highest level of functioning. The pattern of differences on full scale IQ basically mirrored the verbal IQ findings. At Wave 4, no overall or individual IQ differences were present.

Temperament

Significant temperament differences were present across the four groups in the early school years. At Wave 2, differences were found on attention span and emotion reactivity. The vulnerable group had the shortest attention span compared to all the other groups. The resilient and troubled groups had similar scores, and the nonchallenged group had the highest attention span. Post hoc Tukey tests indicated that the vulnerable group was significantly different from the nonchallenged group. The vulnerable group was the most emotionally reactive group compared to other groups, followed by the troubled group, the resilient group, and the nonchallenged group. Post hoc Tukey tests showed that the vulnerable and troubled groups were significantly different from the nonchallenged group, whereas the resilient group was not. No differences were observed for activity level, approach/withdrawal, or rhythmicity.

Self-Esteem

In the early school years, no differences were present. However, in later childhood (ages 9–11), there was a small but significant difference in self-esteem, with the vulnerable group being lowest. Interestingly, paralleling the internalizing findings of later ages, the resilient group was next lowest, followed in increasing esteem order by the troubled and nonchallenged groups. The two extreme risk groups (vulnerable and nonchallenged) were the only ones that were individually reliably different.

Academic Achievement

Information on academic achievement was available from the early school years on and showed increasing patterns of differentiation with increasing age. Small but significant overall group differences in arithmetic achievement were present at Wave 2, but no individual group differences were significant. At Wave 3, the groups were different in reading achievement but not in spelling or arithmetic. Again, post hoc comparisons showed that there were no individual group differences, although the same pattern observed at Wave 2 continued to be present. At Wave 4, the groups were different in all three achievement areas. The posthoc tests showed that the vulnerable group performed less well than both the resilient and nonchallenged groups on reading. Differences in spelling and arithmetic existed between the vulnerable and nonchallenged groups. In addition, by early adolescence the resilient group performed almost as well as the nonchallenged group in reading and spelling.

RISK AND PROTECTIVE FACTORS IN THE DEVELOPMENT OF RESILIENCE

Until now, the analyses we have used have involved a person-centered approach. We turn now to a variable-centered approach to examine what risk and protective factors may affect the development of resilience in these children. The sample was divided into two groups: COAs and non-COAs. Hierarchical multiple regression analyses were used to identify variables that predicted behavioral problems at Wave 4 and self-esteem at Wave 3 for each group. Behavioral problems and self-esteem were chosen as dependent variables because a lack of behavioral problems and a high level of self-esteem are indicators of good adjustment under conditions of adversity. In addition, as noted earlier, both externalizing and internalizing problems are good proxy indicators of the risk for later problem use of alcohol and other drugs.

Table 4.2 shows the results of the hierarchical multiple regression models of factors predicting outcomes in early adolescence. In the model predicting externalizing problems, Wave 1 externalizing problems were entered into the analysis first to control for baseline variation. Then fathers' and mothers' ASPD diagnoses (0 = absence, 1 = presence) were entered to control for persistence of parent psychopathology effects over time. Our Wave 2 protective indicators, intelligence and temperament, were entered in the next step. Finally, Wave 2 and Wave 3 academic performance were entered in the model as potentially protective characteristics related to coping and social achievement that might affect the later behavioral outcome.

Among COAs, even after controlling for Wave 1 externalizing problems, mother antisocial personality diagnosis was still a predictor of Wave 4 externalizing problems. Wave 2 verbal IQ was negatively related to later externalizing behavior, indicating its protective role in the development of externalizing among the COAs. Wave 2 reactivity had a marginally significant positive relationship with the externalizing outcome. That is, being emotionally reactive was a risk factor. Among non-COAs, other than the continued influence of early childhood (baseline) externalizing problems, the only marginally significant risk factor was Wave 2 reactivity.

In the model for internalizing behavior, the same predictors were used except that Wave 1 internalizing problems was used to control for baseline variations. Among COAs, mother ASPD was again positively associated with the presence of internalizing symptoms in early adolescence. Conversely, Wave 2 verbal IQ had a negative relationship with the internalizing outcome, indicating that high verbal ability was protective against later internalizing problems. Among non-COAs, Wave 2 (middle childhood) reactivity was positively related to the outcome; that is, a higher level increased the likelihood of having a larger number of internalizing problems in early adolescence.

In the model predicting self-esteem in middle childhood (Wave 3), parent ASPD was entered in the first step to control for the persistence and potential invasiveness of parent psychopathology effects. The same

TABLE 4.2. *Hierarchical Multiple Regression Analysis Predicting Resilience Indicators*

Block of Predictors	Ages 12–14 Internalizing Problems				Ages 12–14 Externalizing Problems				Ages 9–11 Self-Esteem			
	COA		Non-COA		COA		Non-COA		COA		Non-COA	
	β	$R^2\Delta$[b]	β	$R^2\Delta$[b]	β	$R^2\Delta$[b]	β	$R^2\Delta$[b]	β	$R^2\Delta$[b]	β	$R^2\Delta$[b]
1. Age 3–5 internalizing problems	0.22[a]	.05	.26*	.07	.55***	.30	.57***	.33	.01	.01	−.09	.01
Age 3–5 externalizing problems												
2. Age 3–5 father ASPD	.15	.10	−.03	.00	.06	.11	.06	.00	−.12			
Age 3–5 mother ASPD	.28*				.34**							
3. Age 6–8 Verbal IQ	−.28*	.14	.00	.21	−.23*	.10	.07	.15	−.03	.21	−.08	.12
Age 6–8 Performance IQ	.15		−.18		.01		−.20		.35**		.25[a]	
Age 6–8 activity level	.18		.05		.03		−.10		.00		−.20	
Age 6–8 attention	−.07		.23		−.09		−.10		−.08		.21	
Age 6–8 approach-withdrawal	−.10		−.13		.04		.02		.33**		.02	
Age 6–8 rhythmicity	−.12		−.14		−.11		−.03		.01		−.05	
Age 6–8 reactivity	.10		.40**		.22[a]		.27[a]		−.14		.11	
4. Age 6–8 reading performance	.07	.02	.26	.03	.21	.03	.32	.08	−.23	.04	.47*	.11
Age 6–8 spelling performance	−.23		−.06		−.04		.09		.35*		−.14	
Age 6–8 arithmethic performance	−.02		−.03		−.09		−.12		−.13		−.29[a]	
5. Age 9–11 reading performance	.13	.03	.12	.01	−.19	.01	−.08	.01	.17	.01	.32	.08
Age 9–11 spelling performance	−.27		−.10		.06		−.05		−.02		.13	
Age 9–11 arithmethic performance	.16		.16		.12		.02		.06		−.08	
TOTAL R^2		.34*		.32		.55***		.57***		.27*		.32*

[a] $p < .10$, * $p < .05$, ** $p < .01$, *** $p < .001$.
[b] R^2 change values associated with the block.
ASPD, Antisocial Personality Disorder.

set of Wave 2 and Wave 3 predictors used in previous analyses was used here. Among COAs, performance IQ, that is, better coping and problem-solving skills, as well as a higher approach temperament at school entry (Wave 2), were significant predictors. A high level of performance skill, along with a tendency to approach rather than avoid new circumstances, contributed to the development of a positive self-image. Wave 2 spelling performance was also a significant predictor. Among non-COAs, Wave 2 performance IQ was a marginally significant predictor of self-esteem. Reading performance in school at Wave 2 was also positively related to later self-esteem. Similar to COAs, performance IQ was a predictor of self-esteem among the non-COAs. But unlike the COAs, reading performance in school affected the self-image of the non-COAs more than did spelling performance.

These variable-centered analyses, which obscure individual differences, are highly suggestive of a traitlike model of positive and negative adaptation, and there is little evidence that experience plays much of a role over the longer term. Among both COAs and non-COAs, the significant predictors of both externalizing and internalizing problem outcomes, IQ and temperament, are factors that have a substantial constitutional component. The same kind of variable network was predictive of positive self-esteem in middle childhood, with the exception that two social achievement variables (reading and spelling achievement) also had a significant effect. In contrast, the person-centered analyses are suggestive of a more dynamic process, especially for the resilient children. We elaborate on this point in the next section.

CONCLUSIONS

We started this exploration with several questions; we now deal with each of them in turn and then move to the more general issue of what appears to be protective and what not. We close with some observations about the prevention implications of our work and about the issue of resilience.

1. Early in life, are resilient children distinguishable from their less resilient peers in attributes other than the ones that define them as resilient? Our findings indicate that they are, with the resilient children falling in the upper range of the overall group in intellectual functioning and not being distinguishably different from their nonchallenged counterparts, who scored highest in intellectual functioning. The groups also differed in temperament during this preschool period, with resilient children showing less emotional reactivity than both of the low-adaptation groups (i.e., the troubled and vulnerable children). In contrast, the vulnerable group, the one with the greatest challenges, was most strongly differentiated from the high-functioning nonchallenged children in the areas of activity (theirs was higher), attention span (lower), and emotional reactivity (higher).

2. Over time, what characteristics distinguish resilient children from their less well functioning vulnerable peers who come from similarly adverse environments? Are any pattern differences distinguishable between these two groups over the span between middle childhood and early adolescence? If one inspects the findings in Table 4.1 from a pattern perspective, it is clear that there are some obvious differences. One is that the grouping is highly effective in differentiating these developmentally important domains. Among 30 possible comparisons, more than half (60%) show differences. In addition, and not at all surprisingly, among the 18 comparisons where individual group differences were strong enough to be statistically reliable, all of them differentiated the children with the lowest personal and familial risk burden (the nonchallenged children) from those with the greatest risk burden (the vulnerable children).

What about specific differences between resilient and vulnerable children? There are relatively few, but those are revealing: Resilient children were less externalizing in their behavior in both middle childhood and adolescence, and they had better reading skills. To reframe this slightly, the resilient children were less likely to show conduct problems and they were more likely to demonstrate achievement skills in an area that is an essential base for so much other academic, occupational, and social development.

3. What characteristics distinguish the resilient children from their more advantaged nonchallenged peers? To understand this picture more completely, it is also helpful to examine the findings pertinent to this question. The answer is again that there are relatively few, but the ones that exist are indicative of a complex set of processes. As noted by Luthar and Cicchetti (2000), "even when at-risk individuals reflect exemplary, socially conforming behavioral profiles, many struggle with considerable distress" (p. 877). As noted earlier, and as shown in Figures 4.2 and 4.3, the resilient children were a bit more active than their nonchallenged counterparts and also were somewhat more externalizing in both middle childhood and early adolescence. But the dramatic difference is the substantially higher level of internalizing problems at early adolescence. In all other domains, no differences were present. The lack of differences here, in conjunction with the many differences occurring between the nonchallenged and vulnerable groups, indicates that the resilient children's functioning is intermediate between that of the least risk-burdened children and those with the heaviest burden. Moreover, inspection of the magnitude of the differences among the groups in Table 4.1 indicates that the resilient children are closer in functioning to their nonchallenged counterparts, except for their emerging internalizing difficulties. This conclusion is also suggested by the findings pertinent to question 2.

4. Do any differences exist between the troubled and vulnerable groups? Although not explicitly a part of our earlier inquiry, this question is also of considerable importance. Here the obverse question is being examined, namely, whether the later adaptation of children initially at the same level of difficulty is distinguishable, given that they are exposed to environments of strikingly different adversity over the course of development. The quantitative analyses indicate that no differences exist. And with the exception of internalizing symptomatology among the resilient children, the findings are strongly indicative of a pattern of autostability of developmental trajectories over substantial periods of time, irrespective of the challenge of familial adversity (Figures 4.2 and 4.3). Given the general parallelism of the trajectories shown between these groups, the evidence is suggestive of the operation of a set of diatheses, most probably biologically based, that would appear to provide developmental stability in the face of substantial differences in rearing environment.

At the same time, it would be remiss to ignore the suggestive evidence that the developmental matrix is more complex. For one, the comparisons tested here are between the two groups with the smallest *n* values; if there are underpowering effects in these analyses, this is the most likely place for them to be present. For another, a qualitative analysis of the 33 mean differences between the two groups is also instructive. Although these differences are small, the preponderance of them (67%) show the vulnerable group with poorer functioning. That is, the weight of the evidence is that there are differences in the direction of a higher risk burden leading to a poorer adaptational outcome; but such differences are small.

A Longer-Term Developmental Perspective on the Findings

Given that the study on which we are reporting has not yet fully passed the early adolescent way point in these children's lives, the story we tell needs to be regarded as very much of a work in progress. The study is only just reaching the point where we will be able to examine the relationship of these early grouping characteristics to the psychosexual and psychopathological outcomes of adolescence, in particular those of alcohol and other drug use and abuse.

Nonetheless, in contrast to the earlier work in this area that has looked primarily at relational factors, the information that is most complete in this account pertains to early and middle childhood, and in particular to issues of psychosocial adaptation, symptomatic outcomes, cognitive functioning, and academic achievement. Our findings indicate that (1) the concept of resilience, and its contrast adaptations, have relevance not only to psychosocial functioning but also to cognitive development and its sequelae of academic achievement. To the extent that this is so, the construct would appear to have applicability to a wide range of later psychosocial tasks that require more than socioemotional maturity for their mastery. (2) There also is strong evidence that early identifiers of successful psychosocial adaptation are predictive of both psychosocial and achievement outcomes some 10 years down the line from preschool, and that identifiers of poor early adaptation are likewise predictive of poorer later outcomes. (3) Findings also suggest that if interaction effects exist between early individual characteristics and environmental adversity, the magnitude of such effects upon later psychosocial and achievement outcomes is quite modest for most children, but it may be significant for that subset where there is the potential for greatest hope.

Conclusions and Implications for Prevention

In evaluating these findings, it is important to emphasize that the level of adversity experienced by the resilient and vulnerable children in this study is quite significant and comes close to that found among treatment samples. A variety of benchmark statistics indicate that the level of antisocial behavior and alcoholism among the parents in the high-adversity group is lower than that found among prison populations but is substantially greater than that found in the general U.S. population of alcohol abusing/dependent men. The lifetime comorbidity rate for any DSM-III-R disorder among alcoholic men is 44% in the general population (Helzer et al., 1991), 52% among the alcoholic fathers in our study, and 67% among the Epidemiologic Catchment Area (ECA) 5–site prison sample (Regier, et al., 1990), indicating that the general level of psychiatric disorder is very substantial. Lifetime comorbidity of ASPD in alcoholic prisoners is 74%; among the alcoholic fathers in this study the rate is 27%, and in the general U.S. male alcohol abuse/dependence population it is 15%. Thus, these findings should have direct relevance for child outcomes in of families where the level of adversity approximates that found in treatment settings. It is also possible that the lower levels of adversity that found in less severely troubled families would lead to more child variation over time and that the apparent continuity trajectory would be less apparent.

It should also be emphasized that the work being presented here was not an intervention study but rather an experiment of nature, as is true of all prospective studies. Within that framework, the present results provide only suggestive evidence for moderating effects as a function of child–environment interactions. Other work by our group indicates that moderation is attenuated in natural settings because of the nested nature of child risk in high-risk family structures (Wong et al., 1999; Zucker et al., 2000a). In other words, the vulnerable children are more likely to come from high-adversity families. In fact, some of the increasing behavioral difficulty observed among these children as they grow older has been explained as a function of familial exposure to spanking, persistent parent negative affect, and other negative family interactions (Wong et al., 1999).

At the same time, the nested nature of risk that is present among these families leaves open the possibility that the exacerbation of behavioral problems is a function of indirect genetic effects. The variable network we currently have at our disposal makes it impossible to evaluate these two plausible, and not necessarily competing, hypotheses about mechanisms.

NEXT STEPS

It is important for prevention designers to be aware that what nature produces by its own experiments does not provide the limits within which human experimenters can operate. An increasing number of investigators have been able to demonstrate how focused family- and parent-based interventions can be brought to bear to modify such highly adverse environments, with successful longer-term outcomes for the children (Hogue & Liddle, 1999; Kumpfer, 1998; Luthar & Suchman, 2000; Nye, Zucker, & Fitzgerald, 1999). The challenge remains that of identifying the most efficacious mechanism(s) for bringing about changes in this system, and also identifying the most critical timing points for the intervention. In that regard, our findings suggest the need for bifurcated intervention programs. For vulnerable and troubled children, the evidence points to the need for a multilevel intervention regimen that is based upon a chronic disease model. Such programming would involve initial evaluation and dosing, addressed to the child's difficulties as well as the difficulties of the family in which he or she is growing up. Periodic checkups, which provide an opportunity for renewed intervention when called for, would also be part of such a regimen. It would also be expected that such programming would be available over a substantial portion of the childhood life course (Zucker et al., 2000b). For resilient children, our findings suggest a different intervention strategy. The timing of the rise in internalizing symptoms, in the early elementary school years, suggests that truly preventive intervention dosing should begin at that point, not at the time when it reaches full symptomatic bloom in early adolescence. How long such a developmentally timed intervention would need to be in place is an empirical question. However, the presence of other coping skills (e.g., reading) in this group suggests that the intervention would be facilitated by the child's own orthogenic competence and that the dosing would not need to be as prolonged.

Two remaining issues warrant some comment. First, the work we have presented focuses heavily on the characterization of outcomes that occur among resilient and nonresilient children over relatively long spans of childhood. The work is highly inferential concerning the mechanisms that might be sustaining these effects. As already noted, other work by our group has implicated parent behavior and childrearing practices (Wong et al., 1999), individual differences in neurocognitive development that interact with level of familial adversity (Poon et al., 2000), and even genetic differences in regulation of the serotonergic system (Twitchell et al., 2001). It is imperative that the relationship among these influencing structures be better understood.

It is equally important to understand the long-term capability of the resilient group to fare under challenging circumstances. If resilience is truly in operation, then under conditions of acute adversity there should be a greater capacity to recover and reattain the successful adaptation that existed prior to the challenge (Luthar, Cicchetti, & Becker, 2000). Our analyses do not address this issue at the microlevel at which resilient activity takes place. They need to. Should a better recovery not be observed, then it is more likely that our initial grouping is better described as the initial "luck of the draw," in terms of having a better starting set of characteristics (determined by temperament, early family experiences, or both), which wear down with the increasing assault of an adverse environment. This issue remains a critical one for researchers to address. We plan to do so as the current study progresses.

Note

1. This recruitment involved 3-to 11-year-old daughters in the families. The majority of these girls joined the study at ages 6 to11, thus missing the Wave 1 assessment period. At the time the present data were analyzed, only 11 girls were available who had information at all three data waves. The literature

suggests that boys and girls may differ in their developmental trajectories of internalizing and externalizing problems (e.g., Achenbach, 1991; Zahn-Waxler, Klimes-Dougan, & Slattery, 2000). Due to the small girl *n*, we could not conduct any statistical analysis on gender differences. We therefore decided to exclude them. The ongoing study is currently recruiting an additional sample of girls that begins at Wave 1. Those data will be reported on as soon as they become available.

References

Achenbach, T. (1991). *Manual for the child behavior checklist/4–18 and 1991 profile.* Burlington: University of Vermont Department of Psychiatry.

Alterman, A., Searles, J., & Hall, J. (1989). Failure to find differences in drinking behavior as a function of familial risk for alcoholism: A replication. *Alcoholism: Clinical and Experimental Research, 10,* 305–310.

Bates, M., & Pandina, R. (1992). Familial alcoholism and premorbid cognitive deficit: A failure to replicate subtype differences. *Journal of Studies on Alcohol, 53,* 320–327.

Berlin, R., & Davis, R. B. (1989). Children from alcoholic families: Vulnerability and resilience. In T. F. Dugan & R. Coles (Eds.), *The child in our times* (pp. 107–123). New York: Brunner/Mazel.

Caspi, A., Moffitt, T. E., Newman, D. L., & Silva, E. A. (1996). Behavioral observations at age 3 years predict adult psychiatric disorders: Longitudinal evidence from a birth cohort. *Archives of General Psychiatry, 53,* 1033–1039.

Chassin, L. (1994). Studying individual-level factors for adolescent alcohol problems: The example of adolescent temperament. In R. A. Zucker, G. Boyd, & J. Howard (Eds.), *The development of alcohol problems: Exploring the biopsychosocial matrix of risk* (NIH Publication No. 94–3742, pp. 109–121). Bethesda, MD: National Institute on Alcohol Abuse and Alcoholism.

Chassin, L., Rogosch, F., & Barrera, M. (1991). Substance use and symptomatology among adolescent children of alcoholics. *Journal of Abnormal Psychology, 100,* 449–463.

Finn, P. R., Sharkansky, E. J., Viken, R., West, T. L., Sandy, J., & Bufferd, G. (1997). Heterogeneity in the families of sons of alcoholics: The impact of familial vulnerability type on offspring characteristics. *Journal of Abnormal Psychology, 106,* 26–36.

Fitzgerald, H. E., Sullivan, L. A., Ham, H. P., Zucker, R. A., Bruckel, S., & Schneider, A. M. (1993). Predictors of behavioral problems in three-year-old sons of alcoholics: Early evidence for onset of risk. *Child Development, 64,* 110–123.

Gillen, R., & Hesselbrock, V. (1992). Cognitive functioning, ASP, and family history of alcoholism in young men at risk for alcoholism. *Alcoholism: Clinical and Experimental Research, 16,* 206–214.

Goodwin, D. (1979). Alcoholism and heredity: A review and a hypothesis. *Archives of General Psychiatry, 36,* 57–62.

Grant, B. F. (2000). Estimates of U.S. children exposed to alcohol abuse and dependence in the family. *American Journal of Public Health, 90,* 112–115.

Harter, S. (1979). *Manual for perceived competence scale for children.* Denver: University of Denver Press.

Harter, S. (1982). The perceived competence scale for children. *Child Development, 53,* 87–97.

Henry, B., Feehan, M., McGee, R., Stanton, W., Moffitt, T. E., & Silva, P. (1993). The importance of conduct problems and depressive symptoms in predicting adolescent substance use. *Journal of Abnormal Child Psychology, 21,* 469–480.

Hogue, A., & Liddle, H. A. (1999). Family-based preventive intervention: An approach to preventing substance use and antisocial behavior. *American Journal of Orthopsychiatry, 69,* 278–293.

Huang, L. X., Cerbone, F. G., & Gfroerer, J. C. (1998). Children at risk because of substance abuse. In Office of Applied Studies, Substance Abuse and Mental Health Services Administration (Eds.), *Analyses of substance abuse and treatment need issues* (DHHS Pub. Doc. No. (SMA) 98–3227, Chapter 1, pp. 5–18). Rockville, MD: Author.

Hussong, A. M., & Chassin, L. (1994). The stress-negative affect model of adolescent alcohol use: Disaggregating negative affect. *Journal of Studies on Alcohol, 55,* 707–718.

Jacob, T., & Leonard, K. (1986). Psychosocial functioning in children of alcoholic fathers, depressed fathers and control fathers. *Journal of Studies on Alcohol, 47,* 373–380.

Jansen, R., Fitzgerald, H. E., Ham, H. P., & Zucker, R. A. (1995). Pathways into risk: Temperament and behavior problems in 3–5 year old sons of alcoholics. *Alcoholism: Clinical and Experimental Research, 19,* 501–509.

Jastak, S., & Wilkinson, G. S. (1984). *The Wide Range Achievement Test-revised: Administration manual.* Wilmington, DE: Jastak Associates.

Jessor, R., & Jessor, S. L. (1977). *Problem behavior and psychosocial development: A longitudinal study of youth.* New York: Academic Press.

Kumpfer, K. (1998). Selective preventive interventions: The Strengthening Families program. In R. S. Asher, E. B. Robertson, & K. L. Kumpfer (Eds.), *Drug abuse prevention through family interventions* (National Institute on Drug Abuse: Research Monograph No.177., pp. 160–207). Rockville, MD: National Institute on Drug Abuse.

Lerner, J. V., & Vicarey, J. R. (1984). Difficult temperament and drug use: Analyses from the New York Longitudinal Study. *Journal of Drug Education, 14,* 1–8.

Lerner, R. M., Palermo, M., Spiro, A., & Nesselroade, J. (1982). Assessing the dimensions of temperament individuality across the lifespan: The Dimensions of Temperament Survey. *Child Development, 53,* 149–159.

Luthar, S. S., & Cicchetti, D. (2000). The construct of resilience: Implications for interventions and social policies. *Development and Psychopathology, 12,* 857–885.

Luthar, S. S. , Cicchetti, D., & Becker, B. (2000). The construct of resilience: A critical evaluation and guidelines for future work. *Child Development, 71,* 543–562.

Luthar, S. S., & Suchman, N. E. (2000). Relational psychotherapy mothers' group: A developmentally informed intervention for at-risk mothers. *Development and Psychopathology, 12,* 235–253.

Magnusson, D. (1988). *Individual development from an interactional perspective: A longitudinal study.* Hillsdale, NJ: Erlbaum.

McCord, J. (1988). Identifying developmental paradigms leading to alcoholism. *Journal of Studies on Alcohol, 49,* 357–362.

Mun, E.-Y., Fitzgerald, H. E., Puttler, L. I., Zucker, R. A., & von Eye, A. (2000). Temperamental characteristics as predictors of externalizing and internalizing behavior problems in the contexts of high and low parental psychopathology. *Infant Mental Health Journal, 22,* 393–415.

Nye, C. L., Zucker, R. A., & Fitzgerald, H. E. (1999). Early family-based intervention in the path to alcohol problems: Rationale and relationship between treatment process characteristics and child and parenting outcomes. *Journal of Studies on Alcohol, Supplement No. 13,* 10–21.

Pandina, R. J., & Johnson, V. (1989). Familial drinking history and a predictor of alcohol and drug consumption among adolescent children. *Journal of Studies on Alcohol, 50,* 245–254.

Poon, E., Ellis, D. A., Fitzgerald, H. E., & Zucker, R. A. (2000). Intellectual, cognitive and academic performance among sons of alcoholics during the early elementary school years: Differences related to subtypes of familial alcoholism. *Alcoholism: Clinical and Experimental Research, 24,* 1020–1027.

Puttler, L. I., Zucker, R. A., Fitzgerald, H. E., & Bingham, C. R. (1998). Behavioral outcomes among children of alcoholics during the early and middle childhood years: Familial subtype variations. *Alcoholism: Clinical and Experimental Research, 22,* 1962–1972.

Regier, D. A., Farmer, M. E., Rae, D. S., Locke, B. Z., Keith, S. J., Judd, L. L., & Goodwin, F. K. (1990) Comorbidity of mental disorders with alcohol and other drug abuse. Results from the Epidemiologic Catchment Area (ECA) Study. Journal of the American Medical Association, 264, 2511–2518.

Robins, L. N., Helzer, J. E., Croughan, J. L., & Ratcliff, K. S. (1980). *The NIMH Diagnostic Interview Schedule: Its history, characteristics and validity.* St. Louis: Washington University School of Medicine.

Russell, M. (1990). Prevalence of alcoholism among children of alcoholics. In M. Windle (Ed.), *Children of alcoholics: Critical perspectives* (pp. 9–38). New York: Guilford Press.

Rutter, M. (1987). Psychosocial resilience and protective mechanisms. *American Journal of Orthopsychiatry, 57,* 316–331.

Selzer, M. L., Vinokur, A., & van Rooijen, L. (1975). A self-administered Short Michigan Alcoholism Screening Test (SMAST). *Journal of Studies on Alcohol, 36,* 117–126.

Sher, K. J. (1991). *Children of alcoholics: A critical appraisal of theory and research.* Chicago: University of Chicago Press.

Tarter, R. E. (1988). Are there inherited traits that predispose to substance abuse? *Journal of Consulting and Clinical Psychology, 56,* 189–196.

Terman, L. M., & Merrill, M. A. (1973) *Stanford-Binet Intelligence Scale – Manual for the third revision. Form L-M.* Chicago: Riverside Publishing.

Twitchell, G. R., Hanna, G. L., Cook, E. H., Stoltenberg, S. F., Fitzgerald, H. E., & Zucker, R. A. (2001). Serotonin transporter promoter polymorphism (5-HTTLPR) genotype is associated with behavioral disinhibition and negative affect in children of alcoholics. *Alcoholism: Clinical and Experimental Research, 25,* 953–959.

Wechsler, D. (1974). *Wechsler Intelligence Scale for Children – Revised.* New York: Psychological Corp.

Werner, E. E. (1986). Resilient offspring of alcoholics: A longitudinal study from birth to age 18. *Journal of Studies on Alcohol, 47,* 34–40.

West, M. O., & Prinz, R. J. (1987). Parental alcoholism and childhood psychopathology. *Psychological Bulletin, 102,* 201–218.

Windle, M. (1991). Salient issues in the development of alcohol abuse in adolescence. *Alcohol and Alcoholism, Supplement 1,* 499–504.

Wong, M. M., Zucker, R. A., Puttler, L. I., & Fitzgerald, H. E. (1999). Heterogeneity of risk aggregation for alcohol problems between early and middle childhood: Nesting structure variations. *Development and Psychopathology, 11,* 727–744.

Zahn-Waxler, C., Klimes-Dougan, B., & Slattery, M. J. (2000). Internalizing problems of childhood and adolescence: Prospects, pitfalls, and progress in understanding the development of anxiety and depression. *Development and Psychopathology, 12,* 443–466.

Zucker, R. A. (2000). Alcohol involvement over the life course. In National Institute on Alcohol Abuse and Alcoholism, *Tenth Special Report to the U.S. Congress on Alcohol and Health: Highlights from current research* (pp. 28–53). Bethesda, MD: U.S. Department of Health and Human Services.

Zucker, R. A., Chermack, S. T., & Curran, G. M. (2000a). Alcoholism: A lifespan perspective on etiology and course. In A. J. Sameroff, M. Lewis, & S. Miller (Eds.), *Handbook of developmental psychopathology* (2nd ed., pp. 569–587). New York: Plenum.

Zucker, R. A., Ellis, D. A., Bingham, C. R., & Fitzgerald, H. E. (1996a). The development of alcoholic subtypes: Risk variation among alcoholic families during early childhood. *Alcohol Health and Research World, 20,* 46–54.

Zucker, R. A., Ellis, D. A., Fitzgerald, H. E., Bingham, C. R., & Sanford, K. (1996b). Other evidence for at least two alcoholisms II: Life course variation in antisociality and heterogeneity of alcoholic outcome. *Development and Psychopathology, 8,* 831–848.

Zucker, R. A., & Fitzgerald, H. E. (1991). Early developmental factors and risk for alcohol problems. *Alcohol Health and Research World, 15,* 18–24.

Zucker, R. A., Fitzgerald, H. E., & Noll, R. B. (1990). Drinking and drug history (rev. ed., version 4). Unpublished instrument. East Lansing: Michigan State University.

Zucker, R. A., Fitzgerald, H. E., Refior, S. K., Puttler, L. I., Pallas, D. M., & Ellis, D. A. (2000b). The clinical and social ecology of childhood for children of alcoholics: Description of a study and implications for a differentiated social policy. In H. E. Fitzgerald, B. M. Lester, & B. S. Zuckerman (Eds.), *Children of addiction: Research, health, and policy issues* (pp. 109–141). New York: Routledge Falmer.

Zucker, R. A., Noll, R. B., Ham, H. P., Fitzgerald, H. E., & Sullivan, L. S. (1994). *Assessing antisociality with the Antisocial Behavior Checklist: Reliability and validity studies.* East Lansing and Ann Arbor: Michigan State University and University of Michigan.

5

Maternal Drug Abuse versus Other Psychological Disturbances

Risks and Resilience among Children

Suniya S. Luthar, Karen D'Avanzo, and Sarah Hites

The primary thesis of this chapter is one that flies in the face of rampant stereotypes: that maternal drug abuse is not necessarily more damaging to children's social-emotional well-being than are other maternal psychiatric disorders. It is widely believed that women who abuse illicit drugs are not just dissolute as individuals but also deplorable as parents, with children who, more so than offspring of parents with other mental illnesses, are disruptive, disturbed, or dysphoric. Empirical evidence supporting such beliefs, however, is tenuous at best. In this chapter, we present data from our own ongoing research to elucidate adjustment patterns among children whose mothers have histories of drug abuse. Our primary objective is to disentangle the degree to which risks to children accrue from maternal histories of drug abuse per se, rather than from various other adversities with which this disorder typically coexists.

A second objective is to determine the degree to which different forces, at the levels of the community, family, and child, might mitigate or exacerbate the risks faced by children of drug abusers – an exercise of pragmatic value in light of the magnitude of the risks. It is estimated that approximately 3 million American women regularly use illicit drugs such as cocaine and opioids (e.g., National Center on Addiction and Substance Abuse, 1996). Furthermore, most of these women retain responsibility for their minor children and negotiate the everyday challenges

Preparation of this chapter was made possible by support from the National Institutes of Health (RO1-DA10726 and RO1-DA11498) and the William T. Grant Foundation. The authors are grateful for comments on an earlier draft of this chapter from Sydney Hans, Thomas McMahon, and members of our research laboratory at Teachers College.

of parenting in the context of not only other psychiatric disorders (co-occurring with their addiction) but also scarce financial and emotional resources (McMahon & Luthar, 2000). Given the constellation of adversities confronting most children of drug-abusing mothers, research-based knowledge of salient risk modifiers could be valuable in informing interventions (Luthar, Cicchetti, & Becker, 2000).

In pursuing our two broad objectives, we begin this chapter with an overview of existing empirical evidence relevant to each. Following this, we present findings from our ongoing research involving school-age and adolescent children of mothers with (1) psychiatric diagnoses of cocaine or heroin abuse, (2) diagnoses of depressive or anxiety disorders, and (3) none of these disorders. In the concluding section of the chapter, we distill implications of our empirical findings for contemporary perspectives on maternal psychiatric disorders, as well as for future work across the spheres of research, interventions, and social policies.

MATERNAL DRUG ABUSE AND COEXISTING PROBLEMS: DISENTANGLING RISKS TO CHILDREN

Although adjustment difficulties among addicts' children are typically assumed to derive directly from their mothers' substance abuse, coexisting psychiatric disorders, particularly those in the affective and anxiety domains, may be substantially implicated. As a group, heroin- and cocaine-abusing women report high depression, low self-regard, and pervasive pessimism. For many of these women, exposure to traumatic life experiences also exacerbates vulnerability to anxiety problems such as Posttraumatic Stress Disorder. Studies have shown that depressive or anxiety diagnoses can occur in as many as 9 out of 10 women with lifetime histories of cocaine or opioid addiction (see Luthar, Cushing, Merikangas, & Rounsaville; 1998; Weissman et al., 1999).

There is a large body of convergent evidence on risks associated with maternal depression. In interactions with their children, depressed women are less attentive than others, show less reciprocity and synchronicity, and alternate between disengagement and intrusiveness. They are also more likely to display hostility and aggression in parenting and make negative attributions about their children (for a review, see Hammen, this volume). In parallel with these maternal problems, children of depressed mothers have been found to show poorer adjustment than comparison youth of similar socioeconomic backgrounds, with greater maladjustment confirmed among different developmental stages and across diverse domains of functioning (Hammen, this volume).

Although there have been fewer studies involving maternal anxiety disorders compared to depression, the two diagnoses frequently coexist and are highly overlapping in symptoms; extant evidence also suggests comparable risks to children. Based on their meta-analysis of 46 observational studies, Lovejoy and her colleagues argued that the various behavior disturbances of depressed parents are best conceptualized not as correlates of their depression per se, but rather as stemming from more generalized negative affect, that is, "aversive mood states including distress, anger, upset, guilt, and anxiety" (Lovejoy, Graczyk, O'Hare, & Neuman, 2000, p. 564). Support for this argument is seen in research evidence on children of parents with anxiety disorders, depressive disorders, both depressive and anxiety disorders, and neither of these. The first three of these groups of children were no different from each other, and all were significantly more likely than the fourth to have diagnosable mental disorders (Beidel & Turner, 1997).

Contrasting with the relatively strong evidence of risks linked with maternal negative affect, findings involving maternal substance abuse have been more equivocal. In comparisons of drug-exposed children and nonexposed children of the same socioeconomic status (SES), the former have sometimes shown more problems in specific neurological or cognitive domains (Mayes & Bornstein, 1997), but on psychological or behavioral dimensions, group differences have often been negligible. Summarizing the results of 46 studies on behavioral outcomes of young children prenatally exposed to drugs, Carta et al. (1994) reported significant effects for only half of the outcomes examined, and the majority of these were among infants less than 1 month old and were chiefly in the neurodevelopmental domain.

Relatively few studies have involved school-age children of addicts and comparison youth of the same SES, and those that exist suggest somewhat greater psychopathology among the former, although interpretations are complicated due to possible confounds. In a study of 4- to 18-year-old children of opioid abusers and of normal controls, Wilens and colleagues (1995) found higher levels of both internalizing and externalizing symptoms among the former. However, child symptoms were assessed solely by parent report and thus could have been inflated by parents' own distress. Similar potential for biases might apply in findings reported by de Cubas & Field (1993). In this case, 6- to 13-year-old children of substance-abusing mothers scored higher than matched controls on most dimensions assessed by mothers' reports, but for assessments conducted with the children themselves, differences were found on only 4 of the 16 group comparisons conducted.

The possibility that maternal substance abuse may be no more inimical than maternal affective disturbances – in fact, may even be less so – is suggested by findings of research involving different types of parent problems. Johnson and colleagues (1999) summarized results of 20 investigations on children exposed to crack/cocaine and over 40 studies of children exposed to maternal depression, stress, or low social support. They concluded that the psychological and behavioral difficulties identified among drug-exposed children are by no means unique to this population but occur also among youth exposed to the other risks examined. Similarly, Luthar and colleagues (1998) reported that 61% of the children of drug-abusing mothers in their study had at least one lifetime psychiatric disorder. These authors cited other research indicating *higher* rates (82%) among children of mothers with unipolar depression (see Hammen, this volume).

Within-study comparisons also indicate relatively weak effects of maternal substance abuse compared to other maternal problems. Among low-income toddlers, Johnson and colleagues (1999) found that adjustment problems did not differ as a function of drug exposure but did vary according to maternal stress and depression. In a 10-year study of low-income children first assessed at birth, concurrent maternal opioid abuse had nonsignificant links to children's psychopathology at age 10 years, whereas maternal psychological symptoms *other than* substance abuse were linked to various child outcomes (Wakschlag & Hans, 1999). Several other studies have shown that among children of heroin or cocaine abusers, psychopathology tends to be particularly high among those whose parents have coexisting depressive problems (e.g., Hans, Bernstein, & Henson, 1999; Weissman et al., 1999).

Relative Risks: Maternal Drug Abuse versus Affective Disturbances

In our research, we appraised the relative risks linked with mothers' drug abuse, versus their depressive or anxiety diagnoses, via two strategies. First, we compared the magnitude of links between the presence of each type of maternal illness with levels of children's adaptation in *each of* many psychological and behavioral domains. Second, we considered positive adaptation *across* multiple domains, as at-risk youth can excel in particular spheres while at the same time experiencing considerable trouble in others (Luthar et al., 2000). In both sets of analyses we expected, based on prior evidence, that drug abusers' offspring would show comparable or better adjustment than children of depressed or anxious mothers.

In operationalizing *positive adaptation*, we focused on adjustment dimensions likely to be strongly affected by the focal risks under consideration (mothers' serious psychopathology) and used cutoffs reflecting average or better levels of functioning (see Luthar et al., 2000). As in our past work (Luthar et al., 1998; Luthar & Cushing, 1999), we considered lifetime *psychiatric diagnoses* of both a disruptive and an internalizing nature; *symptom levels* of recent internalizing and externalizing problems; and levels of *social competence* in everyday life. Decisions to define resilience in terms of average rather than superior levels of adaptation were based on the seriousness of the risks confronting these children: maternal histories of substance abuse and other serious psychopathology, along with life in the context of urban poverty.

PROTECTIVE AND VULNERABILITY PROCESSES

In pursuing our second broad research objective, our selection of risk modifiers for empirical scrutiny was based in knowledge of forces generally salient (1) in urban poverty and (2) during later childhood through adolescence. These dual considerations, in turn, stemmed from defining characteristics of participants in our research. Our studies of parental substance abuse have focused on families in urban poverty – where drug problems are typically most concentrated – and on children older than 8 years old – an age group more likely than preschoolers to show elevated psychopathology, yet rarely considered in extant research on addicted mothers. In ensuing discussions, we overview relevant evidence on the child-, family-, and community-level protective and vulnerability indices we considered.

Among children in poverty, vulnerability associated with both *gender* and *age* varies, depending on the outcome considered (see Luthar, 1999, for reviews of findings on each). Consistent with findings in the developmental literature, boys are more likely to manifest externalizing disorders, whereas girls are more vulnerable to internalizing problems. Findings on age show that older children living in poverty are more likely to display counterconventional behavior patterns, whereas their younger counterparts tend to be more vulnerable to depressive problems (possibly because of fewer resources or less mature coping strategies).

High *intelligence* is among the most widely cited factors protecting children against various stressors, including family poverty (Masten & Powell, this volume). In terms of underlying mechanisms, a high IQ may imply superior coping abilities as well as the benefits of a history of academic success. Although high *academic success* in itself may also serve protective functions, its benefits may be attenuated for inner-city adolescents given deep-seated beliefs that this, in itself, can do little to ensure access to good jobs in mainstream society (see Cauce et al., this volume). Personal *attitudes toward deviance*, by contrast, are likely to be highly significant in affecting disturbance among adolescents in poverty: Urban high school students with high intolerance for deviance fare better than others in terms of engagement at school as well as avoidance of problem behaviors (Jessor, Turbin, & Costa, 1998).

With regard to familial influences, various types of maternal psychopathology can affect children's adjustment, but *severity of mothers' depressive symptoms* is likely to be particularly influential. As indicated earlier, reviews have established that the effects of depressive affect on parenting can be insidious and pervasive, with the potential to exacerbate mothers' emotional withdrawal and neglect, as well as irritability and aggressiveness. In a similar vein, feelings of *stress in the parenting role* can affect functioning in multiple domains, impairing mothers' ability to manage, attend to, and provide support to their children (Crnic & Acevedo, 1995). Qualitative and quantitative studies confirm the influence of both *positive and negative parenting behaviors* for youth in high-risk environments (see Luthar, 1999, for reviews), including levels of limit-setting, warmth (Cauce et al., this volume), and neglect or abuse (Bolger & Patterson, this volume).

Unlike these various aspects of mothers' functioning, maternal *ethnicity and single-parent of status* both tend to be more equivocal in relation to psychopathology among children in poverty (see Luthar, 1999, for reviews of studies on each). Minority ethnicity may be associated with a heightened risk for some child problems, but these effects tend to be weak *within* cohorts of low SES. Similarly, single-parent family status has shown modest links with child psychopathology, but this is by no means inevitable, particularly among ethnic minority families.

Among the community-level forces, *affiliation with deviant peers* is likely to be critical in conduct disturbances of youth in areas of urban poverty (Seidman & Pedersen, this volume). The isolation of poor urban neighborhoods from mainstream society, and the dearth of opportunities for youth to achieve goals in socially approved ways, jointly serve to promote bonding with antisocial peers, which in turn fosters deviant behavior patterns. Additionally, *exposure to community violence* can result in serious disturbances of both an internalizing and an externalizing nature (see Gorman-Smith & Tolan, this volume, for a review).

SUMMARY OF RESEARCH QUESTIONS

Based on evidence described here, we considered the following hypotheses in this study: (1) The ill effects of mothers' drug abuse is comparable to or less than the effects of maternal depressive and anxiety disorders; this will be evident in terms of child adjustment within particular domains as well as resilience across multiple spheres. (2) Children's maladjustment varies as a function of their intelligence, academic achievement, and tolerance of deviance; their mothers' dysthymia, parenting stress, and positive and negative parenting behaviors; and the levels of peers' delinquency and exposure to community violence.

METHODS

The mother–child dyads on whom we report here constitute a subset of the sample of an ongoing study aimed at disentangling the risks accruing from maternal drug abuse, other maternal disorders, and family poverty. To achieve variability on relevant dimensions, we recruited mothers from outpatient treatment facilities for substance abuse and for other mental health problems (chiefly depression and anxiety), as well as from community settings such as churches, neighborhood stores, and primary health care facilities.

The presence of *lifetime psychiatric disorders* was assessed based on structured interviews: the Diagnostic Interview Schedule for mothers (DIS-IV; Robins, 1995) and the Diagnostic Interview Schedule for Children (C-DISC-IV) and the C-DISC (NIMH DISC-IV Editorial Board, 1995). Maternal disorders were considered to be present only if they occurred during the lifetime of the child in the study, and child disorders were considered to be present if either the mother or the child endorsed them. Among both mothers and children, affective and anxiety lifetime diagnoses were considered in a single category for the analyses conducted here; to reduce confusion concerning the labels used in this report, however, we refer to this category as "Affective/Anxiety" among mothers and "Internalizing" among children. Similarly, children's lifetime disruptive behavior diagnoses (conduct, oppositional defiant, and attention deficit) were considered in a single category, referred to here as "Disruptive diagnoses." In assessing *dimensional child outcomes,* internalizing problems were measured based on child reports of depressive symptoms, whereas both externalizing symptoms and behavioral competence were assessed via mothers' reports.

Sociodemographic disadvantage was measured in terms of maternal education rather than SES given its greater stability as an indicator of disadvantage among substance abusers (whose monthly income can fluctuate substantially). With the exception of child intelligence and achievement, both of which were assessed by standardized tests, all other *vulnerability and protective factors* were measured by questionnaires administered to mothers and children in interview format. Children and mothers were interviewed concurrently in separate rooms, and child interviewers were unaware of mothers' psychiatric status. Preliminary analyses established the reliability of the assessments, with alpha coefficients ranging between .72 and .93.

Sample: Descriptive Data

At the time of this chapter was written, data on a total of 227 mothers were available for analysis. About half of these women ($n = 119$) had lifetime diagnoses of abuse of, or dependence on, cocaine, opiates, or both, and the rest had no history of drug abuse ($n = 108$). Both groups of mothers had educational levels of high school completion on average, with means of 12.4 and 12.0 years, respectively (these did not differ significantly). At the time of their assessments, average socioeconomic levels of both fell in the lowest category: unemployed or unskilled workers. The two groups were also comparable in gender representation and average age of their children participating in the study, with 55% and 54% of daughters in the two groups, respectively, and a mean child age of 12.0 and 12.1 years.

Although both groups of mothers included more ethnic minorities than Caucasians, minority representation was lower among the 119 drug abusers (56%) than the drug-free women (80%). This disproportionate representation stems, in part, from our efforts to match the groups as closely as possible on SES, as family poverty, regardless of ethnicity, confers significant risks for child psychopathology, whereas effects of minority ethnicity, with income held constant, are less consistent (Luthar, 1999). As noted earlier, the drug-abusing women in our study (as in others) were generally poor, with a high school education on average. Given contemporary demographic trends and uneven opportunities for social mobility

(Philips, Brooks-Gunn, Duncan, Klebanov, & Crane, 1998) in the general population of mothers *without* a history of serious psychiatric illness, this level of disadvantage tends to occur disproportionately among ethnic minority families. Although we will oversample for impoverished Caucasian mothers with no lifetime substance abuse in the remaining years of this study, in the analyses reported here, statistical controls were used to rule out any biases due to disproportionate minority representation.

RESULTS

Maternal Drug Abuse versus Affective/Anxiety Disorders

Group Comparisons: Categorical and Continuous Indicators
Table 5.1 provides profiles of adjustment of mothers and children, presented separately according to the presence of the two sets of maternal disorders of central interest in this study: drug abuse and affective/anxiety disorders. Of the 119 women with histories of drug abuse, about one in three ($n = 37$) had no lifetime affective/anxiety disorders (labeled as "Drug Only" in Table 5.1), whereas two-thirds did ("Comorbid"). Of the 108 drug-free mothers, approximately 41% ($n = 44$) had affective/anxiety disorders ("Affective/Anxiety Only"), and about 59% had neither diagnosis ("Neither").

In terms of problems among the mothers themselves, the four groups differed in the frequency of coexisting diagnoses (Table 5.1), with alcoholism being highest in the Comorbid group and antisocial personality disorder (ASPD) being highest in the Drug Only and Comorbid groups. (With regard to the latter, it should be noted that behaviors directly related to substance use, such as theft or prostitution to acquire drugs, were *not* excluded in making ASPD diagnoses, as they often are [see Luthar, Cushing, & Rounsaville, 1996], as we used summary scores from the computerized version of the DIS for purposes of this report. In the future, we will examine the degree to which elimination of drug-related behaviors reduces diagnosed rates of ASPD diagnoses.)

In comparing the groups on continuous variables, we conducted a preliminary multivariate analysis of variance (significant at $p < .0001$) and followed this up with univariate analyses of variance and posthoc comparisons of means. Results indicated that the Affective/Anxiety and Comorbid mothers generally reported significantly poorer functioning than the Neither group. In addition, the Affective/Anxiety mothers fared more poorly than the Drug Only mothers on several negative dimensions.

TABLE 5.1. *Characteristics of Mothers and Children According to Four Groups Based on Mothers' Diagnoses of Drug Abuse and Affective/Anxiety disorders: Drug Only; Comorbid; Affective/anxiety Only; And Neither*

Maternal Indices — Groups of Mothers by Diagnoses

Categorical	Drug Only n=37 n/%	Comorbid n=82 n/%	Affective/Anxiety Only n=44 n/%	Neither n=64 n/%	p	Eta sq
Minority ethnicity	22/60%	45/55%	34/77%	53/83%		
Alcoholism	11/30%	43/52%	9/21%	7/11%	** *	
Antisocial personality*	31/84%	71/87%	28/64%	26/41%	** * *	
Any disorder	32/87%	72/88%	31/71%	28/44%	** *	
Continuous (Means)						
Dysthymia[a]	13.65	27.74$_N$	22.01$_N$	3.85	** *	.10
Parenting stress[b]	78.73	86.82$_N$	90.69$_{D,N}$	68.65	** *	.14
Limit-setting[c]	48.83	47.50$_N$	50.44	53.51	*	.05
Communic/involvmnt[c]	49.73	47.49	49.35	51.36		.03
Low warmth/affection[c]	24.86	26.42	27.31$_N$	24.47	*	.04
Aggression/hostility[c]	23.79	26.90$_{D,N}$	28.76$_{D,N}$	22.80	** * *	.13
Neglect/indifference[c]	27.29	29.49	31.56$_{D,N}$	27.44	** * *	.10
Rejection[c]	14.69	16.07$_N$	17.76$_{D,N}$	12.77	** * *	.17
Low warmth/affection[d]	29.66	28.13	31.65	29.08		.01
Aggression/hostility[d]	21.62	21.57	24.88	22.77		.02
Neglect/indifference[d]	30.30	29.06	32.57$_{D,N}$	31.01	*	.04
Rejection[d]	15.95	15.41	17.10	16.08		.01

Child Indices — Groups of Mothers by Diagnoses

Categorical	Drug Only n=37 n/%	Comorbid n=82 n/%	Affective/Anxiety Only n=44 n/%	Neither n=64 n/%	p	Eta Sq.
Gender: Girls	20/54%	45/56%	25/57%	33/52%		.04
Affective/anxiety	8/22%	32/39%	20/46%	17/27%	*	
Disruptive	8/22%	23/28%	20/46%	5/8%	***	
Substance use	3/8%	10/12%	5/11%	2/3%		
Any disorder	17/46%	46/56%	31/71%	21/33%	**	
Continuous (Means)						
Depressive symptoms[e]	5.73	7.24	9.69$_D$	8.07	*	.04
Externalizing[f]	53.90$_N$	55.60$_N$	57.95$_N$	43.47	**	.12
Competence[f]	45.49	44.77	43.82	48.01		.02
Intelligence[g]	91.95	93.60	87.37	89.65		.03
Achievement[h]	88.15	91.66	88.27	88.89		.01
Intolerance deviance[i]	34.88	34.59	35.21	35.40		.01
Peer delinquency[j]	10.66	8.85	12.42	8.69		.02
Exposure to violence[k]	23.27	23.82	22.68	20.99		.02

Note: Superscripts represent instances where means differed at $p < .01$ from the Neither group (denoted with subscript N) and from the Drug group (subscript D); differences between the Comorbid and Affective/Anxiety groups were not significant on any dimension. For univariate F tests, * $p < .05$; ** $p < .01$; *** $p < .001$. Continuous variables in italics are based on child reports; others are based on mothers' reports. Measures included: [a]Millon Clinical Multiaxial Inventory–III (Millon, 1994); [b]Parenting Stress Index/Short Form (Abidin, 1990); [c]Parent–Child Relationship Inventory (Gerard, 1994); [d]Parental Acceptance/Rejection Questionnaire (Rohner, 1991); [e]Children's Depression Inventory (Kovacs, 1995); [f]Behavioral Assessment System for Children (Reynolds & Kamphaus, 1992); [g]Kaufman Brief Intelligence Test (Kaufman & Kaufman, 1990); [h]Wide Range Achievement Test (Wilkinson, 1993); [i]Attitudinal Intolerance for Deviance (Jesser, Donovan, & Costa, 1989; [j]Peer Delinquency Scale (Loeber, 1989); [k]Survey of Exposure to Community Violence (Richters & Saltzman, 1990).

Similar patterns were seen on children's psychiatric diagnoses. Both internalizing and disruptive disorders were highest among offspring of the Affective/Anxiety mothers, followed by the Comorbid and Drug Only groups. Children of the Affective/Anxiety mothers also had the highest self-reported depressive symptoms and mother-reported externalizing problems. Finally, children of Affective/Anxiety and Comorbid women reported poorer parenting by mothers on two of the four negative dimensions.

Given the uneven minority representation across the four groups, these group comparisons were all reexamined with mother's minority ethnicity status covaried at the outset (i.e., a Multivariate Analysis of Covariance Followed by Analyses of Covariance). Results were essentially identical to those presented in Table 5.1, based on comparisons of raw means.

Group Comparisons: Resilient Adaptation

In Figure 5.1, we display the proportions of children who manifested risk evasion (by criteria detailed later) across different adjustment domains, showing patterns separately for children defined on the basis of maternal drug abuse and affective/anxiety disorders. The three bars in each set represent, in turn, (1) the proportions of youth who had no disruptive

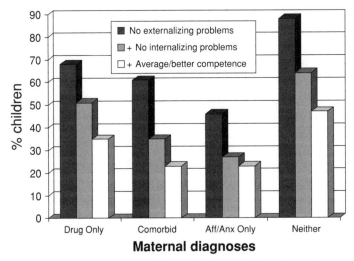

FIGURE 5.1 Percentage of children showing positive adaptation across multiple domains, by mothers' psychiatric diagnoses of drug abuse and affective/anxiety disorders.

psychiatric diagnoses *and* had externalizing symptom levels below the clinical cutoff (*T* score of 60); (2) of this subset, the proportion who also had no lifetime internalizing diagnoses *and* had depressive symptom levels below the clinical cutoff for that age and gender group; and (3) of this remaining subset, the proportion who had at least average competence scores (*T* score of 60 or higher). Results showed that among children whose mothers had neither drug abuse nor affective/anxiety disorders – the Neither group – about half met all three criteria for positive adjustment. In the Drug Only group, the proportion was a little over one third, and in the two groups with affective/anxiety disorders (with or without substance abuse, only about one-quarter of the children demonstrated positive adaptation across all domains. Group comparisons of these proportions showed that the differences were statistically significant, $\chi^2_{(3)}$ 11.40, $p < .01$. Follow-up comparisons of pairs of groups showed that the proportions of manifestly resilient children (in the final bar within each set) were no different in the Drug Only versus the Neither group $\chi^2_{(1)}$ 1.2, n.s., but were significantly in the Comorbid versus Neither ($\chi^2_{(1)}$ 9.06, $p < .003$; and Affective/Anxiety versus Neither groups $\chi^2_{(1)}$ 6.5, $p < .01$.

Maternal Drug Abuse versus Affective/Anxiety Disorders: Variable-Based Analyses

To supplement these person-based analyses (based on groups of children defined by maternal disorders), we conducted variable-based analyses to ascertain the degree to which maternal drug abuse and affective/anxiety disorders were each linked with the five child outcomes: disruptive disorders, internalizing disorders, depressive symptoms, externalizing symptoms, and competence. Logisitic and hierarchical multiple regressions were conducted for the categorical and continuous outcome variables, respectively, with controls for demographics (minority status, mother's education level, and child age and gender) at the outset. These variables were followed by presence/absence of maternal drug abuse, followed by maternal affective/anxiety disorders and then by two other diagnoses that also tend to co-occur with maternal addiction: alcoholism and ASPD. Findings showed that drug abuse was linked with significant risk ($p < .01$) for only externalizing symptoms, accounting for 3% of the variance. Conversely, maternal affective/anxiety diagnosis was associated with significant risk in three of the five domains: children's disruptive and affective/anxiety diagnoses and externalizing symptoms, respectively, accounting for 5%, 4%, and 5% of the variance. When these analyses were rerun with mothers' affective/anxiety disorders entered before drug use, the single effect detected earlier for drug abuse (with externalizing symptoms) became nonsignificant ($p < .10$). Thus, even the modest association between maternal drug abuse and child externalizing symptoms was partly explained by comorbid affective/anxiety diagnoses among these mothers.

In sum, our analyses on specificity of risks were consistent with expectations. In this generally low SES sample, risks unique to maternal drug abuse were smaller in magnitude than those linked with maternal affective/anxiety disorders.

Vulnerability and Protective Processes

In the interest of determining the specificity of vulnerability and protective processes, we examined them separately among children of mothers with drug abuse and those whose mothers had no lifetime history of addiction.[1] Separate analyses per group were considered preferable to using interaction terms in regressions, as interaction effects tend to be small in magnitude and highly unstable (Owens & Shaw, this volume; Rutter, this volume).

Preliminary examination of zero-order correlations showed (as expected) that within this economically disadvantaged sample, minority status had small, nonsignificant associations with all five child outcomes in both the Drug and No Drug groups. Similarly, given the narrow socioeconomic range in the sample as a whole, maternal educational status was not correlated with any child outcome, nor was single-parent status (see also Luthar et al., 1998). To conserve statistical power in our regression analyses, therefore, these maternal indices were excluded (supplementary analyses showed that their inclusion made no difference to the central findings).

In hierarchical multiple regression analyses, we entered child gender and age at the outset. Among the predictors, we gave priority to blocks of variables encompassing child and community indices, as these tend to have more significance than aspects of maternal functioning for children in the later childhood and adolescence years (see Luthar & Cushing, 1999; Owens & Shaw, this volume). Among the maternal characteristics, dysthymia and stress were entered in one block before the set of parenting behaviors, as global affective states are more likely to affect discrete maternal behaviors than the reverse. Within the block of parenting dimensions, we included the overall maltreatment score from the Parental Acceptance/Rejection Questionnaire (PARQ) measure rather than the four subscale scores, using children's reports of mothers' negative behaviors. Within each block of predictors, order of entry was allowed to vary with decreasing tolerance.

Major findings, presented in order of strength of associations, were as follows (see Table 5.2):

1. Parenting stress had strong associations with child outcomes – even though entered relatively late in the regression equations – with the number and magnitude of significant links being somewhat lower in the Drug than in the No Drug group. In the Drug group, this variable accounted for 19% of the variance in children's disruptive diagnoses and 16% of the variation in externalizing symptoms; parallel values in the No Drug group were 30% and 24%. In addition, among comparison children, maternal stress was related to child competence and depressive symptoms, with R^2 changes of 19% and 4%, respectively.

2. Child intelligence was linked with mothers' reports of both externalizing problems and competence in the Drug group and only with competence in the No Drug group.

3. Intolerance of deviance was significantly linked with disruptive diagnoses and depressive symptoms in the Drug group but with neither in the No Drug group.

4. Gender had significant effects only in the No Drug group, with girls having a greater risk for affective/anxiety disorders.

5. After considering all child and community indices, children's reports of mothers' maltreating behaviors were linked with self-reported depression among both Drug and comparison groups and, among the latter, with disruptive disorders as well.

6. Mothers' reports of their own limit-setting was linked with their ratings of fewer externalizing symptoms in the Drug group, and reports of high communication were associated with high competence in both groups.

DISCUSSION

Within this sociodemographically disadvantaged cohort, maternal drug abuse was linked with a lower unique risk for child psychopathology than were maternal depressive and anxiety disorders. In parallel, children's capacity to maintain successful adaptation across multiple domains seemed to be better among drug abusers' offspring than among children of mothers with affective or anxiety disorders. In our analyses of vulnerability and

TABLE 5.2. *Vulnerability and Protective Indices: Associations with Adjustment Outcomes among Children of Women with and without Lifetime Diagnoses of Drug Abuse*

Child Outcomes (Assessment Source)	Disruptive Disorders (Child and Mother Report)		Internalizing Disorders (Child and Mother Report)		Depressive Symptoms (Child Report)		Externalizing Symptoms (Mother Report)		Competence (Mother Report)	
Maternal Diagnostic Group	Drug[a] $R^2\Delta$	No Drug[a] $R^2\Delta$	Drug R^2	No Drug $R^2\Delta$	Drug $R^2\Delta$	No Drug $R^2\Delta$	Drug $R^2\Delta$	No Drug $R^2\Delta$	Drug $R^2\Delta$	No Drug $R^2\Delta$
Child indices										
Gender	.02	.02	.00	.09**	.00	.01	.01	.00	.01	.01
Age	.02	.02	.02	.00	.04*	.00	.01	.01	.04*	.02
Intelligence	.00	.00	.01	.02	.02	.01	.04*	.01	.09***	.05*
Achievement	.00	.01	.00	.01	.01	.04*	.00	.00	.00	.00
Intolerance of deviance	.04*	.00	.00	.00	.07**	.03	.02	.01	.00	.00
Community indices										
Peer delinquency	.02	.02	.00	.00	.00	.07**	.00	.03+	.00	.00
Community violence	.00	.01	.00	.00	.00	.01	.00	.00	.00	.00
Maternal indices										
Parenting stress	.19***	.30***	.01	.01	.02	.04*	.16***	.24***	.01	.19***
Dysthymia	.00	.00	.00	.00	.00	.00	.01	.03*	.01	.00
Maltreatment	.00	.03*	.01	.01	.05**	.07**	.00	.00	.00	.00
Limit setting	.01	.02	.01	.05[b]	.00	.00	.08***	.01	.01	.02
Communication	.02	.05[b]	.00	.01	.01	.00	.00	.00	.10***	.06**
TOTAL R^2	.32	.47	.06	.20	.23	.28	.34	.34	.26	.35

Note: Gender: girls = 0, boys = 1.

[a] The "Drug" group includes mothers with drug abuse alone, as well as those with drug abuse and affective/anxiety disorder (comorbid) (total $n = 119$). The "No Drug" group includes women without drug abuse, regardless of the presence or absence of affective/anxiety disorders ($n = 108$).

[b] These associations are not interpreted, as they probably represent suppressor effects; links are opposite in direction from those in zero-order correlations. Associations that are negative in direction are underlined; * $p < .05$; ** $p < .01$; *** $p < .001$.

118

protective factors, among the strongest associations found were those involving maternal stress in the parenting role. More modest effects were found for children's intelligence, their attitudes toward deviance, and the delinquency levels of their peers. The major findings are discussed in turn.

Maternal Psychiatric Disorders: Specificity of Effects

Most mothers with histories of drug abuse also have lifetime depressive or anxiety disorders, and when both sets of problems are considered, the latter seem to carry greater risks for child psychopathology. In this study, the incidence of psychopathology was found to be highest among children whose mothers had affective/anxiety diagnoses *without* coexisting drug abuse. Among these children, rates of any psychiatric diagnosis were one and a half times as high as those among youth in the Drug Only group (71% vs. 46%) and almost twice as high as those in the Neither maternal disorder group (71% vs. 33%). In parallel, we found that *evasion* of psychopathology – or the maintenance of cross-domain resilience – was lowest among children whose mothers had affective/anxiety disorders, in this case, with or without coexisting substance use.

Results of our variable-based analyses were consistent. After considering children's demographic characteristics such as age, ethnicity, and gender, regression analyses showed that maternal drug abuse was linked with child psychopathology only on one of the five outcomes considered: externalizing behaviors as perceived by their mothers. Even this one link became negligible when mothers' depressive and anxiety diagnoses were taken into account. By contrast, maternal affective/anxiety disorders were linked with risk across three of the five indices – children's diagnoses both in the disruptive and internalizing categories (based on mothers' and children's reports) as well as mothers' reports of externalizing symptoms. Furthermore, mothers with affective/anxiety disorders themselves reported more problems than others, both in personal adjustment and in parenting behaviors.

To some degree, these findings replicate prior findings on parental substance abuse coexisting with depression while at the same time yielding some fresh insights. In their family-genetic research, Weissman and colleagues (1999) have shown that children of opioid abusers manifest greater psychopathology in the presence, versus the absence, of comorbid depression in their parents. Building upon this work, the present findings suggest further that within the combination of parental substance abuse and depression, it is the latter more than the former that seems to be the more "active ingredient" in conferring risks to children (see also Rende & Weissman, 1999).

Support for this speculation about maternal depression is seen in prior findings that affective disturbances can have particularly pervasive and enduring effects on mothers' everyday functioning. As noted by Lovejoy and colleagues (2000) in their review, negative emotional states can engender a variety of negative maternal behaviors ranging from irritability, hostility, and aggression to withdrawal, apathy, and general lack of responsiveness. Furthermore, these authors note that negative parenting behaviors can persist even when a mother's depression is in remission, that is, between episodes of active symptoms. To date, there is no comparable evidence, to our knowledge, establishing such ubiquitous, tenacious, and robust ill effects on parenting as a result of a substance abuse diagnosis at some prior point in a mother's life.[2]

The apparently greater psychopathology in the Affective/Anxiety group may also partly derive from relatively negative – or relatively realistic – perceptions among mothers. Self-criticism and a low threshold for tolerating stress are hallmarks of internalizing disorders, such that slight "transgressions" by the mothers themselves (e.g., harsh parenting) or children (disruptiveness) could come to assume large proportions in the mothers' minds. This suggestion of pronounced negative appraisals among depressed mothers is consistent with our finding that group differences were far greater when it was mothers rather than their children who were rating their negative parenting behaviors. Effect sizes of group comparisons in Table 5.1 ranged from 4% to 17% in the former instance and from 1% to 4% in the latter.

Finally, social-cognitive aspects of the children's perceptions of their mothers may also play a role in explaining differential risk levels. To some degree, maternal disorders such as alcoholism or drug abuse carry a tangible "cause" of the problem, in that there is the potential for children to make associations between mothers' drinking (or being out late at night) and the erratic or disordered behavior that follows. By contrast, when mothers' presentation is one of lassitude and listlessness, or fearfulness and anxiety, the causes of the problem, as well as their onset and cessation, are all far more nebulous. Children may often fear that they have caused the mother's depression, and concomitantly feel driven to find some way to improve her spirits. Consistent with these speculations, Beardslee and colleagues have demonstrated that children's cognitive understanding of their parents' depression is a key treatment component

(Beardslee, Versage, Salt, & Wright, 1999), and Hammen (this volume) describes youth who at an early age assume the role of emotional care-takers of their depressed mothers. In sum, then, cognitive uncertainty, confusion, and a sense of pressure to rectify the problem may jointly con-tribute to particularly high vulnerability among children of dysphoric, apathetic mothers.

Vulnerability and Protective Processes

In our consideration of vulnerability and protective factors, by far the strongest associations found were those between maternal stress and both diagnostic and symptom indicators of children's externalizing behaviors. By itself, maternal stress explained 19% and 30% of variability in rates of disruptive diagnoses among children of drug abusers and comparison children, respectively, and 16% and 24% of variability in their external-izing symptoms. These associations are noteworthy not only because of their magnitude, but also because stress was entered relatively late in re-gression equations, that is, after considering overlapping effects of many child and community characteristics.

Whereas such findings can, in theory, be largely artifactual due to as-pects of data analysis or measurement, we found little evidence of this in our study. One possibility we considered, for example, was that associa-tions involving stress were stronger than others only because preceding variables in regressions were psychometrically weak. As reported earlier, however, all measures had good reliability coefficients, and simple cor-relations attested to their validity (e.g., correlation coefficients among intolerance of deviance, peer delinquency, and community violence, all preceding stress in regressions, were statistically significant with a median absolute value of .35). Similarly, we examined whether these links sim-ply reflected shared variance due to measurement of both by maternal report, but found that maternal stress was also significantly related to children's diagnoses based solely on children's own reports.

In terms of underlying mechanisms, it is quite possible that links be-tween maternal stress and child problems were bidirectional in nature. Children may often have acted out in reaction to maternal stress, which, as noted earlier, can pervade multiple aspects of mothers' everyday func-tioning. Equally, however, mothers may have reacted negatively to their children's obstreperous and delinquent behaviors. Cross-lagged associa-tions in future longitudinal research could help illuminate the relative strength of these associations.

One of our goals was to explore the specificity of vulnerability and protective processes – their differential salience among drug abusers' children versus others – and in interpreting our regression results, we focus here only on instances of recurrent, mutually consistent findings. The first of these differences concerned parenting stress, which was linked with more child outcomes in the No Drug than in the Drug group. To some degree, this difference may derive from the narrower range of stress scores among the latter. The No Drug group included the two subgroups of mothers in this sample who had the lowest and highest levels, respectively, of parenting stress (the Neither and Affective/Anxiety groups; see Table 5.1). The wide range of almost two standard deviations between the average stress scores of these two groups probably increased the likelihood of detecting significant links with other constructs.

Children's *attitudes toward deviance* had somewhat stronger links with disruptive disorders and depression among children in the Drug group than the others, and these findings may partly reflect the high social deviance of mothers with histories of drug abuse (i.e., more so than that of mothers with other types of mental illness). In other words, our findings may indicate buffering or vulnerability effects, wherein a child's personal intolerance of deviance was particularly helpful (or tolerance of deviance was particularly deleterious) when it co-occurred with illegal behavior patterns in the mother. Considering alternative directional influences, it is possible also that child psychopathology operated as a vulnerability-reactive factor, wherein depression, for example, led to high child tolerance of deviance chiefly when it occurred in the context of high maternal deviance. The assumption common to each of these speculations is that maternal deviance, as a proxy for the syndrome of illegal behaviors linked with substance abuse, might catalyze or potentiate the effects of negative attributes including high levels of psychopathology among children or their personal endorsement of deviance among others.

A third construct to show somewhat "selective" associations was intelligence: This was more strongly linked with both mother-rated child outcomes (externalizing symptoms and competence) in the Drug than in the No Drug group. Similar findings were obtained in a previous study involving substance abusers' offspring (Luthar et al., 1998), wherein children's receptive vocabulary scores were related to mothers' reports of low child psychopathology and high competence – but with no child-rated outcomes. These findings collectively raise the possibility that to some degree, drug-abusing mothers may be as reactive to their children's functioning as the converse. Stated differently, intelligence may in fact serve protective functions for drug abusers' children, but given the absence of links with children's *self-reported* adjustment, it is possible that drug-abusing mothers, many of whom rely on their children for emotional support and companionship (Luthar & Suchman, 2000), may also have particularly positive views of their more intelligent children.

As with the community indices discussed previously, the relative lack of links for maternal dysthymia or specific parenting behaviors in our regressions does not suggest their unimportance, but rather probably derives from their substantial overlap with other constructs preceding them in equations. Zero-order correlations showed significant associations, as expected, between dysthymia and stress; between each of these and the various parenting behaviors; and between dsythymia, parenting behaviors, and the different child outcomes. In all probability, therefore, the high overlap across these various constructs rendered it difficult for each to achieve statistical significance when entered into the same hierarchical multiple regression analysis.

In contrast to these indices, gender was unrelated to child psychopathology even though entered first in the regression equations – again, a finding obtained in prior studies of substance abusers' children (e.g., Luthar et al., 1998). This lack of gender differences may partly reflect the high general levels of disturbance in drug abusers' families, which may cause girls to develop not only the typically "female" disorders such as depression, but also the more commonly "male" diagnoses such as conduct problems (and the converse for males).

Limitations, Implications, and Conclusions

Several limitations qualify the conclusiveness of our findings, the first of which is that they are based on cross-sectional data. Psychiatric diagnoses were based on retrospective reports of lifetime problems, which can be subject to recall biases. Inferences about causality are precluded; in addition to bidirectional links between constructs (e.g., maternal psychopathology leads to child disorder and the converse), third variables, such as family life in chronic poverty, could account for variations in levels of each. Our suggestions about possible differences in adjustment processes among children of drug users versus others are entirely speculative, being based in exploratory analyses rather than in testing of a priori hypotheses. Finally, the imbalanced ethnic composition of our subgroups constitutes another limitation, notwithstanding the statistical controls we employed in the analyses presented here.

Aside from these limitations, it is worthwhile to emphasize two important caveats in considering our findings on maternal drug abuse, the first of which is that they do not by any means suggest that this is a low-risk parental problem. More than half of the drug abusers' children (53%) in this sample had at least one lifetime psychiatric diagnosis themselves by the average age of 12 years – a statistic far from trifling. Additionally, most of the children had not yet reached midadolescence, a period of sharp escalation in many problems including conduct disturbances, depressive disorders, and (most significantly from the standpoint of this sample) substance use. Finally, our comparison group was also clearly a troubled one, composed mostly of poor mothers in inner-city neighborhoods, 4 in 10 of whom also had at least one psychiatric disorder. Similarity to the children of these mothers is in no way reassuring about the levels of disturbance we found among children in the Drug group.

The second caveat is that our data pertain only to women's substance abuse at some period during the lifetimes of their children, and not to their current abuse of cocaine or heroin. Most of the women in this study were in treatment, and many, if not most, had achieved some level of abstinence. It is quite plausible that if we had a sample of women with contemporary problems of drug abuse, then their children would in fact have shown more problems than SES-matched others.

Although the analyses reported here encompass lifetime and not current heroin or cocaine abuse, we do believe that our findings have implications for both policies and public sentiments about addiction, for even mothers who are stable in drug programs face attitudes that are wary at best and criminalizing at worst. Perhaps more so than any other psychiatrically disordered group, mothers with histories of drug addiction confront condemnation and censure from the lay public as well as policy makers (see Garrity-Rokous, 1994; Luthar & Suchman, 2000). Whereas mothers with histories of depression are frequently often seen as victims, those with prior drug dependence are usually judged as having willfully jeopardized their families' well-being. With relapses into active symptomatology, the former rarely confront the punitive measures that are commonly meted out to the latter, such as revocation of parental rights. As we weigh such disparities in attitudes, it is worthwhile to consider that drug dependence is not a lifestyle that would be volitionally chosen by anyone. This is a mental illness, and among many mothers, it is an illness that emerges in response to years of distress, isolation, and alienation. By the same token, it is also an illness that can show considerable improvement with therapeutic attention to the women's personal well-being (e.g., Luthar & Suchman, 2000).

It is precisely these aspects of mothers' psychological adjustment that we believe require concerted attention in future interventions for drug-abusing mothers. Although these women are often described as being refractory to treatment, programs currently available for them are typically limited in scope: For the 9 of every 10 drug-abusing mothers who have serious disturbances of affect (Luthar et al., 1998), there is usually little or no attention to these psychological problems in their drug clinics. Accumulating research evidence points to the urgent need for integrative approaches to treatment, where the vital relapse-prevention components of drug treatment are supplemented by therapies for psychological and parenting concerns. This could be done by incorporating, within outpatient drug programs, not only supportive psychotherapies developed for addicted mothers but also other widely tested treatments originally developed for at-risk mothers in general, such as Olds's Nurse Home Visitation Program (Olds et al., 1998), Lieberman's Toddler-Parent Psychotherapy (Lieberman, Weston, & Pawl, 1991).

Lest the preceding recommendations be countered with protests that most drug-abusing mothers do in fact receive enough attention for other mental health and parenting problems, several obstacles bear brief mention. First, treatment services for substance abuse and other psychiatric disorders continue to be splintered, despite increasing calls for their provision under one roof (e.g., Knitzer, Yoshikawa, Cauthen, & Aber, 2000; McMahon & Luthar, 1998). Second, there are considerable logistical problems for any mother committed to daily trips to methadone clinics (in the context of poverty and, often, sole responsibility for minor children) to undertake quests for additional treatment in other settings. Third, even if such additional treatment were sought, the service providers would, in all likelihood, be less than welcoming, for community mental health clinics are often reluctant to accept as patients individuals already attending drug treatment clinics. The long and short of this issue, then, is that the emotions subsumed under the high-risk *negative affect* pattern (Lovejoy et al., 2000) – depression, anxiety, parenting stress, and guilt – are inordinately high among mothers with prior addiction, yet receive no attention in the typical substance abuse clinic – and thus remain neglected altogether, with the potential for accruing risks to children over time.

Beyond these treatment implications for treating drug-abusing mothers, our findings clearly underscore the need for attention to emotional distress and stress more generally among women in poverty. The non-trivial effect sizes for these constructs within our analyses, and their potential to become implicated in mutually aggravating cycles with child psychopathology, jointly point to the urgency of this need. It is vital too that mental health service providers, as well as policy makers, recognize their far lower concern with maternal disturbances of this nature – which are relatively covert and affect mostly the women themselves – compared to disorders that are more blatant and impinge upon those in mainstream society (such as a woman's law-breaking or disruptive behaviors). Addressing depression among mothers in poverty can no longer be seen as a luxury to be considered only after the "more pressing" disorders have been cured. Even if it is only to minimize psychopathology in the next generation, community service providers must directly address the stress and distress experienced by many mothers of young children living in conditions of poverty.

In conclusion, the findings of this study indicate that among economically disadvantaged families, a mother with a prior history of drug abuse is no more inimical for her children's well-being than her counterpart who has been drug-free. This by no means implies that children of poor, drug-abusing mothers are psychologically robust; it simply implies that difficulties are still more pronounced among their counterparts whose mothers have experienced depressive or anxiety disorders. Of the vulnerability and protective factors we have examined here, the most robust effects were found for mothers' stress in the parenting role. Our analyses did suggest modest associations for some nonmaternal indices, such as children's attitudes toward deviance or intelligence, but maternal stress was linked with multiple dimensions of child adaptation, even after considering the effects of various child and community forces.

Implications for future health care policies are clear: There must be specific treatment of mothers' distress and parenting problems within substance abuse treatment facilities and concerted attention to these issues more generally among women living in urban poverty. To be sure, we could plan simply to treat the children of these high-risk mothers as and when they, as adults themselves, come to manifest disruptive or illegal behaviors that inconvenience society. Rather than planning for punitive or rehabilitative strategies at that late stage, however, the more prudent course would seem to be to focus proactively on prevention. From the standpoints of reducing emotional suffering, fostering resilient adaptation, and maximizing the cost efficacy of social programs, there is urgent need for interventions targeting what is clearly critical to maximize children's potential: the emotional well-being of their primary caretakers and the capacities of these adults to maintain supportive, efficacious, and consistent patterns of parenting in their everyday lives.

Notes

1. Sample size restrictions precluded separate regression analyses for the four groups in Table 5.1, defined based on the presence/absence of maternal drug abuse *and* affective/anxiety disorders.
2. In other analyses, consideration of the women's treatment histories (e.g., length of psychiatric treatments) did not affect the group differences that we found.

References

Abidin, R. R. (1990). *Parenting Stress Index: Manual* (2nd ed.). Charlottesville, VA: Pediatric Psychology Press.

Beardslee, W. R., Versage, E. M., Salt, O., & Wright, E. (1999). The development and evaluation of two intervention strategies for children of depressed parents. In D. Cicchetti & S. L. Toth (Eds.), *Rochester symposium on developmental psychopathology: Vol 9. Developmental approaches to prevention and intervention* (pp. 111–151). Rochester, NY: University of Rochester Press.

Beidel, D. C., & Turner, S. M. (1997). At risk for anxiety: I. Psychopathology in the offspring of anxious parents. *Journal of the American Academy of Child and Adolescent Psychiatry, 36*, 918–924.

Carta, J. J., Sideridis, G., Rinkel, P., Guimaraes, S., Greenwood, C., Baggett, K., Peterson, P., & Atwater, J. (1994). Behavioral outcomes of young children prenatally exposed to illicit drugs: Review and analysis of experimental literature. *Topics in Early Childhood Special Education, 14*, 184–216.

Crnic, K., & Acevedo, M. (1995). Everyday stresses and parenting. In M. H. Bornstein (Ed.), *Handbook of parenting, Vol. 4: Applied and practical parenting* (pp. 277–297). Mahwah, NJ: Erlbaum.

de Cubas, M. M., & Field, T. (1993). Children of methadone-dependent women: Developmental outcomes. *American Journal of Orthopsychiatry, 63*, 266–276.

Garrity-Rokous, F. E. (1994). Punitive legal approaches to the problem of prenatal drug exposure. *Infant Mental Health Journal, 15*, 218–237.

Gerard, A. B. (1994). *Parent–child relationship Inventory (PCRI) manual.* Los Angeles: Western Psychological Services.

Hans, S. L., Bernstein, V. J., & Henson, L. G. (1999). The role of psychopathology in the parenting of drug-dependent women. *Development and Psychopathology, 11*, 957–977.

Jessor, R., Donavan, J. E., & Costa, F. M. (1989). *School Health Study.* Boulder: Boulder Institute of Behavioral Science, University of Colorado.

Jessor, R., Turbin, M. S., & Costa, F. M. (1998). Risk and protection in successful outcomes among disadvantaged adolescents. *Applied Developmental Science, 2*, 194–208.

Johnson, H. L., Nusbaum, B. J., Bejarano, A., & Rosen, T. S. (1999). An ecological approach to development in children with prenatal drug exposure. *American Journal of Orthopsychiatry, 69*(4), 448–456.

Kaufman, A. S., & Kaufman, N. L. (1990).*Kaufman Brief Intelligence Test.* Circle Pines, MN: American Guidance Service.

Knitzer, J., Yoshikawa, H., Cauthen, N. K., & Aber, J. L. (2000). Welfare reform, family support, and child development: Perspectives from policy analysis and developmental psychopathology. *Development and Psychopathology, 12,* 619–632.

Kovacs, M. (1995). *Children's depression inventory manual.* New York: Multi-Health Systems.

Lieberman, A., Weston, D., & Pawl, J. H. (1991). Preventive intervention and outcome with anxiously attached dyads. *Child Development, 62,* 199–209.

Loeber, R. (1989). *Life history studies.* Pittsburgh, PA: Western Psychiatric Institute and Clinic.

Lovejoy, M. C., Graczyk, P. A., O'Hare, E., & Neuman, G. (2000). Maternal depression and parenting behavior: A meta-analytic review. *Clinical Psychology Review, 20,* 561–592.

Luthar, S. S. (1999). *Poverty and children's adjustment.* Thousand Oaks, CA: Sage.

Luthar, S. S., Cicchetti, D., & Becker, B. (2000). The construct of resilience: A critical evaluation and guidelines for future work. *Child Development, 71,* 543–562.

Luthar, S. S., & Cushing, G. (1999). Neighborhood influences and child development: A prospective study of substance abusers' offspring. *Developmental Psychology, 11,* 763–784.

Luthar, S. S., Cushing, G., Merikangas, K., & Rounsaville, B. J. (1998). Multiple jeopardy: Risk/protective factors among addicted mothers' offspring. *Development and Psychopathology, 10,* 117–136.

Luthar, S. S., Cushing, G., & Rounsaville, B. J. (1996). Gender differences among opioid abusers: Pathways to disorder and profiles of psychopathology. *Drug and Alcohol Dependence, 43,* 179–189.

Luthar, S. S., & Suchman, N. E. (2000). Relational Psychotherapy Mothers' Group: A developmentally informed intervention for at-risk mothers. *Development and Psychopathology, 12,* 235–253.

Mayes, L. C., & Bornstein, M. H. (1997). The development of children exposed to cocaine. In S. S. Luthar, J. Burack, D. Cicchetti, & J. R. Weisz (Eds.), *Developmental psychopathology: Perspectives on adjustment, risk, and disorder* (pp. 166–188). New York: Cambridge University Press.

McMahon, T. J., & Luthar, S. S. (1998). Bridging the gap for children as their parents enter substance abuse treatment. In R. L. Hampton, V. Senatore, & T. P. Gulotta (Eds.), *Substance abuse, family violence, and child welfare: Bridging perspectives. Issues in children's and families' lives* (Vol. 10., pp. 143–187). Thousand Oaks, CA, Sage.

McMahon, T. J., & Luthar, S. S. (2000). Women in treatment: Within-gender differences in the clinical presentation of opioid-dependent women. *Journal of Nervous and Mental Disease, 188,* 679–687.

Millon, T. (1994). *Millon Clinical Multiaxial Inventory-III.* Minneapolis: National Computer Systems.

National Center on Addiction and Substance Abuse at Columbia University. (1996). *Substance abuse and the American woman.* New York: Author.

NIMH DISC-IV Editorial Board. (1995). *The NIMH diagnostic interview schedule for children.* Unpublished manuscript, Columbia University, New York.

Olds, D., Henderson, C., Kitzman, G., Eckenrode, J., Cole, R., & Tatelbaum, R. (1998). The promise of home visitation: Results of two randomized trials. *Journal of Community Psychology, 26,* 5–21.

Philips, M., Brooks-Gunn, J., Duncan, G. J., Klebanov, P., & Crane, J. (1998). Family background, parenting practices, and the Black–White test score gap. In C. Jencks & M. Phillips (Eds). *The Black–White test score gap* (pp. 103–145). Washington, DC: Brookings Institution.

Rende, R., & Weissman, M. M. (1999). Sibling aggregation for psychopathology in offspring of opiate addicts: Effects of parental comorbidity. *Journal of Clinical Child Psychology, 28,* 342–348.

Reynolds, C. R., & Kamphaus, R. W. (1992). *BASC: Behavioral assessment system for children.* Circle Pines, MN: American Guidance Service.

Richters, J. E., & Saltzman, W. (1990). *Survey of exposure to community violence.* Bethesda, MD: National Institute of Health.

Robins, L. (1995). *Announcing DIS IV: A major revision.* Unpublished manuscript, Washington University School of Medicine.

Rohner, P. R. (1991). *Handbook for the study of parental acceptance and rejection.* Storrs: Center for the Study of Parental Acceptance and Rejection, University of Connecticut.

Wakschlag, L. S., & Hans, S. L. (1999). Relation of maternal responsiveness during infancy to the development of behavior problems in high-risk youths. *Developmental Psychology, 35*(2), 569–579.

Weissman, M. M., McAvay, G., Goldstein, R. B., Nunes, E. V., Verdeli, H., & Wickramaratne, P. J. (1999). Risk/protective factors among addicted mothers' offspring: A replication study. *American Journal of Drug and Alcohol Abuse, 25,* 661–679.

Wilens, T. E., Biederman, J., Kiely, K., Bredin, E., & Spencer, T. J. (1995). Pilot study of behavioral and emotional disturbance in the high-risk children of parents with opioid dependence. *Journal of the American Academy of Child Adolescent Psychiatry, 34,* 779–785.

Wilkinson, G. S. (1993). *WRAT3: Wide Range Achievement Test.* Wilmington, DE: Wide Range.

6

Resilience to Childhood Adversity

Results of a 21-Year Study

David M. Fergusson and L. John Horwood

INTRODUCTION

There has been a large amount of research on the contributions of childhood and familial factors to the development of psychopathology in children and young people (for reviews see, e.g., Farrington et al., 1990; Hawkins, Catalano, & Miller, 1992; Loeber, 1990; Patterson, DeBaryshe, & Ramsey, 1989; Rutter & Giller, 1983). This research has established that young people reared in disadvantaged, dysfunctional, or impaired home environments have increased risks of a wide range of adverse outcomes that span mental health problems, criminality, substance abuse, suicidal behaviors, and educational underachievement. Although popular and policy concerns have often focused on the role of specific factors such as child abuse, poverty, single parenthood, family violence, parental divorce, and the like, the weight of the evidence suggests that the effects of specific risk factors in isolation on later outcomes often tend to be modest (Fergusson, Horwood, & Lynskey, 1994; Garmezy, 1987; Rutter, 1979; Sameroff, Seifer, Barocas, Zax, & Greenspan, 1987). What distinguishes the high-risk child from other children is not so much exposure to a specific risk factor but rather a life history characterized by multiple familial disadvantages that span social and economic disadvantages; impaired parenting; a neglectful and abusive home environment; marital conflict; family instability; family violence; and high exposure to adverse family life events (Blanz, Schmidt, & Esser, 1991; Fergusson et al., 1994; Masten,

This research was funded by grants from the Health Research Council of New Zealand, the National Child Health Research Foundation, the Canterbury Medical Research Foundation, and the New Zealand Lottery Grants Board.

Morison, Pellegrini, & Tellegen, 1990; Sameroff & Seifer, 1990; Shaw & Emery, 1988; Shaw, Vondra, Hommerding, Keenan, & Dunn, 1994).

Despite the often strong relationship between exposure to cumulative adversity and developmental outcomes, this relationship is by no means deterministic, and it has been well documented that children exposed to extremely adverse environments appear to avoid developing later problems of adjustment (Garmezy, 1971; Rutter & Madge, 1976; Werner & Smith, 1992). Observations of this type have led investigators and theorists to propose that failure to develop problems in the face of adversity is evidence of some (nonobserved) form of resilience that protects against or otherwise mitigates the effects of exposure to adversity (Garmezy, 1985; Rutter, 1985).

The identification of individuals who exhibit an ability to transcend exposure to adversity, in turn, raises important issues about the processes that lead to this resilience. There have been two general approaches to describing the factors that contribute to resilience. The first approach has been to suggest the presence of various protective factors that act to mitigate the effects of exposure to adversity. The concept of *protective factors* was first developed systematically by Rutter (1985), who argued that to be meaningful, it was necessary for protective factors to be something more than the converse of risk factors. To address this issue, Rutter proposed a conceptualization of protective factors that implied an interactive relationship between the protective factor, the risk exposure, and the outcome. This relationship was assumed to be such that exposure to the protective factor had beneficial effects on those exposed to the risk factor but did not benefit those not exposed to the risk factor.

Although Rutter's conceptualization of protective factors succeeds in drawing a distinction between risk and protective factors, the overuse of this conceptualization may prove to be a barrier to understanding the origins of resilience because not all factors that contribute to resilience will conform to the interactive model that Rutter implies is a feature of protective factors (Luthar, 1993). To provide a simple illustration of this point, consider a situation in which concerns focus on the question of the factors that distinguish children who escape the effects of family adversity from those who do not. The available evidence suggests that one such factor is childhood intelligence because research suggests that above-average IQ is often a defining feature of children who transcend adversity (e.g., Fergusson & Lynskey, 1996; Herrenkohl, Herrenkohl, & Egolf, 1994). Although childhood IQ may be a factor that leads to resilience, there is no compelling reason why the relationship between family adversity, child IQ, and adverse outcome should be interactive and conform to the definition of protective factors suggested by Rutter. Thus, in discussing the origins of resilience, it becomes useful to distinguish between two types of processes that may lead to resilience in the face of exposure to a specific risk factor or set of risk factors:

> *Protective processes* in which the exposure to the resilience factor is beneficial to those exposed to the risk factor but has no benefit (or less benefit) for those not exposed to the risk factor.
> *Compensatory processes* in which the resilience factor has an equally beneficial effect on those exposed and those not exposed to adversity.

The essential difference between protective and compensatory processes thus lies with the statistical model that describes the linkages between the resilience factors, the risk factor, and the outcome. In the case of protective factors, there is an interactive relationship between the risk factor and the protective factor. In the case of compensatory factors, the data will fit a main effects model in which the compensatory factor is equally beneficial for those exposed and not exposed to the risk factor. In this chapter we use the term *resilience factor* to describe factors that may serve as either protective or compensatory factors.

Beyond the issue of testing for compensatory and protective effects, there is also a need to develop prior theory and evidence to identify those factors and processes that may confer resilience to children who are exposed to childhood adversity. The research literature in this area has suggested a range of family, individual, and peer factors that may confer resilience to children reared in high-risk environments. These factors have included:

1. *Intelligence and problem-solving abilities.* A finding that has emerged from several studies is that resilient young people appear to be characterized by higher intelligence or problem-solving skills than their nonresilient peers (Fergusson & Lynskey, 1996; Herrenkohl et al., 1994; Kandel et al., 1988; Masten et al., 1988; Seifer, Sameroff, Baldwin, & Baldwin, 1992).

2. *Gender.* There have been a number of suggestions in the literature that gender may influence or modify responses to adversity. Specifically, a number of studies of the effects of marital discord or divorce have suggested that females may be less reactive to family stress than males (Emery & O'Leary, 1982; Hetherington, 1989; Porter & O'Leary, 1980; Wallerstein & Kelly, 1980).

3. *External interests and affiliations.* A number of studies have suggested that children from high-risk backgrounds who either develop strong interests outside the family or form attachments with a confiding adult outside their immediate family may be more resilient to the effects of family adversity (Jenkins & Smith, 1990; Werner, 1989).

4. *Parental attachment and bonding.* A further factor that may increase resilience in children from high-risk backgrounds is the nature of parent–child relationships. Specifically, it has been suggested that a warm, nurturant, or supportive relationship with at least one parent may act to protect against or mitigate the effects of family adversity (Bradley et al., 1994; Gribble et al., 1993; Herrenkohl et al., 1994; Jenkins & Smith, 1990; Seifer et al., 1992; Werner, 1989; Wyman, Cowen, Work, & Parker, 1991).

5. *Early temperament and behavior.* There has also been some evidence to suggest that temperamental and behavioral factors may be associated with resilience to adversity (Werner, 1989; Wyman et al., 1991).

6. *Peer factors.* A number of researchers have pointed to the fact that positive peer relationships may contribute to resilience (Benard, 1992; Davis, Martin, Kosky, & O'Hanlon, 2000; Fergusson & Lynskey, 1996; Werner, 1989).

The issues raised by these suggestions clearly require the development of statistical models that describe the linkages between childhood outcomes, exposure to childhood adversity, and the resilience factors listed previously to examine which of these factors may contribute to childhood resilience and whether the effects of these factors are compensatory (main effects) or protective (interactive).

In the present analysis, we use data gathered over a 21-year longitudinal study to examine a series of issues relating to the topic of resilience to childhood adversity. The key issues to be addressed include:

1. To what extent is cumulative exposure to family adversity during childhood (0–16 years) associated with the development of psychopathology in adolescence and young adulthood (16–21 years)?
2. How many young people with high exposure to family adversity avoid developing later psychopathology?
3. What mechanisms underlie this escape from adversity?

METHOD

The data reported here were gathered during the course of the Christchurch Health and Development Study (CHDS). The CHDS is a longitudinal study of an unselected birth cohort of 1,265 children born in the Christchurch (New Zealand) urban region during a 4-month period in mid-1977. This cohort has been studied at birth, 4 months, 1 year, at annual intervals to age 16 years, and at ages 18 and 21 years. Data have been collected from a combination of sources including parental interviews, self-reports, psychometric tests, teacher reports, medical records, and police records. A more detailed description of the study and an overview of the study findings have been provided by Fergusson, Horwood, Shannon, and Lawton (1989) and Fergusson and Horwood (2001). The following measures were used in this analysis.

Measures of Psychosocial Adjustment (16–21 Years)

At ages 18 and 21 years, cohort members were administered a comprehensive mental health interview that assessed various aspects of the individual's mental health and adjustment over the periods 16–18 years and 18–21 years, respectively (Fergusson, Horwood, & Woodward, 2001; Horwood & Fergusson, 1998). This information was used to construct the following measures of individual adjustment over the period 16–21 years.

Major Depression

At each interview, sample members were questioned about their depressive symptomatology since the previous assessment, using items from the Composite International Diagnostic Interview (CIDI) (World Health Organization, 1993). Using these data, DSM-IV (American Psychiatric Association, 1994) criteria were used to construct diagnoses of major depression for each sample member in each interview period.

Anxiety Disorders

Sample members were also questioned using items from the CIDI to assess DSM-IV criteria for anxiety disorders, including generalized anxiety disorder, simple phobia, specific phobia, agoraphobia, and panic disorder.

Conduct/Antisocial Personality Disorders

DSM-IV symptom criteria for these disorders were assessed using a combination of items from the Self Report Delinquency Instrument (SRDI) (Elliott & Huizinga, 1989) supplemented by custom-written survey items for the assessment of antisocial personality.

Alcohol/Illicit Drug Dependence

At each interview, sample members were questioned about their use of alcohol, cannabis, and other illicit drugs since the previous assessment. As part of this questioning, items from the CIDI were used to assess DSM-IV symptom criteria for alcohol dependence and illicit drug dependence.

Suicidal Behaviors

At each interview, sample members were questioned about the frequency and timing of any suicidal thoughts occurring in the interval since the previous assessment. Respondents who reported having suicidal thoughts were also asked whether they had made a suicide attempt during the interval, and about the timing, nature, and outcome of any such attempt(s).

Criminal Offending

Young people were questioned concerning their involvement in criminal offending and their frequency of offending using an instrument based on the SRDI (Elliott & Huizinga, 1989). This information was used to construct two measures of criminal offending over the period 16–21 years: (a) *violent crime*: whether the young person reported committing multiple (two or more) violent offenses including assault, fighting, use of a weapon, or threats of violence against a person and (b) *property crime*: whether the young person reported committing multiple (two or more) property offenses including theft, burglary, breaking and entering, vandalism, or fire setting and related offenses.

Measures of Childhood Adversity (0–16 Years)

To assess the extent of exposure to adverse childhood and family risk factors, the following variables were selected from the database of the study. These variables were chosen to span the potential array of risk exposures and also on the basis of prior knowledge of the variables in the database that had been shown to be consistently related to psychosocial outcomes in adolescence.

Measures of Socioeconomic Adversity

(a) *Family socioeconomic status* at the time of the survey child's birth was assessed using the Elley–Irving (1976) scale of socioeconomic status for New Zealand. (b) *Parental education*: Both maternal and paternal education levels were assessed at the time of the survey child's birth using a three-level classification system reflecting the highest level of educational attainment (no formal qualifications; high school qualifications; tertiary qualifications). (c) *Standard of living*: At each assessment from age 1 to age 12 years, interviewer ratings of the family's standard of living were obtained using a 5-point scale that ranged from "obviously affluent" to "obviously poor/very poor." To provide a measure of exposure to consistently low living standards, these ratings were used to construct a count measure of the number of years in which the family was rated as having a below-average standard of living.

Measures of Parental Change and Conflict

Comprehensive data on family placement and changes of parents were collected at annual intervals from birth to age 16 years. This information was used to construct two measures of family stability over the period 0–16 years: (a) *Single-parent family*: This measure was based on whether the child had ever spent time in a single-parent family before age 16 either as a result of entering a single-parent family at birth or as a result of parental separation/divorce. (b) *Changes of parents*: An overall measure of family instability was constructed on the basis of a count of the number of changes of parents experienced by the child before age 16 years. Information on family instability was supplemented by a further measure of parental conflict. (c) *Interparental violence*: At age 18, sample members were questioned using items from the Conflict Tactics Scale (Straus, 1979) to assess the extent to which they had witnessed incidents of physical violence or serious threats of physical violence between their parents during childhood.

Measures of Child Abuse Exposure

At ages 18 and 21 years, sample members were questioned concerning their experience of child abuse prior to age 16 years. (a) *Parental use of physical punishment*: Young people were asked to describe their parents' use of physical punishment on a 5-point scale ranging from "parent never used physical punishment" to "parent treated me in a harsh and abusive way" (Fergusson & Lynskey, 1997). The questioning was conducted separately for the mother and the father. For the purposes of the present analysis, the young person was defined as having been exposed to physical child abuse if she or he reported at either 18 or 21 years that either parent had used physical punishment too often or too severely or had treated the respondent in a harsh and abusive manner during childhood. (b) *Childhood sexual abuse*: Young people were also questioned at 18 and 21 years concerning their experience of sexual abuse in childhood ranging in severity from episodes of noncontact abuse to various forms of sexual penetration (Fergusson, Lynskey, & Horwood, 1996). For the purposes of the present analysis, the young person was classified as having experienced sexual abuse if she or he reported at either 18 or 21 years any episode of sexual abuse involving physical contact with the perpetrator.

Measures of Parental Adjustment
(a) *Parental alcohol problems*: When sample members were age 15 years, parents were questioned about whether there was a history of alcohol problems for any parent. (b) *Parental criminality*: Also at age 15, information was obtained from parents on whether any parent had a history of criminal offending. (c) *Parental illicit drug use*: When sample members were age 11, information was obtained from parents concerning their history of illicit drug use.

Measures of Resilience Factors (0–16 Years)

On the basis of the literature on resilient adolescents, a range of family, individual, and related factors believed to be associated with resilience to adversity was included in the analyses. In all cases, these measures were assessed at or before age 16 years.

Family Factors
(a) *Parental attachment*: This was assessed at age 15 years using the parental attachment scale developed by Armsden and Greenberg (1987). The full scale score was used in the present analysis, and this scale was found to have good reliability ($\alpha = .87$). (b) *Parental bonding*: To measure the quality of parental bonding during childhood, the maternal and paternal care and protection scales of the Parental Bonding Instrument (PBI) (Parker, Tupling, & Brown, 1979) were administered to sample members at age 16 years. The reliability of these scales was good, with coefficient α values ranging from .85 to .91.

Child Factors
(a) *Gender*. The young person's gender was assessed at the initial (birth) interview. (b) *Attentional problems (8 years)*: At age 8 years, sample members were assessed on their tendency to restless/inattentive/hyperactive behaviors using a measure that combined items from the Rutter, Tizard, and Whitmore (1970) and Conners (1969, 1970) parent and teacher behavior rating scales. For the purposes of the present analysis, the parent and teacher reports were combined to provide an overall measure

of childhood attentional problems. The resulting measure had good reliability ($\alpha = .88$). (c) *Childhood conduct problems (8 years):* The extent to which the child exhibited conduct-disordered or oppositional behaviors at age 8 years was also assessed using items from the Rutter and Conners parent and teacher questionnaires. For the purposes of the present analysis, the parent and teacher reports were combined to produce an overall measure of the extent to which the child exhibited tendencies to conduct problems. This scale had excellent reliability ($\alpha = .93$). (d) *Child neuroticism (14 years):* A measure of the child's tendency to neuroticism was obtained at age 14 years using a short-form version of the Eysenck Personality Inventory Neuroticism Scale (Eysenck & Eysenck, 1964). The scale score was found to have moderate reliability ($\alpha = .80$). (e) *Novelty seeking:* At age 16 years, sample members were administered the novelty seeking subscale of the Tridimensional Personality Questionnaire (TPQ) (Cloninger, 1987). The resulting scale score had moderate reliability ($\alpha = .76$). (f) *Self-esteem (15 years):* This was assessed using the Coopersmith Self Esteem Inventory (Coopersmith, 1981). The full scale score was used in this analysis and was found to have good reliability ($\alpha = .80$).

Peer Factors

Peer affiliations (16 years): At age 16 years, sample members and their parents were questioned on a series of items concerning the extent to which the young person's friends used tobacco, alcohol, or illicit drugs, were truant, or broke the law. These items were combined to produce separate self-report and parental report scales of the extent to which the young person affiliated with substance-using or delinquent peers. These scales had moderate reliability ($\alpha = .74$ for the self-report and $\alpha = .79$ for the parental report).

School Factors

Two measures of schooling/academic attainment were used. (a) *School retention:* Sample members who left school at age 16 or earlier were classified as early school leavers. (b) *School Certificate passes:* The School Certificate is a national series of examinations that is taken by the majority of students in their third year of high school. Students may take examinations in any number of subjects (typically four or five), and performance in each subject is graded from A to E, with a grade of C or better implying a "pass" in that subject. An overall measure of academic attainment for each young person was obtained by summing the number of pass grades achieved in all School Certificate examinations.

Sample Size and Sample Bias

The analyses reported here are based on a sample of 991 sample members for whom data on risk exposure to age 16 years and psychosocial outcomes from 16 to 21 years were available. This sample represents 78.3% of the original cohort. To examine the effects of sample losses on the representativeness of the sample, the 991 subjects included in the analysis were compared with the remaining 274 subjects on a series of measures of sociodemographic characteristics assessed at the point of birth. These comparisons suggested that there were slight tendencies for the obtained sample to underrepresent children from socially disadvantaged families characterized by low parental education, low socioeconomic status, or single parenthood.

To address this issue, all analyses were repeated using the data-weighting method described by Carlin, Wolfe, Coffey, and Patton (1999) to adjust for possible selection effects resulting from the pattern of sample attrition. These analyses produced essentially identical conclusions to those based on the unweighted data. Because the two sets of results were consistent, in the interests of simplicity the results reported here are based on the unweighted sample.

FINDINGS

The Prevalence of Childhood Adversity

Table 6.1 shows the percentages of the cohort who were exposed to various forms of childhood and family adversity during the period 0–16 years. Measures of adversity are classified into four groups of related measures: (1) measures of socioeconomic adversity; (2) measures of parental change and conflict; (3) measures of child abuse; and (4) measures of parental adjustment problems. The table shows the following:

1. *Socioeconomic adversity.* In the region, one child in four came from a family characterized by low socioeconomic status, and in one-third of the families both parents lacked formal educational qualifications. Just over 10% of the cohort were rated repeatedly as having below-average living standards.

2. *Parental change and conflict.* There was a relatively high rate of family instability in the cohort, with over one-third of cohort members having experienced the separation of their parents before the age of 16 or having entered a single-parent family at birth. One in

TABLE 6.1. *Rates (%) of Childhood and Family Adversity (0–16 Years)*

Measure	% of Sample
Socioeconomic Adversity	
Family of semiskilled/unskilled socioeconomic status	25.0
Both parents lacked formal educational qualifications	33.5
Family rated as having below-average living standards on three or more occasions	10.3
Parental Change and Conflict	
Experienced parental separation or entered single-parent family at birth	34.2
Experienced three or more changes of parents	19.7
Physical violence or threats of physical violence between parents	22.0
Child Abuse	
Experienced harsh or severe physical punishment	6.4
Experienced contact sexual abuse	11.6
Parental Adjustment	
Parental history of problems with alcohol	12.1
Parental history of criminal offending	13.3
Parental history of illicit drug use	24.8

five cohort members had experienced three or more changes of home circumstances by the age of 16, and over 20% of the cohort reported acts of physical violence or threats of physical violence between their parents.

3. *Child abuse.* Just over 6% of the cohort described their parents' use of physical punishment as either harsh or overly severe, and 12% of the cohort reported experiencing contact sexual abuse by the age of 16.

4. *Parental adjustment.* In approximately one in eight families, there was a reported history of parental alcohol problems or criminality. In 25% of families, there was a reported history of parental illicit drug use.

The variables described in Table 6.1 tended to be positively correlated, reflecting the tendency for childhood and family adversities to co-occur. To describe the overall exposure of the cohort to childhood adversity, a simple unweighted score was constructed by counting for each childhood. Over half of the cohort had experienced either no or one childhood adversity, whereas at the other extreme, just over 9% of the cohort had experienced six or more adversities.

TABLE 6.2. *Rates (%) of (a) Externalizing Behaviors (16–21 Years) by Childhood Adversity Score (0–16 Years) and (b) Internalizing Behaviors (16–21 Years) by Childhood Adversity Score (0–16 Years)*

(a) Externalizing Responses

	Adversity Score				
Measure	0, 1 ($N = 503$)	2, 3 ($N = 260$)	4, 5 ($N = 136$)	6+ ($N = 92$)	p
Alcohol dependence	5.8	12.3	15.4	14.1	<.0001
Illicit drug dependence	6.4	10.4	11.8	23.9	<.0001
Conduct/antisocial personality disorder	3.8	8.1	8.1	15.2	<.0001
Repeated (2+) violence offenses	9.2	16.2	16.9	30.4	<.0001
Repeated (2+) property offenses	12.1	20.4	17.7	29.4	<.0001
At least one of the preceding	20.5	31.9	36.0	50.0	<.0001
Mean number (rate) of externalizing behavior problems	0.37	0.67	0.70	1.13	<.0001

(b) Internalizing Responses

	Adversity Score				
Measure	0, 1 ($N = 503$)	2, 3 ($N = 260$)	4, 5 ($N = 136$)	6+ ($N = 92$)	p
Major depression	25.5	35.4	50.0	48.9	<.0001
Anxiety disorder	17.9	23.5	30.9	43.5	<.0001
Suicidal ideation	17.1	24.6	28.7	38.0	<.0001
Suicide attempt	3.2	5.8	8.8	19.6	<.0001
At least one of the above	38.8	50.8	61.8	68.5	<.0001
Mean number (rate) of internalizing problems	0.64	0.89	1.18	1.50	<.0001

Table 6.2 shows the relationship between the childhood adversity score and rates of externalizing behaviors (Table 6.2a) and internalizing behaviors (Table 6.2b). In this table, the association between childhood adversities and each outcome is tested for statistical significance using the Mantel Haenszel chi square test of linearity.

Table 6.2a shows that with increases in childhood adversity, there were corresponding and significant increases in rates of: conduct/antisocial personality disorder, violent crime, property crime, and alcohol and illicit drug dependence. Overall, those exposed to six or more adversities during childhood had risks of externalizing problems that were 2.4 times higher than those with low exposure (50.0% vs. 20.5%). Similarly, the rate of externalizing problems was 3.1 times higher among those exposed to high adversity compared with those exposed to low adversity (1.13 vs. .37).

There are similar, but perhaps less marked, relationships between exposure to childhood adversity and measures of internalizing behaviors (Table 6.2b). Those exposed to six or more childhood adversities had risks of internalizing disorders that were 1.8 times higher than those not exposed to adversity (68.5% vs. 38.8%) and overall rates of internalizing problems that were 2.3 times higher (1.50 vs. .64).

Modeling Resilience Processes

Because not all of those exposed to high levels of childhood adversity developed externalizing or internalizing problems, the results in Table 6.2 suggest the presence of nonobserved resilience processes that act to mitigate the effects of high exposure to childhood adversity. To examine this issue, an exploration was undertaken of the relationships between (1) exposure to childhood adversity; (2) the family, individual, peer, and school resilience factors described in Methods; and (3) risks of externalizing and internalizing responses. This analysis involved two stages.

1. Examination of bivariate associations: In the first stage of the analysis, the relationships between each of the resilience factors and the risks of externalizing and internalizing were examined. This analysis showed that:

(i) Risks of externalizing responses were related to parental attachment ($p < .0001$); parental bonding ($p < .001$); gender ($p < .001$); attention deficit symptoms at 8 years ($p < .001$); conduct problems at 8 years ($p < .001$); self-esteem at 15 years ($p < .001$); novelty seeking at 16 years ($p < .001$); deviant peer affiliations at 16 years ($p < .001$); early school leaving ($p < .001$); and success in School Certificate examinations ($p < .001$).

(ii) Risks of internalizing responses were related to parental attachment ($p < .001$); parental bonding ($p < .001$); gender ($p < .001$); neuroticism at age 14 ($p < .001$); self-esteem at 15 years ($p < .001$); novelty seeking at 16 years ($p < .005$); deviant peer affiliations ($p < .001$); and early school leaving ($p < .05$).

2. Fitting logistic models: Following the exploration of bivariate associations, logistic regression models were fitted to risks of (a) externalizing responses and (b) internalizing responses. The model fitted was:

$$\text{Logit } Yi = B0 + B1\,X1 + \Sigma\,Bj\,Zj + \Sigma\,B1\,j\,(X1 \times Zj)$$

where logit Yi was the log odds of the ith outcome (externalizing; internalizing), $X1$ was the measure of exposure to childhood adversity shown in Table 6.2, Zj were the resilience factors, and ($X1 \times Zj$) was a set of multiplicative interaction terms.

For both analyses (externalizing and internalizing), all resilience factors and interaction terms were entered into an initial model, and this model was then refined successively to identify significant factors.

The fitted model for externalizing identified five factors that made contributions to risks of externalizing. These factors were exposure to childhood adversity ($p < .0001$); gender ($p < .001$), deviant peer affiliations ($p < .001$), novelty seeking ($p < .001$), and self-esteem ($p < .005$). These results showed that, independently of childhood adversity, females, those with low novelty seeking, those without delinquent peer affiliations, and those with high self-esteem were less likely to display externalizing responses in adolescence and young adulthood.

The fitted model for internalizing also identified five significant factors. These factors were exposure to childhood adversity ($p < .0001$), gender ($p < .001$), neuroticism ($p < .001$), novelty seeking ($p < .001$), and parental attachment ($p < .001$). These results suggested that males, those with low levels of neuroticism and novelty seeking, and those with high levels of parental attachment were less likely to develop internalizing responses in adolescence and young adulthood.

The results for both externalizing and internalizing fit a main effects model, and there was no evidence of significant interactions between exposure to childhood adversity and the resilience factors described earlier. Further model checking including cross-tabulation and plotting of results failed to produce evidence of interactive associations between childhood adversity and the resilience factors.

To explore the implication of the results of the logistic regression a little further, these results were used to create vulnerability/resilience scores for externalizing and internalizing responses. These scores were created by weighting the resilience factors in each regression by their regression coefficients to obtain scores representing the extent to which:

1. Individuals were exposed to the factors that may mitigate (female gender, low novelty seeking, avoidance of delinquent peer affiliations, high self-esteem) or exacerbate (male gender, high novelty seeking, affiliations with delinquent peers, low self-esteem) risks of subsequent externalizing.

TABLE 6.3. *Rates (%) of Later Adjustment Problems by Childhood Adversity and Resilience Score*

(a) Externalizing Problems

Resilience Score (Quartile)	Childhood Adversity Score				
	0, 1	2, 3	4, 5	6+	Total
Q1 (high)	6.0	7.6	5.3	18.2	6.9
	(9/149)	(4/53)	(1/19)	(2/11)	(16/232)
Q2	13.6	13.8	21.9	16.7	15.0
	(17/125)	(8/58)	(7/32)	(3/18)	(35/233)
Q3	21.2	30.0	31.4	61.1	28.1
	(25/118)	(18/60)	(11/35)	(11/18)	(65/231)
Q4 (low)	51.1	63.9	66.7	70.3	60.5
	(45/88)	(46/72)	(24/36)	(26/37)	(141/233)
TOTAL	20.0	31.3	35.2	50.0	27.7
	(96/480)	(76/243)	(43/122)	(42/84)	(257/929)

(b) Internalizing Problems

Resilience Score (Quartile)	Childhood Adversity Score				
	0, 1	2, 3	4, 5	6+	Total
Q1 (high)	26.7	25.0	31.8	44.4	27.5
	(39/146)	(14/56)	(7/22)	(4/9)	(64/233)
Q2	35.7	35.0	54.2	64.7	39.7
	(45/126)	(21/60)	(13/24)	(11/17)	(90/227)
Q3	39.8	53.6	61.8	63.2	48.5
	(47/118)	(30/56)	(21/34)	(12/19)	(110/227)
Q4 (low)	58.6	81.2	82.9	75.7	72.2
	(51/87)	(56/69)	(34/41)	(28/37)	(169/234)
TOTAL	38.2	50.2	62.0	67.1	47.0
	(182/477)	(121/241)	(75/121)	(55/82)	(433/921)

2. Individuals were exposed to the factors that may mitigate (male gender, low novelty seeking, low neuroticism, high parental attachment) or exacerbate (female gender, high novelty seeking, high neuroticism, low parental attachment) risks of subsequent internalizing responses.

The associations between the vulnerability/resilience scores described previously, exposure to childhood adversity, and rates of externalizing and internalizing responses are shown in Table 6.3. This table shows the vulnerability/resilience scores divided into quartiles that range from those with high resilience to those with low resilience and cross-tabulated with the childhood adversity scores. The cells of the tables show the percentages of the group who developed subsequent externalizing responses (Table 6.3a) and internalizing responses (Table 6.3b).

The table shows that risks of subsequent externalizing or internalizing responses were modified substantially by the resilience scores. This may be seen by examining the ways in which variations in the resilience scores modify risks of externalizing and internalizing responses among those exposed to high levels of family adversity (six or more). The table shows that:

1. Among those with high resilience to externalizing who were exposed to high family adversity, only 18% developed subsequent externalizing responses. In contrast, among those with low resilience to externalizing who were exposed to high childhood adversity, 70% developed subsequent externalizing.

2. Among those with high resilience to internalizing who were exposed to high family adversity, 44% developed subsequent internalizing responses. In contrast, among those with low resilience to internalizing who were exposed to high childhood adversity, 76% developed subsequent internalizing responses.

DISCUSSION

In this chapter, data from a 21-year longitudinal study have been used to examine the relationships between childhood adversity and subsequent externalizing and internalizing responses. This study had a number of features that made it highly suitable for examining the factors that may contribute to resilience in the face of childhood adversity. These features included:

1. Use of a representative population study with high rates of sample retention.
2. Longitudinal study of the cohort from birth to young adulthood.
3. Assessment of a wide range of childhood or family adversities.
4. Assessment of both externalizing and internalizing responses using standardized and validated questionnaires.
5. Assessment of a wide range of factors that may influence resilience or vulnerability to adversity.

The key issues and themes to emerge from this analysis are summarized here.

Resilience and the Cumulative Effects of Childhood
Family Adversity

A composite measure of exposure to childhood adversity was constructed
by summing items from a number of domains of family functioning
including socioeconomic advantage/disadvantage, family change and
conflict, and exposure to child abuse and parental adjustment. In agreement with previous findings from this study and in agreement with other
research provided previously, there was evidence that with increasing
exposure to childhood adversity, there were corresponding increases in
rates of both externalizing and internalizing disorders. Those exposed
to six or more adverse factors during childhood had rates of externalizing disorders that were 2.4 times higher than those with low exposure to
adversity and rates of internalizing disorders that were 1.8 times higher.
However, it was also clear that even at high levels of exposure to adversity,
not all those exposed developed problems. These finding are suggestive
of the presence of resilience processes that mitigated the effects of exposure to adversity.

Modeling Resilience

Statistical modeling of resilience factors led to two sets of conclusions
about the factors and processes that may contribute to resilience to childhood adversity. First, in all cases, the data fitted a main effects model,
and there was no evidence of interactive relationships in which the relationships between the risk factors and outcomes were modified by the
resilience factors. These results suggested that the resilience factors produced their effects by compensating for childhood adversity rather than
by acting in a protective role.

Second, the models for externalizing and internalizing identified a
similar set of resilience factors. These factors included the following:

Gender
The models for externalizing and internalizing showed that gender had
quite opposite effects in compensating for the effects of childhood adversity. Being female reduced the risk of developing externalizing, whereas
being male reduced the risk of developing internalizing responses. These
results suggest the presence of gender-specific strengths and vulnerabilities that may act to mitigate or exacerbate the effects of family adversity
on risks of problems in adolescence. The finding that gender plays a role

in resilience is consistent with previous literature on this topic (Emery & O'Leary, 1982; Hetherington, 1989; Porter & O'Leary, 1980; Rutter, 1990; Wallerstein & Kelly, 1980). However, this previous literature has tended to emphasize the role of female gender as a protective or compensatory factor and has paid less attention to male gender as a source of resilience. When externalizing and internalizing in adolescence are considered, it is apparent that each sex has what appear to be gender-specific strengths and vulnerabilities, with femaleness providing resilience to externalizing but vulnerability to internalizing and maleness providing vulnerability to externalizing but resilience to internalizing. These findings also illustrate the point that in the analysis of resilience it is important to distinguish between resilience to externalizing responses and resilience to internalizing responses. The results show that what may confer resilience to one outcome may increase vulnerability to another.

Personality and Related Factors
The analyses of both externalizing and internalizing responses suggest that personality factors may exacerbate or mitigate the effects of exposure to childhood adversity. For externalizing responses, both novelty seeking and self-esteem were resilience factors, with low novelty seeking and high self-esteem mitigating the effects of exposure to childhood adversity. In the case of internalizing responses, novelty seeking and neuroticism were resilience factors, with low novelty seeking and low neuroticism mitigating the effects of exposure to childhood adversity. These finding are generally consistent with a literature that has suggested that personality or temperamental factors may play an important role in determining resilience in the face of adversity (Luthar, 1991; Werner & Smith, 1992; Wyman et al., 1991).

A clear limitation of the present study is that it provides no insight into the processes by which personality factors contribute to vulnerability or resilience. However, it seems likely that there are two general routes by which personality factors may act to increase vulnerability or resilience. First, these factors may influence the threshold at which the individual reacts to environmental adversity. For example, in the case of neuroticism, it is likely that those with low neuroticism are less likely to react to environmental adversity by developing internalizing responses. Second, these factors may influence individual behavior and choices that may act to increase or decrease rates of problem outcomes. For example, low novelty seeking may inhibit individuals from the high risk-taking behaviors that are a characteristic prelude to externalizing problems.

Affiliations and Attachments

The final measures that played a role in influencing resilience to adversity related to the nature of attachment and affiliation relationships. For externalizing, the avoidance of affiliations with delinquent peers proved to mitigate the effects of exposure to family adversity, whereas in the case of internalizing, the formation of strong parental attachment proved to mitigate the effects of exposure to family adversity. These findings are generally consistent with the view that the nature of parent–child attachment and peer relationships may play a role in determining vulnerability or resilience in the face of adversity (Benard, 1990, 1992; Davis et al., 2000; Fonagy, Steele, Steele, Higgitt, & Target, 1994).

Again, the study does not make clear the processes by which parental attachment influenced subsequent internalizing or peer affiliations influenced subsequent externalizing. However, the findings on parental attachment are consistent with evidence and theorizing that secure attachment lays the foundations for resilience to adversity (Fonagy et al., 1994). The present results suggest that this may apply to internalizing but not externalizing, again highlighting the fact that the factors that confer resilience to externalizing may differ from the factors that confer resilience to internalizing.

The findings on the role of delinquent peer affiliations are clearly consistent with a large literature that has linked these affiliations to increases in externalizing behaviors in adolescence (Farrington et al., 1990; Fergusson & Horwood, 1996; Fergusson, Horwood, & Lynskey, 1995; Hawkins et al., 1992; Quinton, Pickles, Maughan, & Rutter, 1993).

Cumulative Effects of Resilience Factors

Because the data fitted main effects models, the resilience factors outlined previously combined additively to mitigate or exacerbate the effects of child/family adversity on risks of externalizing and internalizing. These cumulative effects were illustrated by examining the relationships between family adversity and risks of externalizing or internalizing for quartiles of the cumulative resilience scores. This analysis showed that differences in the resilience factors had quite dramatic effects on rates of problem development among children exposed to high family adversity. For externalizing, of those in the top quartile of resilience (i.e., females, low novelty seeking, high self-esteem, low affiliation with delinquent peers), only 18% of those exposed to high childhood or family adversity exhibited later externalizing. In contrast, of those in the lowest quartile of resilience (male, high novelty seeking, low self-esteem, high affiliations with delinquent peers), over 70% of those exposed to high childhood of family adversity exhibited later externalizing. For internalizing, variations in resilience scores were associated with similar but less marked trends for rates of internalizing to vary, depending on levels of resilience. Both sets of results illustrate the ways in which accumulations of resilience factors may act to mitigate the effects of accumulations of childhood adversities on the risks of later internalizing or externalizing.

Omitted Factors

It is clearly possible to suggest a number of factors that were omitted from the analysis that, if included, may have explained further resilience. The most important of these factors are likely to be nonobserved genetic factors that may shape the individual's predisposition to respond to environmental adversity. The possible role of such genetic factors is clearly suggested by the fact that important resilience factors identified in the analysis included personality factors such as neuroticism and novelty seeking, both of which have relatively high heritability (Heath, Cloninger, & Martin, 1994). These considerations highlight the need for future research into resilience to employ genetically informative research designs that have the capacity to separate the roles of nature and nurture in response to environmental adversity.

Risk and Resilience

In recent years, there has been a growing interest in the issue of resilience. This interest appears to derive from the view that whereas studies of risk factors emphasize negative features, studies of resilience emphasize positive features. For this reason, it has often been suggested that resilience research differs fundamentally from risk research because of the focus of resilience research on positive aspects of human development (Davis, 1999; Werner & Smith, 1992). This emphasis has also been incorporated into models of program development through the so-called strengths perspective that emphasizes the need for programs to build on individual, family or community strengths rather than focusing on individual, family, or community deficits or risk factors (Werner & Smith, 1992).

Although there have been attempts to draw sharp distinctions between risk factor and resilience research, the extent to which these distinctions can be justified will depend critically on the type of statistical model that describes linkages between risk factors, resilience factors, and outcome measures. If these variables are linked by an additive main effects model, then risk and resilience will prove to be opposite sides of the same coin. Thus (under a main effects model), if low self-esteem is a factor that contributes to increased risk (vulnerability), then high self-esteem can be said to contribute to reduced risk (resilience). Under the main effects model, any risk factor can be represented as a resilience factor, and any resilience factor is a risk factor simply by reversing the interpretation of the factor.

As Rutter (1985) has pointed out in his now classic essay on protective factors, to distinguish between risk and protective factors, it is necessary for protective factors to be something more than the opposites of risk factors. From this position, Rutter developed the view that protective factors were defined by an interactive process in which exposure to the protective factor modified the effects of the risk factor on the outcome.

In this study, we have used longitudinal data gathered on a birth co-hort studied into young adulthood to examine the ways in which a large number of individual, family, peer, and school factors may act to mitigate the effects of exposure to childhood adversity. Despite extensive analy-sis, we have been unable to uncover the types of interactive processes that meet Rutter's definition of protective factors. The results of our sta-tistical analyses suggest a main effects model in which factors such as gender, personality, attachment, and peer relationships act additively in ways that may mitigate or exacerbate the effects of exposure to childhood adversity. There are two important implications of the main effects model identified in this research.

First, a sharp distinction between risk and resilience research was not possible using the data gathered in the CHDS. For these data, risk and re-silience proved to be opposite sides of the same coin, and whether results are described in terms of risk or resilience depends on the perspective applied to a main effects model.

Second, the main effects model did provide a means of (at least par-tially) explaining why not all children exposed to high adversity went on to develop problems in adolescence. The main effects model identified the presence of a series of personal, family, and peer factors that could either exacerbate risks of later problems or mitigate these risks.

In summary, the results of this study suggest three general conclu-sions about the relationship between childhood adversity, adolescent out-comes, and resilience factors.

First, there was clear evidence to suggest that with increasing expo-sure to childhood adversities, there were marked increases in rates of both internalizing and externalizing problems in adolescence and young adulthood. However, not all of those exposed to high levels of adversity developed later externalizing or internalizing, suggesting the presence of resilience processes.

Second, the effects of exposure to childhood adversity on later outcomes were modified by a series of factors that acted to mitigate or exacerbate these risks.

Third, in all cases the data fitted main effects models, suggesting that the factors that contributed to resilience among those exposed to high levels of childhood adversity were equally beneficial for those not exposed to these adversities.

References

American Psychiatric Association. (1994). *Diagnostic and statistical manual of mental disorders* (4th ed.). Washington, DC: American Psychiatric Association.

Armsden, G. C., & Greenberg, M. T. (1987). The inventory of parent and peer attachment: Individual differences and their relationship to psychological well-being in adolescence. *Journal of Youth and Adolescence, 16*, 427–454.

Benard, B. (1990). The case for peers. In *The corner on research*. Portland, OR: Far West Laboratory for Educational Research and Development.

Benard, B. (1992). Peer programs: A major strategy for fostering resiliency in kids. *The Peer Facilitator Quarterly, 9*(3).

Blanz, B., Schmidt, M. H., & Esser, G. (1991). Familial adversities and child psychiatric disorders. *Journal of Child Psychology and Psychiatry, 32*, 939–950.

Bradley, R. H., Whiteside, L., Mundfrom, D. J., Casey, P. H., Keller, K. J., & Pope, S. K. (1994). Early indicators of resilience and their relation to experiences in the home environments of low birthweight, premature children living in poverty. *Child Development, 65*, 346–360.

Carlin, J. B., Wolfe, R., Coffey, C., & Patton, G. C. (1999). Tutorial in biostatistics. Analysis of binary outcomes in longitudinal studies using weighted estimating equations and discrete-time survival methods: Prevalence and incidence of smoking in an adolescent cohort. *Statistics in Medicine, 18*, 2655–2679.

Cloninger, C. R. (1987). A systematic method for clinical description and classification of personality variants. A proposal. *Archives of General Psychiatry, 44*, 573–588.

Conners, C. K. (1969). A teacher rating scale for use in drug studies with children. *American Journal of Psychiatry, 126*, 884–888.

Conners, C. K. (1970). Symptom patterns in hyperkinetic, neurotic and normal children. *Child Development, 41*, 667–682.

Coopersmith, S. (1981). *SEI – Self esteem inventories*. Palo Alto, CA: Consulting Psychologists Press.

Davis, C., Martin, G., Kosky, R., & O'Hanlon, A. (2000). *Early intervention in the mental health of young people: A literature review.* Canberra: Australian Early Intervention Network for Mental Health in Young People.

Davis, N. J. (1999). *Resiliency: Status of the research and research-based programs – working paper draft.* Washington, DC: Substance Abuse and Mental Health Services Administration, Center for Mental Health Services.

Elley, W. B., & Irving, J. C. (1976). Revised socio-economic index for New Zealand. *New Zealand Journal of Educational Studies, 11,* 25–36.

Elliott, D. S., & Huizinga, D. (1989). Improving self-reported measures of delinquency. In M. W. Klein (Ed.), *Cross-national research in self-reported crime and delinquency* (pp. 155–186). Dordrecht: Kluwer Academic.

Emery, R. E., & O'Leary, K. D. (1982). Children's perceptions of marital discord and behavior problems of boys and girls. *Journal of Abnormal Child Psychology, 10,* 11–24.

Eysenck, H. M., & Eysenck, S. B. G. (1964). *Manual of the Eysenck personality inventory.* London: London University Press.

Farrington, D. P., Loeber, R., Elliott, D., Hawkins, J. D., Kandel, D. B., Klein, M. W., McCord, J., Rowe, D. C., & Tremblay, R. E. (1990). Advancing knowledge about the onset of delinquency and crime. In B. B. Lahey & A. E. Kazdin (Eds.), *Advances in clinical child psychology* (Vol. 13, pp. 383–442). New York: Plenum Press.

Fergusson, D. M., & Horwood, L. J. (1996). The role of adolescent peer affiliations in the continuity between childhood behavioral adjustment and juvenile offending. *Journal of Abnormal Child Psychology, 24,* 205–221.

Fergusson, D. M., & Horwood, L. J. (2001). The Christchurch Health and Development Study: Review of findings on child and adolescent mental health. *Australian and New Zealand Journal of Psychiatry, 35*(3), 287–296.

Fergusson, D. M., Horwood, L. J., & Lynskey, M. T. (1994). The childhoods of multiple problem adolescents: A 15-year longitudinal study. *Journal of Child Psychology and Psychiatry and Allied Disciplines, 35,* 1123–1140.

Fergusson, D. M., Horwood, L. J., & Lynskey, M. T. (1995). The prevalence and risk factors associated with abusive or hazardous alcohol consumption in 16-year-olds. *Addiction, 90,* 935–946.

Fergusson, D. M., Horwood, L. J., Shannon, F. T., & Lawton, J. M. (1989). The Christchurch Child Development Study: A review of epidemiological findings. *Paediatric and Perinatal Epidemiology, 3,* 278–301.

Fergusson, D. M., Horwood, L. J., & Woodward, L. J. (2001). Unemployment and psychosocial adjustment in young adults: Causation or selection? *Social Science and Medicine, 53,* 305–320.

Fergusson, D. M., & Lynskey, M. T. (1996). Adolescent resiliency to family adversity. *Journal of Child Psychology and Psychiatry and Allied Disciplines, 37,* 281–292.

Fergusson, D. M., & Lynskey, M. T. (1997). Physical punishment/maltreatment during childhood and adjustment in young adulthood. *Child Abuse and Neglect, 21,* 617–630.

Fergusson, D. M., Lynskey, M. T., & Horwood, L. J. (1996). Childhood sexual abuse and psychiatric disorder in young adulthood: I. Prevalence of sexual abuse and factors associated with sexual abuse. *Journal of the American Academy of Child and Adolescent Psychiatry, 35,* 1355–1364.

Fonagy, P., Steele, M., Steele, H., Higgitt, A., & Target, M. (1994). The Emanuel Miller memorial lecture 1992: The theory and practice of resilience. *Journal of Child Psychology and Psychiatry, 35*, 231–257.

Garmezy, N. (1971). Vulnerability research and the issue of primary prevention. *American Journal of Orthopsychiatry, 41*, 101–116.

Garmezy, N. (1985). Stress-resistant children: The search for protective factors. In J. E. Stevenson (Ed.), *Recent research in developmental psychopathology. Journal of Child Psychology and Psychiatry Book Supplement No. 4* (pp. 213–233). Oxford: Pergamon Press.

Garmezy, N. (1987). Stress, competence, and development: Continuities in the study of schizophrenic adults, children vulnerable to psychopathology, and the search for stress-resistant children. *American Journal of Orthopsychiatry, 57*, 159–174.

Gribble, P. A., Cowen, E. L., Wyman, P. A., Work, W. C., Wannon, M., & Raoof, A. (1993). Parent and child views of parent–child relationship qualities and resilient outcomes among urban children. *Journal of Child Psychology and Psychiatry, 34*, 507–520.

Hawkins, J. D., Catalano, R. F., & Miller, J. Y. (1992). Risk and protective factors for alcohol and other drug problems in adolescence and early adulthood: Implications for substance abuse prevention. *Psychological Bulletin, 112*, 64–105.

Heath, A. C., Cloninger, C. R., & Martin, N. G. (1994). Testing a model for the genetic structure of personality: A comparison of the personality systems of Cloninger and Eysenck. *Journal of Personality and Social Psychology, 66*, 762–775.

Herrenkohl, E. C., Herrenkohl, R. C., & Egolf, B. (1994). Resilient early school-age children from maltreating homes: Outcomes in late adolescence. *American Journal of Orthopsychiatry, 64*, 301–309.

Hetherington, E. M. (1989). Coping with family transitions: Winners, losers and survivors. *Child Development, 60*, 1–14.

Horwood, L. J., & Fergusson, D. M. (1998). *Psychiatric disorder and treatment seeking in a birth cohort of young adults* . Wellington, New Zealand: Ministry of Health.

Jenkins, J. N., & Smith, M. A. (1990). Factors protecting children living in disharmonious homes: Maternal reports. *Journal of the American Academy of Child and Adolescent Psychiatry, 29*, 60–69.

Kandel, E., Mednick, S. A., Kirkegaard-Sorenson, L., Hutchings, B., Knop, J., Rosenberg, R., & Schulsinger, F. (1988). IQ as a protective factor for subjects at high risk for antisocial behavior. *Journal of Consulting and Clinical Psychology, 56*, 224–226.

Loeber, R. (1990). Development and risk factors of juvenile antisocial behavior and delinquency. *Clinical Psychology Review, 10*, 1–41.

Luthar, S. S. (1991). Vulnerability and resilience: A study of high-risk adolescents. *Child Development, 62*, 600–616.

Luthar, S. S. (1993). Annotation: Methodological and conceptual issues in research on childhood resilience. *Journal of Child Psychology and Psychiatry, 34*, 441–453.

Masten, A. S., Garmezy, N., Tellegen, A., Pellegrini, D. S., Larkin, K., & Larsen, A. (1988). Competence and stress in school children: The moderating effects of individual and family qualities. *Journal of Child Psychology and Psychiatry, 29,* 745–764.

Masten, A. S., Morison, P., Pellegrini, D., & Tellegen, A. (1990). Competence under stress: Risk and protective factors. In J. Rolfe, A. S. Masten, D. Cicchetti, K. H. Nuechterlein, & S. Weintraub (Eds.), *Risk and protective factors in the development of psychopathology* (pp. 236–256). New York: Cambridge University Press.

Parker, G., Tupling, H., & Brown, L. B. (1979). A parental bonding instrument. *British Journal of Medical Psychology, 52,* 1–10.

Patterson, G. R., DeBaryshe, B. D., & Ramsey, E. (1989). A developmental perspective on antisocial behavior. *American Psychologist, 44,* 329–335.

Porter, B., & O'Leary, K. D. (1980). Marital discord and childhood behavior problems. *Journal of Abnormal Child Psychology, 8,* 287–295.

Quinton, D., Pickles, A., Maughan, B., & Rutter, M. (1993). Partners, peers and pathways: Assortative pairing and continuities in conduct disorder. *Development and Psychopathology, 5,* 763–783.

Rutter, M. (1979). Protective factors in children's response to stress and disadvantage. In J. S. Bruner & A. Garden (Eds.), *Primary prevention of psychopathology* (Vol. 3, pp. 49–74). Hanover, NH: University Press of New England.

Rutter, M. (1985). Resilience in the face of adversity: Protective factors and resistance to psychiatric disorder. *British Journal of Psychiatry, 147,* 598–611.

Rutter, M. (1990). Psychosocial resilience and protective mechanisms. In J. Rolfe, D. Masten, D. Cicchetti, K. Neuchterlein, & S. Weintraub (Eds.), *Risk and protective factors in the development of psychopathology* (pp. 316–331). New York: Cambridge University Press.

Rutter, M., & Giller, H. (1983). *Juvenile delinquency: Trends and perspectives.* Harmondsworth, U.K.: Penguin Books.

Rutter, M., & Madge, N. (1976). *Cycles of disadvantage: A review of research.* London: Heinemann.

Rutter, M., Tizard, J., & Whitmore, K. (1970). *Education, health and behaviour.* London: Longmans.

Sameroff, A. J., & Seifer, R. (1990). Early contributors to developmental risk. In J. Rolf, A. S. Masten, D. Cicchetti, K. H. Nuechterlein, & S. Weintraub (Eds.), *Risk and protective factors in the development of psychopathology* (pp. 52–66). New York: Cambridge University Press.

Sameroff, A., Seifer, R., Barocas, R., Zax, M., & Greenspan, A. (1987). Intelligence quotient scores of 4-year-old children: Social environmental risk factors. *Pediatrics, 79,* 343–350.

Seifer, R., Sameroff, A. J., Baldwin, C. P., & Baldwin, A. (1992). Child and family factors that ameliorate risk between 4 and 13 years of age. *Journal of the American Academy of Child and Adolescent Psychiatry, 31,* 893–903.

Shaw, D. S., & Emery, E. E. (1988). Chronic family adversity and school-age children's adjustment. *Journal of the American Academy of Child and Adolescent Psychiatry, 27,* 200–206.

Shaw, D. S., Vondra, J. I., Hommerding, K. D., Keenan, K., & Dunn, M. (1994). Chronic family adversity and early child behaviour problems: A longitudinal study of low income families. *Journal of Child Psychology and Psychiatry, 35,* 1109–1122.

Straus, M. A. (1979). Measuring intrafamily conflict and violence: The Conflict Tactics (CT) Scales. *Journal of Marriage and the Family, February, 41*, 75–88.

Wallerstein, J. S., & Kelly, J. B. (1980). *Surviving the breakup: How children and parents cope with divorce.* London: Grant McIntyre.

Werner, E. E. (1989). High risk children in young adulthood: A longitudinal study from birth to 32 years. *American Journal of Orthopsychiatry, 59*, 72–81.

Werner, E. E., & Smith, R. S. (1992). *Overcoming the odds: High-risk children from birth to adulthood.* Ithaca, NY: Cornell University Press.

World Health Organization. (1993). *Composite international diagnostic interview (CIDI).* Geneva: World Health Organization.

Wyman, P. A., Cowen, E. L., Work, W. C., & Parker, G. R. (1991). Developmental and family milieu correlates of resilience in urban children who have experienced major life stress. *American Journal of Community Psychology, 19*, 405–426.

7

Sequelae of Child Maltreatment

Vulnerability and Resilience

Kerry E. Bolger and Charlotte J. Patterson

To grow into competent and productive adults, children must learn to regulate their emotions and their behavior, to form a coherent, positive sense of self, and to form and maintain relationships with other people. A substantial body of evidence indicates that consistent, responsive parenting contributes to children's ability to master these developmental tasks (Lord, Eccles, & McCarthy, 1994; Raver, 1996). In maltreating families, however, parental care does not meet children's basic needs for physical sustenance and protection, emotional security, and social interaction. Thus, maltreatment constitutes a significant deviation from the average expectable or species-typical environment, as defined by community norms and by medical, legal, and social scientific standards (National Research Council, 1993). Developmental theory on the influence of early caregiving predicts that such conditions predispose children to a variety of difficulties in adjustment and adaptation (Cicchetti & Lynch, 1995; Scarr, 1992).

Empirical evidence supports this contention: Maltreatment during childhood is associated with an increased risk for internalizing problems, such as depression and anxiety (Lynch & Cicchetti, 1998; McGee, Wolfe, & Wilson, 1997; Toth, Manly, & Cicchetti, 1992), and externalizing problems including aggression, delinquency, and antisocial behavior (Herrenkohl, Egolf, & Herrenkohl, 1997; Widom, 1989). Maltreated

Support for this research was provided by grants from the Office on Child Abuse and Neglect, the Children's Bureau, U.S. Department of Health and Human Services. The authors wish to thank Janis B. Kupersmidt, Pamela C. Griesler, and Nancy Vaden-Kiernan for their contributions to the Charlottesville Longitudinal Study.

children encounter more difficulties in developing autonomy and self-esteem (Egeland, Sroufe, & Erickson, 1983) and in relationships with others, including peers (Cicchetti, Lynch, Shonk, & Manly, 1992; Rogosch, Cicchetti, & Aber, 1995; Salzinger, Feldman, Hammer, & Rosario, 1993). Thus, maltreatment in childhood has been identified as a significant risk factor for a range of emotional, behavioral, and social adjustment problems.

These elevated rates of difficulties in emotional and behavioral self-regulation, self-concept, and peer relationships among maltreated children are cause for concern not only because they reflect current adjustment, but also because they predict continued problems later in life. For example, internalizing problems in childhood and adolescence are associated with depression and anxiety disorders in adulthood (Kovacs & Devlin, 1998). Aggression and antisocial behavior tend to show stability during childhood and adolescence and continuity into adulthood (Huesmann, Eron, Lefkowitz, & Walder, 1984). Peer rejection during childhood is associated with an increased risk of subsequent school failure, delinquency, and psychopathology (Parker & Asher, 1987). Thus, these aspects of impaired functioning in maltreated children may be avenues through which abuse and neglect in childhood lead to poor adaptation across the lifespan.

In addition to illuminating risk processes, research on maltreated children can address fundamental questions about resilience. Children who have experienced harsh or inadequate parental care and yet maintain or recover positive functioning offer compelling evidence of the possibilities for human growth and mastery. Increased understanding of the processes that enable these children to adapt successfully, and of the limitations on successful coping in such adverse environments, can provide insight into principles underlying human development, and can guide prevention and intervention efforts to promote children's positive adjustment.

Resilient adaptation may be unlikely among maltreated children, however, for several reasons. Cicchetti and Lynch (1995) observed that "maltreating families fail to provide many of the expectable experiences that theoretically are required for normal development." Child maltreatment also tends to co-occur with other environmental threats to children's well-being, including parental conflict, parental psychopathology, community violence, and poverty (Eckenrode, Ganzel, Henderson, et al., 2000; Lynch & Cicchetti, 1998). Moreover, disturbances within the family and the parent–child relationship, the most proximal level of the child's social ecology, may serve as a conduit through which effects of more distal stresses such as economic hardship are conveyed to children (Belsky, 1980; McLoyd, 1998). Another reason that resilience may be rare among maltreated children is the lack of protective factors in these children's environments. For example, previous research on resilience has identified parenting quality as a protective factor for children exposed to adverse experiences and conditions (Masten & Coatsworth, 1998), but maltreated children are by definition unlikely to receive good-quality parenting.

Evidence that maltreatment undermines the likelihood of resilience in the face of stress can be drawn from several studies that followed maltreated and comparison children over time. In such studies, relatively few individuals have been found to meet empirical definitions of resilience, such as the absence of significant adjustment problems or sustained adaptive functioning over time (Egeland, Carlson, & Sroufe, 1993). In their longitudinal study of high-risk children, Farber and Egeland (1987) found that of 44 children identified as maltreated, *none* maintained competent functioning across the period from infancy to preschool. Herrenkohl, Herrenkohl, and Egolf (1994) found that 25 (13%) of the maltreated children in their longitudinal sample were functioning well during elementary school, but many were not able to sustain a high level of adaptation over time. By late adolescence, a substantial number of the maltreated children who appeared resilient in elementary school showed significant problems related to academic achievement, aggressive behavior, intimacy, and individuation. For example, 39% had dropped out of high school before graduation. Cicchetti and Rogosch (1997) examined resilience in a sample of 213 maltreated and nonmaltreated low-income, disadvantaged children tested at three annual assessments. On a composite measure of adaptive functioning over time, maltreated children were significantly more likely than nonmaltreated children to be classified as low functioning and significantly less likely to be classified as high functioning. Only 9.8% of maltreated children were ever classified as high functioning during any of the assessment time points; only 1.5% were classified as high functioning across time.

Despite evidence that resilience is rare among maltreated children, some maltreated children achieve higher levels of adaptive functioning than others (Cicchetti & Rogosch, 1997). This variation in outcomes has prompted efforts to identify profiles of resilient adaptation among maltreated children and to ascertain why some children achieve better than expected adjustment, given their experiences of adversity. One possible explanation rests on the heterogeneity of maltreatment experiences – that is, more well adjusted children were actually exposed to fewer stresses, such as less severe or pervasive maltreatment, older age at onset, or shorter duration of maltreatment over time. Another possible explanation is that protective factors (such as advantageous personal characteristics, positive relationships with alternate caregivers, or attitudes that encourage a more optimistic view of life) enabled some children to achieve positive adaptation despite high risk (Masten & Coatsworth, 1998; Werner & Smith, 1992).

Based on prior research, we identified two domains with high potential to protect children against the ill effects of maltreatment. The first of these is perceived internal control. *Perceived control* refers to beliefs about the sources of one's successes and failures (e.g., in attaining academic and social goals). Children with high levels of perceived *internal* control tend to believe that their own attributes or actions bring about their successes and failures, whereas those with high levels of perceived *external* control believe that other factors (e.g., powerful other people or unknown causes) account for these outcomes (Connell, 1985). Previous research has identified perceived control as a potential protective factor among individuals exposed to high levels of psychosocial stress. Luthar (1991) found that locus of control operated as a protective factor in a sample of inner-city adolescents: Those with a more internal locus of control showed less decline in functioning in response to negative life events. Moran and Eckenrode (1992) reported that maltreated adolescent girls with a more internal locus of control were less depressed on average than those with a more external locus of control. Notably, girls maltreated beginning in adolescence were more likely to have this protective attribute than were girls maltreated earlier, beginning in childhood. Banyard (1999) found that among women who had been maltreated in childhood, those with a more internal locus of control reported fewer depressive symptoms than those with a more external locus of control. In each of these studies, locus of control interacted with stress to predict individual outcomes, thus offering support for the role of perceived control as a protective factor. Other aspects of self-functioning that have been found to predict more positive outcomes among maltreated children include ego resilience, ego control, and self-esteem (Cicchetti & Rogosch, 1997; Cicchetti, Rogosch, Lynch, & Holt, 1993).

The confluence of several lines of theory and research lead us to focus on friendship as a second potentially important protective factor among maltreated children. Previous research on positive adjustment despite risk highlights the role of supportive personal relationships in the resilience process (Egeland, Jacobvitz, & Sroufe, 1988; Rutter & Quinton,

1984; Werner & Smith, 1992). Developmental theory and research suggest that friendships contribute uniquely to children's social adjustment and sense of well-being (Hartup & Stevens, 1999; Parker & Asher, 1993). Friendships may play a particularly important role in the development of maltreated children (Price, 1996). Positive, reciprocal, and stable friendships may enhance children's sense of emotional security (Cicchetti et al., 1992) and provide a setting in which to learn and practice social skills, which may be especially crucial for maltreated children, whose families offer fewer opportunities for positive interaction (Price, 1996). With regard to self-esteem, friendships characterized by trust and acceptance could offer a context for maltreated children to develop more positive models of themselves (Price, 1996).

In this chapter, we review issues of vulnerability and resilience among maltreated children based on evidence from our program of research in this area. We begin by providing an overview of the research from which this evidence is drawn. We then present our major findings on the prevalence and stability of resilience among maltreated children; risks associated with different dimensions of maltreatment; pathways implicated in their effects; and protective factors that moderate the influence of maltreatment. We conclude with discussions of the implications of our research findings for theory and research on resilience as well as for intervention and policy.

VIRGINIA LONGITUDINAL STUDY OF CHILD MALTREATMENT

Sources of Data

The Virginia Longitudinal Study of Child Maltreatment (Bolger & Patterson, 2001a, 2001b; Bolger, Patterson, & Kupersmidt, 1998b) was conducted to study risk and resilience among children who had been maltreated by their parents or caregivers. The Virginia Longitudinal Study grew out of the Charlottesville Longitudinal Study (CLS; Patterson, Griesler, Vaden, & Kupersmidt, 1992), which employed a prospective longitudinal design to examine psychosocial risk and resilience in a community sample of children attending public schools in Charlottesville, Virginia. Subsequently, children in the CLS sample who had been maltreated were identified, according to procedures described later and in previous reports (Bolger & Patterson, 2001a, 2001b; Bolger et al., 1998b). This group of maltreated children comprised the focal sample of children for the Virginia Longitudinal Study of Child Maltreatment.

Research Aims

A major aim of the Virginia Longitudinal Study of Child Maltreatment was to identify associations between specific aspects of maltreatment and patterns of children's adjustment, including their levels of self-esteem, the degree of both internalizing and externalizing problems, and the quality of their peer relationships. In addition, we sought to identify mediating pathways that would help to account for linkages between maltreatment and specific aspects of children's adjustment. A third major aim was to identify predictors of better than expected outcomes among some maltreated children.

Participating Children

The CLS began in 1986 with three cohorts of participating children who were in second, third, and fourth grades; their modal ages were 8, 9, and 10 years, respectively. An additional cohort of second graders was added in 1987 and followed in 1988. The study was conducted during an intervention program as part of the school's curriculum. Over 95% of registered students in the target grades participated; thus, the sample was therefore not only representative, but also nearly exhaustive, of the population from which it was drawn. In all, 1,920 children participated at one or more annual occasions of measurement. Data were collected annually from 1986 through 1989.

Identification of Maltreated Children

Subsequent to collection of data for the CLS, information from state social service records made it possible to identify children in the CLS sample who had been maltreated by their parents or caregivers. This information was obtained from the statewide central registry of substantiated child maltreatment cases in Virginia (Bolger & Patterson, 2001a, 2001b; Bolger et al., 1998b). After maltreated children were identified from among CLS participants, we reviewed their case records in local departments of social services in the City of Charlottesville and in other localities in Virginia where participating children had lived and had been identified as maltreated. Of the 139 children identified as maltreated, 107 had been abused and/or neglected before or during the years they participated in the CLS. These 107 children comprised the focal sample of maltreated children in subsequent data analyses.

The 107 maltreated children did not differ significantly from the CLS sample as a whole on gender (52 girls and 55 boys) or on ethnicity (among both maltreated and nonmaltreated children, approximately 60% of were European American and 40% were African American). Maltreated children, though, were much more likely to have experienced low family incomes: 99 of 107 maltreated children (92%) had low family incomes (as defined by participation in the federal free and reduced-price school lunch program) in at least one year of the CLS compared to 40% of nonmaltreated children.

Children's Experiences of Maltreatment

In addition to examining children's adjustment as a function of maltreatment status, we investigated the sequelae of maltreatment dimensions including specific types (neglect, physical and emotional abuse, and sexual abuse), age at onset, and chronicity. The goal of these analyses was to build upon previous resilience studies not only by examining maltreatment as a global construct but also by studying, in a more fine-grained way, particular aspects of maltreatment as indices of adversity. We hypothesized that children's risk of maladjustment would be exacerbated by maltreatment that (1) was more extensive (e.g., involving more types of abuse and neglect), (2) began earlier in life, and (3) was more chronic (i.e., took place over a longer period of time).

Based on information in local social service case files, each child's experiences of maltreatment were rated according to the Maltreatment Classification System developed by Barnett, Manly, and Cicchetti (1993). This nosological system provided criteria to rate the presence and severity of multiple types of maltreatment, including neglect (including lack of supervision and failure to provide), harsh parenting (including physical abuse and emotional maltreatment), and sexual abuse. Among the 107 maltreated children, 74% were neglected, 64% experienced harsh parenting, and 30% were sexually abused. The three types of maltreatment were relatively distinct but not mutually exclusive: 55 of the 107 maltreated children experienced more than one type of maltreatment, and 18 children experienced all three types (Bolger & Patterson, 2001a). Age at onset of maltreatment was coded as the child's chronological age when maltreatment began. Maltreatment chronicity was coded as the length of time between maltreatment onset and the date when maltreatment ended or the case was closed.

Assessment of Children's Adjustment

To assess maltreated children's adjustment, we focused on stage-salient tasks of middle childhood. During this period of development, children need to regulate their emotions; to modulate their behavior and adapt to the school environment (e.g., by refraining from aggression against peers); to form positive relationships with peers; and to achieve and maintain a positive sense of self. We employed measures of children's competence in each of these areas.

Behavioral and Emotional Adjustment

Measures of children's externalizing and internalizing problems were collected via teacher, peer, and self-reports during each year of the CLS. In individual interviews, teachers rated students' behavior problems on a standardized scale adapted from the Classroom Adjustment Rating Scales (Cowen, Lorion, & Caldwell, 1975). Factor analysis yielded scores for internalizing (e.g., shy, anxious) and externalizing (e.g., aggressive, acting out) problems. Peer reports of aggression and social withdrawal, respectively, were obtained via sociometric nominations (Coie, Dodge, & Coppotelli, 1982). Children's self-reports of internalizing and externalizing problems were obtained from relevant subscales of the Youth Self-Report (Achenbach, 1991), which is valid for children aged 11 to 18 and was therefore administered only during the 1988 and 1989 assessments.

Peer Relationships

During group sociometric testing in each year of the study, children nominated three peers whom they liked most and three whom they liked least. The difference between standardized liked most and liked least scores were computed; when this *social preference* score was one standard deviation or more below the mean, the child was classified as rejected (Coie et al., 1982).

During data collection in 1986, 1987, and 1988, children were asked to report whether they had a best friend (Patterson et al., 1992). Children's best friend choices were compared to each other to determine whether or not they were reciprocated.

Self-Esteem

In each year of the CLS, children completed the Self-Perception Profile (Harter, 1985). The global self-worth subscale, which asks children how happy they feel about themselves and how they are leading their lives, was employed as an indicator of self-esteem.

Academic Achievement

Standardized tests of academic achievement were administered by the school system during each year of the CLS. Schools administered the

Science Research Associates (SRA) Achievement Series during 1986 and 1987 and the Iowa Test of Basic Skills during 1988 and 1989. For both the SRA and Iowa tests, the child's reading, language, and math composite scores were computed. Scores were converted to percentiles to increase comparability across tests.

Assessment of Potential Protective Factors

Perceptions of Control

The Multidimensional Measure of Children's Perceptions of Control (Connell, 1985) was administered during the 1987 and 1988 assessments. This questionnaire measures children's beliefs about sources of their successes and failures as internal, powerful other people, or unknown factors. Children's scores on powerful others' control and unknown control correlated highly and were therefore averaged to create a summary score for external control (Bolger & Patterson, 2001b).

Friendship Reciprocity and Quality

As described previously, children reported whether they had a best friend, and their choices were compared to each other to determine whether or not they were reciprocated. Children were also rated on the qualities of their best friendship using the Network of Relationships Inventory (NRI; Furman & Buhrmester, 1985). Questionnaire items on affection, instrumental aid, companionship, intimacy, and satisfaction with the friendship loaded highly on a single common factor and were summed to create a friendship quality score (Bolger et al., 1998; Patterson et al., 1992). Friendship reciprocity and friendship quality complement each other as indices of children's friendship: Friendship quality reflects positive aspects, rather than the mere existence, of the relationship, whereas friendship reciprocity validates the dyadic nature of the relationship.

Vulnerability and Resilience among Maltreated Children

Here we describe our major findings related to vulnerability and resilience among maltreated children. These are organized into five sections. First, we present findings regarding the prevalence and stability of resilient adaptation. Second, we describe findings regarding sequelae of maltreatment across domains of children's adjustment, including peer relationships, behavioral and emotional adjustment, and self-esteem. Third, we present evidence regarding mediating pathways linking maltreatment to a heightened risk of adjustment problems in specific domains. Fourth, we describe findings regarding protective factors associated with more positive adjustment among maltreated children. Fifth, we present estimates of the likelihood of resilience among maltreated children as a function of presence versus absence of protective factors.

Prevalence of Resilience among Maltreated Children

To assess resilient adaptation, we identified children who were well accepted by peers, showed competent behavior in their school environment, and were successful academically, as indexed by high social preference scores, low scores on teacher ratings of internalizing and externalizing problems, and high scores on standardized academic achievement tests, respectively. Using these measures, we implemented two alternative strategies to estimate the prevalence of resilience among maltreated children. For each strategy, we determined (1) how many maltreated children showed positive adaptation at each time point and (2) how many showed resilience, as defined by sustained positive adaptation over time (i.e., at all time points of participation in the longitudinal study).

The first strategy was to identify maltreated children who showed highly positive adjustment in at least one of the four domains (peer acceptance, internalizing, externalizing, and academic achievement) without doing very poorly in any domain. This strategy embodies the view that resilient children excel in one or more, though not necessarily all, domains of adjustment (Luthar, 1993). Highly positive adjustment was defined as one standard deviation better than the mean, and very poor adjustment as one standard deviation worse than the mean, compared to the CLS sample as a whole. Based on these criteria, nine maltreated children were classified as well adjusted during at least one year of the study. However, only one child met these criteria across all time points of participation in the study. Thus, based on this approach, only one maltreated child was identified as resilient in terms of sustained positive adaptation over time.

The second strategy was to identify maltreated children who had a high score on a composite measure of adaptation (Cicchetti et al., 1993). This strategy reflects the view that resilient children can function competently despite greater difficulties in some domains compared to others. Factor analysis was applied to derive a composite variable based on internalizing, externalizing, peer acceptance, and academic achievement scores at each time point of the CLS. At each time point, any child whose score on this composite was at or above the median for the CLS sample as a whole was classified as competent. Twenty-three of the 107 maltreated children met this criterion during at least one year of the study, but only 5 children did so during all years they participated in the study. These five children were therefore classified as resilient in terms of sustained positive adaptation over time.

Overall, results indicated that relatively few maltreated children showed high levels of positive adaptation at any time point, and fewer still sustained positive adjustment over time.

Sequelae of Maltreatment: Risks for Different Adjustment Domains

To examine sequelae of maltreatment, we conducted two sets of analyses for each adjustment domain. The first set of analyses tested for differences in adjustment between maltreated children and their peers with no known history of maltreatment, with sex of child and low family income (as indexed by participation in the federal school lunch program; Bolger et al., 1998b) entered as covariates. For each domain in which maltreatment was found to be associated with adjustment problems, a follow-up analysis was conducted to examine sequelae of specific aspects of maltreatment. Five aspects of maltreatment were entered as predictors in this second analysis: neglect, harsh parenting, sexual abuse, age at onset, and chronicity. Maltreatment timing variables (onset and chronicity) were relevant only for maltreated children; planned contrasts were therefore employed to make it possible to analyze these variables within models including both maltreated and nonmaltreated children. Sex of child and low family income were also entered as covariates in this model. Analyses were conducted using growth curve modeling, which permitted examination of individual differences and change over time associated with maltreatment status and with specific aspects of maltreatment (for additional details, see Bolger & Patterson, 2001a, 2001b; Bolger et al., 1998b).

PEER RELATIONSHIPS. Maltreated children experienced significantly more problems in peer relationships than their nonmaltreated classmates. On average, maltreated children were less popular than their nonmaltreated peers and more likely to be rejected by peers across all years of the study. Maltreated children were also significantly less likely than nonmaltreated children to have a best friendship that was reciprocal in nature (Bolger et al., 1998b).

Analyses focusing on sequelae of specific aspects of maltreatment revealed that chronic maltreatment, in particular, was associated with problems in peer relationships. Chronically maltreated children were especially unpopular with peers and more likely than other children to be rejected by peers repeatedly across multiple years from childhood to early adolescence (Bolger & Patterson, 2001a). Chronically maltreated children were also significantly less likely than other children to have a reciprocal best friendship.

EXTERNALIZING PROBLEMS. According to teacher ratings, peer nominations, and self-reports, maltreated children exhibited more aggressive behavior and externalizing problems across the years from elementary to middle school. Thirty-one percent of maltreated girls and 24 percent of maltreated boys reported externalizing problems in the clinical range. Results of analyses focusing on sequelae of specific aspects of maltreatment revealed that chronic maltreatment, in particular, was associated with elevated levels of aggressive behavior and externalizing problems (Bolger & Patterson, 2001a).

INTERNALIZING PROBLEMS. Based on their reports of anxiety, depression, withdrawal, and somatic complaints (Achenbach, 1991), maltreated children were also experiencing more internalizing problems than nonmaltreated children (Bolger & Patterson, 2001b). Thirty-four percent of maltreated girls and 24 percent of maltreated boys reported internalizing problems in the clinical range. Results of analyses focusing on sequelae of specific aspects of maltreatment revealed main effects of neglect and sexual abuse on internalizing problems, qualified by a significant interaction between these two types of maltreatment: Neglect and sexual abuse were associated with higher levels of internalizing problems, especially among children who experienced *both* of these types of maltreatment.

SELF-ESTEEM. Maltreated children reported significantly lower levels of self-esteem than children who had not been maltreated. Results of analyses focusing on sequelae of specific aspects of maltreatment indicated that sexual abuse and early onset of maltreatment were each associated with significantly lower mean levels of self-esteem across all years of the study. Results also revealed that chronic maltreatment was associated with a decrease over time in children's self-esteem (Bolger et al., 1998b).

Pathways to Maladjustment among Maltreated Children
To examine developmental pathways that linked maltreatment to problems in major domains of children's adjustment, we conducted two sets of mediation analyses. These analyses were conducted to test specific a priori hypotheses related to more overt behavioral aspects of adjustment

and to less overt cognitive-emotional indices, respectively, as mediators of the effects of maltreatment on particular domains of children's adjustment. The first of these analyses, described in the following subsection, addressed the question "What processes link experiences of maltreatment with increased risk of peer rejection?" The second set of analyses described addressed the question "What processes link experiences of maltreatment with increased risk of internalizing problems?"

PATHWAYS FROM MALTREATMENT TO PEER REJECTION. Developmental theorists have proposed both aggression and social withdrawal as mediators of the association between maltreatment and peer rejection (Dodge, Pettit, & Bates, 1997; Mueller & Silverman, 1989). We examined whether each of these aspects of children's functioning mediated the link from specific dimensions of maltreatment to increased risk of peer rejection (Bolger & Patterson, 2001a). Results revealed that children's aggressive behavior substantially mediated the link between chronic maltreatment and increased risk of rejection by peers, accounting for a substantial portion (27% of variance) of the association between chronic maltreatment and peer rejection. Socially withdrawn behavior, in contrast, did not significantly mediate the relation between chronic maltreatment and peer rejection association. Thus, findings revealed a specific pathway, via aggressive behavior, by which chronic maltreatment was associated with peer rejection.

PATHWAYS FROM MALTREATMENT TO INTERNALIZING PROBLEMS. We hypothesized that maltreated children would perceive less internal control and more external control than nonmaltreated children, and that these differences in perceived control would increase the risk of internalizing problems among maltreated children. To test this hypothesis, we conducted analyses to examine internal and external control, respectively, as mediators of the relation between specific types of maltreatment and children's internalizing problems (Bolger & Patterson, 2001b). Results showed that children who had been neglected had higher levels of perceived *external* control. This main effect of neglect on perceived external control was qualified by a significant sexual abuse –neglect interaction: Sexual abuse was associated with higher levels of perceived *external* control among children who had also been neglected. Results of mediation analyses indicated that perceived *external* control accounted substantially for the associations of neglect and sexual abuse with children's internalizing problems. Of the variance in internalizing problems accounted for by the main effect of neglect, 23% was mediated by perceived external control, and of the variance accounted for by the neglect – sexual abuse interaction, 21% was mediated by perceived external control. Perceived internal control scores, on the other hand, were not related to neglect, harsh parenting, or sexual abuse. These findings suggest that perceptions of external control function as a significant pathway linking maltreatment (particularly neglect and sexual abuse) with increased risk of internalizing problems.

Protective Factors among Maltreated Children

PERCEIVED CONTROL. Theory and research suggest that perceptions of control can play a moderating as well as mediating role with regard to the development of internalizing problems. Consistent with previous research on resilience (Banyard, 1999; Luthar, 1991; Moran & Eckenrode, 1992; Werner & Smith, 1982), we hypothesized that among maltreated children, those who believed they could control the things that happened to them (i.e., who had high perceived internal control) would be less likely to experience internalizing problems. Low levels of perceived internal control, on the other hand, might act as a vulnerability factor among maltreated children by reducing motivation and increasing the tendency to experience depressed and anxious emotional states (Abramson, Seligman, & Teasdale, 1978; Peterson & Seligman, 1984).

To examine the proposed protective role of perceptions of control, we tested whether perceived internal control interacted with maltreatment to predict internalizing problems (Bolger & Patterson, 2001b). Results revealed that internal control interacted significantly with maltreatment, such that greater perceived internal control was associated with lower levels of internalizing problems among maltreated children, though not among children who were not maltreated. Thus, findings supported the hypothesis that internal control functioned as a protective factor against the development of internalizing problems among maltreated children.

In follow-up analyses, we explored the developmental roots of this protective attribute. Consistent with the findings of Moran and Eckenrode (1992), we found that children who had been maltreated earlier in life reported lower levels of perceived internal control than children maltreated later. This finding suggests that early onset of maltreatment reduces the chances of resilient adaptation among maltreated children by altering their beliefs about their ability to control their own successes and failures.

FRIENDSHIP. We hypothesized that friendship could function as a protective factor with regard to self-esteem among maltreated children. To test this hypothesis, we conducted growth curve analyses to examine

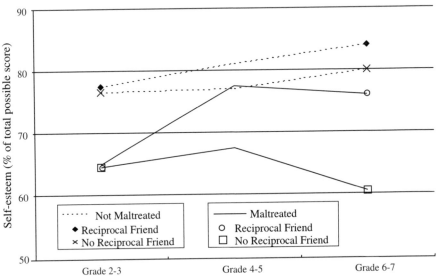

FIGURE 7.1 Self-esteem over time as a function of maltreatment and reciprocated friendship.

friendship reciprocity and quality, respectively, as moderators of the association between maltreatment and self-esteem (Bolger et al., 1998b).
Results supported the protective factor hypothesis: On average, maltreated children who did not have a reciprocal best friend experienced
a decline in self-esteem over the years from early elementary school to
middle school; in contrast, maltreated children who had a reciprocal
best friend reported an increase in self-esteem during this time period
(see Figure 7.1). In contrast, nonmaltreated children reported, on average, an increase over time in self-esteem regardless of whether or not they
had a reciprocal best friend. Analyses examining friendship quality produced a similar pattern of results, thus providing additional evidence for
friendship as a protective factor among maltreated children. Conceivably,
a positive, reciprocal friendship could have led to increased self-esteem
via decreases in loneliness, increases in perceived acceptance, improvement in social skills, and changes in working models of attachment, each
of which could be especially valuable for children who have been maltreated.

Results of additional analyses, conducted subsequently to examine
friendship as a moderator of specific aspects of maltreatment (neglect,
harsh parenting, sexual abuse, chronicity, and onset age), revealed that
reciprocated friendship was associated with a greater increase over time in

self-esteem among chronically maltreated children and among physically abused children. High friendship quality was associated with a greater increase over time in self-esteem among chronically maltreated children. These findings suggest that the protective role of friendship was especially important for children who were maltreated over a long period of time and for those who were physically abused (Bolger et al., 1998b).

After examining friendship as a protective factor with regard to self-esteem, we investigated whether the protective role of friendship extended to other aspects of children's adjustment, including teacher and peer reports of children's classroom adjustment and behavior. Results of these analyses indicated no statistically significant interactions of friendship quality and reciprocity, respectively, with teacher ratings and peer reports of children's internalizing and externalizing behavior problems (Bolger et al., 1998a).

In summary, findings provided support for the role of friendship as a protective factor with regard to self-esteem among maltreated children. However, this protective effect did not generalize broadly to other aspects of children's adjustment such as internalizing and externalizing behavior problems.

The Likelihood of Resilience as a Function of Protective Factors

We next examined the likelihood of resilience as a function of the two protective factors, perceived internal control and reciprocal friendship. Only maltreated children were included in these analyses. The criterion variable was whether the child was classified as competent during at least one year of the study. (We did not use sustained competence over time as a criterion because so few maltreated children met that standard.) Separate logistic regression models were estimated for each of the two alternative methods for identifying resilience, that is, (1) a high score on the adaptive functioning composite (based on internalizing, externalizing, peer acceptance, and academic achievement scores) and (2) highly positive adjustment in at least one domain without very poor adjustment in any domain.

As shown in Table 7.1, maltreated children who had a friendship that was reciprocal were over three times more likely than those who did not have a reciprocal friendship to be classified as resilient during at least one time point. For analyses of perceived control, each child was classified as having *relatively internal* control (if the child's standardized score for perceived internal control was higher than for external control) or *relatively external* control (if the child's z-score was higher for perceived

TABLE 7.1. *Resilience among Maltreated Children as a Function of Protective Factors*

	Resilience Criterion	
Protective Factor	Adaptive Functioning Composite $\geq$ Median	Highly Positive Functioning in *Some* Domain without Very Poor Functioning in *Any* Domain
Reciprocal Friendship		
% of children with/without this protective factor classified as resilient at at least one time point	42% / 16%	19% / 6%
$\chi^2(1)$	5.01*	2.32[†]
Odds ratio	3.90	3.69
Internal Perceived Control		
% of children with/without this protective factor classified as resilient at at least one time point	50% / 20%	18% / 8%
$\chi^2(1)$	6.33**	1.67[†]
Odds ratio	4.00	2.57

**$p < .01$, *$p < .05$, [†]p $< .10$.

external control than for internal control). Maltreated children with relatively internal perceptions of control were over twice as likely as those with relatively external perceptions of control to be classified as resilient during at least one time point (see Table 7.1). Thus, results supported the hypotheses that friendship and perceived internal control functioned as protective factors that were associated with increased odds of resilient adaptation among maltreated children.

OVERVIEW AND IMPLICATIONS

Overall, our findings provide evidence regarding risk, vulnerability, and resilience among maltreated children. Maltreatment was associated with a range of adjustment problems across domains of peer relationships, conduct, and self-concept. Compared to their peers who had not been abused or neglected, maltreated children were significantly less popular with peers, more likely to be rejected by them, and less likely to have a best friend. Maltreated children experienced more internalizing problems, including symptoms of depression and anxiety, and displayed more externalizing problems, such as aggression and acting out in the classroom. On average, maltreated children were more unhappy with themselves and how they were leading their lives, and were more likely than their nonmaltreated peers to believe that external forces, such as other people or unknown causes, controlled their successes and failures.

Prevalence and Stability over Time of Resilience among Maltreated Children

Results of our research revealed that resilience was neither common nor likely to be stable among maltreated children. Procedures to identify profiles of resilient adaptation yielded estimates that between 6% and 21% of maltreated children were functioning competently during at least one time point from middle childhood to early adolescence. A bleaker picture emerged from analyses of the stability of resilient adaptation over time: Fewer than 5% of maltreated children were functioning well consistently over time, attesting to the dynamic nature of resilience and the importance of multiple assessments over time. This evidence of low prevalence and instability of resilient coping is consistent with results of previous longitudinal studies of maltreated children (Cicchetti & Rogosh, 1997; Farber & Egeland, 1987; Herrenkohl et al., 1994). These findings support the proposition that disturbances within the parent–child relationship, the most proximal level of the child's social ecology, diminish the odds of resilience.

Processes Underlying Vulnerability and Resilience

Findings from this research also offer evidence about factors that contribute to vulnerability and to resilience among maltreated children. Variations in experiences of maltreatment, including the types and timing of abuse and neglect, helped to account for individual differences in children's adjustment. For example, neglect and sexual abuse were associated with higher levels of internalizing problems and lower levels of perceived control, especially among children who experienced both of these forms of maltreatment.

The negative sequelae of *chronic* maltreatment were especially striking: Children who were maltreated over a longer period of time had more problems with peers (e.g., they were less popular, more likely to be rejected, and less likely to have a reciprocal best friendship), showed more aggression and externalizing problems, and had lower self-esteem than other children. These findings suggest that the enduring nature of the maltreatment these children experienced exacerbated its effects, producing particularly strong negative consequences for children's development. Early onset of maltreatment also appeared to heighten its negative consequences: Children who were maltreated early in life had lower self-esteem across all time points of the study and were less likely to have a sense of internal control. Our findings add to a growing body of evidence of the deleterious influences of early and chronic maltreatment. Aguilar, Sroufe, Egeland, and Carlson (2000) showed that children who experienced maltreatment that began early and continued into adolescence were more likely to show early-onset, persistent behavior problems. Eckenrode et al. (2001) found that children whose maltreatment persisted during childhood and into adolescence engaged in more early-onset problem behaviors (e.g., early sexual activity, alcohol and drug use, arrests and criminal convictions) than children who experienced no maltreatment or maltreatment that did not continue into adolescence. Thus, maltreatment is likely to pose a particularly serious threat to children's development when it begins early and continues over a long period of time.

Our findings also yielded insights into potential pathways or mechanisms that are implicated in adjustment trajectories of maltreated youth. To illustrate, we found that chronic maltreatment was associated with more aggressive behavior, which in turn was linked with subsequent peer rejection. By the time they reach school age, chronically maltreated children typically have experienced a long history of punitive and unresponsive care within their families. When parents use coercive behavior, and fail to encourage their children's prosocial behavior and to discourage their coercive behavior effectively via nonphysical means, children become more likely to use coercive means in their interactions with others (Patterson, 1995; Patterson, Reid, & Dishion, 1998). Chronically maltreated children are more likely to have witnessed aggressive behavior by parents and less likely than other children to have learned nonaggressive ways to solve conflicts. Each of these pathways could contribute to the development of heightened levels of aggressive behavior, which in turn could engender dislike of the child by peers.

Finally, our analyses highlighted variables that might protect children against the adverse effects of maltreatment. Specifically, higher levels of perceived internal control were associated with a reduced risk of internalizing problems among maltreated children, suggesting that a sense of internal control operated as a protective factor for these children.

Children with a stronger sense of internal control are less likely to accept aversive situations passively and more likely to apply effort to meet challenges (Werner & Smith, 1982). In concert with findings from other research regarding the protective role of internal control (e.g., Moran & Eckenrode, 1992) and with evidence that ego resilience, ego control, and positive self-esteem enhance the odds of resilience among maltreated children (Cicchetti & Rogosch, 1997; Cicchetti et al., 1993), these findings suggest that active coping and effortful control are involved in the processes by which some maltreated children are able to adapt more successfully than others.

Our findings also extend previous research on the role of close relationships in promoting resilience. Previous research has identified a consistent, supportive relationship with an adult as a protective factor for maltreated children (Egeland et al., 1988; Herrenkohl et al., 1994). Our findings suggest that friendship, though not a substitute for adult caregiving, may play a protective role for some maltreated children. Among maltreated children (especially those who were chronically maltreated and those who were physically abused), having a positive, reciprocal friendship was associated with an increase over time in self-esteem. With regard to potential underlying mechanisms, it is possible that a positive reciprocal friendship could lead to decreases in loneliness, increases in perceived acceptance, improved social skills, and changes in working models of attachment; these in turn could result in improved self-perceptions and more prosocial behavior over time (Price, 1996).

Implications for Intervention and Policy

Our findings attest to the crucial role of parent–child relationships in promoting children's competence, and suggest the need for theoretically informed, community-supported interventions to promote positive parenting and prevent child maltreatment. How might this best be accomplished? Intervention could fruitfully occur at several levels, including, at the more distal level, approaches that recognize and address the strong linkages between child maltreatment, on the one hand, and family economic hardship, on the other. In our sample of maltreated children, over 90% experienced family economic hardship (as defined by participation in the federal free and reduced-price lunch program), and 70% experienced chronic family economic hardship. These data are consistent with findings that nationally, the incidence of child maltreatment is many times higher in families with low incomes than in those with greater economic resources (Sedlak & Broadhurst, 1996). The causal links between poverty and child maltreatment are likely to be complex; however, considerable research suggests that economic hardship can lead to problems in family functioning via factors such as parents' increased psychological distress and decreased capacity for sensitive, consistent childrearing (Conger et al., 1992; Elder, Nguyen, & Caspi, 1985). Effective programs to reduce poverty (Vinokur, Schul, Vuori, & Price, 2000) are therefore important policy priorities for preventing and reducing child maltreatment.

Interventions at the more proximal level of the family, that is, those targeting parents at social and economic risk (e.g., low-income, unmarried teenagers; Olds & Kitzmann, 1993) and parents with mental health difficulties, are also needed. Among families in poverty, rates of child maltreatment tend to be elevated among parents with histories of serious psychiatric disorders such as substance abuse and depressive diagnoses (Chaffin, Kelleher, & Hollenberg, 1996; Egami, Ford, Greenfield, & Crum, 1996; Luthar, 1999; Mayes & Truman, 2002; Sameroff, Seifer, & Bartko, 1997). Preventive interventions for these parents are also critical, therefore, in preventing child maltreatment. Results of our research indicate that being maltreated early in life may increase children's vulnerability to adjustment problems, and that early maltreatment that is sustained over time (chronic maltreatment) tends to have especially serious sequelae. These findings, along with evidence that parent training may be more effective in families with younger children (Dishion & Patterson, 1992), underscore the importance of early intervention to prevent child maltreatment. Examples of promising strategies include home visiting (Olds & Kitzmann, 1993), group-based, relationship-oriented interventions (Luthar & Suchman, 2000), and programs that incorporate both of these approaches (Erickson & Egeland, 1999).

In addition to the crucial goal of prevention, efforts to reduce the consequences of abuse and neglect are needed. Interventions aimed at improving maltreated children's relationships are particularly promising in this regard. Examples are therapeutic foster care (Fisher, Gunnar, Chamberlain, & Reid, 2000); programs to match children with adult mentors who provide a supportive, consistent relationship outside the family (Grossman & Tierney, 1998); and interventions that pair maltreated children with well-functioning peers, which have been shown to increase positive interactive peer play among maltreated children (Fantuzzo et al., 1996). Our findings regarding the significant role of perceived control in outcomes for maltreated children also suggest that programs that increase maltreated children's experiences of mastery, whether in academics, athletics, arts, or other activities, may be beneficial (Gilligan, 1999). Further research is needed to evaluate the effectiveness of these and other interventions with maltreated children.

In summary, findings of our research show that maltreatment by parents and caregivers during childhood is associated with greater vulnerability to adjustment difficulties and a reduced probability of resilience. Chronic maltreatment, maltreatment early in life, and specific types of maltreatment were closely associated with decreased odds of positive adaptation. Personal characteristics, such as perceptions of internal control, and good relationships with others, such as supportive peer friendships, were associated with more positive adaptation. Our findings attest to the crucial role of maltreatment in influencing children's development, and strongly underscore the need for effective interventions to promote positive parenting and prevent child maltreatment.

References

Abramson, L. Y., Seligman, M. E. P., & Teasdale, J. D. (1978). Learned helplessness in humans: Critique and reformulation. *Journal of Abnormal Psychology, 87,* 49–74.

Achenbach, T. M. (1991). *Manual for the Youth Self-Report and 1991 Profile.* Burlington: University of Vermont Department of Psychiatry.

Aguilar, B., Sroufe, L. A., Egeland, B., & Carlson, E. (2000). Distinguishing the early-onset/persistent and adolescent-onset antisocial behavior types: From birth to 16 years. *Development and Psychopathology, 12,* 109–132.

Banyard, V. L. (1999). Childhood maltreatment and the mental health of low-income women. *American Journal of Orthopsychiatry, 69,* 161–171.

Barnett, D., Manly, J. T., & Cicchetti, D. (1993). Defining child maltreatment: The interface between policy and research. In D. Cicchetti & S. L. Toth (Eds.), *Child abuse, child development, and social policy* (pp. 7–74). Norwood, NJ: Ablex.

Belsky, J. (1980). Child maltreatment: An ecological integration. *American Psychologist, 35,* 320–335.

Bolger, K. E., & Patterson, C. J. (2001a). Developmental pathways from child maltreatment to peer rejection. *Child Development, 72*(2), 549–568.

Bolger, K. E. & Patterson, C. J. (2001b). Pathways from child maltreatment to internalizing problems: Perceptions of control as mediators and moderators. *Development and Psychopathology. 13,* 913–940.

Bolger K. E., Patterson, C. J., & Kupersmidt, J. B. (1998a, July). *Friendship as a moderator of the relation between maltreatment and childern's adjustment.* Poster presented at the meetings of the International Society for the Study of Behavioural Development, Berne, Switzerland.

Bolger, K. E., Patterson, C. J., & Kupersmidt, J. B. (1998b). Peer relationships and self-esteem among children who have been maltreated. *Child Development, 69,* 1171–1197.

Chaffin, M., Kelleher, K., & Hollenberg, J. (1996). Onset of physical abuse and neglect: Psychiatric, substance abuse, and social risk factors from prospective community data. *Child Abuse and Neglect, 20,* 191–203.

Cicchetti, D., & Lynch, M. (1995). Failures in the expectable environment and their impact on individual development: The case of child maltreatment. In D. Cicchetti & D. J. Cohen (Eds.), *Developmental psychopathology, Vol. 2: Risk, disorder, and adaptation* (pp. 32–71). New York: Wiley.

Cicchetti, D., Lynch, M., Shonk, S., & Manly, J. T. (1992). An organizational perspective on peer relations in maltreated children. In R. D. Parke & G. W. Ladd (Eds.), *Family–peer relationships: Modes of linkage* (pp. 345–383). Hillsdale, NJ: Erlbaum.

Cicchetti, D., & Rogosch, F. A. (1997). The role of self-organization in the promotion of resilience in maltreated children. *Development and Psychopathology, 9,* 797–815.

Cicchetti, D., Rogosch, F. A., Lynch, M., & Holt, K. (1993). Resilience in maltreated children: Processes leading to adaptive outcome. *Development and Psychopathology, 5,* 629–647.

Coie, J. D., Dodge, K. A., & Coppotelli, H. (1982). Dimensions and types of social status: A cross-age perspective. *Developmental Psychology, 18,* 557–570.

Conger, R. D., Conger, K. J., Elder, G. H., Lorenz, F. O., Simons, R. L., & Whitbeck, L. B. (1992). A family process model of economic hardship and adjustment of early adolescent boys. *Child Development, 63,* 526–541.

Connell, J. P. (1985). A new multidimensional measure of children's perceptions of control. *Child Development, 56,* 1018–1041.

Cowen, E. L., Lorion, R. P., & Caldwell, R. A. (1975). Nonprofessionals' judgments about clinical interaction problems. *Journal of Consulting and Clinical Psychology, 43,* 619–625.

Dishion, T. J., & Patterson, G. R. (1992). Age effects in parent training outcome. *Behavior Therapy, 23,* 719–729.

Dodge, K. A., Pettit, G. S., & Bates, J. E. (1997). How the experience of early physical abuse leads children to become chronically aggressive. In D. Cicchetti & S. L. Toth (Eds.), Developmental perspectives on trauma: Theory, research, and intervention. *Rochester symposium on developmental psychology* (Vol. 8, pp. 263–288). Rochester, NY: University of Rochester Press.

Eckenrode, J., Ganzel, B., Henderson, C. R., Smith, E., Olds, D. L., Powers, J., Cole, R., Kitzman, H., & Sidora, K. (2000). Preventing child abuse and neglect with a program of nurse home visitation: The limiting effects of domestic violence. *Journal of the American Medical Association, 284,* 1385–1391.

Eckenrode, J., Zielinski, D., Smith, E., Marcynyszyn, L. A., Henderson, C. R., Kitzman, H., Cole, R., Powers, J., & Olds, D. L. (2001). Child maltreatment and the early onset of problem behaviors: Can a program of nurse home visitation break the link? *Development and Psychopathology. 13,* 873–890.

Egeland, B., Carlson, E., & Sroufe, L. A. (1993). Resilience as process. *Development and Psychopathology, 5,* 517–528.

Egami, Y., Ford, D. E., Greenfield, S. F., & Crum, R. M. (1996). Psychiatric profile and sociodemographic characteristics of adults who report physically abusing or neglecting children. *American Journal of Psychiatry, 153,* 921–928.

Egeland, B., Jacobvitz, D., & Sroufe, L. A. (1988). Breaking the cycle of abuse. *Child Development, 59,* 1080–1088.

Egeland, B., Sroufe, L. A., & Erickson, M. (1983). The developmental consequences of different patterns of maltreatment. *Child Abuse and Neglect, 7,* 459–469.

Elder, G. H., Nguyen, T., & Caspi, A. (1985). Linking family hardship to children's lives. *Child Development, 56,* 361–375.

Erickson, M. F., & Egeland, B. (1999). The STEEP program: Linking theory and research to practice. In M. F. Erickson & R. A. Weinberg (Eds.), *Zero to three* (Vol. 20, pp. 11–16). Washington, D C: Zero to Three: National Center for Infants, Toddlers, and Families.

Fantuzzo, J., Sutton-Smith, B., Atkins, M., Stevenson, H., Coolahan, K., Weiss, A., & Manz, P. (1996). Community-based resilient peer treatment of withdrawn maltreated preschool children. *Journal of Consulting and Clinical Psychology, 64,* 1377–1386.

Farber, E. A., & Egeland, B. (1987). Invulnerability in abused and neglected children. In E. J. Anthony & B. J. Cohler (Eds.), *The invulnerable child* (pp. 253–288). New York: Guilford Press.

Fisher, P. A., Gunnar, M. R., Chamberlain, P., & Reid, J. B. (2000). Preventive intervention for maltreated preschool children: Impact on children's behavior, neuroendocrine activity, and foster parent functioning. *Journal of the American Academy of Child and Adolescent Psychiatry, 39,* 1356–1364.

Furman, W., & Buhrmester, D. (1985). Children's perceptions of the personal relationships in their social networks. *Developmental Psychology, 21,* 1016–1024.

Gilligan, R. (1999). Enhancing the resilience of children and young people in public care by mentoring their talents and interests. *Child and Family Social Work, 4,* 187–196.

Grossman, J. B., & Tierney, J. P. (1998). Does mentoring work? An impact study of the Big Brothers Big Sisters program. *Evaluation Review, 22,* 403–426.

Harter, S. (1985). *Manual for the Self-Perception Profile for Children.* Denver: Department of Psychology, University of Denver.

Hartup, W. W., & Stevens, N. (1999). Friendships and adaptation across the lifespan. *Current Directions in Psychological Science, 8,* 76–79.

Herrenkohl, R. C., Egolf, B. P., & Herrenkohl, E. C. (1997). Preschool antecedents of adolescent assaultive behavior: A longitudinal study. *American Journal of Orthopsychiatry, 67,* 422–432.

Herrenkohl, E. C., Herrenkohl, R. C., & Egolf, B. P. (1994). Resilient early-school-age children from maltreating homes: Outcomes in late adolescence. *American Journal of Orthopsychiatry, 64,* 301–309.

Huesmann, L. R., Eron, L. D., Lefkowitz, M. M., & Walder, L. O. (1984). Stability of aggression over time and generations. *Developmental Psychology, 20,* 1120–1134.

Kovacs, M., & Devlin, B. (1998). Internalizing disorders in childhood. *Journal of Child Psychology and Psychiatry and Allied Disciplines, 39,* 47–63.

Lord, S. E., Eccles, J. S., & McCarthy, K. A. (1994). Surviving the junior high school transition: Family processes and self-perceptions as protective and risk factors. *Journal of Early Adolescence, 14,* 162–199.

Luthar, S. S. (1991). Vulnerability and resilience: A study of high-risk adolescents. *Child Development, 62,* 600–616.

Luthar, S. S. (1993). Annotation: Methodological and conceptual issues in research on childhood resilience. *Journal of Child Psychology and Psychiatry and Allied Disciplines, 34,* 441–453.

Luthar, S. S. (1999). *Poverty and children's adjustment.* Thousand Oaks, CA: Sage.

Luthar, S. S., & Suchman, N. E. (2000). Relational Psychotherapy Mothers' Group: A developmentally informed intervention for at-risk mothers. *Development and Psychopathology, 12,* 235–253.

Lynch, M., & Cicchetti, D. (1998). An ecological-transactional analysis of children and contexts: The longitudinal interplay among child maltreatment, community violence, and children's symptomatology. *Development and Psychopathology, 10,* 235–257.

Masten, A. S., & Coatsworth, J. D. (1998). The development of competence in favorable and unfavorable environments: Lessons from research on successful children. *American Psychologist, 53,* 205–220.

Mayes, L. C., & Truman, S. D. (2002). Substance abuse and parenting. In M. Bornstein (Ed.), *Handbook of parenting* (3rd ed., Vol. 4, pp. 329–359). Mahwah, NJ: Erlbaum.

McGee, R. A., Wolfe, D. A., & Wilson, S. K. (1997). Multiple maltreatment experiences and adolescents' behavior problems: Adolescents' perspectives. *Development and Psychopathology, 9,* 131–149.

McLoyd, V. C. (1998). Socioeconomic disadvantage and child development. *American Psychologist, 53,* 185–204.

Moran, P. B., & Eckenrode, J. (1992). Protective personality characteristics among adolescent victims of maltreatment. *Child Abuse and Neglect, 16,* 743–754.

Mueller, E., & Silverman, N. (1989). Peer relations in maltreated children. In D. Cicchetti & V. Carlson (Eds.), *Child maltreatment: Theory and research on the causes and consequences of child abuse and neglect* (pp. 529–578). New York: Cambridge University Press.

National Research Council (U. S.) Panel on Research on Child Abuse and Neglect (1993). *Understanding child abuse and neglect.* Washington, DC: National Academy of Sciences.

Olds, D. L., & Kitzman, H. (1993). Review of research on home visiting for pregnant women and parents of young children. *The Future of Children, 3,* 53–92.

Parker, J. G., & Asher, S. R. (1987). Peer relations and later personal adjustment: Are low-accepted children at risk? *Psychological Bulletin, 102,* 357–389.

Parker, J. G., & Asher, S. R. (1993). Friendship and friendship quality in middle childhood: Links with peer group acceptance and feelings of loneliness and social dissatisfaction. *Developmental Psychology, 29,* 611–621.

Patterson, C. J., Griesler, P. C., Vaden, N. A., & Kupersmidt, J. B. (1992). Family economic circumstances, life transitions, and children's peer relations.

In R. D. Parke & G. W. Ladd (Eds.), *Family–peer relationships: Modes of linkage* (pp. 385–424). Hillsdale, NJ: Erlbaum.

Patterson, G. R. (1995). Coercion as a basis for early age of onset for arrest. In J. McCord (Ed.), *Coercion and punishment in long-term perspecive* (pp. 81–105). Cambridge: Cambridge University Press.

Patterson, G. R., Reid, J. B., & Dishion, T. J. (1998). Antisocial boys. In J. M. Jenkins, K. Oatley, et al. (Eds.), *Human emotions: A reader* (pp. 330–336). Malden, MA: Blackwell.

Peterson, C., & Seligman, M. E. (1984). Causal explanations as a risk factor for depression: Theory and evidence. *Psychological Review, 91,* 347–374.

Price, J. M. (1996). Friendships of maltreated children and adolescents: Contexts for expressing and modifying relationship history. In W. M. Bukowski & A. F. Newcomb (Eds.), *The company they keep: Friendships in childhood and adolescence* (pp. 262–285). New York: Cambridge University Press.

Raver, C. C. (1996). Relations between social contingency in mother–child interaction and 2-year-olds' social competence. *Developmental Psychology, 32,* 850–859.

Rogosch, F. A., Cicchetti, D., & Aber, J. L. (1995). The role of child maltreatment in early deviations in cognitive and affective processing abilities and later peer relationship problems. *Development and Psychopathology, 7,* 591–609.

Rutter, M., & Quinton, D. (1984). Long-term follow-up of women institutionalized in childhood: Factors promoting good functioning in adult life. *British Journal of Developmental Psychology, 2,* 191–204.

Salzinger, S., Feldman, R. S., Hammer, M., & Rosario, M. (1993). The effects of physical abuse on children's social relationships. *Child Development, 64,* 169–187.

Sameroff, A. J., Seifer, R., & Bartko, W. T. (1997). Environmental perspectives on adaptation during childhood and adolescence. In S. S. Luthar, J. A. Burack, D. Cicchetti, & J. R. Weisz (Eds.), *Developmental psychopathology: Perspectives on adjustment, risk, and disorder* (pp. 507–526). New York: Cambridge University Press.

Scarr, S. (1992). Developmental theories for the 1990s: Development and individual differences. *Child Development, 63,* 1–19.

Sedlak, A. J., & Broadhurst, D. D. (1996). *Third National Incidence Study of Child Abuse and Neglect, final report.* Washington, DC: U.S. Department of Health and Human Services.

Toth, S. L., Manly, J. T., & Cicchetti, D. (1992). Child maltreatment and vulnerability to depression. *Development and Psychopathology, 4,* 97–112.

Vinokur, A. D., Schul, Y., Vuori, J., & Price, R. H. (2000). Two years after a job loss: Long-term impact of the JOBS program on reemployment and mental health. *Journal of Occupational Health Psychology, 5,* 32–47.

Werner, E., & Smith, R. S. (1992). *Overcoming the odds: High risk children from birth to adulthood.* Ithaca, NY: Cornell University Press.

Widom, C. S. (1989). Does violence beget violence? A critical examination of the literature. *Psychological Bulletin, 106,* 3–28.

8

Risk and Resilience in Children Coping with Their Parents' Divorce and Remarriage

E. Mavis Hetherington and Anne Mitchell Elmore

In the past 50 years in the United States, marriage has become a more optional, less permanent institution. Marriage is being delayed, rates of marital formation are decreasing, and divorce, births to single mothers, and cohabitation have increased. The divorce rate has more than doubled since 1950, and although in the past two decades it has declined modestly and stabilized, still about 45% of contemporary marriages are expected to fail (Teachman, Tedrow, & Crowder, 2000; U.S. Bureau of the Census, 1998). As the divorce rate increased in the 1970s, the remarriage rate for women began to decline. About 65% of women and 75% of men now remarry. However, divorces occur more rapidly and frequently in remarriages, especially in those involving stepchildren (Cherlin & Furstenberg, 1994; Tzeng & Mare, 1995).

The general long-term pattern of a rising divorce rate over the past 50 years and a decreasing remarriage rate starting in the 1980s holds for non-Hispanic whites, African Americans, and Hispanic whites, but the absolute levels differ for the three groups. Compared to non-Hispanic and Hispanic whites, African Americans wait longer and are less likely to marry and also are more likely to separate and divorce, to remain separated without a divorce, and less likely to remarry (Teachman et al., 2000).

As parents move in and out of intimate relationships, their children are exposed to the changes, challenges, and stresses associated with multiple family transitions. It is estimated that about 40% of children will experience their parents' divorce, with about 80% of them placed primarily in the physical custody of their biological mother. This usually is a short-lived situation because half of divorced adults remarry within 4 years. One-third of American children will eventually become members of a stepfamily, with 86% of these stepfamilies composed of a biological mother and a stepfather (U.S. Census Bureau, 1998). Considering only divorce and remarriage as transitions underestimates the number of family reorganizations encountered by children, as cohabitation has become an increasingly common antecedent or alternative to marriage and remarriage (Seltzer, 2001). Almost one-third of adults have cohabited before a first marriage and 75% before a remarriage.

What is striking following divorce and remarriage is not the inevitability but the diversity in the experiences and outcomes for parents and children. In this chapter, we will describe vulnerability factors that increase the likelihood of adverse outcomes and protective factors that buffer children or foster resilience in coping with their parents' marital transitions. Some of the vulnerability or protective processes that are catalyzed by stresses associated with parental divorce or remarriage lie in individual characteristics of the child, some in family relationships, and some in experiences and relationships external to the family.

THE ADJUSTMENT OF CHILDREN IN DIVORCED AND REMARRIED FAMILIES

There is considerable agreement in the research literature that children in divorced and remarried families are at increased risk for the development of psychological, behavioral, social, and academic problems in comparison to those in two-parent nondivorced families (for reviews see Amato, 2001; Amato & Keith, 1991a, 1991b; Emery, 1999; Hetherington, Bridges, & Insabella, 1998) and that the risk is greatest for children who have experienced multiple marital transitions (Capaldi & Patterson, 1991; Kurdek, Fine, & Sinclair, 1995). There is less consensus on the size than on the presence of the differences between the adjustments of children in divorced and remarried families with those in nondivorced families. In a meta-analysis of the effects of divorce on children's adjustment, Amato and Keith (1991a) report that for externalizing disorders, where the largest differences usually are obtained, the effect size is only about one-third of a deviation unit. However, much larger effect sizes have been reported in some studies using multiple measures including observations and composite indices (Bray, 1999; Hetherington & Clingempeel, 1992; Hetherington, Cox, & Cox, 1985; Hetherington, Henderson, & Reiss, 1999; Simons & Associates, 1996).

In the immediate aftermath of a parental divorce or remarriage, most children experience emotional distress and behavior problems, including anger, resentment, demandingness, noncompliance, anxiety, and depression, as they cope with the confusion and apprehension stemming from changing relationships in the family and shifts in their life situation. In most children, these responses begin to diminish in the second year following divorce and the third to fifth year following remarriage (Hetherington & Stanley-Hagan, 2002). However, some children may show severe, enduring adjustment difficulties and other children show delayed effects, appearing to adapt well in the early stages following divorce but showing problems at a later time.

Large-scale survey studies using nationally representative samples and more intensive psychological studies using such measures as clinical cutoff scores on the Child Behavior Checklist (Achenbach, 1991) generally have found that about 20–25% of children in divorced and remarried families, compared to 10% of children in nondivorced families, demonstrate severe emotional and behavioral problems (Hetherington, 1991a, 1993; Hetherington & Clingempeel, 1992; Hetherington & Jodl, 1994; McLanahan, 1999; Simons & Associates, 1996; Zill, Morrison, & Coiro, 1993) and that differences between divorced and nondivorced families are less marked for African American than for white children and adolescents (McLanahan, 1999).

The largest and most consistently reported effects of marital transitions on children's adjustment have been in the domains of externalizing behavior, social responsibility, and academic and economic attainment (Amato, 2001; Bray, 1999; Dunn et al., 1998; Emery, 1999; Hetherington & Clingempeel, 1992; Hetherington et al., 1999). On average, preadolescent children in divorced and remarried families, compared to children in two-parent, nondivorced families, show increased levels of aggression, conduct disorders, noncompliance, disobedience, and decreased self-regulation and social responsibility, as well as poorer classroom conduct and academic performance and an increase in the frequency of school suspensions.

Children in divorced and remarried families also show an increased risk for internalizing problems, including higher levels of depression and anxiety, and lower levels of self-esteem compared to children in nondivorced families, although the associations between family structure and internalizing problems are generally weaker and less consistently found than those for externalizing and achievement (Amato, 2001; Deater-Deckard & Dunn, 1999; Hetherington, 1993; Hetherington & Clingempeel, 1992; Hetherington et al., 1999). In addition, children's relationships with parents, siblings, and peers are adversely affected by their parents' marital transitions and are characterized by increased negativity, conflict, aggression, and coercion (Amato, 2001; Amato & Keith, 1991a; Hetherington, 1989, 1993; Hetherington & Clingempeel, 1992; Simons & Associates, 1996).

Although the intensity of adverse responses to their parents' marital transitions tends to diminish over time following divorce, even in adolescence and young adulthood offspring from divorced and remarried families function less well than those from nondivorced families (Amato, 1999, 2001; Amato & Keith, 1991b; Hetherington, 1999a; Hetherington & Kelly, 2002). Adolescents from divorced and remarried families compared to those from nondivorced families show a two- to threefold increase in risk for psychological and behavioral problems, including school dropout, early sexual activity, having children out of wedlock, unemployment, substance abuse and delinquent activities, and involvement with antisocial peers (Amato, 2000, 2001; Amato & Keith, 1991a; Hetherington & Clingempeel, 1992; McLanahan, 1999; McLanahan & Sandefur, 1994; Simons & Associates, 1996; Zill et al., 1993).

Although conduct disorders decline in young adulthood, substance abuse, alcoholism, and troubles with the law remain higher in youths from divorced and remarried families. In comparison to young adults from nondivorced families, adult offspring from divorced and remarried families also experience lower socioeconomic and educational attainment and are more likely to be on welfare. In addition, they have more problems with family members, in intimate relations, in marriage, and in the workplace. Their divorce rate is higher, and their reports of general well-being and life satisfaction are lower (Amato, 1999, 2001; Amato & Booth, 1997; Amato & Keith, 1991a; Hetherington, 1999a; Hetherington & Kelly, 2002).

There is recent evidence to suggest that many offspring in divorced and remarried families may experience more subtle, less perceptible forms of pain or distress that may not be detected on standardized measures. Long after a divorce, although most young adults report that the divorce in the long run may have been a good thing, still regrets about relationships with their fathers, about family loyalty and conflicts and a tendency to blame problems they encounter or lack of well being on the divorce may persist (Emery, 1999; Laumann-Billings & Emery, 2000).

There is greater variability in the adjustment of offspring from divorced and remarried families than those from nondivorced families. Cluster analyses indicate that children, adolescents and young adults whose parents have gone through marital transitions are overrepresented both in multiproblem clusters and in high competency clusters (Hetherington, 1989, 1993, 1999a; Hetherington & Kelly, 2002). A subgroup of girls in divorced, mother-headed families are especially likely to be exceptionally well adjusted and socially responsible, although for some this competence comes at a cost and is accompanied by low self-esteem and elevated anxiety and depression.

Although children and adolescents in divorced and remarried families compared to those in nondivorced families are at increased risk for psychological and behavioral problems, resilience is the normative outcome for children who are faced with the stresses and adaptive challenges associated with their parents' marital transitions. This is not to underestimate the apprehension, painful feelings, and grief that many children experience in response to the end of their parent's marriage or their entry into remarriage. However, in the absence of new stresses and adversity, the vast majority of offspring are able to cope with their new life situation and eventually emerge as reasonably competent, well-adjusted adults (Amato, 1999, 2000, 2001; Hetherington, 1993, 1999a; McLanahan, 1999; Zill et al., 1993).

CHALLENGES AND CHANGES IN EXPERIENCES OF CHILDREN IN DIVORCED AND REMARRIED FAMILIES

The challenges for children accompanying parental divorce and remarriage differ. Many of the difficulties associated with divorce are related to the exit of a parent, those in remarriage with the entrance of a new parent and sometimes new siblings. Although children report both types of transitions to be accompanied by high rates of negative life events, remarriage is reported also to have more positive life changes than divorce (Anderson, Greene, Hetherington, & Clingempeel, 1999; Bray, 1999; Hetherington & Jodl, 1994).

Children in divorced families often encounter stressors that put them at risk for developing problems in adjustment such as high interparental conflict, loss of or intermittent contact with one parent, usually the father, problems in the mental and physical health of parents, and nonauthoritative parenting. In addition, those in mother-custody families often confront problems associated with poverty, such as multiple moves into high-risk neighborhoods with inadequate schools, delinquent, low-achieving peer groups, and high rates of unemployment, single-parent families, and substance abuse (Amato, 2001; Hetherington et al., 1998; McLanahan, 1999). Still, a divorce also can offer parents and children in some families an escape from an unhappy, conflictual, or abusive family situation and a move to a more harmonious, gratifying life with greater opportunities to form new, more fulfilling relationships and for personal growth and individuation.

Remarriage is the fastest route out of poverty for divorced mothers and their children. The presence of a stepparent also offers possible emotional, practical, and social support for both biological parents and children. Yet the adjustment of children in divorced single-parent households and in stepfamilies is remarkably similar (Cherlin & Furstenberg, 1994; Deater-Deckard & Dunn, 1999; Hetherington, 1993, 1999a; Hetherington & Clingempeel, 1992; Hetherington & Jodl, 1994). Some investigators have argued that the new stresses encountered in stepfamilies in trying to develop positive relations between stepparents and stepchildren and between stepsiblings, in attempting to build a strong marital relationship in the presence of children, and in balancing relationships within the household and outside of it with the noncustodial parent counter the benefits that children might receive in a stepfamily (Bray, 1999; Hetherington & Jodl, 1994). Other researchers have suggested that the negative effects of divorce and life in a single-parent family may be intense, persistent, and difficult to eradicate by the resources in a stepfamily (Anderson et al., 1999; Cherlin & Furstenberg, 1994). This seems unlikely to be the sole explanations for problems in the adjustment of children in stepfamilies because problems in new stepfamilies are greater than those in stabilized divorced, single-parent families and they diminish in longer-established stepfamilies (Bray, 1999; Hetherington & Clingempeel, 1992; Hetherington et al., 1999).

PROBLEMS PRECEDING DIVORCE

Problems in the adjustment of parents and children and in disrupted, inept parenting practices are present long before a divorce occurs (see Amato, 2001, for a review). Higher rates of alcohol and substance abuse, antisocial behavior, depression, economic problems, and stressful life events are found in adults who will later divorce (Capaldi & Patterson, 1991; Davies, Aveson, & McAlpine, 1997; Hope, Power, & Rodgers, 1999; Kitson, 1992; Kurdek, 1990). In their interactions with marital partners, they have poor problem-solving skills and exhibit escalation and reciprocation of negative affect, contempt, denial, withdrawal, and negative attributions about their spouses' behavior, which in turn significantly increase their risk for marital dissolution and multiple divorces

(Bradbury & Fincham, 1990; Fincham, Bradbury, & Scott, 1990; Gottman, 1993, 1994; Gottman & Levenson, 1992; Gottman & Notarius, 2001; Hetherington, 1999a, 1999b; Matthews, Wickrama, & Conger, 1996). More conflict, negativity, and irritability and less warmth and control also are found in the parenting of mothers and fathers who will later divorce compared to those who remain married (Amato, 2001; Amato & Booth, 1996; Block, Block, & Gjerde, 1988; Hetherington, 1999b). Their children also exhibit more problems before the marital breakup such as conduct disorders (Amato & Booth, 1996; Cherlin et al., 1991), substance abuse (Doherty & Needle, 1991; Hetherington, 1996), internalizing, and diminished social competence, self-esteem and achievement (Aseltine, 1996; Hetherington, 1999b).

It is not surprising that living in an unhappy marriage and in what often is a conflictual family situation may have taken its toll on the well-being of family members before a marital breakup occurs. Furthermore, the presence of a difficult child with behavior disorders may undermine a fragile marital relationship and contribute to the divorce. However, selection processes also must be considered. People who have adjustment problems such as antisocial behavior, impulsivity, and depression are more likely to encounter stressful life events, to have problems in interpersonal relationships, to be inept parents, to have difficulty building successful intimate relationships, and to divorce. Furthermore, antisocial individuals are more likely to select an antisocial partner (Amato, 2001; Hetherington & Kelly, in press).

It has been argued that there may be an underlying genetic substrate to divorce that links personality problems in parents, inadequate parenting practices, and behavior problems in children. The concordance for divorce and similarity on personality characteristics such as antisocial or impulsive behavior that erodes marriage and parent–child relationships is greater in identical than fraternal twins (Jockin, McGue, & Lykken, 1996; McGue & Lykken, 1992). Therefore, children from divorced families may have more problems both because they have inherited these characteristics from their parents and because of their exposure to genetically influenced inept parenting, not because of divorce. These partially genetically based personality traits in adults and problems in interpersonal interactions are likely to carry over and contribute to difficulties in a remarriage.

Selection and genetic factors may contribute to divorce, but longitudinal studies also show that an unhappy marriage, divorce, and remarriage at least temporarily increase adjustment problems in adults and children and lead to less authoritative parenting (Amato, 2001; Bray, 1999; Hetherington, 1993; Hetherington & Clingempeel, 1992; Hetherington & Jodl, 1994; McLanahan, 1999).

VULNERABILITY AND PROTECTIVE FACTORS IN CHILDREN ADJUSTING TO DIVORCE AND REMARRIAGE

We now turn to the discussion of risk and protective mechanisms at the individual, familial, and extrafamilial levels that serve to moderate or mediate children's responses to the stresses associated with parental divorce and life in a single-parent, divorced family.

Individual Characteristics as Vulnerability and Protective Factors

Age
Although children's gender and age at the time of parental divorce and remarriage have been extensively studied in relation to adaptation to divorce, the results of these studies are largely inconsistent. It has been hypothesized that due to their developmental status, younger children may be less cognitively equipped than older children to accurately appraise the circumstances surrounding their parents' marital disruption, and therefore may be particularly prone to fears of abandonment by parents and feelings of self-blame and guilt over their parents' divorce. In addition, young children are less able than older children to seek supportive social relationships outside the family that may protect them from the stresses associated with their parents' marital transition. Older children, especially adolescents, in contrast to younger children, have more opportunities to disengage from a troubled family life and seek comfort and support from individuals and institutions outside of the family environment. Supportive relationships outside of the family with peers and other individuals, such as teachers, coaches, friends' parents, and extended family, may protect older children from the negative outcomes associated with divorce. Moreover, academic, social, artistic, athletic, and extracurricular attainments, activities, and skills may serve to buffer children from the adverse consequences of divorce.

Support for the hypothesis that divorce would have more adverse effects on younger children compared to older children, however, has not been forthcoming, perhaps because studies to date have failed to disentangle the confounding influences of children's current age, children's age at the time of marital disruption, and the amount of time since the marital disruption (Emery, 1999). Some studies have reported more negative consequences of divorce for younger children (Allison & Furstenberg, 1989), and other studies have found equally negative consequences for older children and adolescents (Amato & Keith, 1991a).

There is some evidence that early adolescence may be an especially difficult time in which to have a remarriage occur (Hetherington & Clingempeel, 1992; Hetherington & Jodl, 1994). Early adolescent children and those who have spent more time in a divorced, single-parent household show more resistance to the entry of a stepparent than do either younger children or older adolescents, and their externalizing behavior and problems with cognitive competence and social competence may be exacerbated by their parent's remarriage.

Gender

Early studies commonly reported more deleterious effects of divorce for boys and remarriage for girls. Boys in single-mother, divorced households were more likely than girls to be overrepresented in a subset of children showing particularly maladaptive patterns of adjustment following parental divorce, including increased externalizing behaviors in multiple settings and poorer school functioning (Hetherington, 1989).

However, more recent studies have reported less pronounced and consistent gender differences in response to divorce, and these effects are usually found with younger children and not with adolescents (Amato, 2001; Amato & Keith, 1991a; Aseltine, 1996; Simons & Associates, 1996). The decline in gender effects may reflect recent trends of greater father involvement following divorce, including higher rates of father custody, joint custody, and contact with noncustodial fathers, and this increased involvement of fathers may be especially beneficial to the adjustment of boys compared to girls (Amato & Keith, 1991a; Clarke-Stewart & Hayward, 1996; Hetherington et al., 1998).

Although some researchers have found that divorce is associated with greater externalizing behavior for boys and greater internalizing behavior for girls in adolescence (Emery, 1982), other researchers have reported that male and female adolescents from divorced families exhibit higher levels of both externalizing and internalizing behaviors compared to adolescents in nondivorced families (Hetherington, 1993; Hetherington & Clingempeel, 1992). More consistent gender differences have been found for educational attainment, with adolescent females from divorced or remarried families being less likely to complete high school and college compared to adolescent males. Teenage parenthood is equally likely to occur among male and female adolescents from divorced families. However, single parenthood has more adverse consequences for females than males, including economic decline in adulthood due to lower educational attainment and the sequelae of teenage motherhood (Hetherington, 1999a; McLanahan & Sandefur, 1994). There is more evidence for gender differences in response to remarriage, with girls being more likely than boys to resist the entry of a stepparent and less likely to benefit from the presence of a stepfather (Amato & Keith, 1991a; Hetherington & Kelly, 2002; Hetherington & Jodl, 1994; Hetherington et al., 1998).

Interestingly, studies have revealed gender differences in positive outcomes following divorce. Some girls in divorced, mother-headed households emerge as exceptionally resilient individuals, enhanced by confronting the challenges and responsibilities that follow divorce when they have the support of a competent, caring adult (Hetherington, 1989, 1991b; Hetherington & Kelly, 2002). Many divorced mothers also report greater personal growth, autonomy, and attainments and decreased depression in comparison to those who have remained in unhappy marriages (Acock & Demo, 1994; Hetherington, 1993; Hetherington & Kelly, 2002; Riessman, 1990). Such enhancement effects are less likely to be found in boys or fathers in divorced families.

Temperament and Personality Characteristics

The temperamental and personality characteristics of children also may serve to moderate children's responses to the stresses associated with divorce and remarriage. In general, children with a positive constellation of individual characteristics, such as an easy temperament, physical attractiveness, normal or above-average intelligence and self-esteem, and a sense of humor, are more likely to evoke positive responses and support from others, and are better able to adapt to the stresses and challenges associated with divorce, life in a single-parent family, and remarriage (Amato, 2001; Hetherington, 1989, 1991; Werner, 1999). Children with difficult temperaments and less attractive individual characteristics are more adversely affected by divorce, particularly those who exhibited behavior problems prior to divorce (Hetherington, 1989, 1991b). Therefore, differences in the adjustment of children with positive or negative temperaments and personality characteristics prior to divorce tend to become more marked in the adaptation to parental divorce.

The associations between temperament and children's adjustment to divorce are modified by children's gender and levels of family stress and maternal support. Temperamentally difficult boys are more likely than girls to evoke and be the target of negative exchanges with their divorced custodial mothers, and are more likely to exhibit higher levels of externalizing behavior and lower levels of social competence, particularly under conditions of high family stress and low availability of social support from mothers. Under supportive conditions and moderate levels of family stress, females with an easy temperament may actually be enhanced by their successful negotiation of the transition to divorce and living in a single-parent family, and may emerge as individuals with exceptional social competence and low levels of externalizing behavior. This is not found for temperamentally difficult children, nor is it found for temperamentally easy females under conditions of extremely high or low levels of family stress (Hetherington, 1989, 1991b). Children do not learn to cope with stress in too benign an environment and, even with support, can be overwhelmed by high levels of multiple stressors in harsh environments. A *steeling* or *inoculation* effect occurs when children's controlled exposure and successful adaptation to current stressors enhances their ability to cope with later stressors (Rutter, 1987).

Cognitions and coping styles also contribute to children's responses to divorce and remarriage. Children who have low self-efficacy and an external locus of control (Kim, Sandler, & Jenn-Yum, 1997), who blame themselves for the divorce (Bussell, 1995; Healy, Stewart, & Copeland, 1993), and who rely on distraction or avoidance rather than more active coping skills such as problem solving and gaining social support (Sandler, Tein, & West, 1994) have more difficulty coping with their parents' marital transitions and are more likely to exhibit a wide range of problems such as low self-esteem and internalizing and externalizing disorders.

Family-Level Vulnerability and Protective Factors

Financial Status
There is some controversy in the literature regarding the role of economic factors in the adjustment of children to parental divorce. Some researchers have argued that as much as half of the psychological, behavioral, and academic differences observed between children from single-parent, divorced families and two-parent families can be attributed to the significant economic decline that custodial mothers typically experience in the aftermath of divorce due to father absence (McLanahan, 1999; McLanahan & Sandefur, 1994). Indeed, despite more recent changes in the legal enforcement of child support payments from noncustodial

fathers and the increased participation of women in the labor force, custodial mothers retain only about 50–75% of their predivorce income compared to the 90% retained by noncustodial fathers (Bianchi, Subaiya, & Kahn, 1997).

In addition, these researchers estimate that another quarter of the differences in children's adjustment can be attributed to greater residential mobility and the loss of social capital among custodial mothers. In response to income loss and instability, custodial mothers often must break supportive neighborhood ties and move to more affordable and usually less desirable neighborhoods with poorer schools, higher crime rates, more deviant peer groups, and fewer resources that make successful parenting and raising competent children more difficult (McLanahan, 1999; McLanahan & Sandefur, 1994). According to the perspective of these researchers, therefore, children can be protected from many of the negative consequences associated with divorce when there is greater economic investment in offspring on the part of noncustodial fathers following divorce.

There is some research evidence to suggest that children benefit from the economic advantage that fathers provide. Children in mother-custody families who receive child support payments from their fathers view their fathers more favorably, have higher levels of academic attainment, and have fewer conduct disorders (Emery, 1999). There have been some inconsistent reports of better adjustment of children in father-custody families, and when this has been found, it is usually attributed to the economic advantage fathers have over mothers following divorce (Amato & Keith, 1991a). However, although few differences usually are found in the adjustment of children in father- and mother-custody homes, a recent small study with a nonrepresentative sample reported that even with income controlled for, children, especially boys, show greater well-being in father-custody arrangements compared to mother-custody arrangements (Clarke-Stewart & Hayward, 1996). Because father-custody arrangements are relatively rare (less than 20% of custody arrangements), these findings may reflect a select group of fathers who are exceptionally involved in the lives of their children.

A range of studies suggest that although poverty following divorce puts children at risk for a variety of life stresses, the effects of income are not primary and are largely indirect. Some researchers have shown that differences in the adjustment of children in single-parent, divorced families compared to two-parent families remain, although they are reduced, when custodial mothers' income is statistically controlled for

(Amato, 1993). Other researchers have found that the effects of economic decline on the adjustment of children are more indirect and are largely mediated by correlates of income loss, such as increased negative life events, parental distress, and deterioration in the quality of parent–child relationships (Amato, 2001; Hetherington, 1993; Hetherington & Jodl, 1994; Simons & Associates, 1996). Finally, both remarriage and, to a lesser extent, cohabitation increase the household income of divorced mothers and their children, yet this economic improvement is not reflected in the academic attainments or improved adjustment in children (Amato, 2001; Cherlin & Furstenberg, 1994; Coleman, Ganong, & Fine, 2001; Hetherington & Jodl, 1994; Seltzer, 2001).

Interparental Conflict

A common question in the divorce literature is whether it is better for parents who are involved in conflict-ridden, acrimonious, and unsatisfying marriages to stay together for the well-being of their children or to divorce. Conflict between parents, whether it occurs in a nondivorced, divorced, or remarried family, is associated with a wide range of deleterious outcomes for children, including higher levels of depression, anxiety, and externalizing behaviors and lower levels of self-esteem and social and academic competence (Amato, 2001; Amato & Keith, 1991b; Bray, 1999; Cowan & Cowan, 1990; Davies & Cummings, 1994; Gottman & Katz, 1989; Hetherington, 1999b).

Not all types of parental conflict are equally detrimental to children's adjustment, nor are all children equally vulnerable to conflict. Encapsulated conflict to which children are not directly exposed has no effect on their adjustment. However, parental conflict that is about the child or directly involves the child, conflict that is physically violent, threatening, or abusive, and conflict in which the child feels caught in the middle has the most adverse consequences for the well-being of children (Buchanan, Maccoby, & Dornbusch, 1996; Davies & Cummings, 1994; Hetherington, 1999b; Johnston, Kline, & Tschann, 1989; Maccoby, Depner, & Mnookin, 1990). The type of conflict, rather than the frequency of conflict, has been shown to be more influential in children's adjustment.

Not all children are similarly affected by parental conflict Hetherington, 1999b). Children with an easy temperament, who are intelligent and socially responsible and mature, and who have an internal locus of control are better able to cope with parental conflict and divorce than are children who do not possess these characteristics (Hetherington, 1989, 1999b). In addition, preadolescent boys may be more vulnerable to the deleterious effects of conflict between couples than preadolescent girls, although gender differences diminish in adolescence (Hetherington, 1989).

To some extent, children's perception of conflict and changes in conflict also influence children's response to divorce. Children who perceive their parents' marriage as high in conflict show better long-term adjustment if parental divorce occurs than if it does not. Conversely, children who view their parents' marriage as having low levels of conflict show poorer long-term adjustment if divorce occurs than if it does not (Amato, Loomis, & Booth, 1995). When divorce is associated with a move to a more harmonious, less stressful home environment with an authoritative parent, children in divorced families are similar in adjustment to children in low-conflict, nondivorced families and demonstrate better adjustment than children in high-conflict, nondivorced families (Amato et al., 1995; Hetherington, 1999b). However, high levels of conflict have been found to have more negative consequences for children in divorced families than in nondivorced families, perhaps because children in divorced households lack the possible protective influence of a second residential parent or because of the compounding adverse effects of higher levels of stressful life events in single-parent families following divorce (Hetherington, 1999b).

In remarried families, marital conflict, especially conflict about stepchildren, undermines the stepparents' authority and their chances of playing a constructive role in the stepchild's development (Bray, 1999; Hetherington & Jodl, 1994; Hetherington, 1991b). Conflict and competition between noncustodial mothers and stepmothers also can make stepchildren less likely to accept the stepmother and lessen the possible benefits that might have accrued to a positive relationship with a stepmother.

Parent–Child Relationships

On average, parenting deteriorates and becomes less authoritative immediately after a divorce or remarriage as parents are preoccupied with dealing with the many life changes and stresses confronting them. Parenting in both types of families gradually improves, and in stabilized stepfamilies with a supportive spouse, few differences are found between the relationships of biological mothers and their children and those in nondivorced families. However, problems often remain in the parenting of single, divorced, custodial parents (see Hetherington & Stanley-Hagan, 2002, for a review).

In the immediate aftermath of divorce, custodial mothers and fathers experience similar concerns and problems, such as worries about their adequacy as a parent, task overload, and psychological distress, including anxiety, depression, feelings of isolation, and health problems associated with lowered immune functioning (Hetherington, 1989, 1993; Kiecolt-Glaser et al., 1988; Simons & Associates, 1996). These stresses and psychological and physical changes may compromise their ability to parent effectively and place children at risk for adjustment problems (Amato, 2001; Forgatch, Patterson, Ray, 1995; Hetherington, 1993; Simons & Associates, 1996). Psychological well-being and health improve markedly with the formation of a satisfying new intimate relationship or a remarriage (Amato, 2001; Coleman et al., 2001; Hetherington & Kelly, 2002). Parenting during the early period following divorce is often characterized by increased irritability and coercion, as well as diminished communication, affection, consistency, control, and supervision (Hetherington, 1993; Hetherington & Kelly, 2002; Simons & Associates, 1996), but the parenting of both custodial mothers and fathers improves after the first year following divorce.

The quality of parenting plays an important role in protecting children or making them more vulnerable to adverse consequences from the stresses associated with parental divorce and remarriage (Amato, 2001; Deater-Deckard & Dunn, 1999; Hetherington et al., 1998; Hetherington & Stanley-Hagan, 2002). In all types of families, authoritative parents who are warm, supportive, communicative, and responsive to their children's needs, and who exert firm, consistent, and reasonable control and close supervision, provide the optimal environment for the healthy and competent development of children. The protective function of authoritative parenting is particularly salient for children in families going through their parents' marital transitions and other situations involving multiple stressors (Amato, 2001; Amato & Keith, 1991a; Hetherington 1993; Hetherington & Clingempeel, 1992; Hetherington et al., 1999; Simons & Associates, 1996; Werner, 1999).

Approximately 84% of children reside in the custody of their mothers following divorce (Seltzer, 1994). Children in the custody of their fathers are more likely to be boys, to be older, and to have mothers with lower levels of education and socioeconomic attainment and who are less involved with their children and more psychologically impaired (Fox & Kelly, 1995; Maccoby & Mnookin, 1992). Although the experiences of children in mother-custody, father-custody, and joint-custody families vary, there is little consistent evidence of the superiority of any of these arrangements for children's adjustment. There is some evidence that adolescents may benefit more from being in the custody of a same-sex parent than an opposite-sex parent (Lindner-Gunnoe, 1993). However, research is mixed (Downey, Ainsworth-Darnell, & Dufur, 1998), and both boys and girls can develop well in any type of custodial arrangement with low conflict and an involved, authoritative parent.

Although there are many similarities in the concerns about parenting voiced by custodial mothers and fathers and in their less authoritative parenting in comparison to those in nondivorced families, some differences between fathers and mothers remain. Custodial fathers tend to have fewer problems with control or discipline and report less childrearing stress than do mothers, but they communicate and self-disclose less openly with their children and are less competent in monitoring their children's activities. Poor monitoring by custodial fathers is associated with more delinquent activities in adolescence (Buchanan et al., 1996; Hetherington & Stanley-Hagen, 2002).

Although problems in control and coercive exchanges between mothers and sons may endure (Hetherington, 1991a), preadolescent girls often develop close, supportive, companionate, and confiding relationships with their divorced mothers. However, in adolescence, there is a notable increase in conflict in these relationships, particularly between early-maturing daughters and their mothers (Hetherington, 1991a; Hetherington & Clingempeel, 1992).

It has been noted that children in divorced, single-parent households seem to "grow up faster" (Weiss, 1979). This has been attributed, in part, to greater autonomy due to lack of adult supervision, more independent decision making, and greater responsibility at a younger age. In addition, the instrumental and emotional parentification of children who assume more adultlike roles in the family, including performing household tasks and taking care of siblings, and serving as an emotional support, advisor, or confidant to distressed parents, may contribute to early maturity among children in divorced families (Hetherington, 1999b). Moderate levels of responsibility and the nurturing of others are associated with greater social competence and resilience among girls in divorced families. However, excessive task demands that exceed children's capabilities and high emotional parentification by mothers are associated with elevated anxiety and depression, low social competence and self-esteem, and a lurking sense of failure and inadequacy among girls in adulthood (Hetherington, 1989, 1999a). Among boys, moderate levels of maternal emotional and instrumental parentification are associated with greater social responsibility in adolescence and adulthood; however, very high levels of instrumental parentification leads to resistance and lower social responsibility in boys. In addition, excessive emotional parentification by fathers, but not mothers, is associated with greater internalizing behavior in boys and alienation of boys from their fathers. Children view extreme emotional neediness in men as inappropriate and embarrassing (Hetherington, 1999a, 1999b).

Coparenting

In the aftermath of divorce and remarriage, the ideal environment for the shared parenting of children, and the one most advantageous to children's adjustment, is one in which there is minimal conflict and supportive, cooperative parenting based on mutual consent and trust. About one-quarter of divorced spouses are able to achieve this ideal. The majority of divorced spouses, however, develop patterns of disengaged, parallel parenting that involve little communication or cooperation, but also little undermining of the other parent, and another quarter of divorced spouses experience sustained and, in some cases, increased conflict (Buchanan et al., 1996; Maccoby & Mnookin, 1992; Tschann, Johnston, Kline, & Wallerstein, 1990). Continued conflict following divorce in a subset of parents may partially explain the research finding that joint custody arrangements provide relatively few benefits for children compared to sole custody arrangements (Hetherington, 1999a, 1999b; Maccoby & Mnookin, 1992).

Noncustodial Parents

Following divorce, contact with noncustodial mothers and fathers declines rapidly. Although over 25% of children have weekly visits with their noncustodial fathers, about 20% of children have no contact with their noncustodial fathers or see them only a few times a year (Amato, 2001; Hetherington et al., 1998). Decreased parental involvement is related to residential distance, low socioeconomic status, and parental remarriage. When the child is a boy, when there is low conflict between divorced spouses, when mediation is used, or when noncustodial fathers feel they have some control over decisions in the lives of their children, parental contact and child support payments are more likely to be maintained (Amato, 2001; Braver et al., 1993; Maccoby & Mnookin, 1992; Seltzer, 1994). Noncustodial mothers are more likely than noncustodial fathers to sustain contact with their children and to rearrange living arrangements to facilitate children's visits, and are less likely to completely drop out of their children's lives or to diminish contact when either parent remarries. They are more supportive, sensitive, and responsive to their children's needs, are more adept at controlling and monitoring their children's behavior, and are more influential in the adjustment of their children, particularly girls, than are noncustodial fathers. In addition, children report feeling closer to noncustodial mothers than noncustodial fathers (Furstenberg & Nord, 1987; Hetherington, 1993; Hetherington & Stanley-Hagan, 2002; Lindner-Gunnoe, 1993).

Benefits of contact with noncustodial parents depend less on the amount of time spent together than on the quality of the relationship between the two parents, and between the noncustodial parent and the child. Under conditions of low spousal conflict, contact with competent, supportive, authoritative noncustodial parents can have protective effects for children, especially when the custodial parent is incompetent or rejecting (Hetherington, 1989). Although some researchers have found these effects to be more marked for noncustodial parents and children of the same sex (Lindner-Gunnoe, 1993), others have not found such evidence (Amato & Gilbreth, 1999). Children, especially boys who have a close relationship with an authoritative nonresidential father, exhibit higher levels of academic achievement and lower levels of internalizing and externalizing behaviors (Amato & Gilbreth, 1999; Hetherington, 1993; Lindner-Gunnoe, 1993). However, under conditions of high spousal conflict following divorce, frequent contact with noncustodial parents may exacerbate children's adjustment problems (Johnston et al., 1989; Kline, Johnston, & Tschann, 1991). Noncustodial fathers who engage in authoritative practices and who are involved in the everyday activities of their children's lives, such as helping their children with homework and talking over their children's personal problems, have greater influence in promoting children's positive adjustment than do "entertainment" fathers who primarily engage in recreational activities with their children, such as going to movies and restaurants (Amato & Gilbreth, 1999; Emery, 1999).

Stepparents
Although it has been suggested that because of their different family histories and experiences, functional relationships between parenting and child adjustment should differ in nondivorced, divorced, and remarried families, evidence supports the hypothesis that these associations are similar in different family types. If a stepparent can form a close, authoritative relationship with a stepchild, this is associated with improved child

well-being and adjustment (see Coleman et al., 2001; Hetherington et al., 1998; Hetherington & Stanley-Hagan, 2002, for reviews). Unfortunately, because of child resistance and lack of biological ties, such relationships are often difficult to establish, especially with early adolescents (Anderson et al., 1999; Bray, 1999; Coleman et al., 2001; Fine, Coleman & Ganong, 1999; Hetherington & Clingempeel, 1992; Hetherington & Jodl, 1994). The precocious independence and power of children in single-parent families frequently makes the assertion of control by a stepparent difficult. The most successful strategy for stepparents may be to build a warm, involved relationship with the child, support the biological parents' discipline, and move in gradually to establish control (Bray, 1999; Coleman et al., 2001; Hetherington & Jodl, 1994). Stepmothers often do not have this option bacause many custodial fathers who remarry expect their new wives to take over many of the parenting responsibilities. Hence, relationships between stepmothers and stepchildren are more difficult, and children are less likely to feel close to stepmothers than to stepfathers (Coleman et al., 2001; Hetherington & Kelly, 2002).

Relationships between stepdaughters and stepfathers are more problematic than those with stepsons perhaps because the relationship between single mothers and daughters has often been so close. Thus, boys are more likely than girls to benefit from the presence of a stepfather with increased achievement and decreased antisocial behavior in comparison to boys in divorced, mother-headed, single-parent families (Amato & Keith, 1991a; Hetherington & Jodl, 1994). However, most stepfathers remain less involved and communicative with stepchildren, are less nurturing and warm, exert less control, and have less positive perceptions of their relationships with their stepchildren (Amato, 2001; Bray, 1999; Coleman et al., 2001; Fine et al., 1999; Hetherington & Clingempeel, 1992; Hetherington & Jodl, 1994; Hetherington et al., 1999). These problems are most marked in complex stepfamilies where the siblings have differing patterns of relationships to their mothers and fathers, for example in blended families where children come from both the mother's and father's previous relationships or in families with a stepchild and a new child born to the remarriage (Hetherington et al., 1999).

Sibling Relationships
There is growing evidence that siblings play an important role in the social, emotional, behavioral, and cognitive development of children and adolescents, and that sibling relationships in divorced families are more

negative and less positive than those in nondivorced families, particularly among boys (Hetherington, 1989, 1999a; Hetherington & Clingempeel, 1992; MacKinnon, 1989).

Sibling relationships in stepfamilies are more complex and are related to the structure of the stepfamilies. Early in a remarriage, sibling relationships look much like those in divorced families, with biologically related full siblings from a mother's previous marriage in a stepfamily showing greater negativity and less positivity than those in nondivorced families (Hetherington, 1993; Hetherington & Clingempeel, 1992; Hetherington & Jodl, 1994). In longer-established stepfamilies, it is the biological relationship between siblings rather than the type of family that is important. There is greater affective intensity involving both affection and positive involvement and negativity, rivalry, and quarreling in biologically related siblings, whether they are full siblings in nondivorced families or full and half-siblings in stepfamilies than in stepsiblings (Hetherington, 1999a; Hetherington & Kelly, 2002; Hetherington et al., 1999).

A few studies suggest that siblings, particularly female siblings, may serve to protect children from the adverse consequences associated with family conflict and disharmony (Jenkins, 1992; Jenkins & Smith, 1990) and parental divorce (Hetherington, 1989; Kempton, Armistead, Wierson, & Forehand, 1991). Positive relationships with siblings in divorced and remarried families lead to increased social competence and negative relationships to increased externalizing in both divorced and remarried families (Hetherington & Clingempeel, 1992; Hetherington et al., 1999). In divorced and remarried families as well as in nondivorced families, early sexuality, childbearing, and substance abuse in older siblings are more likely to promote these behaviors in younger siblings than the reverse (Hetherington & Kelly, 2002; Hetherington et al., 1999).

Grandparents
Many divorced mothers turn to their parents for economic and emotional support and child care following divorce. In white families, economic support is most likely to be forthcoming, whereas in African American families, help in services is most likely to be given.

Research findings regarding the role of grandparents in protecting children from the deleterious effects of parental divorce have been mixed. Although early studies of African American families provided evidence that children may benefit from the presence of a grandmother in mother-headed households (Kellam, Adams, Brown, & Ensminger, 1982; Kellam, Ensminger, & Turner, 1977), other studies have suggested that the presence of a grandmother also may contribute to family stress as grandmothers and daughters struggle over issues related to shared control of children, discipline, and the divorced mother's social life and loss of independence (Hetherington, 1989). Conflict between grandmothers and divorced single mothers has been associated with increased externalizing behaviors in boys (Hetherington, 1989). When positive effects are obtained, they tend to be indirect and are mediated by grandmothers' support, leading to improved maternal parenting (Hetherington, 1989). There is some evidence that the involvement of a grandfather may have beneficial effects on the prosocial behavior and academic achievement of boys in single-mother, divorced families (Hetherington, 1989). However, when support comes with costs and restrictions and unwanted advice from grandparents, neither parents nor children benefit (Amato, 2001; Cherlin & Furstenberg, 1994; Hetherington, 1989; Kitson, 1992; Miller, Smerglia, Gaudet, & Kitson, 1998).

Extrafamilial Vulnerability and Protective Factors

Risk and protective factors outside of the family become increasingly important with age. In addition, they often interact with individual and family factors to moderate children's responses to the stresses associated with divorce and remarriage.

Peer Relationships
As children enter the adolescent years, extrafamilial factors such as peers and schools play an increasingly salient role in children's adjustment to their parents' marital transitions. Peer rejection has been shown to exacerbate the negative consequences associated with divorce. However, a supportive relationship with a single friend may help to buffer children from the deleterious effects of both peer rejection and marital disruption (Hetherington, 1989).

Adolescents from divorced and remarried families are less socially competent (Hetherington & Clingempeel, 1992) and more vulnerable to peer influence than those in nondivorced families (Hetherington, 1993; Hetherington & Jodl, 1994; Steinberg, 1987). Their susceptibility to peer influence is due in part to their precocious independence, early physical maturing, and lower levels of adult supervision and authoritative parenting (Amato, 2001; Avenoli, Sessa, & Steinberg, 1999; Hetherington, 1991b, 1993; Hetherington & Jodl, 1994; Hetherington et al., 1998).

About one-third of adolescents in divorced families, particularly boys, disengage from the family unit, spending little time at home and avoiding interactions, activities, and communication with family members (Hetherington, 1993). When disengagement from family relationships is associated with increased involvement in a delinquent peer group, adolescents are at greater risk for the development of antisocial behavior and academic problems, particularly in families lacking adequate adult supervision (Hetherington, 1993; Patterson, DeBaryshe, & Ramsey, 1989). However, if disengagement is associated with greater involvement with a caring adult outside of the family home, including parents of a friend, a coach or teacher, or some other adult mentor, then disengagement may be a positive alternative to an unstable, conflicted family environment (Hetherington, 1993).

The distancing hypothesis proposes that stressful family environments such as those found in divorced and remarried families promote early physical maturing (Belsky, Steinberg, & Draper, 1991). Girls in divorced and remarried families attain puberty earlier and are more likely to become involved with older male peers. This, in combination with nonauthoritative parenting and, in single-parent families with a sexually active mother, is associated with earlier and more promiscuous sexual activities and teenage pregnancy (Hetherington, 1993). Early maturing and involvement with older peers is also associated with early alcohol and drug use in both adolescent boys and girls (Hetherington, 1993; Hetherington & Jodl, 1994).

Schools
Schools and teachers with an authoritative approach to children's education may have salutary effects on children from divorced and remarried families. School environments characterized by defined schedules, rules, and regulations, and the use of warm, consistent, discipline and expectations for mature behavior have been associated with enhanced social and cognitive development in children from divorced and remarried families (Hetherington, 1989; Hetherington & Jodl, 1994). These protective effects are particularly marked among boys, children with difficult temperaments, children experiencing multiple stressful life events, and those with no authoritative parent in the home. In addition, greater academic achievement and, for boys, greater athletic achievement have been associated with fewer behavior problems among children in high-risk families (Hetherington, 1989, 1993; Hetherington & Jodl, 1994; Patterson, Reid, & Dishion, 1992; Simons & Associates, 1996).

Chaotic schools characterized by disorder, punitive erratic discipline, lack of control, responsiveness and support, low expectations by teachers, and a mutual lack of respect by teachers and students undermine the achievement of students and increase conduct disorders. The children who suffer most from such schools are those exposed to multiple stressors, such as those accompanying poverty and marital transitions, and those who have no authoritative parent in the home (Hetherington, 1993; Rutter, 1985a, 1985b).

Legal and Therapeutic Interventions
The increase in joint custody and mediation has led to greater sustained involvement of divorced fathers with their children, increased payment of child support, and greater satisfaction of fathers in their relationships with their children (Emery, Kitzmann, & Waldron, 1999; Maccoby & Mnookin, 1992). Women are less satisfied with joint custody and the outcomes of mediation because they feel they have lost some control over their child and rights that they might otherwise have retained. Furthermore, these legal innovations seem to have had little impact on the adjustment of children, although children usually enjoy the greater involvement of fathers (Buchanan et al., 1996; Emery et al., 1999).

Therapy seems to be more difficult and to have more modest effects with divorced than nondivorced families, perhaps because of the many stresses they encounter (Emery et al., 1999; Lee, Picard, & Blain, 1994). A meta-analysis noted a small average effect size of .27 of therapy influencing a variety of child adjustment domains, and most studies focus on extremely short-term follow-ups (Lee et al., 1994). School-based programs and child-focused interventions appear to be more successful in changing children's views of divorce and reducing their distress than in eliminating such things as conduct disorders in school (see Emery et al., 1999, for a review).

Programs focused on parents and parenting interventions are more successful in showing changes in parent adjustment and parenting practices than in child adjustment (Beuhler, Betz, Ryan, Legg, & Trotter, 1992; Braver, Salem, Pearson, & DeLuse, 1996). However, those few adult intervention studies that also found changes in child adjustment showed that the parent–child relationship and parenting skills were important mediators of change (Emery et al., 1999; Wolchik et al., 1993).

In comparison to the intervention research on divorced families, that on stepfamilies is meager, although clinical reports suggest that programs that help family members validate their lives, strengthen the marital relationship, and develop a parenting coalition may be helpful (Visher & Visher, 1996). More systematic empirical studies are needed before conclusions about the efficacy of such programs can be drawn.

In a recent paper studying long-term adult outcomes of children who had confronted a variety of risks in childhood including divorce, inept incompetent parents, and poverty, Emmy Werner concluded that *talk therapies* were relatively ineffective in contributing to resilience (Werner, 1999). Resilient adults rated mental health professionals as having helped little in dealing with the challenges they confronted over the course of their lives.

SUMMARY

In spite of accumulating research findings, a fierce debate continues about the impact of contemporary family life and marital transitions on the well-being of adults and children. Some family scholars see the break-down of the traditional family as destroying the basic fabric of American society and contributing to a vast array of social problems that will carry on into future generations (Popenoe, Elshtain, & Blankenhorn, 1996). Others view diversity in families and shifting family relationships as op-portunities for choice, new chances for fulfillment, individuation, and happier intimate relationships, and the escape from an unsatisfying, aver-sive family situation (Demo, Allen, & Fine, 2000). Both positions hold some truth but are simplistic. It is the diversity, not the inevitability of life paths following divorce and remarriage, that is striking (Amato, 2000; Hetherington, & Kelly, 2002). Although, on the average, children and adults in divorced and remarried families may confront more stresses and show more problems in family relations and personal adjustment than those in nondivorced families, especially in the early years following a marital transition, the vast majority are resilient and able to cope with or even benefit from their new life situation.

Adverse effects of parental marital transitions are most often found in increased externalizing behaviors and in decreased social responsi-bility and academic attainments. Not all children are similarly affected. Preadolescent boys seem somewhat more vulnerable to divorce and girls to remarriage, and enhancement or *steeling* effects of divorce are more likely to be found in girls and mothers than in boys and fathers. Protective effects have been found for an easy temperament, an internal locus of control, and active coping styles. Low conflict and supportive relation-ships within the family and positive relationships outside of the family with mentors, school personnel, and peers also help buffer children from the stresses encountered during parents' marital transitions. A close relationship with a supportive adult, most often an authoritative parent, plays a critical role in promoting the well-being of children in all families, but seems to be especially salient for children confronting the challenges of divorce and life in a single-parent family or stepfamily.

References

Achenbach, T. M. (1991). *Integrative guide for the 19991 CBCL/4–18, YSR, and TRF profiles.* Burlington: Department of Psychiatry, University of Vermont.

Acock, A. C., & Demo, D. H. (1994). *Family diversity and well-being.* Thousand Oaks, CA: Sage.

Allison, P., & Furstenberg, F. F., Jr. (1989). How marital dissolution affects children: Variations by age and sex. *Development Psychology, 25,* 540–549.

Amato, P. R. (1993). Children's adjustment to divorce: Theories, hypotheses, and empirical support. *Journal of Marriage and the Family, 55,* 23–38.

Amato, P. R. (1999). Children of divorced parents as young adults. In E. M. Hetherington (Ed.), *Coping with divorce, single parenting and remarriage: A risk and resiliency perspective* (pp. 147–164). Mahwah, NJ: Erlbaum.

Amato, P. R. (2000). The consequences of divorce for adults and children. *Journal of Marriage and the Family, 62,* 1269–1287.

Amato, P. R. (2001). The consequences of divorce for adults and children. In R. M. Milardo (Ed.), *Understanding families into the new millennium: A decade in review* (pp. 488–506). Minneapolis: National Council on Family Relations.

Amato, P. R., & Booth, A. (1996). A prospective study of divorce and parent–child relationships. *Journal of Marriage and the Family, 58,* 356–365.

Amato, P. R., & Booth, A. (1997). *A generation at risk: Growing up in an era of family upheaval.* Cambridge, MA: Harvard University Press.

Amato, P. R., & Gilbreth, J. G. (1999). Nonresident fathers and children's well-being: A meta-analysis. *Journal of Marriage and the Family, 61,* 557–575.

Amato, P. R., & Keith, B. (1991a). Parental divorce and the well-being of children: A meta-analysis. *Psychological Bulletin, 110,* 26–46.

Amato, P. R., & Keith, B. (1991b). Parental divorce and adult well-being: A meta-analysis. *Journal of Marriage and the Family, 53,* 43–58.

Amato, P. R., Loomis, L. S., & Booth, A. (1995). Parental divorce, marital conflict, and offspring well-being in during early adulthood. *Social Forces, 73,* 895–915.

Anderson, E.R., Greene, S. M., Hetherington, E. M., & Clingempeel, W. G. (1999). The dynamics of parental remarriage: Adolescent, parent, and sibling influences. In E. M. Hetherington (Ed.), *Coping with divorce, single parenting and remarriage: A risk and resiliency perspective* (pp. 295–319). Mahwah, NJ: Erlbaum.

Aseltine, R. H. (1996). Pathways linking parental divorce with adolescent depression. *Journal of Health and Social Behavior, 37,* 133–148.

Avenoli, S., Sessa, F. M., & Steinberg, L. (1999). Family structure, parenting practices, and adolescent adjustment: An ecological examination. In E. M.

Hetherington (Ed.), *Coping with divorce, single parenting and remarriage: A risk and resiliency perspective* (pp. 65–90). Mahwah, NJ: Erlbaum.

Belsky, J., Steinberg, L., & Draper, P. (1991). Childhood experience, interpersonal development and reproductive strategy: An evolutionary theory of socialization. *Child Development, 62,* 647–670.

Beuhler, C., Betz, P., Ryan, C. M., Legg, B. H., & Trotter, B. B. (1992). Description and evaluation of the orientation for divorcing parents: Implications for postdivorce prevention programs. *Family Relations, 41,* 154–162.

Bianchi, S. M., Subaiya, L., & Kahn, J. (1997, March). *Economic well-being of husbands and wives after marital disruption.* Paper presented at the annual meeting of the Population Association of America, Washington, DC.

Block, J., Block, J. H., & Gjerde, P. E. (1988). Parental functioning and the home environment in families of divorce: Prospective and concurrent analyses. *Journal of the American Academy of Child and Adolescent Psychiatry, 27,* 207–213.

Booth, A., & Dunn, J. (1994). *Stepfamilies: Who benefits? Who does not?* Hillsdale, NJ: Erlbaum.

Bradbury, T. N., & Fincham, F. D. (1990). Attributions in marriage: Review and critique. *Psychological Bulletin, 107,* 3–33.

Braver, S. L., Salem, P., Pearson, J., & DeLuse, S. R. (1996). The content of divorce education programs: Results of a survey. *Family and Conciliation Courts Review, 34,* 41–59.

Braver, S. L., Wolchik, S. A., Sandefur, I. N., Sheets, V. L., Fogas, B., & Bay, R. C. (1993). A longitudinal study of noncustodial parents: Parents without children. *Journal of Family Psychology, 7,* 9–23.

Bray, J. H. (1999). From marriage to remarriage and beyond: Findings from the Developmental Issues in Stepfamilies Research Project. In E. M. Hetherington (Ed.), *Coping with divorce, single parenting and remarriage: A risk and resiliency perspective* (pp. 253–271). Mahwah, NJ: Erlbaum.

Buchanan, C. M., Maccoby, E. E., & Dornbusch, S. M. (1996). *Adolescents after divorce.* Cambridge, MA: Harvard University Press.

Bussell, D. A. (1995). A pilot study of African American children's cognitive and emotional reactions to parental separation. *Journal of Divorce and Remarriage, 25,* 3–15.

Capaldi, D. M., & Patterson, G. R. (1991). Relation of parental transitions to boys' adjustment problems: I. A linear hypothesis. II. Mothers at risk for transitions and unskilled parenting. *Developmental Psychology, 27,* 489–504.

Cherlin, A. J., & Furstenberg, F. F. (1994). Stepfamilies in the United States. *Review of Sociology, 20,* 359–381.

Cherlin, A. J., Furstenberg, F. F., Chase-Lansdale, P., Kiernan, K. E., Robins, P. K., Morrison, D. R., & Tietler, J. O. (1991). Longitudinal studies of the effects of divorce on children in Great Britain and the United States. *Science, 252,* 1386–1389.

Clarke-Stewart, K. A., & Hayward, C. (1996). Advantages of father custody and contract for the psychological well-being of school-age children. *Journal of Applied Developmental Psychology, 17,* 239–270.

Coleman, M., Ganong, L., & Fine, M. (2001). Reinvestigating remarriage: Another decade of progress. In R. M. Milardo (Ed.), *Understanding families into the new millennium: A decade in review* (pp. 508–526). Minneapolis: National Council on Family Relations.

Cowan, P. A., & Cowan, C. P. (1990). Becoming a family: Research and intervention. In I. Sigel & G. A. Brody (Eds.), *Family research* (pp. 246–279). Hillsdale, NJ: Erlbaum.

Davies, L., Avison, W. R., & McAlpine, D. D. (1997). Significant life experiences and depression among single and married mothers. *Journal of Marriage and the Family, 59,* 294–308.

Davies, P. T., & Cummings, M. E. (1994). Marital conflict and child adjustment: An emotional security hypothesis. *Psychological Bulletin, 116,* 387– 411.

Deater-Deckard, K., & Dunn, J. (1999). Multiple risks and adjustment in young children growing up in different family settings. In E. M. Hetherington (Ed.), *Coping with divorce, single parenting and remarriage: A risk and resiliency perspective* (pp. 47–64). Mahwah, NJ: Erlbaum.

Demo, D. H., Allen, K. R., & Fine, M. A. (Eds.). (2000). *The handbook of family diversity.* New York: Oxford University Press.

Doherty, W. J., & Needle, R. H. (1991). Psychological adjustment and substance use among adolescents before and after a parental divorce. *Child Development, 62,* 328–337.

Downey, D. B., Ainsworth-Darnell, J. W., & Dufur, M. J. (1998). Sex of parent and children's well-being in single-parent households. *Journal of Marriage and the Family, 60,* 878–893.

Dunn, J., Deater-Deckard, K., Pickering, K., O'Connor, T., Golding, J., & the ALSPAC Study Team (1998). Children's adjustment and pro-social behavior in step, single and nonstep settings: Findings from a community study. *Journal of Child Psychology and Psychiatry, 39,* 1083–1095.

Emery, R. E. (1982). Interparental conflict and the children of discord and divorce. *Psychological Bulletin, 92,* 310–330.

Emery, R. E. (1999). *Marriage, divorce, and children's adjustment* (2nd ed.). Thousand Oaks, CA: Sage.

Emery, R. E., Kitzmann, K. M., & Waldron, M. (1999). Psychological interventions for separated and divorced families. In E. M. Hetherington (Ed.), *Coping with divorce, single parenting and remarriage: A risk and resiliency perspective* (pp. 332–344). Mahwah, NJ: Erlbaum.

Fincham, F. D., Bradbury, T. N., & Scott, C. K. (1990). Cognition in marriage. In F. D. Finchman & T. N. Bradbury (Eds.), *The psychology of marriage* (pp. 118–149). New York: Guilford Press.

Fine, M. A., Coleman, M., & Ganong, L. H. (1999). A social constructonist multimethod approach to understanding the stepparent role. In E. M. Hetherington (Ed.), *Coping with divorce, single parenting and remarriage: A risk and resiliency perspective* (pp. 273–294). Mahwah, NJ: Erlbaum.

Forgatch, M. S., Patterson, G. R., & Ray, J. A. (1995). Divorce and boys' adjustment problems: Two paths with a single model. In E. M. Hetherington & E. A. Blechman (Eds.), *Stress, coping, and resiliency in children and families* (pp. 67–105). Mahwah, NJ: Erlbaum.

Fox, G. L., & Kelly, R. F. (1995). Determinants of child custody arrangements at divorce. *Journal of Marriage and the Family, 57,* 693–708.

Furstenberg, F. F., Jr., & Nord, C. W. (1987). Parenting apart: Patterns of childrearing after marital disruption. *Journal of Marriage and the Family, 47*, 893–904.

Gottman, J. M. (1993). A theory of marital dissolution and stability. *Journal of Family Psychology, 7*, 57–75.

Gottman, J. M. (1994). *What predicts divorce?* Hillsdale, NJ: Erlbaum.

Gottman, J. M., & Katz, L. F. (1989). Effects of marital discord on young children's peer interaction and health. *Developmental Psychology, 25*, 373–381.

Gottman, J. M., & Levenson, R. W. (1992). Marital processes predictive of later dissolution: Behavior, physiology, and health. *Journal of Personality and Social Psychology, 63*, 221–223.

Gottman, J. M., & Notarius, C. T. (2001). Decade review: Observing marital interaction. In R. M. Milardo (Ed.), *Understanding families into the new millennium: A decade in review* (pp. 146–166). Minneapolis: National Council on Family Relations.

Healy, J. M., Stewart, A. J., & Copeland, A. P. (1993). The role of self-blame in children's adjustment to parental separation. *Personality and Social Psychology Bulletin, 19*, 279–289.

Hetherington, E. M. (1989). Coping with family transitions: Winners, losers, and survivors. *Child Development, 60*, 1–14.

Hetherington, E. M. (1991a). Families, lies, and videotapes. *Journal of Research in Adolescence, 1*, 323–348.

Hetherington, E. M. (1991b). The role of individual differences and family relationships in children coping with divorce and remarriage. In P. Cowan & E. M. Hetherington (Eds.), *Family transitions* (pp. 165–174). Hillsdale, NJ: Erlbaum.

Hetherington, E. M. (1993). An overview of the Virginia Longitudinal Study of Divorce and Remarriage with a focus on early adolescence. *Journal of Family Psychology, 7*, 39–56.

Hetherington, E. M. (1999a). Social capital and the development of youth from nondivorced, divorced, and remarried families. In A. Collins (Ed.), *Relationships as developmental contexts: The 29th Minnesota Symposium on Child Psychology* (Vol. 30, pp. 177–210). Hillsdale, NJ: Erlbaum.

Hetherington, E. M. (1999b). Should we stay together for the sake of our children? In E. M. Hetherington (Ed.), *Coping with divorce, single parenting and remarriage: A risk and resiliency perspective* (pp. 93–116). Mahwah, NJ: Erlbaum.

Hetherington, E. M., & Blechman, E. A. (Eds.). (1996). *Stress, coping, and resiliency in children and families.* Hillsdale, NJ: Erlbaum.

Hetherington, E. M., Bridges, M., & Insabella, G. M. (1998). What matters? What does not? Five perspectives on the association between marital transitions and children's adjustment. *American Psychologist, 53*, 167–184.

Hetherington, E. M., & Clingempeel, W. G. (1992). Coping with marital transitions: A family systems perspective. *Monographs of the Society for Child Development* (Serial No. 227, *57*, Nos. 2–3).

Hetherington, E. M., Cox, M., & Cox, R. (1985). Long-term effects of divorce and remarriage on the adjustment of children. *Journal of the American Academy of Child Psychiatry, 24*, 518–530.

Hetherington, E. M., Henderson, S. H., & Reiss, D. (1999). Adolescent siblings in stepfamilies: Family functioning and adolescent adjustment. *Monographs for the Society for Research in Child Development, 64*(4), 222.

Hetherington, E. M., & Jodl, K. M. (1994). Stepfamilies as settings for child development. In A. Booth & J. Dunn (Eds.), *Stepfamilies: Who benefits? Who does not?* (pp. 55–79). Hillsdale, NJ: Erlbaum.

Hetherington, E. M., & Kelly, J. (2002). *For better or for worse: Divorce reconsidered.* New York: Norton.

Hetherington, E. M., & Stanley-Hagan, M. (2002). Parenting in divorced and remarried families. In M. Bornstein (Ed.), *Handbook of parenting* (2nd ed.). Mahwah, NJ: Erlbaum.

Hope, S., Power, C., & Rodgers, B. (1999). Does financial hardship account for elevated psychological distress in lone mothers? *Social Science and Medicine, 29,* 381–389.

Jenkins, J. M. (1992). Sibling relationships in disharmonious homes: Potential difficulties and protective effects. In F. Boer & J. Dunn (Eds.), *Children's sibling relationships: Developmental and clinical issues* (pp. 125–138). Hillsdale, NJ: Erlbaum.

Jenkins, J. M., & Smith, M. A. (1990). Factors protecting children living in disharmonious homes: Maternal reports. *Journal of the American Academy of Child and Adolescent Psychiatry, 29,* 60–69.

Jockin, V., McGue, M., & Lykken, D. T. (1996). Personality and divorce: A genetic analysis. *Journal of Personality and Social Psychology, 71,* 288–299.

Johnston, J. R., Kline, M., & Tschann, J. (1989). Ongoing post-divorce conflict in families contesting custody: Effects on children of joint custody and frequent access. *American Journal of Orthopsychiatry, 59,* 576–592.

Kellam, S. G., Adams, R. G., Brown, C. H., & Ensminger, M. A. (1982). The long-term evolution of the family structure of teenage and older mothers. *Journal of Marriage and the Family, 4,* 539–554.

Kellam, S. G., Ensminger, M. A., and Turner, R. J. (1977). Family structure and the mental health of children: Concurrent and longitudinal community-wide studies. *Archives of General Psychiatry, 34,* 1012–1022.

Kempton, T., Armistead, L., Wierson, M., & Forehand, R. (1991). Presence of a sibling as a potential buffer following parental divorce: An examination of young adolescents. *Journal of Clinical Child Psychology, 20,* 434–438.

Kiecolt-Glaser, J. K., Kennedy, S., Malkoff, S., Fisher, L. D., Speicher, C. E., & Glaser, R. (1988). Marital discord and immunity in males. *Psychosomatic Medicine, 50,* 213–229.

Kim, L., Sandler, I. N., & Jenn-Yun, T. (1997). Locus of control as a stress moderator and mediator in children of divorce. *Journal of Abnormal Child Psychology, 25,* 145–155.

Kitson, G. C. (1992). *Portrait of divorce: Adjustment to marital breakdown.* New York: Guilford Press.

Kline, M., Johnson, J. R., & Tschann, J. M. (1991). The long shadow of marital conflict: A model of children's postdivorce adjustment. *Journal of Marriage and the Family, 53,* 297–309.

Kurdek, L. A. (1990). Divorce history and self-reported psychological distress in husbands and wives. *Journal of Marriage and the Family, 52,* 701–708.

Kurdek, L. A., Fine, M. A., & Sinclair, R. J. (1995). School adjustment in sixth graders: Parenting transitions, family climate, and peer norm effects. *Child Development, 66,* 430–445.

Laumann-Billings, L., & Emery, R. E. (2000). Distress among young adults from divorced families. *Journal of Family Psychology, 14,* 671–687.

Lee, C. M., Picard, M., & Blain, M. D. (1994). A methodological and substantive review of intervention outcome studies for families undergoing divorce. *Journal of Family Psychology, 8,* 3–15.

Lindner-Gunnoe, M. (1993). *Noncustodial mothers' and fathers' contributions to the adjustment of adolescent stepchildren.* Unpublished doctoral dissertation, University of Virginia.

Maccoby, E. E., Depner, C. E., & Mnookin, R. H. (1990). Co-parenting in the second year after divorce. *Journal of Marriage and the Family, 52,* 141–155.

Maccoby, E. E., & Mnookin, R. H. (1992). *Dividing the child: Social and legal dilemmas of custody.* Cambridge, MA: Harvard University Press.

MacKinnon, C. E. (1989). An observational investigation of sibling interactions in married and divorced families. *Developmental Psychology, 25,* 36–44.

Matthews, L. S., Wickrama, K. A. S., & Conger, R. D. (1996). Predicting marital instability from spouse and observer reports of marital interaction. *Journal of Marriage and the Family, 58,* 641–655.

McGue, M., & Lykken, D. T. (1992). Genetic influence on risk of divorce. *Psychological Science, 6,* 368–373.

McLanahan, S. (1999). Father absence and the welfare of children. In E. M. Hetherington (Ed.), *Coping with divorce, single parenting and remarriage: A risk and resiliency perspective* (pp. 117–146). Mahwah, NJ: Erlbaum.

McLanahan, S., & Sandefur, G. (1994). *Growing up with a single parent: What hurts, what helps.* Cambridge, MA: Harvard University Press.

Miller, N. B., Smerglia, V. L., Gaudet, D. S., & Kitson, G. C. (1998). Stressful life events, social support, and the distress of widowed and divorced women. *Journal of Family Issues, 19,* 181–203.

Patterson, G. R., DeBaryshe, B., & Ramsey, E. (1989). A developmental perspective on antisocial behavior. *American Psychologist, 44,* 329–335.

Patterson, G. R., Reid, J. B., & Dishion, T. J. (1992). *Antisocial boys.* Eugene, OR: Castalia.

Popenoe, D., Elshtain, J. B., & Blankenhorn, D. (Eds.). (1996). *Promises to keep: Decline and renewal of marriage in America.* Langham, MD: Rowman & Littlefield.

Riessmann, C. K. (1990). *Divorce talk: Women and men make sense of personal relationships.* New Brunswick, NJ: Rutgers University Press.

Rutter, M. (1985a). Family and school influences on behavioral development. *Journal of Child Psychology and Psychiatry, 26,* 349–368.

Rutter, M. (1985b). Family and school influences on behavioral development. *Journal of Child Psychology and Psychiatry, 26,* 369–398.

Rutter, M. (1987). Psychosocial resilience and protective mechanism. *American Journal of Othorpsychiatry, 5,* 315–331.

Sandler, I. N., Tein, J. Y., & West, S. G. (1994). Coping, stress, and the psychological symptoms of children of divorce: A cross-sectional and longitudinal study. *Child Development, 65,* 1744–1763.

Seltzer, J. A. (1994). Consequences of marital dissolution for children. *Annual Review of Sociology, 20,* 235–266.

Seltzer, J. A. (2001). Families formed outside of marriage. In R. M. Milardo (Ed.), *Understanding families into the new millennium: A decade in review* (pp. 466–487). Minneapolis: National Council on Family Relations.

Simons, R. L., & Associates (Eds.). (1996). *Understanding differences between divorced and intact families: Stress, interaction, and child outcome.* Thousand Oaks, CA: Sage.

Steinberg, L. (1987). Single parents, stepparents, and the susceptibility of adolescents to antisocial peer pressure. *Child Development, 58,* 269–275.

Teachman, J. D., Tedrow, L. M., & Crowder, K. D. (2000). The changing demography of America's families. *Journal of Marriage and the Family, 62,* 1234–1246.

Tschann, J. M., Johnston, J. R., Kline, M., & Wallerstein, J. (1990). Conflict, loss, change, and parent–child relationships: Predicting children's adjustment during divorce. *Journal of Divorce and Remarriage, 13,* 1–22.

Tzeng, J. M., & Mare, R. D. (1995). Labor market and socioeconomic effects on marital stability. *Social Science Research, 24,* 329–351.

U.S. Bureau of the Census (1998). *Current population reports, Marital Status and Living Arrangements: March 1998 (Update)* (P20–514). Washington, DC: U.S. Department of Commerce, Economics and Statistics Administration.

Visher, E. B., & Visher, J. S. (1996). *Therapy with stepfamilies.* New York: Brunner Mazel.

Weiss, R. S. (1979). Growing up a little faster: The experience of growing up in a single-parent household. *Journal of Social Issues, 35,* 97–111.

Werner, E. (1999, September 24). *The Children of Kauai: Multiple pathways from birth to midlife.* Paper presented at the Annual Conference of the Life History Research Society, Kauai, Hawaii.

Wolchik, S. A., West, S. G., Westover, S., Sandler, I. N., Martin, A., Lustig, J., Tein, J., & Fisher, J. (1993). The children of divorce parenting intervention. *American Journal of Community Psychology, 21,* 293–331.

Zill, N., Morrison, D. R., & Coiro, M. J. (1993). Long-term effects of parental divorce on parent–child relationships, adjustment, and achievement in young adulthood. *Journal of Family Psychology, 7,* 91–103.

9

Correlational and Experimental Study of Resilience in Children of Divorce and Parentally Bereaved Children

Irwin Sandler, Sharlene Wolchik, Caroline Davis, Rachel Haine, and Tim Ayers

This chapter presents research on resilience of children and adolescents who have experienced two major disruptions of the nuclear family, parental divorce and parental bereavement. The two research programs share a common research paradigm in which there is an iterative relationship between correlational and experimental studies (Sandler, Wolchik, MacKinnon, Ayers, & Roosa, 1997). Correlational studies are used to identify protective and vulnerability factors, particularly those that may be modifiable by planned interventions. Experimental studies are designed on the basis of the *small theory* that changing these factors in the desirable direction will promote resilience. Randomized experimental trials of the interventions are conducted to test whether the intervention has changed these vulnerability and protective factors and reduced negative outcomes and whether change in negative outcomes is mediated by change in the vulnerability and protective factors (Sandler et al., 1997). The mediational analysis within the randomized trial provides a stronger test of the causal role of the vulnerability and protective factors to influence negative outcomes than is provided by the correlational studies, and thus contributes to theory about resilience (Rutter, Pickles, Murray, & Eaves, 2001).

The chapter first presents a theoretical framework that specifies alternative models of the influence of vulnerability and protective factors on the resilience of children experiencing significant adversities. We then discuss correlational research on key constructs in the theoretical

Support for this research was provided by National Institute of Mental Health Grants P30 MH439246, R01 MH49155, and R01 MH57013, which are gratefully acknowledged.

framework: adversity, and child and family protective and vulnerability factors. Finally, experimental studies of resilience are presented, which test the effects of changing these protective and vulnerability factors to reduce negative mental health outcomes. Although the research programs on bereavement and divorce were not specifically designed as comparative, findings that indicate common pathways to resilience, as well as pathways that are unique to each adversity, will be discussed.

THEORETICAL FRAMEWORK FOR VULNERABILITY
AND PROTECTIVE MECHANISMS

The next important step for resilience research is to shift the focus from predicting positive outcomes for children in adversity to studying mechanisms by which these outcomes are achieved (Wyman, Sandler, Wolchik & Nelson, 2000). Our general theoretical model of the mechanisms of resilience has been described previously (Sandler, 2001), so it will be reiterated only briefly here. The model specifies that the impact of adversities and resources is mediated through two common mechanisms, the development of age-appropriate competencies and the satisfaction of basic needs and goals. Adversities are conceptualized as relations between the person and the environment that threaten the satisfaction of these needs and competencies and thereby lead to disorder. Resources are conceptualized as characteristics of individuals, families, or communities, such as coping style, parenting, and community efficacy. Where resources promote satisfaction of needs and competencies, they are called *protective factors*, and where they have a negative effect, they are called *vulnerability factors*. Resources and adversities are seen as dynamically affecting each other over time.

The joint influence of adversities and resources on outcomes can be specified in terms of main effects, interactive effects, and mediating effects models (for alternative models see Luthar, Cicchetti, & Becker, 2000). We are interested in positive outcomes such as developmental competence as well as mental health problems, and we believe that these influence each other. In the main effects model, there are additive direct effects of adversities and resources on outcomes (Figure 9.1A). In an interactive model, the effects of resources condition the effects of adversity (Figure 9.1B) and can be either a protective or a vulnerability factor. In the interactive protective model, the adversity has a weaker relation to problem outcomes when the level of the resource is higher. In the interactive vulnerability model, the relation between the adversity and

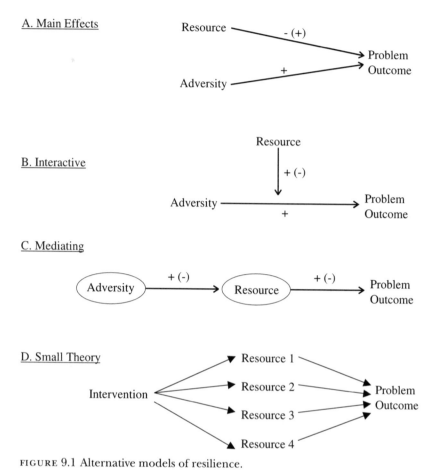

FIGURE 9.1 Alternative models of resilience.

the problem outcome is stronger when the level of the resource is higher. Finally, the resource may be affected by the adversity and may mediate the relations between the adversity and the problem outcome (Figure 9.1C). In the deterioration form of mediation, the occurrence of adversities decreases the ability of an individual, family, or community to function effectively. For example, adversities may create a sense of helplessness, make parenting more difficult, or decrease community efficacy. In the mobilization form of mediation, adversities may lead to the mobilization of individual, family, or community resources. For example, individuals may engage in effective coping, parents may facilitate effective coping on the part of their children, or communities may organize to meet threats. Our research with children of divorce and bereaved children has studied these alternative models as pathways by which adversities and resources relate to mental health outcomes for which these children are at risk (e.g., Lutzke, Ayers, Sandler, & Barr, 1997; Sandler, 2001).

ADVERSITIES FOR BEREAVED CHILDREN AND CHILDREN OF DIVORCE

Parental divorce and parental death are both major adversities that disrupt parent–child relationships and lead to restructuring of the family. However, there is great variability in the adversities experienced by children in these situations. Felner, Terre, and Rowlison (1988) proposed a transitional events model in which the major stressor was conceptualized as leading to a series of other stressors as the family restructured. In some cases the family disruption may lead to a prolonged period of instability, conflict, and economic strain, whereas in other cases, the family structure may become stable, supportive, and relatively low in conflict. The study of resilience requires careful assessment of adversities in order to assess whether the resources have main effects over and above adversities, interact with adversities, or mediate the effects of adversities.

We have developed several approaches to assessing the adversities of bereaved children and children of divorce. One approach has been to use life events methodology to assess recent stressful events. We developed "tailor-made" stressful events measures to assess the specific discrete events that may follow divorce or parental bereavement. Based on the reports of bereaved children and adults, we developed a measure of bereavement-related stressors (Parent Death Event List, PDEL) and classified them into four categories: environmental changes (e.g., a new adult starts taking care of you), expectations of the child's behavior (e.g., you're told to be the man/woman of the house), parental distress (e.g., your parent acted worried, upset, or sad), and death reminders (e.g., your relatives said your mom/dad is watching you). Li, Lutzke, Sandler, and Ayers (1995) found that events classified as parental distress and death reminders each had unique relations with children's mental health problems. Similarly, we used knowledgeable informants to develop the Divorce Events Schedule for Children (DESC; Sandler, Wolchik, Braver, & Fogas, 1986). Using the ratings of divorced parents, children of divorce, and clinicians, we found that the most stressful events for children of divorce involved blaming the child for the divorce, derogation of the parents, and interparental conflict (Wolchik, Sandler, Braver, & Fogas, 1986). We also assessed stressful events that are not unique to children of divorce or bereaved children but that may be increased by these family disruptions (e.g., family fights, seeing a parent drunk). We found that higher levels of such stressful events were positively associated with mental health problems for bereaved children in both cross-sectional (West et al., 1991) and longitudinal analyses (Sandler et al., 1992).

A second approach to assessing adversity measures ongoing aspects of the child's environment that threaten the child's well-being – for example, the mental health of the caregivers (e.g., demoralization, depression, grief, substance abuse), economic hardship in the household, or, in the case of divorce, ongoing interparental conflict. In separate samples of bereaved children, we found significant relations between parent demoralization and children's mental health problems using both cross-sectional (West et al., 1991) and longitudinal analyses (Sandler et al., 1992). Sandler, Tein, Mehta, Wolchik, and Ayers (2000) developed a multimeasure and multireporter aggregate measure of adversity for children of divorce that included parental demoralization, economic hardship, recent stressful events, and interparental conflict and found that it was associated with higher internalizing and externalizing problems in a cross-sectional analysis.

RESOURCES FOR CHILDREN OF DIVORCE AND BEREAVED CHILDREN

Our research has focused on the assessment of individual and family resources and on testing alternative main effect, interactive, and mediation pathways by which resources and adversities affect outcomes. Because of our interest in developing interventions to promote resilience, we focused primarily on resources that are potentially modifiable by relatively brief interventions.

Individual Child Resources

We have studied multiple characteristics of children as sources of resilience, including beliefs about control and self-worth, cognitive appraisal of stressors, coping, affect regulation, and temperament. We have studied the effects of these resources individually and how they influence each other or act in combination to influence outcomes.

Beliefs about Control

There is considerable evidence that control beliefs affect adaptation for children exposed to a wide range of adversities (Seifer, Sameroff,

Baldwin, & Baldwin, 1992). However, a close examination of this literature identifies two issues that have not been well studied: (1) What theoretical model (i.e., main effects, interaction, or mediation) best accounts for the protective effects of control beliefs? and (2) Are there subdimensions of control beliefs and, if so, which subdimensions are responsible for the protective effects? Because attempting to directly control uncontrollable situations often has negative effects (Janoff-Bulman & Brickman, 1980), the issue of what dimensions of children's control beliefs are protective is particularly complicated for children of divorce and bereaved children.

We initially investigated whether there was support for a protective interaction effect of control beliefs across children experiencing different adversities and across age and gender (Kliewer & Sandler, 1992). We used a sample of children and adolescents (ages 8–16) who had experienced three different stressors – parental divorce, bereavement, or asthma – and a group that had experienced none of these stressors. We found that the covariance matrix for the bereavement group was significantly different from that of the other three groups, so the bereavement group was dropped from these analyses and studied separately. The analyses with the remaining three groups found evidence for an interactive protective effect: The relations between negative events and total mental health problems were weaker for children with more internal control beliefs than for children who had more external control beliefs. An alternative plausible theoretical model is a mediational pathway, in which exposure to uncontrollable stressful events teaches children that events in their lives are beyond their control, and these external control beliefs lead to greater mental health problems (Janoff-Bulman, 1992). Fogas et al. (1992) found support for a mediational model for a sample of children of divorce, in which the relation between divorce-related stressors and self-reported internalizing problems was mediated by their control beliefs. We did not find any support for the mediational or moderational models with the bereaved children who were dropped from the prior analysis (Haine, Ayers, Sandler, Wolchik, & Lutzke, 2001).

Several studies have shown that a dimension labeled *known versus unknown control* (which reflects children's belief that they understand why events occur), as well as the internal versus external control dimension, is associated with children's depression and other mental health problems (Weisz et al., 1989). Theoretically, it may be that the dimension of known versus unknown control might be particularly relevant to children's secondary control, or their ability to adapt to uncontrollable situations by having a coherent understanding of what is happening (Rothbaum, Weisz, & Snyder, 1982). In a series of studies (Kim, Sandler, & Tein, 1997), we found that unknown control beliefs mediated the relations between stress and higher levels of children's mental health problems, although the mediational effect was not significant in the prospective longitudinal model for bereaved children. In addition, known versus unknown control beliefs had a protective interaction effect on mental health problems for children of divorce but not for bereaved children. In a second study, Sandler, Kim-Bae, and MacKinnon (2000) found that negative appraisals of stressful events accounted for the relations between unknown control beliefs and mental health problems. It may be that having a sense of understanding why things happen is protective because it reduces the likelihood of interpreting events in negative ways. The lack of an interactive protective effect for bereaved children may reflect the fact that parental death is more unambiguously uncontrollable for children, so that the secondary control provided by known versus unknown control is necessary for healthy adjustment across levels of stressful events. For parental divorces that involve lower levels of stressful events, children may more easily have a sense of secondary control because parents provide them with reassuring and less personally threatening ways of understanding the situation.

Self-Worth

There is considerable evidence that adversities have a negative impact on people's sense of self-worth (Sandler, Miller, Short, & Wolchik, 1989) and that a positive sense of self moderates the negative effects of exposure to adversity (Werner & Smith, 1992). In three separate samples of bereaved children and children of divorce, we have found that self-worth mediated the relations of ongoing adversity (e.g., parental mental health problems, poverty, stressful events) and symptom levels (see Sandler, Kwok, Ayers, & Wolchik, 2001, for a summary). Adversity had a negative effect on self-worth, which in turn was related to problem outcomes among children. Across all three samples, only a single protective interaction effect was found for high self-worth, and this held only among girls.

Coping and Coping Efficacy

We conceptualize coping as including children's cognitive or behavioral efforts to deal with adversities. We used a four-dimensional model of coping (Ayers, Sandler, West, & Roosa, 1996) to study the effects of coping on mental health problems in a sample of children of divorce and in a sample of bereaved children. The four dimensions were active coping, avoidance, distraction, and support seeking.[1] For children of divorce aged 8–12, we found that avoidance coping mediated the relations between stressful events and children's mental health problems in the cross-sectional analysis. Stressful events led to higher avoidant coping, which, in turn, led to higher levels of depression, anxiety, and conduct problems. A protective interactive effect was found for active coping on conduct problems in the cross-sectional analysis. In the prospective analyses (over 5 months), we found main effects for active and distraction coping related to lower levels of symptoms at time 2.

We postulated that, as a consequence of multiple experiences, children make a general judgment concerning their efficacy in dealing with problems in their lives (Bandura, 1997). We studied two models of how coping efficacy beliefs influence mental health problems in children of divorce and bereaved children, a coping mediation and a protective interactive model. There was consistent evidence for efficacy to mediate the relations between coping and mental health problems for both bereaved children and children of divorce. For active coping, in both cross-sectional and longitudinal models there was support for a positive mobilization model: Active coping leads to increased coping efficacy, which in turn leads to lower levels of mental health problems (Sandler, Ayers, Tein, & Wolchik, 1999; Sandler et al., 2000). For avoidant coping, there was evidence from the cross-sectional but not the longitudinal model for a negative mobilization model in which avoidant coping leads to lower efficacy, which in turn leads to higher internalizing problems (Sandler et al., 2000, 2001). No evidence was found for efficacy to moderate the relations between coping and mental health problems for either children of divorce or bereaved children.

Appraisal of Stressful Situations
Theoretically, the meanings people construct for stressful situations have a powerful effect on their adaptation (Janoff-Bulman, 1992). In our research with children of divorce,[2] we have examined appraisals in two ways; appraisals for specific stressful events and biases to appraise events either positively or negatively.

Our first set of questions concerned assessing appraisals for stressful events, that is, the reasons children felt events were threatening to their well-being (Sheets, Sandler, & West, 1996). Using confirmatory factor analysis of self-report responses, we found that the dimensional structure of appraisals became more differentiated with age. Whereas a one-dimensional model provided an adequate fit for children aged 8–10, a three-dimensional model provided the best fit for children aged 11–12. The dimensions were labeled *threat to self, other threat,* and *material loss.* There were also important age differences in the relations between appraisals and mental health problems. For older children only, threat to self predicted higher internalizing problems in both cross-sectional and prospective longitudinal analyses controlling for the effects of all other appraisals.

A second approach to studying appraisals is based on the proposition that children have biases or stylistic propensities to appraise stressful events either positively or negatively. Positive cognitions have included self-enhancement, optimism, and control and have been related to better outcomes for adults facing health stressors (Taylor & Brown, 1988). Negative cognitions have included overgeneralizing, personalizing, and catastrophizing and have been associated with depression, anxiety, and conduct problems (Kaslow & Racusin, 1990). Mazur, Wolchik, and Sandler (1992) developed a measure in which children of divorce rated how much they would have positive or negative thoughts in scenarios representing prototypical stressors experienced by children of divorce, such as parental arguments, a parent missing visits, and so on. There was only a weak correlation between the positive and negative cognitions.[3] As predicted, positive cognitions had a main effect on lower mental health problems and negative cognitions had a main effect on higher mental health problems over and above the effects of recent stressful events. In a second study using a larger sample, Mazur, Wolchik, Virdin, Sandler, and West (1999) found significant stress interaction effects for negative and positive cognitions. For older children but not younger children, there was a vulnerability interaction effect in which the relation between stressful events and mental health problems was stronger at higher levels of negative cognitions. For positive cognitions, there was a stress protective interaction effect in predicting children's reports of depressive symptoms and, for older children, in predicting parent reports of externalizing problems.

Expression of Emotion

Although we had studied emotional regulation strategies in our coping research (e.g., positive reframing, distraction), critical unanswered questions came to the fore in our research with bereaved children. Recent empirical research with adults (Bonanno & Kaltman, 1999) has challenged the traditional *grief-work* proposition that expression of grief-related feelings is critical for healthy mourning, in favor of a *social-functional* proposition that suppression of negative emotions may sometimes facilitate adaptation by strengthening social ties or improving management of affect. However, there is little empirical research on these issues and none with bereaved children. We differentiated and developed reliable measures of three aspects of emotional expression: inhibition of emotional expression, talking with others about one's emotions, and feeling that others understand one's emotions. We found that inhibition of emotional expression had a main effect on higher internalizing and externalizing problems of bereaved children in both cross-sectional and prospective longitudinal analyses (Ayers, Sandler, Wolchik, & Haine, 2000). We also found that talking about one's feelings with members of the family and feeling understood by the primary caregiver in the family were related to lower mental health problems. Our data indirectly support the grief-work model in that *inhibition of expression* of felt emotions is related to higher mental health problems. In addition, consistent with a social-functional perspective, expressing feelings to intimate family members and feeling understood by them is related to better mental health.[4]

Temperament

Several studies have demonstrated that temperament relates to resilience in children of divorce[5] (Hetherington, 1989; Kurdek, 1988). For those concerned with potentially modifiable correlates of resilience, this raises the issue of how to deal with relatively stable, physiologically based individual differences such as temperament. We approached this issue by studying how temperament acted jointly with two potentially modifiable responses to stress, appraisal and coping. Lengua and Sandler (1996) found that the temperament dimension of approach/flexibility moderated the relations between active and avoidant coping and mental health outcomes. Active coping related to lower mental health problems only for high-approach/flexibility children, whereas avoidant coping related to higher mental health problems only for children who were lower on approach/flexibility. It may be that temperament sets the boundary conditions for who can effectively use different coping strategies. Using a separate data set, Lengua, Sandler, West, Wolchik, and Curran (1999) found that the temperament dimension of negative emotionality had an indirect relation to mental health problems through increasing threat appraisal. The findings from these two studies indicate that changing coping and appraisal is a pathway by which at least part of the effects of temperament on resilience may be influenced.

Summary of Individual-Level Resources

These studies provide correlational evidence for following potentially modifiable individual-level resources to promote positive outcomes for bereaved children and children of divorce: beliefs about control, self-worth, coping, coping efficacy, and appraisals of stressful events. Whereas some of these resilience resources, such as coping efficacy, appear to operate the same way for children of divorce and bereaved children, others, such as control beliefs, may operate differently. The studies also find that stable personal characteristics of temperament and control beliefs may impact mental health problems of children in these stressful situations by affecting the more proximal processes of adaptation, such as coping and stress appraisals. Finally, it is notable that there is support for main effect, interactional, and mediational models. Some individual resources, such as coping efficacy and self-worth, show robust mediation or main effects across groups. Other resources, such as control beliefs and cognitive appraisals, show interaction effects in children of divorce; however, these interactions have not yet been shown to generalize to bereaved children.

Family Resources

Some family resilience resources, such as parental warmth and parental discipline, involve the dyadic-level relationship between the parent and child, whereas others are family-level constructs such as family support, family cohesion, stable positive events, and positive family routines. We have examined main effect, interactive models, and mediational models of how these family resources relate to mental health outcomes. We have also examined more complex models, which involve the interplay between these family resources and individual child factors such as temperament, appraisal of stressful events, and individual beliefs about satisfaction of basic needs.

Parent–Child Relationships: Parental Warmth

Parental warmth is conceptualized to include the positive affective and emotionally supportive relationship between parents and children that conveys to children the belief that their parent values and thinks highly of them and can be counted on to care for them in the future. There is consistent evidence that adversities are associated with changes in the affective nature of the parent–child relationship and that high-quality parent–child relationships serve to protect children from the effects of exposure to adversity (Amato, 2000; Masten, 2001).

In cross-sectional and longitudinal analyses with bereaved children, we have found that parental warmth has a main effect on lowering parent and child reports of mental health problems (Sandler et al., 1992; West, Sandler, Pillow, Baca, & Gersten, 1991). Ayers et al. (2000) found a prospective longitudinal main effect for children's reports that their parent was understanding of their feelings at time 1 to predict lower mental health problems 3 months later. Sandler, Kwok, Ayers, and Wolchik, 2001) found that parental warmth mediated the relations between the mental health problems of bereaved parents and children's mental health problems.

In our work with divorced families, we have examined both main effect and interactive models of the relations between parental warmth and mental health problems, as well as potential mediators of these relations. Given that 80% of children reside primarily with their mothers after divorce (U.S. Census Bureau, 1998), our work has focused on the mother–child relationship. Wolchik, Wilcox, Tein, and Sandler (2000) found support for main effects as well as protective interactive effects of maternal warmth. The main effects of both mother and child reports of warmth were significant in predicting lower levels of internalizing and externalizing problems. The plot of the Stress × Warmth interaction indicated that although maternal warmth (as reported by mothers) was associated with lower mental health problems across the levels of stress, the difference was stronger when the level of stress was higher, indicating a protective interactive effect. For child reports of maternal warmth, the interaction with stress was further moderated by consistent discipline, which will be discussed later when we consider other evidence of the combined effects of parental warmth and discipline. We also examined whether high maternal warmth had a protective interactive effect to mitigate the negative effects of one highly stressful aspect of children's postdivorce environments: interparental conflict (Lutzke, Wolchik, & Braver, 1996). Although there was a main effect for maternal warmth to predict lower mother and child reports of mental health problems, there was no support for a protective interactive effect.

We have begun to investigate individual child variables that either mediate or moderate the protective effects of parental warmth on mental health problems. Theoretically, a mediational model tests whether the effects of parental warmth on mental health problems might be accounted for by characteristics of children, such as their beliefs, feelings, cognitions, and behaviors. From the perspective of our general theoretical model, it is predicted that the effects of parenting would be mediated through satisfaction of children's basic needs and developmental competencies. Wolchik, Tein, Sandler, and Wilcox (2001) found that the prospective longitudinal relation between maternal warmth and internalizing and externalizing problems was mediated by children's fears that they would not be taken care of by their parents. This model is consistent with the proposition that maternal warmth reduces children's fears about not being cared for by their parents, which in turn affects their mental health problems. Similarly, Dawson, Cohen, Tein, Wolchik, and Mazur (1999), in a study with children of divorce, found that negative cognitions partially mediated the relation between maternal warmth and child and mother reports of internalizing as well as externalizing problems. We have also found support for a mediational role of perceived competence. Studying children of divorce, Nelson, Wolchik, and Sandler (1997) found that perceived academic and peer competence partially mediated the cross-sectional relations between child report of warmth and internalizing and externalizing problems. Analyses using mother report of warmth provided support for the mediational role of academic competence in predicting internalizing and externalizing problems.

A moderational model tests whether the effects of parenting differ as a function of individual differences of children. Lengua, Wolchik, Sandler, and West (2000) found that the relation between maternal rejection (an aspect of low maternal warmth) and mental health problems differed, depending on one aspect of children's temperament: positive emotionality. Rejection was more strongly related to conduct problems and depression for children low in positive emotionality than for those high in positive emotionality. This indicates that low positive emotionality may create vulnerability to the effects of maternal rejection and that interventions to reduce rejection may be particularly important for children who are low on positive emotionality.

Parent–Child Relationships: Discipline

Parents' ability to be effective disciplinarians can be diminished by the psychological distress associated with death or divorce, as well as by decreases in the time they are able to spend monitoring their children's behavior. In our work with children of divorce, we have investigated both main effect and stress interactive models of the effects of consistent discipline on mental health problems. Similar to the findings for warmth, Wolchik et al. (2000) found that the findings differed across reporting of parenting. Main effects occurred for mother report of consistency of discipline for both internalizing and externalizing problems. For child report of consistency of discipline, stress and gender interacted to predict internalizing problems, with a protective interactive effect occurring for girls but not boys. In research with parentally bereaved children, Sandler et al. (2001) found that consistency of discipline mediated the effects of parental mental health problems on child report of internalizing problems.

We have begun to explore individual child variables that may moderate or mediate the effects of consistency of discipline on mental health problems. Lengua et al. (2000) found that the relation between maternal rejection and mental health problems was dependent on the level of child impulsivity. Maternal rejection was more strongly related to both depression and conduct problems for children high in impulsivity than for those low in impulsivity. Exploring mediational relations, Dawson et al. (1999) found that negative cognitions partially mediated the relation between inconsistency of discipline and mother as well as child reports of internalizing problems and child reports of externalizing problems.

Parent–Child Relationships: Warmth and Discipline

Warmth and discipline can also be seen to work in combination, with optimum parenting involving high levels of warmth combined with appropriate and consistent discipline. Studying the joint influence of consistent discipline and maternal warmth in a large sample of children of divorce, Wolchik et al. (2000) found a significant three-way interaction of Stress × Child Report of Consistency of Discipline × Warmth in predicting both internalizing and externalizing problems. The interaction indicated that children who reported inconsistent discipline and low warmth were the most vulnerable to the negative effects of stress.

Family-Level Resources

Our work with bereaved families has focused on three aspects of family-level resources: cohesion; stable positive events, such as family outings and positive time with parents; and satisfaction with family support. The stressors associated with bereavement put a strain on most families, which negatively affects these resources. West et al. (1991) found that parental death was related to lower parent reports of family cohesion and lower child reports of stable positive events, and that these family resources significantly mediated the relation between stressful events and children's mental health problems. Sandler et al. (1992), using a separate sample of bereaved children, found support for the cross-sectional relation between mental health problems and parent and child reports of stable positive events and family cohesion, as well as child reports of family social support. In a third sample, Ayers et al. (2001) developed a measurement model of children's seeking of social support from the family and found that it was significantly related to lower mental health problems.

In our work with divorced families, we have focused on family social support and family routines. Because many children of divorce move, change schools, and spend less time with one or both parents as well as extended family members, changes in social support are likely to occur. Defining support as the total number of support functions (i.e., recreation, advice, goods/services, emotional support, and positive feedback) provided by nuclear and extended family members, we examined main and interactive models separately for support provided by child and adult family members (Wolchik, Ruehlman, Braver, & Sandler, 1989). The analyses provided support for a protective interactive effect for support given by family adults for child report but not parent report of mental health problems. The interaction indicated that children who reported low support from family adults were most vulnerable to the negative effects of stress. Support provided by children was not predictive of either child or mother report of mental health problems.

Several researchers have speculated that divorce disrupts the occurrence of family routines or regular, predictable family-level interactions such as eating meals together. Examining main and protective interactive models of family routines, Cohen, Taborga, Dawson, and Wolchik (2000) found support for both models, depending on the reporter. When mother report of routines was used, main effects occurred for both child and mother reports of internalizing problems and mother report of externalizing problems. A significant three-way interaction (Age × Stressful Divorce Events × Routines) occurred for child report of externalizing problems, with routines mitigating the effects of stress on externalizing problems for older but not younger children. For child report of routines and mental health problems, routines had a main effect in predicting externalizing problems and interacted with gender to predict internalizing problems, with routines being protective for girls but not boys. Child report of routines was not predictive of mother report of internalizing or externalizing problems.

These family-level resources may exert their protective effects by affecting individual child variables, parent–child relationship variables, or both. It is plausible that these resources create a context in which parental warmth and consistent discipline occur and that these parent–child relationship variables affect mental health outcomes. Alternatively, these family-level resources may directly affect individual child variables. For example, family support may enhance children's self-worth and promote effective coping efforts. Family routines and positive stable events also may promote a sense of stability and reduce fear of abandonment. The satisfaction of these basic needs may affect mental health problems. The identification of pathways through which family-level resources affect mental health outcomes is an important direction for future research that can provide guidance for preventive interventions.

Summary of Parent–Child Relationship and Family-Level Resources
Our programs of research with bereaved and divorced families have provided support for the protective role of several family resources. For some resources, the nature of the protective effect differed, depending on whether the parent or child reported on the family resource. When the parent reported on the resource, main effects were more likely to occur than interactive effects and the resource was often predictive of child as well as parent report of mental health problems. Some of the analyses using child report of the family resource provided support for a protective interactive model, with some of these interactive effects being qualified by age, gender, or another family resource. Further, these protective interactive effects were often significant for child report of mental health problems only, which raises concerns about whether they reflect shared reporter method variance. Although not surprising given the small correlation between parent and child reports of most family resources, the discrepancy in findings across reporters highlights the importance of research that examines the meanings that children and parents attach to these family resources.

Interventions as Experimental Studies of Resilience

The correlational studies just reviewed provide our best empirical basis for a *theory* of an intervention to promote resilience. In this theory, the variables that show main effects, protective interactions, or stress-mediation effects are potential resilience resources. Tests of the effects of experimentally induced changes in these resilience resources to reduce negative outcomes in a randomized experimental trial would rule out attributing these effects to third variables and provide strong evidence of the causal role of the resilience resource (Rutter et al., 2001). We have conducted experimental trials of interventions to strengthen resilience resources for bereaved children and children of divorce, which we conceptualize as experimental studies of resilience.

Small Theory of Resilience

Wyman et al. (2000) described a cumulative protection model in which resources at multiple levels protect children from the negative effects of adversities. In designing the interventions, we selected potentially changeable child and family-level resources that we believed were protective for bereaved children or children of divorce, and developed an additive main effect model in which change in these resources is • predicted to contribute to improving outcomes (Figure 9.1D). This additive model constitutes what Lipsey (1990) has termed the *small theory* of the intervention.[6] The term small theory is used to indicate that this is the conceptual theory underlying the construction of a specific intervention, rather than a more general theory of all processes that might affect the outcomes. There are three aspects of the theory of the intervention (Chen, 1990). First is the action theory, which states that the intervention will change each of the resilience resources in the model. Second is that the intervention will change the mental health outcomes. Third is that change in the resilience resources in the small theory will mediate the effects of the program on mental health outcomes.

New Beginnings Program for Children of Divorce

We have conducted two randomized experimental trials of interventions designed to improve mental health outcomes for children of divorce. Our first intervention employed the custodial mother as the change agent and targeted five variables (Wolchik, West, Westover, Sandler, Martin, Lustig, Tein, & Fisher, 1993). The evaluation was designed to address three questions of critical relevance to resilience research. First, are resilience resources malleable due to our intervention? The question of malleability is critical in determining the implications of our theory of resilience for prevention programming, and indeed, some resilience factors may not be malleable or may be very difficult to change (e.g., temperament). The results of this trial indicated that we were successful in changing child and mother reports of maternal warmth and mother report of consistency of discipline. Importantly, some of these effects were Intervention × Baseline interactions in which the positive program benefits on the resilience resource were found for those families that scored lower on this resource at the pretest. There was also a significant program effect to reduce child and mother reports of divorce-related negative events and a marginally significant effect on mother and child reports of interparental conflict, again with the program effect being seen for families with higher levels on these variables at the pretest. Although program participants improved in their attitudes toward children's contact with their fathers, there were no significant effects on reports of actual contact. Interestingly, there was also an unexpected effect of the program to reduce the amount of support children reported from nonparental adults. Although this is the opposite of the program's intent, we interpret the findings as being due to mothers spending more time with their children, thus leaving the children less time to be with nonparental adults.

The second question concerns whether the intervention affects mental health outcomes. The results indicated a Program × Baseline interaction on parent report of total behavior problems, in which the program benefited children who had higher levels of behavior problems at baseline. The third question concerns whether the effects of the program on mental health outcomes were mediated by the resilience resources. We tested this model using structural equation modeling in which each of the resilience resources that were impacted by the program were tested as potential mediators of program effects on total behavior problems. The results found support for quality of maternal warmth as a mediator of program effects. No significant mediation effect was found for the other candidate mediating variables: consistency of discipline, negative events, or interparental conflict.

In a second trial, we attempted to replicate the effects of the parenting program for custodial mothers and to test the additive effects of a second intervention component that worked with the children (Wolchik, West, et al., 2000). The mother component was slightly modified based on the effects of the first trial to target four resilience resources: maternal warmth, discipline, father–child relationship, and interparental conflict. The child component was designed to change four resilience resources that it was believed could be impacted by children: active coping, avoidant coping, negative appraisal of divorce stressors, and quality of the mother–child relationship. An additive design was used in which the effects of three groups were compared: mother program alone, mother program plus child program, and a self-study comparison group using a randomized experimental design.

The posttest results indicated that compared with the self-study condition, the mother program led to significantly greater improvement on maternal warmth (for those with lower maternal warmth at time 1), mother's attending to child's conversation, mother's validation of the child's conversation content, consistent discipline, and mother's attitude toward the noncustodial father–child relationship. At the posttest, the mother program had a significant effect on reducing internalizing problems. There was also a significant program effect on reducing externalizing problems for those who were high on externalizing problems at the pretest. Tests for mediation were conducted for each of the six resources impacted by the program (Tein, Sandler, MacKinnon, & Wolchik, 2002). These tests found support for maternal warmth and discipline as mediators of the program effects on children's externalizing and internalizing problems at posttest. Parental warmth mediated program effects on both internalizing and externalizing, whereas discipline mediated program effects only on externalizing problems. Interestingly, the mediation effects were found for children who were higher on mental health problems and lower on maternal warmth or discipline at time 1. Although the child program showed some evidence of improving knowledge of coping and threat appraisal, there was no evidence that it improved mental health problems compared to the mother program.

At the 6-month follow-up, the mother program was found to have a significant program effect on reducing externalizing problems for those who were higher on externalizing problems at time 1. Mediational analyses found that program effects on externalizing problems at the 6-month follow-up for those who were high on externalizing at pretest were mediated by program effects on parental warmth and discipline at immediate posttest. This was a prospective mediation effect in which program-induced improvements on the parenting resources at immediate posttest led to change in externalizing problems 6 months later (Tein et al., 2002).

The two intervention trials provide evidence that experimentally induced change in maternal warmth led to a reduction in mental health problems. Although effective discipline was found to be a significant mediator of program effects only in the replication study, it should be noted that the initial study did not test effects on internalizing and externalizing separately, that the replication study had considerably greater power to detect mediation effects, and that discipline was a significant mediator of program effects on externalizing problems at both posttest and the 6-month follow-up in the replication study. The results of these mediational analyses provide experimental evidence of parenting as a resilience resource for children of divorce.

Family Bereavement Program

We have conducted two randomized experimental trials of interventions designed to prevent mental health problems in bereaved children aged 7–17. The first trial (Sandler et al., 1992) targeted four resilience resources for bereaved children that were supported by existing studies at that time: demoralization of the surviving parent, warmth of the relationship between the surviving parent and the child, stable positive family events, and stressful events. In addition, the program attempted to improve parents' satisfaction with their social support as a mechanism for improving parental demoralization and family coping to deal with stressful events. The intervention included a family grief workshop and a home visiting family adviser program to build these resilience resources.

Program effects were tested using a randomized experimental design in which families were assigned to the Family Bereavement Program (FBP) and a self-study control condition. The results showed that parents in the intervention improved more on parental warmth and support satisfaction than those in the comparison group. In addition, parents in the program reported less of a decrease in discussions of grief-related issues than those in the control group. In terms of mental health problems, the program improved depressive symptoms and conduct problems in older adolescents but not younger children. Finally, a test of mediation found support for parental warmth to mediate the effects of the program on adolescents' mental health problems.

Although the results were encouraging, the program was redesigned to accomplish the following two objectives (Ayers et al., 2002): (1) To account for more recent findings on putative resilience resources, an expanded list of resources was targeted for change, including caregiver warmth, discipline, child's exposure to negative events, caregiver's mental health, child's inhibition of feeling expression, appraisal of threat from stressful events, positive coping, feeling understood by the caregiver, self-esteem, and control beliefs. (2) The format of the program was changed to include a group designed for the caregiver and for the child/adolescent, with five joint activities that involved both caregivers and children. In addition, there were two family meetings to individualize program activities to meet family needs.

The experimental trial of the program involved random assignment of families to the program or a literature comparison condition (Sandler et al., in press). Participants were assessed before entering the program, immediate afterward, and 11-months after completing the program. At posttest, families in the program were found to improve more than controls on multiple resilience resources, including a composite measure of caregiver warmth and discipline, negative events, coping, inhibition of feelings, caregiver mental health problems, and behavioral observation of positive affect in caregiver–child interactions. However, there was only one program effect on children's mental health problems; teachers reported that total behavior problems were lower for program compared to control children who began the program with higher levels of problems. At the 11-month follow-up however, there were significant program effects of lower caregiver report of internalizing problems for children who had higher levels of internalizing problems at time 1, and, for girls, of lower internalizing and externalizing problems. Preliminary results of the mediational analyses indicate that program effects on mental health problems are mediated by the program's impact to improve caregiver warmth, discipline, children's belief that their caregiver understands their feelings, reduction in children's exposure to stressful events, inhibition of emotional expression, and reduction in unknown control beliefs (Tein, Ayers, Sandler, Wolchik, & Newton, 2002). These studies provide the first experimental evidence in the literature that multiple resilience resources are malleable for parentally bereaved children and that an intervention program reduces the mental health problems of these children. The results of the mediational analyses in both experimental trials with bereaved children replicate the findings from the study with children of divorce that experimentally induced changes in parenting reduce children's mental health problems.

Implications for Developmental Theory

These complementary correlational and experimental studies have implications for preventing the mental health problems of children of divorce and bereaved children, and they also contribute to our understanding of the theoretical processes that lead to better adaptation. Theoretically, we conceptualize resilience as a dynamic process of adaptation in which there is reorganization of the individual microsystems and macrosystems that impact developmental outcomes (Sameroff & Fiese, 2000). Our studies converge on identifying the critical role of parenting as a resilience resource for both bereaved children and children of divorce. The studies provide evidence that (1) parenting has main effects to lower levels of mental health problems for children exposed to these stressors, (2) that it has protective interaction effects to reduce the impact of negative events that follow parental divorce and bereavement, and (3) that experimentally improving parenting reduces the mental health problems of children who experience these stressors. The consistent role of parenting as a resource for children of divorce and bereaved children may be important because both of these stressors involve a disruption in the family system. It may be that parenting that involves high levels of warmth and effective discipline enables children to satisfy basic needs (such as a sense of belonging) and to succeed at developmental tasks (such as academic success) that are threatened by the disruption in their family system.

On the other hand, the evidence is more limited or inconsistent concerning the effects of individual-level resilience resources. For example, for bereaved children and children of divorce, coping efficacy seems to mediate the effects of stress and accounts for the effects of coping efforts on mental health outcomes. However, we do not yet have experimental evidence that changing efficacy affects the mental health outcomes of these children. The findings are more complicated still for another individual-level resource: children's beliefs about control. Our correlational studies with children of divorce and bereaved children both indicate the importance of children believing that they understand why events occur (i.e., unknown control). For both bereaved children and children of divorce, unknown control beliefs mediate the relations between stressful events and mental health problems. However, there is also evidence of a stress protective interaction effect for unknown control beliefs for children of divorce but not for bereaved children. These findings are based on cross-sectional analyses, and longitudinal analyses will be needed to better understand their implications for resilience. However, the differential pattern across bereaved children and children of divorce indicates that resilience resources may operate differently in different stressful contexts.

The most important limitation of our theoretical research on resilience factors is that it has not sufficiently investigated the role of broader contextual factors. We expect that neighborhood, culture, and poverty may have important influences on how resources impact resilience because they influence the possible ways in which people satisfy their needs and achieve competencies under conditions of stress. For example, the effects of active coping may be affected by living in the inner city (Gonzales, Tein, Sandler, & Friedman, 2001), where active coping has diminished benefits for children with very high levels of stress exposure.

The most important implication of our studies may be that they provide support for the proposition that resilient processes are malleable, at least in the short term. Resilience is not simply a fixed characteristic of individuals (Luthar et al., 2000); it is a process that can be modified. The critical test of malleability, however, will come as we follow our samples over time and across developmental transitions and learn more about the pathways by which short-term changes in resilience resources or mental health problems affect longer-term trajectories of development.

Notes

1. We are continuing to study alternative models of the support-seeking dimension of coping, and recent findings indicate that a model based on the providers of support may provider a better fit than one based on emotion- vs. problem-focused functions.
2. We have not yet investigated threat appraisal for bereaved children, so this presentation will focus on our work with children of divorce.
3. In these papers the positive cognitions were called *illusions* following from the work of Taylor, Collins, Skokan, and Aspinwall (1989), whereas the negative cognitions were called *cognitive errors* following from the work of Beck (1991). However, to avoid comparisons with an unknown reality, we use the more descriptive terms *positive cognitions* and *negative cognitions* here.
4. The finding that inhibition of emotional expression relate to higher mental health problems is consistent with other laboratory-based research on the negative effects of emotional inhibition (Gross & Munoz, 1995). These results refer to the subjective experience of hiding or inhibiting the expression of felt emotion. The focus on *inhibition* of emotional expression differs from other research that finds that the discrepancy between autonomic and verbal emotion relates to lower levels of prolonged grief (e.g., Bonanno, 2001). It may be that the active process of inhibiting emotional expression differs from the simple discrepancy between autonomic and verbal emotion and is the component that leads to negative mental health outcomes. It may not be whether bereaved people express negative emotion per se that is important, but whether they feel that they are doing the work of inhibiting or hiding the emotion they experience.
5. We have not yet conducted research on the temperament of bereaved children, so this section will focus only on our work with children of divorce.
6. The additive model of the intervention makes it difficult to derive clear causal statements about the effects of changing each *specific* variable in the model, particularly if the intervention is successful in changing multiple variables. Although it is possible to construct interventions that systematically target one or another resource and systematically test their effects (West & Aiken, 1997), the desire to develop maximally powerful prevention programs as rapidly as possible led us to begin with a model that included multiple plausible mediators. Alternative data analysis and design strategies can be used, such

as mediational analysis or more complex factorial designs, to further refine our tests of which resilience resource accounts for program effects (West & Aiken, 1997).

References

Amato, P. R. (2000). The consequences of divorce for adults and children. *Journal of Marriage and the Family, 62,* 1269–1287.

Ayers, T. S., Sandler, I. N., West, S. G., & Roosa, M. W. (1996). A dispositional and situational assessment of children's coping: Testing alternative models of coping. *Journal of Personality, 64,* 923–958.

Ayers, T. S., Sandler, I. N., Wolchik, S. A., & Haine, R. (2000, June). *Emotional expression and mental health problems of bereaved children.* Presented at the annual meeting of the Society for Prevention Research, Montreal, Canada.

Ayers, T. S., Twohey, J. L., Sandler, I. N., Wolchik, S. A., Luztke, J. R., Padgett-Jones, S., Weiss, L., Cole, E., & Kriege, G. (2002). *The Family Bereavement Program: Description of a theory-based prevention program for parentally-bereaved children and adolescents.* Tempe: Prevention Research Center, Arizona State University.

Bandura, A. (1997). *Self-efficacy: The exercise of control.* New York: W. H. Freeman.

Beck, A. T. (1991). Cognitive therapy as integrative therapy. *Journal of Psychotherapy Integration, 1*(3), 191–198.

Bonanno, G. A. (2001). Grief and emotion: A social-functional perspective. In M. S. Stroebe, R. O. Hansson, W. Stroebe, & H. Schut. (Eds.), *Handbook of bereavement research: Consequences, coping and care* (pp. 493–517). Washington, DC: American Psychological Association.

Bonanno, G. A., & Kaltman, S. (1999). Toward an integrative perspective on bereavement. *Psychological Bulletin, 125*(6), 760–776.

Chen, H.-T. (1990). *Theory-driven evaluations.* Newbury Park, CA: Sage.

Cohen, J. M., Taborga, M., Dawson, S., & Wolchik, S. (2000, June). *Do family routines buffer the effects of stressful divorce events on children's symptomatology?* Presented at the annual meeting of the Society for Prevention Research, Montreal, Canada.

Dawson, S. R., Cohen, J. M., Tein, J.-Y., Wolchik, S. A., & Mazur, E. (1999, June). *Children's cognitions as a mediator of parenting and postdivorce adjustment.* Poster presented at the biennial meeting of the Society for Community Research in Action, New Haven, CT.

Felner, R. D., Terre, L., & Rowlison, R. T. (1988). A life transition framework for understanding marital dissolution and family reorganization. In S. A. Wolchik & P. Karoly (Eds.), *Children of divorce: Empirical perspectives on adjustment* (pp. 35–65). New York: Gardner Press.

Fogas, B. S., Wolchik, S. A., Braver, S. L., Freedom, D. S., & Bay, C. (1992). Locus of control as a mediator of negative divorce-related events and adjustment problems in children. *American Journal of Orthopsychiatry, 62,* 589–598.

Gonzales, N. A., Tein, J.-Y., Sandler, I. N., & Friedman, R. J. (2001). On the limits of coping: Interaction between stress and coping for inner-city adolescents. *Journal of Adolescent Research, 16,* 372–395.

Gross, J. J, & Munoz, R. F. (1995). Emotion regulation and mental health. *Clinical Psychology: Science and Practice, 2,* 151–164.

Haine, R. A., Ayers, T. S., Sandler, I. N., Wolchik, S. A., & Luztke, J. R. (2001). *Locus of control and self-esteem as moderators or mediators of the relation between negative life events and mental health problems in parentally bereaved children.* Manuscript submitted.

Hetherington, E. M. (1989). Coping with family transitions: winners, losers, and survivors. *Child Development, 60*(1), 1–14.

Janoff-Bulman, R. (1992). *Shattered assumptions: Towards a new psychology of trauma* (Vol. 12). New York: Free Press.

Janoff-Bulman, R., & Brickman, P. (1980). Expectations and what people learn from failure. In T. Feather (Ed.), *Expectance, incentive and action* (pp. 207–272). Hillsdale, NJ: Erlbaum.

Kaslow, N. J., & Racusin, G. R. (1990). Childhood depression: Current status and future directions. In A. S. Bellack, M. Hersen & A. E. Kazdin (Eds.), *International handbook of behavioral modification and therapy* (2nd ed., pp. 649–667). New York: Plenum Press.

Kim, L. S., Sandler, I. N., & Tein, J. Y. (1997). Locus of control as a stress moderator and mediator in children of divorce. *Journal of Abnormal Child Psychology, 25,* 181–199.

Kliewer, W., & Sandler, I. N. (1992). Locus of control and self-esteem as moderators of stressor symptom relations in children and adolescents. *Journal of Abnormal Child Psychology, 20,* 393–413.

Kurdek, L. A. (1988). Cognitive mediators of children's adjestment to divorce. In S. A. Wolchik & P. Karoly (Eds.), *Children of divorce: Empirical perspectives on adjustment* (pp. 233–267). New York: Gardner.

Lengua, L. J., & Sandler, I. N. (1996). Self-regulation as a moderator of the relation between coping and symptomatology in children of divorce. *Journal of Abnormal Child Psychology, 24,* 681–701.

Lengua, L. J., Sandler, I. N., West, S. G., Wolchik, S. A., & Curran, P. J. (1999). Emotionality and self-regulation, threat appraisal, and coping in children of divorce. *Development and Psychopathology, 11,* 15–37.

Lengua, L. J., Wolchik, S. A., Sandler, I. N., & West, S. G. (2000). The additive and interactive effects of parenting and temperament in predicting problems of children of divorce. *Journal of Clinical Child Psychology, 29*(2), 232–244.

Li, S., Lutzke, J., Sandler, I. N., & Ayers, T. S. (1995, June). *Structure and specificity of negative life event categories for bereaved children.* Presented at the Biennial Conference of the Society for Community Research and Action, Chicago.

Lipsey, M. W. (1990). Theory as method: Small theories of treatments. In L. Sechrest, E. Perrin, & J. Bunker (Eds.), *Research methodology: Strengthening causal interpretations of nonexperimental data* (Vol. DHHS Publication No. 90–3454, pp. 33–51). Washington, DC: U.S. Government Printing Office.

Luthar, S. S., Cichetti, D., & Becker, B. (2000). Research on resilience: Response to commentaries. *Child Development, 71*(3), 573–575.

Lutzke, J. R., Wolchik, S. A., & Braver, S. L. (1996). Does the quality of mother–child relationships moderate the effect of postdivorce interparental conflict on children's adjustment problems? *Journal of Divorce and Remarriage, 25,* 15–37.

Masten, A. S. (2001). Ordinary magic: Resilience processes in development. *American Psychologist, 56*(3), 227–238.

Mazur, E., Wolchik, S. A., & Sandler, I. N. (1992). Negative cognitive errors and positive illusions for negative divorce events: Predictors of children's psychological adjustment. *Journal of Abnormal Child Psychology, 20*, 523–542.

Mazur, E., Wolchik, S. A., Virdin, L., Sandler, I. N., & West, S. G. (1999). Cognitive moderators of children's adjustment to stressful divorce events: The role of negative cognitive errors and positive illusions. *Child Development, 70*, 231–245.

Nelson, K., Wolchik, S., & Sandler, I. (1997, May). *Competence as a mediator between quality of the mother-child relationship and children's adjustment to divorce.* Presented at the Biennial Conference on Community Research and Action, Columbia, SC.

Rothbaum, F., Weisz, J. R., & Snyder, S. S. (1982). Changing the world and changing the self: A two-process model of perceived control. *Journal of Personality and Social Psychology, 42*, 5–37.

Rutter, M., Pickles, A., Murray, R., & Eaves, L. (2001). Testing hypotheses on specific environmental causal effects on behavior. *Psychological Bulletin, 127*, 291–324.

Sameroff, A. J., & Fiese, B. H. (2000). Models of development and developmental risk. In C. H. J. Zeanah (Ed.), *Handbook of infant mental health* (2nd ed., Vol. 17, pp. 3–19). New York: Guilford Press.

Sandler, I. N. (2001). Quality and ecology of adversity as common mediators of risk and resilience. *American Journal of Community Psychology, 29*, 19–63.

Sandler, I. N., Ayers, T. S., Tein, J. Y., & Wolchik, S. A. (1999, April). Perceived coping efficacy as a mediator of the effects of coping efforts. In I. N. Sandler & B. Compas (Chair), *Beyond simple models of coping: Advance in theory and research.* Symposium conducted at the biennial meeting of the Society for Research in Child Development, Albuquerque, New Mexico.

Sandler, I. N., Ayers, T. S., Wolchik, S. A., Tein, J.-Y., Kwok, O.-M., Haine, R. A., Twohey, J. L., Suter, J., Lin, K., Padgett-Jones, S., Lutzke, J. R., Cole, E., Kriege, G., & Griffin, W. A. (in press). The Family Bereavement Program: Efficacy evaluation of a theory-based prevention program for parentally-bereaved children and adolescents. *Journal of Consulting and Clinical Psychology.*

Sandler, I. N., Kim-Bae, L., & MacKinnon, D. P. (2000). Coping and appraisal as mediators of the effects of locus of control beliefs on psychological symptoms for children of divorce. *Journal of Clinical Child Psychology, 29*, 336–347.

Sandler, I. N., Kwok, O. M., Ayers, T. S., & Wolchik, S. A. (2001, March). *Impact of parental grief, parenting and depression on bereaved children.* Presented at the 23rd Annual Conference of the Association for Death Education and Counseling, Toronto, Canada.

Sandler, I. N., Miller, P., Short, J., & Wolchik, S. A. (1989). Social support as a protective factor for children in stress. In D. Belle (Ed.), *Children's social networks and social supports* (pp. 277–307). New York: Wiley.

Sandler, I. N., Tein, J. Y., Mehta, P., Wolchik, S. A., & Ayers, T. S. (2000). Coping efficacy and psychological problems of children of divorce. *Child Development, 71*, 1099–1118.

Sandler, I. N., West, S. G., Baca, L., Pillow, D. R., Gersten, J., Rogosch, F., Virdin, L., Beals, J., Reynolds, K., Kallgren, C., Tein, J., Krieg, G., Cole, E., &

Ramirez, R. (1992). Linking empirically based theory and evaluation: The Family Bereavement Program. *American Journal of Community Psychology, 20,* 491–521.

Sandler, I. N., Wolchik, S. A., Braver, S. L., & Fogas, B. S. (1986). Significant events of children of divorce: Toward the assessment of risky situations. In S. M. Auerbach & A. L. Stolberg (Eds.), *Crisis intervention with children and families* (Vol. 20, pp. 65–83). Washington, DC: Hemisphere.

Sandler, I. N., Wolchik, S. A., MacKinnon, D., Ayers, T. S., & Roosa, M. W. (1997). Developing linkages between theory and intervention in stress and coping processes. In S. A. Wolchik & I. N. Sandler (Eds.), *Handbook of children's coping: Linking theory and intervention* (pp. 3–40). New York: Plenum Press.

Seifer, R., Sameroff, A. J., Baldwin, C. P., & Baldwin, A. L. (1992). Child and family factors that ameliorate risk between 4 and 13 years of age. *Journal of the American Academy of Child and Adolescent Psychiatry, 31*(5), 893–903.

Sheets, V., Sandler, I. N., & West, S. G. (1996). Appraisals of negative events by preadolescent children of divorce. *Child Development, 67,* 2166–2182.

Taylor, S. E., & Brown, J. D. (1988). Illusion and well-being: A social psychological perspective on mental health. *Psychological Bulletin, 103*(2), 193–210.

Taylor, S. E., Collins, R. L., Skokan, L. A., & Aspinwall, L. G. (1989). Maintaining positive illusions in the face of negative information: Getting the facts without letting them get to you. *Journal of Social and Clinical Psychology, 8*(2), 114–129.

Tein, J.-Y., Ayers, T. S. Sandler, I. N., Ayers, T. S., & Wolchik, S. A. (2002). *Mediational processes of a preventive intervention for parentally bereaved children.* Manuscript in preparation.

Tein, J. Y., Sandler, I. N., MacKinnon, D. P., & Wolchik, S. A. (2002). Testing of mediation when program effects interact with pretest mediator or outcome variables. In J. Y. Tein (Chair), *Mediational models.* Symposium conducted at the eighth annual meeting of the Society for Prevention Research, Montreal, Canada.

U.S. Census Bureau. (1998). *Marital status and living arrangements: March 1998* (update) (P20–514). Washington, DC: U.S. Census Bureau.

Weisz, J. R., Stevens, J. S., Curry, J. F., Cohen, R., Craighead, W. E., Burlingame, W. V., Smith, A., Weiss, B., & Parmelee, D. X. (1989). Control-related cognitions and depression among inpatient children and adolescents. *Journal of the American Academy of Child and Adolescent Psychiatry, 28*(3), 358–363.

Werner, E. E., & Smith, R. S. (1992). *Overcoming the odds: High risk children from birth to adulthood.* Ithaca, NY: Cornell University Press.

West, S. G., & Aiken, L. (1997). Toward understanding individual effects in multicomponent prevention programs: Design and analysis strategies. In K. J. Bryant, M. Windle, & S. G. West (Eds.), *The science of prevention: Methodological advances in alcohol and substance abuse research* (pp. 167–211). Washington, DC: American Psychological Association.

West, S. G., Sandler, I. N., Pillow, D. R., Baca, L., & Gersten, J. (1991). The use of structural equation modeling in generative research: Toward the design of a preventive intervention for bereaved children. Special Issue: Preventive Intervention Research Centers. *American Journal of Community Psychology, 19*(4), 459–480.

Wolchik, S. A., Ruehlman, L. S., Braver, S. L., & Sandler, I. N. (1989). Social support of children of divorce: Direct and stress buffer effects. *American Journal of Community Psychology, 17,* 485–501.

Wolchik, S. A., Tein, J. Y., Sandler, I. N., & Doyle, K. W. (in press). *Fear of abandonment s a mediator of the relations between divorce stressors and mother–child relationship quality and children's mental health problems. Journal of Abnormal Child Psychology.*

Wolchik, S. A., West, S. G., Sandler, I. N., Tein, J.-Y., Coatsworth, D., Lengua, L., Weiss, L., Anderson, E. R., Greene, S. M., & Griffin, W. (2000). The New Beginnings Program for Divorced Families: An experimental evaluation of theory-based single-component and dual-component programs. *Journal of Consulting and Clinical Psychology, 68,* 843–856.

Wolchik, S. A., Wilcox, K. L., Tein, J. Y., & Sandler, I. N. (2000). Maternal acceptance and consistency of discipline as buffers of divorce stressors on children's psychological adjustment problems. *Journal of Abnormal Child Psychology, 28*(1), 87–102.

Wyman, P. A., Sandler, I. N., Wolchik, S. A., & Nelson, K. (2000). Resilience as cumulative competence promotion and stress protection: Theory and intervention. In D. Cicchetti, J. Rappaport, I. N. Sandler, & R. P. Weissberg (Eds.), *The promotion of wellness in children and adolescents* (Vol. 26, pp. 133–184). Washington, DC: Child Welfare League of America Inc.

PART II

EXOSYSTEMIC AND SOCIODEMOGRAPHIC RISKS

10

Rethinking Resilience

A Developmental Process Perspective

Tuppett M. Yates, Byron Egeland, L., and Alan Sroufe

Children's talent to endure stems from their ignorance of alternatives
(Maya Angelou, 1969)

INTRODUCTION

A central tenet of contemporary developmental psychopathology is that
our understandings of normative and abnormal development mutually
inform one another (Cicchetti, 1990, 1993; Cicchetti & Cohen, 1995;
Sroufe & Rutter, 1984). Historically, however, research has focused on
the determinants of psychopathology and maladaptation to the relative
exclusion of elucidating factors that contribute to the initiation and maintenance of adaptive developmental pathways. More recently, a strong and
growing literature has emerged identifying factors that enable individuals
to achieve adaptive developmental outcomes despite adversity.

The study of risk and resilience derived from the observation that some
individuals in populations exposed to incontrovertible adversity nevertheless achieve adaptive developmental outcomes (e.g., Garmezy, 1974;
Murphy & Moriarty, 1976; Rutter, 1979; Sameroff & Seifer, 1983; Werner
& Smith, 1992). These individuals exemplify resilience, "the process of,
capacity for, or outcome of successful adaptation despite challenging or

Preparation of this work was supported in part by a grant from the National Institute of
Mental Health (MH0864) awarded to the second and third authors. The first author was
supported by the National Science Foundation's Graduate Research Fellowship.

The authors wish to thank Benjamin Aguilar, Karen Appleyard, Elizabeth Carlson, Glenn
Roisman, Megan Sampson, and Gloria Whaley for their comments on an earlier draft of
this chapter.

threatening circumstances" (Masten, Best, & Garmezy, 1990, p. 426). Over the past 25 years, research on a variety of at-risk populations has identified factors that moderate the relation between risk and competence, namely, protective and vulnerability factors (Masten & Coatsworth, 1998). More recently, however, increasing attention has been directed toward identifying and refining the methodological and theoretical frameworks within which resilience is conceptualized and studied in order to clarify the processes that underlie adaptive development in the context of adversity (e.g., Luthar, Cicchetti, & Becker, 2000; Sameroff, 2000).

In this chapter, we emphasize the importance of a theoretically grounded approach to the study of resilience, using the literature on children reared in poverty to illustrate our central arguments. Adopting an organizational perspective on development, we argue that a developmental history of consistent and supportive care engenders early competence, which, in turn, plays a critical role in later adaptation, one that has been heretofore underappreciated in the prevailing literature on resilience. We begin with a review of the extant literature on the deleterious effects of poverty on children's development. We then outline the organizational model of development and its theoretical application to the study of risk and resilience. The third section presents the current state of knowledge regarding salient protective factors for children reared in poverty. Next, we suggest that, because of the transactional nature of development, an early history of positive adaptation is a powerful source of enduring influence on children's adaptation. Current empirical support for the salience of an early history of competence as a protective resource, its operational definition within an organizational framework, and the theoretical basis for its construction in early childhood are also discussed. In closing, we offer process-oriented suggestions for intervention and prevention efforts, with a focus on interventions aimed at fostering early developmental competence in the parent–child relationship.

CHILDREN IN POVERTY

One-fifth of American children reside in families with incomes below the federal poverty line (U.S. Bureau of the Census, 1997). Although socioeconomic status is, in and of itself, a poor indicator of early adversity, it is a powerful correlate of multiple risk factors that act in concert to thwart positive adaptation. A cumulative risk model asserts that multiple risk factors across several levels of influence contribute significant explanatory power to child outcomes (Rutter, 1979; Sameroff, 2000; Sameroff

& Seifer, 1983; Seifer & Sameroff, 1987). From this perspective, poverty is a distal risk factor whose effects are mediated by proximal risk factors such as parenting behaviors, family structure, community variables, and the broader social networks within which the child and her or his family are embedded (Egeland, Carlson, & Sroufe, 1993).

The negative impact of socioeconomic instability on parenting behavior is a primary mediator of the effect of poverty on children's development. In comparison to higher-income families, poor families are more likely to be led by a young, single parent who has low educational attainment and significant periods of unemployment (Brooks-Gunn & Duncan, 1997; Brooks-Gunn, Duncan, & Maritato, 1997). Faced with a barrage of needs to be filled and inadequate resources with which to meet them, low-income families are disproportionately affected by parental depression and substance use disorders (Belle, 1990; Hall, Williams, & Greenberg, 1985). "Poverty and economic loss diminish the capacity for supportive, consistent, and involved parenting" (McLoyd, 1990, p. 312). Poverty and its associated negative life experiences contribute to poor parental emotional well-being, insufficient child-directed attention, and harsh, intrusive, and punitive parenting (Brooks-Gunn et al., 1997; Sampson & Laub, 1994).

In a study of the development of premature infants, Escalona (1987) found that, although poor infants often received an adequate amount of nurturance and affection, these expressions of caring were administered independent of the infant's cues or needs; care was offered in an unpredictable fashion, depending on who, if anyone, was available at a given point in time. Similar studies have shown that economically disadvantaged infants are subject to less stable caregiving patterns and daily routines (Halpern, 1993). Erratic, unpredictable caregiving may foster a child's early conceptions of the world as frightening, unstable, and unpredictable (Minuchin, 1967). These expectations may be subsequently confirmed by experiences in the parent–child relationship (e.g., child maltreatment: Jones & McCurdy, 1992; Luthar, 1999) and in the broader community (e.g., community violence: Limber & Nation, 1998).

Socioeconomic disadvantage has a deleterious impact on children's cognitive, intellectual, social, and emotional development. Children raised in poverty perform below their higher-income peers on assessments of cognitive development, physical health, academic achievement, and emotional well-being (Brooks-Gunn et al., 1997; Halpern, 1993). Family poverty impedes children's cognitive development as assessed by IQ, verbal ability, and achievement tests (Duncan, Brooks-Gunn, &

Klebanov, 1994; Seifer & Sameroff, 1987; Smith, Brooks-Gunn, & Klebanov, 1997). Moreover, these cognitive effects are significant above and beyond the contributions of maternal education, maternal IQ, and family structure (Brooks-Gunn et al., 1997; McLoyd, 1998; Smith et al., 1997). Academically, poverty increases the likelihood of placement in special education programs (Egeland & Abery, 1991), grade retention (Jimerson, Carlson, Rotert, Egeland, & Sroufe, 1997), and school dropout (Jimerson, Egeland, Sroufe, & Carlson, 2000). With respect to socioemotional development, poor children are at greater risk for psychiatric disorders (Costello, Farmer, Angold, Burns, & Erkanli, 1997), and receive higher scores on parent and teacher ratings of behavioral and emotional problems (Bolger, Patterson, Thompson, & Kupersmidt, 1995; Egeland, Kalkoske, Gottesman, & Erickson, 1990; McLeod & Shanahan, 1993).

Despite the preponderance of evidence indicating a strong association between poverty and negative developmental outcomes, the developmental courses of low-income children are variable. Indeed, a significant proportion of impoverished youth manage to achieve adaptive developmental outcomes (Garmezy, 1981). These children meet the two criteria on which resilience is predicated (Luthar et al., 2000; Wyman, Cowen, Work, & Parker, 1991). First, they have been exposed to significant adversity in the form of poverty and its associated stresses. Second, they have achieved positive developmental outcomes despite these adverse experiences. Thus, children who are at risk due to the deleterious consequences of poverty and its associated threats to adaptive development have been a popular focus of risk and resilience research over the past several decades.

THE ORGANIZATIONAL MODEL OF DEVELOPMENT

Although research has contributed to identifying and understanding specific protective and vulnerability factors, it remains a challenge to integrate these data into a theoretical framework capable of structuring and explaining the central features of the extant literature. The construct of resilience has been conceptualized within several, often overlapping, theoretical models (see Luthar et al., 2000, for a review). As the need for a developmental perspective on risk and resilience becomes increasingly apparent (Glantz & Sloboda, 1999; Windle, 1999), the organizational model of development (Sroufe, 1979) is gaining popularity in the risk and resilience literature (Cicchetti & Schneider-Rosen, 1986).

The organizational model conceptualizes development as a hierarchically integrative process in which earlier patterns of adaptation provide a framework for, and are transformed by, later experiences to yield increasing complexity, flexibility, and organization (Egeland et al., 1993; Sroufe & Rutter, 1984). Through this series of qualitative reorganizations, prior experience is not lost, but instead is incorporated into new patterns of adaptation (Werner & Kaplan, 1964). Interpreted within this framework, *adaptation* refers to qualitative features of the individual's negotiation of developmentally salient issues, and *competence* is the adaptive use of both internal and external resources to enable the successful negotiation of such issues (Cicchetti & Schneider-Rosen, 1986; Waters & Sroufe, 1983). Because it affects the way in which subsequent experiences are integrated into the system, early experience is a salient consideration for understanding later adaptive strategies.

Thus, development constitutes a patterning of adaptation across time such that prior levels of adaptation are probabilistically, rather than deterministically, related to later levels of functioning (Egeland et al., 1993; Sroufe & Rutter, 1984). Competence in one developmental period provides the child with a foundation that enables successful encounters with subsequent stage-salient issues. Conversely, maladaptation at a prior stage of development may compromise the child's capacity for subsequent effective engagement with developmental challenges (Cicchetti & Schneider-Rosen, 1986; Sroufe, 1997; Sroufe & Rutter, 1984). In this way, developmental patterns are magnified across time by virtue of the coherence with which both maladaptive and adaptive behaviors are organized. A corollary to this principle is that the longer an individual is on a particular developmental pathway, the less likely it becomes that she or he will deviate from that course (Bowlby, 1973; Cicchetti, 1993; Sroufe, 1997).

There are, however, notable cases of discontinuity in patterns of adaptation. The organizational model allows for the exploration of processes that mediate continuity in adaptation, as well as of those mechanisms that precipitate changes in functioning over time. Moreover, the probabilistic nature of associations among successive levels of adaptation allows for heterogeneity among developmental pathways such that the same developmental origin can yield divergent outcomes (multifinality), and different beginnings may converge on a single developmental endpoint (equifinality; see Cicchetti & Rogosch, 1996, for discussion).

A CLASSICAL VIEW OF PROTECTIVE FACTORS

Risk and resilience research has proposed three domains of resources that serve to protect children in the face of adversity: (1) child characteristics, (2) family characteristics, and (3) community characteristics (Garmezy,

1991; Masten et al., 1990; Rutter, 1979; Sameroff, Seifer, Zax, & Barocas, 1987; Werner & Smith, 1992). Children who are able to develop flexible coping strategies and a locus of control that allows them to attribute negative experiences to external factors, while retaining the capacity to value their own strengths and assets, fare better in the face of adversity (Luthar, 1991; Murphy & Moriarty, 1976; Werner, 1995). Intelligence and a good sense of humor are associated with flexible problem-solving skills, as well as with academic and social competence (Masten, 1986; Masten et al., 1988, 1999; Werner, 1990). Children who thrive in the face of adversity tend to be socially responsive and are able to elicit positive regard and warmth from their caregivers (Farber & Egeland, 1987; Werner, 1993). At the level of the family, these children emerge from warm, sensitive, and cohesive intrafamilial exchanges (Cowen, Work, & Wyman, 1997; Pianta & Egeland, 1990; Smith & Prior, 1995; Zaslow et al., 1999) and similarly nurturant kinship networks (Cowen, Wyman, Work, & Parker, 1990). Protective resources in the community may derive from high-quality educational milieus, nurturing and attentive teacher–child relationships (Brooks, 1994; Rutter, 1979; Werner, 1995), safe housing and neighborhoods (Brooks-Gunn, 1995), and available adult models of prosocial involvement (e.g., mentors; Freedman, 1993).

Because the majority of research on resilience has focused on middle childhood and adolescence, an early history of developmental competence is typically absent from discussions of protective factors. Moreover, studies that do examine factors in early childhood are often based on retrospective parent reports (e.g., Grizenko & Pawliuk, 1994). Notable exceptions include the Kauai Longitudinal Study (Werner & Smith, 1992), Murphy and Moriarty's (1976) study of vulnerability and coping, and the Minnesota Longitudinal Study of Parents and Children (Egeland & Brunnquell, 1979). Nevertheless, more prospective investigations of the early and core capacities that enable children to develop protective resources within themselves and to utilize sources of protection in their environment are needed.

For example, the ability to regulate emotional arousal is critical for behavioral and attentional control, thereby fostering academic and social competence (Eisenberg et al., 1997; Rubin, Coplan, Fox, & Calkins, 1995). Regulatory skills may be especially important for at-risk youth, who likely experience high levels of emotional intensity and negativity (Eisenberg et al., 1997). Thus, a key aim of developmental resilience research is to identify the processes by which children acquire adaptive emotion regulation strategies in high-risk environments.

Similarly, a protective mentoring relationship with an older individual is most likely to be helpful for children who are able to trust and engage in productive, reciprocal social interaction. Ultimately, children cannot benefit from our protective efforts unless they possess the capacity to effectively engage their psychosocial environments. Research adopting a developmental process perspective aims to explore the experiences through which children acquire the capacity for resilience. Developmental research is needed to clarify the processes by which children *become* flexible problem solvers, effective social actors, and self-preserving attribution makers. Toward this end, the organizational model of development conceptualizes resilience as a developmental process (Egeland et al., 1993; Sroufe, Carlson, Levy, & Egeland, 1999).

THE PLACE OF DEVELOPMENTAL HISTORY IN RESILIENCE RESEARCH

As applied to the study of risk and resilience, the organizational theory of development allows for interdependent relations among multiple levels of risk and protection that reciprocally influence one another to yield the qualitative features of a child's adaptation in the context of current situational and developmental demands. Adaptive outcomes at given stages of development derive from transactional exchanges between the child and her or his current environment, as well as from the developmental history that the child brings to these exchanges (Bowlby, 1973; Sroufe & Egeland, 1991). In this view, resilience is itself a developmental concept that characterizes the dynamic transactional processes that enable the organization and integration of experience in functionally adaptive ways. As development progresses, the salient components of the child's environment evolve from an exclusive focus on the parent–child caregiving relationship to include other contexts such as peer, school, and community milieus (Carlson & Sroufe, 1995; Wyman, Sandler, Wolchik, & Nelson, 2000). Thus, the organizational model supports the investigation of multiple domains of adaptation across several different time points in order to clarify the underlying capacities that enable competent negotiation of salient issues at each developmental stage and in each domain of adaptation. Resilience always encompasses more than the individual and always reflects a process over time.

In our view, *resilience* refers to an ongoing process of garnering resources that enables the individual to negotiate current issues adaptively and provides a foundation for dealing with subsequent challenges, as well as for recovering from reversals of fortune. Resilience doesn't *cause* children to do well in the face of adversity. Rather, resilience reflects the developmental process by which children acquire the ability to use both internal and external resources to achieve positive adaptation despite prior or concomitant adversity. Developmental history plays a key role in resilience; it is relevant to the acquisition of coping capacities as well as to the ability to draw upon resources from the environment. Thus, our understanding of resilience will be greatly advanced by recognizing and exploring the influential contribution of developmental history to the qualitative features of later adaptation.

Data from the Minnesota Longitudinal Study of Parents and Children, a 25-year study of impoverished mothers and their first-born children, suggest that a developmental history of support, and the competent functioning with which it is associated, is a major contributor to positive adaptation in the face of continuing or prior adversity. Social competence, well-regulated emotion and a sense of self-efficacy, each characteristic of children who achieve adaptive developmental outcomes, are predicted by a child's history of consistent, supportive care (e.g., Elicker, Englund, & Sroufe, 1992; Sroufe, 1983). Even child characteristics, such as IQ, are related to positive support and may change as environmental supports improve or decline (Pianta & Egeland, 1994). Moreover, many aspects of adaptation under stress, such as school completion, are better predicted by an early history of emotional support than by IQ (Carlson et al., 1999; Jimerson et al., 1997). Where we observe positive adaptation in the face of adversity, we routinely find an underlying foundation of positive adaptation and environmental supports that foster the development of the child's capacity to surmount adversity.

For example, Egeland and Kreutzer (1991) identified a group of children with a developmental history of support and positive adaptation. Early positive adaptation was operationalized as (1) secure mother–child attachment in infancy; (2) effective, persistent, and enthusiastic problem solving by the mother and child at 24 and 42 months; and (3) the child's demonstration of self-esteem, flexibility, creativity, frustration tolerance, and positive affect in response to a problem-solving situation at 42 months. The poverty sample was divided on the basis of maternal life stress reports to yield a high-stress risk sample and a low-stress risk sample. A history of positive adaptation was a significant protective factor against the negative effects of maternal life stress for the high-stress risk sample, as reflected by teacher ratings of behavior problems, social competence, and academic achievement in grades 1 and 3.

Additional research points to the salience of an early history of support, and the competence it enables, not only as a contributor to later positive adaptation but also as an important self-righting resource during intermittent regressions to maladaptive behavior patterns. Sroufe and colleagues (1990) identified two groups of high-risk children, both of whom consistently demonstrated poor adaptation during the preschool period but who differed with respect to the quality of their prior functioning. Children with early histories of secure attachment in infancy and generally supportive care in the first 2 years demonstrated a greater capacity to rebound from a period of poor adaptation in comparison to children who had not evidenced early positive adaptation. Children with positive developmental histories scored significantly higher on teacher ratings of peer competence and emotional health during the elementary school years in comparison to those with less supportive early histories, despite having demonstrated comparable levels of maladaptation during the preschool period. As confirmed by regression analyses, an early history of positive adaptation predicted elementary school performance above and beyond the contribution of more contemporaneous indices of support (Sroufe et al., 1990). Notably, without early developmental data, the recovery of positive functioning may have appeared to be due to inherent characteristics of resilient children, rather than the outcome of a transactional developmental process.

We have recently extended these findings to later childhood and adolescence (Sroufe et al., 1999). Among groups of children who exhibited comparable levels of behavior problems during the elementary school period, the qualitative features of the children's early developmental histories again predicted both psychopathology and competence in adolescence. Consistent with findings from the preschool period (Sroufe et al., 1990), children who exhibited positive transitions from maladaptation in middle childhood to competence in adolescence were able to draw on a positive foundation of early support and positive adaptation.

Together, these data indicate that resilience reflects a developmental process. Consider the alternative interpretation that an early history of positive adaptation reflects an underlying individual trait called resilience. In this view, some of these children were resilient, then were not, and then were again. Our interpretation of these data is that the process of resilience is manifest in the entire developmental trajectory. Children who were troubled in middle childhood and later rebounded drew, in large part, upon an early history of supportive and consistent care. Children who are competent are indeed more likely to manifest resilience at some point; however, competence is a characterization of functioning at a particular point in time, whereas resilience is a developmental process over time.

An early foundation of support engenders positive adaptation at later time points despite intervening maladaptation. Just as maladaptation may lie dormant for periods of time only to affect later adaptation (Sroufe & Rutter, 1984), so, too, may early competence influence later functioning above and beyond the contribution of intervening adaptation. Thus, "early resilience will not be 'extinguished'; although it may go underground for a while, it will later present itself as surprising and unexpected strengths in the behavior of the older individual" (Anthony, 1987, p. 33). The goal, then, must be to foster early competence in the parent–child relationship in light of its contribution to later adaptation.

CHARACTERIZING EARLY COMPETENCE

Within the organizational model of development, an early history of competence is characterized by the adaptive negotiation of specific developmental issues in the infant and toddler years. The salient developmental issues for these periods are (1) the formation of an effective attachment relationship; (2) the development of autonomous functioning; and (3) the acquisition of flexible problem-solving skills enabled by adequate behavioral and emotional self-regulation (Carlson & Sroufe, 1995; Cicchetti & Schneider-Rosen, 1986; Sroufe, 1989). These capacities develop through transactional exchanges between the infant and her or his environment, most notably in relation to the primary caregiver. In a transactional exchange, the child and the environment are actively engaged with one another, both participate as agents of change, and both are transformed by the interaction (Sameroff & Chandler, 1975). "Where the mutual regulation of the individual and context succeeds, a healthy, happy child develops; where the system regulation fails, deviancy appears" (Sameroff & Seifer, 1983, p. 1265).

The capacities for autonomy, self-regulation, and the ability to garner support from important others in the psychosocial milieu develop in the context of reciprocal and supportive exchanges between the child and her or his caregiver (Werner, 1990). Children who rise above adversity have histories of interaction that instill in them an expectation that adults can be turned to for nurturance, support, guidance, and need fulfillment, as well as other promotive factors (Musick, Stott, Spencer, Goldman, & Cohler, 1987; Sameroff, 2000). Children with internalized representations of self-worth, available protection, and sensitive care may be more responsive to the positive features of their environment and better equipped with the regulatory capacities to effectively engage and benefit from such resources (Sroufe et al., 1990). As observed prospectively by Werner (1993), children who have developed the capacity to trust both themselves and others select or construct environments that, in turn, reinforce and sustain their positive expectations of the social world and reward their competencies. Retrospectively, resilient youth report more positive and nurturant relationships with early caregivers and hold more positive expectations of future educational, employment, and interpersonal opportunities (Wyman et al., 1992). Nevertheless, the following question remains: What specific aspects of the child's early experience contribute to, and enable, the *process* of resilience?

There are several features of the early caregiving relationship that foster children's developing understandings of causation, trust, and self. These characteristics include responsiveness, positive affect, contingency, and cooperativeness in the caregiver–child relationship. Early encounters with sensitive caregiving contribute to children's beliefs that their needs will be fulfilled when they signal for care, that they are social actors capable of effecting change in their environment and interpersonal milieu, and that they are worthy of responsive care and attention. Coordinated affective exchanges between the caregiver and infant foster the infant's goal-directed activities in terms of both exploration and achievement (Tronick, 1989). Infants who trust in the availability of sensitive and appropriate care will explore their environments with greater confidence, signal their needs more effectively, and respond to caregiver intervention more readily than infants who have developed expectations of the world as harsh and unpredictable, and of themselves as ineffective and undeserving of care (Sroufe, 1989). Thus, even in the first several months of life, the child is an active participant in her or his development, interpreting and organizing behavioral responses to novel situations in accordance with her or his developmental history.

Poverty and life stress are associated with decrements in parental sensitivity in both the infancy and early childhood periods (Crittenden & Bonvillian, 1984; Pianta & Egeland, 1990; Pianta, Sroufe, & Egeland, 1989). Insensitive caregiving provides insufficient scaffolding for the child's emerging regulatory capacities, thereby fostering insecurity, both in the child's expectations of the social world and in her or his sense of self. Insensitive and intrusive caregiving is associated with conduct, attentional, and other behavior problems in later childhood (Egeland, Pianta, & O'Brien, 1993).

This is not to say that children in these environments are not cared for or tended to; indeed, gross neglect or maltreatment is the exception, not the rule, in these families. Most of these parents are well intentioned but lack the necessary resources to provide sensitive care, including time, flexibility, and, in many cases, their own developmental history of positive experience (Pianta, Hyatt, & Egeland, 1986; Sroufe & Fleeson, 1986). Nevertheless, the uncued, inconsistent, and noncontingent nature of the caregiving offered can warp the child's developing notions of trust, self-worth, and social reciprocity, just as the absence of care can. In this way, the insensitively nurturing parent is "depriving even when [she or he] is manifestly giving" (Anthony, 1987, p. 30).

Our data consistently show that a responsive, supportive, structured, and affectively stimulating environment in early childhood contributes to children's feeling of self-worth, empathic involvement with others, social competence, self-confidence, curiosity, and positive affective expression (Elicker et al., 1992; Englund, Levy, Hyson, & Sroufe, 2000; Sroufe, 1983; Sroufe, Schork, Motti, Lawroski, & LaFreniere, 1984). For example, in Farber and Egeland's (1987) study of maltreated children, maternal sensitivity emerged as the only significant discriminator between secure and insecure attachments among maltreated infants. Similarly, mothers who were maltreated in childhood and who broke the cycle of violence when rearing their own children reported a history of available care by an alternative parental figure. In contrast, mothers with histories of abuse who grew up to mistreat their own children did not report a positive history of alternate care (Egeland, Jacobvitz, & Sroufe, 1988).

We argue that the core of a developmental history of positive adaptation is a sensitive and emotionally responsive early caregiving relationship. These exchanges foster the development of children's positive expectations of the social world, and of their self-concepts as potent agents of change within that world. It is within a framework of available care and positive self-regard that the child develops adaptive emotion regulation patterns, flexible problem-solving skills, and an expectation of success in the face of adversity. Research suggests that not only is regulation of emotion "practiced" in early dyadic exchanges, but also that such exchanges are vital for the tuning of excitatory and inhibitory systems in the brain itself (Shore, 1994). Thus, competent adaptation in early childhood, particularly with respect to the parent–child relationship, is a prime target for prevention and intervention efforts aimed at fostering the process of resilience among economically and/or psychosocially disadvantaged youth.

IMPLICATIONS FOR PREVENTION AND INTERVENTION

Prevention and intervention programs are putative tools for preventing developmental deviations from adaptive pathways *and* for righting developmentally misguided pathways. Several features of the organizational model of development support the assertion that these efforts should originate in early childhood (Egeland, Weinfield, Bosquet, & Cheng, 2000; Ramey & Ramey, 1998). First, early experience is a salient influence on later adaptation. Second, it is easier to precipitate desistance on a newly emerging pattern of maladaptation than it is to alter a deeply ingrained pattern of behavior. Finally, preventing derailment from a positive adaptive pathway is more effective than attempting to reroute a child once she or he has embarked on a maladaptive trajectory. In addition, recent advances in neurodevelopment and neural plasticity further support the disproportionate salience of early experience for behavioral and neurological development (Dawson, Ashman, & Carver, 2000).

Prevention and intervention programs targeting families living in poverty have typically focused on either children *or* parents. More recently, programs for disadvantaged families have been broadened to include both parents *and* children in *two-generation programs* (Smith, 1995). Many of these programs involve home visitation and have been patterned after the work of David Olds's Nurse Home Visitation Program (Olds, Henderson, Tatelbaum, & Chamberlin, 1988). These programs have many goals, including the promotion of good parenting skills, the prevention of child abuse, and the promotion of healthy child development. However, relatively few programs aim to improve the quality of the parent–child relationship, particularly with respect to the parent–child attachment relationship.

In our view of resilience as a process, the successful negotiation of early developmental issues (i.e., secure parent–child attachment in infancy) provides the foundation for positive adaptation among children exposed to adversity. Therefore, we believe that prevention and intervention programs designed to promote resilience need to begin in the early years and should involve attachment-oriented interventions. Programs aimed at fostering secure parent–infant attachment relationships are varied, with specific programs emphasizing different antecedents of a secure attachment (see Egeland et al., 2000, for review).

Perhaps the most commonly used approach attempts to alter the negative beliefs, mental representations, and expectations that the parent carries over into the caregiving situation from her or his own childhood experiences (Egeland et al., 2000). Selma Fraiberg was one of the first to talk about early experience and its impact on parenting in the next generation, calling these unrecognized influences of early experiences *ghosts in the nursery* (Fraiberg, Adelson, & Shapiro, 1980). Fraiberg developed a set of intervention strategies based on psychodynamic principles. Since then, infant–parent psychotherapy has been used with some success to promote secure attachment and attachment-related behavior (i.e., maternal empathy, goal-directed partnerships; Barnard et al., 1988; Cicchetti, Toth, & Rogosch, 1999; Egeland & Erickson, 1993; Lieberman, Weston, & Pawl, 1991).

A second approach to attachment-based intervention aims to enhance parental sensitivity. Using a sample of irritable infants, van den Boom (1995) developed a short-term intervention that focused on mothers' attention to, and perception of, their infants' signals. Mothers who participated in the intervention were more sensitive to their infants' cues and had a greater number of securely attached infants compared to the control group. Finally, approaches aimed at reducing maternal depressive symptomatology (Cooper & Murray, 1997; Lyons-Ruth, Connell, & Grunebaum, 1990) and providing social support (Beckwith, 1988) have had a positive impact on a number of parenting variables, though they have had limited success with respect to differences in attachment security between treatment and control groups.

In a recent review of the literature in this area, we concluded that existing attachment interventions for high-risk poverty samples do not yield significant changes in attachment classification (Egeland et al., 2000). Parents in high-risk samples are often dealing with multiple challenges in their lives that need to be addressed before they can devote themselves to improving their relationship with their infants. Many parents living in poverty struggle to ensure basic shelter, nutrition, and safety for their families; poor parents are often young and single, lack social support, and suffer from the emotional scars of their own troubled childhood. Therefore, comprehensive and successful intervention efforts aimed at disadvantaged youth and their families should target the parent–child attachment relationship in the context of a family-focused, multipronged, interdisciplinary program (Black & Krishnakumar, 1998; Rolf & Johnson, 1999; Schorr, 1988).

Just as risk research has emphasized the multiplicative salience of several concomitant risks, so, too, has intervention research begun to recognize the powerful effect of providing children with multiple protective resources to foster competence across several domains. A cumulative model of positive influence (Bradley et al., 1994; Jessor, Turbin, & Costa, 1998; Zaslow et al., 1999) supports interventions that strive to ameliorate multiple risks while promoting successful adaptation in several settings (Coie et al., 1993; Masten & Wright, 1998; Wyman et al., 2000; Yoshikawa, 1994). It is essential that the varied needs of the high-risk family be addressed in order for parents to participate fully in and benefit from a relationship-based program. Ideally, a parent intervention program serving high-risk families should include medical, mental health, social, and chemical dependency services, as well as flexibility within the program itself to meet the unique needs of each family (Egeland et al., 2000).

In addition to a comprehensive approach, it is imperative that prevention and intervention efforts aimed at poor families adopt an empowerment model in order to optimize responsiveness and openness to intervention and to attenuate the demoralization that poverty precipitates. Programs that incorporate culturally congruent values and norms will be more readily accepted, utilized, and integrated into the community structure (Black & Krishnakumar, 1998). Successful prevention and intervention programs will focus not only on deficits in need of restorative attention, but also on the child's, family's, and community's intact or better-developed resources that may enable the development of compensatory abilities (Luthar & Cicchetti, 2000; Masterpasqua, 1989; Werner, 1990). Adopting a strengths-oriented perspective, these programs should include local community leaders and culturally specific resources (e.g., extended kinship networks and religious organizations; Luthar & Cicchetti, 2000; Rolf & Johnson, 1999). Finally, an empowerment model recognizes the veridical challenges of rearing children in poverty and validates the impact of social constructions of gender and race on impoverished families, which are led predominantly by single, often minority, women.

CONCLUSIONS AND IMPLICATIONS FOR FUTURE RESEARCH

Working within an organizational model of development, we have argued that the successful negotiation of early developmental issues provides a foundation for the process of resilience among disadvantaged youth. This process originates in early transactional exchanges between the child and her or his caregiver that scaffold the child's developing capacities for adaptive emotion regulation, social engagement, and positive expectations of the social world and of the self. We suggest that prevention and intervention programs aimed at developing strong, supportive, responsive, and successful early parent–child relationships are critical to fostering the process of resilience in high-risk populations. Moreover, such efforts should begin early and should be offered in the context of a multipronged, support-based intervention program. Finally, given that evaluations of developmentally sensitive intervention efforts can serve to confirm or disconfirm our hypotheses about developmental processes (Cicchetti & Toth, 1992), we encourage the pursuit of carefully executed evaluation research aimed at ascertaining the features of relationship-based interventions that appear to be most efficacious.

A history of adaptive negotiation of salient developmental issues endows children with the capacity to adaptively engage psychosocial stressors. Resilience, then, is not an outcome in and of itself. Rather, it is a dynamic developmental process that enables children to achieve positive adaptation despite prior or concomitant adversity. Therefore, resilience cannot be dissociated from the child's developmental history, nor can it be studied independently of the child's current developmental context. Only by understanding the salient features of a child's developmental history and her or his psychosocial context can we begin to develop and implement effective prevention and intervention programs that foster the raising of successfully adapting youth within at-risk populations.

References

Anthony, E. J. (1987). Risk, vulnerability, and resilience: An overview. In E. J. Anthony & B. J. Cohler (Eds.), *The invulnerable child* (pp. 3–48). New York: Guilford Press.

Barnard, K. E., Magyary, D., Sumner, G., Booth, C. L., Mitchell, S. K., & Spieker, S. (1988). Prevention of parenting alterations for women with low social support. *Psychiatry, 51,* 248–254.

Beckwith, L. (1988). Intervention with disadvantaged parents of sick preterm infants. *Psychiatry, 51,* 242–247.

Belle, D. (1990). Poverty and women's mental health. *American Psychologist, 45*(3), 385–389.

Black, M. M., & Krishnakumar, A. (1998). Children in low-income, urban settings: Interventions to promote mental health and well-being. *American Psychologist, 53*(6), 635–646.

Bolger, K. E., Patterson, C. J., Thompson, W. W., & Kupersmidt, J. B. (1995). Psychosocial adjustment among children experiencing persistent and intermittent family economic hardship. *Child Development, 66,* 1107–1129.

Bowlby, J. (1973). *Attachment and loss: Vol. 2: Separation*. New York: Basic Books.

Bradley, R. H., Whiteside, L., Mundfron, D. J., Casey, P. H., Kelleher, K. J., & Pope, S. K. (1994). Early indications of resilience and their relation to experiences in the home environments of low birthweight, premature children living in poverty. *Child Development, 65*, 346–360.

Brooks, R. B. (1994). Children at risk: Fostering resilience and hope. *American Journal of Orthopsychiatry, 64*(4), 545–553.

Brooks-Gunn, J. (1995). Children in families and communities: Risk and intervention in the Bronfenbrenner tradition. In P. Moen, G. H. Elder, & K. Luscher (Eds.), *Examining lives in context* (pp. 467–451). Washington, DC: American Psychological Association.

Brooks-Gunn, J., & Duncan, G. J. (1997). The effects of poverty on children. *The Future of Children, 7*(2), 55–71.

Brooks-Gunn, J., Duncan, G. J., & Maritato, N. (1997). Poor families, poor outcomes: The well-being of children and youth. In G. J. Duncan & J. Brooks-Gunn (Eds.), *Consequences of growing up poor* (pp. 1–17). New York: Russell Sage Foundation.

Carlson, E. A., & Sroufe, L. A. (1995). The contribution of attachment theory to developmental psychopathology. In D. Cicchetti & D. Cohen (Eds.), *Developmental processes and psychopathology: Vol. 1. Theoretical perspectives and methodological approaches* (pp. 581–617). New York: Cambridge University Press.

Carlson, E. A., Sroufe, L. A., Collins, W. A., Jimerson, S., Weinfield, N., Hennighausen, K., Egeland, B., Hyson, D., Anderson, F., & Meyer, S. (1999). Early environmental support and elementary school adjustment as predictors of school adjustment in middle adolescence. *Journal of Adolescent Research, 14*, 72–94.

Cicchetti, D. (1990). A historical perspective on the discipline of developmental psychopathology. In J. Rolf, A. S. Masten, D. Cicchetti, K. H. Nuechterlein, & S. Weintraub (Eds.), *Risk and protective factors in the development of psychopathology* (pp. 2–28). New York: Cambridge University Press.

Cicchetti, D. (1993). Developmental psychopathology: Reactions, reflections, projections. *Developmental Review, 13*, 471–502.

Cicchetti, D., & Cohen, D. J. (1995). Perspectives on developmental psychopathology. In D. Cicchetti & D. J. Cohen (Eds.), *Developmental psychopathology, Vol. 1: Theory and methods* (pp. 3–17). New York: Wiley.

Cicchetti, D., & Rogosch, F. A. (1996). Equifinality and multifinality in developmental psychopathology. *Development and Psychopathology, 8*, 597–600.

Cicchetti, D., & Schneider-Rosen, K. (1986). An organizational approach to childhood depression. In M. Rutter, C. E. Izard, & P. B. Read (Eds.), *Depression in young people: Developmental and clinical perspectives* (pp. 71–134). New York: Guilford Press.

Cicchetti, D., & Toth, S. L. (1992). The role of developmental theory in prevention and intervention. *Development and Psychopathology, 4*, 489–493.

Cicchetti, D., Toth, S. L., & Rogosch, F. A. (1999). The efficacy of toddler–parent psychotherapy to increase attachment security in offspring of depressed mothers. *Attachment and Human Development, 1*(1), 34–66.

Coie, J. D., Watt, N. F., West, S. G., Hawkins, J. D., Asarnow, J. R., Markman, H. J., Ramey, S. L., Shure, M. B., & Long, B. (1993). The science of prevention: A conceptual framework and some directions for a national research program. *American Psychologist, 48,* 1013–1022.

Cooper, P. J., & Murray, L. (1997). The impact of psychobiological treatments of postpartum depression on maternal mood and infant development. In L. Murray & P. J. Cooper (Eds.), *Postpartum depression and child development* (pp. 201–220). New York: Guilford Press.

Costello, E. J., Farmer, M. Z., Angold, A., Burns, B. J., & Erkanli, A. (1997). Psychiatric disorders among American Indian and White youth in Appalachia: The Great Smoky Mountains Study. *American Journal of Public Health, 87,* 827–832.

Cowen, E. L., Work, W. C., & Wyman, P. A. (1997). The Rochester Resilience Project (RCRP): Facts found, lessons learned, future directions divined. In S. S. Luthar, J. A. Burack, D. Cicchetti, & J. R. Weisz (Eds.), *Developmental psychopathology: Perspectives on adjustment, risk, and disorder* (pp. 527–547). New York: Cambridge University Press.

Cowen, E. L., Wyman, P. A., Work, W. C., & Parker, G. R. (1990). The Rochester Child Resilience Project: Overview and summary of first year findings. *Development and Psychopathology, 2,* 193–212.

Crittenden, P. M., & Bonvillian, J. D. (1984). The relationship between maternal risk status and maternal sensitivity. *American Journal of Orthopsychiatry, 54*(2), 250–262.

Dawson, G., Ashman, S. B., & Carver, L. J. (2000). The role of early experience in shaping behavioral and brain development and its implications for social policy. *Development and Psychopathology, 12,* 695–712.

Duncan, G. J., Brooks-Gunn, J., & Klebanov, P. K. (1994). Economic deprivation and early childhood development. *Child Development, 65,* 296–318.

Egeland, B., & Abery, B. (1991). A longitudinal study of high-risk children: Educational outcomes. *International Journal of Disability, Development, and Education, 38*(3), 271–287.

Egeland, B., & Brunnquell, D. (1979). An at-risk approach to the study of child abuse: Some preliminary findings. *Journal of the American Academy of Child Psychiatry, 18,* 219–235.

Egeland, B., Carlson, E., & Sroufe, L. A. (1993). Resilience as process. *Development and Psychopathology, 5*(4), 517–528.

Egeland, B., & Erickson, M. F. (1993). Attachment theory and findings: Implications for prevention and intervention. In S. Kramer & H. Parens (Eds.), *Prevention in mental health: Now, tomorrow, ever?* (pp. 21–50). Northvale, NJ: Aronson.

Egeland, B., Jacobvitz, D., & Sroufe, L. A. (1988). Breaking the cycle of abuse. *Child Development, 59*(4), 1080–1088.

Egeland, B., Kalkoske, M., Gottesman, N., & Erickson, M. F. (1990). Preschool behavior problems: Stability and factors accounting for change. *Journal of Child Psychology and Psychiatry, 31*(6), 891–909.

Egeland, B., & Kreutzer, T. (1991). A longitudinal study of the effects of maternal stress and protective factors on the development of high risk children. In E. M. Cummings, A. L. Greene, & K. H. Karraker (Eds.), *Life-span developmental psychology: Perspectives on stress and coping* (pp. 61–85). Hillsdale, NJ: Erlbaum.

Egeland, B., Pianta, R. C., & O'Brien, M. A. (1993). Maternal intrusiveness in infancy and child maladaptation in early school years. *Development and Psychopathology, 5(3)*, 359–370.

Egeland, B., Weinfield, N. S., Bosquet, M., & Cheng, V. K. (2000). Remembering, repeating, and working through: Lessons from attachment-based interventions. In J. D. Osofsky & H. E. Fitzgerald (Eds.), *Infant mental health in groups at high risk. WAIMH handbook of infant mental health* (Vol. 4, pp. 35–89). New York: Wiley.

Eisenberg, N., Guthrie, I. K., Fabes, R. A., Reiser, M., Murphy, B. C., Holgren, R., Maszk, P., & Losoya, S. (1997). The relations of regulation and emotionality to resiliency and competent social functioning in elementary school children. *Child Development, 68(2)*, 295–311.

Elicker, J., Englund, M., & Sroufe, L. A. (1992). Predicting peer competence and peer relationships in childhood from early parent–child relationships. In R. Parke & G. Ladd (Eds.), *Family–peer relationships: Modes of linkage* (pp. 77–106). Hillsdale, NJ: Erlbaum.

Englund, M., Levy, A., Hyson, D., & Sroufe, L. A. (2000). Adolescent social competence: Effectiveness in a group setting. *Child Development, 71*, 1049–1060.

Escalona, S. (1987). *Critical issues in the early development of premature infants.* New Haven, CT: Yale University Press.

Farber, E. A., & Egeland, B. (1987). Invulnerability among abused and neglected children. In E. J. Anthony & B. Cohler (Eds.), *The invulnerable child* (pp. 253–288). New York: Guilford Press.

Fraiberg, S., Adelson, E., & Shapiro, V. (1980). Ghosts in the nursery: A psychoanalytic approach to the problems of impaired infant–mother relationships. In S. Fraiberg (Ed.), *Clinical studies in infant mental health* (pp. 164–196). New York: Basic Books.

Freedman, M. (1993). *The kindness of strangers.* San Francisco: Jossey-Bass.

Garmezy, N. (1974). The study of competence in children at risk for severe psychopathology. In E. J. Anthony & C. Koupernik (Eds.), *The child in his family: Children at psychiatric risk* (Vol. 3, pp. 77–97). New York: Wiley.

Garmezy, N. (1981). Children under stress: Perspectives on antecedents and correlates of vulnerability and resistance to psychopathology. In A. I. Rabin, J. Aronoff, A. M. Barclay, & R. Zucker (Eds.), *Further explorations in personality* (pp. 196–269). New York: Wiley Interscience.

Garmezy, N. (1991). Resiliency and vulnerability to adverse developmental outcomes associated with poverty. *American Behavioral Scientist, 34(4)*, 416–430.

Glantz, M. D., & Sloboda, Z. (1999). Analysis and reconceptualization of resilience. In M. D. Glantz & J. L. Johnson (Eds.), *Resilience and development: Positive life adaptations* (pp. 109–126). New York: Kluwer Academic/Plenum.

Grizenko, N., & Pawliuk, N. (1994). Risk and protective factors for disruptive behavior disorders in children. *American Journal of Orthopsychiatry, 64(4)*, 534–544.

Hall, L. A., Williams, C. A., & Greenberg, R. S. (1985). Supports, stressors, and depressive symptoms in low-income mothers of young children. *American Journal of Public Health, 75*, 518–522.

Halpern, R. (1993). Poverty and infant development. In C. H. Zeanah (Ed.), *Handbook of infant mental health* (pp. 73–86). New York: Guilford Press.

Jessor, R., Turbin, M. S., & Costa, F. M. (1998). Risk and protection in successful outcomes among disadvantaged adolescents. *Applied Developmental Science, 2*(4), 194–208.

Jimerson, S., Carlson, E. A., Rotert, M., Egeland, B., & Sroufe, L. A. (1997). A prospective, longitudinal study of the correlates and consequences of early grade retention. *Journal of School Psychology, 35*(1), 3–25.

Jimerson, S., Egeland, B., Sroufe, L. A., & Carlson, E. A. (2000). A prospective, longitudinal study of high-school dropouts: Examining multiple predictors across development. *Journal of School Psychology, 38*(6), 525–549.

Jones, E. D., & McCurdy, K. (1992). The links between types of maltreatment and demographic characteristics of children. *Child Abuse and Neglect, 16*, 201–215.

Lieberman, A. F., Weston, D. R., & Pawl, J. H. (1991). Preventive intervention and outcome with anxiously attached dyads. *Child Development, 62*, 199–209.

Limber, S. P., & Nation, M. A. (1998). Violence within the neighborhood and community. In P. K. Trickett & C. J. Schellenbach (Eds.), *Violence against children in the family and the community* (pp. 171–209). Washington, DC: American Psychological Association.

Luthar, S. S. (1991). Vulnerability and resilience: A study of high-risk adolescents. *Child Development, 62*, 600–616.

Luthar, S. S. (1999). *Poverty and children's adjustment* (Vol. 41). Thousand Oaks, CA: Sage.

Luthar, S. S., & Cicchetti, D. (2000). The construct of resilience: Implications for interventions and social policies. *Development and Psychopathology, 12*, 857–885.

Luthar, S. S., Cicchetti, D., & Becker, B. (2000). The construct of resilience: A critical evaluation and guidelines for future work. *Child Development, 71*(3), 543–562.

Lyons-Ruth, K., Connell, D. B., & Grunebaum, H. U. (1990). Infants at risk: Maternal depression and family support services as mediators of infant development and security of attachment. *Child Development 61*(1), 85–98.

Masten, A. (1986). Humor and competence in school-age children. *Child Development, 57*, 461–473.

Masten, A. S., Best, K. M., & Garmezy, N. (1990). Resilience and development: Contributions from the study of children who overcome adversity. *Development and Psychopathology, 2*, 425–444.

Masten, A. S., & Coatsworth, J. D. (1998). The development of competence in favorable and unfavorable environments. *American Psychologist, 53*(2), 205–220.

Masten, A. S., Garmezy, N., Tellegen, A., Pellegrini, D. S., Larkin, K., & Larsen, A. (1988). Competence and stress in school children: The moderating effects of individual and family qualities. *Journal of Child Psychology and Psychiatry, 29*(6), 745–764.

Masten, A. S., Hubbard, J. J., Gest, S. D., Tellegen, A., Garmezy, N., & Ramirez, M. (1999). Competence in the context of adversity: Pathways to resilience and maladaptation from childhood to late adolescence. *Development and Psychopathology, 11*, 143–169.

Masten, A. S., & Wright, M. O. (1998). Cumulative risk and protection models of child maltreatment. *Journal of Aggression, Maltreatment and Trauma, 2*(1), 7–30.

Masterpasqua, F. (1989). A competence paradigm for psychological practice. *American Psychologist, 44*(11), 1366–1371.

McLeod, J. D., & Shanahan, M. J. (1993). Poverty, parenting, and children's mental health. *American Sociological Review, 58*, 351–366.

McLoyd, V. C. (1990). The impact of economic hardship on black families and children: Psychological distress, parenting and socioemotional development. *Child Development, 61*, 311–346.

McLoyd, V. C. (1998). Socioeconomic disadvantage and child development. *American Psychologist, 53*(2), 185–204.

Minuchin, S. (1967). *Families of the slums.* New York: Basic Books.

Murphy, L. B., & Moriarty, A. E. (1976). *Vulnerability, coping and growth: From infancy to adolescence.* New Haven, CT: Yale University Press.

Musick, J. S., Stott, F. M., Spencer, K. K., Goldman, J., & Cohler, B. J. (1987). Maternal factors related to vulnerability and resiliency in young children at risk. In E. J. Anthony & B. J. Cohler (Eds.), *The invulnerable child* (pp. 229–252). New York: Guilford Press.

Olds, D. L., Henderson, C. R. J., Tatelbaum, R., & Chamberlin, R. (1988). Improving the life-course development of socially disadvantaged mothers: A randomized trial of nurse home visitation. *American Journal of Public Health, 78*, 1436–1445.

Pianta, R. C., & Egeland, B. (1990). Life stress and parenting outcomes in a disadvantaged sample: Results of the Mother–Child Interaction Project. *Journal of Clinical Child Psychology, 19*(4), 329–336.

Pianta, R. C., & Egeland, B. (1994). Predictors of instability in children's mental test performance at 24, 48, and 96 months. *Intelligence, 18*(2), 145–163.

Pianta, R. C., Hyatt, A., & Egeland, B. (1986). Maternal relationship history as an indicator of developmental risk. *American Journal of Orthopsychiatry, 56*(2), 385–398.

Pianta, R. C., Sroufe, L. A., & Egeland, B. (1989). Continuity and discontinuity in maternal sensitivity at 6, 24, and 42 months in a high risk sample. *Child Development, 60*(2), 481–487.

Ramey, C. T., & Ramey, S. L. (1998). Early intervention and early experience. *American Psychologist, 53*(2), 109–120.

Rolf, J. E., & Johnson, J. L. (1999). Opening doors to resilience intervention for prevention research. In M. D. Glantz & J. L. Johnson (Eds.), *Resilience and development: Positive life adaptations* (pp. 229–249). New York: Kluwer Academic/Plenum.

Rubin, K. H., Coplan, R. J., Fox, N. A., & Calkins, S. D. (1995). Emotionality, emotion regulation, and preschoolers' social adaptation. *Development and Psychopathology, 7*, 49–62.

Rutter, M. (1979). Protective factors in children's responses to stress and disadvantage. In M. W. Kent & J. E. Rolf (Eds.), *Primary prevention of psychopathology: Social competence in children* (pp. 49–74). Hanover, NH: University Press of New England.

Sameroff, A. J. (2000). Dialectical processes in developmental psychopathology. In A. J. Sameroff, M. Lewis, & S. Miller (Eds.), *Handbook of developmental psychopathology* (2nd ed., pp. 23–40). New York: Kluwer Academic/Plenum.

Sameroff, A. J., & Chandler, M. J. (1975). Reproductive risk and the continuum of caretaking casualty. In F. D. Horowitz, M. Hetherington, S. Scarr-Salapatek, & G. Siegel (Eds.), *Review of child development research* (Vol. 4, pp. 187–243). Chicago: University of Chicago Press.

Sameroff, A. J., & Seifer, R. (1983). Familial risk and child competence. *Child Development, 54*, 1254–1268.

Sameroff, A. J., Seifer, R., Zax, M., & Barocas, R. (1987). Early indicators of developmental risk: Rochester Longitudinal Study. *Schizophrenia Bulletin, 13*(3), 383–394.

Sampson, R. J., & Laub, J. H. (1994). Urban poverty and the family context of delinquency: A new look at structure and process in a classic study. *Child Development, 65*, 523–540.

Schorr, L. (1988). *Within our reach: Breaking the cycle of disadvantage.* New York: Anchor Press.

Seifer, R., & Sameroff, A. J. (1987). Multiple determinants of risk and vulnerability. In E. J. Anthony & B. J. Cohler (Eds.), *The invulnerable child* (pp. 51–69). New York: Guilford Press.

Shore, A. N. (1994). *Affect regulation and the origin of the self: The neurobiology of emotional development.* Hillsdale, NJ: Erlbaum.

Smith, J. R., & Prior, M. (1995). Temperament and stress resilience in school-age children: A within families study. *Journal of the American Academy of Child and Adolescent Psychiatry, 34*(2), 168–179.

Smith, J. R., Brooks-Gunn, J., & Klebanov, P. K. (1997). Consequences of living in poverty for young children's cognitive and verbal ability and early school achievement. In G. J. Duncan & J. Brooks-Gunn (Eds.), *Consequences of growing up poor* (pp. 132–189). New York: Russell Sage Foundation.

Smith, S. (1995). *Two generation programs for families in poverty: A new intervention strategy* (Vol. 9). Norwood, NJ: Ablex.

Sroufe, L. A. (1979). The coherence of individual development: Early care, attachment, and subsequent developmental issues. *American Psychologist, 34*(10), 834–841.

Sroufe, L. A. (1983). Infant–caregiver attachment and patterns of adaptation in preschool: The roots of maladaptation and competence. In M. Perlmutter (Ed.), *Minnesota symposium in child psychology* (Vol. 16, pp. 129–135). Hillsdale, NJ: Erlbaum.

Sroufe, L. A. (1989). Pathways to adaptation and maladaptation: Psychopathology as developmental deviation. In D. Cicchetti (Ed.), *The emergence of a discipline: Rochester symposia on developmental psychopathology* (Vol. 1, pp. 13–40). Hillsdale, NJ: Erlbaum.

Sroufe, L. A. (1997). Psychopathology as an outcome of development. *Development and Psychopathology, 9*, 251–268.

Sroufe, L. A., Carlson, E. A., Levy, A. K., & Egeland, B. (1999). Implications of attachment theory for developmental psychopathology. *Development and Psychopathology, 11*, 1–13.

Sroufe, L. A., & Egeland, B. (1991). Illustrations of person and environment interaction from a longitudinal study. In T. Wachs & R. Plomin (Eds.), *Conceptualization and measurement of organism-environment interaction* (pp. 68–84). Washington, DC: American Psychological Association.

Sroufe, L. A., Egeland, B., & Kreutzer, T. (1990). The fate of early experience following developmental change: Longitudinal approaches to individual adaptation in childhood. *Child Development, 61*, 1363–1373.

Sroufe, L. A., & Fleeson, J. (1986). Attachment and the construction of relationships. In W. Hartup & Z. Rubin (Eds.), *Relationships and development* (pp. 51–71). Hillsdale, NJ: Erlbaum.

Sroufe, L. A., & Rutter, M. (1984). The domain of developmental psychopathology. *Child Development, 55*, 17–29.

Sroufe, L. A., Schork, E., Motti, F., Lawroski, N., & LaFreniere, P. (1984). The role of affect in social competence. In C. E. Izard, J. Kagan, & R. Zajonc (Eds.), *Emotions, cognition, and behavior* (pp. 289–319). New York: Plenum.

Tronick, E. Z. (1989). Emotions and emotional communication in infants. *American Psychologist, 44*(2), 112–119.

U.S. Bureau of the Census. (1997). *Statistical abstract of the United States: 1997*. Washington, DC: U.S. Government Printing Office.

Van den Boom, D. C. (1995). Do first-year intervention effects endure? Follow-up during toddlerhood of a sample of Dutch irritable infants. *Child Development, 66*, 1798–1816.

Waters, E., & Sroufe, L. A. (1983). Social competence as developmental construct. *Developmental Review, 3*, 79–97.

Werner, E. E. (1990). Protective factors and individual resilience. In S. J. Meisels & J. P. Shonkoff (Eds.), *Handbook of early childhood intervention* (pp. 97–116). New York: Cambridge University Press.

Werner, E. E. (1993). Risk, resilience, and recovery: Perspectives from the Kauai Longitudinal Study. *Development and Psychopathology, 5*, 503–515.

Werner, E. E. (1995). Resilience in development. *Current Directions in Psychological Science, 4*(3), 81–85.

Werner, E. E., & Smith, R. S. (1992). *Overcoming the odds*. Ithaca, NY: Cornell University Press.

Werner, H., & Kaplan, B. (1964). *Symbol formation: An organismic-developmental approach to language and the expression of thought*. New York: Wiley.

Windle, M. (1999). Critical conceptual and measurement issues in the study of resilience. In M. D. Glantz & J. L. Johnson (Eds.), *Resilience and development: Positive life adaptations* (pp. 161–176). New York: Kluwer Academic/Plenum.

Wyman, P. A., Cowen, E. L., Work, W. C., & Parker, G. R. (1991). Developmental and family milieu interview correlates of resilience in urban children who have experienced major life stress. *American Journal of Community Psychology, 19*, 405–426.

Wyman, P. A., Cowen, E. L., Work, W. C., Raoof, A., Gribble, P. A., Parker, G. R., & Wannon, M. (1992). Interviews with children who experienced major life stress: Family and child attributes that predict resilient outcomes. *Journal of the American Academy of Child and Adolescent Psychiatry, 31*(5), 904–910.

Wyman, P. A., Sandler, I., Wolchik, S., & Nelson, K. (2000). Resilience as cumulative competence promotion and stress protection: Theory and intervention. In D. Cicchetti, J. Rappaport, I. Sandler, & R. P. Weissberg (Eds.), *The promotion of wellness in children and adolescents* (pp. 133–184). Washington, DC: Child Welfare League of America.

Yoshikawa, H. (1994). Prevention as cumulative protection: Effects of early family support and education on chronic delinquency and its risks. *Psychological Bulletin, 115*(1), 28–54.

Zaslow, M., Dion, M. J., Robin, M., Morrison, D. R., Weinfield, N., Ogawa, J., & Tabors, P. (1999). Protective factors in the development of preschool-age children of young mothers receiving welfare. In E. M. Hetherington (Ed.), *Coping with divorce, single parenting, and remarriage: A risk and resiliency perspective* (pp. 193–223). Mahwah, NJ: Erlbaum.

11

Poverty and Early Childhood Adjustment

Elizabeth B. Owens and Daniel S. Shaw

Childhood poverty appears to be an enduring and entrenched problem, resistant to most social and economic policies intended to lift families above the poverty line. Although rates of poverty among families of pre–school-age children initially declined during the 1960s, when antipoverty programs directed at children and families were initiated, rates rose throughout the 1970s and 1980s and leveled off in the 1990s, with the consequence that young children continue to experience poverty at alarmingly high rates. In fact, in 1999 about one in five infants and preschool-age children in the United States lived in families whose incomes fell below the poverty threshold (U.S. Census Bureau, 2000a). Poverty is considered a pervasive and nonspecific stressor, rather than a bounded one, because it negatively affects many aspects of individual and family functioning; yet at the same time, many impoverished children are positively adjusted (Garmezy, 1991; Luthar, 1999; Werner & Smith, 1992). How is it that some children are vulnerable to the effects of poverty, whereas others demonstrate positive adjustment (i.e., resilience)? Attempts to answer this question are at the core of this chapter. Our primary objective is twofold: to summarize findings from relevant literatures regarding factors associated with better or worse adjustment

The authors would like to thank the mothers and their sons who generously donated their time to participate in this research project. This project was sponsored by a National Research Service Award from the National Institutes of Health to the first author (#MH 12792) and both R01 (#MH 50907) and K awards (#MH 01666) from the National Institutes of Health to the second author.

Send correspondence to Elizabeth Owens, Institute of Human Development, Tolman Hall, mc1690, University of California, Berkeley, CA, 94720-1690.

among young impoverished children, and to showcase one effort toward the identification of such factors using data from the Pitt Mother and Child Project, a longitudinal study of adjustment and psychopathology among young boys from low-income families. In addition to identifying predictive factors, we will consider whether they are associated with outcomes among all children in the sample or just those at highest risk. We will also test the limits of resilient adjustment across time, and will discuss implications our findings have for both basic developmental science and early intervention programs.

POVERTY AS A RISK FACTOR FOR EARLY CHILDHOOD DEVELOPMENT

To be established as a risk factor, a variable must temporally precede the negative outcome with which it is associated and must have a meaningful association with that outcome (Kraemer et al., 1997). Early childhood poverty, by which we mean living in a family prior to the age of 5 whose income falls below a specified level necessary for minimum coverage of basic expenses (usually the federal poverty thresholds set by the U.S. Census Bureau), clearly meets these criteria. Numerous researchers in recent decades have documented the negative child outcomes associated with living under the poverty threshold (see Brooks-Gunn & Duncan, 1997, for review), especially when poverty is experienced during the first 5 years of life (Duncan, Yeung, Brooks-Gunn, & Smith, 1998). The detrimental outcomes are many but can be grouped into three categories: poor physical health (e.g. Jason & Jarvis, 1987; Pollitt, 1994), lower intellectual attainment and poor school performance (e.g. Dubow & Ippolito, 1994; Guo, 1998), and increased likelihood of social, emotional, and behavioral problems (e.g. Dubow & Ippolito, 1994; Duncan, Brooks-Gunn, & Klebanov, 1994). In terms of effect sizes, Brooks-Gunn and Duncan (1997) document the following odds ratios for these outcomes associated with living compared to not living in childhood poverty: In the health domain, the risk for low birth weight is 1.7, for child mortality 1.7, and for lead poisoning 3.5; in the achievement domain, the risk for grade retention is 2.0; in the social/emotional/behavior domain, the risk for parent-reported behavior problems is 1.3.

Of note too is that children who live in extreme or enduring poverty have the worst outcomes (Duncan et al., 1994; Guo, 1998; Korenman, Miller, & Sjaastad, 1995). This is an important finding, as it suggests that although income poverty is typically operationalized as a static, dichotomous construct, there may be linear effects of the level of family income or duration of impoverishment. Explaining variations in child adjustment may have more to do with the severity or chronicity of poverty than with its presence or absence.

CONCEPTUALIZING POSITIVE ADJUSTMENT AMONG YOUNG IMPOVERISHED CHILDREN

Developmentalists have adopted various methods of operationalizing child positive adjustment, one of which involves the creation of indices reflecting the achievement of stage-salient developmental tasks. For example, Farber and Egeland (1987), in their study of resilient outcomes among maltreated young children, developed composite measures of positive adjustment or resilience at different ages that depended on achievement of developmentally appropriate tasks. At 18 months, secure attachment was considered resilient; at 24 months, autonomy and problem solving were; at 42 months, measures of self-regulation, success with peers, and level of self-awareness contributed to their measure of resilience. The appeal of this approach is its developmental sensitivity and inclusion of the concept of fit. Adjustment is conceptualized in different ways across development that are defined according to both the changing capacities of the child and changing environmental demands and expectations.

Operationalizing positive adjustment among impoverished children could also be guided by consideration of those domains in which they are at greatest risk for a poor outcome. This approach suggests that assessing physical health, intellectual attainment and school performance, and/or social/emotional/behavioral adjustment (the three primary domains of impairment for impoverished children) would be the best way to determine successful adjustment among these children. Children experiencing poverty might be considered positively adjusted if they are physically healthy, demonstrate the achievement of age-appropriate cognitive skills or receive good grades at school, or do not display social, emotional, or behavioral problems.

In assessing adjustment, some investigators have considered outcome domains individually, whereas others considered them collectively. In their study of maltreated children, Cicchetti, Rogosch, Lynch, and Holt (1993) measured seven indicators of competent adjustment in the following domains: aspects of interpersonal behavior with peers, indicators of psychopathology, and school difficulties. Children were defined as resilient when four or more of the indicators were present. Similarly, Radke-Yarrow and Sherman (1990) provide an example of this cross-domain approach to defining positive adjustment. In their study of children at risk due to serious psychopathology in parents, they chose a group of *survivors* (those functioning adequately) who had no psychiatric diagnoses, were performing at grade level, related well to peers and to adults at school and home, and had a positive self-concept.

We have conceptualized positive adjustment (also called resilience) as a dynamic process that is reflected in a measurable outcome and indicates competent functioning despite the experience of significant adversity (Luthar, Cicchetti, & Becker, 2000). Our focus is on social and behavioral adjustment. In our own research, impoverished children were considered positively adjusted if they displayed levels of total behavior problems at age 8 within the normal range (within .5 standard deviation above the sample median) *and* displayed levels of social skills greater than those of the sample median. In this way, positive adjustment was considered average or better adaptation in the domains of both psychopathology and social competence but not necessarily exceptional functioning. Pragmatically too, although our sample is large by some standards, we felt that it might be difficult to find many at-risk children with exceptional outcomes, and thus identified children as positively adjusted if they demonstrated at least average functioning at a particular time point.

FACTORS ASSOCIATED WITH POSITIVE ADJUSTMENT

We turn next to a brief review of factors potentially associated with positive social and behavioral adjustment among young children in poverty. As there have been relatively few studies specifically focused on adjustment patterns of this group, we also draw upon developmental theory and findings regarding adjustment of both preschool-age and school-age children at risk due to exposure to other chronic psychosocial stressors.

Within the resilience framework, factors associated with positive adjustment among at-risk children can be organized according to child, family, and community domains (Luthar & Zigler, 1991; Masten, Best, & Garmezy, 1990). In this chapter we will consider factors in the child and family domains. We do not mean to deemphasize the importance of the community domain, by which we mean extrafamilial factors such as peer relationships, relationships with adults outside of the family, and community resources. Theoretically, a number of these factors might be related to positive adjustment in young at-risk children. We chose to focus only on child and family factors because we believed that the child's own characteristics and characteristics of the parents and family environment would likely be more influential than extrafamilial factors during the early childhood period.

Child

Among the potentially most important factors affecting the adjustment of all children is the quality of attachment to their primary caregivers.[1] Bowlby's (1969) attachment theory suggests that attachment security should be related to later social and behavioral adjustment. It is thought that primarily through its impact on a child's internal working model, attachment security influences thoughts and feelings about oneself in relationship with others, and about others in relationship with one-self (Bretherton & Munholland, 1999). These thoughts and feelings are hypothesized to influence interpersonal behavior, including social competence and behavior problems that occur within relationships (e.g., noncompliance and aggression).

Infant attachment security has, in fact, been shown to predict various developmental outcomes among young children from low-income families and families with high levels of psychosocial problems (see Greenberg, 1999, for review). In particular, insecurely attached infants from such families tend to show higher levels of emotional and behavioral problems (particularly aggression) as children (Erickson, Sroufe, & Egeland, 1985; Lyons-Ruth, Alpern, & Repacholi, 1993; Renken, Egeland, Marvinney, Mangelsdorf, & Sroufe, 1989; Shaw, Owens, Vondra, Keenan, & Winslow, 1996). In one large sample of low socioeconomic status (SES) children, infant attachment security was predictive of psychopathology at ages 10–11 (Urban, Carlson, Egeland, & Sroufe, 1991). Urban et al. (1991) also reported more dependence, less ego resilience, and less social competence at follow-up among their insecurely attached infants.

A second potentially important predictive factor is child temperament. It is possible that temperament and later adjustment are linked because an underlying biological process contributes to both. It is also possible that temperamentally difficult children may elicit certain caregiver responses, such as inconsistent or harsh discipline, that then lead to later maladjustment (Bates, 1980). As predicted, certain temperamental attributes reflecting whether a child is difficult or easygoing have been shown to predict adjustment among at-risk young children. Werner and Smith (1982) described their resilient children as agreeable, cheerful, friendly, relaxed, and sociable as toddlers. Tschann, Kaiser, Chesney, Alkon, and Boyce (1996) found teacher-rated easy temperament to protect preschoolers in high-conflict families from developing teacher-rated externalizing problems. Radke-Yarrow and Sherman (1990), in their sample exposed to parental psychopathology, described the resilient young children as socially engaging and charming. Alertness, high activity, and curiosity have been found to predict resilient outcome in infants and young children exposed to multiple psychosocial stressors (Egeland & Sroufe, 1981; Farber & Egeland, 1987). Similar findings are noted among school-age children at risk, in which positive temperamental attributes have been shown to predict resilience (O'Keefe, 1994; Radke-Yarrow & Brown, 1993; Smith & Prior, 1995).

Intelligence is another attribute widely documented to protect against adversity (Luthar & Zigler, 1991; Masten & Coatsworth, 1998). Intelligent children may have an easier time learning social skills or responding to certain parental socialization efforts, such as reasoning. Perhaps IQ is associated with aspects of behavioral adjustment such as compliance because intelligent children may better understand, and therefore be able to follow, rules and procedures. It is also possible that children with higher IQs are better able to use internal verbal mediation strategies in order to regulate negative emotions, or are better able to use verbal strategies in conflict situations in order to avoid resorting to aggressive or disruptive behavior.

Among at-risk preschoolers, developmental quotients and language test scores have been found to predict positive adjustment (Erickson et al., 1985; Pianta, Egeland, & Sroufe, 1990; Werner & Smith, 1982). A number of researchers have also found child IQ to be negatively associated with disruptive behavior and school failure in their at-risk samples (Masten et al., 1990; Smith & Prior, 1995). Radke-Yarrow and Brown (1993) found high IQ to be associated with the lack of a psychiatric diagnosis. However, childhood intelligence has not consistently been found to be associated with positive adjustment (Cicchetti et al., 1993; Egeland, Kalkoske, Gottesman, & Erickson, 1990). Furthermore, among older children, it has been argued that although intelligent but stressed youth may be relatively well adjusted, they can lose their overall advantage because of greater sensitivity to negative forces in their lives (Luthar, 1999).

Given this accumulation of theory and evidence, in our own work we have explored whether infant attachment security, level of negative emotionality, and child IQ might be predictive of positive adjustment among young impoverished children.

Family

Developmental theories suggest diverse ways in which family factors might be predictive of adjustment. For example, Patterson's (1982) coercion theory carefully details patterns of reinforcement among certain negative and ineffective disciplinary strategies (e.g., giving in to a child's disruptive behavior or hitting the child) and child noncompliance and aggression. Negative and rejecting parenting may also be a model for disruptive and angry child behavior and/or could contribute to a child's low self-esteem, which may also produce behavioral maladjustment in children. Rohner (1986) argues for a biologically based need for positive interactions with caretakers and states that maladjustment is a response to rejection from caregivers. There is evidence to support such posited associations between negative parental behaviors, including criticism, punitiveness, neglect, and rejection, and different dimensions of child maladjustment in low-SES samples (Dodge, Pettit, & Bates, 1994; Shaw et al., 1998) and impoverished samples (Conger, Ge, Elder, Lorenz, & Simons, 1994; McLoyd, Jayaratne, Ceballo, & Borquez, 1994; Sampson & Laub, 1994), although much of the work with impoverished samples has involved adolescents rather than young children.

Positive parental behaviors, particularly responsiveness and acceptance, may also be associated with child adjustment (Rohner, 1986; Shaw & Bell, 1993). Such behaviors should have the opposite effect of negative and rejecting behavior in that responsiveness and acceptance may enhance the parent–child relationship and increase the effectiveness of socialization attempts. Evidence shows that among at-risk children, positive parental behaviors and parent–child relationship quality are linked with social/behavioral adjustment. Early maternal sensitivity and responsiveness (Bradley et al., 1994; Egeland & Sroufe, 1981; Erickson et al., 1985; Farber & Egeland, 1987; Shaw, Keenan, & Vondra, 1994), acceptance of child behavior (Bradley et al., 1994), and involvement (Erickson et al., 1985; Werner & Smith, 1982) have been associated with secure attachment and low levels of behavior problems in at-risk samples. Werner and Smith (1982) also reported that emotional supportiveness was associated with resilience in young at-risk children. Among school-age children, Fisher, Kokes, Cole, Perkins, and Wynne (1987) found active, warm, and reciprocal parent–child relationships to predict measures of competence in boys with psychiatrically ill parents. Mother–child warmth and relationship quality have been associated with a lack of behavior problems in children exposed to stressful life events and family violence (O'Keefe, 1994; Smith & Prior, 1995). Masten et al. (1990) found interviewer ratings of parenting quality to be protective for girls (not boys) under stress, although parenting quality was not precisely defined. A positive parent–child relationship and parental involvement have been found to be protective among at-risk children (Cowen, Wyman, Work, & Parker, 1990), and Stouthamer-Loeber et al. (1993) found a positive relationship with parents to predict nondelinquency.

Theoretically, parental personality traits and psychopathology should also be related to child adjustment. It is possible that whatever genetic influences are partly responsible for parental personality or psychopathology are passed on to children, who express those genes as behavior problems. These influences may also be environmentally mediated in that they have an impact on parental behavior and the parent–child relationship. Patterson and Capaldi (1991) found mothers with aggressive personality styles to be less effective parents and to monitor their children less well. Angry mothers might also, through modeling, teach their children to be aggressive. Mothers who are hostile and/or depressed are more likely to use inconsistent, permissive, harsh and punitive, or coercive discipline (Gelfand & Teti, 1990; Kochanska, Kuczynski, & Maguire, 1989; Peterson, Ewigman, & Vandiver, 1994). Depressed parents may be more likely to disengage from the parenting role, to withdraw emotionally from their children, and to neglect their parenting responsibilities (Gelfand & Teti, 1990; Osofsky & Thompson, 2000). Harnish, Dodge, and Valente (1995) found the association between maternal depressive symptomatology and child behavior problems for the whites in their sample to be partially mediated by poor mother–child interaction quality (i.e., low enjoyment and sensitivity, high controllingness).

However, links between parental personality and dimensions of child adjustment have been somewhat inconsistent, at least among very young children. Some find predictions in at-risk samples from negative personality traits including aggressivity and hostility (Renken et al., 1989; Shaw, Vondra, Hommerding, Keenan, & Dunn, 1994), but others do not

(Egeland & Sroufe, 1981; Egeland et al., 1990) or report relations only for girls (Pianta et al., 1990). On the other hand, evidence clearly exists for relations between maternal psychopathology, especially depression, and child behavioral adjustment (Leadbeter & Bishop, 1994; Osofsky & Thompson, 2000; Pannacione & Wahler, 1986; Rose, Rose, & Feldman, 1989; Shaw & Vondra, 1995).

Furthermore, many have argued that family factors are the primary mechanisms by which poverty influences child social and behavioral development (see *Child Development*, 1994, *65*(2), special issue on Children and Poverty). It is suggested that the strains of living in poverty negatively affect parental adjustment and behavior, for example, by increasing parental dysphoria and use of rejecting or inconsistent discipline (Brody et al., 1994; Conger et al., 1994; Dodge et al., 1994; McLoyd et al., 1994; Sampson & Laub, 1994) or by decreasing parent–child relationship quality and warmth (Dodge et al., 1994; Sampson & Laub, 1994), which may then contribute to child maladjustment.

Given this accumulation of theory and evidence, we tested whether maternal rejection, acceptance, and responsivity, mother–child relationship quality, maternal aggressive/hostile personality, and maternal depressive symptoms showed relations with social/behavioral adjustment among the impoverished children in our sample.

THE PITT MOTHER AND CHILD PROJECT

Participants and Procedures

The Pitt Mother and Child Project is an ongoing study of developmental precursors of antisocial behavior among boys from low-income families in the Pittsburgh, Pennsylvania, metropolitan area. A total of 310 infant boys and their mothers were recruited from Women, Infant, and Children (WIC) nutritional supplement clinics when the boys were approaching 1.5 years of age. Sixty percent of the mothers are white, and 40% are black. Almost two-thirds of the mothers had 12 or fewer years of education, and about 60% were married or living with partner. At 18 months, two-thirds of the families were living below the poverty threshold, and by age 6, about half were. Forty percent of the families were living below the poverty threshold at all visits between 18 months and 5 years.

Boys and their mothers have been seen at 1.5, 2, 3.5, 5, 5.5, 6, and 8 years of age in the home and/or in the lab for $1^1/_2$ to $3^1/_2$ hours. They participated in a series of developmentally appropriate unstructured and semistructured interaction tasks, many of which were videotaped for later coding. At each visit, mothers also completed questionnaires and interviews regarding demographic variables, their own adjustment, family functioning, and child behavior. Typically, 280 to 300 of the families were seen at each of the visits (after 1.5 years), so that attrition at each age was usually less than 10%.

Measures

Early Childhood Poverty

Early childhood poverty was indexed using maternal report of monthly family income and the number of people living at home at each of the 1.5-, 2-, 3.5-, and 5-year visits. Poverty thresholds were established for households of different sizes in the different years in which data were collected (U.S. Census Bureau, 2000b), and it was determined whether each boy was living in a family that was above or below the poverty threshold at each of the four visits at or before age 5. A total score ranging from 0 to 4 reflected the number of assessments at which the family was living below the poverty threshold. Eighteen percent of families never lived in poverty, 11% families lived in poverty at one visit, 12% lived in poverty at two visits, 19% lived in poverty at three visits, and 40% lived in poverty at all four visits.

Positive Adjustment

Positive adjustment was indexed using total scores from the Child Behavior Checklist (CBCL; Achenbach, 1991), completed by the mother, and the Social Skills Rating System (SSRS; Gresham & Elliot, 1989), completed by the teacher. Both instruments were administered when the child was approximately 8 years old. Both are widely used and possess satisfactory psychometric properties. The total score from the CBCL is based on both internalizing and externalizing problems; the total score from the SSRS reflects cooperation, assertiveness, and self-control with peers and adults.

In our analyses, a dichotomous score reflecting the presence or absence of positive adjustment was created. Children were considered positively adjusted if (1) their total behavior problem score from the CBCL was well within the normal range (i.e., a T score below 55, which is within .5 standard deviation above both the normative and sample median of 50) and (2) their total social skills score was higher than average (i.e., higher than the sample median of 37). Children who did not meet both of these criteria were not considered to be positively adjusted (although they were not necessarily maladjusted either). Of the 207 children with CBCL and SSRS scores, 83 (40%) were considered positively adjusted and 124 (60%) were not.

Child Factors Tested for Association with Adjustment
Infant attachment security was measured at 1.5 years using the Strange Situation procedure (Ainsworth & Wittig, 1969). Children were classified as avoidant, secure, ambivalent, or disorganized by reliable, trained raters. For these analyses, children were categorized as secure or insecure (avoidant, ambivalent, or disorganized). Child negative emotionality was measured at 1.5 years by reliable, trained raters who viewed videotapes of the hour-long lab visits and rated the frequency, duration, and intensity of child fussing and crying. Child intelligence was measured at 5.5 years using prorated Verbal and Performance scores derived from a four-scale short form of the Wechsler Preschool and Primary Scale of Intelligence – Revised (Wechsler, 1989).

Family Factors Tested for Association with Adjustment
Maternal rejection was derived at 1.5, 2, and 3.5 years from videotaped observations of a clean-up task (Winslow, Shaw, Bruns, & Kiebler, 1995), with scores averaged across age. Maternal acceptance and responsivity were derived from the Acceptance and Emotional/Verbal Responsivity subscales of the HOME Inventory (Caldwell & Bradley, 1984), an observer-report measure of maternal behavior and quality of the home environment that was completed at the age 2 visit. Parent–child relationship quality was measured using maternal report on a parent adaptation of the Teacher–Child Relationship Scale (Pianta & Steinberg, 1991), administered at 5 and 6 years. Scores from the Openness and Conflicted/Angry (negative) scales at both assessment points were averaged to create a score for mother–child relationship quality. Maternal depressive symptoms were self-reported using the total score from the Beck Depression Inventory (BDI; Beck, Ward, Mendelson, Mock, & Erbaugh, 1961) administered at 1.5, 2, 3.5, and 5 years. The average of these four scores was used in analyses. Maternal aggressive/hostile personality was measured using the Aggression subscale of the Jackson Personality Research Form (Jackson, 1967), administered at 1.5 years, and the Overt Anger subscale from the Handling Anger Questionnaire (Spielberger et al., 1985), administered at 3.5 years. Scores from these two measures

were averaged to create a single score for maternal aggressive/hostile personality.

Results

Analyses were conducted in four stages: (1) testing of associations between each child and family factor and positive adjustment among those children living below the poverty threshold at one or more visits between 1.5 and 5 years of age, (2) exploring joint effects of significant child and family factors identified at stage 1, (3) testing of main versus interactive effects of child and family factors, and (4) ascertaining cross-time limits to positive adjustment.

Stage 1

Although all children in our sample were from low-income families, some were not impoverished. Only those who were impoverished at one or more of the four visits between 1.5 and 5 years were considered at risk ($n = 235$, 82% of the original 310), and only those in this at-risk group with available CBCL *and* SSRS data at age 8 ($n = 167$, 54% of the original 310) were used in the primary analyses. Impoverished children with ($n = 66$, 40% of those analyzed) and without ($n = 101$, 60% of those analyzed) positive adjustment, according to their CBCL and SSRS total scores, were compared using a series of t-tests, and the results are presented in Table 11.1. Because these analyses were largely exploratory (few have investigated the factors associated with adjustment among young impoverished children), the only procedure chosen to control the Type I error rate was the use of two-tailed tests. Of note too is that among the 101 children without positive adjustment, 61 had either CBCL total *or* SSRS total scores that met the criteria for adjustment, whereas 40 did not meet the criteria in either domain.

Two child factors were associated with positive adjustment. Impoverished children with secure attachments at 18 months were 2.5 times more likely to be positively adjusted at age 8 compared to those with insecure infant attachments (odds ratio = 2.48; 95% CI = 1.29 to 4.80). Child Verbal IQ at age 5.5 was positively associated with positive adjustment, and the size of the IQ effect in children with versus without positive adjustment was moderate (Cohen's $d = .43$). Two family factors also showed significant associations with positive adjustment. Mothers of impoverished children who were positively adjusted at age 8 were more likely to describe

TABLE 11.1. *Comparisons between Those with and without Positive Adjustment: Differences on Child and Family Factors*

	Impoverished (n = 167; 66 Adjusted, 101 Not)		Not Impoverished (n = 40; 17 Adjusted, 23 Not)		Chronically Impoverished (n = 75; 28 Adjusted, 47 Not)	
	Test	Effect Size	Test	Effect Size	Test	Effect Size
Child Factors						
Secure attachment[a]	7.52**	2.48	.18	1.30	.35	1.33
Negative emotionality[b]	.26	.04	1.57	.51	−1.49	.36
Verbal IQ[b]	2.68**	.43	−.66	.22	.82	.25
Performance IQ[b]	1.68^	.31	1.90^	.66	1.02	.27
Family Factors						
Maternal rejection[b]	−1.88^	.30	−.01	.00	−2.58*	.63
Maternal acceptance[b]	1.66^	.28	.37	.12	.85	.21
Maternal responsivity[b]	−.51	.10	.00	.00	.52	.13
Mother–child relationship quality[b]	3.17**	.51	1.08	.39	3.43**	.85
Maternal aggressive personality[b]	−3.02**	.48	.89	.29	−2.00*	.47
Maternal depressive symptoms[b]	−1.27	.20	.26	.08	−2.55*	.59

[a] Inferential statistic is χ^2, and effect size is odds ratio.
[b] Inferential statistic is a two-tailed t-test, and effect size is Cohen's d.
^ $p < .10$, * $p < .05$, ** $p < .01$.

their relationships with their children as open and relatively free of conflict at ages 5 and 6. These same mothers also reported lower aggressive/hostile personality scores when their children were ages 1.5 to 3.5 compared to mothers of children who were not positively adjusted. The size of each of these effects was moderate (Cohen's $d = .51$ and .48, respectively).

Stage 2
In order to test joint effects while controlling for collinearity among these four child and family factors, a logistic regression equation was computed in which these factors were entered stepwise, with presence or absence of positive adjustment employed as the dependent variable. We did not enter all child and family predictors at this point in order to preserve the power to detect significant effects and chose a stepwise entry procedure due to our interest in empirically identifying those child and family factors most strongly and uniquely related to outcome. Maternal aggressive/hostile personality (Wald $= 4.43$, $p = .04$; odds ratio $= .58$, 95% CI $= .35$ to .96), infant attachment security (Wald $= 7.36$, $p = .01$; odds ratio $= 2.88$, 95% CI $= 1.34$ to 6.20), and mother–child relationship quality (Wald $= 6.25$, $p = .01$; odds ratio $= 2.04$, 95% CI $= 1.17$ to 3.59) each emerged as a statistically significant and unique predictor of child positive adjustment. (The statistics presented here are from the final step once all significant variables were entered into the equation.) Once these factors were in the equation, the relation between child Verbal IQ and positive adjustment was not significant. Therefore, with the exception of Verbal IQ, the factors individually associated with outcome continued to show unique and significant associations with positive adjustment even when considered jointly.

Stage 3
A key question is whether associations between child and family factors and positive adjustment exist only or to a greater degree in at-risk children compared to children not at risk. Statistically, the question is whether factors exert main effects (present regardless of level of risk) or interactive effects (present only or to a greater degree among children at risk). Although knowledge regarding factors associated with positive adjustment across all children is valuable, identifying factors that operate specifically under conditions of risk furthers our understanding of the concept of resilience (the process and outcome of positive adaptation despite adversity

[Luthar et al., 2000]), and some argue that only under such conditions would a factor associated with a good outcome be considered protective (Rutter, 1985).

Our sample is not ideal for testing such a question because of its restricted continuum of risk (i.e., all participants were low-income). However, we conducted analyses comparing children who were not living below the poverty threshold at *any* visit to those who were living below the poverty threshold at *every* visit. Although the proportion of positively adjusted children was not very different in these two groups (37% versus 43%, respectively), at least theoretically, chronic poverty between the ages of 1.5 and 5 years should pose greater risks to adaptive development in the long term than low family income in the absence of poverty. And despite the comparable rates of positive adjustment in these two groups, some evidence suggests that the chronically impoverished group was in fact worse off. Within both groups of children (never impoverished and chronically impoverished) who were not positively adjusted, almost all (83% and 84%, respectively) were at or below the median on social skills. However, whereas only 26% of the never impoverished children were also high on behavior problems, 53% of the chronically impoverished children showed elevated levels of behavior problems.

Hierarchical logistic regressions would typically be used to test main and interactive effects of putative predictive factors on the presence or absence of positive adjustment. In these cases, risk would be entered first, and the predictor and its interaction with risk would then be entered either stepwise or hierarchically. However, we believed that this analytic strategy was not optimal for our purposes. Entering risk on step 1 allows for tests of the effects of predictive factors once the effect of risk has been statistically controlled for, but not for tests of predictor effects within varying risk contexts. Additionally, given that statistical tests of interactions are generally low powered (Smith & Sechrest, 1991), interactions can be difficult to detect when independent variables are normally distributed (McClelland & Judd, 1993), and not all interaction effects are best represented by multiplicative interaction terms (Rutter, 1983); we instead split the sample according to high- or low-risk status. Then relations between predictors and positive adjustment were tested using *t*-tests and effect sizes within each group.

Associations between child and family factors and the presence or absence of positive adjustment in the never impoverished and chronically impoverished groups are presented in Table 11.1. As can be seen, maternal rejection, maternal depressive symptoms, and mother–child relationship quality were significantly associated with lower rates of positive adjustment only among the chronically impoverished children. Furthermore, effect sizes were notably larger among the chronically impoverished children (.63, .59, and .85, respectively) compared to effect sizes among the not impoverished children (.00, .08, and .39, respectively). Maternal aggressive/hostile personality was also significantly associated with lower rates of positive adjustment only among the chronically impoverished children, but the effect size difference between the theoretically most at-risk and low-risk groups was smaller (.78 versus .49).

Because of collinearity among predictors, relations between family factors and positive adjustment in the chronically impoverished group were probably not unique. In this group, the largest correlation among predictors was .38 between maternal depressive symptoms and aggressive personality. Absolute values of all other correlations among these four predictors were in the range of .20 to .30 (i.e., shared variance of 4% to 9%), with the exception of the .06 correlation between maternal rejection and depressive symptoms. Given the relatively small number of subjects in the never impoverished and chronically impoverished groups, logistic regressions accounting for collinearity among variables by including all predictors were notably underpowered to detect significant effects and were not computed. Therefore, our findings suggesting that less maternal rejection and depression, and better-quality mother–child relationships, were associated with positive adjustment primarily among those presumably at highest risk, a suggestion that must be interpreted with the collinearity among these predictors in mind.

Stage 4

In order to explore the cross-time stability of positive adjustment among our participants, children who were impoverished and positively adjusted at age 8 were selected ($n = 66$). Forty of these children had CBCL and SSRS ratings available at age 6. Of these 40, 25 met the criteria for positive adjustment at age 6. In other words, 62% of the impoverished children who showed positive adjustment at age 8 and had data available at age 6 showed positive adjustment at age 6. Furthermore, of the entire 112 impoverished children who had CBCL and SSRS data available at ages 6 and 8, 73% showed stability of adjustment across time (positively adjusted or not positively adjusted at both times), whereas 27% were positively adjusted at one time and not at the other. Although the amount of missing data prevents us from drawing firm conclusions, these descriptive statistics suggest stability of adjustment ratings among a majority of children in our sample.

We also investigated which child and family factors were associated with cross-time stability versus instability of positive adjustment in the 112 impoverished children with CBCL and SSRS data at ages 6 and 8. Using a logistic regression equation, we entered all 10 child and family factors stepwise to see which best predicted positive adjustment at ages 6 *and* 8 ($n = 25$) versus positive adjustment at 6 *or* 8 ($n = 30$) among the impoverished children in our sample. Only child Verbal IQ emerged as a statistically significant predictor of stable positive adjustment versus unstable positive adjustment (Wald = 5.98, $p = .01$; odds ratio = 1.09, 95% CI = 1.02 to 1.16). Although given 10 putative predictors this test was underpowered to detect more than one significant effect, results of a series of 10 *t*-tests revealed similar results (only Verbal and Performance IQ were associated with the presence or absence of stable positive adjustment).

SUMMARY AND CONCLUSIONS

We aimed to identify factors associated with positive adjustment at age 8, defined by a lack of behavior problems and above-average social skills, among the impoverished young children participating in the Pitt Mother and Child Project. Our search was guided by developmental theory and empirical evidence regarding factors that might discriminate those who were considered positively adjusted from those who were not. These factors included infant attachment security and temperament, child IQ, mothers' rejection, depressive symptoms, aggressive/hostile personality, acceptance and responsivity, and the quality of the mother–child relationship.

Results indicated unique and moderately strong effects for secure attachment, a good mother–child relationship, and lack of maternal aggression/hostility. Among children who lived below the poverty threshold at some point between the ages of 1.5 and 5 years, those with secure attachment at 18 months were 2.5 times as likely as others to show positive adjustment 5.5 years later. Similarly, the average mother–child relationship quality score at ages 5 to 6 was twice as large, and the early-measured maternal aggressive/hostile personality score was half as large, for children who were positively adjusted at age 8 compared to those who were not. Verbal IQ was also associated with later adjustment but only when considered individually.

These primary findings suggest predictability across stages of child-hood development from infancy to middle childhood. Although predictive factors measured during the infant/preschool period may simply be associated with causal factors not identified, it is possible that certain early experiences have lasting effects. Primary findings also implicate the importance of the child's close relationships and the affective or emotional aspects of the family environment in the prediction of positive adjustment. Exactly how close relationships and the affective nature of a child's immediate environment influence adjustment is not suggested by our findings, but it is possible that the impact is either direct (e.g., modeling of negative affectivity resulting in child behavior problems and poor interpersonal skills) or indirect (e.g., maternal aggressive personality negatively impacting disciplinary behaviors, which then lead to behavior problems).

In order to determine whether a factor was associated with the outcome regardless of risk or to a greater degree among children most at risk, we compared those who were low income but never impoverished to those were who were impoverished throughout their first 5 years of life. Maternal rejection, depressive symptoms, and mother–child relationship quality were significantly related to positive adjustment only among those most at risk, and each showed moderate to large effect size differences across the most and least at-risk groups. This suggests that these family factors interact with risk status in the prediction of positive outcome, rather than exerting primarily main effects regardless of risk status. However, the findings must be interpreted with caution because of our inability to account for collinearity among the predictors.

Such interactive effects may be interpreted as protection afforded by the presence of certain positive family factors (e.g., high-quality mother–child relationship) or as increased vulnerability due to the presence of negative family factors (e.g., low-quality mother–child relationship). Stouthamer-Loeber et al. (1993) drew attention to this issue when they identified a number of *double-edged* variables that contained both protective and risk effects for delinquency. A high-quality mother–child relationship might be protective because, in the context of frequent and intense stressors (often found in the environments of chronically impoverished children), there is a special need for the parent–child relationship to be strong. However, it could also be argued that a high-quality mother–child relationship or low levels of maternal depressive or aggressive symptoms should predict positive adjustment regardless of a child's level of risk and therefore are not best described as protective. Rather, such predictive factors should increase vulnerability by having a greater impact in an already risk-laden situation, as is suggested by a cumulative threshold model. Up to a certain point, family factors appear less influential. However, in the presence of chronic poverty, certain family factors are more important for adjustment. It also may be that chronically impoverished children have few ways to compensate for a poor relationship with their mothers or for the experience of maternal rejection (e.g., they may not have another parent at home or a caring teacher at school to whom to turn), which might explain the greater negative effect of certain family factors.

The stronger associations between mother and child adjustment among the chronically poor children may also have been due to the fact that mothers perhaps were globally maladjusted, that is, when depressed, their own adjustment, their relationship with their children, *and* their ratings of their children's adjustment (which partially determined who was positively adjusted) all looked bleak. Alternatively, perhaps high maternal maladjustment operated as a third variable, leading both to maternal inability to work and subsequent chronic poverty (Knitzer, Yoshikawa, Cauthen, & Aber, 2000) and to high levels of child maladjustment, with effects on children being either environmentally or genetically mediated.

Our findings indicated modest consistency of resilient status across domains and over time. Of the at-risk children who showed positive adjustment at age 8 in at least one of the two domains considered (behavior problems and social skills), about half were well adjusted in both, whereas half did well in one area but not in the other. Almost two-thirds of the impoverished children who met the criteria for positive adjustment at age 8 had also shown positive adjustment at age 6. Family factors did not predict stable versus unstable positive adjustment, but child verbal intelligence did. It is possible that because children leave the confines of home and enter school at around age 6, their own coping abilities (as opposed to parental characteristics and behaviors) come to play a greater role in determining whether they tend to retain the patterns of adjustment shown previously.

Without knowledge of the causal mechanisms underlying associations between child and family factors and positive adjustment, the following implications for early intervention are tentatively suggested. When one's goal is to foster positive adjustment among children in poverty, our findings suggest the need for concerted attention to promoting positive mother–child relationships. This idea is supported by our data on impoverished infants with insecure attachments to their mothers, who were more than twice as likely to manifest subsequent maladjustment compared to those with secure attachments early in life, and our finding that mother–child relationship quality at ages 5 to 6 was associated with the presence of positive adjustment at age 8. The promotion of positive mother–child relationships may be particularly important for those experiencing chronic poverty. As noted previously, perhaps because there are typically frequent and intense stressors in the environments of chronically impoverished children, there is a greater need for the parent–child relationship to be strong. The promotion of a positive mother–child relationship could be achieved through parent–infant psychotherapy (Heinicke et al., 1999; Lieberman & Zeanah, 1999) or multisystemic family therapy (Henggeler, 1990), the latter addressing both proximal and more distal risk factors that compromise the quality of caregiving (Shaw, Bell, & Gilliom, 2000). Aspects of maternal adjustment (aggressive/hostile personality and depressive symptoms) should also be targets of intervention, perhaps especially among chronically impoverished families. Maternal adjustment might be directly treated with individual therapy or medication. As a relevant example, Luthar and Suchman (1999) stressed the importance of using supportive psychotherapy to address maternal comorbid psychopathology and adjustment problems among low-SES substance-abusing mothers when the goal is to improve parenting behaviors and mother–child relationships.

In summary, in our study of impoverished children, we found that positive adjustment at age 8 was associated with secure attachment manifested at 18 months, low maternal aggressive personality at 1.5 to 3.5 years, and positive mother–child relationships at 5 to 6 years. Comparisons between children who experienced chronic poverty and those who were never impoverished (but were nevertheless low-income) suggested that the presence or absence of positive adjustment at age 8 among the former group was more strongly linked with prior maternal rejection, maternal depressive symptoms, and poor mother–child relationship quality than among the latter. Our findings regarding the limits of positive adjustment point to the dangers of assuming that resilience is either absolute across domains or fixed over time. At the same time, our findings underscore the potential benefits of preventive early interventions that foster secure infant attachments and positive mother–child relationships, as well as interventions designed to address maternal adjustment problems, when one's goal is to promote positive social and behavioral adjustment among impoverished children.

Note

1. We have chosen to place attachment in the child domain because, as measured by the Strange Situation, it is fundamentally a measure of the child's behavior, although we acknowledge that theoretically it is presumed to reflect in part the quality of the caregiving environment.

References

Achenbach, T. M. (1991). *Manual for the Child Behavior Checklist/4–18 and 1991 profile.* Burlington: Department of Psychiatry, University of Vermont.

Ainsworth, M. D. S., & Wittig, B. A. (1969). Attachment and exploratory behavior of one-year-olds in a strange situation. In B. M. Foss (Ed.), *Determinants of infant behavior* (Vol. 4, pp. 113–136). London: Methuen.

Bates, J. E. (1980). The concept of difficult temperament. *Merrill-Palmer Quarterly, 26,* 299–319.

Beck, A. T., Ward, C. H., Mendelson, M., Mock, J. E., & Erbaugh, J. K. (1961). An inventory for measuring depression. *Archives of General Psychiatry, 4,* 561–571.

Bowlby, J. (1969). *Attachment and loss: Vol. 1: Attachment.* New York: Basic Books.

Bradley, R. H., Whiteside, L., Mundfrom, D. J., Casey, P. H., Kelleher, K. J., & Pope, S. K. (1994). Early indications of resilience and their relation to experiences in the home environments of low birthweight, premature children living in poverty. *Child Development, 65* (2), 346–360.

Bretherton, I., & Munholland, K. A. (1999). Internal working models in attachment relationships: A construct revisited. In J. Cassidy & P. R. Shaver (Eds.), *Handbook of attachment: Theory, research, and clinical applications* (pp. 89–114). New York: Guilford Press.

Brody, G. H., Stoneman, Z., Flor, D., McCrary, C., Hastings, L., & Conyers, O. (1994). Financial resources, parent psychological functioning, parent co-caregiving, and early adolescent competence in rural two-parent African-American families. *Child Development, 65*(2), 590–605.

Brooks-Gunn, J., & Duncan, G. J. (1997). The effects of poverty on children. *The Future of Children, 7*(2), 55–71.

Caldwell, B. M., & Bradley, R. H. (1984). *Manual for the home observation for measurement of the environment.* Little Rock: University of Arkansas Press.

Cicchetti, D., Rogosch, F. A., Lynch, M., & Holt, K. D. (1993). Resilience in maltreated children: Processes leading to adaptive outcome. *Development and Psychopathology, 5*(4), 629–648.

Conger, R. D., Ge, X., Elder, G. H., Lorenz, F. O., & Simons, R. L. (1994). Economic stress, coercive family process, and development problems of adolescents. *Child Development, 65*(2), 541–561.

Cowen, E. L., Wyman, P. A., Work, W. C., & Parker, G. R. (1990). The Rochester Child Resilience Project: Overview and summary of first year findings. *Development and Psychopathology, 2,* 193–212.

Dodge, K. A., Pettit, G. S., & Bates, J. E. (1994). Socialization mediators of the relation between socioeconomic status and child conduct problems. *Child Development, 65*(2), 649–665.

Dubow, E. F., & Ippolito, M. E. (1994). Effects of poverty and quality of the home environment on changes in the academic and behavioral adjustment of elementary school-age children. *Journal of Clinical Child Psychology, 23*(4), 401–412.

Duncan, G. J., Brooks-Gunn, J., & Klebanov, P. K. (1994). Economic deprivation and early childhood development. *Child Development, 65,* 296–318.

Duncan, G. J., Yeung, W. J., Brooks-Gunn, J., & Smith, J. R. (1998). How much does childhood poverty affect the life chances of children? *American Sociological Review, 63*(3), 406–423.

Egeland, B., Kalkoske, M., Gottesman, N., & Erickson, M. F. (1990). Preschool behavior problems: Stability and factors accounting for change. *Journal of Child Psychology and Psychiatry, 31,* 891–909.

Egeland, B., & Sroufe, L. A. (1981). Attachment and early maltreatment. *Child Development, 52,* 44–52.

Erickson, M. F., Sroufe, L. A., & Egeland, B. (1985). The relationship between quality of attachment and behavior problems in preschool in a high-risk sample. In I. Bretherton & E. Waters (Eds.), Growing points of attachment theory and research. *Monographs of the Society for Research in Child Development, 50*(1–2), 147–167.

Farber, E. A., & Egeland, B. (1987). Invulnerability among abused and neglected children. In E. J. Anthony & B. J. Cohler (Eds.), *The invulnerable child* (pp. 253–288). New York: Guilford Press.

Fisher, L., Kokes, R. F., Cole, R. E., Perkins, P. M., & Wynne, L. C. (1987). Competent children at risk: A study of well-functioning offspring of disturbed parents. In E. J. Anthony & B. J. Cohler (Eds.), *The invulnerable child* (pp. 253–289). New York: Guilford Press.

Garmezy, N. (1991). Resilience and vulnerability to adverse developmental outcomes associated with poverty. *American Behavioral Scientist, 34*(4), 416–430.

Gelfand, D. M., & Teti, D. M. (1990). The effects of maternal depression on children. *Clinical Psychology Review, 10*(3), 329–353.

Greenberg, M. T. (1999). Attachment and psychopathology in childhood. In J. Cassidy & P. R. Shaver (Eds.), *Handbook of attachment: Theory, research, and clinical applications* (pp. 469–496). New York: Guilford Press.

Gresham, F. M., & Elliot, S. N. (1989). *Social Skills Rating System: Parent, teacher, and child forms.* Circle Pines, MN: American Guidance Systems.

Guo, G. (1998). The timing of the influences of cumulative poverty on children's cognitive ability and achievement. *Social Forces, 77*(1), 257–287.

Harnish, J. D., Dodge, K. A., & Valente, E. (1995). Mother–child interaction quality as a partial mediator of the roles of depressive symptoms and socioeconomic status in the development of child behavior problems. *Child Development, 66*(3), 739–753.

Heinicke, C. M., Fineman, N. R., Ruth, G., Recchia, S. L., Guthrie, D., & Rodning, C. (1999). Relationship-based intervention with at-risk mothers: Outcome in the first year of life. *Infant Mental Health Journal, 20*(4), 349–374.

Henggeler, S. W. (1990). *Family therapy and beyond: A multisystemic approach to treating the behavior problems of children and adolescents.* Pacific Grove, CA: Brooks/Cole.

Jackson, D. N. (1967). *Personality Research Form manual.* New York: Research Psychologists Press.

Jason, J. M., & Jarvis, W. R. (1987). Infectious disease: Preventable causes of infant mortality. *Pediatrics, 80,* 335–341.

Knitzer, J., Yoshikawa, H., Cauthen, N. K., & Aber, J. L. (2000). Welfare reform, family support, and child development: Perspectives from policy analysis and developmental psychopathology. *Development and Psychopathology, 12*(4), 619–632.

Kochanska, G., Kuczynski, L., & Maguire, M. (1989). Impact of diagnosed depression and self-reported mood on mothers' control strategies: A longitudinal study. *Journal of Abnormal Child Psychology, 17*(5), 493–511.

Korenman, S., Miller, J. E., & Sjaastad, J. E. (1995). Long-term poverty and child development in the United States: Results from the NLSY. *Children and Youth Services Review, 17,* 127–155.

Kraemer, H. C., Kazdin, E., Offord, D. R., Kessler, R. C., Jensen, P. S., & Kupfer, D. J. (1997). Coming to terms with the terms of risk. *Archives of General Psychiatry, 54,* 337–343.

Leadbeater, B. J., & Bishop, S. J. (1994). Predictors of behavior problems in preschool children of inner-city Afro-American and Puerto Rican adolescent mothers. *Child Development, 65*(2), 638–648.

Lieberman, A. F., & Zeanah, C. H. (1999). Contributions of attachment theory to infant–parent psychotherapy and other interventions with infants and young children. In J. Cassidy & P. R. Shaver (Eds.), *Handbook of attachment: Theory, research, and clinical applications* (pp. 555–574). New York: Guilford Press.

Luthar, S. S. (1999). *Poverty and children's adjustment.* Thousand Oaks, CA: Sage.

Luthar, S. S., Cicchetti, D., & Becker, B. (2000). The construct of resilience: A critical evaluation and guidelines for future work. *Child Development, 71*(3), 543–562.

Luthar, S. S., & Suchman, N. E. (1999). Relational psychotherapy mothers' group: A developmentally informed intervention for at-risk mothers. *Development and Psychopathology, 12,* 235–253.

Luthar, S. S., & Zigler, E. (1991). Vulnerability and competence: A review of research on resilience in childhood. *American Journal of Orthopsychiatry, 61*(1), 6–22.

Lyons-Ruth, K., Alpern, L., & Repacholi, B. (1993). Disorganized infant attachment classification and maternal psychosocial problems as predictors of hostile-aggressive behavior in the preschool classroom. *Child Development, 64*(2), 572–585.

Masten, A. S., Best, K. M., & Garmezy, N. (1990). Resilience and development: Contributions from the study of children who overcome adversity. *Development and Psychopathology, 2,* 425–444.

Masten, A. S., & Coatsworth, J. D. (1998). The development of competence in favorable and unfavorable environments: Lessons from research on successful children. *American Psychologist, 53*(2), 205–220.

McClelland, G. H., & Judd, C. M. (1993). Statistical difficulties of detecting interactions and moderator effects. *Psychological Bulletin, 114*(2), 376–390.

McLoyd, V. C., Jayaratne, T. E., Ceballo, R., & Borquez, J. (1994). Unemployment and work interruption among African American single mothers: Effects on parenting and adolescent socioemotional functioning. *Child Development, 65*(2), 562–589.

O'Keefe, M. (1994). Adjustment of children from maritally violent homes. *Families in Society, 75*, 403–415.

Osofsky, J. D., & Thompson, M. D. (2000). Adaptive and maladaptive parenting: Perspectives on risk and protective factors. In J. P. Shonkoff & S. J. Meisels (Eds.), *Handbook of early childhood intervention* (2nd ed., pp. 54–75). New York: Cambridge University Press.

Pannacione, V., & Wahler, R. (1986). Child behavior, maternal depression, and social coercion as factors in the quality of child care. *Journal of Abnormal Child Psychology, 45*, 747–758.

Patterson, G. R. (1982). *Coercive family processes* (Vol. 3). Eugene, OR: Castalia.

Patterson, G. R., & Capaldi, D. (1991). Relation of parental transitions to boys' adjustment problems: I. A linear hypothesis. II. Mothers at risk for transitions and unskilled parenting. *Developmental Psychology, 27*(3), 489–504.

Peterson, L., Ewigman, B., & Vandiver, T. (1994). Role of parental anger in low-income women: Discipline strategy, perceptions of behavior problems, and the need for control. *Journal of Clinical Child Psychology, 23*(4), 435–443.

Pianta, R. C., Egeland, B., & Sroufe, L. A. (1990). Maternal stress and children's development: Prediction of school outcomes and identification of protective factors. In J. Rolf, A. S. Masten, D Cicchetti, K. H. Nuechterlein, & S. Weintraub (Eds.), *Risk and protective factors in the development of psychopathology* (pp. 215–235). New York: Cambridge University Press.

Pianta, R. C., & Steinberg, M. (1991, April). *Relationships between children and kindergarten teachers: Associations with home and classroom behavior.* Paper presented at the meeting of the Society for Research in Child Development, Seattle, WA.

Pollitt, E. (1994). Poverty and child development: Relevance of research in developing countries to the United States. *Child Development, 65*(2), 283–295.

Radke-Yarrow, M., & Brown, E. (1993). Resilience and vulnerability in children of multiple-risk families. *Development and Psychopathology, 5*(4), 581–592.

Radke-Yarrow, M., & Sherman, T. (1990). Hard growing: Children who survive. In J. Rolf, A. S. Masten, D. Cicchetti, K. H. Nuechterlein, & S. Weintraub (Eds.), *Risk and protective factors in the development of psychopathology* (pp. 97–119). New York: Cambridge University Press.

Renken, B., Egeland, B., Marvinney, D., Mangelsdorf, S., & Sroufe, L. A. (1989). Early childhood antecedents of aggression and passive-withdrawal in early elementary school. *Journal of Personality, 57*(2), 257–281.

Rohner, R. P. (1986). *The warmth dimension: Foundations of parental acceptance-rejection theory.* Beverly Hills, CA: Sage.

Rose, S. L., Rose, S. A., & Feldman, J. F. (1989). Stability of behavior problems in very young children. *Development and Psychopathology, 1*(1), 5–19.

Rutter, M. (1983). Statistical and personal interactions: Facets and perspectives. In D. Magnusson & V. L. Allen (Eds.), *Human development: An interactional perspective* (pp. 295–319). New York: Academic Press.

Rutter, M. (1985). Resilience in the face of adversity: Protective factors and resistance to psychiatric disorder. *British Journal of Psychiatry, 147*, 598–611.

Sampson, R. J., & Laub, J. H. (1994). Urban poverty and the family context of delinquency: A new look at structure and process in a classic study. *Child Development, 65*(2), 523–540.

Shaw, D. S., & Bell, R. Q. (1993). Developmental theories of parental contributors to antisocial behavior. *Journal of Abnormal Child Psychology, 21*(5), 493–518.

Shaw, D. S., Bell, R. Q., & Gilliom, M. (2000). A truly early starter model of antisocial behavior revisited. *Clinical Child and Family Psychology Review, 3*, 155–172.

Shaw, D. S., Keenan, K., & Vondra, J. I. (1994). Developmental precursors of externalizing behavior: Ages 1 to 3. *Developmental Psychology, 30*, 355–364.

Shaw, D. S., Owens, E. B., Vondra, J. I., Keenan, K., & Winslow, E. B. (1996). Early risk factors and pathways in the development of early disruptive behavior problems. *Development and Psychopathology, 8*, 679–699.

Shaw, D. S., & Vondra, J. I. (1995). Infant attachment security and maternal predictors of early behavior problems: A longitudinal study of low-income families. *Journal of Abnormal Child Psychology, 23*(3), 335–357.

Shaw, D. S., Vondra, J. I., Hommerding, K. D., Keenan, K., & Dunn, M. (1994). Chronic family adversity and early child behavior problems: A longitudinal study of low income families. *Journal of Child Psychology and Psychiatry, 35*(6), 1109–1122.

Shaw, D. S., Winslow, E. B., Owens, E. B., Vondra, J. I., Cohn, J. F., & Bell, R. Q. (1998). The development of early externalizing problems among children from low-income families: A transformational perspective. *Journal of Abnormal Child Psychology, 26*, 95–107.

Smith, J., & Prior, M. (1995). Temperament and stress resilience in school-age children: A within-families study. *Journal of the American Academy of Child and Adolescent Psychiatry, 34*(2), 168–179.

Smith, B., & Sechrest, L. (1991). Treatment of aptitude X treatment interactions. *Journal of Consulting and Clinical Psychology, 59*(2), 233–244.

Spielberger, C. D., Johnson, E. H., Russell, S. F., Crane, R. J., Jacobs, G. A., & Worden, T. J. (1985). The experience and expression of anger: Construction and validation of an anger expression scale. In M. A. Chesney & R. H. Rosemann (Eds.), *Anger and hostility in cardiovascular and behavioral disorders* (pp. 5–30). New York: Hemisphere/McGraw-Hill.

Stouthamer-Loeber, M., Loeber, R., Farrington, D. P., Zhang, Q., van Kammen, W., & Maguin, E. (1993). The double edge of protective and risk factors for delinquency: Interrelations and developmental patterns. *Development and Psychopathology, 5*, 683–702.

Tschann, J. M., Kaiser, P., Chesney, M. A., Alkon, A., & Boyce, W. T. (1996). Resilience and vulnerability among preschool children: Family functioning, temperament, and behavior problems. *Journal of the American Academy of Child and Adolescent Psychiatry, 35*(2), 184–192.

Urban, J., Carlson, E., Egeland, B., & Sroufe, L. A. (1991). Patterns of individual adaptation across childhood. *Development and Psychopathology, 3*(4), 445–460.

U.S. Census Bureau. (2000a). *Poverty in the United States: 1999* [On-line]. Available at http://www.census.gov/hhes/www/povty99.html

U.S. Census Bureau (2000b). *Historical poverty tables* [On-line]. Available at http://www.census.gov/hhes/poverty/histpov/hstpov1.html

Werner, E., & Smith, R. (1982). *Vulnerable but invincible: A longitudinal study of resilient children and youth.* New York: McGraw-Hill.

Weschler, D. (1989). *Weschler Preschool and Primary Scale of Intelligence – Revised.* San Antonio, TX: Psychological Corp.

Winslow, E. B., Shaw, D. S., Bruns, H., & Kiebler, K. (1995, March). *Parenting as a mediator of child behavior problems and maternal stress, support, and adjustment.* Paper presented at the meeting of the Society for Research in Child Development, Indianapolis, IN.

12

Emerging Perspectives on Context Specificity of Children's Adaptation and Resilience

Evidence from a Decade of Research with Urban Children in Adversity

Peter A. Wyman

To what extent are the processes that promote children's competence and their resilience *universal* (i.e., comparable for children across populations) or *specific* (i.e., different in their effectiveness according to a child's social context and individual endowment)? On the one hand, reviews of research comparing diverse populations of children underscore that there are common adaptive systems (e.g., sound intellectual functioning; secure parent–child attachment relationships) that promote positive developmental outcomes for children across favorable and unfavorable environments (e.g., Masten, 2001; Masten & Coatsworth, 1998). On the other hand, there is building empirical evidence pointing to the context specificity of many protective processes. For example, some emotion-regulation processes that enhance resilience among maltreated children are not associated with resilience in other populations of children (Cicchetti & Rogosch, 1997). Those investigators found that maltreated children who showed enhanced adjustment had more restrictive emotional self-regulation styles and drew on fewer relational resources compared to poor, nonmaltreated children who also demonstrated positive adjustment over time. Studies of children with depressed parents also point to context-specific coping and adaptation. Children with depressed parents benefit from gaining age-appropriate knowledge about depression and from using that knowledge to develop skills for

This chapter is dedicated to Emory L. Cowen (1926–2000) in admiration of his leadership in developing a conceptual framework for children's positive well being. I wish also to thank the William T. Grant Foundation for support of the Rochester Child Resilience Project and the families who have generously given their time so that we may learn about their lives.

maintaining psychological separateness from a parent's illness (Beardslee & Podorefsky, 1988).

Those contrasting perspectives demonstrate the need for more knowledge of how contexts influence (and are influenced by) positive developmental processes and resilience. Contexts include differences in communities (e.g., availability of mentors), family settings (emotional tone, cohesion), and within children (e.g., temperament). Greater attention to contexts in studies of risk and resilience can help illuminate which adaptive strategies and protective resources tend to promote positive development for most children (i.e., are universal) and which are selectively beneficial for some children (i.e., are context-specific).

This chapter reviews highlights from a decade of research with urban children (Rochester Child Resilience Project) to contrast the explanatory power of studies guided by two perspectives on context-specific adaptation. Specifically, this chapter examines whether several child-based attributes (e.g., affective responsiveness and efficacy beliefs) that were identified as beneficial to adaptation for aggregated samples of at-risk children have differential effects on adaptation for children in varying contexts. This chapter is selective and considers only a few context differences in an effort to provide some insights on how future studies of risk and resilience may benefit from more attention to context specificity. The present focus is on several context differences in social settings (e.g., level of family functioning, peer group influences) and in individuals (e.g., degree of children's conduct disturbance) that are salient for urban children.

CONTEXT SPECIFICITY AND PROCESSES OF RESILIENCE

Lessons from Developmental Psychopathology

Knowledge of how contexts influence processes that promote children's well-being is not well developed. However, studies of social contexts and the development of psychopathology offer some direction (e.g., Boyce et al., 1998; Cicchetti & Aber, 1998). For example, studies from developmental psychopathology underscore the importance of contexts in determining the meaning and function of behavior. As a case in point, the extent to which a child's individual level of aggression in first grade predicts later conduct problems depends, in part, on the level of aggression in that child's first-grade classroom (Kellam, Ling, Merisca, Brown, & Ialongo, 1998). The implication for research on risk and resilience is that studies should investigate differences in the *protectiveness* of social resources and competencies based on how those factors serve children in specific contexts to reduce dysfunctional processes and enhance children's coping and mastery. Another lesson from developmental psychopathology is that maturing children enter more differentiated social contexts, which often mediate the effects of other systems on the genesis of problems. For example, there is evidence that some effects of lax parental discipline on children's conduct problems are mediated through the choices children make about peer group affiliations (Boyce et al., 1998). Similarly, studies of risk and resilience should clarify how family systems promote children's access to community resources, such as mentors, and other opportunities that promote well-being.

A Proposed Conceptual Framework for Studying Resilience in Context

We have identified several transactional-developmental concepts to be useful in expanding our research with urban children to include a focus on contexts.

1. First, achieving healthy development in adverse environments (e.g., high conflict families, violent neighborhoods) requires that children traverse between risks that disrupt adaptation (e.g., reducing their exposure to violence) and toward resources necessary for developing competence (e.g., establishing relationships with stable adults). The implication is that children in adversity are more likely to enter positive developmental trajectories when the "fit" between their development and environment reduces the impact of risk factors over time and enhances their ability to draw on potential, embedded resources. This idea suggests that when we identify qualities of "fit" between protective factors and contexts we will clarify positive developmental processes.

2. Children's adaptation and resilience depend on the integration of competencies across multiple developmental systems, which include affect and behavior regulation, and interpersonal competence. The implication is that child-level resources at one level of functioning (e.g., positive efficacy beliefs) may promote resilience for some children, but not for other children, depending on how those resources integrate with other systems of functioning (e.g., whether positive efficacy beliefs are matched by executive functioning necessary to achieve goals). Thus, we expect to clarify resilience processes when we investigate patterns of competencies across more than one developmental system, rather then studying single competence systems.

3. Finally, children face distinctive adaptive challenges in chronically adverse settings (e.g., highly discordant or neglecting families) because of the intertwining of risk processes and development of competencies. Some effective adaptations that children make to reduce their distress and risk exposure (e.g., affective and interpersonal distancing) may, paradoxically, decrease their ability to draw on potential resources (e.g., limit skills for developing intimate, supportive relationships in new environments). The implications are these: (a) the range of potentially adaptive "fits" between children's development and environment may be narrower in highly adverse compared to more favorable contexts, and (b) different definitions of children's competence may be required in highly adverse settings.

Evaluating Two Perspectives on Context-Specific Adaptation among Urban Children

Findings from more than a decade of research within the Rochester Child Resilience Project (RCRP) provide an opportunity to contrast the explanatory power of different perspectives on context-specific adaptation and resilience (e.g., Cowen & Work, 1988; Wyman & Forbes-Jones, 2000). Since 1987 the RCRP has investigated two cohorts of ethnically diverse urban children, one 10- to 12-year-olds and the other 7- to 9-year-olds. A special focus has been on children of families in chronic adversity (e.g., high rates of poverty, violence, family discord, and substance use problems). A subgroup of cohort 1 (10- to 12-year-olds) participated in a 2-year follow-up evaluation. The second cohort, originally enrolled as 7- to 9-year-olds, is the focus of an ongoing 10-year longitudinal study, and some initial findings from the 6-year follow-up at ages 13–15 are now available.

Table 12.1 summarizes the research topics and studies in the two phases of research. The first wave of research studies tested a *universal developmental assets* perspective. Using a social-learning model of resilience (Cowen & Work, 1988), these early studies evaluated how well a common set of child-centered and social resources predicted adaptation and mastery among large samples of children in adversity. The first section of this chapter reviews (a) the conceptual model, (b) how chronic family adversities were assessed and used to define groups at high risk for psychopathology, and (c) findings from studies evaluating that model.

A second wave of RCRP studies has evaluated a perspective emphasizing *context-specific adaptation and processes of resilience.* This perspective

TABLE 12.1. *Two Phases of Research in the Rochester Child Resilience Project (1988–2001)*

Phase 1: Studies Evaluating a Universal Developmental Assets Perspective

---

A. Description of a social-learning model of resilience outlining child- and family-centered resources promoting adaptation in chronic adversity (Cowen & Work, 1988)

B. Measurement of family stress processes and identification of children at high risk for psychopathology in two urban cohorts (10- to 12-year-olds and 7- to 9-year-olds) (Kilmer, Cowen, Wyman, Work & Magnus, 1998; Work, Cowen, Parker & Wyman, 1990)

C. Studies focusing on child-centered competencies

Children's control attributions, mastery beliefs, and social-emotional competencies: relationships to resilience in 10- to 12-year-olds (Parker, Cowen, Work, & Wyman, 1990)

Development of a measure of children's realistic control attributions about family adversities (Wannon, 1990)

Development of a measure of children's perceived self-efficacy: relationships to adjustment in several urban samples (Cowen et al., 1991)

Children's future expectations and resilience (10- to 12-year-olds) (Wyman et al., 1992)

Future expectations predicting school engagement and social adjustment at 2-year follow-up (ages 12–14) (Wyman, Cowen, Work, & Kerley, 1993)

Children's empathy and social problem solving: predictors of school competence at 2-year follow-up (Kerley, 1997)

Children's realistic control, efficacy, and social-emotional competencies: Relationships to resilience in 7- to 9-year-children (Hoyt-Meyers et al., 1995)

D. Studies focusing on family-based resources

Parent–child relationships, discipline, and parent psychosocial resources: relationships to resilience in 10- to 12-year-old children (Wyman, Cowen, Work & Parker, 1991)

Youth reports of family environment resources: relationships to resilience (10- to 12-year-olds) (Wyman et al., 1992)

Family and parent resources: Relationships to resilience in 7- to 9-year-old children and test of social learning vs. attachment-based effects (Wyman et al., 1999a)

E. Evaluation of a school-based intervention to promote competencies and resilience among 8- to 10-year-old-urban, at-risk children (Cowen, Wyman, Work & Iker, 1994; Iker, 1990)

(continued)

TABLE 12.1 *(continued)*

Phase 2: Studies Evaluating Context-Specific Processes of Resilience

---

A. Description of an organizational-developmental model for resilience: specifying protective and development-enhancing processes (Wyman, Sandler, Wolchik, & Nelson, 2000)

B. Studies based on 6-year follow-up of cohort 2 youths (ages 13–15)

Children's context-specific emotion regulation and adaptation in high-adversity families (Wyman et al., 2002)

Accuracy of children's perceptions of competence and levels of disruptive behavior at ages 10–12 and ages 13–15 (Forbes-Jones, Wyman, Cowen, & Kaufmann, 2001)

Youth-specific differences in relationships between positive future expectations and adjustment (Wyman & Forbes-Jones, 2001)

Involvement in structured activities and levels of conduct problems: specificity of protective effects (Kaufmann, Wyman, Cowen, & Forbes-Jones, 2001)

---

suggests that adaptive strategies and protective resources vary for children, depending on individual qualities and on the specific risks and opportunities they face. The second section of this chapter describes some modifications to the project's conceptual model (Wyman, Sandler, Wolchik, & Nelson, 2000) and then reviews selected findings from recent studies investigating (a) context-specific emotional regulation and resilience in high adversity families, (b) youth-specific differences in relationships between self-evaluations and adjustment, and (c) peer group contexts and protective effects of afterschool activities.

EARLY RCRP STUDIES: INVESTIGATING UNIVERSAL DEVELOPMENTAL ASSETS

Social-Learning Model for Children's Resilience

The design and objectives of initial RCRP studies were derived from a conceptual model of resilience (Cowen & Work, 1988) based on social-learning and efficacy principles (Bandura, 1977). This model contrasted adaptation processes for children in adverse environments who demonstrated positive adjustment (deemed *stress-resilient*) with a trajectory for children demonstrating dysfunctional behavioral and social-emotional outcomes (deemed *stress-affected*). The intent of this framework was not to account for all sources of developmental variability (e.g., biologically based differences) but rather focused on capacities of young children that were potentially modifiable in interventions.

Cowen and Work's (1988) model proposed that children who acquire age-specific competencies and a growing sense of mastery associated with effective coping are better able to surmount ongoing adversities and manifest resilience (i.e., mastery of positive developmental objectives under ongoing life stress). Similar to qualities linked to *hardiness* in adults (Kobasa, Maddi, & Kahn, 1982), children's resilience was proposed to derive from a sense of internal control, self-perceptions of competence and coping efficacy, and affective and social-cognitive competencies (e.g., empathy) necessary for establishing supportive relationships. Competent adults (e.g., an involved parent, extended family member, or mentor) were posited to model adaptive cognitive and social coping strategies for children, and through effective parenting practices, to ameliorate some of the adverse consequences of life stressors. In contrast, children for whom adult models were ineffective or dysfunctional would fail to acquire coping strategies and remain unprotected from adverse stress consequences.

Design of Studies and Selection of Cohorts

The first phase of the RCRP research studies evaluated the project's initial conceptual model by (a) enrolling samples of urban children at high risk for psychopathology based on chronic family stress processes; (b) creating indices of children's behavioral and social-emotional adjustment, including classifying children into groups reflecting divergent adjustment trajectories; and (c) identifying child-centered competencies and family resources linked to differences in children's quality of adaptation (both cross-sectionally and longitudinally).

Measuring Family Stress Processes

Designating children in RCRP cohorts as at high risk for psychopathology used the criteria of exposure to four or more psychosocial adversities, focusing on chronic adverse processes (e.g., parent substance use or psychiatric disorder, ongoing discord). The criteria of four or more adversities was based on research demonstrating that a child's risk for psychopathology increased markedly as the number of lifetime risk factors increased (Rutter, 1990). The focus on chronic stressors was based on research suggesting that negative conditions extending over time were the crucial dimension of life stress with etiological significance for children's behavioral and emotional dysfunction (Gersten, Langer, Eisenberg, & Simcha-Fagen, 1977).

A 32-item parent-report measure was developed to assess cumulative stressors for each child (Kilmer, Cowen, Wyman, Work, & Magnus, 1998; Work, Cowen, Parker, & Wyman, 1990). This measure focused on three constellations of adverse processes based on evidence pointing to those conditions as predisposing to maladjustment in substantial proportions of children: (a) poverty and/or serious deficiencies in the physical environment; (b) impairment of a child's parent or guardian (e.g., psychiatric disorder, substance abuse); and (c) chronic family discord (e.g., Emery, 1982). Other adversities assessed by the measure (e.g., death of a parent) were drawn from research linking those events and conditions to adverse health and psychological outcomes in children (e.g., Kornberg & Caplan, 1980).

The primary caregiver of each child in the RCRP reported which family stressors had occurred since the child's birth, either within the family or pertaining to "a close family member in the child's home." The focus of assessment was on adverse processes within a child's *microsystem* (Bronfenbrenner, 1979) of intimate relationships, which for many urban children includes grandparents, and other extended family members.

Rates and patterns of family adversities reported by families enrolling in the RCRP over 14 years (total N of 1,179) underscore the interconnection of poverty, community violence, and family stress processes (Kilmer et al., 1998). For example, over one-quarter (i.e., 26.3%) of parents reported that a family member had a problem with alcohol or substance abuse, 30.7% reported chronic discord in their families, and 19% had a close family member arrested or in jail. Rates of children's exposure to community violence were high: 25.9% of parents indicated that their neighborhoods were unsafe, and 10% of children had seen someone get badly hurt. Across study cohorts, the median number of family adversities since birth of the enrolled child was approximately 4.5. The median number of adversities for children designated high risk in study subgroups was nearly double that number.

Cohort Selection and Subgroup Designation
Early RCRP studies drew on several samples of urban children. However, the majority of studies focused on two cohorts. The first cohort of 10- to 12-year-old children was selected from fourth- to sixth-grade classrooms in nine urban schools (1987–8). From a potential sample of 2,069 children,

656 enrolled. To create subgroups representing distinct adaptive trajectories, selected children who met high-risk criteria (i.e., four or more adversities since birth) were further classified into subgroups based on their quality of adjustment from multisource (parent, teacher) ratings: (a) children demonstrating competent adjustment in multiple spheres (stress-resilient) and (b) a group demonstrating problems of adaptation across multiple spheres (stress-affected). To be classified as stress resilient, a child had to rate in the top one-third on at least two of three adjustment screening measures and no lower than the middle one-third on the remaining measure. Conversely, to classify as stress affected, a child had to be ranked in the bottom one-third on at least two of the same three screening measures and no higher than the middle one-third on the other. Using the above criteria, 75 children were classified as stress resilient and 72 as stress-affected (Work et al., 1990). The two subgroups were predominantly poor (median family incomes in both groups of $600 to $900 per month) and racially diverse (58% minority).

A second cohort of 7- to 9-year-old children was selected 4 years later (1998–9) from the same urban school district, using the same screening and classification criteria (Hoyt-Meyers et al., 1995). In this case, 758 (37.1%) families enrolled of 2,063 contacted from second- to third-grade classrooms in 11 schools; from the high-risk portion of the sample 85 children were classified as stress resilient and 74 children as stress affected. A third subgroup was classified, composed of children demonstrating intermediate levels of behavioral and emotional adjustment. That subgroup has been included in follow-up evaluations of this cohort. Compared to the first cohort, the second cohort had a higher proportion of minority families (48% African American; 20% Hispanic) and families below the poverty level.

Assessments of children and families in both RCRP cohorts included self-report measures administered to children in schools, home interviews with an adult identified as the child's primary caregiver, and collection of school record data relevant to children's behavioral and social adjustment and educational progress.

Child-Centered Resources Predicting Competence in Adversity

The first questions addressed by the RCRP studies focused on identifying child-centered competencies associated with resilience for the sample of 10- to 12-year-old children. The cohort of younger (7- to 9-year-old) children provided an opportunity to assess the replicability of those findings with an independent sample and to investigate developmentally focused questions. For example, at what typical age does cognitive development enable children to differentiate between controllable and uncontrollable family problems, and when does that capacity predict resilience? Two short-term follow-up evaluations of each cohort afforded the opportunity to investigate the extent to which early competencies initiated, or sustained, adaptive processes. Some RCRP studies used the person-level designation of stress-resilient versus stress-affected status as the outcome variable; other studies used variables-based indices of functioning (e.g., level of classroom behavior control) as dependent variables. Because findings from different analytic strategies were generally consistent, they are reviewed together in the summary to follow.

Realistic Control Attributions about Family Adversity

Prior to the RCRP, most research on children's beliefs about their personal control focused on internal versus external control, and studies generally reported that greater internal control correlated with positive adjustment (e.g., Nowicki & Strickland, 1973). In applying the concept of control attributions to children's coping and resilience, RCRP studies focused on children's beliefs about their ability to influence family and personal problems (e.g., family discord, divorce, substance use). Several studies tested the hypothesis that the protective effects of children's expectations for controlling problems (e.g., arguments, substance use) should vary according to the likelihood of children's typical age-appropriate ability to influence those outcomes. Thus, selective, *realistic* control attributions (i.e., perceptions that some problems are controllable, whereas others are not) were expected to be more adaptive for children than undifferentiated beliefs in internal control, particularly in tumultuous environments.

Indeed, evidence from studies with both RCRP cohorts supported the view that differentiated, realistic control beliefs predicted children's adaptation better than undifferentiated beliefs in personal control. On a self-report measure developed for the Cohort 1 study (Wannon, 1990), realistic control was computed as a ratio of low control expectations for uncontrollable events (e.g., parental divorce) and high control expectations for controllable events (e.g., academic problems). As hypothesized, children classified as stress resilient (versus stress affected) were more likely to report that children their age had less ability to change family processes such as parent alcohol use and family arguments (deemed uncontrollable events) and more ability to alter events such as whether they had conflicts with others or substance use problems (deemed controllable) (Parker,

Cowen, Work, & Wyman, 1990). Importantly, the degree of realistic control predicted several indices of children's positive adjustment (e.g., level of school engagement) above and beyond the variance accounted for in adjustment by a measure of undifferentiated internal control (Wannon, 1990).

A study with the cohort of 7- to 9-year-olds also demonstrated that (a) many children within the younger age group had the cognitive capacity to differentiate the degree of controllability of family problems and their ability to influence those conditions, and (b) the ability to make that differentiation predicted more positive adaptation (Hoyt-Meyers et al., 1995). At both age groups, no consistent gender or race differences were found in relationships between children's control attributions and adjustment (Kim, Cowen, & Wyman, 1997).

Personal Mastery: Efficacy, Perceived Competence, and Future Expectations
The initial RCRP model emphasized that children who acquired positive mastery beliefs from effective coping would be more likely to sustain positive adaptation. That hypothesis was based on evidence from research with adults showing that positive efficacy expectations promoted the initiation and persistence of positive coping behaviors (Bandura, 1977). In the RCRP studies, three dimensions of children's self-perceptions were evaluated.

First, a self-report measure was developed for the cohort 1 study assessing children's efficacy expectations (i.e., the belief that they could achieve desired outcomes) for three types of challenges: difficult situations, problems with people, and new experiences (Cowen et al., 1991). Consistent with hypotheses from the RCRP model, 10- to 12-year-old children's positive efficacy expectations in all three domains predicted better behavioral adaptation and classification as stress resilient. Among the 7- to 9-year-old children in cohort 2, more positive efficacy expectations for problems with people, but not in other domains, predicted greater resilience (Hoyt-Meyers et al., 1995). Similarly, children's perceptions of their competence (e.g., academic ability, social skills, and acceptance) predicted greater resilience in both age cohorts.

Second, a measure of children's future expectations was developed for an interview with the 10- to 12-year-old sample (Wyman et al., 1992). Although research prior to the RCRP suggested that *expecting well* was an important characteristic of resilient children, children's future expectations had not been systematically assessed or evaluated across time in those studies (e.g., Werner & Smith, 1982). Consistent with the RCRP model, children in cohort 1 who reported more positive and more differentiated expectations for their future life outcomes (e.g., educational attainment, satisfaction with relationships) were more likely to be identified as resilient than as stress affected. Additional analyses demonstrated that positive future expectations predicted lower anxiety, higher school achievement, and better classroom behavior control (Wyman, Cowen, Work, & Kerley, 1993).

Findings from a 2-year follow-up evaluation of cohort 1 suggested that children's expectations for a better future promoted ongoing adaptive processes. Specifically, more positive future expectations at ages 10–12 predicted higher school engagement and social adjustment ratings of their adjustment by teachers 2 years later, above and beyond the effects of earlier school adjustment ratings and beyond the effects of intervening family stressors (Wyman et al., 1993).

Pilot investigations with younger children found that 7- to 9-year-olds could not reliably ascertain the concept of the future or of a changing self over time. Therefore, future expectations were not assessed in cohort 2 studies.

Social-Emotional Competencies

In studies with both RCRP cohorts (10- to 12-year-olds and 7- to 9-year-olds), positive school adaptation and functioning was associated with children's self-reports of (a) affective responsiveness and empathy (e.g., feeling sad when other children are sad) and acceptance of other children's emotional expressiveness and (b) prosocial preferences for solving common interpersonal problems involving other children (Cowen et al., 1992; Hoyt-Meyers et al., 1995). Those findings supported the contention from the initial RCRP model that affective competence and prosocial skills promoted resilience by enhancing children's ability to satisfy relational needs in environments characterized by discord and interpersonal instability. Indeed, longitudinal findings with cohort 1 demonstrated that those competencies predicted more positive behavior adaptation at school and social adjustment 2 years later at ages 12–14, beyond the significant effects on adjustment from early life and ongoing family stressors (Kerley, 1997).

Family Resources Predicting Competence

The second principal focus of early RCRP studies was on identifying family-based protective resources and on clarifying mechanisms linking those resources with children's acquisition of competencies. The body of evidence from studies with both RCRP cohorts demonstrated that (a) functional family environments were strongly protective for children in buffering them from many chronic adversities, and (b) children's competence in adversity often but not always, reflected considerable resilience of a parent or family system. Those broad-band conclusions were supported by findings that parents who maintained emotionally responsive, structured environments for their children, despite chronic adversity (e.g., poverty coupled with family substance use problems), provided conditions that strongly favored children's acquisition of competencies and their mastery of normative developmental tasks (Wyman, Cowen, Work, & Parker, 1991; Wyman et al., 1992, 1999a).

In both RCRP cohorts, indices of children's well-being and resilience were predicted by parents' reports of more time spent in emotionally responsive interactions with their children, more consistent discipline practices, and use of language-based versus physical-based discipline practices. Positive parent functioning was enhanced by extended family support, including more involvement by fathers (in cohort 1) in their child's care (although fewer than 40% resided with their children). Parents' resources also predicted their children's positive adjustment status. Parents of resilient children reported having more positive personal efficacy (e.g., confidence in being a parent), adaptive emotion-focused coping strategies, and self-views on an amalgam of characteristics including "potency" and life satisfaction. For a significant number of children (about 12%), fathers, grandparents, or relatives other than a biological or adoptive mother provided continuity of caregiving for children.

Children in cohort 1 (10–12 years old) identified a similar array of protective family resources. For example, children classified as resilient reported more emotionally close relationships with their primary caregivers, more frequently endorsed items such as "I can talk to my parent about things that worry me" and reported more consistent family discipline. One gender difference noted was that children's perceptions of valued qualities of their mothers predicted positive adjustment for girls but not for boys. This difference suggested the intriguing possibility that girls' identification with mothers was an additional benefit for girls living with a competent parent. For boys, parent involvement and structure appeared more protective (Wyman et al., 1992).

Social-Learning versus Attachment-Based Models of Parent Protection
A test of social-learning vs. attachment models using data from studies with the cohort 2 sample suggested that the attachment-based model more accurately described how parents' resources positively influenced

children's development in the sample. Specifically, the positive association between parents' competencies (combining adaptive coping skills, efficacy, and education) and their children's competence was mediated through (Baron & Kenny, 1986) a set of variables indicating parents' use of emotionally responsive, developmentally appropriate caregiving practices. Those findings suggested that emotionally responsive parenting practices helped establish a positively regulated parent–child relationship, which in turn facilitated children's emotional and behavioral self-regulation, and on that foundation children developed more differentiated competencies (Wyman et al., 1999).

Preventive Intervention: Promoting Child Competencies

The first phase of RCRP research included the development and evaluation of a school-based intervention to promote young urban children's coping competencies and self-efficacy. Because this intervention was short-term and exclusively child-focused (i.e., did not include intervention with parents), expectations for effects on children's adaptation were modest. However, the initiative served to test the extent to which competencies identified in the RCRP research could be promoted in children in a short-term, school-based intervention and the impact on their adjustment. The intervention targeted 10- to 12-year-old children who (a) were evidencing nascent adjustment problems (e.g., aggression, social withdrawal) and (b) were from families experiencing one or more major family stressors (e.g., parent incarceration, serious family illness). Two adult leaders facilitated the 12-week program guided by a structured curriculum in three phases: (a) promoting social competencies, (b) learning realistic control, and (c) applying skills (e.g., role plays) to increase perceptions of self-efficacy (Iker, 1990).

Empirical evaluation found that children who participated in the 12-week intervention demonstrated increases in perceived self-efficacy and knowledge of realistic control about family problems, but they did not show significant changes in short-term classroom behavior (Cowen, Wyman, Work, & Iker, 1994). Process evaluations (with group leaders, teachers, and children) were informative about the strengths and limitations of the program. First, children benefited from very different coping strategies according to life conditions, which a curriculum-based program did not always ideally accommodate. For example, a girl whose parent was acutely ill with acquired immune deficiency syndrome (AIDS)-related illness benefited from sharing her sadness and anger. Other children experiencing chronic family discord benefited from strategies of emotional structuring and focus on controllable aspects of their families. Second, many children had lost parents through incarceration, death, or impairment (illness, substance use), and program leaders observed that many children sought more individual adult attention than the group program could provide.

Early RCRP Studies: Contributions and Limitations
The first phase of RCRP studies contributed to knowledge of child-based competencies associated with positive developmental processes for poor urban children in adversity. Children as young as 6–7 years of age demonstrated an impressive array of cognitive, affective, and social skills, including the ability to differentiate adverse processes that they can and cannot control. Longitudinal findings demonstrated that many of those capacities predicted children's well-being several years later. Those findings suggested that emotional competence, effective coping skills, and perceptions of efficacy play an important role in promoting children's ongoing adaptation. Domains of competencies associated with adaptation were generally comparable for boys and girls and for children of different race/ethnicity. The early RCRP findings also underscored the strong protective function of positive attachment relationships for children in families experiencing turmoil and frequent disruptions.

Because the RCRP cohorts were composed of high-risk families, the studies were not designed to compare low- and high-adversity groups, which would have been useful in identifying factors that enhanced adaptation specifically for children at highest risk. However, early RCRP findings point to numerous other questions about development in adversity. For example, although early studies pointed to the protective function of parenting competence and functional family systems, that generalized conclusion may not apply to all children. For example, those findings did not ascertain whether different resources and adaptive processes promoted well-being for children in families unable to provide effectively for children's needs.

RECENT RCRP STUDIES EVALUATING CONTEXT-SPECIFIC ADAPTATION

Modifications in the RCRP Conceptual Model

The focus of studies from the first to the second phase of RCRP research shifted from (a) investigating predictors of positive adaptation for whole samples of at-risk children, toward (b) investigating variations in children's self-righting processes and in protective factors. This shift reflected several reformulations of the project's guiding framework (Wyman et al., 2000), including the view that resilience reflects a diverse set of processes that alter children's transactions with adverse life conditions to reduce negative effects and promote mastery of normative developmental tasks. The efficacy of some processes that promote resilience was posited to be context specific, according to the specific risks children face and the child's capacity to draw on those resources.

Several studies based on a 6-year follow-up of the second RCRP cohort have investigated context-specific adaptation. Before reviewing those studies, the follow-up of cohort 2 families will be briefly described

Lives in Progress: A 6-Year Follow-up of Cohort 2 Youths

Nearly 85% of the children and parents initially enrolled in cohort 2 ($n = 199$) participated in follow-up evaluations 6 years later when the children were ages 13–15 (Wyman & Forbes-Jones, 2000; Wyman, Kilmer, Forbes-Jones, Spomer, & Cowen, 1999b). Four domains of variables were assessed: (a) *risk factors*: the degree to which each youth and family was exposed to psychosocial adversities in the intervening 6 years (e.g., poverty, discord, violence); (b) *youth adjustment:* current behavioral, scholastic, and social-emotional functioning, including behaviors of emerging importance to adolescents (e.g., sexual activity); (c) *family/community resources*: degree of family involvement (e.g., support/monitoring) and extrafamilial resources (e.g., activities, adult mentors); and (d) *youth-centered competencies*: cognitive, affective, and social functioning (e.g., efficacy beliefs).

Large proportions the sample reported ongoing, severe hardships. Nearly 50% of the families reported incomes at or below the poverty line, and one in six youths had lived with two or more parent-guardians due to family disruptions (e.g., 30% had a family member arrested or in jail, and 42% had a family member with a substance abuse problem). Many youths were victims of violence. For example, 21% of youths had been threatened by someone holding a weapon. Most striking was the finding that 24% of youths reported that a family member (immediate or extended) had been murdered.

To evaluate the large body of information about youths' adjustment, *variable-centered* approaches have been used to study levels of adjustment in discrete areas (e.g., conduct problems). *Person-centered* approaches have been used to identify groups who demonstrate meaningfully distinctive patterns of adaptation (representing a *gestalt* of functioning) (Cairns &

Cairns, 1994). For example, about 30% of the sample demonstrated an *engaged-thriving* pattern, that is, positive academic and social functioning and low rates of problem behaviors (Wyman et al., 2002). Another group was *antisocial-academic disengaged*, that is, delinquency behaviors coupled with academic problems and truancy. Girls who were above average on problem behaviors (e.g., substance use, delinquency) were less likely than boys who were above average on those problems to show serious academic problems.

The next section reviews three emerging areas of RCRP studies investigating context-specificity of adaptation and resilience.

Emotion Regulation and Competence in High vs. Low Adversity Families

For children in families that lack the capacity to provide *average expectable* parenting, or that pose ongoing threats to their well-being, emotion regulation strategies that promote well-being may be different from those in more favorable family settings (Cicchetti & Rogosch, 1997). In those contexts a restrictive emotional regulation style (e.g., reduced empathy, less flexible affective responsiveness) may be adaptive to buffer children from chronic emotional distress. In contrast, children in most family environments may be better served by a more open, affective, and social form of responsiveness, which also promotes other social connections.

Many children in the RCRP cohort resided in chronically disturbed families with minimal resources necessary to meet children's age-appropriate needs. For example, one in six children in the cohort had lived with multiple guardians in the 5 years preceding the follow-up evaluation due to parent substance abuse problems, incarcerations, and other changes. Two salient questions were raised by those observations: (a) To what extent did children in high-adversity families demonstrate positive development? (b) Were more restrictive patterns of emotional self-regulation predictive of competence in high-adversity families?

Several findings with the cohort 2 sample supported context-specific hypotheses about emotion regulation (Wyman et al., 2002). First, a modest number of youths were identified who demonstrated enhanced adaptation over the 6-year follow-up period in high-adversity, low-resource families. Youths in that group were contrasted with youths in other family contexts on several measures of functioning, including indices of affect and emotional regulation. Of principal interest were comparisons of youths who demonstrated positive adaptation in more favorable family contexts.

In brief summary, the group of children who demonstrated enhanced adjustment in high-adversity families reported low levels of affective responsiveness to others' feelings and low acceptance of others' affect expressiveness compared to competent youths in more favorable settings. They also reported minimal engagement and emotional involvement with their primary caregivers. In contrast, they reported positive beliefs in their own competence and had positive expectations for their futures. Those findings were consistent with the hypothesis that more restrictive affective management strategies would help children to reduce distress associated with family turmoil and disappointment over unmet emotional needs. Firm psychological boundaries in relationships with adult family members (e.g., limited expectations) may have enabled them to experience competence in other avenues. In contrast, positive adaptation for children in more favorable family climates was associated with emotional responsiveness and with skills for promoting and maintaining close emotional connections with family.

Mastery Beliefs and Adjustment: Effects of Youth-Specific Contexts

The first phase of RCRP research identified positive relationships between children's personal mastery beliefs (e.g., self-efficacy, future expectations, perceived competence) and their behavioral and social adjustment. However, those main-effects relationships may have masked important distinctions and variations in the meaning and function of children's self-evaluations. First, the accuracy of children's perceptions of their abilities may determine whether those beliefs promote adaptive cognitive processes. Several studies have demonstrated that aggressive children tend to overrate their own competence to a greater extent than do nonaggressive children (e.g., Cairns & Cairns, 1994), and that the degree of inflated perceptions of competence predicted interpersonal aggression (Hughes, Cavell, & Grossman, 1997). A second, related issue concerns how children's mastery beliefs fit with other aspects of their functioning (e.g., quality of behavioral control). Variations in youth contexts may influence whether children's appraisals of personal competence stimulate effective behaviors and social transactions.

Accuracy of Self-Evaluations of Competence

Forbes-Jones, Wyman, Cowen, and Kaufmann (2001) tested the extent to which distortions in youths' self-appraisals of competence predicted poorer behavior control and aggression for youths in the cohort 2 sample. First, youths' self-ratings of their competence were compared to the ratings provided by parents and teachers. In addition, children's perceptions of their academic competence were indexed to their current grade point averages. Based in those comparisons indices were created for each youth in cohort 2 at the first and second follow-up evaluations (i.e., ages 10–12 and 13–15). The accuracy of self-appraisals was examined in relation to children's degree of classroom behavioral control and levels of delinquent behaviors.

As predicted by Forbes-Jones et al. (2001), children's overestimation of their competence was associated with higher levels of aggressive behavior at school (reported by teachers) and with higher rates of delinquent behaviors (reported by parents). Those relationships were found at both age periods (10–12 and 13–15 years). Importantly, the link between children's inflated self-appraisals and higher aggression was found above and beyond the effects of other variables known to be associated with conduct problems, including a child's gender, current family income, and levels of parent monitoring of their activities. This study's findings with a high-risk urban sample add to the growing body of evidence suggesting that inflated self-appraisals characterize aggressive children. Rather than promoting effective behavior and adaptation, inflated self-views reflect a *protective avoidant* information processing style that impedes youths' ability to benefit from evaluative feedback about their behavior (Hughes et al., 1997).

Future Expectations and Adjustment: Effects of Behavior Functioning

Another recent study investigated whether youths' positive future expectations stimulated productive behavior also depend on individual context. Wyman and Forbes-Jones (2001) tested the hypothesis that adolescent youths' positive expectations for their futures (e.g., completing education) would predict adaptive functioning if those expectations were built on a foundation of behavior regulation skills necessary to sustain planning.

For the full sample of youths, Wyman and Forbes-Jones (2001) found low to moderate relationships between positive expectations and three indices of current adjustment: (a) school behavior competence (teacher ratings), (b) social-emotional functioning (youth and parent ratings), and (c) lower problem behaviors (youth and parent ratings).

However, in support of study hypotheses some meaningful differences in patterns of relationships between expectations and adjustment indices were identified for youths according to *individual contexts*. Specifically, for a subgroup of youths that had above-average problems (e.g., conduct problems, substance abuse problems), more positive future expectations predicted lower ratings of school behavior competence and academic engagement by teachers. Thus, positive future expectations promoted engaged behaviors if those beliefs were "built" on an adequate base of skills such as the capacity to delay gratification and to plan. Conversely, if youths lacked those concurrent skills, positive future expectations appeared to reflect wishful thinking or a process of protective avoidance (Hughes et al., 1997) used to disavow knowledge of potentially distressing problems.

Peer Group Contexts and Protective Effects of Afterschool Activities

Studies of youths' conduct problems have shown that social contexts (e.g., peer group behavior norms, prosocial influences) are influential in determining whether conduct problems are stable over time, escalate, or diminish (Loeber & Stouthamer-Loeber, 1998). The RCRP follow-up provided an opportunity to evaluate peer and community influences on conduct problems in this cohort and to test the context specificity of those influences.

Due to their high levels of poverty, chronic family disruptions, and community violence, the RCRP sample is a group at high risk for behavior problems. Indeed, a substantial proportion of the sample was showing school conduct problems when recruited at ages 7–9. As expected, rates of serious delinquent behaviors (e.g., stealing, assault, property destruction) had increased at the follow-up point (ages 13–15). However, the majority of youths in the cohort did not have serious conduct problems or other behavior problems (e.g., substance abuse) disrupting their school and social adjustment.

Kaufmann, Wyman, Cowen, and Forbes-Jones (2001) assessed the degree to which involvement in structured activities (e.g., organized sports, musical activities, volunteer work) was linked to lower levels of conduct problems and how context specific that relationship was. Although prior studies with at-risk samples of children have reported that youths who participate in more prosocial activities have fewer conduct problems (e.g., Mahoney, 2000), less is known about which groups of youths benefit from those protective processes.

Kaufmann et al. (2001) hypothesized that youths' involvement in activities would reduce the risk for conduct problems that was attributable to their affiliation with delinquent peers for two reasons. First, involvement in activities increases supervised time and reduces opportunities for engagement in problem behaviors that are often done in the company of peers (including substance abuse, which is a substantial stimulus for delinquency). Second, more structured activities would expand youths' social networks to include more peers with behaviors and attitudes that do not reinforce aggression. Two indices of behavior at the 6-year follow-up point were examined: (a) *conduct problems*, combining parent, teacher, and youth self-ratings of youth aggression, and (b) *delinquency behaviors*, combining parent and youth reports of the number of antisocial behaviors (e.g., destruction of property, fighting) committed in the prior year.

As expected, youths with more antisocial peers (e.g., friends with legal problems, who regularly used drugs, and were sexually active) had higher overall levels of both conduct problems and delinquency behaviors. In fact, degree of antisocial peer affiliations predicted youths' behavior problems above and beyond the effects of children's prior aggression (at ages 8–10) and children's gender, ethnicity, and family income. Conversely, more involvement in structured activities predicted lower levels of behavior problems. The focal question tested by Kaufmann et al. (2001) was whether youths' involvement in structured activities was specifically protective for youths with high exposure to antisocial peers. Indeed, evidence supported that hypothesis in a regression model predicting youths' levels of delinquent behaviors. Specifically, a significant interaction (Prosocial Activities × Antisocial Peer Associations) predicted delinquency behaviors above and beyond the main effect of those variables. Elucidation of that interaction term showed that more involvement in activities predicted lower levels of delinquency behaviors for youths who reported above-average contacts with antisocial peers (Kaufmann et al., 2001) but not for youths with below-average contacts.

SUMMING UP: PERSPECTIVES ON CONTEXT SPECIFICITY OF CHILDREN'S ADAPTATION

Early findings from the RCRP identified child-centered attributes in areas of cognitive, affective, and social functioning associated with well-being and resilience for groups of urban children at high risk for psychopathology. Those attributes included realistic control attributions about family stress processes, feelings of self-efficacy to master challenges, positive future expectations, and empathy. Protective effects for children were also found in parents' competencies, including their positive emotion-focused coping strategies, feelings of self-efficacy, and provision of emotionally responsive, structured home environments.

More recent findings based on studies with our second cohort in later childhood and early adolescence showed that many effects of those competencies and resources on children's adaptation vary, depending on context. Whereas interpersonal and affective distancing and low expectations for parent involvement were generally associated with poorer child adaptation, those qualities were adaptive for children in highly dysfunctional families. Similarly, positive future expectations and perceptions of competence were not uniformly salutary. In fact, adolescents with unrealistically high perceptions of competence were at elevated risk for conduct problems. Similarly, positive future expectations were associated with academic disengagement for a group of adolescents with conduct disturbances. Finally, involvement in structured afterschool activities was protective for adolescents with many antisocial friends by lowering their risk for delinquent behavior but that protective function was not found for adolescents with few antisocial friends.

Collectively, recent RCRP findings underscore the importance of contextual specificity of protective and vulnerability processes. In our future efforts to investigate resilience trajectories – and in our efforts to promote them – we should remain attentive to the fact that processes that are beneficial to children in one context may be neutral, or even deleterious, in another.

References

Bandura, A. (1977). Self-efficacy: Toward a unifying theory of behavioral change. *Psychological Review, 84,* 191–215.

Baron, R. M., & Kenny, D. A. (1986). The moderator–mediator variable distinction in social psychological research: Conceptual, strategic, and statistical consideration. *Journal of Personality and Social Psychology, 51,* 1173–1182.

Beardslee, W. R., & Podorefsky, D. (1988). Resilient adolescents whose parents have serious affective and other psychiatric disorders: Importance of self-understanding and relationships. *American Journal of Psychiatry, 145(1),* 63–69.

Boyce, W. T., Frank, E., Jensen, P. S., Kessler, R. C., Nelson, C. A., Steinberg, L., & The MacArthur Foundation Research Network on Psychopathology and Development. (1998). Social context in developmental psychopathology: Recommendations for future research from the MacArthur Network on Psychopathology and Development. *Development and Psychopathology, 10,* 143–164.

Bronfenbrenner, U. (1979). *The ecology of human development: Experiments by nature and design.* Cambridge, MA: Harvard University Press.

Cairns, R. B., & Cairns, B. (1994). *Lifelines and risks: Pathways of youth in our time.* New York: Cambridge University Press.

Cicchetti, D., & Aber, J. L. (1998). Contextualism and developmental psychopathology. *Development and Psychopathology, 10,* 137–141.

Cicchetti, D., & Rogosch, F. A. (1997). The role of self-organization in the promotion of resilience in maltreated children. *Development and Psychopathology, 9,* 797–815.

Cowen, E. L., & Work, W. C. (1988). Resilient children, psychological wellness and primary prevention. *American Journal of Community Psychology, 16,* 591–607.

Cowen, E. L., Work, W. C., Hightower, A. D., Wyman, P. A., Parker, G. R., & Lotyczewski, B. S. (1991). Toward the development of a measure of perceived self-efficacy in children. *Journal of Clinical Child Psychology, 20,* 169–178.

Cowen, E. L., Work, W. C., Wyman, P. A., Parker, G. R., Wannon, M., & Gribble, P. A. (1992). Test comparisons among stress-affected, stress-resilient and non-classified fourth through sixth grade urban children. *Journal of Community Psychology, 20,* 200–214.

Cowen, E. L., Wyman, P. A., Work, W. C., & Iker, M. R. (1994). A preventive intervention for enhancing resilience among young highly stressed urban children. *Journal of Primary Prevention, 15,* 247–260.

Emery, R. E. (1982). Interpersonal conflict and the children of discord and divorce. *Psychological Bulletin, 92,* 310–330.

Forbes-Jones, E. L., Wyman, P. A., Cowen, E. L., & Kaufmann, D. R. (2001, August). *Inflated self-perceptions: Its relationship to aggression and family variables in highly stressed adolescents.* Poster presented at the American Psychological Association's annual meeting, San Francisco.

Gersten, J., Langer, T. S., Eisenberg, J. G., & Simcha-Fagen, O. (1977). An evaluation of the etiologic role of stressful life-change events in psychological disorder, *Journal of Health and Social Behavior, 18,* 228–244.

Hoyt-Meyers, L. A., Cowen, E. L., Work, W. C., Wyman, P. A., Magnus, K. B., Fagen, D. B., & Lotyczewski, B. S. (1995). Test correlates of resilient outcomes among highly stressed 2nd and 3rd grade urban children. *Journal of Community Psychology, 23,* 326–338.

Hughes, J. N., Cavell, T. A., & Grossman, P. B. (1997). A positive view of self: Risk or protection for aggressive children? *Development and Psychopathology, 9,* 75–94.

Iker, M. R. (1990). *Evaluation of a school-based preventive intervention for at-risk urban children.* Unpublished doctoral dissertation, University of Connecticut.

Kaufmann, D. K., Wyman, P. A., Cowen, E. L., & Forbes-Jones, E. L. (2001, August). *The stability and course of aggressive conduct and delinquent behavior.* Poster presented at the American Psychological Association's annual meeting, San Francisco.

Kellam, S. G., Ling, X., Merisca, R., Brown, C. H., & Ialongo, N. (1998). The effect of the level of aggression in the first grade classroom on the course and malleability of aggressive behavior in middle school. *Development and Psychopathology, 10,* 165–185.

Kerley, J. A. (1997). *Social competence and life stress as predictors of school adjustment in urban early adolescents: A prospective-longitudinal study*. Unpublished doctoral dissertation, The Fielding Institute.

Kilmer, R. P., Cowen, E. L., Wyman, P. A., Work, W. C., & Magnus, K. B. (1998). Differences in stressors experienced by urban African-American, White and Hispanic children. *Journal of Community Psychology, 26*, 415–428.

Kim, J. Y., Cowen, E. L., & Wyman, P. A. (1997, March). *Gender and stress-resilience: A comparisons of child test indicators*. Poster presented at the biennial meeting of the Society for Research in Child Development, Washington, D.C.

Kobasa, S. C., Maddi, S. R., & Kahn, S. (1982). Hardiness and health: A prospective study. *Journal of Personality and Social Psychology, 42*, 168–177.

Kornberg, M. S., & Caplan, G. (1980). Risk factors and preventive intervention in child therapy: A review. *Journal of Prevention, 1*, 71–133.

Loeber, R., & Stouthamer-Loeber, M. (1998). Development of juvenile aggression and violence: Some common misconceptions and controversies. *American Psychologist, 53*(2), 242–259.

Mahoney, J. L. (2000). School extracurricular activity participation as a moderator in the development of antisocial patterns. *Child Development, 71*, 502–516.

Masten, A. S. (2001). Ordinary magic: Resilience processes in development. *American Psychologist, 56*, 227–238.

Masten, A. S., & Coatsworth, J. D. (1998). The development of competence in favorable and unfavorable environments: Lessons from research on successful children. *American Psychologist, 53*, 205–220.

Nowicki, S., & Strickland, B. R. (1973). A locus of control scale for children. *Journal of Consulting and Clinical Psychology, 40*, 148–154.

Parker, G. R., Cowen, E. L., Work, W. C., & Wyman, P. A. (1990). Test correlates of stress resilience among urban school children. *Journal of Primary Prevention, 11*, 19–35.

Rutter, M. (1990). Psychosocial resilience and protective mechanisms. In J. Rolf, A. S. Masten, D. Cicchetti, K. H. Neuchterlein, & S. Weintraub (Eds.), *Risk and protective factors in the development of psychopathology* (pp. 181–214). New York: Cambridge University Press.

Wannon, M. (1990). *Children's control beliefs about controllable and uncontrollable events: Their relationship to stress resilience and psychosocial adjustment*. Unpublished doctoral dissertation, University of Rochester.

Werner, E. E., & Smith, R. S. (1982). *Vulnerable but invincible: A study of resilient children*. New York: McGraw-Hill.

Work, W. C., Cowen, E. L., Parker, G. W., & Wyman, P. A. (1990). Stress resilient children in an urban setting. *Journal of Primary Prevention, 11*, 3–17.

Wyman, P. A., Forbes-Jones, E. F., Cowen, E. L., Kilmer, R. P., Kaufmann, D. R., Barry, J., Spomer, M., & Montes, G. (2002). Trajectories of competence and antisocial behavior among urban youths in adversity: Contributions of family contexts and youth resources from childhood to adolescence. Manuscript submitted.

Wyman, P. A., Cowen, E. L., Work, W. C., Hoyt-Meyers, L. A., Magnus, K. B., & Fagen, D. B. (1999a). Caregiving and developmental factors differentiating young at-risk urban children showing resilient versus stress-affected outcomes: A replication and extension. *Child Development, 70,* 645–659.

Wyman, P. A., Cowen, E. L., Work, W. C., & Kerley, J. H. (1993). The role of children's future expectations in self-system functioning and adjustment to life-stress. *Development and Psychopathology, 5,* 649–661.

Wyman, P. A., Cowen, E. L., Work, W. C., & Parker, G. R. (1991). Developmental and family milieu interview correlates of resilience in urban children who have experienced major life-stress. *American Journal of Community Psychology, 19,* 405–426.

Wyman, P. A., Cowen, E. L., Work, W. C., Raoof, A., Gribble, P. A., Parker, G. R., & Wannon, M. (1992). Interviews with children who experienced major life stress: Family and child attributes that predict resilient outcomes. *Journal of the American Academy of Child and Adolescent Psychiatry, 31,* 904–910.

Wyman, P. A., & Forbes-Jones, E. L. (2001). Creative adaptation to life adversities: Deriving meaning from the past and expectations for the future. In B. Bloom & T. Gullotta (Eds.), Hartman monograph series: Creativity across the life span (pp. 157–190). Washington, DC: CWLA Press.

Wyman, P. A., Kilmer, R. P., Forbes-Jones, E. L., Spomer, M. L., & Cowen, E. L. (1999b, August). *Long-term follow up of urban, stress-exposed adolescents: Examining adjustment stability.* Poster presented at the American Psychological Association, Annual Meeting, Boston.

Wyman, P. A., Sandler, I. N., Wolchik, S., & Nelson, K. (2000). Resilience as cumulative competence promotion and stress protection: Theory and intervention. In D. Cicchetti, J. Rappaport, I. N. Sandler, & R. P. Weissberg (Eds.), *The promotion of wellness in children and adolescents* (pp. 133–184). Thousand Oaks, CA: Sage.

13

Holistic Contextual Perspectives on Risk, Protection, and Competence among Low-Income Urban Adolescents

Edward Seidman and Sara Pedersen

What are the characteristic ways in which risk, vulnerability, protection, and competence have been studied? What are the implicit assumptions underlying this body of research and scholarship? This chapter addresses these questions in the domain of adolescent development, with an emphasis on how a set of alternative assumptions and related research and data analytic strategies can both enrich our understanding of youth well-being and increase our ability to promote positive developmental outcomes.

RISK, PROTECTION, AND COMPETENCE

We define the central phenomena of interest: risk, vulnerability, protection, and competence. Either an individual or a population can be at increased risk for some form of negative developmental outcome, be it delinquency, drug use, depression, schizophrenia, school dropout, or unemployment. Multiple risk or vulnerability factors increase the likelihood that an individual or a population will manifest negative developmental outcomes. Many studies indicate that it is not any single risk factor that

Work on this chapter was supported in part by grants from the National Institutes of Mental Health (MH43084) and the Carnegie Corporation (B4850) awarded to Edward Seidman, J. Lawrence Aber, LaRue Allen, and Christina Mitchell. We express our appreciation to the adolescents and schools whose cooperation made this study possible and to Suniya Luthar, Laura Lambert, Tracey A. Revenson, and Hirokazu Yoshikawa for their penetrating and constructive comments on earlier drafts of the manuscript.

Address correspondence to Edward Seidman, Adolescent Pathways Project, Psychology Department, New York University, 6 Washington Place, Room 277, New York, NY 10003. Phone (212) 998-7794, Fax (212) 998-7781, or <edward.seidman@nyu.edu>.

is problematic, but the accumulation of multiple risks (e.g., Sameroff & Seifer, 1990). Protective factors are defined as experiences that ameliorate the negative impact of risks. Some investigators have operationalized protective and vulnerability factors in conjunction with each other as part of a multiple risk index (Sameroff & Seifer, 1990), whereas other scholars have argued that protective *processes* are set in motion only in the presence of adverse risk factors (Rutter, 1990).

Our program of research deals with a population placed at risk because it is exposed to poverty and consequently to a cascading set of related distal risk factors, including dangerous neighborhoods, under-resourced schools, large families, and low parental education. Yet, the proximal and daily experiences of poverty-associated vulnerability and protective circumstances, such as interpersonal conflict and daily hassles or social support from and engagement with family, peer, school, work, and neighborhood microsystems may be more determinative of developmental outcomes than poverty per se. As will become evident, we believe that within the context of poverty, it is the *particular constellation of proximal vulnerability and protective circumstances* within and across proximal social settings that places individuals at risk for, and protects them against, adverse developmental outcomes. At the same time, this proximal configuration of vulnerability and protective circumstances can enhance the probability of experiencing positive developmental outcomes. In a classic study, Sameroff, Seifer, Barocas, Zax, and Greenspan (1987) found that an index of multiple risk and protective factors was associated with negative developmental outcomes, although they failed to find an association between different family constellations of structural risk and protective factors and these same outcomes. Nevertheless, our research focuses more on the constellation of perceived psychosocial processes than on structural factors and indices.

The meaning and utility of the different but related concepts of invulnerability, resilience, and competence have been subjected to considerable scrutiny (e.g., Luthar, Cicchetti, & Becker, 2000; Masten & Coatsworth, 1998). Consistent with the views of many of these scholars, we are interested in understanding under what adverse conditions and by which processes positive adaptation or competence unfolds. Theoretically, competence has been defined as the "complex interactions between a child and his or her environment; thus, it will change as a child develops and changes or when the context changes. A child is a living system, embedded within many other systems, such as families and schools" (Masten & Coatsworth, 1998, p. 206). Thus, the concept of competence directs our attention toward ongoing transactional processes *between* people and their social contexts.

Research on competence (and resilience), however, has most often focused on functioning in a single social context, such as academic achievement or peer competence. Yet, to truly grasp the holistic meaning of a person's competence, one must examine the "package" or pattern of responses across multiple proximal social contexts (Yoshikawa & Seidman, 2000). We refer to this as *contextual competence*. We will provide empirical evidence supporting this construct of contextual competence as well as related holistic perspectives on proximal vulnerability and protective circumstances later in this chapter, drawing on data from a study of urban adolescents living in poverty.

GUIDING RESEARCH TENETS

Four tenets guide the research presented here and distinguish it from much of the earlier mainstream research. First, this research is anchored in an attempt to examine developmental phenomena from both holistic and dynamic perspectives and, consequently, takes as its unit of analysis the individual-in-context. Second, this research places a premium on intensive, within-group studies of at-risk populations. Third, it is important to explicitly consider positive outcomes, and not just indices of maladjustment among groups traditionally thought of as at risk. Fourth, pattern-centered data analytic techniques are congruent with a holistic approach to understanding the individual-in-context. These guiding tenets challenge the traditional assumptions inherent in mainstream research design and data analytic strategies (Seidman, 1978).

Holistic, Individual-in-Context Perspective

The earliest studies of risk, protection, and developmental outcomes were guided by trait theories in which person-centered dimensions were the exclusive points of departure. These dimensions took the form of biological predispositions such as temperament, cognitive abilities such as intelligence, and behaviors such as bullying. More recently, such person-centered dimensions have been examined in interaction with each other or with contextual dimensions. Most studies now also go beyond examining the (risk or protective) influence of single variables on single outcomes. Multivariate investigations have become the mode, allowing for the assessment of additive and interactive models.

From a developmental contextual perspective, risk, protection, and competence cannot be ascertained by simply examining person-centered characteristics (Lerner & Simi, 2000). As Magnusson (2000) states: "The recognition of the interactive character of dynamic processes means that the models highlight the concept of context. The role of context is important for understanding individual development and functioning at all levels of the total system.... The behavior of an individual cannot be understood without reference to the environment with which he or she has to deal, and systems at different levels function and develop in an interdependent way" (p. 40). Conceptually, this perspective is not new to developmental science or community psychology, but empirically, it has infrequently been examined.

The true meaning and impact of risk and protection unfold in the complex and multivariate transactions of individuals with a particular context, like their family or peers. From this perspective, the influence of these factors can best be fully understood in terms of the *pattern* of critical transactions youths have with that context in terms of salient dimensions of their experience. For example, the vulnerability and protective nature of adolescents' transactions with their families may be evaluated in terms of such salient dimensions as daily hassles, social support, and involvement. Similarly, competence cannot be fully grasped by simply examining individuals' transactions with a single social context. Competence unfolds simultaneously in multiple proximal social contexts (Yoshikawa & Seidman, 2000), and there is critical interdomain variation among contexts (Luthar & Burack, 2000). In other words, competence can best be understood as multivariate *and* as manifested differently in relationship to different social contexts, like peer groups, schools, athletics, and religion.

A holistic, individual-in-context tenet questions the dominant canon of searching for *universal laws of behavior*. It is easy for unique phenomena to be overlooked when the investigation is driven by the search for common, generalizable laws. This social science assumption steers us toward trying to understand the unique expression of phenomena in different contexts and cultures.

Importance of Intensive Within-Group Samples

Understanding a phenomenon in context requires intensive within-group studies in contrast to representative and heterogeneous samples. The use of representative and heterogeneous samples almost ensures the finding that those in the sample at greatest risk, usually those participants low in socioeconomic resources that are often confounded with racial/ethnic minority group membership, are afforded the least protection and fall victim to the worst developmental outcomes. Not surprisingly, such studies commonly have revealed that low-income, and often Black and Latina/o, youths manifested higher rates and levels of severity of maladaptive developmental outcomes, such as, delinquency, substance abuse, teenage pregnancy, school failure, and dropout. These findings reflected average differences among income or race/ethnic groups. As a consequence, the wide range of variation in developmental outcomes among youths subjected to poverty was often ignored (Luthar & McMahon, 1996).

More specifically, the expression and meaning of competence or the processes that foster it may take different forms in low- versus middle-income populations or in different racial/ethnic groups. For example, it appears that authoritarian parenting facilitates competent developmental outcomes among Blacks but not Whites (Steinberg, Mounts, Lamborn, & Dornbusch, 1991). Often, it is precisely these *boundary conditions* to generalizability that we need to identify (Seidman, 1989). Indeed, understanding a phenomenon in context – for example, the racial, ethnic, or socioeconomic context – may hold the critical key for generating and designing innovative ameliorative, preventive, and promotive interventions (Hughes, Seidman, & Williams, 1993).

Fortunately, during the past decade, research in developmental psychopathology increasingly has involved the selection of populations homogeneous on a particular risk condition, be it poverty, parental mental illness, alcohol abuse, divorce, or teenage pregnancy (as illustrated in many of the chapters on resilience research in this volume). This type of homogeneity allows for a better understanding of the processes of resilience or competence within the sampled population. To examine and understand the meaning of such variability and the phenomenon's multiple forms of expression, a high-powered microscope is needed. Large samples of homogeneous groups are one form of a high-powered microscope.

The Need to Examine Positive Developmental Outcomes

All youths growing up in economically precarious circumstances do not end up as school dropouts, pregnant teenagers, delinquents, or substance abusers. They have diverse outcomes, and many of these are positive outcomes. In recent years, we have seen a return toward a positive psychology, as evidenced in a recent special issue of the *American Psychologist* (Seligman & Csikszentmihalyi, 2000). Clearly, there is a movement away from the more dominant and exclusive focus on psychopathology and social deviance. Yet, many of these efforts continue to focus on person-centered experiences and attributes. Nevertheless, Seligman and Csikszentmihalyi's (2000) third thread of a positive psychology recognizes "that people and experiences are embedded in a social context" (p. 8). In this vein, we pursue the positive notion of contextual competence.

The Congruence of Pattern-Centered Data Analytic Strategies

How can we tap the multiple holistic ways in which a family or peer network places youth at risk for, or offers them protection against, maladaptive outcomes? Similarly, how can we understand the multiple holistic expressions of competence as embedded in the social context? In addition to using large, homogeneous samples of youths living in poverty with subsamples from different racial/ethnic groups, we need to challenge the assumptions of our traditional linear and variable-based data analytic strategies if we are to understand the full gestalt and its effects. Pattern-based methods are tools that allow us to examine co-occurrence (or complex interactions) more easily and make it possible to search for and identify multiple holistic expressions of socially embedded risk, protection, and competence (Bergman, 2000; Cairns, 2000).

RISK, PROTECTION, AND CONTEXTUAL COMPETENCE AMONG LOW-INCOME URBAN ADOLESCENTS

In the remainder of this chapter, we explore the utility of a holistic, individual-in-context perspective using homogeneous samples and pattern-based data analytic strategies to explore competence as well as vulnerable and protective circumstances in a population of urban adolescents living in poverty. We describe the sample, its design, cascading risks of poverty, and several studies bearing on vulnerable and protective family and peer circumstances and their associated developmental outcomes as well as contextual competence and their associated outcomes.

The Adolescent Pathways Project (APP)

The APP followed two cohorts of urban youth from the public schools of New York City, Washington, D.C., and Baltimore (Seidman, 1991).

The younger cohort (YC; $N = 907$) was assessed initially at the end of the spring semester of their last year of elementary school (fifth or sixth grade). The older cohort (OC; $N = 531$) was assessed initially at the end of the spring semester of their last year of intermediate or junior high school (eighth or ninth grade). Three annual waves of data were collected from both cohorts. A fourth wave of data was collected on the YC youths approximately 5 years after the initial wave of data was collected. The sample of 1,438 consists of 27% Black, 23% White, and 40% Latina/o youths. The subgroups constituting the remaining 10% of the sample are each too small in number to examine uniquely. The Black subsample consists of youth from primarily African American and Caribbean American families, the White subsample consists of youth from primarily Italian and Greek immigrant families, and the Latina/o subsample consists of youth from primarily Dominican and Puerto Rican families.

The Cascading Nature of Poverty into Proximal Social Contexts

Poverty is our central risk condition of interest. However, poverty is far more than a simple economic variable. The effects of poverty are numerous and correlated – financial, structural, social, and psychological. The magnitude and nature of these poverty effects cascade into the neighborhoods, schools, peer groups, and families, affecting the daily lives and experiences of the youths.

The APP was created in response to the fact that through the 1980s, the bulk of the knowledge base about urban poor teens, and especially teens of color, was generated from cross-sectional studies of heterogeneous samples (Seidman, 1991). The APP focuses on the longitudinal development of poor, urban public school youths, looking at pathways to maladaptation *and* adaptation. Instead of sampling individuals, we endeavored to find public schools that contained the highest percentages of poor children in New York City, Washington, D.C., and Baltimore. These schools were more likely to have students who grew up in neighborhoods characterized by economic adversity. To do this, we chose schools with the highest percentages of children receiving reduced-price/free lunch (R/FL). We chose schools whose student bodies were predominantly Black and Latina/o (80% or more), where at least 80% of the students were on R/FL, and predominantly White (50% or more), where at least 60% of the students were on R/FL. Given the strong confound between race/ethnicity and poverty in urban communities, it was not surprising that in those public schools with higher concentrations of White students, we had to accept a slightly lower percentage of the student body who were receiving R/FL.

By examining large samples of different racial/ethnic groups, we can test whether the findings are common across racial/ethnic groups and which are unique to each group. We also can examine multiple ways in which vulnerability, protection, and contextual competence are expressed in a homogeneously low-income yet racially and ethnically heterogeneous sample.

For us, sampling students from schools with high concentrations of poor children was a proxy for the cascading nature of poverty; it was reflected in structural (including material and financial resources) ways not only in the schools we sampled, but in the neighborhoods and families of the youths as well. In addition to enrolling high percentages of students on R/FL, the schools we sampled were overcrowded and lacked financial and material resources. For example, the New York City elementary schools in our sample had an average of 1,050 pupils compared to a citywide average of 750 and a nationwide average of well under 500. Sixty percent of the APP youth lived in neighborhoods with federal designations as poverty neighborhoods (i.e., 20% or more of the nonelderly residents in that census track live below the official poverty line). For the Black and Latina/o youths, 79% live in poverty neighborhoods. These neighborhood poverty differences reflect the fact that the White sample can best be described as *working-class poor*, in contrast to the much lower economic status of the Black and Latina/o youths' families.

Not surprisingly, APP youths often reside in households with limited finances, often indexed by a one-parent household. The percentage of youths residing in a one-parent household differs dramatically by race/ethnicity. For example, across racial/ethnic groups, 28% of the YC reported living alone with one biological parent, whereas for the Black subsample this figure rises to 48%.

The cascading effects of poverty also unfold in the psychosocial climates of the proximal social contexts – family, peer group, school, and neighborhood – that youths inhabit. How they experience daily hassles and social support, and the degree to which they participate with each of these microsystems, are impacted, as well as the prosocial versus antisocial values of the peers with whom they associate. Yet poverty in itself does not lead families or peer groups to subject youths to a uniform set of psychosocial risk processes. Instead, unique constellations of these salient psychosocial processes that transpire within youths' families, peer groups, schools, and neighborhoods place them differentially at risk for (and protect them against) various negative outcomes and enhance the possibility of positive developmental outcomes.

Pattern-based methods can identify critical configurations of salient dimensions both within and across contexts. To this end, we employ cluster analyses to identify the multiple ways, for example, within family or peer networks that perceived daily transactions protect or place youth at risk and the multiple forms in which competence can be expressed across varying social contexts.

Context-Based Vulnerable and Protective Circumstances: Nature and Outcomes

In this section, we describe the holistic and contextual manner in which we examine adolescents' perceptions of their transactions with their proximal microsystems. What follows is our examination of family and peer profiles of perceived transactions as they relate to psychological and behavioral outcomes (Roberts et al., 2000; Seidman et al., 1999). Within the family system, we also present temporal profiles of change or stasis across the span of early adolescence (Lambert, 2003).

Profiles of Perceived Family Transactions

To understand the different ways in which families can protect against or place youth at risk for different developmental outcomes, we utilized student self-reports of the intensity of daily hassles, social support, and involvement with their families (Seidman et al., 1999). Employing the full APP sample at Wave 1, six different profiles were uncovered; these are illustrated in Table 13.1.

Two profiles – Dysfunctional and Functional-Involving – are mirror images of each other. In families perceived as Dysfunctional, hassles were high, whereas support and involvement were low, and vice versa for those perceived as Functional-Involving. These profiles are consistent with the endpoints of what one would expect from previous theory and research using variable-centered data analytic strategies. However, four other unexpected and nuanced perceived family profiles were also uncovered. The Functional-Uninvolving profile bears a strong resemblance to the Functional-Involving profile, but involvement was low. A fourth profile is labeled Detaching because students perceived their relationship to their family as moderately low in hassles, support, and involvement. The configurations of the two final profiles – Hassling and Enmeshing – can also be observed in Table 13.1.

TABLE 13.1. *Perceived Family Transactional Profiles, Distribution by Subsample, and Developmental Outcomes (N = 1,160)*

		Family Profiles					
		Functional-Involving	Functional-Uninvolving	Detaching	Hassling	Enmeshing	Dysfunctional
Perceived transactional dimension (standardized scores)	Daily hassles	−0.58	−0.68	−0.49	1.25	0.61	1.25
	Social support	0.74	+0.85	−0.68	0.39	−0.50	−1.50
	Involvement	1.01	−0.48	−0.49	−0.34	1.50	−0.67
Distribution of profiles within full/demographic subsamples	Full sample	20%	20%	25%	15%	9%	11%
	Older cohort	13%	20%	32%	13%	6%	16%
	Younger cohort	24%	20%	21%	15%	11%	9%
	Females	19%	17%	25%	16%	10%	13%
	Males	23%	25%	25%	12%	7%	8%
	Blacks	18%	18%	29%	11%	11%	13%
	Whites	20%	28%	22%	15%	6%	9%
	Latina/os	23%	16%	21%	18%	11%	11%
Outcome (adjusted means)	Self-esteem[1]	3.16	3.14	2.91	2.66	2.80	2.48
	Depression[2]	0.43[e]	0.45[d]	0.51[c]	0.64[b]	0.64[b]	0.77[a]
	Antisocial behavior[3]	0.64[b]	0.58[b]	0.69[b]	0.97[a]	0.98[a]	0.92[a]

[1] Self-esteem analyses used only the Younger Cohort subsample (N = 635). Significant planned comparisons: Functional Involving, Functional Uninvolving > all other profiles; Detaching > Hassling, Enmeshing, Dysfunctional; Enmeshing, Hassling > Dysfunctional.
[2] Significant posthoc comparisons (Bonferroni correction): a > b > c, d, e; c > e.
[3] Significant posthoc comparisons (Bonferroni correction): a > b.

327

Overall, the same six constellations of hassles, support, and involvement were apparent in each racial/ethnic group, gender, and cohort; thus, the profiles are not unique to each group. There were, however, several noteworthy differential rates of association between profiles and race/ethnicity, gender, and cohort. White teens were more likely to depict their families as Functional-Uninvolving than the other racial/ethnic groups. Boys were more likely to portray their family transactions as Functional-Uninvolving, whereas girls were more likely to perceive their family transactions as Dysfunctional. The YC, compared to the OC, was more likely to perceive their family transactions as Functional-Involving and Enmeshing and less likely to depict them as Dysfunctional and Detaching. The latter finding indicates a differential likelihood of occurrence of perceived family profiles during early and middle adolescence and may suggest changes within individuals' perceptions of their family's influence over this span of time.

Are these various constellations of perceived family transactions associated with psychological and behavioral outcomes, controlling for gender, race/ethnicity, and cohort? (See Table 13.1.) Not surprisingly, youths who experienced their families as Dysfunctional, Hassling, and Enmeshing – the maladaptive patterns – were at greatest risk for engaging in antisocial behavior, whereas Functional-Involving as well as Functional-Uninvolving families – the adaptive patterns – reported protection against engaging in antisocial behavior. Somewhat surprisingly, those who perceived their families as Detaching were also protected against engaging in antisocial behavior. For depression, identification with the Dysfunctional profile and the Functional-Involving profile was associated with the greatest and least risk, respectively. The Functional-Uninvolving profile youths were also protected from depression, as were youths in the Detaching family transactional constellation. In terms of self-esteem in the YC, the two functional or adaptive profiles were protective in comparison to all others, whereas Detaching was more protective than Dysfunctional, Hassling, and Enmeshing (Roberts et al., 2000). Overall, the Detaching profile seemed to offer a surprising amount of protection/enhancement in both young and old cohorts. It appears that a pattern of detaching transactions from families subjected to the stresses of adverse economic conditions may have adaptive value for the adolescent.

The preceding cross-sectional study revealed multiple constellations of perceived family processes with different developmental outcome correlates. It is also possible to examine these issues and the same constructs in a more dynamic and temporal fashion. In that vein, in her dissertation,

Lambert (2003) examined the changing patterns of perceived family transactions across the first three waves of data collection in the YC, that is, during early adolescence. This is a time when the responsivity of the family to an adolescent's changing ecology, biology, cognitive needs, and social needs is critical for future adaptation (Eccles et al., 1993).

Eight temporal profiles or trajectories were identified. Based on prior literature, these trajectories of perceived family transactions can be viewed as representing either a good or a poor developmental fit for early adolescents (Combrinck-Graham, 1985). Profiles that depict a pattern of perceptions of ongoing beneficial family relationships (the Engaging and Supportive profiles) or movement toward better family relationships (the Responsive-Involved and Evolving-Fit profiles) represent a good developmental fit. Given that our cross-sectional investigation (Seidman et al., 1999) uncovered a Detaching profile that, surprisingly, was associated with positive developmental outcomes, the corresponding temporal profile also was expected to be adaptive. In contrast, profiles that depicted high rates of perceived conflict, whether stable (Conflictual-Static) or unstable (the Evolving-Misfit and Transitional-Upheaval profiles), were expected to represent a poor developmental fit and to be maladaptive. A planned contrast between the adaptive and maladaptive profiles, controlling for the respective dependent measure at Wave 1, proved to be significant at Wave 3 for antisocial behavior, depression, and self-esteem.

Several other empirically and theoretically driven planned contrasts were studied; only one of these yielded a consistent pattern of findings, albeit contrary to our expectations. This contrast compared the Transitional-Upheaval trajectory, characterized by a perceived maladaptive familial response after the transition to junior high school and, 1 year later, a perceived reduction in the maladaptive familial response, with the Evolving-Misfit trajectory, characterized by a continuous maladaptive familial response across the three waves of data. The contrast was again significant in the full and racial/ethnic subgroup analyses for depression and self-esteem, but in a surprising direction: Adolescents who perceived deterioration in their family processes over the course of early adolescence (Evolving-Misfit) reported more favorable well-being outcomes than adolescents who perceived their family transactions to recover (Transitional-Upheaval). It may be that families who experienced enormous difficulty in coping with their child's transition to junior high school had a longer-term effect on the youth's psychological adjustment.

Profiles of Perceived Peer Transactions

The identification of different constellations of perceived peer transactions, and their contemporaneous associations with developmental outcomes, paralleled those for the families of these youths, as previously described. Here, we employed not only daily hassles, social support, and social involvement with peers, but also social acceptance by peers and peer values (pro- versus antisocial) (Seidman et al., 1999). Again, six different profiles were uncovered; these are illustrated in Table 13.2.

A classic adaptive perceived peer profile revealed itself. The Prosocial-Engaging profile was high in social support, involvement, acceptance, and prosocial peer values and low in hassles. Another very similar profile appeared, with the exception that its members reported quite antisocial peer values, and it was labeled Antisocial-Engaging. The coexistence of popularity and antisocial aspects bears some similarities to both configural (Rodkin, Farmer, Pearl, & Van Acker, 2000) and nomothetic (Luthar & McMahon, 1996) research with poor adolescents. A third profile was high in social support and involvement but, paradoxically, quite high in hassles and was labeled Entangling. The small Rejecting and Neglecting profiles were consistent with much prior literature. Both of these profiles manifested low social support and involvement, as did the Disengaging-Accepting profile. However, it revealed high acceptance and moderately prosocial peer values as well.

Although each perceived peer profile appeared within each gender, racial/ethnic group, and cohort, there were a few noteworthy differences in terms of the degree of association. Boys and YC youths were more likely to depict their perceived peer transactions as Disengaging-Accepting and least likely to depict them as Antisocial-Engaging, whereas girls and OC youths were more likely to exhibit the opposite pattern of association. White youths most often classified their transactions as Antisocial-Engaging and least often as Neglecting, whereas Black youths most often perceived their transactions as Rejecting.

Are these various constellations of perceived peer relationships associated with different degrees of risk and protection, controlling for gender, race/ethnicity, and cohort? (See Table 13.2.) One might expect that the two profiles depicted as engaging are highly protective. Or, perhaps, the directional reversal on peer values' for the Antisocial-Engaging cluster might erode the protective effect for the latter profile in terms of antisocial behavior. Indeed, the Prosocial-Engaging peer profile was protective against depression and enhancing of self-esteem, but only modestly protective against antisocial behavior (Roberts et al., 2000;

TABLE 13.2. *Perceived Peer Transactional Profiles, Distribution by Subsample, and Developmental Outcomes (N = 1,016)*

		Peer Profiles					
		Disengaging-Accepting	Prosocial-Engaging	Antisocial-Engaging	Entangling	Neglecting	Rejecting
Perceived transactional dimension (standardized scores)	Daily hassles	−0.33	−0.53	−0.40	1.45	−0.28	1.88
	Social support	−1.12	0.53	0.51	0.55	−0.27	−0.67
	Involvement	−0.57	0.24	0.52	0.51	−0.50	−0.60
	Acceptance	0.51	0.58	0.34	0.23	−1.28	−1.06
	Peer values	0.36	0.66	−1.22	0.15	0.18	0.14
Distribution of profiles within full/demographic subsamples	Full sample	17%	24%	20%	13%	17%	9%
	Older cohort	11%	23%	36%	10%	14%	6%
	Younger cohort	20%	25%	12%	14%	19%	10%
	Females	14%	23%	23%	14%	16%	10%
	Males	22%	27%	15%	10%	19%	7%
	Blacks	18%	20%	18%	15%	17%	12%
	Whites	14%	30%	28%	10%	12%	6%
	Latina/os	18%	25%	18%	13%	18%	8%
Outcome (Adjusted Means)	Self-esteem[1]	3.15	3.12	2.87	2.74	2.88	2.46
	Depression[2]	0.47[c]	0.46[c]	0.49[c]	0.67[b]	0.59[b]	0.78[a]
	Antisocial Behavior[3]	0.68[d]	0.81[c]	1.08[a]	0.90[b]	0.68[d]	0.65[d]

[1] Self-esteem analyses used only the Younger Cohort subsample (N = 635). Significant planned comparisons: Disengaging-Accepting, Prosocial-Engaging, Antisocial-Engaging > all other profiles; Prosocial-Engaging > Antisocial-Engaging.

[2] Significant posthoc comparisons (Bonferroni correction): a > b > c.

[3] Significant posthoc comparisons (Bonferroni correction): a > c, d; b > d.

Seidman et al., 1999). The Antisocial-Engaging profile served to protect against depression and, at the same time, placed its constituents at greatest risk for behaving in an antisocial fashion. The Disengaging-Accepting profile was protective against both depression and antisocial behavior. The Entangling profile manifested the highest risk of any peer profile for depression and the second highest risk for antisocial behavior. Not surprisingly, those who perceived their peer network as Rejecting were at greatest risk for depression.

Holistic Patterns of Contextual Competence: Nature and Outcomes

In assessing contextual competence, our assumptions about how adaptation is embedded in the everyday transactions youths experience with their social contexts become even more salient. As previously indicated, most research has examined competence in terms of cognitive and interpersonal dimensions. School and peer settings are vital and primary locations in which adolescents can demonstrate competence. Are they, however, sufficient in scope to capture different manifestations of contextual competence?

Often, adolescents are engaged in other salient domains of experience, such as athletics, employment, and religion, that might foster the development of different competencies. For many young people, particularly those from ethnic minority backgrounds, their cultural connection (identification with their racial/ethnic group) takes on added importance as well. Individually, connection to one or another of these settings is represented in the literature as having powerful risk or protective effects on developmental outcomes. So, for example, religion has almost uniformly been represented as a protective context for youth development and has been found to have protective effects against maladaptive outcomes that fall under the problem behavior rubric (Weaver et al., 1998). Similarly, adolescent employment for more than 15 or 20 hours per week has been shown to place youth at greater risk for maladaptive outcomes (Steinberg, Fegley, & Dornbusch, 1993). However, are the developmental outcomes different for youth who heavily engage in employment *and* strongly connect to other settings, such as school, in contrast to those who only heavily engage in work? This question suggests the possibility of multiple forms of competence with different meanings and outcomes. Thus, understanding competence *within and across* settings is imperative. Competence defined and assessed from a multidimensional and contextual standpoint is both more comprehensive and holistic.

In order to explore further the utility of a multidimensional and contextual framework for assessing youth competence, we became interested in capturing adolescents' *engagement* and *quality of performance* in multiple salient domains of youth experience (Pedersen et al., 2001). The contextual domains chosen for study were the peer group, academics, athletics, religion, employment, and culture. The nature and quality of familial connections were excluded because we were most interested in examining the development of competence in contexts that become more salient during adolescence and reflect youths' growing connections to settings outside the family system during this developmental stage. Here we utilized the YC participants at Wave 4 when their mean age was 16.5 (0.99); at this age, we could attain a fuller assessment of their competence through our in-depth individual interviews. A principal component analysis of a variety of indices tapping both engagement (e.g., involvement, attendance, hours worked) and quality of performance dimensions (e.g., grade point average, attachment, honors) in each social context, except in the case of work, where only indices of involvement were included, revealed six context-based factors. In addition, academic efficacy expectations and social efficacy expectations did not load on the school and peer components, as anticipated, but instead "hung" together as a separate component labeled *self-efficacy*.

Nine intriguing profiles of contextual competence emerged from the cluster analyses, and these are shown in Table 13.3. We describe each profile with an eye toward identifying interesting profile comparisons that may elucidate the benefits of measuring competence as holistic patterns of engagement and performance across salient settings. We also identify patterns of associations among the clusters and demographic variables, such as race/ethnicity, gender, and age. Finally, we explore the extent to which planned profile comparisons reveal differential associations between profiles and three frequently studied adolescent developmental outcomes – delinquency, depression, and self-esteem (for further details, see Pedersen et al., 2003).

Two profiles emerged that represented differing forms of *pan-competence* – generally high engagement and quality across most settings. For example, the Engaged Nonworker profile represents youths who reported moderate to high engagement and quality across all domains except employment. A contrasting configuration was the Engaged Worker profile. Youths in this group, although also reporting high athletic and religious engagement, strongly endorsed engagement in employment activities.

TABLE 13.3. *Contextual Competence Profiles, Distribution by Subsample, and Developmental Outcomes (N = 530)*

		Contextual Competence Profiles								
		Engag. Non-worker	Engag. Worker	Engag. Non-athlete	Strong Relig. Connec.	Cultur. Diseng. Athlete	Acad. Diseng. Athlete	Worker	Low-Effic. Acad.	Disconnected
Context (standardized scores)	Efficacy	0.64	0.38	0.67	−0.16	−0.31	0.24	−0.10	−0.90	−0.68
	Peer	0.42	0.23	0.63	0.14	−0.64	0.19	−0.66	0.09	−0.71
	Academic	0.57	0.48	0.08	−0.56	−0.08	−0.69	−0.18	0.56	−0.48
	Athletics	0.54	0.58	−0.91	−0.20	0.65	0.74	−0.11	−0.35	−0.93
	Religion	0.47	0.32	−0.35	0.91	−0.19	−0.34	−0.42	−0.21	−0.38
	Employment	−0.53	1.01	0.06	−0.37	−0.22	−0.10	1.10	−0.46	−0.41
	Culture	0.67	0.31	0.29	−0.08	−1.00	0.20	−0.28	0.23	−0.65
Distribution of profiles within full/demographic subsamples	Full sample	10%	10%	10%	12%	9%	13%	14%	13%	9%
	Female	14%	11%	18%	11%	5%	5%	7%	17%	12%
	Male	14%	14%	5%	9%	13%	18%	13%	8%	6%
	Blacks	20%	12%	15%	12%	8%	9%	5%	8%	11%
	Whites	11%	22%	13%	5%	10%	14%	9%	11%	5%
	Latina/os	11%	9%	12%	11%	8%	12%	13%	15%	9%
Outcome (adjusted means)	Self-esteem[1]	3.50	3.26	3.45	3.18	3.12	3.19	3.16	3.13	2.62
	Depression[2]	1.31	1.38	1.35	1.39	1.40	1.32	1.41	1.51	1.63
	Delinquency[3]	1.95	2.37	2.32	2.16	2.63	2.41	2.16	2.20	1.94

Note: In every presentation of our cluster analytic findings that follow, the findings are reliable in that they were replicated on random subsets of the entire sample and account for significantly more variance than a set of random solutions. For further details, see each article that is referenced.

[1] Significant planned comparisons: Engaged Nonworker, Engaged Worker, and Engaged Nonathlete > all other profiles; Disconnected < Strong Religious Connection, Culturally Disengaged Athlete, Academically Disengaged Athlete, Disengaged Worker, and Low Efficacy Academic profiles.

[2] Significant planned comparisons: Engaged Nonworker, Engaged Worker, and Engaged Nonathlete > all other profiles; Disconnected < Strong Religious Connection, Culturally Disengaged Athlete, Academically Disengaged Athlete, Disengaged Worker, and Low-Efficacy Academic profiles; Strong Religious Connection, Low-Efficacy Academic > Worker, Academically Disengaged Athlete, and Culturally Disengaged Athlete profiles; Low-Efficacy Academic > Strong Religious Connection profiles.

[3] Significant planned comparisons: Disconnected < all other profiles; Strong Religious Connection, Low-Efficacy Academic, Engaged Nonworker, Engaged Nonathlete < Worker, Academically Disengaged Athlete, Engaged Worker, Culturally Disengaged Athlete profiles. Worker < Culturally Disengaged Athlete profiles.

Two additional profiles characterized youths with similarly strong high-quality connections to the athletic domain. However, the importance of examining the youths' experiences holistically, rather than simply investigating the role of athletic engagement in youth development, was reflected in the extent to which youths who fit these profiles were differentially engaged with other social settings. The Culturally Disengaged Athlete profile reflects a pattern of competence marked by a positive peak for athletic engagement/quality but very low endorsements on the ethnic identity and peer dimensions. A second configuration, the Academically Disengaged Athlete profile, was again marked by a positive peak on the athletic domain but very low engagement/quality of performance in academics.

Similarly, religious involvement seems central to the experience of members of two clusters. However, the context in which religion assumes importance is different for each. The Engaged Nonworker profile (described previously) was marked by a moderately strong connection to religion in the context of high engagement along most other dimensions. In contrast, the Strong Religious Connection profile was marked by high religious involvement and commitment but only moderate or below-average engagement, quality, and performance in each of the remaining contexts.

Employment is one type of experience that has often been considered risky during adolescence. Two profiles emerged during our cluster analysis in which youths reported very high involvement in the work force, but with very different patterns of engagement in other contexts. One such constellation of youth competence, the Engaged Worker profile, as described previously, characterizes youths reporting above-average competence in multiple settings, including employment and athletics. In contrast, youths in the other high employment profile, or Worker constellation, reported consistently low engagement and achievement in the remaining dimensions, particularly in their peer relationships and ethnic identity development.

The Engaged Nonathlete profile appeared to represent youths who experienced a particularly strong connection to the peer group in combination with high efficacy expectations. However, these youths reported very low levels of engagement in the athletic domain.

An additional profile emerged that was characterized by engagement only in academics, but very low self-efficacy expectations, the Low Efficacy Academic profile. These youths reported high engagement in and preparedness for school-related activities. Finally, one profile emerged that was characterized by consistently low endorsements across all domains, the Disconnected profile.

Although each profile of contextual competence appeared within each gender and racial/ethnic group, there were a few noteworthy differences. Not surprisingly, there was an overrepresentation of males in profiles depicting high versus low engagement in athletics (the Academically and Culturally Disengaged Athletic profiles versus the Engaged Nonathletic profile). Females were overrepresented in the Low Efficacy Academic and Disconnected profiles. The most frequently occurring profile among Blacks was the Engaged Nonworker profile, whereas for Whites it was the Engaged Worker profile. Whites were underrepresented in the Strong Religious Connection and Disconnected profiles, whereas Latina/os were overrepresented in the Low Efficacy Academic and Worker profiles.

Turning to the relationships of these competence profiles to delinquency, depression, and self-esteem, our findings demonstrate that those profiles marked by positive youth experience in multiple settings (i.e., two or more) were associated with less depression, and greater self-esteem than were the profiles marked by high-quality engagement with only one domain or negative endorsements within all domains. (See Table 13.3.). In particular, we found that youths who reported positive engagement with multiple contexts (the Engaged Worker, Engaged Nonworker, and Engaged Nonathlete profiles) reported greater self-esteem and less depression than those who reported disengagement/negative experiences in all or almost all contexts (Strong Religious Connection, Culturally Disengaged Athlete, Academically Disengaged Athlete, Worker, and Low Efficacy Academic profiles).

In contrast, engagement in particular settings (e.g., athletics and employment) was associated with more serious delinquency. For example, youths in the Disconnected profile indicated the lowest levels of delinquency, while youths in the Culturally Disengaged Athletic profile reported the highest level of delinquency.

Revisiting the Guiding Tenets

By examining a population that is relatively homogeneous in terms of socioeconomic resources, we had the opportunity to uncover multiple constellations of perceived psychosocial processes *within* the family and peer contexts. The different risk/protective family and peer constellations that were revealed took advantage of both a holistic and a transactional worldview. The pattern-centered cluster analyses were critical in achieving these ends. Even if somehow one could overcome the difficult power problems in detecting complex interactions in field studies with regression techniques or other nomothetic methods (McClelland & Judd, 1993), imagine the difficulty of trying to uncover such richly textured understanding of such configurations of individual–family and individual–peer perceived psychosocial transactions. The configurations we identified here were meaningfully related to psychological and behavioral outcomes, both concurrently and prospectively. Moreover, the resulting family and peer profiles and the associated outcomes represent considerable variation among a sample of poor urban youth. Contrary to prevailing myths, there are many different patterns of vulnerability and protective processes in families and peers, and many of these configurations were associated with adaptive outcomes.

These findings underscore the importance of using within-group designs, because in large samples that are heterogeneous in economic status, these same youths would likely be found to be problematic, and the considerable variation in their relationships with family and peers, as well as in their associated psychological and behavioral outcomes, would be obscured. Additionally, our findings indicate that there can be few straightforward universal laws of behavior. Finally, when both perceived family and peer profiles are examined, important differences are revealed. Whereas perceived family profiles revealed uniform effects in terms of antisocial behavior, depression, and self-esteem, perceived peer profiles revealed differential effects on each outcome. For perceived transactions with peers, there is no gold standard of adaptation. Different peer configurations are differentially associated with psychological versus behavioral adaptation.

Our holistic orientation was also applied when we looked *across* social contexts at competence. A surprising diversity of forms of contextual competence was revealed in our sample of poor urban youths. These diverse forms of contextual competence too would probably have been obscured had we not employed a sample homogeneous in economic status. The idea of examining competence both within and across contexts proved to be both novel and fruitful.

The findings on contextual competence counter common myths, such as the singularly protective value of religious engagement and the risk of long hours of employment. As we have demonstrated, the benefits or risks associated with experiences generally framed as either positive or negative in the literature depend to an enormous degree on patterns of engagement and quality with other contexts in these youths' lives. For example, athletic engagement seems to be risky for youth development when experienced in the absence of a connection to other important settings. However, athletic participation in combination with employment, religious, and/or cultural involvement is associated with adaptive outcomes, such as higher self-esteem, less depression, and less serious delinquent acts. Most important, high and positive engagement with more than one experiential context is related to greater adaptation in terms of both self-esteem and depression. Again, it seems unlikely that a variable-centered analysis would have revealed such a richly textured portrait with meaningful relationships to competence and well-being as did these pattern-centered profiles of contextual competence.

Yet, we do not know what mechanisms are responsible for youths' appearing more competent when they are positively engaged with more than one setting. Is it because they have more opportunities to get involved in a relationship with a caring, supportive adult or engaged in more structured and/or supervised afterschool activities (Mahoney & Stattin, 2000)? This is a critical question for future research. Moreover, future theorizing and research would do well to systematically question many of the implicit background assumptions that typify much psychological research, such as a sole focus on variable-centered research, and seek alternative frameworks that might guide research in more fruitful directions.

The multiple profiles and their related outcomes also make it harder to accept uncritically the naive canon that there are generalizable laws about behavior. If there are generalizable laws, they must be sought at a meta-level. So for example, in thinking about the numerous findings of contextual competence, one could suggest that what is generalizable is the fact that competence may be related to developmental processes and outcomes only if one is positively engaged with more than one setting, no matter how powerful each individual setting is viewed in its own right.

FUTURE DIRECTIONS FOR RESEARCH AND INTERVENTION

To date, most of our work has been cross-sectional with regard to both setting-based risk and protection profiles and contextual competence. The Lambert (2001) study of trajectories of perceived family transactions is both an exception and an important first step. We need to continue to examine risk and protection profiles across time as well as across settings, as we did with contextual competence. We have also begun to test how peer profiles might mediate the effects of family profiles on developmental outcomes (Roberts et al., 2000). In the future, we will examine the stability of the family and peer profiles over time and their long-term relationships to profiles of contextual competence. Longitudinal analyses will give us increased power to elucidate how these microsystem profiles might moderate or mediate each other in the prediction of both positive and negative developmental outcomes.

When we turn to interventions, we can see that the implications of research findings, even our own, are a function of the level of analysis upon which we choose to focus. At the most macro level, we might choose to focus upon poverty in terms of economic policy and income inequality. This would probably not be a pragmatic or judicious use of our time and energy as psychologists, particularly in today's political climate. Nevertheless, reducing poverty and income inequality might reduce not only the structural and material inequities but also the cascading effects of psychosocial stressors within and across proximal social contexts of youths' lives.

Our work on competence directs us toward both preventive and promotive interventions at the level of settings. Positive engagement with only a single setting appears insufficient to enhance positive or inhibit negative psychological outcomes. On the other hand, positive engagement with two or more settings enhances positive and reduces negative developmental outcomes. Knowing the value of enhancing connection to two or more settings, unfortunately, does not tell us how to intervene without more knowledge of the potential mechanisms. Definitive intervention strategies will need to await the accumulation of this knowledge.

Speculatively, our findings on contextual competence suggest the need to create or enhance the ability of multiple settings to engage youths positively, whether religious, academic, athletic, or community-based organizations. Connections to several settings seem important for every child (Resnick et al., 1997). In settings where staff is able to communicate a sense of relatedness and foster autonomy, youth are most likely to become engaged (Allen, Kuperminc, Philliber, & Herre, 1994). More supervised and structured activities may also transpire. Here, favorable developmental outcomes may be enhanced and negative ones minimized. We need to find ways to implement such processes across a wide array of social settings in which youth participate.

Our investigations of the risk and protective functions of the family and peer profiles also suggest intervening at the microsystem level. Among inner-city teenagers, daily family hassles were critical in distinguishing between those well versus poorly adjusted – regardless of whether adjustment was measured in terms of depression or in terms of levels of antisocial behavior. These findings point to the value of reducing everyday family hassles as one potential route to promoting the well-being of youth in poverty. However, the findings also suggest that interventions designed to promote adolescent well-being should target the totality of the family system or peer group, rather than only a single element of one of these microsystems. For example, interventions that seek to foster peer popularity without considering other dimensions of peer functioning may, in fact, have serious iatrogenic effects. To help adolescents become engaged with and accepted by age-mates may be beneficial in reducing their depression levels. However, high status among peers may also inadvertently promote conduct disturbances – unless the peer group also supports the youth's engagement in prosocial behaviors.

CONCLUSION

We have endeavored to bring to bear a more holistic and contextual approach to the study of risk/protection and competence than has characterized prior person-centered research. This has enabled us to uncover multiple and different patterns of perceived psychosocial processes in families and peer networks that are differentially related to positive and negative developmental outcomes. Similarly, with these new assumptions and methods, we were able to uncover multiple forms of contextual competence. The central finding of this research suggests the need to engage youth positively with two or more settings.

References

Allen, J. P., Kuperminc, G., Philliber, S., & Herre, K. (1994). Programmatic prevention of adolescent problem behaviors: The role of autonomy, relatedness, and volunteer service in the Teen Outreach Program. *American Journal of Community Psychology, 22*(5), 617–638.

Bergman, L. R. (2000). The application of a person-centered approach: Types and clusters. In L. R. Bergman, R. B. Cairns, L. Nilsson, & L. Nystedt (Eds.), *Developmental science and the holistic approach* (pp. 137–1540. Mahwah, NJ: Erlbaum.

Cairns, R. B. (2000). Developmental science: Three audacious implications. In L. R. Bergman, R. B. Cairns, L. Nilsson, & L. Nystedt (Eds.), *Developmental science and the holistic approach* (pp. 49–62). Mahwah, NJ: Erlbaum.

Combrinck-Graham, L. (1985). A developmental model for family systems. *Family Process, 24*, 139–150.

Eccles, J. S., Midgley, C., Wigfield, A., Buchanan, C. M., Reuman, D., Flanagan, C., & MacIver, D. (1993). Development during adolescence: The impact of stage–environment fit on young adolescents' experiences in schools and in families. *American Psychologist, 48,* 90–101.

Hughes, D., Seidman, E., & Williams, E. (1993). Cultural phenomena and the research enterprise: Toward a cuturally-anchored methodology. *American Journal of Community Psychology, 21,* 687–703.

Lambert, L. (2003). *Evolving family processes and well-being among urban early adolescents.* Unpublished doctoral dissertation, New York University.

Lerner, R. M., & Simi, N. L. (2000). A holistic, integrated model of risk and protection in adolescence: A developmental contextual perspective about research, programs, and policies. In L. R. Bergman, R. B. Cairns, L. Nilsson, & L. Nystedt (Eds.), *Developmental science and the holistic approach* (pp. 421–443). Mahwah, NJ: Erlbaum.

Luthar, S. S., & Burack, J. A. (2000). Adolescent wellness: In the eye of the beholder? In D. Cicchetti, J. Rappaport, I. Sandler, & R. Weissberg (Eds.), *The promotion of wellness in children and adolescents* (pp. 29–57). Washington, DC: Child Welfare League of America.

Luthar, S. S., Cicchetti, D., & Becker, B. (2000). The construct of resilience: A critical evaluation and guidelines for future work. *Child Development, 71,* 543–562.

Luthar, S. S., & McMahon, T. J. (1996). Peer reputation among inner-city adolescents: Structure and correlates. *Journal of Research on Adolescence, 6*(4), 581–603.

Magnusson, D. (2000). The individual as the organizing principle in psychological inquiry: A holistic approach. In L. R. Bergman, R. B. Cairns, L. Nilsson, & L. Nystedt (Eds.), *Developmental science and the holistic approach* (pp. 33–47). Mahwah, NJ: Erlbaum.

Mahoney, J. L., & Stattin, H. (2000). Leisure activities and adolescent antisocial behavior: The role and structure of social context. *Journal of Adolescence, 23*(2), 113–127.

Masten, A., & Coatsworth, D. (1998). The development of competence in favorable and unfavorable environments: Lessons from research on successful children. *American Psychologist, 53,* 205–220.

McClelland, G. H., & Judd, C. M. (1993). Statistical difficulties in detecting interactions and moderator effects. *Psychological Bulletin, 114,* 376–390.

Pedersen, S., Seidman, E., Yoshikawa, H., Rivera, A. C., Allen, L., & Aber, J. L. (2003). *Contextual competence: Multiple manifestations among urban adolescents.* Unpublished manuscript.

Resnick, M. D., Bearman, P. S., Blum, R. W., Bauman, K. E., Harris, K. M., Jones, J., Tabor, J., Beuhring, T., Sieving, R. E., Shew, M., Ireland, M., Bearinger, L. H., & Urdry, J. R. (1997). Protecting adolescents from harm: Findings from the National Longitudinal Study of Adolescent Health. *Journal of the American Medical Association, 278,* 823–832.

Roberts, A., Seidman, E., Pedersen, S., Chesir-Teran, D., Allen, L., Aber, J. L., Duran, V., & Hsueh, J. (2000). Family and peer perceived transactions and self-esteem among urban early adolescents. *Journal of Early Adolescence, 20,* 68–92.

Rodkin, P. T., Farmer, T. W., Pearl, R., & Van Acker, R. (2000). Heterogeneity of popular boys: Antisocial and prosocial configurations. *Developmental Psychology, 36*(1), 14–24.

Rutter, M. (1990). Psychosocial resilience and protective mechanisms. In J. Rolf, A. S. Masten, D. Cicchetti, K. H. Nuechterlein, & S. Weintraub (Eds.), *Risk and protective factors in the development of psychopathology* (pp. 181–214). New York: Cambridge University Press.

Sameroff, A. J., & Seifer, R. (1990). Early contributions to developmental risk. In J. Rolf, A. S. Masten, D. Cicchetti, K. H. Nuechterlein, & S. Weintraub (Eds.), *Risk and protective factors in the development of psychopathology* (pp. 52–66). New York: Cambridge University Press.

Sameroff, A. J., Seifer, R., Barocas, R., Zax, M., & Greenspan, S. (1987). Intelligence quotient scores of 4 year old children: Social-environmental risk factors. *Pediatrics, 79*, 343–350.

Seidman, E. (1978). Justice, values and social science: Unexamined premises. In R. J. Simon (Ed.), *Research in law and sociology* (Vol. 1, pp. 175–200). Greenwich, CT: JAI Press.

Seidman, E. (1989). A preferred route to substantive theorizing. *American Journal of Community Psychology, 17*, 555–560.

Seidman, E. (1991). Growing up the hard way: Pathways of urban adolescents. *American Journal of Community Psychology, 19*, 169–205.

Seidman, E., Chesir-Teran, D., Friedman, J. L., Yoshikawa, H., Allen, L., Roberts, A., & Aber, J. L. (1999). The risk and protective functions of perceived family and peer microsystems among urban adolescents in poverty. *American Journal of Community Psychology, 27*, 211–237.

Seligman, M. E. P., & Csikszentmihalyi, M. (2000). Positive psychology: An introduction. *American Psychologist, 55*(1), 5–14.

Steinberg, L., Fegley, S., & Dornbusch, S. M. (1993). Negative impact of part-time work on adolescent adjustment: Evidence from a longitudinal study. *Developmental Psychology, 29*(2), 171–180.

Steinberg, L., Mounts, N. S., Lamborn, S. D., & Dormbusch, S. M. (1991). Authoritative parenting and adolescent adjustment across varied ecological niches. *Journal of Research on Adolescence, 1*, 19–36.

Weaver, A. J., Kline, A. E., Samford, J. A., Lucas, L. A., Larson, D. B., & Gorsuch, R. L. (1998). Is religion taboo in psychology? A systematic analysis of research on religion in seven major American psychological journals: 1991–1994. *Journal of Psychology and Christianity, 17*, 220–232.

Yoshikawa, H., & Seidman, E. (2000). Competence among urban adolescents in poverty: Multiple forms, contexts, and developmental processes. In R. Montemayor, G. R. Adams, & R. P. Gullotta (Eds.), *Advances in adolescent development: Vol. 10. Cultural and economic diversity in adolescent development* (pp. 9–42). Newbury Park, CA: Sage.

14

Overcoming the Odds?

Adolescent Development in the Context of Urban Poverty

Ana Mari Cauce, Angela Stewart,
Melanie Domenech Rodriguez, Bryan Cochran,
and Joshua Ginzler

Adolescence, a time of rapid biological, emotional, and social changes, brings with it a heightened developmental risk (McCord, 1997). This risk may be highest for adolescents growing up in poverty within our country's inner cities. In addition to the normative stress of adolescence, poor inner-city youth face multiple stressors and adversities including crowded housing, poor-quality schools, inadequate nutrition, and the presence of violence and drugs in their neighborhoods (Sampson, Morenoff, & Earls, 1999). These factors, in turn, have been linked to a host of negative outcomes (Brooks-Gunn & Duncan, 1997; Gorman-Smith & Tolan, this volume). Nonetheless, some inner-city youth survive these circumstances, overcoming adversity to become productive members of society. This chapter will highlight research that helps us understand the dynamic process of risk and resilience during this difficult transition in an even more difficult context.

We begin this chapter with a definition of adolescence and urban poverty and then lay out a rationale for focusing on two outcomes, school achievement and dropout and behavior problems of an internalizing or externalizing nature. We then identify salient factors that increase vulnerability or protective processes for youth growing up in urban poverty. We end with a discussion of resilience, emphasizing the limits of resilient adaptation and implications of this for theory and research on resilience, as well as for interventions that may better the lives of these vulnerable youth.

ADOLESCENCE AND URBAN POVERTY

The definitions of adolescence and urban poverty have been subject to so much controversy that entire papers have been written about how to best define them. Although a detailed presentation of these arguments is beyond the scope of this chapter, we do not want to skirt them entirely.

Adolescence

The definition of adolescence has shifted over time due to both biological and societal changes. Once neatly marked by the "teen" years (13–19), such that *adolescent* and *teenager* were interchangeable terms, the traditional starting point of adolescence, puberty, is beginning earlier than ever. This is especially the case for girls. One large study of girls in pediatric practices found that by the age of 10, almost 70% of white girls and 95% of African American girls show evidence of breast development and pubic hair. A quarter of African American girls start breast development by age 8 (Herman-Giddens et al., 1997).

Whereas puberty is beginning earlier, the endpoint of adolescence, traditionally marked by independence from parents and economic self-sufficiency, is happening later. Finishing high school is no longer a ticket to employment that can lead to establishing an independent residence and supporting a family. An increasing number of college-bound youth experience extended adolescence, maintaining an economically dependent relationship with their parents well beyond their teens.

Some youth may not experience adolescence at all, defined as a protected space between childhood and adulthood. Numerous factors, including structural inconsistencies in the definition of adolescent roles, age-condensed families and blurred intergenerational boundaries, an accelerated life course, and culture-specific definitions of successful developmental outcomes, combine to place these adolescents either in adultlike or developmentally ambiguous roles from very early ages (Burton, Obeidallah, & Allison, 1996). Youths who experience an adolescence extended at the tail end are more likely to be white and middle- or upper-class. Those who do not experience adolescence at all are more likely to be African American or Latino, urban, and poor. As such, the very definition of adolescence and the nature of this developmental transition may depend on youths' levels of poverty and their neighborhood environments.

Urban Poverty

At the turn of the millennium, 17% of children below the age of 18 in the United States were living in families with incomes below the federal poverty line. More than twice as many children (39%) live in or *near* poverty (Dalaker & Proctor, 2000). Those under 18 years of age are more likely to be poor than any other age group.

There are also vast disparities in rates of poverty across ethnic groups. The poverty rate in 1999 was 24% for African Americans, 23% for Hispanics, 11% for Asian/Pacific Islanders, 8% for non-Hispanic whites, and 26% for American Indians and Alaska Natives. Clearly, children and adolescents of color are overrepresented among the poor (Dalaker & Proctor, 2000).

The ability of older adolescents to obtain lawful work does not seem to significantly affect these disparities in ethnic poverty rates. Among working adolescents, 6% of white non-Hispanic adolescents were poor compared to 20% of working black adolescents and 18% of working Latino adolescents.

Poverty rates also vary by the type of neighborhood youths live in. When we refer to the *urban poor*, we mean those living within central cities in neighborhoods of concentrated poverty, defined by census tracts in which more than 40% of the residents are poor. Although a quarter of poor African Americans live in neighborhoods characterized by concentrated poverty, only 3% of whites do so (Jargowsky, 1997). Inner-city neighborhoods are primarily African American and/or Latino, although we know extremely little about the neighborhoods characterized by the latter.

Other important issues in deriving a clear understanding of adolescents in poverty and the impact that this may have in the long term are the duration of poverty and whether they have grown up in persistent poverty. Here again, ethnic disparities are evident. Among nonblack children, 20% spent 1–4 years in poverty, 5% spent 5–9 years in poverty, and 1% spent 10 or more years in poverty. In contrast, for African American children the statistics are bleaker, with 32% living in poverty for 1–4 years, 18% in poverty for 5–9 years, and 29% in poverty for 10 years or more. Only 21% of the African American children followed over time lived above the poverty threshold for their entire childhood (Lewit, 1993). These disparities are significant because, although virtually no studies account for this factor, the amount of time spent in poverty is related to child outcomes (Brooks-Gunn & Duncan, 1997).

In sum, neither adolescence nor urban poverty is a homogeneous phenomenon. Unfortunately, few research studies provide the details necessary to calculate family poverty status or neighborhood income characteristics. For this reason, we chose to review studies that were relevant to the questions at hand, even when they never precisely specified that youths in the study were part of the urban poor or when definitions of urban poverty were loose or vague. In addition, given the confound between urban poverty and ethnicity, we sometimes drew upon research on African American adolescents within metropolitan areas, even when it was not clear whether the sample was primarily poor.

ADOLESCENT PROBLEM BEHAVIORS AND OUTCOMES

As Luthar and colleagues have stated in their theoretical examination and reformulation of risk and resilience, we cannot address either issue adequately without tying them to specific outcomes (Luthar & Cichetti, 2000; Luthar, Doernberger, & Zigler, 1993). We must specifically address risk, or resilience for specific problems.

We report on studies that examine school achievement or behavior problems of an internalizing or externalizing nature, such as depression, delinquency, or aggression. We chose to focus on these problems because they are associated with life in neighborhoods of concentrated poverty, are either first initiated, detected, or exacerbated during adolescence, and have serious consequences for later life outcomes (McCord, 1997).

VULNERABILITY AND PROTECTIVE MECHANISMS
FOR POOR URBAN ADOLESCENTS

Early models of risk typically attributed the vulnerability of inner-city youth, and more specifically African American inner-city youth, to the *tangle of pathology* created by their culture and their families (see Cauce, Coronado, & Watson, 1998). More recent, sophisticated research and theory consider the neighborhood as the cradle of risk (Booth & Crouter, 2001). There is a great deal of evidence supporting this latter position. These risks are especially high for adolescents, given their increasing mobility and autonomy. Although it is difficult to protect youth from the dangers of the inner city at any age, families of young children are better able to create risk-free lacunae within their homes and immediate vicinity.

From among the vast array of potential risk factors in poor inner cities, we have chosen to focus on violence and victimization. Violence and the threat of victimization are two of the most dramatic risks associated with inner-city life. They also fall disproportionately upon youth. Furthermore, there is increasing evidence that the aftereffects of exposure to violence are more than transitory and may directly affect the developmental outcomes we are most interested in. On the positive side, we examine the role of youth serving community organizations as sources of protection in low-income urban neighborhoods.

Moving from the neighborhood to a more proximal center for vulnerability or protection, we next examine the family and the peer group. We focus on the role of harsh/punitive parenting and a delinquent peer group as vulnerability factors and on parenting that combines warmth and firm discipline as a protective factor. We have chosen not to focus on characteristics within the adolescent. Environmental factors are so salient and overwhelming for inner-city youth that there has not been much recent research that focuses on the individual as the locus for risk or protection. Characteristics such as intelligence, an easy temperament, or a positive life outlook can help youth cope with adversity, and the converse might heighten stress. However, this is the case whether one lives in a wealthy suburb or an inner city; we found no consistent empirical evidence that individual characteristics uniquely contribute to coping with the risks of inner-city life. In light of an earlier body of work that placed blame on inner-city youth and their families for their own problems, a focus on the individual without compelling evidence seemed inappropriate.

It is also worth noting that studies focusing on risk among poor inner-city youth typically draw upon an ecological model of development in which more distal risks, such as those in the neighborhood, are filtered through the more proximal environments of the family and the peer group before they result in youth vulnerability. These studies attempt to identify mediational mechanisms, rather than searching for moderators of risk. Studies that focus on mediation better help us understand how risk translates into vulnerability. Those that focus on moderation best help us understand resilience processes. Thus, more than a review of the literature, this chapter serves as a call for more sophisticated research in this area.

NEIGHBORHOOD INFLUENCES

Violence and Victimization

Our nation's poor urban youth are particularly vulnerable to the high incidence of violence in this country. Crime rates in our nation's urban locales were 74% higher than those in rural areas and 37% higher than those in suburban areas during the period 1993–1998. Urbanites experienced the highest rates of rape and sexual assault, robbery, aggravated assault, simple assault, and personal theft. Moreover, community violence was especially high in inner-city neighborhoods characterized by poverty. Across all urban, suburban, and rural locales, lower annual income was associated with a higher incidence of violence. Households supported by less than $7,500 a year were twice as likely to report victimization of a family member than households with annual incomes above $75,000. And victimization rates among the urban poor were 41% higher than those among the poor living in rural locations (Duhart, 2000).

Media representations of youth violence have focused disproportionately on them as perpetrators and relatively rarely on them as victims. Portrayals of violent adolescents are readily accessible and direct public attention away from their risk of victimization (Hashima & Finkelhor, 1999). Stereotypes notwithstanding, victimization rates among adolescents were twice the national average. Adolescents between the ages of 12 and 15 were more often victims of crime than any other age group; although youth 12 to 24 years old represented less than a quarter of the U.S. population (1992 to 1994), they experienced nearly half of all violent victimizations (Perkins, 1997).

Among adolescents living in extremely disadvantaged inner cities, violence has been described as common and their neighborhoods have been compared to war zones (Dubrow & Garbarino, 1989). Available data lend credence to such descriptions across numerous urban settings and age groups. In a Chicago area study, more than half of inner-city early adolescents reported that within the past year, they had witnessed a violent attack and stayed home out of fear of violence (Attar, Guerra, & Tolan, 1994). Mothers in New Orleans reported that over 25% of their 9- to 12-year-old children had witnessed a shooting, and 20% had witnessed a stabbing (Osofsky, Wevers, Hann, & Fick, 1993). In a sample of Detroit youth aged 14–23, about 40% had seen someone shot or stabbed, and over 20% had seen someone killed (Schubiner, Scott, & Tzelepis, 1993). In a sample of low-income 7- to 14-year-old African American urban youth, almost half had witnessed a murder, and nearly 75% had seen someone shot or shot at (Fitzpatrick & Boldizar, 1993).

In addition to the experience of witnessing violence, referred to as *covictimization,* inner-city youth are often the direct recipients of violence. A child living in the inner city is more apt to die from violence than from any other single cause. One study found that 75% of urban youth had been beaten up, stabbed, or shot, almost twice the rate of their suburban counterparts (Campbell & Schwarz, 1996). Moreover, havens safe from violence are hard to identify. Only 17% of mothers of preadolescents and early adolescents in New Orleans rated hanging out or playing in the neighborhood as very safe, and only 30% rated school as safe (Osofsky et al., 1993).

In addition to poverty and urban dwelling, certain ethnic groups are at increased risk for victimization related to gang activity. Compared to their white counterparts, poor African American and Latino students are more likely to report the presence of gang activity in their schools and to fear attack while coming to or leaving school. Students who attended schools with gangs were more likely to be afraid of violence near or around their school and were more likely to alter their behavior for protection (Bastain & Taylor, 1991).

The relationship between victimization and covictimization with adjustment difficulties is well established. There are strong associations between violence exposure and victimization, on the one hand, and levels of aggression, anxiety, or depression, on the other (see Gorman-Smith & Tolan, this volume). There is also some evidence that living in poor inner cities may strengthen the link between exposure to violence and aggression. In a longitudinal study of inner-city African American and Latino preadolescents, exposure to violence was associated with peer-rated aggression, but only for youth in areas of high neighborhood disadvantage (Attar et al., 1994).

Exposure to community violence has also been linked to school-related problems. Students exposed to violence were more likely to show evidence of compromised cognitive functioning, to have lowered academic achievement and school attendance, and to have higher rates of school dropout (Shakoor & Chalmers, 1991). A national telephone survey of adolescents aged 10–16 likewise found that youth who reported being victimized had more school difficulties, as indicated by having trouble with a teacher (Boney-McCoy & Finkelhor, 1995).

In sum, there is a great deal of evidence that adolescents in inner-city neighborhoods, compared to similar youths of other ages or similarly aged youths from more affluent settings, are exposed to elevated rates of violence, whether as a witness or as a victim. There is also a growing body of research linking this exposure or experience to internalizing and externalizing behavior and to school underachievement. When examined directly, these associations generally account for a modest to moderate amount of variance in internalizing or externalizing behaviors.

Community Organizations and Youth-Serving Agencies

What factors within inner-city neighborhoods might help youth stay out of trouble or recover from trouble? Churches, community centers, and neighborhood youth-serving organizations, such as girls' and boys' clubs, Little League, and YM/YWCAs have been found to influence youth positively (Masten & Coatsworth, 1998). Adolescents involved in voluntary activities and services are less likely to participate in problem behaviors like assault, stealing, and vandalism (Hart, Atkins, & Ford, 1998).

Community youth organizations have often been described as *urban sanctuaries*, serving as sources of hope and support in the lives of many inner-city youths (McLaughlin, Irby, & Langman, 1994). There are countless anecdotal accounts to this effect, and there are many studies indicating positive associations between participation in neighborhood organizations and social competence or reduced problem behavior. For example, one study found that in the Chicago Area Projects, in which two youth organizations provided services and organized activities aimed at delinquency prevention, youth in treatment neighborhoods, compared to comparison neighborhoods, had lower delinquency rates (Schlossman & Sedlak, 1983). Unfortunately, there are few studies like this one that have utilized random assignment procedures, leaving open the interpretation that youth who participate in such organizations are more competent or display less problem behavior to begin with. Thus, although community organizations may serve as safe havens to ameliorate the risks of inner-city lives, the empirical evidence for this remains thin. Moreover, we could find no evidence that the positive effects of community involvement were unique for youth in urban neighborhoods.

Peer and Family Influences

In this section we highlight research on vulnerability and protective factors within the peer and family microsystems. We begin by presenting research demonstrating that adolescent problem behavior is associated with participation in delinquent peer groups and harsh parenting practices. We then move to research suggesting that warmth and support from family members, and parenting styles that include firm control and close monitoring, may mitigate the effects of both negative neighborhood and peer group factors.

Delinquent Peer Groups

A recent review suggests that the peer group may represent the primary agent through which neighborhood socialization adversely affects child outcomes (Leventhal & Brooks-Gunn, 2000). Within inner-city neighborhoods and schools, the peer culture often reflects the violence in the larger community. Adolescents growing up in high-crime, dangerous neighborhoods are exposed to more delinquent peer groups than other youth (Wikstrom, 1998), and a large body of evidence implicates delinquent peers in the development of adolescent behavior problems (Dryfoos, 1990).

Moreover, the personal characteristics valued by peers on inner-city streets are often not consistent with success in the more conventional mode (Jarrett, 1999). The link between peer popularity and academic performance is not as strong as that between peer group pressure and externalizing behaviors, but both empirical and ethnographic studies have suggested that it is hard for inner-city African American youths to find peers who are supportive of school achievement (Fordham & Ogbu, 1986; Luthar, 1995).

Social relations on the streets in impoverished inner-city communities have been described as "individualistic and predatory," with "getting over" and "hustling" considered valid ways of gaining access to limited resources (Jarrett, 1999). The potentially negative role of inner-city peers was nicely illustrated by a recent study with a sample of mostly African American and Latino adolescents attending low-income inner-city schools in Baltimore, Washington D.C., and New York City (Seidman et al., 1999; see also Seidman & Pedersen, this volume). Using a pattern-based analytic approach, Seidman and colleagues identified six experiential peer clusters and examined their risk or protective functions vis-à-vis depression and antisocial behavior. The most protective of these clusters for both depression and antisocial behavior was labeled *disengaging-accepting*. This cluster of adolescents had relationships with peers characterized by high levels of perceived social acceptance or popularity but not much support per se. Instead, actual relationships with peers were described as "marginal." The study authors suggest that this marginality may have provided them with a safe haven from the antisocial values common among their peer group (p. 16).

Harsh and Punitive Parenting

Parents bringing up youth in low-income inner cities find themselves in a difficult position. They are responsible for protecting their children, but living in the inner city can feel anything but safe. A study examining the link between exposure to violence and parenting, albeit with younger children, found that about a fifth of inner-city mothers who witnessed violence did not feel safe and curtailed the neighborhood activities of their

children (Taylor, 1997). Another study, also of young children, found that
parents reported being more vigilant and more regulating of their children's experiences when they perceived the neighborhood as less safe
(Parke & O'Neill, 1999). Under such conditions, parents are more likely
to adopt discipline styles characterized by restrictive and punitive methods (Garbarino, Kostelny, & Dubrow, 1991; McLoyd, 1997). In her excellent review of parenting among the poor and disadvantaged, McLoyd
(1990) noted that a lack of financial resources combined with the cascading stresses typical of inner-city life leads to "quick and decisive" disciplinary strategies that can be described as harsh and are typically linked
to adolescent problem behaviors, especially those of an externalizing
nature.

Although the extant research has consistently found that parenting
practices among poor, especially minority, families are power assertive
or harsh, some have suggested that this may be an adaptive response
to the dangers of the inner city. The argument of these investigators is
that under these circumstances, a more controlling parenting style may
result in more positive outcomes for young people. There is some, albeit
limited, evidence in support of this assertion. We present this evidence
in the next section, as we review the literature on parental support and
child protection strategies.

Parental Support and Protection
During the adolescent years, family roles are reorganized to accommodate the adolescent's increasing need for independence. During this
period, conflict between children and their parents is at its height
(Steinberg, 1990), and developing effective parenting strategies that combine warmth and nurturance with appropriate discipline is always a challenge. The inner-city environment, where collective socialization strategies or collective efficacy is especially weak (Sampson et al., 1999), makes
the challenge even greater. But even within the inner city, some parents
manage to rise to the occasion, developing strategies that both support
and protect their young.

The ethnographic work of Jarrett (1997, 1999) offers powerful descriptions of how some parents persist in their parenting efforts even in
the worst community conditions. The child protection strategies that she
has identified include child monitoring, parental resource seeking, and
in-home learning.

CHILD MONITORING. The core of the youth monitoring strategy
is restricting the association between an adolescent and undesirable

neighbors or peers. The most common ways to do this are through isolation and chaperonage. *Isolation* refers to confining children, such as not allowing them out of the house after school or allowing them to go only to certain places. *Chaperonage* involves having a family member or a family friend accompany a child during routine or high-risk activities. For example, a mother may have her adolescent son take his younger brother with him when he goes to his girlfriend's house when her parents are not around.

Part of the task of monitoring entails maintaining clear generational role boundaries and demanding respect from children. Although some mothers attempt to be friends with their daughters, Cauce and colleagues (1996) described how, when an urban African American adolescent called her mother "pal" during a mother–daughter interaction task, the mother immediately replied, "I'll give you pal in the mouth. I'm *not* your pal." Time and again during these interactions, mothers were found to listen to daughters, show respect for their opinions, and encourage them to behave in a more autonomous fashion while also reminding their daughters that when "push comes to shove, *they* [the mothers] were in charge" (p. 110).

PARENTAL RESOURCE SEEKING. Jarrett's work also identifies *community-bridging* parents who create "insulated and enriching developmental niches" (Jarrett, 1999, p. 48) for their children. Astute parents help their children identity safe spaces within the neighborhood and more desirable neighbors and peers. For example, James Comer (1989), a doctor and dean of the Yale Medical School, described how his mother, a domestic worker, helped to connect him with a doctor whose house she cleaned.

Ethnographic studies have also highlighted ways in which groups of affiliated relatives or extended kin networks can assist children and youth in navigating around the risks in inner-city neighborhoods. Sometimes these kin were of higher economic status and provided families and youth with valuable resources. These kin can also fill in for each other and share roles (Jarrett, 1997). Extended kin networks and role flexibility have often been considered among the unique strengths of African American families.

IN-HOME LEARNING. This strategy, specific to intellectual development, involves devising learning activities that can be carried out at home and that reinforce school expectations. For example, parents may look for teachable moments to reinforce what a child is learning in a history or civics class. Rewarding a child for good school performance, such as attaching privileges to school grades, is another variation of this strategy.

The rich ethnographic research, briefly described earlier, elucidates the creative strategies that families use to both support and protect their young in risky circumstances. Although the nature of the work does not allow us to clearly tie these strategies to child or adolescent outcomes, the findings of several empirical investigations corroborate Jarrett's observations while forging stronger links with adolescent adjustment. More specifically, these studies suggest that parental disciplinary strategies that are higher in control may be most adaptive for urban African American youths. These are also among the relatively few studies of primarily low-income urban adolescents that examine the moderation effects most often associated with a resilience perspective. Several of them are based on the work of the same study team: Mason, Gonzales, Cauce, and their colleagues (Gonzales, Cauce, Friedman, & Mason, 1996; Mason, Cauce, Gonzales, & Hiraga, 1994, 1996). These studies all draw upon data from an investigation of primarily low-income, urban African American adolescents aged 12 to 14. The adolescents were followed for a 3-year period, and all the studies cited used prospective designs in which outcomes from year 1 were controlled for before looking at the predictors of behavior in year 2.

The first of these studies focused on maternal warmth, or the affective quality of the adolescent–mother relationship, examining whether a close and warm relationship between an adolescent and his or her mother could counteract the negative influences of father absence and a delinquent peer group. Results indicated that, as expected, participation in a more delinquent peer group was a vulnerability factor for adolescent externalizing problem behavior. This vulnerability was exacerbated by father absence. Maternal warmth, conversely, not only served to buffer the negative effects of a delinquent peer group, it served to substantially mitigate the combined negative effects of a delinquent peer group and father absence. In other words, adolescent externalizing behavior was especially elevated for youths with delinquent peers in a mother-only household when their relationship with their mother was distant and lacked affection. However, when the relationship between adolescent and mother was close and warm, the effects of a delinquent peer group and father absence were close to negligible. These results strongly suggest that the relationship between a mother and her adolescent child can serve a protective function, even under conditions of multiple risk (Mason et al., 1996).

The next set of studies focused on another aspect of mother–adolescent relationships: maternal control or a mother's disciplinary style. The first of these studies examined school achievement as an outcome and found that within neighborhoods that adolescents perceived as more risky (e.g. with more vandalism, gang activity, crime), they attained better grades when mothers exercised higher levels of restrictive control. The opposite was true for adolescents who described their neighborhoods as more low risk. They attained better grades when their mothers exercised lower levels of restrictive control (Gonzales et al., 1996).

That the effects of maternal control vary by context was further corroborated by the third study in this set. This study found a curvilinear relationship between maternal control, whether restrictive or behavioral, and externalizing problem behavior: Optimal levels of adolescent behavior were found when parental control was neither overly harsh nor overly lenient. Furthermore, this window of optimal control was particularly narrow for youths at risk due to a negative peer environment. This condition was referred to as the need for *precision parenting*, a term that underscores the difficulty of parenting adolescents in risky environments (Mason et al., 1996).

The results of the ethnographic and empirical studies just summarized suggest that parents who cultivate close and warm relationships with their adolescent children, who monitor their whereabouts and provide firm discipline, neither overly harsh and punitive nor overly lenient and lax, can have a positive impact on the behavior of their children. Moreover, parenting of this sort has not only been shown to have a direct effect upon adolescent behavior, it also serves to moderate or buffer the negative effects of a risky neighborhood or peer environment. Thus, effective parenting can make a difference in high-risk environments.

This research is quite clear about the best strategies for childrearing in these tough environmental settings. It also indicates that, in such circumstances, this type of parenting is difficult. The toll is especially high for precisely those parents least able to pay it. Cauce et al. (1996) referred to parents of urban African American youth as "between a rock and a hard place," and one parent described her efforts to exercise just the right amount of control as akin to "threading a needle in the dark."

We believe that it is still premature to conclude, as did the National Research Council (1993), that high-risk urban environments swamp the effects of parents or other potential protective factors. But there is at least one study indicating that, within the very worst inner-city neighborhoods, this may be the case. Results of the Chicago Youth Development

Study (Gorman-Smith, Tolan, & Henry, 1999), which focused on early adolescent African and Latino American males from either inner-city, underclass neighborhoods or otherwise urban, poor neighborhoods, found that among the latter, parenting had little impact on problem behavior of a delinquent or externalizing nature. When hierarchical regressions were conducted to examine the social predictors of delinquency for boys within urban poor but not underclass neighborhoods, family cohesion, beliefs about families, and family disciplinary practices were all significant predictors that also mediated the impact of life stress upon adjustment. On the other hand, within inner-city underclass neighborhoods, those where more that 40% of the residents were poor, only stress predicted adolescent male delinquency. None of the family or parenting variables had any effect. As the authors note, the variation in predictive relationships by neighborhood type is particularly striking because there were no differences between groups on level of stress experienced, family relationships, parenting practices, or beliefs about families. Thus, like previous studies, this one also indicates that the challenges for inner-city parents are great. But its results are more sobering and suggest that resilience may be hard to find in the most difficult of these environments.

LIMITS OF RESILIENT ADAPTATION AND IMPLICATIONS FOR INTERVENTION

In this chapter, we have tried to shed light upon resilience processes among adolescents in the context of poverty by focusing on both vulnerability and protective factors. We identified one vulnerability factor at the community level, community violence, and one protective factor, the presence of youth-serving community organizations. At the microsystem level, we identified two vulnerability factors, delinquent peer groups and harsh and punitive parenting, and one protective factor, parental support and firm discipline.

We tried to be balanced in our focus on risk and protection, but this task proved impossible. Identifying vulnerability factors was easy. The competition among constructs for salience was keen. For example, we could have easily focused on the vulnerability of youths growing up in single-parent families or on the vulnerability that comes from attending poor-quality and underresourced schools. We could also have focused on racial discrimination as a risk factor because so many youths who are urban and poor are also members of ethnic minorities. Lastly, a great deal has been written on the role of stress in inner-city environments, a construct that cuts across several of these risk factors. It would not be hard to make the case that youths growing up in this difficult environment are vulnerable largely because of the confluence of stresses in their lives (Attar et al. 1994; Gorman-Smith et al., 1999). Space limitations not only constrained us from presenting the full range of variables that have been identified as posing risks to youths growing up in the inner city, they also constrained us from presenting more fully all the research supporting their status as risk factors. Indeed, although we may not fully understand the mechanisms by which community violence, delinquent peers, or harsh parenting affect behavioral adjustment, there is little question about whether their impact is negative.

Conversely, our identification of protective factors was constrained not by space limitations, but by the research literature. We struggled to identify protective factors, and the research literature supporting the protective function of those factors we did identify was difficult to locate. These constraints likely reflect those posed by the neighborhood environment surrounding inner-city youth, especially if one focuses on inner-city neighborhoods characterized by concentrated poverty. Put bluntly, although there is much research still to be done, the empirical evidence in support of protection and resilience in such settings is quite thin. It is undoubtedly the fact that some youths survive the rigors of the inner city and emerge intact. There is also much room for resilience research that identifies the strengths of inner-city youths, which exist alongside the many problems that have been identified. Indeed, such research is especially important because it can help us identify areas that we can build upon when developing intervention or prevention programs. For example, in their work with poor, urban, substance-abusing mothers, Luthar and Suchman (2000) were able to harness strengths such as their strong concern for their children in motivating them to make good use of a relationally based intervention.

Still, it is important to acknowledge that relatively few empirical studies have identified factors in the community, family, or peer group that actually mitigate the negative effects of inner-city life. In light of the strong evidence for the presence of potent and multiple risks in the inner city and the relatively weak evidence suggesting that there are clearly identifiable protective factors that counteract these risks, there is a surprising amount of resistance to labeling these environments as toxic. In part because so many inner-city residents are black and brown, there is a legitimate fear that so labeling these environments might lead to stigmatizing the people who live in them. Perhaps for this reason, in the past several years it has been more fashionable to issue calls for research focusing on those youths who manage to do well in these environments than to rail against a social structure that allows children to grow up in such toxic circumstances. Indeed, it has become almost a cliché to say that despite the tremendous obstacles they face, many poor inner-city youths are doing just fine. Yet, a hard, sober look at the research literature suggests that, much as we'd like to think otherwise, this may not be the case.

In one study of poor, inner city sixth and seventh graders, 21% of the boys and 2% of the girls reported that they had carried a gun; 21% of the boys and 16% of the girls reported that they had initiated a fist fight or shoving match three or more times, and a full 67.7% had hit someone "because they didn't like what they said or did," all within the previous 6 months. Although resilience processes were not explicitly examined, there is reason to believe that the search for resilience would not have turned up much. Only about a third (35.5%) of these youths were found to be without serious problem behaviors, either delinquency, school failure, high-risk sexual behavior, or substance abuse. Indeed, almost a third of all youth (30.3%) had serious problem behaviors in at least three of these areas. And they were barely teenagers (Barone et al., 1995).

Another study of 13- to 17-year-old African American boys growing up in three of the higher-crime areas in Washington, D.C., found that fewer than one-fourth of these youths (22%) failed to self-report an act that could be considered criminal. Morever, within the past 6 months, even these "nonoffenders" committed, on average, more than one act that could be considered a juvenile offense, like underage drinking or running away from home (Washington, D.C., Juvenile Violence Research Study, cited by the Office of Juvenile Justice and Delinquency Prevention, 1999).

When making pronouncements about resilience among poor urban youth, it is important to keep in mind that the bulk of the research that has identified resilience processes among poor, minority, or urban adolescents has not focused exclusively on those growing up in inner-city neighborhoods characterized by *concentrated* poverty. Instead, youths in most of these studies have represented a range of socioeconomic backgrounds and a range of urban neighborhoods (Seidman, 1991). For example, the studies by Mason, Gonzales, Cauce, and colleagues were conducted with urban African American youths living in Seattle, where there are very virtually no neighborhoods that are truly underclass. Moreover, although the youths came primarily from families of modest means, with about 40% in poverty or near poverty, almost 20% were at least lower middle class. There was no significant association between income and problem behavior in these studies, but this does not rule out the fact that the processes associated with resilience in these studies (e.g., a warm relationship between adolescent and mother, an adequate amount of parental control) were confounded with economic status, neighborhood residence, or exposure to risk. For example, the mothers most able to monitor their adolescents adequately and provide them with adequate, but not too much, control may have been those living in the better neighborhoods with access to more resources.

The evidence suggests that such confounds are common; the riskier the setting, the less likely we are to find protective factors. As we have already alluded to, the type of protective parenting described in our review is probably most difficult to sustain in inner-city neighborhoods. The very nature of inner-city neighborhoods, the dangers they pose, and the sheer grind of living day in and day out under an onslaught of poverty-related stress militate against just the type of parenting that is most apt to deflect their effects upon children. Indeed, the difficulty of these circumstances is most apt to lead to harsh and punitive parenting styles that serve to magnify neighborhood risks.

By the same token, although strong youth-serving community organizations may provide some protection from neighborhood violence, such organizations are rare in precisely those neighborhoods in which we are apt to find the highest level of violence. Ironically, those neighborhoods with the greatest need for such organizations typically don't command the resources, political or economic, to sustain high-quality youth-serving organizations (Connell & Aber, in press). Rates of participation in organized afterschool activities are lower for youth in low-income families compared to their more privileged counterparts. Such activities are less available in poor communities because they are generally locally funded, including reliance on fees for service (Quinn, 1999).

Thus, whether it is politically correct to say so or not, when we focus on inner-city neighborhoods with a high poverty concentration, the limits of resilience are all too obvious. Although it may not be impossible, it is certainly hard for the researcher with open eyes, just as it is hard for an adolescent living in these neighborhoods, not to be overwhelmed by risk.

The primary implication of this review for intervention is that although we undoubtedly should and need to focus on and identify the strengths and resilience processes that do exist among inner-city underclass youths, it is equally important to work on diminishing the risks these youths are exposed to. History suggests that it is not possible to create an environment so oppressive as to totally vanquish the human spirit and eliminate the capacity of some to survive and overcome, but some environments come close. If one limits oneself to environments that one is likely to encounter in everyday life in the United States, inner-city neighborhoods characterized by high concentrations of poverty perhaps comes closest. We might do well to acknowledge this more readily and to focus our resources not only on reinforcing factors that may mitigate toxicity, but also on making these environments less toxic. This is not a new point. It has been made more eloquently by previous resilience researchers (see Luthar & Cicchetti, 2000), but in an environment where public policies aimed at providing a safety net for the poor are increasingly being cut back, it is a point well worth repeating.

Note

1. The census data provide this information only for 16- and 17-year-olds.

References

Attar, B. K., Guerra, N. G., & Tolan, P. (1994). Neighborhood disadvantage, stressful life events, and adjustment in urban elementary school children. *Journal of Clinical Child Psychology, 23,* 391–400.

Barone, C., Weissberg, R. P., Kasprow, W., Voyce, C., Arthur, M. W., & Shriver, T. P. (1995). Involvement in multiple problem behaviors of young urban adolescents. *Journal of Primary Prevention, 15,* 261–283.L

Bastian, L. D., & Taylor, B. M. (1991). *School crime: A national crime victimization report.* Washington, DC: Bureau of Justice Statistics.

Boney-McCoy, S., & Finkelhor, D. (1995). Psychosocial sequelae of violence victimization in a national youth sample. *Journal of Consulting and Clinical Psychology, 63,* 726–736.

Booth, A., & Crouter, A. C. (Eds.). (2001). *Does it take a village? Community effects on children, adolescents, and families.* Mahwah, NJ: Erlbaum.

Brooks-Gunn, J., & Duncan, G. J. (1997). The effects of poverty on children. *The Future of Children, 7*(2), 55–71.

Burton, L. M., Obeidallah, D. A., & Allison, K. (1996). Ethnographic insights on social context and adolescent development among inner-city African-American teens. In R. Jessor & A. Colby (Eds.), *Ethnography and human development: Context and meaning in social inquiry* (pp. 395–418). Chicago: University of Chicago Press.

Campbell, C., & Schwarz, D. F. (1996). Prevalence and impact of exposure to interpersonal violence among suburban and urban middle school students. *Pediatrics, 98,* 396–402.

Cauce, A. M, Coronado, N., & Watson, J. (1998). Conceptual and methodological issues in conducting culturally competent research. In M. Hernandez &

R. Isaacs (Eds.), *Promoting cultural competence in children's mental health services* (pp. 305–329). Brookes.

Cauce, A. M., Hiraga, Y., Graves, D., Gonzales, N., Ryan-Finn, K., & Grove, K. (1996). African American mothers and their adolescent daughters: Closeness, conflict, and control. In B. J. Leadbeater & N. Way (Eds.), *Urban girls: Resisting stereotypes, creating identities* (pp. 100–116). New York: New York University Press.

Comer, J. (1989). *Maggie's dream: The life and times of a black family.* New York: New American Library.

Connell, J. P., & Aber, J. L. (in press). How do urban communities affect youth? Using social science research to inform the design and evaluation of comprehensive community initiatives. In J. Brooks-Gunn, G. J. Duncan, & J. L. Aber (Eds.), *Neighborhood poverty: Context and consequences for children* (Vol. 1). New York: Russell Sage Foundation.

Dalaker, J., & Proctor, B. D. (2000). *Poverty in the United States:* 1999 (U.S. Census Bureau Report Series P60-210). Washington, DC: U.S. Government Printing Office.

Dryfoos, J. (1990). *Adolescents at risk.* New York: Oxford University Press.

Dubrow, N. F., & Garbarino, J. (1989). Living in the war zone: Mothers and young children in a public housing development. *Child Welfare, 68,* 3–20.

Duhart, D. T. (2000). *Urban, suburban, and rural victimization, 1993–98.* Washington, DC: Bureau of Justice Statistics.

Fitzpatrick, K. M., & Boldizar, J. P. (1993). The prevalence and consequences of exposure to violence among African-American youth. *Journal of the American Academy of Child and Adolescent Psychiatry, 32,* 424–430.

Fordham, S., & Ogbu, J. U. (1986). Black students' school success: Coping with the "burden of acting white." *Urban Review, 18,* 176–206.

Garbarino, J., Kostelny, K., & Dubrow, N. (1991). What children can tell us about living in danger. *American Psychologist, 46,* 376–383.

Gonzales, N., Cauce, A. M., Friedman, R., & Mason, C. (1996). Family, peer, and neighborhood influences on academic achievement among African American adolescents: One year prospective effects. *American Journal of Community Psychology, 24,* 365–387.

Gorman-Smith, D., Tolan, P., & Henry, D. (1999). The relation of community and family to risk among urban-poor adolescents. In P. Cohen, C. Slomkowski, & L. Robins (Eds.), *Historical and geographical influences on psychopathology* (pp. 349–367). Mahwah, NJ: Erlbaum.

Hart, D., Atkins, R., & Ford, D. (1998). Urban America as a context for the development of moral identity in adolescence. *Journal of Social Issues, 54,* 513–530.

Hashima, P. Y., & Finkelhor, D. (1999). Violent victimization of youth versus adults in the national crime victimization survey. *Journal of Interpersonal Violence, 14,* 799–820.

Herman-Giddens, M. E., Slora, E. J., Wasserman, R. C., Bourdony, C. J., Bhapkar, M. V., Koch, G. G., & Hasemeir, C. M. (1997). Secondary sexual characteristics and menses in young girls seen in office practices: A study from the Pediatric Research in Office Settings network. *Pediatrics, 99,* 505–512.

Jargowsky, P. (1997). *Poverty and place.* New York: Russell Sage Foundation.

Jarrett, R. L. (1997). African American family and parenting strategies in impoverished neighborhoods. *Qualitative Sociology, 20,* 275–288.

Jarrett, R. L. (1999). Successful parenting in high-risk neighborhoods. *The Future of Children: When School Is Out, 9,* 45–50.

Leventhal, T. L., & Brooks-Gunn, J. (2000). The neighborhoods they live in: The effects of neighborhood residence upon child and adolescent outcomes. *Psychological Bulletin, 126,* 309–337.

Lewit, E. M. (1993). Children in poverty. *The Future of Children, 3,* 176–182.

Luthar, S. S. (1995). Social competence in the school setting: Prospective cross-domain association among inner-city teens. *Child Development, 66,* 416–429.

Luthar, S. S., & Cicchetti, D. (2000). The construct of resilience: Implications for interventions and social policies. *Development and Psychopathology, 12,* 857–885.

Luthar, S. S., Doernberger, C. H., & Zigler, E. (1993). Resilience is not a unidimensional construct: Insights from a prospective study of inner-city adolescents. *Development and Psychopathology, 5,* 703–717.

Luthar, S. S., & Suchman, N. E. (2000). Relational psychotherapy mothers' group: A developmentally-informed intervention for at-risk mothers. *Development and Psychopathology, 12,* 235–253.

Mason, C. A., Cauce, A. M., Gonzales, N., & Hiraga, Y. (1994). Adolescent problem behavior: The effect of peers and the moderating role of father absence and the mother–child relationship. *American Journal of Community Psychology, 22,* 723–743.

Mason, C. A., Cauce, A. M., Gonzales, N., & Hiraga, Y. (1996). Neither too sweet nor too sour: Problem peers, maternal control, and problem behavior in African American adolescents. *Child Development, 67,* 2115–2130.

Masten, A. S., & Coatsworth, D. J. (1998). The development of competence in favorable and unfavorable environments: Lessons from research on successful children. *American Psychologist, 53,* 205–220.

McCord, J. (1997). *Violence and childhood in the inner-city.* Cambridge: Cambridge University Press.

McLaughlin, M. W., Irby, M., & Langman, J. (1994). *Urban sanctuaries: Neighborhood organizations in the lives and futures or inner-city youth.* San Francisco: Jossey-Bass.

McLoyd, V. C. (1990). The impact of economic hardship on black families and children: Psychological distress, parenting, and socioemotional development. *Child Development, 61,* 311–346.

McLoyd, V. C. (1997). The impact of poverty and low socioeconomic status on the socioemotional functioning of African-American children and adolescents: Mediating effects. In R. W. Taylor & M. C. Wang (Eds.), *Social and emotional adjustment and family relations in ethnic minority families* (pp. 7–34). Mahwah, NJ: Erlbaum.

National Research Council. (1993). *Losing generations: Adolescents in high-risk settings.* Washington, DC: National Academy of Science.

Office of Juvenile Justice and Delinquency Prevention. (1999). *Report to Congress on juvenile violence research* (NCJ176976). Retrieved October 16, 2001, from http://ojjdp.ncjrs.org/pubs/jvr

Osofsky, J. D., Wewers, S., Hann, D. M., & Fick, A. C. (1993) Chronic community violence: What is happening to our children? *Psychiatry: Interpersonal and Biological Processes, 56*, 36–45.

Parke, R. D., & O'Neill, P. (1999) Social relationships across contexts: Family–peer linkages. In W. A. Collins & B. Laursen (Eds.), *Relationships in developmental contexts: The Minnesota symposium on child psychology* (Vol. 30, pp. 211–239). Mahwah, NJ: Erlbaum.

Perkins, C. A. (1997). *Age patterns of victims of serious violent crime.* Washington, DC: Bureau of Justice Statistics.

Quinn, J. (1999). Where need meets opportunity: Youth development programs for early teens. *The Future of Children: When School Is Out, 9,* 96–116.

Sampson, R., Morenoff, J., & Earls, F. (1999). Beyond social capital: Spatial dynamics of collective efficacy for children. *American Sociological Review, 64,* 633–660.

Schlossman, S., & Sedlak, M. (1983). The Chicago Area Project revisited. *Crime and Delinquency, 29,* 398–462.

Schubiner, H., Scott, R., & Tzelepis, A. (1993). Exposure to violence among inner-city youth. *Journal of Adolescent Health, 14,* 214–219.

Seidman, E. (1991). Growing up the hard way: Pathways of urban adolescents. *American Journal of Community Psychology, 19,* 173–205.

Seidman, E., Chesir-Teran, D., Friedman, J., Yoshikawa, H., Allen, L., & Roberts, A. (1999). The risk and protective functions of perceived family and peer microsystems among urban adolescents in poverty. *American Journal of Community Psychology, 27,* 211–237.

Shakoor, B. H., & Chalmers, D. (1991). Co-victimization of African-American children who witness violence: Effects on cognitive, emotional, and behavioral development. *Journal of the National Medical Association, 83,* 233–238.

Steinberg, L. (1990). Autonomy, conflict, and harmony in the family relationship. In S. S. Feldman & G. R. Elliott (Eds.), *At the threshold: The developing adolescent* (pp. 255–276). Cambridge, MA: Harvard University Press.

Taylor, R. (1997). The effects of economic and social stressors on parenting and adolescent adjustment in African-American families. In R. W. Taylor & M. C. Wang (Eds.), *Social and emotional adjustment and family relations in ethnic minority families.* Mahwah, NJ: Erlbaum.

Wikstrom, P. (1998). Communities and crime. In M. H. Tonrey (Ed.), *The handbook of crime and punishment* (pp. 269–304). New York: Oxford University Press.

15

Adaptation among Youth Facing Multiple Risks

Prospective Research Findings

Arnold Sameroff, Leslie Morrison Gutman,
and Stephen C. Peck

The high prevalence of mental health problems among children in the United States has continued to stimulate service-oriented professionals to seek targets for preventive intervention. In a 1999 survey of youth risk behavior during the previous year (Centers for Disease Control and Prevention, 2000), 28% of high school children felt blue or hopeless, 19% had considered suicide, and 8% had made an attempt. In terms of aggression, 36% had been in a physical fight. Academic problems were equally serious, with 30% of Hispanics dropping out before high school graduation compared to 14% of African Americans and 8% of whites. Although the majority of youth do not have such problems, the number who do is substantial.

Understanding the pathways that have led to such problem behavior is an important precursor of any successful intervention. Prevention is intimately connected to developmental concerns because there is an expected time course in which activities in the present will influence activities in the future. Where the problem seems to be in the family, school, or peer group, intuitively interventions should take place in those settings and should have immediate impact. Unfortunately, most interventions in single domains have not produced major reductions in problem behavior. It appears that children typically experience multiple risks in multiple social contexts; consequently, it is unlikely that a "magic bullet" for prevention or intervention will be found (Masten & Coatsworth, 1998). Prevention and intervention efforts emerging from this realization utilize combinations of protective efforts to target multiple rather than single risk factors (Coie et al., 1993). Outcomes of lack of academic success or mental illness in the present or lack of financial independence or marital problems in the future appear to have many determinants. Increasingly, attention must be given to the multiple social subsystems that play important roles in producing or reducing social and academic competence.

In this chapter, we will examine a model for predicting developmental competence based on an ecological analysis of the child's social surroundings as well as the child's capacities. Although it is important to understand the specific processes that lead to specific maladjustments, from an epidemiological standpoint the best predictors of problem behaviors seem to be a cumulative risk score that reflects statuses in the full range of ecological subsystems of the child. Moreover, the kind of risk appears to be secondary to the number of negative factors. When the strengths of the individual youth are added to the predictive model, they do not overcome the effects of high environmental risk.

ASSESSING RISKS

Where scientists usually see their task as a search for causes, research on risk factors may appear to be a substitute for a more basic understanding of why individuals succeed or fail. Risks are probabilistic where causes are thought to be deterministic. However, the history of research into the etiology of biological disorders has demonstrated that there are no single sufficient causes. The term *risk factors* itself arose from epidemiological research seeking the cause of heart disease (Costello & Angold, 2000). In the most comprehensive of these efforts, the Framingham Study, it was found that no one factor was either necessary or sufficient (Dawber, 1980). Hypertension, obesity, lack of exercise, and smoking all made significant contributions to heart disease at the population level, but for any single affected individual there was a different combination of these factors. We shall discover a similar result in our search for the causes of developmental problems in children and adolescents. It is not a single factor that causes such difficulties, but an accumulation of adversity that reduces developmental competence.

The emerging field of prevention science (Coie et al., 1993; Mrazek & Haggerty, 1994) is much concerned with the universality of risk factors. Common findings are that the same risk factors affect multiple outcomes, such as depression, conduct disorder, or substance abuse, and that each disorder has multiple risk factors (Coie, Miller-Johnson, & Bagwell, 2000). In studies of single risks and single outcomes, this fact would be missed. The comprehensiveness and the unity of the developmental process require studies of multiple risks and multiple outcomes to avoid a distorted view of the importance of any single risk.

REPRESENTATIVE RISK FACTORS

Let us turn for a moment to research aimed at identifying representative risk factors in the development of cognitive and social-emotional competence. Such child competencies have been found to be strongly related to family mental health and especially social class. In an investigation of a sample of families with a high level of maternal psychopathology, children were followed from birth through high school in the Rochester Longitudinal Study (RLS). When the effects of the mother's mental health and social status on the child's preschool intelligence and mental health were compared, socioeconomic status (SES) had a greater influence (Sameroff, Seifer, & Zax, 1982). However, to better understand the role of SES, more differentiated views of environmental influences were necessary. The measures of parents' educational and occupational achievement that constituted SES scores needed to be transformed into variables that would have a conceptually more direct influence on the child and would illuminate the differences in experiences of children raised in different socioeconomic environments.

Although SES was the best single variable for predicting children's cognitive competence, and an important predictor of social-emotional functioning, the circumstances of families within the same social class differed markedly. SES impacts parenting, parental attitudes and beliefs, family interactions, and the availability of institutions in the surrounding community. From the early data available in the RLS, a set of variables were chosen that were related to economic circumstance but were not the same as SES (Sameroff, Seifer, Barocas, Zax, & Greenspan, 1987). The 10 environmental risk variables identified were (1) a history of maternal mental illness, (2) high maternal anxiety, (3) parental perspectives that reflected rigidity in the attitudes, beliefs, and values that mothers had in regard to their child's development, (4) few positive maternal interactions with the child observed during infancy, (5) head of the household in an unskilled occupation, (6) minimal maternal education, (7) disadvantaged minority status, (8) single parenthood, (9) stressful life events, and (10) large family size. Each of these risk factors has a large literature documenting its potential for deleterious developmental effects (Cichetti & Cohen, 1995; Damon & Eisenberg, 1998; Sameroff, Lewis, & Miller, 2000, Zeanah, 2000).

Where there was no intuitive definition of risk, such as a single parent, the 25% of the sample with the worst scores were labeled as high risk. We then tested whether poor cognitive and social-emotional development was related to the risk factors associated with low socioeconomic circumstances. Each of these variables was a risk factor for preschool competence. For both cognitive and mental health outcomes, the high-risk group for each factor had worse scores than the low-risk group. However, these group differences were not large enough to provide the specificity necessary to identify specific individuals as needing intervention; most children with only a single risk factor did not have a major developmental problem.

CUMULATIVE RISK STUDIES

As children often experience many risks and recurring stressors, focusing on a single risk factor does not address the reality of most children's lives. To increase specificity, it is necessary to take a broader perspective when examining the factors that may be targeted for intervention efforts. Multiple settings and multiple systems must be examined simultaneously because risk factors tend to cluster in the same individuals (Bronfenbrenner, 1979, 1994). Conversely, indices of successful adaptation also tend to cluster (Carnegie Council, 1995). As children often experience many risks and recurring stressors, focusing on a single risk factor does not address the reality of most children's lives.

In improving predictive power, Rutter (1979) argued that it was no particular risk factor but the number of risk factors in a child's background that led to psychiatric disorder. Psychiatric risk for a sample of 10-year-olds rose from 2% in families with zero or one risk factors to 20% in families with four or more. The six risk factors considered included severe marital distress, low SES, large family size or overcrowding, paternal criminality, maternal psychiatric disorder, and placement of the child in foster care. Similarly, Williams, Anderson, McGee, and Silva (1990) related a cumulative disadvantage score to behavioral disorders in 11-year-olds, and Ferguson, Horwood, and Lynsky (1994) to adolescent mental health problems. In each study, the more risk factors, the more behavioral problems.

In the Rochester study, we created a multiple risk score that was the total number of risks for each family (Sameroff et al., 1987). Using this strategy, major differences were found on mental health and intelligence measures between those children with few risks and those with many.

On the intelligence test, children with no environmental risks scored more than 30 points higher than children with eight or nine risks. No preschooler in the zero-risk group had an IQ below 85, whereas 26% of those in the high-risk group did. On average, each risk factor reduced the child's IQ score by 4 points. Four-year-olds in the high-risk group (five or more risk factors) were 12.3 times more likely to be rated as having clinical mental health symptoms.

Statistically, use of the multirisk strategy sacrifices some information on variability in risk indices (e.g., Burchinal, Roberts, Hooper, & Zeisel, 2000; Hooper, Burchinal, Roberts, Zeisel, & Neebe, 1998), yet at the same time it has the advantage of permitting simultaneous consideration of multiple risks in relatively small samples. In general, maximal explanatory power is attained when conducting regression analyses that consider the associations of each of multiple risk variables with a particular outcome. In situations where 20 or 30 risk indices are considered, however, it is often impractical to have this large number of predictor variables included in a single regression analysis. Particularly when sample sizes are limited, therefore, it is often preferable to dichotomize the continuum of scores on each adversity condition into two groups, representing the presence (1) or absence (0) of risk, and then adding all the resultant scores (Sameroff, Seifer, Baldwin, & Baldwin, 1993).

If the primary interest is in some developmental process relating single predictors and outcomes, then the multirisk score provides a good summary of background variables without sacrificing degrees of freedom. An example of this is the Ackerman, Izard, Schoff, Youngstrom, and Kogos (1999) study examining the relation between contextual risk and problem behaviors of 6- and 7-year-old children from economically disadvantaged families. Eleven indicators were used to index contextual risk, but they excluded proximal family variables of specific interest. The investigation found an interaction where more positive caregiver emotionality buffered the influence of higher cumulative risk.

Quality versus Quantity

Another question about the multirisk strategy is whether the negative effects on developmental outcomes are the result of the accumulation of risk factors or the action of a specific risk factor. We had examined this question in the analysis of the 4-year IQ data in the Rochester study (Sameroff et al., 1987). Data from the families that had a moderate multiple risk score (3 to 5 out of 10) were analyzed to determine which risk factors occurred together and whether specific combinations had worse effects than others. The families fell into five groups with different combinations of high-risk conditions. Despite these differences, developmental competencies were the same for children in the five groups. If there were the same number of risk factors, it didn't matter which ones they were. As in the Framingham study of heart disease (Dawber, 1980), no single variable was either a necessary or a sufficient determinant of good or bad outcomes. It was not the quality of the risky environment but the number of risk factors that was affecting the development of children.

In another study contrasting regression and add-em-up strategies, Deater-Deckard, Dodge, Bates, and Pettit (1998) found that multirisk scores were successful outcome predictors, but they explained only about two-thirds of the variance predicted by regressions. In addition, they followed up on the quantity versus quality issue and found that different combinations of risks led to similar outcomes. This means that it is unlikely that the same intervention will work for all children. For every family situation, a unique combination of risk factors will require a unique set of intervention strategies embedded within a developmental model.

Multiple Outcomes and Multiple Risks

To measure the prevalence of risk factors and their association with developmental outcomes, a study is required with a large representative sample and a clearly conceptualized model of risk. Unfortunately, no such epidemiological study has been performed. Moreover, most studies of the effects of risk on development have not applied an ecological perspective in their conceptualization. Attention in the planning has not been given to family, school, peer, and community variables simultaneously. It is only after the fact that risk analyses have been considered.

An example is an analysis of the progress of several thousand young children from kindergarten to third grade using community samples from 30 sites (Peck, Sameroff, Ramey, & Ramey, 1999). From the data collected, 14 risk factors were chosen that tapped ecological levels ranging from parent behavior to neighborhood characteristics. The risk factors were summed, and the expected linear relations were found between the multiple environmental risk scores and school outcomes of academic achievement and social competence supporting the findings from the RLS. Although this study used a large sample at multiple sites, the children were not a representative sample of the community, and the risk factors were selected from available data rather than planned in advance.

Another set of data on the effects of multiple environmental risks on child development was provided by a study of adolescents in a group of Philadelphia families (Furstenberg, Cook, Eccles, Elder, & Sameroff, 1999). Mothers, fathers, and offspring were interviewed in almost 500 families where there was a youth between the ages of 11 and 14. Although not a representative sample, the families varied widely in SES and racial composition.

An advantage of the Philadelphia project was that a more conceptual approach was taken to the design so that environmental measures were available at a number of ecological levels. For the analyses of environmental risk, variables were grouped and examined within subsystems that affected the adolescent, from microsystems (Bronfenbrenner, 1979) in which the child was an active participant to those more distal to the child, where any effect had to be mediated by more proximal variables.

To approximate an ecological model, six groupings of 20 environmental risk variables reflecting different relations to the adolescent were built into the design (Sameroff, Bartko, Baldwin, Baldwin, & Seifer, 1998) (see Table 15.1). The intention was to include multiple factors in each

TABLE 15.1. *Risk Variables in the Philadelphia Study*

Domain	Variable
Family process	Support for autonomy
	Discipline effectiveness
	Parental investment
	Family climate
Parent characteristics	Education
	Efficacy
	Resourcefulness
	Mental health
Family structure	Marital status
	Household crowding
	Welfare receipt
Management of community	Institutional involvement
	Informal networks
	Social resources
	Economic adjustment
Peers	Prosocial
	Antisocial
Community	Neighborhood SES
	Neighborhood problems
	School climate

of the six ecological subsystems. Family process was the first grouping and included variables in the family microsystem that were directly experienced by the child and would fit into a category of parent–child interaction. These variables included support for autonomy, behavior control, parental involvement, and family climate. The second grouping was Parent Characteristics, which included mental health, sense of efficacy, resourcefulness, and level of education. The third grouping, Family Structure, included the parents' marital status, and socioeconomic indicators of household crowding and receiving welfare payments. The fourth grouping was Family Management of the Community, composed of institutional involvement, informal networks, social resources, and adjustments to economic pressure. The fifth grouping, Peers, included indicators of another microsystem of the youth, the extent to which the youth was associated with prosocial and antisocial peers. Community was the sixth grouping, representing the ecological level most distal to the youth and the family. It included a census tract variable reflecting the average income and educational level of the neighborhood the family lived in, a parental report of the number of problems in the neighborhood, and the climate of the adolescent's school.

In the Philadelphia study, in addition to the larger number of ecological variables, we had a wider array of youth assessments for interpreting developmental competence. The five outcomes used to characterize successful adolescence were Psychological Adjustment, Self-Competence, Problem Behaviors with drugs, delinquency, and early sexual behavior, Activity Involvement in sports, religious, extracurricular, and community projects, and Academic Performance, as reflected in grades.

To examine the effect of the accumulation of risks, scores were calculated for each adolescent. The result ranged from a minimum of 0 to a maximum of 13 out of a possible 20 risk factors. When the five normalized adolescent outcome scores were plotted against the number of risk factors a very large decline in outcome was found with increasing risk (see Figure 15.1) (Sameroff et al., 1998).

Whether cumulative risk scores meaningfully increase predictive efficiency can be demonstrated by an odds-ratio analyses, involving comparisons of the odds of having a bad outcome in a high-risk versus a low-risk environment. For the typical analysis of relative and attributable risk the outcome variable is usually discrete, either succumbing to a disease or disorder or not. For children, there are few discrete negative outcomes. They are generally too young to have many pregnancies or arrests, and the rate of academic failure is not particularly high. In the Philadelphia

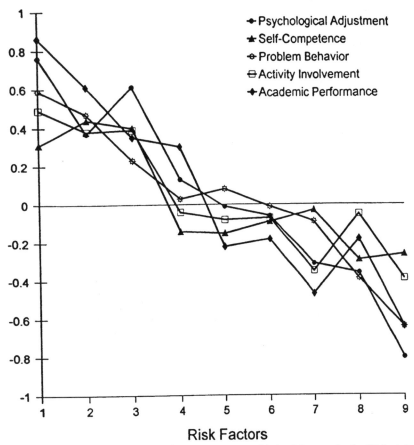

FIGURE 15.1 Relation of five youth outcomes to multiple-risk score in the Philadelphia study.

study, bad outcomes were artificially created by identifying the 25% of adolescents who were doing the most poorly in terms of mental health, self-competence, problem behavior, activity involvement, or academic performance.

The relative risk in the high-risk group (eight or more risks) for each of the bad outcomes was substantially higher than in the low-risk group (three or fewer risks). The strongest effects were for Academic Performance, where the relative risk for a bad outcome increased from 7% in the low-risk group to 45% in the high-risk group, an odds ratio of 6.7. The odds ratios for Psychological Adjustment, Problem Behavior, Self-Competence, and Activity Involvement were 5.7, 4.5, 3.4, and 2.7, respectively. For the important cognitive and social-emotional outcomes of youth, powerful negative effects, seem to result from the accumulation of environmental risk factors.

Our assessments of both multiple risks and multiple outcomes have allowed us to examine another important issue: the degree to which some sets of risks are associated with some outcomes more than with others. Using data from a longitudinal study of African American and white adolescents in a large county in Maryland that included both urban and suburban neighborhoods (Eccles, Early, Frasier, Belansky, & McCarthy, 1997), we examined the pattern of contributions from different ecological subsystems to the mental health, problem behavior, and academic achievement during the eighth grade (Sameroff & Peck, 2001). Because many variables are correlated with each other (e.g., education and income), their contribution to multiple regression equations may not reflect their actual influence. To get around this problem, we entered the set of variables for each ecological subsystem first and last in a series of hierarchical multiple regressions. The variance explained when entered first represents the upper limit and when entered last represents the lower limit, with the truth somewhere in between (Figures 15.2, 15.3, and 15.4).

For each outcome we found a different pattern, with parental mental health being the largest contributor to youth mental health, peers being the largest contributor to problem behavior, and almost every variable contributing to academic achievement. Yet when we used multiple risk scores that equalized the influence of each contextual variable, there were similar relations to each outcome – the more risk factors, the worse the outcome.

Similarly, in the Philadelphia study, the pattern of relations between ecological variables chosen as risk factors and adolescent behavior was different in regression analyses for each outcome (Furstenberg et al., 1999). But again, the more risk factors, the worse the outcome.

RESILIENCE AND PROTECTIVE FACTORS

A major counterpoint to changing the social circumstances of children's lives is the idea of changing the characteristics of the children themselves. Resilience connotes positive adaptation by individuals despite severe adversity. Over the past three decades, studies of resilience have focused on individual variation in response to risky conditions such as stressful life events (Garmezy, Masten, & Tellegen, 1984; Luthar, 1991; Weist, Freedman, Paskewitz, Proescher, & Flaherty, 1995), exposure to

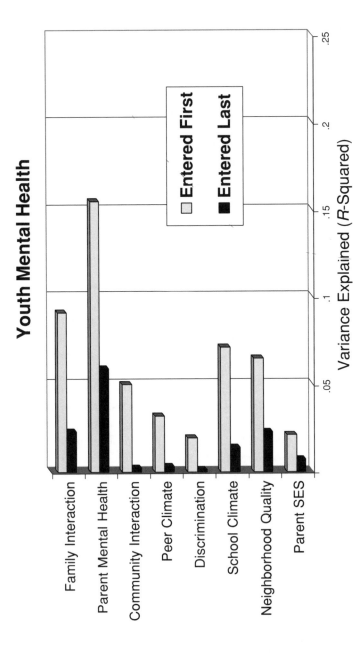

FIGURE 15.2 Proportion of variance explained when sets of variables from various ecological systems are entered first and last in hierarchical linear regression analyses predicting youth mental health, problem behavior, and academic achievement in the Maryland study.

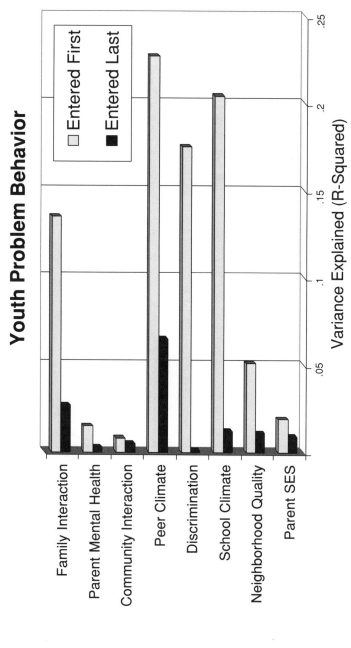

FIGURE 15.3 Caption same as Figure 15.2.

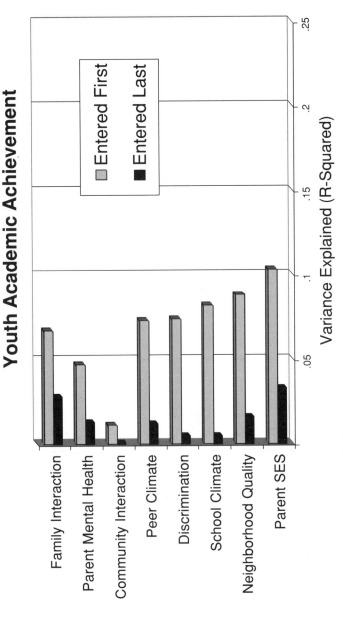

FIGURE 15.4 Caption same as Figure 15.2.

community violence (White, Bruce, Farrell, & Kliewer, 1998) maltreatment (Moran & Eckenrode, 1992), urban poverty (Luthar, 1999), and maternal mental illness (Seifer et al., 1982).

These studies have brought sharper attention to the protective factors that influence stress resistance in children and adolescents. Whereas earlier studies focused primarily on personal attributes, such as high IQ, that were associated with manifestations of competence in children despite exposure to stressful events (Garmezy et al., 1984), later research incorporated protective factors in the social context. For example, Garmezy (1993) identified three broad sets of variables that have been found to operate as protective factors in stress-resistant children: (1) characteristics of the child such as temperament, cognitive skills, and positive responsiveness to others, (2) families marked by warmth, cohesion, and structure, and (3) the availability of external support systems.

Recently, however, there has been sharp criticism concerning the construct of resilience and the methods used by resilience researchers (see Luthar, Cicchetti, & Becker, 2000). One of the main criticisms concerns the absence of a unifying conceptual framework that encompasses its integration across disciplines and specialized areas. A scientific basis for intervention research necessitates precise terminology to built upon earlier classifications and to ensure its continued vitality (Luthar et al., 2000). A consistent and systematic framework is essential to facilitate the work of researchers and practitioners who pursue work in this area, to integrate findings across diverse fields, and to provide guidance for the identification and implementation of age-appropriate, optimal targets for preventive interventions.

Many current research reports use the phrase *protective factors* as a synonym for *competence-enhancing factors*, but early pioneers of resilience research restricted the use of these term to situations where there was an interaction with a risk variable. In this sense, the effect of a protective factor would be minimal in low-risk populations but would be magnified in the presence of one or more risk variables (Garmezy et al., 1984). Protective factors should have meaning only in the face of adversity (Rutter, 1987).

However, other researchers have been using the term *protective factors* to describe variables associated with desirable outcomes independent of the occurrence of social disadvantage or adverse circumstances (McFarlane, Bellissimo, & Norman, 1995; Resnick, et al., 1997). In other studies, protective factors were defined simply as the positive pole of risk factors (Stouthhamer-Loeber et al., 1993). To counter the confusion, Sameroff (1999) proposed that a better term for the positive end of the risk dimension would be *promotive factors* rather than *protective factors*. In this sense, a promotive factor would have a positive effect in both high- and low-risk populations.

PROMOTIVE FACTORS

To examine the different effects of risk and promotive influences, we created a set of promotive factors by cutting each of our risk dimensions at the top quartile rather than the bottom (Sameroff et al., 1998). For example, where a negative family climate had been a risk factor, a positive family climate now became a promotive factor; where a parent's poor mental health was a risk factor, her good mental health became promotive. We then summed these promotive factors and examined their relation to the five Philadelphia outcomes. There was a similar range of promotive factors, from families with none to families with 15 out of a possible 20. The effects of the multiple promotive factor score mirrored the effects of multiple risks. Families with many promotive factors did substantially better than families with few promotive factors. For the youth in the Philadelphia sample, there does not seem to be much difference between the influence of risk and promotive variables. The more risk factors, the worse the outcomes; the more promotive factors, the better the outcomes. In short, when taken as part of a constellation of environmental influences on child development, most contextual variables in the parents, the family, the neighborhood, and the culture at large seem to be dimensional, aiding in general child development at one end and inhibiting it at the other. For intervention purposes, increasing promotive factors has the same effect as reducing risks, because they are on the same dimensions for most children most of the time.

Although most family and social factors seem to have linear effects on child competence, for intervention purposes it is worthwhile to determine if there are some factors that would show an interactive effect. One approach is to determine if some environmental factor would buffer the effects of other risks. Another is to search for factors in the child that would serve such functions.

ENVIRONMENTAL PROTECTIVE FACTORS

Income and Marital Status

On the environmental side, we examined the effect of two risk factors in the Philadelphia study that economists and sociologists have been very concerned about: low income level and single parenthood (Sameroff et al., 1998). Although one would think that these factors should have powerful effects on the fate of children, we did not find such differences when these single variables were put into a broader ecological framework. Differences in effects on child competence disappeared when we controlled for the number of other environmental risk factors in each family. To test the effects of different amounts of financial resources, we split our sample of families into those with high, middle, and low income levels. For the family structure comparison, we split the sample into groups of children living in two-parent versus single-parent families. In each case, there were no differences and no interactions in the relation to child competence when we compared groups of children with the same number of risk factors raised in rich or poor families or families with one or two parents (Sameroff et al., 1998). There are many successful adults who were raised in poverty and unsuccessful ones who were raised in affluence. There are many healthy and happy adults who come from broken homes, and there are many unhappy ones who were raised by two parents.

Again, what our analyses of these data reveal is that it is not single environmental factors that make a difference but rather the constellation of risks in each family's life. Income and marital status seem to make major differences in child development not because they are overarching variables in themselves, but because they are strongly associated with a combination of other risk factors. For example, whereas 39% of poor children lived in high-risk families with more than seven risk factors only 7% of affluent children did. Similarly, whereas 29% of single-parent families lived in high-risk social conditions, only 15% of two-parent families did.

Family Process

In a more recent study, Gutman, Sameroff, and Eccles (2002) did find interactions. We examined the effects of multiple risk and protective factors on the academic outcomes of African American adolescents in our Maryland sample (Eccles et al., 1997; Sameroff & Peck, 2001). Negative demographic and structural variables were defined as risk factors, and parent interaction and social support variables were defined as positive factors to emphasize the interplay between these two sets of influences on adolescent development. A multiple-risk score for each family was calculated based on many of the factors already shown to have deleterious effects on children and adolescents. These included maternal depression, family income, highest occupation in the household, maternal education, marital status, number of children living in the household, family stressful events, percentage of neighborhood poverty, percentage of neighborhood female-headed households, and percentage of neighborhood welfare recipients.

We defined parenting behavior and social support as positive variables to determine whether they had promotive (i.e., direct) and/or protective (i.e., interactive) effects. For the most part, previous studies have focused on how positive factors influence the developmental outcomes of either low-risk or high-risk adolescents. But in many studies of resilience, there has been a confound between high-risk samples and ethnic differences (e.g., the high-risk groups have been primarily African American, whereas the low-risk groups have been primarily white) (Baldwin et al., 1993). Because our sample included African American families with a wide distribution of exposure to risk, both promotive and protective effects could be examined.

Consistent with past research (Rutter, 1979; Sameroff et al., 1987, 1993), we found that the more risk factors adolescents experienced, the worse their academic outcomes were (Gutman et al., 2002). As the number of risk factors increased, adolescents had lower grade point averages, more absences, and lower math achievement test scores. Different promotive and protective factors also emerged as significant contributors, depending on the nature of the achievement-related outcome that was assessed. Factors were identified that were promotive only, such as parental school involvement, and those that had both promotive and protective effects, such as consistent discipline. Both factors had a positive influence on all groups of children, regardless of risk status, but consistent discipline had an additional positive effect on high-risk youth.

There were also factors that were protective only, such as peer support. In particular, peer support was associated with higher math achievement test scores for higher-risk adolescents, but it did not affect the math achievement test scores of lower-risk adolescents. Although peer support for academic success may be limited for African American adolescents (Steinberg, Dornbusch, & Brown, 1992), African American adolescents exposed to multiple risks who perceive that they can depend on their peers for help with their personal and school difficulties may be more likely to experience higher academic outcomes than their counterparts who perceive their peers as less supportive.

A surprise were variables that were thought to be positive but showed negative effects instead, such as democratic decision making. We found that fewer opportunities for adolescent democratic decision making were associated with higher grade point averages and math achievement test scores for African American adolescents with more risks, whereas democratic decision making had little or no effect on the grade point averages and math achievement test scores of adolescents with fewer risks. Although this finding was unexpected, it was less surprising when we considered the values and demands of the larger social context in which each family lives. Parenting practices that emphasize democratic decision making and foster a sense of autonomy may be more suitable for children from low-risk environments, whereas they may be inappropriate for, or even detrimental to, youth living in more risky environments. Children and adolescents who live in more dangerous environments may benefit from high levels of parental control, whereas children living in less risky neighborhoods may experience negative effects of such restrictive control (Baldwin, Baldwin, & Cole, 1990; Baumrind, 1972; Furstenberg et al., 1999; Gonzales, Cauce, Friedman, & Mason, 1996).

We have presented the details of such studies to demonstrate the complexity involved in determining the links between context and child. Comparing the positive and negative effects of social and individual factors is necessary to understand the processes that lead to more or less successful adolescent outcomes. For example, based on the results of the Maryland study, it appears that increasing parental school involvement is important for all African American students (a promotive effect), whereas African American youth exposed to multiple risks may benefit especially from efforts designed to enhance peer networks in early adolescence such as peer mentoring or tutoring programs (a protective effect).

PERSONAL PROTECTIVE FACTORS

Gender and Race

Personal characteristics should be important ingredients in each child's development and can be divided into demographic domains, like gender and race, and behavioral domains, like sense of efficacy. To give some perspective on the relation between individual contributions and the effects of social risk, some child characteristics were included in the Philadelphia study (Furstenberg et al., 1999). The correlations between risk scores and outcomes for separate groups of boys and girls and for blacks and whites were examined, and no differences were found (Sameroff, Seifer, & Bartko, 1997). When the relation between our summary competence measure and risk factors was compared for gender and racial groups, the curves were essentially overlapping; the more risk factors, the worse the developmental outcomes.

Resourcefulness

Like the SES variable on the environmental side, race and gender are not behavioral variables. Therefore, it would be of greater interest to investigate the influence of variables with psychological content. A personality variable that is given great importance in discussions of successful development is resourcefulness. Is it possible that despite social adversity, those children with high levels of *human capital* (Coleman, 1988) are able to overcome the problem of minimal resources at home and in the community to reach levels of achievement comparable to those of children from more highly advantaged social strata?

In the Philadelphia study, we measured this construct of resourcefulness with a set of questions asked of the parent and the child about the youth's capacity to solve problems, overcome difficulties, and bounce back from setbacks. We divided the sample into high- and low-efficacy groups and looked at their adolescent outcomes. High-efficacy youth were more competent than those with low efficacy on our measures of adolescent competence. A sense of personal resourcefulness did seem to pay off.

But what happens to this effect when we take environmental adversity into account? When we matched high- and low-efficacy children on the number of environmental risk factors, the difference in general competence between those in the high and low environmental risk conditions was far greater than that between the high-resourceful and low-resourceful groups (see figure 15.5). High-efficacy adolescents in high-risk conditions did worse than low-efficacy youth in low-risk conditions (Sameroff et al., 1998). For some, it may be a surprise to learn that the ineffective offspring of advantaged families may have a much easier developmental path than that of more resourceful multirisk children.

We did the same analysis using academic achievement as an indicator of competence and examined whether the good work of high-efficacy youth at school was related to better mental health, more engagement in positive community activities, and less involvement in delinquent problem behavior. Again, for every outcome, adolescents with high grades in high-risk conditions did worse than those with low grades in low-risk conditions.

Mental Health

One of the weaknesses of the Philadelphia study is that the data are cross-sectional. Finding causal factors is impossible unless one has longitudinal developmental data, and it is difficult even then. The Rochester study did have a series of developmental assessments that permitted a longitudinal view of the contribution of individual factors to developmental success. We could see how infant competence affected preschool competence and then how preschool competence affected high school competence.

From the Rochester data collected during the first year of life, we created a multiple competence score for each child during infancy that included 12 factors. These were scores from newborn medical and behavioral tests, temperament assessments, and developmental scales. We then divided the sample into groups of high- and low-competent infants and examined as outcomes their 4-year IQ and social-emotional functioning scores. We found no relation between infant competence and 4-year IQ or social-emotional problems. We could not find infant protective factors (Sameroff et al., 1998).

However, infant developmental scales may be weak predictors because they assess different developmental functions than those captured by later cognitive and personality assessments. Perhaps if we move up the age scale, we may find that characteristics of these children at 4 years of age may be protective for later achievement. We divided the 4-year-olds into high and low mental health groups and high and low IQ groups. We then compared these groups on how they did at 18 years on mental health and measures of school achievement. More resourceful children did better on average than less resourceful children, but as in the Philadelphia study, when we controlled for environmental risk, the differences in performance between children with high and low levels of early competence were much less than those between children in high- and low-risk social environments. In each case, we found again that high-competent children in high-risk environments did worse than low-competent children in low-risk environments.

The situation was much the same at 13 years of age. We divided the adolescents into high and low mental health groups and high and low intelligence groups and examined their 18-year behavior. Again, in each case, 13-year-old youths with better mental health and intelligence did better within the same social risk conditions, but competent youths living in high-risk conditions did worse than competent youths in low-risk conditions. However more to our point, they did worse than low-competent children in low-risk environments (Sameroff et al., 1998). The negative effects of a disadvantaged environment seem to be more powerful contributors to child achievement at every age than the personality characteristics of the child.

DEVELOPMENTAL TRAJECTORIES

Although several studies have examined the impact of risk and protective factors on the academic outcomes of children and adolescents, most have either examined a single point in time or change across two time points. Interactive processes between risk and protective factors, however, often rely on chains of connections over time rather than on a multiplicative effect at any single time point (Rutter, 1987). Understanding the factors that influence students' academic trajectories over many time points may help explain why high-risk students either catch up or fall further behind their more advantaged peers as they progress through school.

In the Rochester study, we examined school records and obtained grades and attendance records for the participants from 1st to 12th grades (Gutman, Sameroff, & Cole, submitted). Hierarchical linear modeling (HLM) was used to examine the trajectories of the children throughout their school careers (Bryk & Raudenbush, 1992). We then determined how the growth curves were influenced by early environmental risk, that is, their 4-year multirisk scores. We also determined the degree to which their early mental health and intelligence interacted with environmental risk in a two-level hierarchical linear model where the time points were conceptualizing as nested within children. In other words, in addition to measuring multiple risk factors, we examined the promotive (i.e., direct) and protective (i.e., interactive) effects of intelligence and mental health on grade point average and number of absences using the 12 time points from 1st to 12th grades. We expected that (1) multiple risks would have negative effects on students' academic trajectories; (2) child factors would act as either promotive and/or protective factors, depending on the outcome being assessed; and (3) protective factors would be identified whose effects were magnified in the presence of multiple risks.

Amplifying other studies that examined either one or two points in time, we found that early risk had an adverse effect on academic trajectories from 1st to 12th grades (Gutman et al., submitted). Although high-risk students started out with academic achievement similar to that of average students in first grade, their school grades became lower and

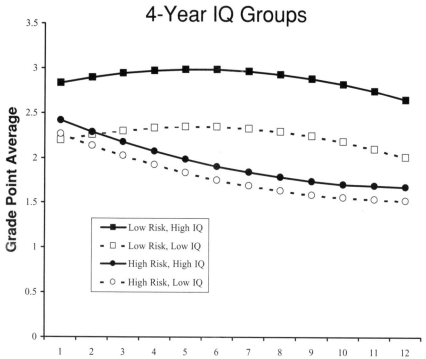

FIGURE 15.5 Effects of 4-year high and low multiple risk and high and low 4-year verbal intelligence on school grades (GPA) from first to twelfth grades.

the number of absences notably higher than those of their low-risk peers as they reached high school. We found preschool promotive effects where both higher intelligence and better mental health had significant direct effects on later school grades but not on absences.

Early intelligence and mental health had significant interactive effects on students' school grades, but these were not the traditional protective effects, as these influences did not help high-risk students; they only maintained the performance of low-risk students. High-competent children, either by virtue of higher 4-year IQ (Figure 15.5) or mental health (Figure 15.6), did well in low-risk environments, but their competence was no benefit if they were at high social risk. High-risk 4-year-olds did poorly throughout the school years whether they were competent or not. Low-competent 4-year-olds in low-risk conditions consistently had higher grade point average than the high-competent children in high-risk conditions.

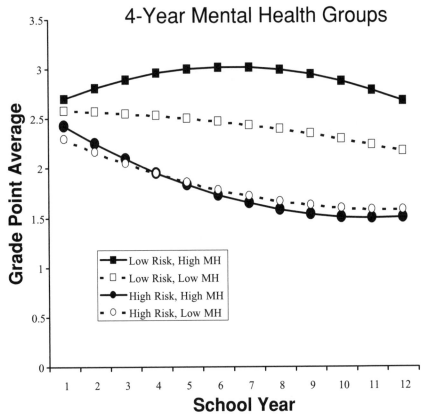

FIGURE 15.6 Effects of 4-year high and low multiple risk and high and low 4-year mental health on school grades (GPA) from first to twelfth grades.

OVERVIEW

Pervasive Effects of Multiple Risks

We have examined the effects of multiple risks across a wide range of studies and have found the accumulation of social risks across the family, peer group, school, and neighborhood to have a consistent by negative effect. The more risks, the worse the outcomes.

Nonspecificity of Risks

A variety of developmental problems and disorders have been studied, and in each case different risk factors have been found to produce the same negative results. Moreover, a similar set of risk factors affect a number of different disorders (Coie et al., 1993; Mrazek & Haggerty, 1994).

Small Effects of Single Risks

Single variables, such as income level and marital status on the family side, and gender, race, efficacy, mental health, and achievement on the personal side, taken alone, may have statistically significant effects on children's behavior, but their effects are small in comparison with the accumulation of multiple negative influences that characterize high-risk groups. The overlap in children's outcomes is substantial for low-income versus high-income families, families with one or two parents, boys versus girls, blacks versus whites, and high-resourceful and low-resourceful youth. But the overlap is far less in comparisons between groups of children reared in conditions of high versus low levels of multiple risks, where the effects of gender, race, resourcefulness, income, and number of parents in the home are accumulated.

Individual Competence Is a Weak Protective Factor

Individual competence is a major candidate for a protective factor in the face of environmental adversity. Indeed, when the level of social risk is controlled for, more competent children do better later on than less competent children. However, more competent children in high-risk conditions consistently do worse than less competent children in low-risk conditions.

Nonuniversality of Protective Factors

We seriously question most efforts to find a universal protective factor for all children. The positive factors that promote competence may vary according to the age of the child and the developmental outcome being targeted. Paradoxically, promotive processes in one context may prove to be risky in another. For example, although democratic, authoritative parenting may be successful in increasing the academic achievement of white, middle-class children, those who live in more dangerous environments may benefit from higher levels of parental control. Conversely, children living in less risky neighborhoods may experience negative effects of such restrictive control (Baldwin et al., 1990; Baumrind, 1972; Furstenberg et al., 1998; Gutman et al., 2002). To truly appreciate the determinants of competence requires attention to the broad constellation of ecological factors in which these individuals and families are embedded.

Necessity of Multiple Interventions to Counter Multiple Risks

A systems perspective requires attention to the multiple influences on child development, ranging from individual competencies to the characteristics of the many social settings in which the child participates. A focus on single characteristics of individuals or families has never explained more than a small proportion of variance in behavioral development. The children at most risk for poor outcomes are those with problems in the longest number of settings. Interventions designed to change the fates of such high-risk children will have to operate in all of these contexts. The proverbial magic bullet may turn out to be as multidimensional as the modern army. The major implication of multiple-risk models is that interventions need to be as complex as development itself.

References

Ackerman, B. P., Izard, C. E., Schoff, K., Youngstrom, E. A., & Kogos, J. (1999). Contextual risk, caregiver emotionality, and the problem behaviors of six- and seven-year-old children from economically disadvantaged families. *Child Development, 70*(6), 1415–1427.

Baldwin, A. L., Baldwin, C., & Cole, R. E. (1990). Stress-resistant families and stress-resistant children. In J. E. Rolf (Ed.), *Risk and protective factors in the development of psychopathology* (pp. 257–280). New York: Cambridge University Press.

Baldwin, A. L., Baldwin, C., Kasser, T., Zax, M., Sameroff, A., & Seifer, R. (1993). Contextual risk and resiliency during late adolescence. *Development and Psychopathology, 5*, 741–761.

Baumrind, D. (1972). An exploratory study of socialization effects on black children: Some black–white comparisons. *Child Development, 43*, 261–267.

Bronfenbrenner, U. (1979). *The ecology of human development.* Cambridge, MA: Harvard University Press.

Bronfenbrenner, U. (1994). Ecological models of human development. In T. Husten & T. N. Postlethwaite (Eds), *International encyclopedia of education* (2nd ed., Vol. 3, pp. 1643–1647). New York: Elsevier Science.

Bryk, A. S., & Raudenbush, S. W. (1992). *Hierarchical linear modeling applications and data analysis methods.* Newbury Park, CA: Sage.

Burchinal, M. R., Roberts, J. E., Hooper, S., & Zeisel, S. A. (2000). Cumulative risk and early cognitive development: A comparison of statistical risk models. *Developmental Psychology, 36*(6), 793–807.

Carnegie Council on Adolescent Development. (1995). *Great transitions: Preparing adolescents for the new century.* New York: Carnegie.

Centers for Disease Control and Prevention. (2000). Youth Risk Behavior Surveillance – United States, 1999. *Morbidity and Mortality Weekly Report, 49* (SS-5), 1–96.

Cicchetti, D., & Cohen, D. (Eds.). (1995) *Developmental psychopathology, Vol 2: Risk, disorder, and adaptation.* New York: Wiley.

Coie, J. D., Watt, N. F., West, S., Hawkins, J. D., Asarnow, J. R., Markman, H. J., Ramey, S. L., Shure, M. B., & Long, B. (1993). The science of prevention. *American Psychologist, 48,* 1013–1022.

Coleman, J. (1988). Social capital in the creation of human capital. *American Journal of Sociology, 94,* S95–S120.

Costello, E. J., & Angold, A. (2000). Developmental epidemiology: A framework for developmental psychopathology. In A. Sameroff, M. Lewis, & S. Miller (Eds.), *Handbook of developmental psychopathology* (pp. 57–73). New York: Plenum.

Damon, W., & Eisenberg, N. (Eds.). (1998). *Handbook of child psychology, Vol. 3: Social, emotional, and personality development* (5th ed.). New York: Wiley.

Dawber, T. R. (1980). *The Framingham Study:* The *epidemiology of coronary heart disease.* Cambridge, MA: Harvard University Press.

Deater-Deckard, K., Dodge, K. A., Bates, J. E., & Pettit, G. S. (1998). Multiple risk factors in the development of externalizing behavior problems: Group and individual differences. *Development and Psychopathology, 10*(3), 469–493.

Eccles, J. S., Early, D., Frasier, K., Belansky, E., & McCarthy, K. (1997). The relation of connection, regulation, and support for autonomy to adolescents' functioning. *Journal of Adolescent Research, 12,* 263–286.

Fergusson, D. M., Horwood, L. J., & Lynsky, M. T. (1994). The childhoods of multiple problem adolescents: A 15-year longitudinal study. *Journal of Child Psychology and Psychiatry, 35,* 1123–1140.

Furstenberg, F. F., Jr., Cook, T., Eccles, J., Elder, G. H., & Sameroff, A. J. (1999). *Managing to make it: Urban families and adolescent success.* Chicago: University of Chicago Press.

Garmezy, N. (1993). Children in poverty: Resilience despite risk. *Psychiatry, 56,* 127–136.

Garmezy, N., Masten, A. S., & Tellegen, A. (1984). The study of stress and competence in children: A building block of developmental psychopathology. *Child Development, 55,* 97–111.

Gonzales, N. A., Cauce, A. M., Friedman, R. J., & Mason, C. A. (1996). Family, peer, and neighborhood influences on academic achievement among African American adolescents: One-year prospective effects. *American Journal of Community Psychology, 24,* 365–388.

Gutman, L. M., Sameroff, A. J., & Cole, R. (submitted). *Academic trajectories from first to twelfth grades: Growth curves according to multiple risk and child factors.* Submitted.

Gutman, L. M., Sameroff, A. S., & Eccles, J. S. (2002). The academic achievement of African-American students during early adolescence: An examination of multiple risk, promotive, and protective factors. *American Journal of Community Psychology, 30,* 367–399.

Hooper, S. R., Burchinal, M. R., Roberts, J. E., Zeisel, S., & Neebe, E. C. (1998). Social and family risk factors for infant development at one year: An application of the cumulative risk model. *Journal of Applied Developmental Psychology, 19*(1), 85–96.

Luthar, S. S. (1991). Vulnerability and resilience: A study of high-risk adolescents. *Child Development, 62,* 600–616.

Luthar, S. S., Cicchetti, D., & Becker, B. (2000). The construct of resilience: A critical evaluation and guidelines for future work. *Child Development, 71,* 543–562.

Masten, A. S., & Coatsworth, J. D. (1998). The development of competence in favorable and unfavorable environments: Lessons from research on successful children. *American Psychologist, 53,* 205–220.

McFarlane, A. H., Bellissimo, A., & Norman, G. R. (1995). The role of family and peers in social self-efficacy: Links to depression in adolescence. *American Journal of Orthopsychiatry, 65,* 402–410.

Moran, P. B., & Eckenrode, J. (1992). Protective personality characteristics among adolescent victims of maltreatment. *Child Abuse and Neglect, 16,* 743–754.

Mrazek, P. G., & Haggerty, R. J. (Eds.). (1994). *Reducing risks for mental disorders: Frontiers for preventive intervention programs.* Washington, DC: National Academy Press.

Peck, S., Sameroff, A., Ramey, S., & Ramey, C. (1999, April). *Transition into school: Ecological risks for adaptation and achievement in a national sample.* Paper presented at the biennial meeting of the Society for Research and Development, Albuquerque, NM.

Resnick, M., Bearman, P., Blum, R., Bauman, K., Harris, K., Jones, J., Tabor, J., Beuhring, T., Sieving, R., Shew, M., Ireland, M., Bearinger, L., & Udry, R. (1997). Protecting adolescents from harm: Findings from the longitudinal study on adolescent health. *Journal of the American Medical Association, 278*(10), 823–832.

Rutter, M. (1979). Protective factors in children's responses to stress and disadvantage. In M. W. Kent & J. E. Rolf (Eds.), *Primary prevention of psychopathology: Vol. 3. Social competence in children* (pp. 49–74). Hanover, NH: University Press of New England.

Rutter, M. (1987). Psychosocial resilience and protective mechanisms. *American Journal of Orthopsychiatry, 57,* 316–331.

Sameroff, A. J. (1999). Ecological perspectives on developmental risk. In J. D. Osofsky & H. E. Fitzgerald (Eds.), *WAIMH handbook of infant mental health: Vol. 4. Infant mental health groups at risk* (pp. 223–248). New York: Wiley.

Sameroff, A. J., Bartko, W. T., Baldwin, A., Baldwin, C., & Seifer, R. (1998). Family and social influences on the development of child competence. In M. Lewis & C. Feiring (Eds.), *Families, risk, and competence* (pp. 177–192). Mahwah, NJ: Erlbaum.

Sameroff, A., Lewis, M., & Miller, S. (Eds.). (2000). *Handbook of developmental psychopathology.* New York: Plenum.

Sameroff, A. J., & Peck, S. (2001, April). Individual and contextual influences on adolescent competence. Symposium presentation at the biennial meetings of the Society for Research in Child Development, Minneapolis.

Sameroff, A. J., Seifer, R., Baldwin, A., & Baldwin, C. (1993). Stability of intelligence from preschool to adolescence: The influence of social and family risk factors. *Child Development, 64,* 80–97.

Sameroff, A. J., Seifer, R., Barocas, B., Zax, M., & Greenspan, S. (1987). IQ scores of 4-year-old children: Social-environmental risk factors. *Pediatrics, 79*(3), 343–350.

Sameroff, A. J., Seifer, R., & Bartko, W. T. (1997). Environmental perspectives on adaptation during childhood and adolescence. In S. S. Luthar, J. A. Barack, D. Cicchetti, & J. Weisz (Eds.), *Developmental psychopathology: Perspectives on risk and disorder* (pp. 507–526). Cambridge, MA: Cambridge University Press.

Sameroff, A. J., Seifer, R., & Zax, M. (1982). Early development of children at risk for emotional disorder. *Monographs of the Society for Research in Child Development, 47*(7, Serial No. 199).

Steinberg, L., Dornbusch, S. M., & Brown, B. B. (1992). Ethnic differences in adolescent achievement: An ecological perspective. *American Psychologist, 47*, 723–729.

Stouthamer-Loeber, M., Loeber, R., Farrington, D. P., Zhang, Q., van Kammen, W., & Maguin, E. (1993). The double edge of protective and risk factors for delinquency: Interrelations and developmental patterns. *Development and Psychopathology, 5*, 683–701.

Weist, M., Freedman, A., Pakewitz, D., Proescher, E., & Flaherty, L. (1995). Urban youth under stress: Empirical identification of protective factors. *Journal of Youth and Adolescence, 24*(6), 705–721.

White, K., Bruce, S., Farrell, A., & Kliewer, W. (1998). Impact of exposure to community violence on anxiety: A longitudinal study of family social support as a protective factor for urban children. *Journal of Child and Family Studies, 7*(2), 187–203.

Williams, S., Anderson, J., McGee, R., & Silva, P. A. (1990). Risk factors for behavioral and emotional disorder in preadolescent children. *Journal of the American Academy of Child and Adolescent Psychiatry, 29*, 413–419.

Zeanah, C. H. (2000). *Handbook of infant mental health.* New York: Guildford press.

16

Positive Adaptation among Youth Exposed to Community Violence

Deborah Gorman-Smith and Patrick H. Tolan

Exposure to community violence threatens the well-being of children in several ways. Living in communities plagued by violence threatens the very core of what is needed for healthy development and is related to a host of short- and long-term developmental problems (Bell & Jenkins, 1993; Cooley-Quill, Boyd, Frantz, & Walsh, 2001; Gorman-Smith & Tolan, 1998; Richters & Martinez, 1993; Schwab-Stone et al., 1995). Unfortunately, although it is possible to list many problems and disorders associated with exposure to community violence, we can say very little based on scientific study about variations in outcome, relations between specific types of exposure and outcome, and mechanisms through which children who are exposed do better or worse. We know that some children appear to suffer symptoms of posttraumatic stress disorder or other types of internalizing disorders, and others seem to react by becoming more aggressive or showing greater behavioral problems. However, we know little about how and why these different reactions occur. We also have few empirically based treatments for children exposed to chronic community violence, and even less work has been conducted on how to protect children from exposure in the first place. So, although it is clear that exposure to community violence can harm children, the scientific knowledge base on promoting positive adaptation among youth exposed to community violence is very sketchy.

This work was supported by funding from the National Institute of Mental Health (R01 MH48248), the National Institute of Child Health and Human Development Centers for Disease Control and Prevention (R01 HD35415), CDC-P (R49 CCR512739), and a Faculty Scholar Award from the William T. Grant Foundation to the first author.

This chapter will use the available research to outline a set of issues and propose a research agenda to advance our knowledge about how best to protect children from exposure and help those who have been exposed. Clearly, part of the difficulty in moving forward is the complexity of the issue. Exposure to community violence can occur in many forms: through victimization, witnessing, or simply hearing about friends' and family members' experience with violence. Also, violence exposure rarely occurs in isolation from other stressors and risk factors. Children living in inner-city neighborhoods are both most likely to be exposed to community violence and to be exposed to multiple chronic stressors, including poverty, familial disruption, inadequate housing, and difficulty accessing social resources

In the following sections, we review the current literature on exposure to community violence, with specific attention to implications for positive adaptation among exposed youth. We first review the extent of the problem (i.e., the number of children exposed) and the associated risks. We then address factors related to differences in outcome, including the mechanisms through which more positive adaptation might occur. With the goal of informing intervention and prevention efforts, we distinguish between those factors through which violence exposure appears to relate to differences in risk outcomes (i.e., mediators or mechanisms through which exposure exerts impact) and those factors associated with the differences found (i.e., moderators, which include characteristics of the child, family, community, or the incident itself). Suggestions for future research are outlined, and implications for intervention and prevention are discussed.

Children in the United States are exposed to a great deal of violence through the media and other sources. However, we focus here on those most likely to be exposed to community violence as a function of where they live – children and families living in inner-city neighborhoods. We do this because most of the research that has been conducted has focused on this population, and this is the group most affected by the problem.

RATES OF EXPOSURE TO VIOLENCE

Community violence comprises incidents of interpersonal violence including murder, shooting, physical assault, rape, and robbery with physical assault that occur in neighborhoods in which children and families live. Victimization may be direct or indirect – for example, witnessing violence or having friends or family members be the victims of violence. Often the violence is chronic (Jenkins & Bell, 1997).

Previous studies have found that 50% to 96% of urban children have witnessed community violence in their lifetimes (Fitzpatrick & Boldizar, 1993; Gorman-Smith & Tolan, 1998; Miller, Wasserman, Neugebauer, Gorman-Smith, & Kamboukos, 1999; Richters & Martinez, 1993; Schwab-Stone et al., 1995). Much of the violence is serious. In a study of 6- to 10-year-old boys in New York City, 35% reported witnessing a stabbing, 33% had seen someone shot, 23% had seen a dead body in their neighborhood, and 25% had seen someone killed (Miller et al., 1999). Further, children living in poor urban communities are often exposed to multiple violent events and to various types of violence. In studies of youth in Chicago, 45% reported having witnessed more than one violent event (Bell & Jenkins, 1993), and 30% had seen three or more such events (Gorman-Smith & Tolan, 1998). In both the Richters and Martinez (1993) sample of fifth and sixth graders and the high school sample of Jenkins and Bell (1994), 70% of the youth witnessing a shooting had seen two or more.

Children are also often close to the individuals whose victimization they witnessed (Jenkins & Bell, 1994). In the Chicago sample, 70% of those witnessing a shooting or stabbing reported that the closest victim was a friend or a family member.

IMPACT OF VIOLENCE EXPOSURE ON CHILDREN

The data clearly show that children exposed to community violence are at risk for a variety of psychological, behavioral, and academic problems (Garbarino, Dubrow, Kostelny, & Pardo, 1992; Kliewer, Leport, Oskin, & Johnson, 1998; Richters & Martinez, 1993), as well as difficulty concentrating, impaired memory, anxious attachments to caregivers, or aggressive behavior (Garbarino et al., 1992). These responses to violence have implications for school performance, relationship development, and overall quality of life.

Posttraumatic Stress and Internalizing Disorders

Much of the work on violence has focused on psychological (internalizing) disturbances, including posttraumatic stress disorder (PTSD), anxiety disorders, and depression. In a sample of low-income African American youth (7–18 years old), victimization and witnessing violence were both associated with symptoms of PTSD, and 27% of the sample met diagnostic criteria for PTSD (Fitzpatrick & Boldizar, 1993). Horowitz, Weine, and Jekel (1995) found a particularly large association between violence exposure and PTSD symptoms in a sample of urban adolescent girls.

Other studies have linked violence exposure to anxiety and depression (Kliewer et al., 1998; Lynch & Cicchetti, 1998), although the results are inconsistent. Singer, Anglin, Song, and Lunghofer (1995) found that witnessing violence and victimization were related to symptoms of PTSD, depression, anxiety, and dissociation. Cooley-Quille and colleagues (2001) found that youth with high levels of community violence exposure reported more fears, anxiety, internalizing behavior, and negative life experience than youth reporting low exposure.

Some studies report differences in outcome based on the type of exposure. In the Martinez and Richters (1993) study, being victimized by or witnessing violence involving family, friends, and acquaintances was associated with depression, whereas violence involving strangers was not. Fitzpatrick (1993) reported that violent victimization, but not witnessing violence, was related to depression among African American youth. In a sample of African American and Latino adolescent males in Chicago, community violence was related to increases in both anxiety and depression, controlling for previous levels (Gorman-Smith & Tolan, 1998).

Externalizing Disorders

In addition to internalizing symptoms, community violence exposure has been linked to externalizing symptoms. Jenkins and Bell (1994) found that for female adolescents, witnessing violence was significantly related to drinking alcohol, using drugs, carrying guns and knives, and having trouble in school. For boys, the strongest relation was between being a victim and similar high-risk behaviors, although witnessing violence was also significantly related to carrying a weapon, fighting, and having trouble in school. Others report that exposure to violence is related to increased aggression and antisocial behavior, even when controlling for previous levels of aggression (Farrell & Bruce, 1997; Schwab-Stone et al., 1995). In a longitudinal study of African American and Latino adolescent boys, Gorman-Smith and Tolan (1998) found exposure to violence related to increases in aggression over a 1- year period. In a follow-up of that study, Miller and colleagues (1999) found the same pattern among a younger inner-city sample (6- to 9-year olds) of African American and Latino boys living in New York City.

Academic Functioning

Problems in academic functioning are often noted among youth exposed to community violence (Dyson, 1990; Schwab-Stone et al., 1995). Most often, decline in academic performance appears to be related to the types of internalizing and externalizing disorders discussed previously. Some suggest that children may be distracted by intrusive thoughts associated with the trauma. Similarly, increased physiological arousal can make it difficult to concentrate (Jenkins & Bell, 1997). Learning problems might also be the result of fatigue or of not getting the rest needed to perform in school because of sleep disturbance (Pynoos & Nader, 1988). Thus, although there is a relation between violence exposure and academic functioning, research is needed to understand the process through which this is likely to occur.

Neurodevelopmental/Biological Effects

There is an increasing focus on how exposure to violence affects children's neurobiology (Perry, 1997; Perry, Pollard, Blakley, Baker, & Vigilante, 1995). The theoretical contention is that exposure, particularly repeated exposure early in development, can fundamentally alter neurological system development. Brain development during the early years of life is seen as particularly sensitive to overarousal, which affects the organization and development of specific brain areas (Perry, 1997). During this critical period, the central nervous system is thought to be particularly responsive to traumatic organizing and structuring experiences (Weiss & Wagner, 1998). Children exposed to trauma may experience abnormal neurological development due to overstimulation of certain brain structures. The extent of the impact depends on the developmental timing of the event(s). Exposure to violence may also affect children's arousal and ability to react appropriately to stress. Perry (1997) reported that children exposed to trauma have increased overall arousal, an increased startle response, sleep disturbance, and abnormalities in cardiovascular regulation (Perry & Pate, 1994).

Summary of Exposure Impact

The studies reviewed suggest that there are many possible outcomes for children exposed to community violence, thus complicating our understanding and development of appropriate intervention (Gorman-Smith & Tolan, 1998; Thornberry, Huizinga, & Loeber, 1995). In addition, there are limited data available to help us understand those differences or make predictions about what a likely outcome might be. Research is needed that assesses multiple outcomes within the same population to begin to understand the processes through which these different outcomes might occur, as well as the extent of comorbidity within a population.

VULNERABILITY AND PROTECTIVE MECHANISMS

Although violence exposure can have serious consequences for children's development, clearly not all children exposed to violence are equally affected. However, surprisingly little research has been conducted specifically on protective processes. The following section reviews the limited empirical research on which factors decrease the associated risks.

Our work and the work of many others in this area is guided by a developmental-ecological model of risk and development (Bronfenbrenner, 1979; Szapocznik & Coatsworth, 1999). A central tenet of developmental-ecological theory is that individual development is influenced by the ongoing qualities of the social settings in which the child lives or participates and by the extent and nature of the interaction between these settings (Bronfenbrenner, 1979, 1988). Child development is influenced by family functioning, peer relationships, schools, communities, and larger societal influences (e.g., the media). There are direct influences of each of these characteristics, as well as interactions among them, that relate to risk and development. Thus, an important aspect of developmental-ecological theory is the presumption that the impact of major developmental influences, such as family functioning, depends on the sociological characteristics of the communities in which youth and families reside (Szapocznik & Coatsworth, 1999; Tolan & Gorman-Smith, 1997). It may be that how families function or how they parent differs, depending on the neighborhood in which they live, and the same level of family functioning may have different effects on risk, depending on neighborhood residence (Furstenberg, 1993; Gorman-Smith, Tolan, & Henry, 2000; Sampson, 1997). In addition to context, a developmental-ecological model incorporates the capacity for change over time. The same factor may have a different impact, depending on the age of the child. Thus, specific to violence exposure, both the risk for exposure and the impact of exposure must be considered within the developmental ecology of the child's life.

We outline this perspective because although the research on potential mediating and moderating processes focuses on one level of the system (e.g., individual, family, peer), we recognize that each is related to others and that it is often difficult to tease apart the effects and consider a single level of system in isolation. Thus, even though we organize the available data within a single level of the system, we recognize that there are probably important interactions that may result in differences in exposure impact (Gorman-Smith et al., 2000).

FACTORS THAT AFFECT THE IMPACT OF VIOLENCE

Proximity and Relationship to the Victim or Perpetrator

Several aspects of violence itself can affect a youth's reaction to it, including proximity and relation to it. A major determinant of impact appears to be the extent of direct exposure to the incident. For example, in a 14-month follow-up of children attending the school where a sniper shot 14 students on the playground, Nader, Pynoos, Fairbanks, and Frederick (1990) found that children on the playground had the most severe symptoms, followed by those in the school building and then those not at school that day.

Another important factor related to the impact of the exposure is the child's relationship to the victim and the perpetrator. Not surprisingly, children are most affected when the victim is someone close to them. Martinez and Richters (1993) found that only those incidents involving people known, as both victims and perpetrators, were significantly related to distress. Jenkins and Bell (1994) found that victimization of family members, whether witnessed or not, was as strongly correlated with psychological distress as was personal victimization.

Individual Characteristics

Age

Much of the research on exposure to community violence has been conducted with adolescent and school-age children. There has been less research on younger children and infants. The limited research available suggests that even in the earliest phases of infant and toddler development, there are clear associations between exposure to violence and posttraumatic stress symptoms and disorder (Osofsky, 1995; Osofsky, Cohen, & Drell, 1995). The work of Perry and colleagues suggests that early childhood is a particularly vulnerable time, and that profound and perhaps permanent brain changes can occur as the result of violent trauma within the first 3 years of life (Perry, 1997; Perry et al., 1995). Indirect effects on the caregiver are also likely to have a greater effect on young children given the essential nature of this relationship in the early years of development (Zeanah & Scheeringa, 1997). Preschool children tend to exhibit passive reactions and regressive symptoms, such as enuresis, decreased verbal skills, and clinging behavior (Garbarino et al., 1992).

School-age children display more aggression and more inhibition in response to exposure to violence. They also develop somatic complaints and cognitive distortions and have problems with learning and academic functioning (Dodge, Bates, & Pettit, 1990, Garbarino et al., 1992; Osofsky, 1995). School-age children often experience increases in anxiety and sleep disturbances (Pynoos, 1993). Adolescents tend to exhibit some of the same problems, but are also more likely to engage in acting out and self-destructive behaviors such as substance abuse, delinquent behavior, and early sexual involvement (Garbarino et al., 1992; Jenkins & Bell, 1997). Our longitudinal study suggests that there is likely continued impact even into adolescence. In the study described previously, we found exposure to violence related to increases in aggression, even after controlling for previous levels of both exposure and aggression (Gorman-Smith & Tolan, 1998).

Gender

A number of studies have found gender differences in children's response to violence exposure. Some studies have found that girls have more serious symptoms, including anxiety, depression, anger, and posttraumatic stress, as both witnesses and victims of violence (Fitzpatrick & Boldizar, 1993; Singer et al., 1995). Jenkins and Bell (1994) found a stronger effect on boys of victimization and on girls of witnessing violence. Also, girls were more psychologically distressed and boys displayed more risk behaviors. For boys, the strongest relationship was between victimization and weapon carrying; however, both boys and girls responded to violence with increased weapon carrying.

Other Stressors

The extent of exposure to other types of stressors (e.g., economic, health, inadequate housing) is also linked to the impact of exposure to violence. Jenkins and Bell (1994) found that high school students in Chicago reported an average of 3.5 non-violence-related stressful events in the previous year. Attar, Guerra, and Tolan (1994) found similar results in a sample of elementary school children. The data show fairly clearly that more severe developmental problems are likely to occur when multiple risks are present in the child's environment (Garmezy, 1993; Rutter, 2000). Thus, for children living in the inner city, intervention and prevention efforts should consider the multiple risks associated with exposure to violence.

Family

Although surprisingly little empirical work has been done regarding the potentially protective role of parents and family, understanding the importance of the caregiver response for children exposed to violence actually dates back to bombing raids on children in World War II (Freud & Burlingham, 1943; Janis, 1951). Studies of children living under these conditions suggest that the emotional state and behavior of the mother were the primary mediators between the child's psychological functioning and the traumatic experience. When the adult caregiver appears calm and effective in the face of danger, while not minimizing the seriousness of the situation, the prognosis is better than when the parent is either not present or is overwhelmed by the situation (Pynoos, 1993).

Although more recent work has begun to look at family factors as potential mediators or moderators of impact, little of this work has focused on process. Much of the work has evaluated demographic variables as markers for process. For example, Martinez and Richters (1993) found that distress symptoms were related to maternal education. However, the process through which this variable affected symptoms was unclear. One interpretation was that maternal education may have an "organizing influence on the family environment" (Cicchetti & Lynch, 1993, p. 100). Families that provide a dependable, organized refuge may mediate the impact of violence exposure.

In a second study, Martinez and Richters (1993) found that characteristics of the children's homes also play a role. Significant problems in both social-emotional functioning and academic functioning increased significantly for children living in unstable or unsafe homes. These investigators concluded that "it was not the mere accumulation of environmental adversities that gave rise to adaptational failure in these children. Rather, it was only when such adversities contaminated or eroded the stability and/or safety levels of the children's homes that the odds of their adaptational failure increased" (Richters & Martinez, 1993, p. 609).

Gorman-Smith and Tolan (1998) found that family structure (level of organization and support within the family) and cohesion (emotional closeness and support) were linked to changes in both aggression and anxiety and depression for those exposed to community violence. These results suggest that the lack of a dependable, supportive refuge, or a lack of emotional connectedness to the family, might be related to an increased risk for problematic outcomes for youth exposed to violence. These family characteristics of organization and support may be particularly important for youth living in urban environments with increased numbers of stressors, fewer resources, and less predictability (Tolan & Gorman-Smith, 1997).

Community

There is increasing evidence that aspects of the community may play an important role in buffering risk for children (Garbarino et al., 1992; Gorman-Smith et al., 2000; Sampson, 2001). In particular, the social processes or organization within the neighborhood seems to be most important (Sampson, Raudenbush, & Earls, 1997; Tolan, Gorman-Smith, & Henry, in press; Wilson, 1987). The social organization of the neighborhood is reflected in processes such as felt social support and cohesion among neighbors, a sense of belonging to the community, supervision and control of children and adolescents by other adults in the community, and participation in formal and voluntary organizations. Even within poor urban communities, there can be variation in the social organization of the neighborhood (Sampson, 2001; Sampson & Morenoff, 1997) and differences in associated risk (Gorman-Smith et al., 2000). These neighborhood social processes seem to help buffer the impact of structural characteristics of the community (e.g., poverty, violence, economic investment) on youth and family risk (Furstenberg, 1993; Garbarino & Sherman, 1980; Sampson et al., 1997).

There is also evidence that both the structural characteristics and social organization of the neighborhood have an influence on family functioning and its relation to risk (Brooks-Gunn, Duncan, & Aber, 1997; Gorman-Smith, Tolan, & Henry, 1999; Sampson, 1997). Studies suggest that across communities with similar structural dimensions such as poverty and single parenthood, neighborhood social organization and networks that relate to differences in the ways families function and how parents manage their children can differ significantly (Furstenberg, 1993; Garbarino & Sherman, 1980; Sampson & Laub, 1994; Sullivan, 1989). For example, in a study of parenting among single mothers in poor urban neighborhoods, Furstenberg (1993) found that those residing in the most dangerous neighborhood adapted by isolating themselves and their families. Although this served to increase the mothers' sense of safety, it also cut them off from potential social supports.

In the study described earlier (Gorman-Smith et al., 2000), we found different relations between family patterns and types of delinquents in different types of neighborhoods. We found that youth from *task-oriented* families, families with relatively high levels of discipline consistency, parental monitoring, and structure in family roles, but low levels of emotional warmth and cohesion and few beliefs about family importance, were at increased risk for serious and chronic (including violent) delinquency. However, this was the case only when the families lived in neighborhoods with low levels of social organization. These findings suggest that if emotional needs such as a sense of belonging and support are met by the neighborhood, the risk carried by the family is minimized. This may indicate an important ecological consideration for prevention or intervention; it may be as useful to help youth connect to neighborhood support as it is to try to improve family functioning (Gorman-Smith, Tolan, Zelli, & Huesmann, 1996; Sampson, 1997).

LIMITS TO RESILIENT ADAPTATION

The focus of this book is on resilience of children in the face of adversity, although it is not always clear what defines resilience or that there can even be such an outcome given the adversities many children must face. We would agree with Perry (1997) that children may be malleable (able to adjust to changing circumstances) but are not necessarily resilient (capable of returning to their previous shape or position; marked by the ability to recover readily). Particularly for children exposed to community violence or living in environments with chronic danger, it is hard to imagine that there are no effects, even when they may adapt to them.

The extent to which we can determine the limits of positive adaptation over the course of development depends on measuring multiple outcomes over time. There may be differences in the number of children who appear to be doing well, depending on the aspect of functioning assessed, and differences if measured at more than one point in time (Luthar, 1991). Thus, resilience seems difficult to identify if adequate functioning across several domains over time is seen as critical (Luthar & Cicchetti, 2000; Luthar, Cicchetti, & Becker, 2000; Luthar, Doernberger, & Zigler, 1993). There has simply not been enough research to provide understanding of both the limits of positive adaptation and the extent to which positive outcomes along multiple dimensions are even possible.

This is not to say that children growing up in these environments cannot do well. Rather, it may take a concentration of protective factors to overcome the risk (Garbarino, 2001).

IMPLICATIONS FOR THEORY AND RESEARCH ON RESILIENCE

The impact of violence exposure can be mitigated by developmental timing, individual and familial capabilities and resources, and expectations about violence (Cicchetti & Rizley, 1981; Gorman-Smith & Tolan, 1998; Pynoos, 1993). However, mapping these risk correlations to development and understanding the effects when violence often occurs simultaneously with other adversities has proved to be a formidable challenge (Garbarino, Kostelny, & Dubrow, 1991; Garmezy & Masten, 1990). A key factor underlying the complexity is that outcomes vary, sometimes greatly, among those similarly exposed (Gorman-Smith & Tolan, 1998; Thornberry et al., 1995). Some children and adolescents seem unharmed by exposure or involvement, whereas others seem quite susceptible to immediate and lasting effects. This suggests the need for more complicated risk models that can take into account the interaction between individual risk and other levels of the system related to increasing or decreasing risk.

A second problem is that the impact of a given risk factor or a given type of involvement seems to vary, depending on the developmental timing of the involvement and the social ecology within which it occurs (Cicchetti & Lynch, 1993; Reese, Vera, Thompson, & Reyes, 2001). The experience of community violence takes place within a larger context of risk for most children (Garbarino, 2001). Children most at risk for exposure to community violence are those who are also at risk for multiple types of stressors, including poverty, fractured families, inadequate housing, and less access to social resources. Thus, one of the major challenges is to understand the effects of exposure to community violence versus the effects of exposure to other types of stressors in the community. Importantly, it may be that the most ecologically valid position will be to evaluate community violence within the context of these other stressors, including family and community factors. Because it is unlikely that these factors occur in isolation, it may be more useful to consider patterns of stress exposure and how different patterns of risk relate to differences in outcome.

Related to this is the need to evaluate multiple outcomes within a single study. A focus on one or two outcomes may misrepresent the extent of the problem. That is, a narrow focus may overestimate the prevalence of children who appear to be unaffected (Luthar, 1991; Luthar et al., 2000). Previous research suggests that children may be capable of coping with low levels of risk, but as the number of risk factors increases, it becomes increasingly difficult for children to overcome this accumulation of risk (Rutter, 1989; Seifer & Sameroff, 1987).

There is also a need to evaluate the long-term impact of violence exposure. Most of the available studies are cross-sectional or follow children only over a few years. Studies that follow children through adolescence and young adulthood are needed before we can begin to understand the long-term implications of exposure. These studies should focus on the processes through which exposure might relate to both risk and positive outcome.

An important area of research is the role of family and other resources in mediating the impact of violence exposure (Gorman-Smith & Tolan, 1998; Miller et al., 1999; Sheidow, Gorman-Smith, Tolan, & Henry, 2001). Although most will concede that the goal should be to reduce or eliminate exposure to violence, there is the pragmatic issue of how to help children and adolescents who live in a society with so much violence, who live with violent parents, or who must navigate threats of violence in going to and from school (Garbarino et al., 1991). Although several studies have identified apparently protective factors, limited research has attempted to place those protective factors in a developmental and ecological framework, that is, to consider children and youth within the complicated ecology of their lives (family, peers, schools, neighborhoods). Such a step is critical to moving away from lists and toward processes that can be the targets of intervention. For example, advancing clinical knowledge of collinearity of exposure and effects on victims versus perpetrators rests on being able to develop measures that can differentiate the extent and type of involvement (Acosta, Albus, Reynolds, Spriggs, & Weist, 2001).

Another issue is the paucity of in-depth qualitative studies of exposure impact. Not only do such reports help deepen understanding of the issue of violence, but they also highlight clinical issues that are unlikely to be distinct or prominent enough to drive statistical associations. Similarly, understanding can be furthered through studies that emphasize patterns of risk factors among samples rather than overall trends (Cairns & Cairns, 1994). For example, we found that family factors related to violence involvement of inner-city adolescents depend on neighborhood characteristics. It was the clustering of characteristics that helped explain differing risk patterns. This information would not be evident in traditional variance-oriented explanations (Gorman-Smith et al., 2000). Such *person-oriented* analyses may be more easily interpreted for their clinical implications because they suggest patterns of person–situation character- istics associated with risk rather than a more abstract notation that occurs with the relative extent of several dimensions.

IMPLICATIONS FOR INTERVENTION

The multiple outcomes associated with exposure to violence and the mul- tiple levels of the system in which this exposure is embedded make the issues of intervention and prevention quite complex. The characteristics of inner-city communities are related not only to increases in violence, but also to families' ability to protect themselves from and buffer the impact of violence exposure (Garbarino et al., 1992; Gorman-Smith et al., 2000; Jenkins & Bell, 1997). The current state of research suggests three poten- tial strategies for intervention in community violence exposure: (1) strate- gies to reduce the occurrence of community violence, (2) working with families to help protect children from exposure and cope with expo- sure and other types of adverse events when they occur, and (3) effective treatment for those exposed.

Community-Level Intervention

One potential method for decreasing children's exposure to violence is to increase connections between families and to promote involve- ment beyond one's immediate family. When parents know the parents of their children's friends, opportunities arise to compare notes and establish norms of behavior, including those related to violence (Cole- man, 1990; Furstenberg & Hughes, 1997). This can occur through sev- eral avenues, including community watch groups and block organiza- tions. In our prevention work, the primary component of the interven- tion is multiple-family group meetings. The substantive focus of these multiple-family groups is parenting and family functioning within the ecological context in which families reside. Important in this method is the creation of groups that can provide informal social support. Groups are organized by neighborhood so that social connections can form be- tween caregivers living in close proximity (Gorman-Smith, Tolan, Henry, Quintana, & Lutovsky, in press).

Other broad-based community efforts designed to reduce youth violence are currently underway. These projects tend to result from coalitions of community groups and agencies (e.g., police, faith-based organizations) working together to address some of the multiple risks associated with violence. For example, Operation Ceasefire in Boston grew out of the Gun Project Working Group and sought to lower youth homicide by directly attacking the illegal gun trade and creating a strong deterrent to gang violence (Braga, Kennedy, Waring & Piehl, 2001; Kennedy, Braga, & Piehl, 1997; Piehl, Kennedy, & Braga, 2000). This occurred through both targeted and strong enforcement by police and the legal system, as well as coalitions providing services and other kinds of help to gang members (e.g., street workers, probation and parole officers, churches, community groups). Violent crime evoked an immediate and intense response from multiple agencies. The intervention targeted the entire city. Therefore, there were no areas of control, and a classic evaluation design was impossible. However, using a one-group time series and a quasi-experimental design comparing Boston to other U.S. cities shows a significant reduction in youth violence over the course of the intervention. After the first year of intervention, the mean number of monthly youth homicides was reduced by 63% (Braga et al., 2001). Also, comparisons with other U.S. cities suggest that the results were distinct when compared with trends in most major U.S. and New England cities.

Family Interventions

Despite data suggesting that caregivers are important in helping to buffer the impact of community violence, there are few empirically evaluated, family-focused interventions. This is true not only for programs focused on community violence exposure, but also for interventions aimed at other types of problems and disorders. Several reviews of youth health promotion programs report a need for comprehensive prevention and intervention programs that include families and caregivers (see, e.g., Catalano, Berglund, Ryan, Lonczak, & Hawkins, 1998; Tolan & Guerra, 1994). Programs that exclusively involve youth, particularly those aimed at reducing violence, are less effective than those that involve parents and caregivers (Farrington & Welsh, 1999; Reese, Vera, Thompson, & Reyes, 2001; Tolan & Guerra, 1994).

One example of a family-focused preventive intervention is the Schools and Families Educating Children (SAFE Children) (Gorman-Smith et al., in press) program, targeting families of first-grade children in inner-city neighborhoods in Chicago. The family-focused intervention is composed of 20 weekly multiple-family group meetings (e.g., four to six families per group) and addresses issues of parenting, family relations, parental involvement and investment in their child's schooling, peer relations, and neighborhood support (Tolan, Quintana, & Gorman-Smith, 1998).

Sessions focus on the internal functioning of the family (e.g., rules and consequences, support, communication), specific developmental challenges for the age group, the developmental challenge of managing peer relations (e.g., communication about selecting and maintaining friends, integrating peers into family life, helping children manage peer relations), demands of managing urban life, and the developmental challenge of moving toward and setting up goals for the future.

Initial results appear positive. Families assigned to the program maintained greater involvement in school, used more effective parenting practices, and had better family relationship characteristics (i.e., organizational structure, cohesion) than control families. In addition, intervention children displayed higher academic functioning (Gorman-Smith et al., in press). It is hypothesized that these individual and family characteristics will relate to decreased exposure to violence and less devastating impact of exposure when it occurs.

Interventions for Those Exposed

As with prevention programs, effective interventions for youth exposed to community violence focus on multiple levels of the system, including the individual child, the family, and the larger setting (e.g., school, neighborhood) (Garbarino et al., 1992; Jenkins & Bell, 1997; Pynoos & Nader, 1988). Services should be directed not only to the individual child, but also to caregivers and other individuals or systems that can provide support for the child.

The work of Pynoos and colleagues provides an example of the type of intervention needed (Pynoos, 1993; Pynoos & Nader, 1988). Their intervention model of *psychological first aid* for children exposed to violence focuses on identifying symptoms by developmental level. The model outlines symptoms and provides concrete responses for each developmental level. The intervention is multifaceted and addresses issues at the individual child, family, classroom, school, group, and community levels. Again, working with the family is key. Particularly in the inner city, caregivers' own experience with violence and other stressors can reduce their capacity to meet the needs of their children.

CONCLUSION

As others before us have said, children are changed by exposure to violence (Bell & Jenkins, 1993; Garbarino et al., 1992; Osofsky, 1995; Pynoos & Nader, 1988). Although children have an amazing ability to cope, and many may go on to do well, their capacity to overcome exposure to multiple events or multiple types of stress is not unlimited. As Werner stated (1990, p. 111), "As long as the balance between stressful life events and protective factors is favorable, successful adaptation is possible. However, when stressful life events outweigh the protective factors, even the most resilient child can develop problems. Intervention may thus be conceived as an attempt to shift the balance from vulnerability to resilience, either by decreasing exposure to risk factors and stressful live events or by increasing the number of available protective factors (e.g., competencies and sources of support) in the lives of children." For youth living in inner-city neighborhoods, the challenge is to increase those protective factors.

Despite the heightened focus on risk associated with exposure to community violence over the past decade, a number of important issues remain. Many of these issues have been outlined in this chapter, and there are likely many more to be considered. It is only with continued empirical focus on these issues that we will be able to develop intervention and prevention programs to affect the factors that are critical to positive adaptation among children exposed to community violence.

References

Acosta, O. M., Albus, K., Reynolds, M. W., Spriggs, D., & Weist, M. D. (2001). Assessing the status of research on violence-related problems among youth. *Journal of Clinical Child Psychology, 30,* 152–160.

Attar, B. K., Guerra, N. G., & Tolan, P. H. (1994). Neighborhood disadvantage, stressful life events, and adjustment in urban elementary-school children. *Journal of Clinical Child Psychology, 23,* 391–400.

Bell, C. C., & Jenkins, E. J. (1993). Community violence and children on Chicago's southside. *Psychiatry, 56,* 46–54.

Braga, A. A., Kennedy, D. M., Waring, E. J., & Piehl, A. M. (2001). Problem-oriented policing, deterrence, and youth violence: An evaluation of Boston's operation ceasefire. *Journal of Research in Crime and Delinquency, 38,* 195–225.

Bronfenbrenner, U. (1979). *The ecology of human development: Experiments by nature and design.* Cambridge, MA: Harvard University Press.

Bronfenbrenner, U. (1988). Interacting systems in human development. Research paradigms: Present and future. In N. Bolger, A. Caspi, G. Downey, & M. Moorehouse (Eds.), *Persons in context: Developmental processes* (pp. 25–49). New York: Cambridge University Press.

Brooks-Gunn, J., Duncan, G. J., & Aber, J. L. (1997). *Neighborhood poverty*. New York: Russell Sage Foundation.

Cairns, R. B., & Cairns, B. D. (1994). *Lifelines and risks: Pathways of youth in our time*. New York: Cambridge University Press.

Catalano, R. F., Berglund, M. L., Ryan, J. A., Lonczak, H. C., & Hawkins, J. D. (1998). *Positive youth development in the U.S.: Research findings of positive youth development programs*. Washington, DC: Department of Health and Human Services, National Institute of Child Health and Human Development.

Cicchetti, D., & Lynch, M. (1993). Toward an ecological/transactional model of community violence and child maltreatment: Consequences for children's development. *Psychiatry, 56*, 96–118.

Cicchetti, D., & Rizley, R. (1981). Developmental perspectives on the etiology, intergenerational transmission, and sequelae of child maltreatment. *New Directions for Child Development, 11*, 31–55.

Coleman, J. S. (1990). Social capital in the creation of human capital. *American Journal of Sociology, 94*, S95–S120.

Cooley-Quille, M., Boyd, R. C., Frantz, E., & Walsh, J. (2001). Emotional and behavioral impact of exposure to community violence in inner-city adolescents. *Journal of Clinical Child Psychology, 30*, 199–206.

Dodge, K. A., Bates, J. E., & Pettit, G. S. (1990). Mechanisms in the cycle of violence. *Science, 250*, 1678–1683.

Dyson, J. (1990). The effects of family violence on children's academic performance and behavior. *Journal of the National Medical Association, 82*, 17–22.

Farrell, A. D., & Bruce, S. E. (1997). Impact of exposure to community violence on violent behavior and emotional distress among urban adolescents. *Journal of Clinical Child Psychology, 26*, 2–14.

Farrington, D., & Welsh, B. (1999). Delinquency prevention using family based interventions. *Children and Society, 13*, 287–303.

Fitzpatrick, K. M. (1993). Exposure to violence and presence of depression among low-income African-American youth. *Journal of Consulting Clinical Psychology, 61*, 528–531.

Fitzpatrick, K. M., & Boldizar, J. P. (1993). The prevalence and consequences of exposure to violence among African-American youth. *Journal of the American Academy of Child Adolescent Psychiatry, 32*, 424–430.

Freud, A., & Burlingham, D. (1943). *War and children*. New York: Ernest Willard.

Furstenberg, F. (1993). How families manage risk and opportunity in dangerous neighborhoods. In W. J. Wilson (Ed.), *Sociology and the public agenda* (pp. 231–258). Newbury Park, CA: Sage.

Furstenberg, F., & Hughes, M. E. (1997). The influence of neighborhoods on children's development: A theoretical perspective and research agenda. In J. Brooks-Gunn, G. J. Duncan, & L. Aber (Eds.), *Neighborhood poverty: Policy implications in studying neighborhoods* (pp. 23–47). New York: Russell Sage Foundation.

Garbarino, J. (2001). An ecological perspective on the effects of violence on children. *Journal of Community Psychology, 29*, 361–378.

Garbarino, J., Dubrow, N., Kostelny, K., & Pardo, C. (1992). *Children in anger*. San Francisco: Jossey-Bass.

Garbarino, J., Kostelny, K., & Dubrow, N. (1991). What children can tell us about living in danger. *American Psychologist, 46,* 376–383.

Garbarino, J., & Sherman, D. (1980). High-risk neighborhoods and high-risk families: The human ecology of maltreatment. *Child Development, 51,* 188–198.

Garmezy, N. (1993). Children in poverty: Resilience despite risk. *Psychiatry: Interpersonal and Biological Processes, 56,* 127–136.

Garmezy, N., & Masten, A. S. (1990). The adaptation of children to a stressful world: Mastery of fear. In L. E. Arnold (Ed.), *Childhood stress. Wiley series in child and adolescent mental health* (pp. 460–473). New York: Wiley.

Gorman-Smith, D., & Tolan, P. H. (1998). The role of exposure to community violence and developmental problems among inner-city youth. *Development and Psychopathology, 10,* 101–116.

Gorman-Smith, D., Tolan, P. H., & Henry, D. B. (1999). The relation of community and family to risk among urban-poor adolescents. In P. Cohen, C. Slomkowski, & L. Robins (Eds.), *Historical and geographical influences on psychopathology* (pp. 349–367). Hillsdale, NJ: Erlbaum.

Gorman-Smith, D., Tolan, P. H., & Henry, D. B. (2000). A developmental-ecological model of the relation of family functioning to patterns of delinquency. *Journal of Quantitative Criminology, 16,* 169–198.

Gorman-Smith, D., Tolan, P. H., Henry, D. B., Quintana, E., & Lutovsky, K. (in press). SAFE children: A preventive intervention for urban families. (In J. Szapocznik, P. Tolan, & S. Sombrano (Eds.), *Preventive interventions for substance use: Preschool through adolescence.*

Gorman-Smith, D., Tolan, P. H., Zelli, A., & Huesmann, L. R. (1996). The relation of family functioning to violence among inner-city minority youths. *Journal of Family Psychology, 10,* 115–129.

Horowitz, K., Weine, S., & Jekel, J. (1995). PTSD symptoms in urban adolescent girls: Compounded community trauma. *Journal of the American Academy of Child and Adolescent Psychiatry, 34,* 1353–1361.

Janis, I. (1951). *Air war and emotional stress.* New York: McGraw-Hill.

Jenkins, E. J., & Bell, C. C. (1994). Violence exposure, psychological distress, and high risk behaviors among inner-city high school students. In S. Friedman (Ed.), *Anxiety disorders in African-Americans* (pp. 76–88). New York: Springer.

Jenkins, E. J., & Bell, C. C. (1997). Exposure and response to community violence among children and adolescents. In J. D. Osofsky (Ed.), *Children in a violent society* (pp. 9–31). New York: Guilford Press.

Kennedy, D. M., Braga, A. A., & Piehl, A. M. (1997). The (un)known universe: Mapping gangs and gang violence in Boston. In D. Weisburd & J. T. McEwen (Eds.), *Crime mapping and crime prevention* (pp. 219–262). New York: Criminal Justice Press.

Kliewer, W., Leport, S. J., Oskin, D., & Johnson, P. D. (1998). The role of social and cognitive processes in children's adjustment to community violence. *Journal of Consulting Clinical Psychology, 66,* 199–209.

Luthar, S. S. (1991). Vulnerability and resilience: A study of high-risk adolescents. *Child Development, 62,* 600–616.

Luthar, S. S., & Cicchetti, D. (2000). The construct of resilience: Implications for interventions and social policies. *Development and Psychopathology, 12,* 857–885.

Luthar, S. S., Cicchetti, D., & Becker, B. (2000). The construct of resilience: A critical evaluation and guidelines for future work. *Child Development, 71,* 543–562.

Luthar, S. S., Doernberger, C. H., & Zigler, E. (1993). Resilience is not a unidimensional construct: Insights from a prospective study of inner-city adolescents. *Development and Psychopathology, 5,* 703–717.

Lynch, M., & Cicchetti, D. (1998). An ecological-transactional analysis of children and contexts: The longitudinal interplay among child maltreatment, community violence, and children's symptomatology. *Development and Psychopathology, 10*(2), 235–257.

Martinez, P., & Richters, J. E. (1993). The NIMH Community violence project: II. Children's distress symptoms associated with violence exposure. In D. Reiss, J. E. Richters, M. Radke-Yarrow, & D. Scharff (Eds.), *Children and violence* (pp. 22–35). New York: Guilford Press.

Miller, L. S., Wasserman, G. A., Neugebauer, R., Gorman-Smith, D., & Kamboukos, D. (1999). Witnessed community violence and anti-social behavior in high-risk urban boys. *Journal of Clinical Child Psychology, 28,* 2–11.

Nader, K., Pynoos, R. S., Fairbanks, L., & Frederick, C. (1990). Childhood PTSD reactions one year after a sniper attack. *Journal of the American Psychiatric Association, 147,* 1526–1530.

Osofsky, J. D. (1995). The effects of exposure to violence on young children. *American Psychologist, 50,* 782–788.

Osofsky, J. D., Cohen, G., & Drell, M. (1995). The effects of trauma on young children: A case of two-year-old twins. *International Journal of Psycho-Analysis, 76,* 595–608.

Perry, B. D. (1997). Incubated in terror: Neurodevelopmental factors in the "cycle of violence." In J. D. Osofsky (Ed.), *Children in a violent society* (pp. 124–149). New York: Guilford Press.

Perry, B. D., & Pate, J. E. (1994). Neurodevelopment and the psychobiological roots of post-traumatic stress disorders. In L. F. Koziol & C. E. Stout (Eds.), *The neuropsychology of mental illness: A practical guide* (pp. 129–147). Springfield, IL: Charles C. Thomas.

Perry, B. D., Pollard, R., Blakley, T., Baker, W., & Vigilante, D. (1995). Childhood trauma, the neurobiology of adaption, and "use-dependent" development of the brain: How "states" become "traits." *Infant Mental Health Journal, 16,* 271–291.

Piehl, A. M., Kennedy, D. M., & Braga, A. A. (2000). Problem solving and youth violence: An evaluation of the Boston gun project. *American Law and Economics Review, 2,* 58–106.

Pynoos, R. S. (1993). Traumatic stress and development psychopathology in children and adolescents. In J. M. Oldham, M. B. Riba, & A. Tasman (Eds.), *Review of psychiatry, 12* (pp. 205–237). Washington, DC: American Psychiatric Press.

Pynoos, R. S., & Eth, S. (1984). Child as a criminal witness to homicide. *Journal of Social Issues, 40,* 87–108.

Pynoos, R. S., & Nader, K. (1986). Children's exposure to violence and traumatic death. *Psychiatric Annals, 20,* 334–344.

Pynoos, R. S., & Nader, K. (1988). Psychological first aid: For children who witness community violence. *Journal of Traumatic Stress, 1*, 445–473.

Reese, L. E., Vera, E. M., Thompson, K., & Reyes, R. (2001). A qualitative investigation of perceptions of youth violence risk factors in low-income African American children. *Journal of Clinical Child Psychology, 30*, 161–171.

Richters, J. E., & Martinez, P. E. (1993). Violent communities, family choices, and children's chances: An algorithm for improving the odds. *Development and Psychopathology, 5*, 609–627.

Rutter, M. (1989). Psychiatric disorder in parents as a risk factor for children. In D. Schaffer, I. Phillips, & N. B. Enzer (Eds.), *Prevention of mental disorders, alcohol and other drug use in children and adolescents* (OSAP Prevention Monograph No. 2, DHHS Pub. No. ADM 89-1646, pp. 16–26). Washington, DC: U.S. Government Printing Office.

Sampson, R. J. (1997). The embeddedness of child and adolescent development: A community-level perspective on urban violence. In J. McCord (Ed.), *Violence and childhood in the inner city* (pp. 31–77). Cambridge: Cambridge University Press.

Sampson, R. J. (2001). How do communities undergird or undermine human development? Relevant contexts and social mechanisms. In A. Booth & A. C. Crouter (Eds.), *Does it take a village? Community effects on children, adolescents, and families* (pp. 3–30). Mahwah, NJ: Erlbaum.

Sampson, R. J., & Laub, J. H. (1994). Urban poverty and the family context of delinquency: A new look at structure and process in a classic study. *Child Development, 65*, 523–539.

Sampson, R. J., & Morenoff, J. (1997). Ecological perspectives on the neighborhood context of urban poverty: Past and present. In J. Brooks-Gunn, G. Duncan, & L. Aber (Eds.), *Neighborhood poverty: Policy implications in studying neighborhoods* (pp. 1–22). New York: Russell Sage Foundation.

Sampson, R., Raudenbush, S., & Earls, F. (1997). Neighborhood and violent crime: A multilevel study of collective efficacy. *Science, 277*, 918–924.

Schwab-Stone, M. E., Ayers, T. S., Kasprow, W., Voyce, C., Barone, C., Shriver, T., & Weissberg, R. P. (1995). No safe haven: A study of violence exposure in an urban community. *Journal of the American Academy of Child and Adolescent Psychiatry, 34*, 1343–1352.

Seifer, R., & Sameroff, A. J. (1987). Multiple determinants of risk and invulnerability. In J. Anthony & B. J. Cohler (Eds.), *The invulnerable child* (pp. 51–69). New York: Guilford Press.

Sheidow, A. J., Gorman-Smith, D., Tolan, P. H., & Henry, D. B. (2001). Family and community characteristics: Risk factors for violence exposure in inner-city youth. *Journal of Community Psychology, 29*, 345–360.

Singer, M. I., Anglin, T. M., Song, L. Y., & Lunghofer, L. (1995). Adolescents' exposure to violence and associated symptoms of psychological trauma. *Journal of the American Medical Association, 273*, 477–482.

Sullivan, M. L. (1989). *Getting paid: Youth, crime and work in the inner-city.* Ithaca, NY: Cornell University Press.

Szapocznik, J., & Coatsworth, J. D. (1999). An ecodevelopmental framework for organizing the influences on drug abuse: A developmental model of risk and protection. In M. Glantz & C. R. Hartel (Eds.), *Drug abuse: Origins and interventions,*(pp. 331–366). Washington, DC: American Psychological Association.

Thornberry, T. P., Huizinga, D., & Loeber, R. (1995). The prevention of serious delinquency and violence: Implications from the Program of Research on the Causes and Correlates of Delinquency. In J. C. Howell, B. Krisberg, J. D. Hawkins, & J. J. Wilson (Eds.), *Sourcebook of serious, violent, and chronic juvenile offenders* (pp. 213–237). Thousand Oaks, CA: Sage.

Tolan, P. H., & Gorman-Smith, D. (1997). Families and the development of urban children. In O. Reyes, H. Walberg, & R. Weissberg (Eds), *Interdisciplinary perspectives on children and youth* (pp. 67–91). Newbury Park, CA: Sage.

Tolan, P. H., Gorman-Smith, D., & Henry, D. B. (in press). Developmental ecology of family and peer influence on delinquency, *Developmental Psychology.*

Tolan, P. H., & Guerra, N. G. (1994). *What works in reducing adolescent violence: An empirical review of the field.* Monograph prepared for the Center for the Study and Prevention of Youth Violence. Boulder: University of Colorado.

Tolan, P. H., Quintana, E., & Gorman-Smith, D. (1998). Prevention approaches for families. In L. L' Abate (Ed.). *Family psychopathology: The relational roots of dysfunctional behavior* (pp. 379–400). New York: Guilford Press.

Weiss, M. J. S., & Wagner, S. H. (1998). What explains the negative consequences of adverse childhood experiences on adult health? Insights from cognitive and neuroscience research. *American Journal of Preventative Medicine, 14,* 356–360.

Werner, E. E. (1990). Protective factors and individual resilience. In S. J. Meisels & J. P. Shonkoff (Eds.), *Handbook of early childhood intervention* (pp. 97–116). New York: Cambridge University Press.

Wilson, W. J. (1987). *The truly disadvantaged.* Chicago: University of Chicago Press.

Zeanah, C. H., & Scheeringa, M. S. (1997). The experience and effects of violence in infancy. In J. D. Osofsky (Ed.), *Children in a violent society* (pp. 97–123). New York: Guilford Press.

17

Perceived Discrimination and Resilience

Laura A. Szalacha, Sumru Erkut, Cynthia García Coll, Jacqueline P. Fields, Odette Alarcón, and Ineke Ceder

On the first day of school, second grader Eduardo's Anglo classmates call him a "dirty Spic" on the playground and won't let him play basketball with them. At a middle school, in a mixed-race classroom, Juanita's teacher, Mr. Smith, yells at her when she does not turn her homework in on time. He tells her she is lazy and irresponsible.

Are Eduardo and Juanita likely to perceive these interactions as acts of racial or ethnic discrimination? Is this a common occurrence for these children? Will their feelings of having been discriminated against serve as a risk factor for poor self-esteem or depression? How do racism and discrimination fit in the overall complex development of resilience?

The past three decades have seen the study of resilience in development progress from its early conceptions of *invulnerable children* (Anthony & Cohler, 1987; Pines, 1975) to our present understandings of mediated and moderated paths toward resilience. We have begun to move from the identification of important individual characteristics of the *invincibles* (Werner & Smith, 1992) to a more systemic approach involving families, schools, and communities; from the identification of risk or protective factors to the understanding of the mechanisms that underlie these factors. Our conception of resilience as a multidimensional construct presently requires that empirical attention be paid not only to adaptational failures

The Puerto Rican Research Program on Children and Youth is funded by Grant R01-HD30592 from the National Institute of Child Health and Human Development and by Grants MCJ-250643 and R40 MC 00161 from the Maternal and Child Health Bureau (Title V, Social Security Act), Health Resources and Services Administration, Department of Health and Human Services.

but also to positive adjustment, "to forces that are protective in nature as well as those that exacerbate vulnerability" in various groups (Luthar & Cicchetti, 2000, p. 878).

In this chapter, we focus on vulnerability and protective factors implicated in the psychosocial adjustment of minority youth. In response to the increasing calls for examining the developmental processes and patterns of resilience that may be unique to particular ethnic groups (e.g., Luthar, 1999; MacPhee, Kreutzer, & Fritz, 1994), several studies have focused on African American and Hispanic youth (though very few have considered other ethnic minorities). As Masten has noted, "the task before us . . . is to delineate how adaptive systems develop, how they operate under diverse conditions and how they work for or against the success for a given child in his or her environmental and developmental context" (2001, p. 235). It is precisely those "diverse conditions," the specific environmental and developmental contexts of differing cultural, ethnic, and racial groups, to which we call attention here, with the goal of elucidating some salient processes implicated in resilient adaptation among minority individuals.

In 1996, García Coll and her colleagues argued for an integrative model for studying the developmental competencies of minority youth. This theoretical model included eight major constructs affecting development: (1) social position variables (e.g., race, social class, gender); (2) racism and discrimination; (3) segregation (residential, economic, social, and psychological); (4) promoting/inhibiting environments (schools, neighborhoods, and health care); (5) adaptive culture (traditions and legacies); (6) child characteristics (age, temperament, and physical characteristics); (7) family values and beliefs; and (8) developmental competencies (cognition, socioemotional development, and biculturalism). By including racism and its derivatives at the core of studies on minority children's normative development, the authors argue that research can illuminate the causal mechanisms in the development of competencies in children of color that have been ignored by other models.

Of the constructs in this integrative model, our focus here is on a subset prominent in – and possibly unique to – the lives of ethnic minority children, that is, the external manifestations of the social mechanisms of racism, discrimination, and prejudice. Heretofore, perceived discrimination has been studied in relation to mental and physical health outcomes (see, e.g., Krieger, 1999, for a review) and has not been routinely specified in analyses of macrosystem influences in resilience, where mediators and moderators of its effects are also explicitly considered. In considering discrimination as a risk factor, our concern in this chapter is with phenomenological experiences of discrimination and not with the more invisible, but potentially more powerful, impact of institutional racism on minority mental health (see Rollock & Gordon, 2000, for a review). As noted by Spencer, "it is not merely experience, but one's perception of experience in culturally diverse contexts," that can have an impact on developmental processes (1999, p. 44). Finally, mainland Puerto Ricans serve as our referent group, as our own research has concentrated on the developmental trajectories of Puerto Rican children and adolescents; however, we believe that the issues we discuss may be applicable to other ethnic and minority groups as well (Ogbu, 1981, 1987).

After providing a brief overview on adjustment patterns among Puerto Rican youth, we review, in turn, research evidence on the negative effects of perceived discrimination, on processes that might underlie (or mediate) its effects, and on vulnerability and protective factors that may moderate its effects. We conclude with suggested directions for future research on the effects of discrimination on ethnic minority youth.

PUERTO RICANS AS A LATINO SUBGROUP

Since 1994, our research has focused on the health and development of mainland Puerto Rican youth as a Latino subgroup. Over the past decade, the Latino population in the United States increased by 58%, from 22.4 million in 1990 to 35.3 million in 2000 (U.S. Census, 2001). Latinos are projected to become the largest minority group in the United States by the mid-21st century. This population growth has not, however, been accompanied by comparable advancement in economic opportunities. Latino children are at greater risk for negative adjustment outcomes across such diverse domains as academic failure, substance use, and depression than even African American children of similar socioeconomic status (e.g., Jessor, Van Den Bos, Vanderryn, Costa, & Turbin, 1995; Sanders-Phillips, Moisan, Wadlington, Morgan, & English, 1995).

Latinos encompass considerable diversity across as well as within different Spanish-speaking subgroups on the mainland. The designation *Hispanic* combines white-collar and professional Cubans who arrived in the United States following the Cuban revolution with the marginally employed Cubans who came with the Mariel boat lift in the 1980s; Central American refugees; Mexican American migrant workers; Spanish-speaking residents of the Southwest (who have populated the area since the arrival of the early Spanish colonizers in the 1600s); Latin Americans, who come from differing mixtures of indigenous, African, and European origins; and Puerto Ricans with their own internal diversity and frequency of immigration to and from the mainland. Therefore, there is large variation among different Latino subgroups with respect to income, marital status, sexual attitudes, fertility patterns, health status, school completion, and women's participation in the labor force (see, e.g., Darabi, 1987; Oboler, 1995; Schur, Bernstein, & Minkler, 1987). In view of the diversity within and across Latino subgroups, Hispanic is not a meaningful research population without further delineation of national origin–based subgroups or of important demographic and social stratification variables. There is a clear need for normative data on different Latino subgroups (Alarcón, Erkut, García Coll, & Vázquez García, 1994).[1]

Resilience research specifically focused on Puerto Rican youth is lacking. Most research has examined Latinos as an undifferentiated group or has focused on Mexican Americans, who make up 59% of the Latino population in the United States. This body of research has examined the relevance of individual characteristics (such as self-concept, problem-solving skills, and academic self-efficacy) and interpersonal variables (such as supportive families and teachers and the role of peers) with academic achievement, sexual activity, and substance use outcomes (Feliz-Ortiz, Villatorio Velazquez, Medina-Mora, & Newcomb, 2001; Gonzalez & Padilla, 1997; Yin, Zapata, & Katims, 1995). For example, Gordon (1996) found that resilient Latino youth (defined as high-scoring on academic, social, and problem-solving skills) were more confident in their academic self-efficacy and maintained connectedness with their school communities. Arellano and Padilla (1996) determined that crucial factors in educational resilience among Latino youth were supportive relationships with teachers and within families. Finally, the consistency of values between youth and their parents was the key predictor of low levels of risky sexual behavior among Latino youth in Liebowitz, Castellano, and Cuellar's (1999) study. Appropriately, *la familia*, a core cultural characteristic of Latino cultures, is beginning to be included in studies of resilience among Latino youth (Falicov, 1996; McNeill et al., 2001). As we cannot ascertain how applicable these findings are to Puerto Rican youth, or to what degree they are relevant, there is a need to examine resilience processes in this subgroup.

Puertorriqueños are native-born American citizens (a technicality of legal status and not necessarily a cultural or identity factor). They are the second largest of the Latino groups on the U.S. mainland, approximately 3.5 million, but have fared the worst economically (Perez y Gonzalez,

2000). In addition to having serious socioeconomic disadvantages concomitant with the task of adjusting to a changing economic base from manufacturing to high technology along the Eastern seaboard, they become a minority when they settle on the mainland. They become *persons of color* by virtue of their culture, language, and skin color, which ranges from ivory to ebony. Given the prevalence of racism in mainstream U.S. society, by and against people of color and those whose first language is not English, there is a very high likelihood that Puerto Rican youth will be subjected to prejudiced interactions at some point while growing up.

PERCEIVED DISCRIMINATION

Researchers, using survey methods, have found ample evidence for the pernicious and deleterious presence of discrimination in the lives of ethnic minority individuals (Brown et al., 2000; Carter, 1993; Tidwell, 1990). A nationwide survey conducted by Kessler, Michelson, and Williams (1999) revealed that 33.5% of adults of all races between ages 25 and 74 reported exposure to major lifetime discrimination (unfair treatment for any reason and that is likely to have major lifetime consequences, such as being turned down for a loan or losing a job), and 61% of the sample reported exposure to day-to-day discrimination (such as being treated with less courtesy than others, being called names, or receiving poor service). Although Kessler et al. (1999) examined discrimination of any kind (as opposed to racial discrimination specifically), 44.4% of the non-Hispanic whites in their sample reported that they had never experienced day-to-day discrimination, in contrast to only 8.8% of the non-Hispanic blacks. Similarly, only 3.4% of the non-Hispanic whites reported experiencing day-to-day discrimination often, compared to 24.8% of the non-Hispanic blacks. In Landrine and Klonoff's (1996) study of African American university students, staff, and faculty, 98% of the sample reported personally having experienced a racist event in the past year and 100% had experienced such an event in their lifetime. Examples of racist events included being treated badly by a variety of people, being accused of doing something wrong, or having one's intentions misunderstood, all because of being black. Expanding the scope of this research, Lang (2001) adapted Landrine and Klonoff's measure (Schedule of Racist Events) for use with a variety of ethnic/racial groups. Among the Hispanics in Lang's study, 94% reported that they had experienced some racist events in the past year; over 70% reported being treated unfairly by people in service jobs; 78% wanted to tell someone off for being racist but did not say anything;

and 50% indicated that their lives would be different if they had not been treated in a racist manner during the past year.

In variant of perceived discrimination, members of disenfranchised groups are less likely to perceive being discriminated against *personally*, although they report that the group to which they belong is a frequent target of discrimination. Taylor, Wright, and Porter's (1993) review demonstrates that college students and other adults consistently rate discrimination directed at their group as a whole to be substantially higher than discrimination aimed at themselves individually, a phenomenon Taylor refers to as *personal/group discrimination discrepancy* (Taylor, Wright, Moghaddam, & Lalonde, 1990). Verkuyten (1998) has also observed this tendency among ethnic minority adolescents in the Netherlands, where he found reports of higher rates of perceived discrimination against their groups than against the adolescents individually.

PERCEIVED DISCRIMINATION AS A RISK FACTOR FOR POOR MENTAL HEALTH

Racial and ethnic discrimination experiences are demeaning and degrading (Delgado, 1982; Feagin, 1991). They can induce stress and loss of control and can evoke frustration, anxiety, and a feeling of injustice (Bowser, 1981; Fernando, 1984; Fisher, Wallace, & Fenton, 2000). Indeed, there is an emerging literature based on survey methodology that links perceived discrimination to poor mental health among racial and ethnic minority groups, particularly African Americans (Brown et al., 2000; Rumbaut & Ima, 1988; Thompson, 1996; Williams, Yu, Jackson, & Anderson, 1997). Kessler et al. (1999) found that reports of day-to-day discrimination were significantly related to general psychological distress, depression, and generalized anxiety. Reports of lifetime perceived discrimination were related to general distress and depression. Similarly, Landrine and Klonoff (1996) found that the majority of the respondents who reported having experienced racist events (recently and over their lifetime) appraised each event as stressful. These experiences were all significantly correlated with obsessive-compulsive symptoms, interpersonal sensitivity, anxiety, depression, and somatization symptoms. Finally, in Lang's study (2001), 96% of the Hispanic American sample reported experiencing stress as a result of a racist event.

Additional evidence for a relationship between perceived discrimination and poor mental health among adults comes from Krieger's (1999) review of the public health literature. Among the 15 studies of racial/ethnic discrimination, 7 out of 8 studies specifically examining mental health outcomes found perceptions of discrimination to be related to psychological distress, depression, and stress. The only study that did not find a relationship between personally perceived discrimination and mental health outcomes (Jackson et al., 1996) nevertheless found that believing that one's *group* is discriminated against (the perception that white people do not care about blacks or that they want to keep blacks down) was associated with increased psychological distress.

Survey research with adolescents corroborates the findings obtained with adults. Fisher and colleagues' (2000) study of adolescents from a variety of racial and ethnic backgrounds found that all of the ethnic minority youth in their sample reported distress associated with instances of perceived racial prejudice encountered in educational contexts, and that their self-esteem scores were negatively correlated with that distress. Rumbaut's (1994) large-scale multiethnic study of first- and second-generation immigrant adolescents found that 55% of the adolescents reported having personally experienced discrimination. These self-reports of perceived discrimination were significantly related to depressive symptoms. In addition, *expecting discrimination* was significantly related to high levels of depression as well as to low self-esteem. Franklin (1993) has called the inner vigilance for racial slights among African Americans a *sixth sense*. The expectation that discrimination is "right around the corner" can create a state of constant vigilance for negative outcomes, such that one is constantly tense and stressed.

In our research, we have examined both perceived discrimination and expectations of discrimination in two longitudinal studies of Puerto Ricans living on the mainland, one involving children in grades 1–3 (Alarcón, 2000), and the other involving 13- to 15-year-old youth (Erkut, Alarcón, & García Coll, 1999). Our results concur with the literature findings indicating that perceiving discrimination is a risk factor for poor mental health. Among the Puerto Rican children, those who believed that they had been discriminated against reported significantly higher levels of depression, stress, and behavioral conduct problems, as well as lower global self-esteem. Additionally, even worrying about discrimination was a risk factor for lower self-esteem. Nearly half of the adolescents in our sample were experienced enough with discrimination to be worried about coming up against it in different situations (outside of their own neighborhoods, in stores and other public places, etc.), and adolescents who were anxious about being discriminated against had lower global self-esteem than others (Erkut et al., 1999).

PROCESSES THAT MEDIATE THE RISK OF
PERCEIVED DISCRIMINATION

In order to be able to design effective prevention and intervention strategies, it is imperative that we move from the identification of risk or protective factors to understanding their underlying processes. It has been postulated that the mechanism underlying the effect of discrimination is the internalization of the negativity encapsulated in a discriminatory experience. Historically, the symbolic interactionist point of view associated with Cooley's (1922) notion of a *looking glass self* and Mead's (1934/1967) concept of the *generalized other* has underscored the social origins of self-identity. Paraphrasing Mead, the symbolic interactionist perspective holds that we are who we think others think we are. Allport (1954/1979) was concerned that members of minority groups would internalize the prejudice emanating from the majority culture in the United States. His question "What would happen to your personality if you heard it said over and over again that you are lazy and had inferior blood?" (p. 42) is an extension of symbolic interactionist views into intergroup relations, specifically identity formation among blacks. Later traditional personality theorists (e.g., Erikson, 1968) also concluded that minority members are expected to internalize negative images.

Aside from internalized negative societal views, another proposed mechanism for how perceived discrimination can be associated with poor mental health is that repeated exposure to personal and others' discrimination experiences gives rise to the anxiety that one will suffer from racism and prejudice again in the future, with unknown consequences. This anxiety about the future is experienced as stress, which in turn can adversely affect mental health, as shown by previously cited studies (Erkut et al., 1999; Franklin, 1993; Rumbaut, 1994).

In our study of Puerto Rican children, we found that the mothers' anxiety over discrimination was associated with the children's mental health as well. Those children with mothers reporting discrimination anxiety had significantly lower self-esteem, higher depression, and higher academic stress, even when controlling for mothers' state and trait anxiety scores.

PROTECTION FROM PERCEIVING DISCRIMINATION

Having provided a brief overview of survey research that demonstrates the relationship between perceived discrimination and poor mental health outcomes, we now examine the research on factors that influence both the ability and the likelihood of perceiving discrimination. Such factors as lacking the requisite cognitive ability and/or a worldview for interpreting unfair treatment as racial/ethnic discrimination, attributional uncertainty, and a need for control may "protect" individuals from perceiving discrimination that may be evident to others.

Age as a Proxy for Cognitive Development

Diverse cognitive skills are required for children to attribute negative outcomes to racial or ethnic discrimination (Aboud, 1988; Bigler & Liben, 1993; Doyle & Aboud, 1995). These include the ability to classify the self and others on multiple dimensions (including race/ethnicity), the capacity to take differing perspectives necessary for understanding the principle of unjust treatment, and formal operational reasoning required to judge whether same behavior elicits different responses from people (holding one variable constant and varying the other).

The case of Eduardo, in the vignette at the beginning of this chapter, being subjected to an ethnic slur is a straightforward instance of name-calling. What Eduardo needs to have acquired to be able to perceive this event as discrimination is the ability to classify himself and others as having multiple characteristics (which include ethnicity) and the moral judgment corresponding to Piaget's (1932/1999) autonomous stage of reciprocity and equality undergirded by concrete operational reasoning: If kids call you a name without a reason and won't let you play with them, then that is not fair.

For Juanita to be able to see her teacher's action as discrimination requires the same ability to classify herself and others, but she also needs the formal operational reasoning skills (Inhelder & Piaget, 1958), which usually develop by early adolescence. She needs to think like a scientist when comparing the teacher's reaction to her with his reaction to other students differing in race or ethnicity (vary "race/ethnicity") who also did not turn their assignments in on time (hold constant "late assignment"). She then needs to examine the evidence to decide if Mr. Smith yells at *all* students who don't turn in assignments on time or only at nonwhite students.

In our research with Puerto Rican youth, we have found that 6- to 8-year-old children have a low likelihood of perceiving discrimination (12% of 296), whereas among 13- and 14-year-olds, nearly half of the sample (49% of 248) reported perceived discrimination (Szalacha et al., in press). Although the two studies in question do not constitute a longitudinal cohort investigation, taken together they suggest that children are less likely than adolescents to perceive discrimination – that is, age is a proxy for cognitive development that is necessary for the ability to perceive discrimination. On the other hand, just as Sigelman and Welch (1991) found with their research on racial discrimination, we need to be cognizant that exposure to discrimination experiences accumulates with age. This suggests that fewer children may be reporting discrimination experiences, in part, because they have not lived long enough to have had significant exposure.

A Shared Worldview of Differential Power for Interpreting Events

If the acquisition of certain cognitive structures were the sole condition necessary for the judgment of discrimination to take place, any case of a child calling another child a name would be perceived as discriminatory by children who have the cognitive skills of classification and perspective taking (Verkuyten, Kinket, & van der Wielen, 1997). Clearly, this is not the case. In their research among Turkish, Moroccan, and Surinamese minority 10- to 13-year-olds and their Dutch peers in the Netherlands, Verkuyten and his colleagues found that another important ingredient in the judgment of discrimination is a shared belief system about power differentials. Both minority and Dutch children were less likely to label name calling discrimination when both the perpetrator and victim were of the same background or when the perpetrator was a minority child and the victim was a Dutch child. The prototypical instance of discrimination was a Dutch child calling a minority child names. The researchers argue that the social cognitive skills of classifying self and others on multiple dimensions and upholding the principle that "giving offense without reason is unjust" were not sufficient to explain the result that the majority-on-minority name calling was the situation most likely to be labeled a discriminatory event. They concluded that, beyond the acquisition of social cognitive skills, shared beliefs that define social reality and help in interpreting it play a role in the perception of discrimination.

Returning to our examples of Eduardo and Juanita, what role do worldviews play in their likelihood of identifying their predicaments as instances of racial and ethnic discrimination? In Eduardo's case, ideologies are likely to play a minimal role, as the ethnic nature of the name-calling is a tip-off that his classmates called him a name because he is Puerto Rican. In Juanita's case, however, what would prompt her to monitor race/ethnicity as a variable relevant to understanding her teacher's behavior? Why would she be more likely to examine the race/ethnicity variable than, for example, being a girl, overweight, unathletic, or any other of the many characteristics on which students can differ? We can surmise that she can monitor race and ethnicity to the extent that she has learned the social reality that race matters in the United States.

Attributional Ambiguity

Attributional ambiguity has been cited as one of the reasons that members of minority groups do not often judge personal mistreatment to be racial and ethnic discrimination (Crocker & Major, 1989). Perceiving that one has been discriminated against because of one's race or ethnicity is a complex attributional process. In a social interaction, a young person needs to perceive the interaction as negative, to further perceive the interaction as unwarranted by his or her own qualities, and to locate the cause of the unearned negativity in the prejudices of the other parties to the interaction before finally labeling the interaction as involving discrimination. In every step of this process, there are possibilities for making other causal attributions.

In Juanita's case, assuming that as a middle school student she has acquired formal operational reasoning, low expectations could lead her to view Mr. Smith's yelling as normal or nothing worse than usual. Even if she acknowledges that the interaction did not go well, she can attribute the yelling to her own behavior (turning in the assignment late). She can attribute the yelling to external causes, unrelated to herself or the teacher – for example, rowdy students upsetting the teacher. She can attribute the cause to Mr. Smith (e.g., his tiredness) but not to his being prejudiced. She can judge that Mr. Smith is prejudiced, but she could believe that he is prejudiced against tall students, girls, or heavy students. For a judgment of racial or ethnic discrimination to occur, the negativity needs to be attributed to the teachers' holding a racial or ethnic prejudice.

Ruggiero and Taylor (1997) report that in two experimental studies of perceived discrimination – one among white women and the other among minority group members (blacks and Asians) – they found a tendency to minimize perceived discrimination whenever there was attributional ambiguity. The likelihood of perceiving discrimination increased only when negative judgments could not be attributed to any source other than prejudice on the part of the person making negative judgments, which was established in experimental conditions where study participants were told that there was a 100% chance that the person rendering judgments was prejudiced. Thus, experimental research suggests that the reluctance of members of stigmatized groups to perceive negative feedback as discrimination may function as a protective factor.

Need to Feel in Control

In experiments, operating alongside attributional ambiguity, the need for control may also reduce the likelihood of perceiving discrimination. Ruggiero and Taylor (1997) suggest that by minimizing discrimination (by not perceiving it), members of disenfranchised groups are able to uphold a sense of control over their performance and their environment. Results of their research supported this contention, showing that the tendency to minimize perceived discrimination was in fact associated with a higher sense of control over their performance and social interactions. In discussing their findings, Ruggiero and Taylor argued that the converse association is also possible, that is, to the extent that people are motivated to maintain a view of themselves as being in control of personal outcomes in their lives (Wallston, Wallston, Smith, & Dobbins, 1987), they will be motivated to minimize perceived discrimination.

PERCEIVING DISCRIMINATION AS PROTECTION FROM THE NEGATIVE IMPACT OF RACISM

There is evidence from experimental research that contradicts the worst fears of the symbolic interactionists that negative views projected onto minority youth by racist others will be internalized. Crocker and her colleagues (Crocker, 1999; Crocker & Major, 1989, 1994; Crocker, Voelkle, Testa, & Major, 1991) have demonstrated that attributing negative feedback to discrimination can have a paradoxically protective effect on the self-esteem of stigmatized groups, such as minority group members and overweight women, when they externalize the negativity. If the person making the judgment is known to be prejudiced, labeling the negative interaction as discrimination makes it possible for members of stigmatized groups to say that the judgment is not about them, but that it says something about the kind of person who is saying bad things about them – in other words, "consider the source." These findings raise the possibility that the ability and tendency to perceive discrimination, that is, the ability to attribute negative feedback to others' prejudice or ignorance, may serve as a resilience factor decreasing one's vulnerability to the negative impact of others' racism.

METHODOLOGICAL ISSUES

As indicated in preceding discussions, survey research has generally shown that perceived discrimination has negative effects, whereas several experiments have shown that it can protect self-esteem. Why this discrepancy?

Our suggestion for reconciling the contradictions is to consider that in an experiment the frame of reference is a single instance of an undesirable outcome, whereas the frame of reference for answering a survey question on perceived discrimination is an accumulation of instances of discrimination. If, in a single instance, the negative feedback is attributed to discrimination by an experimenter or a confederate, the individual's self-esteem would remain unaffected, and even if the single instance is attributed to the self, its adverse effect would probably be temporary. On the other hand, the cumulative effect of many instances of undesirable outcomes, which surveys are likely tapping, can have a more permanent negative effect. This can be so even when unfavorable outcomes are attributed to external causes – that is, to the discriminatory behavior of prejudiced individuals – for the *potency* of perceived discrimination is likely to increase incrementally with greater exposure to it (in terms of frequency of the event over time, as well as the number of people exhibiting prejudice).

Crocker (1999) has made similar arguments, suggesting that negative feedback received by minority youth in a given situation does not necessarily have a lasting effect (see also Ruggiero & Taylor, 1997). She notes that shared worldviews (or collective representations) found among members of subcultures play a role in interpreting the negative feedback so that it does not have the depressive effect on self-esteem that it might otherwise have. Therefore, in experimental studies, when people make internal attributions to themselves to explain negative outcomes, rather than externalizing the cause, this internalization does not go very deep. It affects how one feels at that moment (in that state), but it does not affect the more deeply held sense of one's worth (trait).

Additionally, we speculate that the situational demands of participating in a scientific experiment may artificially suppress attributions to prejudice when there is a degree of uncertainty. This can happen because one does not want to appear to be "jumping to conclusions" in a scientific setting by saying that the negative feedback is due to prejudiced opinions when one is not *absolutely* sure. Similarly, participating in a scientific experiment during which one voluntarily relinquishes control to the experimenter may serve to heighten the desire for more control over one's life.

The differences between experiment and survey findings on the ill effects of prejudice may also reflect biases in the latter, particularly those arising from shared methodological variance. It is possible that survey methods artificially inflate effects of perceived discrimination, as the perceptions of discrimination, and the outcomes of poor mental health or low self-esteem, are all based on the individual's self-report. Further research on methodological artifacts is needed to elucidate the contributions of these various possibilities.

A final source of potential bias pertains to directionality of associations: Whereas survey research suggests that perceived discrimination is linked with poor mental health, directionality cannot be assumed, as most prior work has been cross-sectional. In our own work, our references to discrimination as a risk factor for poor mental health derive from the social interactionist perspective of the social origins of self-identity. We suggest that children and adolescents are likely to internalize *repeated* exposure to negative feedback that they are not likable or that there is something wrong with them, which leads to low self-esteem.

On the other hand, Phinney, Madden, and Santos (1998) have investigated whether psychological variables are causally prior to perceived ethnic discrimination among minority and immigrant adolescents. Using cross-sectional data, they tested a model that predicts perception of discrimination from self-esteem, mastery, depression/anxiety, intergroup competence, and ethnic identity, as well as demographic variables. Their results showed that higher depression/anxiety scores and lower intergroup competence predicted more perceived discrimination. Depression/anxiety and intergroup competence were, in turn, predicted by self-esteem and mastery, respectively. Consequently, Phinney and her colleagues have argued that there are psychological factors that *predispose* people to perceive discrimination.

To begin to address issues of bias stemming from both shared measurement in self-report and bidirectionality of links, there is a need for prospective research studies designed within the framework of sound conceptual models. In such research, for example, links between perceived discrimination at time 1 could be examined in relation to depression at subsequent times, taking into account the shared variance contributed by depression scores at time 1. Concomitantly, baseline depression can be examined in relation to perceived discrimination at later times, controlling for initial tendencies to perceive discrimination. Although even such prospective analyses cannot establish causality (e.g., because third variables might underlie links across time), they are certainly preferable to cross-sectional data in our initial efforts to explore cause–effect associations in this area of research.

VULNERABILITY AND PROTECTIVE FACTORS THAT MODERATE THE RISK OF PERCEIVED DISCRIMINATION

Apart from perceived discrimination, researchers have documented several other substantive vulnerability factors that Puerto Rican youth in particular, and minority youth in general, encounter in the course of development. These factors, both individually and as multiple strains, may well exacerbate the risks associated with perceived discrimination. These include poverty (Garmezy, 1991; Luthar, 1999), fatalism (García Coll & Vasquez García, 1995), limited knowledge of English, and a potential clash between traditional cultural values and the individualistic values of mainstream America (García Coll, Meyer, & Brillon, 1995; Harwood, Schoelmerich, Ventura Cook, Schulze, & Wilson, 1996).

Ironically, in our focus on those aspects likely to be particularly salient in the lives of children of color, we find that the factors that can protect them from the risks associated with perceived discrimination are rooted in race and ethnicity. Ethnic pride (Biggs, 1998), competence in relating to members of different racial/ethnic groups (Phinney et al., 1998), racial socialization (Cross, 1992; García Coll et al., 1995) and biculturalism (Phinney, 1990; Spencer & Markstrom-Adams, 1990) have all been documented as mitigating the negative effects of discrimination. For ethnic minorities, the processes of negotiating their way through two worlds, their own subculture and the dominant culture, may serve as a protective mechanism in the emergence of resilience (Luthar & McMahon, 1996).

FUTURE DIRECTIONS: RESEARCH

Aside from more prospective studies such as those described earlier, we must examine the subjective experiences of discrimination in relation to non-self-reported adjustment difficulties (with controls for self-reported distress), that is, addressing questions of the degree to which, and domains in which, subjectively perceived discrimination might impair individuals' adaptation in areas such as performance at school and work, as well as their physical health status. We require studies specifically examining possible gender differences in reactivity to discrimination, developmental differences in such reactivity from early childhood to adulthood, and in-depth consideration of what seem to be some of the more potent vulnerability and protective factors that alter the likelihood of negative effects (e.g., not knowing English, having high status as an academic/athletic achiever in the school setting).

Sameroff and others have found that a key concern in resilience is not the type of vulnerability factor, but rather the number of cumulative factors and their interactions (Sameroff, Seifer, Zax, & Barocas, 1987; see also Rutter, 1979). Inspired by Bronfenbrenner (1986), we assert that in order to assess adequately the stress from perceived discrimination within a racist society, we require assessments of several variables at various levels of an ecological model. Rather than employ a linear life events model, as traditionally used in stress and coping research (Lazarus & Folkman, 1984), we join with resilience researchers (Garmezy, Masten, & Tellegen, 1984; Luthar, 1991; Sameroff et al., 1987) in advocating the assessment of risk and processes of adaptation by employing an ecological/transactional model.

SUMMARY AND CONCLUSIONS

Racism and discrimination are fundamental aspects of our current social structures and constitute pervasive stressors in the daily lives of many minority individuals. Understanding the normal developmental trajectories of children of color requires that resilience studies pay explicit attention to the unique ecological circumstances (e.g., the pervasive influence of racism) in analyses of macrosystem influences.

Survey research on perceived discrimination and its risks for minority children's mental health identifies two processes that are likely *mediators* of its effects: (1) the internalization of negative feedback and the stress attributable to repeated exposure to discrimination and (2) the associated anxiety that one will be a victim of discrimination. Several factors also have been found to *moderate* the likelihood of perceiving discrimination, including various aspects of cognitive development. Research further demonstrates that social cognitive capacity is necessary but not sufficient. One also needs a worldview of differential power for different subgroups based on their respective ethnicities.

The experimental literature contributes two additional factors, attributional ambiguity and the need for control, that can suppress the likelihood of perceiving discrimination. There is also the counterintuitive finding that the external attribution of negativity to another's prejudice can render discrimination irrelevant to one's self-assessment. The apparent discrepancy between experimental and survey findings may reflect the fact that in the former, perceiving someone as discriminatory is a one-time experience that may affect self-esteem in the short term. By contrast, survey reports probably reflect experiences of perceived discrimination across multiple occasions over time, which in turn have high potential to engender more enduring changes in global self-esteem. Additional research reconciling experimental and survey research findings would be beneficial.

Outside of studies of discrimination, other research with Latina youth has illuminated several factors that can increase their vulnerability to negative outcomes, such as poverty, fatalism, difficulties with the English language, and clashes between subcultural collectivistic values and the more individualistic values of mainstream society. Potential protective factors include ethnic pride and biculturalism. In future research on resilience, it would be useful to examine such vulnerability and protective factors specifically in relation to the degree to which they modify the effects of discrimination. Truly integrative models for the study of developmental competencies in minority children must fully articulate interactions between such processes and sources of ongoing oppression, racism, and discrimination in everyday life.

As a final note, our review could be erroneously misread to assume that the solution lies in helping people to not perceive discrimination. Nothing could be further from our intent. Our goal in elucidating the mental health costs of perceived discrimination is to accentuate the toll that racism, prejudice, and discrimination can take on the well-being of minority children and adolescents. The goal is to eradicate racism, not to "protect" people from perceiving it. In fact, the more it is perceived, the more urgent it is that social forces must be galvanized to work against racism.

Note

1. We use the term *Latino*, as preferred by many academics. When referring to the work of others, including U.S. government publications, we preserve their usage, whether it is *Hispanic* or *Latino*.

References

Aboud, F. (1988). *Children and prejudice.* New York: Basil Blackwell.

Alarcón, O. (2000). *Social context of Puerto Rican Child Health and Growth Study – Final report.* Submitted to the Maternal and Child Health Bureau, U.S. Department of Health and Human Services.

Alarcón, O., Erkut, S., García Coll, C., & Vázquez García, H. A. (1994). *Engaging in culturally sensitive research on Puerto Rican youth* (Working Paper CRW #275). Wellesley, MA: Wellesley Centers for Women.

Allport, G. W. (1979). *The nature of prejudice.* New York: Doubleday Anchor Books. (Original work published 1954.)

Anthony, E. J., & Cohler, B. J. (Eds.). (1987). *The invulnerable child.* New York: Guilford Press.

Arellano, A., & Padilla, A. (1996). Academic invulnerability among a selected group of Latino university students. *Hispanic Journal of Behavioral Sciences, 18,* 485–507.

Biggs, M. A. (1998). *Puerto Rican adolescents' cultural orientation: Contextual determinants and psychosocial outcomes.* Unpublished doctoral dissertation, Boston University.

Bigler, R. S., & Liben, L. S. (1993). A cognitive-developmental approach to racial stereotyping and reconstructive memory in Euro-American children. *Child Development, 64,* 1507–1518.

Bowser, B. J. (1981). Racism and mental illness: An exploration of the racist's illness and the victim's health. In O. Barbarin, P. R. Good, O. M. Pharr, & J. A. Siskind (Eds.), *Institutional racism and community competence* (DHHS Pub. No. (ADM) 81-907, pp. 107–113). Washington, DC: U.S. Government Printing Office.

Bronfenbrenner, U. (1986). Ecology of the family as a context for human development: Research perspectives. *Developmental Psychology, 22,* 723–742.

Brown, T. N., Williams, D. R., Jackson, J. S., Neighbors, H. W., Torres, M., Sellers, S. L., & Brown, K. T. (2000). "Being black and feeling blue": The mental health consequences of racial discrimination. *Race and Society, 2,* 117–131.

Carter, J. H. (1993). Racism's impact on mental health. *Journal of the National Medical Association, 86,* 543–547.

Cooley, C. H. (1922). *Human nature and the social order.* New York: Charles Scribner's Sons.

Crocker, J. (1999). Social stigma and self-esteem: Situational construction of self-worth. *Journal of Experimental Social Psychology, 35,* 89–107.

Crocker, J., & Major, B. (1989). Social stigma and self-esteem: The self-protective properties of stigma. *Psychological Review, 96,* 608–630.

Crocker, J., & Major, B. (1994). Reactions to stigma: The moderating role of justifications. In M. P. Zanna & J. M. Olson (Eds.), *The psychology of prejudice: The Ontario Symposium* (Vol. 7, pp. 289–314). Hillsdale, NJ: Erlbaum.

Crocker, J., Voelkle, K., Testa, M., & Major, B. (1991). Social stigma: The affective consequences of attributional ambiguity. *Journal of Personality and Social Psychology, 60,* 218–228.

Cross, W. E., Jr. (1992). *Shades of blackness*. Philadelphia: Temple University Press.

Darabi, K. F. (1987). *Childbearing among Hispanics in the U.S.: An annotated bibliography*. Westport, CT: Greenwood Press.

Delgado, A. K. (1982). On being black. In F. X. Acosta, J. Yamamoto, & L. A. Evans (Eds.), *Effective psychotherapy for low-income and minority patients* (pp. 109–116). New York: Plenum Press.

Doyle, A. B., & Aboud, F. E. (1995). A longitudinal study of white children's racial prejudice as a social-cognitive development. *Merrill Palmer Quarterly, 41,* 209–228.

Erikson, E. (1968). *Identity: Youth and crisis*. New York: Norton.

Erkut, S., Alarcón, O., & García Coll, C. (1999). *Normative study of Puerto Rican adolescents – Final report* (Special Report #CRW 23). Wellesley, MA: Wellesley Centers for Women.

Falicov, C. J. (1996). Mexican families. In M. McGoldrick, J. Giordano, & J. K. Pearce (Eds.), *Ethnicity and family therapy* (2nd ed., pp. 169–182). New York: Guilford Press.

Feagin, J. R. (1991). The continuing significance of race: Anti-black discrimination in public places. *American Sociological Review, 56,* 101–116.

Feliz-Ortiz, M., Villatorio Velazquez, J. A., Medina-Mora, M. E., & Newcomb, M. D. (2001). Adolescent drug use in Mexico and among Mexican American adolescents in the United States: Environmental influences and individual characteristics. *Cultural Diversity and Ethnic Minority Psychology, 7,* 27–46.

Fernando, S. (1984). Racism as a cause of depression. *International Journal of Social Psychology, 30,* 41–49.

Fisher, C. B., Wallace, S. A., & Fenton, R. E. (2000). Discrimination distress during adolescence. *Journal of Youth and Adolescence, 29,* 679–695.

Franklin, A. J. (1993, July–August). The invisibility syndrome. *Family Therapy Networker,* 32–39.

García Coll, C., Lamberty, G., Jenkins, R., McAdoo, H. P., Crnic, K., Wasik, B. H., & Vázquez García, H. (1996). An integrative model for the study of developmental competencies in minority children. *Child Development, 67,* 1891–1914.

García Coll, C. T., Meyer, E. C., & Brillon, L. (1995). Ethnic and minority parenting. In M. H. Bornstein (Ed.), *Handbook of parenting* (Vol. 2, pp. 198–210). Mahwah, NJ: Erlbaum.

García Coll, C., & Vazquez García, H. (1995). Hispanic children and their families: On a different track from the very beginning. In H. E. Fitzgerald, B. M. Lester, & B. Zuckerman (Eds.), *Children of poverty: Research, health and policy issues* (pp. 57–83). New York: Garland.

Garmezy, N. (1991). Resiliency and vulnerability to adverse developmental outcomes associated with poverty. *American Behavioral Scientist, 34,* 416–430.

Garmezy, N., Masten, A. S., & Tellegen, A. (1984). The study of stress and competence in children: A building block for developmental psychopathology. *Child Development, 55,* 97–111.

Gonzalez, R., & Padilla, A. M. (1997). The academic resilience of Mexican American high school students. *Hispanic Journal of Behavioral Sciences, 19,* 301–317.

Gordon, K. A. (1996). Resilient Hispanic youths' self-concept and motivational patterns. *Hispanic Journal of Behavioral Sciences, 18,* 63–73.

Harwood, R., Schoelmerich, A., Ventura Cook, E., Schulze, P., & Wilson, S. (1996). Culture and class influences on Anglo and Puerto Rican mothers' beliefs regarding long-term socialization goals and child behavior. *Child Development, 67,* 2446–2461.

Inhelder, B., & Piaget, J. (1958). *The growth of logical thinking from childhood to adolescence: An essay on the construction of formal operational structures.* New York: Basic Books.

Jackson, J. S., Brown, T. N., Williams, D. R., Torres, M., Sellers, S. L., & Brown, K. (1996). Racism and the physical and mental health status of African Americans: A thirteen year national panel study. *Ethnicity and Disease, 6,* 132–147.

Jessor, R., Van Den Bos, J., Vanderryn, J., Costa., F. M., & Turbin, M. S. (1995). Protective factors in adolescent problem behavior: Moderator effects and developmental change. *Developmental Psychology, 31,* 923–933.

Kessler, R. C., Michelson, K. D., & Williams, D. R. (1999). The prevalence, distribution, and mental health correlates of perceived discrimination in the United States. *Journal of Health and Social Behavior, 40,* 208–230.

Krieger, N. (1999). Embodying inequality: A review of concepts, measures, and methods for studying health consequences of discrimination. *International Journal of Health Services, 29,* 295–352.

Landrine, H., & Klonoff, E. A. (1996). The Schedule of Racist Events: A measure of racial discrimination and a study of its negative physical and mental health consequences. *Journal of Black Psychology, 22,* 144–168.

Lang, D. L. (2001). *The Schedule of Racist Events-Generic: A measure of perceived racism across ethnic groups.* Unpublished doctoral dissertation, Loma Linda University.

Lazarus, R. S., & Folkman, S. (1984). *Stress, appraisal, and coping.* New York: Springer.

Liebowitz, S. W., Castellano, D. C., & Cuellar, I. (1999). Factors that predict sexual behavior among young Mexican American adolescents: An exploratory study. *Hispanic Journal of Behavioral Sciences, 21,* 470–479.

Luthar, S. S. (1991). Vulnerability and resilience: A study of high-risk adolescents. *Child Development, 62,* 600–616.

Luthar, S. (1999). *Poverty and children's adjustment.* Thousand Oaks, CA: Sage.

Luthar, S. S., & Cicchetti, D. (2000). The construct of resilience: Implications for interventions and social policies. *Development and Psychopathology, 12,* 857–885.

Luthar, S. S., & McMahon, T. J. (1996). Peer reputation among inner-city adolescents: Structure and correlates. *Journal of Research on Adolescence, 6,* 581–603.

MacPhee, D., Kreutzer, J. C., & Fritz, J. J. (1994). Infusing a diversity perspective into human development courses. *Child Development, 62,* 699–715.

Masten, A. (2001). Ordinary magic: Resilience processes in development. *American Psychologist, 56,* 227–238.

McNeill, B. W., Prieto, L. R., Niemann, Y. F., Pizarro, M., Vera, E. M., & Gomez, S. P. (2001). Current directions in Chicana/o psychology. *The Counseling Psychologist, 29,* 5–17.

Mead, G. H. (1967). *Mind, self and society, from the standpoint of a social behavioralist* (C. W. Morris, Ed.). Chicago: University of Chicago Press. (Original work published 1934.)

Oboler, S. (1995). *Ethnic labels, Latino lives.* Minneapolis: University of Minnesota Press.

Ogbu, J. U. (1981). Origins of human competence: A cultural ecological perspective. *Child Development, 52,* 413–429.

Ogbu, J. U. (1987). Variability in minority school performance: A problem in search of an explanation. *Anthropology and Education Quarterly, 18,* 312–334.

Perez y Gonzalez, M. E. (2000). *Puerto Ricans in the United States.* Westport, CT: Greenwood.

Phinney, J. S. (1990). Ethnic identity in adolescents and adults: Review of research. *Psychological Bulletin, 108,* 499–514.

Phinney, J. S., Madden, T., & Santos, L. J. (1998). Psychological variables as predictors of perceived ethnic discrimination among minority and immigrant adolescents. *Journal of Applied Social Psychology, 28,* 937–953.

Piaget, J. (1999). *The moral judgement of the child.* London: Routledge. (Original work published 1932.)

Pines, M. (1975, December). In praise of "invulnerables." *APA Monitor,* p. 7.

Rollock, D., & Gordon, E. W. (2000). Racism and mental health into the 21st century: Perspectives and parameters. *American Journal of Orthopsychiatry, 70,* 5–13.

Ruggiero, K. M., & Taylor, D. M. (1997). Why minority group members perceive or do not perceive the discrimination that confronts them: The role of self-esteem and perceived control. *Journal of Personality and Social Psychology, 22,* 373–389.

Rumbaut, R. (1994). The crucible within: Ethnic identity, self-esteem, and segmented assimilation among children of immigrants. *International Migration Review, 28,* 748–794.

Rumbaut, R., & Ima, K. (1988). *The adaptation of Southeast Asian refugee youth: A comparative study.* Washington, DC: U.S. Department of Health and Human Services, Office of Refugee Resettlement.

Rutter, M. (1979). Protective factors in children's responses to stress and disadvantage. In M. W. Kent & J. E. Rolf (Eds.), *Primary prevention in psychopathology* (pp. 49–74). Hanover, NH: University Press of New England.

Sameroff, A. J., Seifer, R., Zax, M., & Barocas, R. (1987). Early indicators of developmental risk: The Rochester Longitudinal Study. *Schizophrenia Bulletin, 13,* 383–393.

Sanders-Phillips, K., Moisan, P. A., Wadlington, S., Morgan, S., & English, K. (1995). Ethnic differences in psychological functioning among black and Latino sexually abused girls. *Child Abuse and Neglect, 19,* 691–706.

Schur, C. L., Bernstein, A. B., & Minkler, D. (1987). The importance of distinguishing Hispanic subpopulations in the use of medical care. *Medical Care, 25,* 627–641.

Sigelman, L., & Welch, S. (1991). *Black Americans' views of racial inequality: The dream deferred.* Cambridge, MA: Harvard University Press.

Spencer, M. B. (1999). Social and cultural influences on school adjustment: The application of an identity-focused cultural ecological perspective. *Educational Psychology, 34,* 43–57.

Spencer, M. B., & Markstrom-Adams, C. (1990). Identity process among racial and ethnic minority children in America. *Child Development, 61,* 290–310.

Szalacha, L. A., Erkut, S., García Coll, C., Alarcón, O., Fields, J. P., & Ceder, I. (in press). Discrimination and Puerto Rican children and adolescents' mental health. *Cultural Diversity and Ethnic Minority Psychology.*

Taylor, D. M., Wright, S. C., Moghaddam, F. M., & Lalonde, R. N. (1990). The personal/group discrimination discrepancy: Perceiving my group, but not myself, to be a target of discrimination. *Personality and Social Psychology Bulletin, 16,* 254–262.

Taylor, D. M., Wright, S. C., & Porter, L. E. (1993). Dimensions of perceived discrimination: The personal/group discrimination discrepancy. In M. P. Zanna & J. M. Olson (Eds.), *The psychology of prejudice: The Ontario Symposium* (Vol. 7, pp. 233–255). Hillsdale, NJ: Erlbaum.

Thompson, S. V. T. (1996). Perceived experiences of racism and stressful life events. *Community Mental Health Journal, 32,* 233.

Tidwell, B. J. (1990). *The price: A study of the costs of racism in America.* Washington, DC: The Urban Institute.

U.S. Census. (2001, April 2). *Population by race and Hispanic or Latino origin, for all ages and for 18 years and over, for the United States: 2000.* Retrieved September 17, 2001, from http://www.census.gov/population/www/cen2000/phc-t1.html

Verkuyten, M. (1998). Perceived discrimination and self-esteem among ethnic minority adolescents. *Journal of Social Psychology, 138,* 479–495.

Verkuyten, M., Kinket, B., & van der Wielen, C. (1997). Preadolescents' understanding of ethnic discrimination. *Journal of Genetic Psychology, 158,* 97–112.

Wallston, K. A., Wallston, B. S., Smith, S., & Dobbins, C. J. (1987). Perceived control and health. *Current Psychological Research and Reviews, 6,* 5–25.

Werner, E. E., & Smith, R. S. (1992). *Overcoming the odds: High risk children from birth to adulthood.* Ithaca, NY: Cornell University Press.

Williams, D. R., Yu, Y., Jackson, J. S., & Anderson, N. B. (1997). Racial differences in physical and mental health: Socio-economic status, stress and discrimination. *Journal of Health Psychology, 2,* 335–351.

Yin, Z., Zapata, J. T., & Katims, D. S. (1995). Risk factors for substance use among Mexican American school-age youth. *Hispanic Journal of Behavioral Sciences, 17,* 61–76.

18

Promoting Resilience through Early Childhood Intervention

Arthur J. Reynolds and Suh-Ruu Ou

INTRODUCTION

In the past decade, research on resilience has grown dramatically beyond the field of clinical psychology from which it arose. Applications in education, social work, human development, health, and business have expanded the conceptualization of resilience from a psychosocial perspective to a multidimensional one (Wang & Gordon, 1994; Werner & Smith, 1992; Zimmerman & Arunkumar, 1994). Although much of the knowledge base has highlighted measurement and methodology, a major source of the appeal of the resilience concept is to enhance the well-being of individuals through social programs and policies. One major priority is the identification of personal and environmental factors that promote successful adjustment among the most vulnerable young people.

In this chapter, we review evidence about the effects of early childhood interventions in promoting resilience for children who have experienced high levels of social-environmental risk due to economic disadvantage. We address several contemporary issues including the measurement of resilience, interventions as protective factors, and the pathways through which the effects of interventions lead to positive developmental outcomes.

Despite continuing concerns about construct and measurement validity (Luthar, Cicchetti, & Becker, 2000; Tolan, 1996), resilience as a subject of investigation has been a major influence on developmental research. Four characteristics explain its influence. First, resilience is a positive outcome of development and thus provides an alternative perspective to dysfunctional behavior that has long been associated with the field of psychology. Undue focus on individual pathology and disease can have stigmatizing effects, and this is largely avoided with resilience. Second, resilience is a dynamic concept that transcends its roots in clinical research and has wide appeal across the disciplines and among the public at large. Unlike the associated terms *competence, achievement,* and *well-being, resilience* connotes a deeper dimension of experience in human development. A third explanation for the growth of resilience research is the emphasis on nonnormative development or unexpected success in the face of risk, which draws attention to populations most in need and can provide lessons for promoting resilience. A fourth reason for the emergence of resilience as a major conceptual perspective concerns its goal of identifying protective factors that enhance adjustment. Because protective factors have greater effects on individuals and groups who are at high risk, social and educational interventions that strengthen protective factors can contribute to the development of resilience.

This chapter emphasizes this latter perspective by discussing the contributions of intervention research in early childhood to strengthening protective factors and ultimately resilience. Early childhood interventions from birth to the early school grades are receiving widespread attention today as one of the most effective ways to promote children's well-being. The main attraction of early childhood interventions is their potential for prevention and their cost effectiveness, especially when compared to the well-known limits of treatment. Viewed from the perspective of resilience, participation in early childhood intervention is often hypothesized as a protective factor. Because early interventions provide compensatory services, the effects of intervention are believed to be greater for children who are at risk of poor outcomes due to environmental disadvantages or developmental disabilities. In this chapter, early childhood intervention (ECI hereafter) is broadly defined as the provision of educational, family, health, and/or social services during any of the first 8 years of life to children who are at risk of poor outcomes because they face socioenvironmental disadvantages.

ADVANCES IN KNOWLEDGE ABOUT EFFECTIVENESS AND PROTECTION

Three major advances in knowledge about the effects of ECI have occurred over the past decade. First, there is substantial support for the short- and long-term impact of a wide variety of well-implemented programs on a variety of child development outcomes (Barnett & Boocock,

1998; Guralnick, 1997; Karoly et al., 1998). These outcomes include cognitive development, school achievement, reduced need for school remedial services, and educational attainment. Some studies also have found that program participation is associated with lower rates of antisocial behavior, delinquency, and crime (Lally Mangione, Honig, & Wittner, 1988; Reynolds, Chang, & Temple, 1998; Schweinhart, Barnes, & Weikart, 1993) and with employment and economic success in adulthood (Schweinhart et al., 1993). Although the number of well-controlled studies with long-term follow-up is relatively small, findings of positive effects generally hold for both model and large-scale programs. Thus, research supports the conclusion that early childhood intervention is a protective factor among disadvantaged children.

A second major conclusion is that both the timing and the duration of intervention matter. In the past decade, empirical support for these attributes has grown substantially (Ramey & Ramey, 1992, 1998; Yoshikawa, 1995). The most effective programs reported in the literature spanning home visitation to center-based preschool education have been those that began during the first 3 years of life, continue for multiple years, and provide support to families (Weissberg & Greenberg, 1998; Yoshikawa, 1995). These findings are consistent with both ecological and resilience perspectives of development.

Third, a major developmental mechanism of long-term effects of early intervention on child outcomes is the cognitive/scholastic advantage experienced in the program. Although the Consortium for Longitudinal Studies (1983; Lazar, Darlington, Murray, & Snipper, 1982) and Berrueta-Clement Schweinhart, Barnett, Epstein, Weikart, (1984) provided empirical demonstration for the cognitive advantage hypotheses, more recent studies into adulthood (Barnett, Young, & Schweinhart, 1998; Schweinhart et al., 1993) and for contemporary large-scale programs (Reynolds, 2000; Reynolds, Mavrogenes, Bezruczko, & Hagemann, 1996) reinforce the validity of this hypothesis, as well as suggest that family and school support factors contribute to long-run effects.

NEW DIRECTIONS IN INTERVENTION RSEARCH

As much as knowledge has advanced about the effects of ECI, many questions remain unanswered. Two recurrent questions stand out that are directly related to resilience:

1. What are the causal mechanisms and pathways through which the effects of early childhood interventions promote long-term success?

2. For whom are existing programs most effective, and which program features are most associated with success?

These and related questions represent the natural progression of research toward a more complete knowledge base. As discussed by Guralnickt (1997), the main task in the first generation of research was to demonstrate that early intervention can be effective in impacting children's development. The task of the second generation is to address these more refined questions, such as who benefits most and what environmental conditions and mechanisms influence effectiveness. Research on resilience has followed a parallel course (Rutter, Champion, Quinton, Maughan, & Pickles, 1995).

The issue of protective mechanisms (pathways) of effects is central to understanding the process of change over time. Until recently, direct evidence of the mechanisms of effects came from the model projects in the Consortium for Longitudinal Studies (1983), primarily the Perry Preschool Program (Schweinhart et al., 1993). Differential effects by child, family, and program characteristics are an open question (Barnett & Boocock, 1998; Consortium, 1983), and the use of small samples has reduced the power to detect moderator effects. The question of which program components are most associated with children's success has similar difficulties, and findings have often been mixed (Lazar et al., 1982; Schweinhart et al., 1993). Moreover, a clear need exists for more and better evidence of the longer-term effects of large-scale programs (Reynolds, Mann, Miedel, & Smokowski, 1997; U.S. General Accounting Office, 1997).

The greater emphasis on mechanisms of influence that link early childhood experiences and later outcomes has been aided by alternative approaches to evaluation research. One of these is theory-driven evaluation, which is designed to investigate causal explanations of program–outcome relationships rather than causal descriptions. The latter is focused on internal validity whereas the former emphasizes external and construct validity (Cook & Campbell, 1979; Cronbach, 1982). In order to highlight the role of causal explanation in developmental research, we developed a perspective called *confirmatory program evaluation*.

CONTRIBUTIONS OF CONFIRMATORY PROGRAM EVALUATION

Confirmatory program evaluation (CPE; Reynolds, 1998a) is a theory-driven methodology for investigating the effects of social and educational programs. In a theory-driven impact evaluation, the explicit theory of the program is highlighted to establish an a priori model of how the program is hypothesized to exert its impact (Chen, 1990; Lipsey, 1993). Causal uncertainty is reduced through an examination of the pattern of findings against the program theory. Special emphasis is placed on testing causal mechanisms and pathways that contribute to program effectiveness over time. A major tenet of CPE is that the plausibility of an estimated effect can be strengthened through systematic testing of causal mechanisms and other aspects of the program–outcome relationship.

Three key questions addressed in CPE are: (1) Is program participation independently and consistently associated with key outcomes? (2) What are the processes or pathways through which participation leads to children's outcomes? and (3) Are the estimated effects conditional on child and family attributes, or particular program components? Given their emphasis on multivariate prediction, theory-driven evaluations are confirmatory and corroborative approaches. Based on the program theory, for example, an evaluator can explicate or test the following: (1) the size of the program effect, (2) the consistency of effects across subgroups, and (3) the causal mechanisms or pathways through which the estimated effects are manifested.

CPE is aided by the use of six empirically verifiable criteria that strengthen the validity of research findings. Adapted from Susser (1973) and Anderson et al. (1980). Satisfaction or affirmation of these criteria in a CPE strengthens the likelihood that the relationship between program participation and outcomes is causal, and criteria help probe analyses of theory-relevant questions. These criteria are summarized as follows:

Temporality. Program participation precedes in time the outcome or program response.

Size. The stronger the association between program participation and outcome, the more likely the association represents a true effect.

Gradient (dose–response). A causal inference is more warranted if the relationship between program exposure (e.g., number of days or sessions attended) and outcome is monotonic. This is especially the case when experiments are not possible, a common occurrence in intervention research.

Specificity. Causal inference is strengthened if the program–outcome relationship is limited to specific domains of behavior or to particular subgroups (e.g., high-risk children). In social and educational programs, specificity can be predicted on the basis of the program theory. Early childhood interventions focused on educational or cognitive enrichment, for example, should affect literacy skills and educational outcomes more than social skills or psychological factors. Although ECI is based on the assumption that high-risk children can benefit from intervention more than low-risk children, few studies of moderator effects within at-risk samples have been conducted.

Consistency. Consistency of association between program exposure and outcome indicates whether the estimated program effect is similar across sample populations, and is similar at different times and places, under different types of analysis and with different model specifications. The greater the consistency of findings favoring positive effects, the more likely the observed effects are real. There are two dimensions of consistency: within- and between-study. Evidence of within-study consistency is based on the degree to which evaluation data are robust and sensitive to model specification, for example. Evidence for between-study consistency is based on the correspondence of study findings with previous studies.

Coherence. This examines the extent to which the evaluation findings show a clear pattern of effects relative to the causes of behaviors the program is attempting to impact. The coherence criterion investigates whether the hypothesized causal mechanisms (*active ingredients*) provide a coherent explanation of the main-effect findings and the theory of the program. The coherence criterion is especially relevant to prevention and developmental science. Once a direct relation is established between program participation and a longer-term outcome variable, the pathways that produce this estimated effect must be identified. Little attention in the field of early intervention has been given to the developmental pathways or causal mechanisms that promote long-term effects. Yet the study of causal mechanisms is paradigmatic in prevention and developmental research (Coie, Walt, West, and Hawkins, 1993; Ramey & Ramey, 1998).

HYPOTHESIS OF PROTECTIVE MECHANISM IN EARLY INTERVENTION

Identification of the pathways through which the long-run effects of early childhood programs are achieved not only provides a rationale for explaining the observed direct effects of participation, but also helps identify protective mechanisms and processes that can be the focus of intervention for maintaining or enhancing the effects of earlier intervention. Identified pathways also aid program design and improvement by highlighting key components or active ingredients that require special attention. If ECI, for example, influenced later school achievement primarily by enhancing children's early cognitive skills rather than their social skills or their parents' educational development, then program content may be optimally directed toward the development of structured language and cognitive enrichment (while not ignoring family of social development). Moreover, investigation of the pathways of intervention effects can illuminate factors that encourage replication and generalizability of findings to other settings and populations.

Figure 18.1 shows five hypothesized pathways through which ECI may affect competence behaviors in the years after program participation. The consensus outcomes of early childhood programs include school and social competence behaviors. Because the major purpose of early intervention concerns educational enrichment (i.e., school readiness), many outcomes concern children's school performance. Indeed, enhancing school performance and success are the most frequently reported findings in the literature (Karoly et al., 1998).

Derived from the 30-year literature on the effects of early intervention on child outcomes (Consortium for Longitudinal Studies, 1983; Schweinhart et al., 1993; Seitz, 1990), the hypotheses associated with these pathways provide a foundation for developing the knowledge base on how early childhood experiences lead to longer-term effects and the environmental conditions that promote or limit adjustment. As shown, the effects of early intervention may be transmitted through (1) developed cognitive and scholastic abilities (cognitive advantage hypothesis), (2) parents' behavior with or on behalf of children (family support hypothesis), (3) children's motivation or self-efficacy (motivational advantage hypothesis), (4) social development and adjustment (social adjustment hypothesis) and (5) the quality of the school environments children experience after participating in the program (school support hypotheses).

1. *The cognitive advantage hypothesis* indicates that the long-term effects of intervention are initiated by improvements in children's developed abilities in early childhood, usually at the end or close to the end of the program. The cognitive advantage hypothesis is the most frequent explanation for the long-term effects of early intervention (Consortium for Longitudinal Studies, 1983; Lazar et al., 1982; Reynolds et al.,1996; Schweinhart & Weikart, 1980; Schweinhart et al., 1993). It reflects a belief

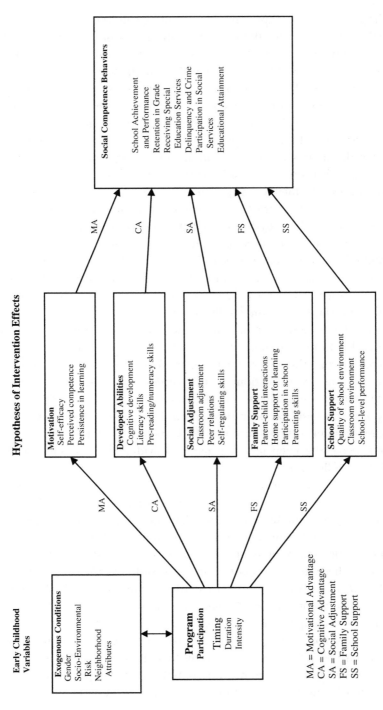

Early Childhood Variables

Hypotheses of Intervention Effects

Exogenous Conditions
Gender
Socio-Environmental Risk
Neighborhood Attributes

Program Participation
Timing
Duration
Intensity

Motivation
Self-efficacy
Perceived competence
Persistence in learning

Developed Abilities
Cognitive development
Literacy skills
Pre-reading/numeracy skills

Social Adjustment
Classroom adjustment
Peer relations
Self-regulating skills

Family Support
Parent-child interactions
Home support for learning
Participation in school
Parenting skills

School Support
Quality of school environment
Classroom environment
School-level performance

Social Competence Behaviors
School Achievement and Performance
Retention in Grade
Receiving Special Education Services
Delinquency and Crime
Participation in Social Services
Educational Attainment

MA = Motivational Advantage
CA = Cognitive Advantage
SA = Social Adjustment
FS = Family Support
SS = School Support

FIGURE 18.1 Alternative paths leading to social competence.

in the *primacy* of early experience in promoting children's success that was a major justification for the Head Start preschool program in the early 1960s. In this perspective, the cognitive and language stimulation experienced in center-based education may directly affect children's cognitive functioning as well as their social and motivational behavior. A major focus of an activity-based educational component is the development of literacy skills through individual and group reading and writing activities, as well as field trips, to promote knowledge and understanding of the world. These systematic educational experiences produce cognitive advantages that initiate a positive cycle of performance culminating in more successful adolescent adjustment.

2. *The family support hypothesis* indicates that longer-term effects of early intervention will occur to the extent that program participation enhances the capacities of parents to support children's learning and development. Parenting behaviors may include those with or on behalf of children such as home support for learning and school support for learning through participation in school-related activities. A central goal of early childhood interventions is to promote family development, often through the provision of family education activities. The family support hypothesis was offered by Bronfenbrenner (1975) as an explanation for the observed dissipating cognitive effects of participation in Head Start. He noted, for example, that family functioning and parent–child relations must be impacted for long-term effects on child development to occur. The family support hypothesis has been the central theory of family-centered programs and interventions since the 1960s and 1970s (Powell, 1999; Seitz, 1990). It has not been tested in many individual studies, especially in long-term follow-ups.

3. *In the motivational advantage hypothesis,* the long-term effects of program participation are due to changes in children's motivational development rather than in their cognitive or language development. *Motivation* is broadly defined to include self-system attributes such as perceived competence, self-concept of ability, self-efficacy, task persistence, and effort. This hypothesis derives, in part, from Zigler and Butterfield's (1968) and Zigler, Abelson, Trickett, and Seitz's (1982) findings that changes in intelligence test scores among low-income children may have a substantial motivational component. Indeed, motivational development was one of the original goals of the Head Start program (Zigler & Styfco, 1993). There have been few direct tests of this hypothesis.

4. The social adjustment hypothesis indicates that improved social development is the major reason that participation in early intervention

leads to long-term program effectiveness. Rather than directly changing children's cognitive status or motivation, participation may enhance children's internalization of social rules and norms, as well as peer relations necessary for successful school adjustment and for negotiating social situations. As a result of participation in the organized activities of early educational intervention, children are expected to learn self-regularity skills such as following directions, working with others, and inhibiting their behavior. This hypothesis of the effects of early intervention has rarely, if ever, been directly tested.

5. In the *school support hypothesis* the effects of program participation persist to the extent that children attend schools of sufficient quality to maintain or enhance the impact of earlier intervention experiences. This hypothesis is the school-based version of the family support hypothesis. It has never been directly tested as an explanation of long-term effects, although there is evidence that postprogram enrollment in poor-quality schools may reduce the persistence of learning gains (Currie & Thomas, 1998; Lee & Loeb, 1995) and that school instability (i.e., school transfer), and the consequent disruptions it may cause, also affects this process (Reynolds et al., 1996). One key issue is whether the school support hypothesis explains intervention effects above and beyond those of the cognitive advantage hypothesis.

Note that the indicators of the hypotheses must be independently associated with both program measures and outcome measures to be valid mechanisms. That is, the arrows on either side of the intervening constructs in Figure 18.1 must be significant. Of course, the hypotheses could work in combination. For example, program participation may affect adolescent social competence through early developed abilities and family support experiences or through a combination of early developed abilities, family support, and school support factors. These and other combinations deserve consideration in studies of these hypotheses. Moreover, empirically supported hypotheses may vary by program and sample characteristics.

INTERVENTION FINDINGS IN THE CHICAGO
LONGITUDINAL STUDY

Three studies of the contributions of early interventions to child and youth development are described for data in the Chicago Longitudinal Study. They provide a foundation for further investigations of early intervention research. The first one investigates participation in early intervention as a protective factor. The second and primary example is an investigation of hypotheses associated with long-term program effects or protective mechanisms. This addresses the coherence of the program–outcome relation. The third illustration examines for whom participation in intervention is most effective. This addresses the specificity of the program–outcome relation.

The Chicago Longitudinal Study (Reynolds, 2000; Reynolds et al., 1997) is an ongoing investigation of the effects of the Child–Parent Center (CPC) Program. The longitudinal quasiexperimental cohort design included 989 low-income mostly African American children who entered the program in preschool and graduated from kindergarten in 1986 from 20 centers and 550 children from similarly disadvantaged neighborhoods who participated in an alternative all-day kindergarten program in the Chicago schools, which was the "treatment as usual" at the time. The groups were well matched on eligibility for intervention, family socioeconomic status, gender, and race/ethnicity. At age 14 (spring 1994), 1,164 children (76% of the original sample) were active in the study sample in the Chicago public schools with no evidence of differential attrition. By age 20 (January 2000), 1,281 sample participants were active in the study, and data on their educational attainment were available. The Chicago project is one of the largest and most extensive studies of the effects of a large-scale early childhood intervention.

The CPC program is a Title I–funded center-based early intervention that provides comprehensive educational and family-support services to economically disadvantaged children from preschool to the early elementary grades (age 3 to 9). It is the second oldest federally funded preschool program (after Head Start) and the oldest extended childhood intervention (Reynolds, 1998). Each site is under the direction of a head teacher and is located adjacent to the elementary school or in a wing of the school. The major features of the program are as follows (see Reynolds, 2000, for details): (1) A structured but diverse set of language-based instructional activities designed to promote academic and social success. An activity-based curriculum called the Chicago EARLY (Chicago Board of Education, 1988) has been used frequently. Field trips are common. (2) A multifaceted parent program that includes participating in parent room activities, volunteering in the classroom, attending school events, and enrolling in educational courses for personal development, all under the supervision of the parent resource teacher. (3) Outreach activities coordinated by the school–community representative include resource mobilization, home visitation, and enrollment of children most in need.

Finally, there is a comprehensive school-age program from first to third grade that supports children's transition to elementary school through reduced class sizes (up to 25 children), the addition of teacher aides in each class, extra instructional supplies, and coordination of instructional activities, staff development, and parent-program activities organized by the curriculum-parent resource teacher.

Program and comparison groups were similar on many child and family characteristics at the follow-up assessment and the beginning of the study. The means of the risk index, a sum of six dichotomous factors associated with lower child health in many previous studies (i.e., low parent education, neighborhood poverty, low family income, single-parent family status, unemployed full- or part-time, and large family size), were equal between the groups (M's $= 3.6$ each). Consistent with developmental research, the risk index provides a summary measure of the cumulative effects of child risk factors on later outcomes. At the follow-up, the CPC preschool group had a higher proportion of girls, parents who had completed high school, and fewer siblings. Alternatively, the preschool group was more likely than the comparison group to reside in higher poverty neighborhoods, as a result of the centers being located in high-poverty neighborhoods (Reynolds, 2000; Reynolds & Temple, 1998).

Protective Effects of Participation in Intervention

We have found consistent evidence in the Chicago study that participation in the CPC program among this economically disadvantaged sample is associated with better performance on a wide variety of competence indicators including school achievement, need for remedial education, delinquency, and educational attainment, as well as resilience more broadly. These findings indicate the protective effects of early intervention over time. Reynolds (2000) analyzed the effects of preschool participation (1 or 2 years) and the duration of program participation (0 to 6 years) for school achievement at age 14 and for prevalence of grade retention under four sequential model specifications: (1) unadjusted mean group difference, (2) adjustments for sex of child and risk status (number of family risk factors such as low parental education), (3) adjustments for parent participation in school, as rated by teachers, and (4) adjustments for school site attributes as measured by 24 site dummy variables. The findings indicated that both preschool participation and years of total program participation were significantly associated with child outcomes under all model specifications. Preschool participation was associated with a 5% to 7% advantage in reading achievement, and an 8% to 10% reduction in the rate of grade retention. Each additional year of program participation was associated with a 2% to 3% advantage in achievement and a 3% to 4% reduction in grade retention. These findings are consistent with those studies using latent-variable and simultaneous-equation models (Reynolds & Temple, 1995, 1998). Such testing of consistency of program effects under different model specifications and analytic techniques is rare in intervention research and shows the value of confirmatory approaches to evaluation.

Evidence for the protective effects of early intervention persisted through adolescence. By age 20, participation in the preschool program was associated with higher rates of high school completion and lower rates of school dropout, above and beyond the risk index, sex of the child, and program sites. For example, Reynolds, Temple, Robertson, & Mann (2001) reported that preschool participants had a higher rate of high school completion than that of the matched comparison group (49.7% vs 38.5%). This translates to an increase of 29% over the comparison group (115%/38.5%). Preschool participants also completed more years of education than the comparison group (10.6 vs. 10.2 years). The mechanisms that produce these observed effects are addressed next.

Mechanisms of Intervention Effects

The theory of CPC intervention is that children's scholastic and social readiness for school will be facilitated by the provision of systematic language learning activities in center-based early intervention and opportunities for family support experiences through direct parent participation in the program. This theory is embodied in the goal statement: "[CPC is] designed to reach the child and parent early, develop language skills and self-confidence, and to demonstrate that these children, if given a chance, can meet successfully all the demands of today's technological, urban society" (cf. Naisbitt, 1968). The key measures to assess this goal include indicators of school achievement, incidence of grade retention and special education placement, and family–school relations.

Based on the conceptualization of protective mechanisms linking early intervention to later social competence in Figure 18.1, we investigated the pathways through which CPC program participation leads to longer-term effects. Results of a LISREL (Linear Structural Relations) model of the plausibility of the five hypotheses are illustrated in Figure 18.2. The

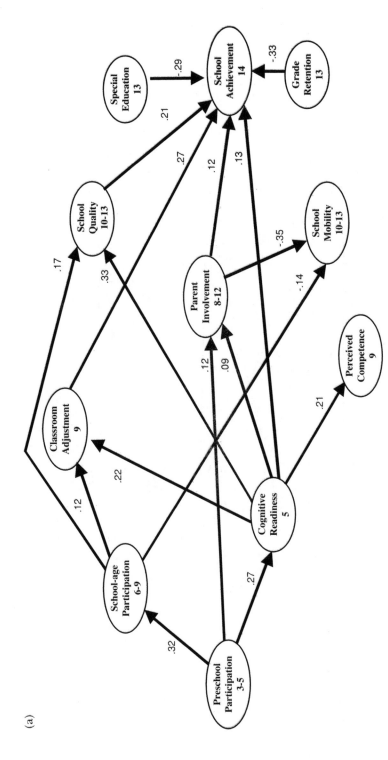

FIGURE 18.2 (a) Pathways from CPC intervention to school achievement by age 14. (b) Pathways from preschool participation and from years of CPC participation to high school dropout. *Note:* Gender and risk status are now shown.

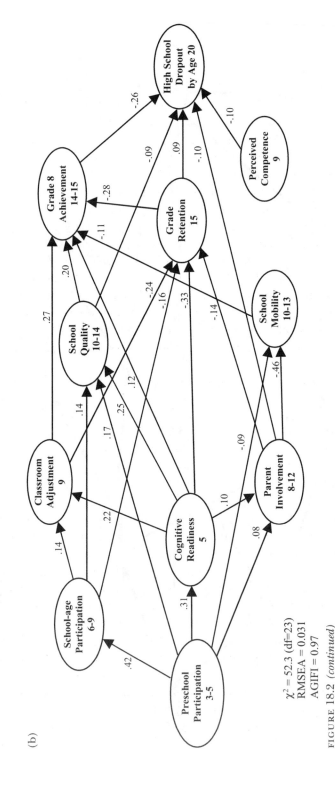

$\chi^2 = 52.3$ (df=23)
RMSEA = 0.031
AGIFI = 0.97

FIGURE 18.2 *(continued)*

(b)

coefficients are standardized and significant at the .01 level. Structural modeling is particularly appropriate for theory-driven tests of hypotheses of causal mediation. The top half of the figure shows the paths of influence from preschool participation to school achievement at age 14; the bottom half shows the paths leading to school dropout at age 20. School achievement was defined by reading comprehension and math achievement scores on the Iowa Tests of Basic Skills (ITBS). As shown, the cognitive advantage hypothesis, measured by the school readiness battery on the ITBS at age 5, provided the best single explanation for the significant relation between preschool participation and school achievement. Preschool participants started kindergarten more cognitively ready to learn than no-preschool participants ($b = .27$), and this advantage directly carried over to later school achievement ($b = .13$), above and beyond the effects of other intervening variables. Apparently, this cognitive advantage diffuses throughout the schooling process by also promoting positive classroom adjustment and by helping to reduce school mobility, grade retention, and special education placement.

Among the other significant pathways contributing to the explanation of preschool effects was the dual mechanism of cognitive readiness and school quality ($b = .019$ or $.27 \times .33. \times .21$). School quality was the number of years children attended schools in which relatively high proportions of students scored at or above the national achievement norms. Parent participation in school also was a pathway through which preschool participation affected school achievement. This provides support for the family support hypothesis. Controlling for other model variables, preschool participants were more likely to have parents who participated in school activities after the end of the program ($b = .12$), and this participation independently contributed to school achievement in adolescence ($b = .12$). As shown in the bottom half of Figure 18.2, the major mechanisms associated with lower rates of school dropout were similar to those for achievement. They included cognitive/scholastic achievement, parent involvement in school, and school quality.

Table 18.1 summarizes the major contributing pathways to the long-term effects of CPC program participation as a proportion of the total indirect effect. The total indirect effect (standardized) denotes the effect of CPC participation through the intervening variables or the hypotheses of program influence. For the most part, the cognitive advantage hypothesis contributed the most to the explanation of CPC effects on school achievement. For preschool participation, the cognitive

TABLE 18.1. *Total Indirect Effects of 2 Program Indicators*

Key Pathways	Age 14 School Achievement	Age 20 High School Dropout
Preschool Participation	.17	−.13
Percentage of Indirect effect Due to:		
Cognitive advantage	21	8
Family support	8	6
Cog adv & sch support	11	7
Cog adv & social adj	9	−
School support	−	12
Cog adv & retention	−	7
Years of Total Participation	.26	−.14
Percentage of Indirect Effect Due to:		
Cognitive advantage	59	36
Family support	5	10
School support	7	14
Cog adv & sch support	4	−
Cog adv & retention	−	6

Note: Cog adv = cognitive advantage.

advantage hypothesis (measured by cognitive readiness at age 5) accounted for 21% of the total indirect effect. This hypothesis contributed an even larger share to the explanation of years of total CPC participation (0 to 6 years).

To demonstrate the variation by outcome, the second column of Table 18.1 shows the contribution of the different hypotheses using high school dropout by age 20 as the dependent variable. Here the hypotheses of program effects were more balanced, as the cognitive advantage, school support, and family support hypotheses contributed to the total indirect effects of program participation (Reynolds, 1999). These and other hypotheses warrant further tests using a variety of indicators.

Our findings concerning the mechanisms of preschool effects in the CPCs are consistent with those of the High/Scope Perry Preschool Project (Berrueta-Clement et al., 1984) and the Consortium for Longitudinal Studies (1983), the only other studies that have investigated pathways of program effects in detail. The three studies reveal a strikingly similar pattern of findings in support of the cognitive advantage hypothesis despite differences in time frame (i.e., two decades), geography, sample composition, program content, and model specification. This degree of consistency strongly indicates the primacy of early cognitive and scholastic skills in maintaining the protective effects of early intervention (see Reynolds, 2000, for comparisons concerning family support and social adjustment pathways).

For Whom Are Intervention Services Most Effective?

Because of the compensatory nature of early interventions, it is often believed that children and families at the highest risk should benefit more from participation than those at less risk. In the relatively few studies that have systematically investigated interactions of program by child characterstics (e.g., gender, race/ethnicity) or family characteristics (e.g., socioeconomic status), no consistent findings have emerged. Many studies have low statistical power due to small sample sizes, limited variation on participant characteristics (e.g., poverty, risk status), and limited range of characteristics investigated (e.g., sex of child, parent education). To investigate this issue, the differential effects of program participation were investigated for the following child-, family-, and program-related variables: (1) sex of the child, (2) parent education, (3) number of risk factors experienced, (4) neighborhood poverty surrounding the centers, (5) parent participation in school, and (6) instructional approach in preschool.

Findings revealed limited support for differential effects on the adolescent outcome of school achievement, incidence of grade retention and special education, delinquency, and parent involvement in children's education. Neighborhood poverty was the most consistent moderator of program effects. Children who attended programs in the poorest neighborhoods (i.e., >60% of children from low-income families) benefited more than children who attended programs in less poor neighborhoods. This was especially true for reading and math achievement.

There was some indication that boys benefited more from preschool, whereas girls benefited more from follow-up intervention. Interestingly, the preschool curriculum approach (teacher-oriented, developmental, undifferentiated) did not lead to consistent differences across outcomes. Children who participated in centers implementing a more structured, basic skills approach had higher achievement test scores and lower rates of grade retention at age 14. An undifferentiated instructional approach (not distinctly teacher-oriented or child developmental) was most associated with lower school competence. In sum, although few subgroup effects were detected, some evidence indicated that children from the poorest neighborhoods benefited most. Risk status was not associated with estimates of program effects across outcomes. This is likely due to the fact that most study children experienced high levels of environmental risk while growing up (Reynolds, 1998b).

CONCLUSION

Intervention research has expanded beyond reliance on main effects to investigations of the mechanisms through which program participation affects later adjustment, as well as which groups benefit most from participation. This trend toward addressing these more refined questions also is occurring in research on resilience. Investigating the processes through which early childhood experiences impact later well-being contributes not only to understanding the nature of developmental change but also to identifying the experiences and behaviors that help maintain the effects of interventions. These experiences can promote resilience and can be a focus of intervention in their own right. The major themes of our chapter were that (1) early childhood experiences, including participation in intervention, contribute positively to later well-being, (2) several protective mechanisms associated with family and school experiences mediate the effects of participation in intervention on child development outcomes, and (3) the effects of intervention are largest for children growing up in the most disadvantaged environments. We will now expand on these themes.

In this chapter, we examined evidence that participation in a comprehensive early childhood intervention is a protective factor in children's development and that several hypothesized mechanisms associated with the program theory promote positive long-term effects. We found that participation in the CPC program was associated with significantly higher levels of adjustment across a variety of outcomes. Irrespective of model specification, program participation appears to be a protective factor in children's scholastic and social development. Given that the program is federally funded and administered by a large urban school district, findings show that established large-scale early childhood programs can be successful for economically disadvantaged children. This appears to be especially the case for children growing up in the highest poverty neighborhoods and for children who experience a relatively structured learning environment.

To put these demonstrated effects in perspective, consider the evidence on the protective effects of participation in the CPC program relative to those of other social programs. Durlak and Wells (1997) reviewed the effects of 177 evaluations of mental health prevention programs for children and youth, and reported an average effect size of .34 standard deviations at the end of the program or soon afterward. Only 25% of the studies reviewed had any follow-up assessment and less than 10% had follow-up assessments beyond one year. Lipsey and Wilson (1993) reviewed 156 meta-analyses of the effects of a wide range of educational, psychological, and behavioral treatments and found a mean effect size of .47 standard deviations. Posttest, short-term, and long-term effects were not distinguished, however. Given the nearly universal binding pattern that the effects of social programs dissipate over time, it is likely that the average short- and long-term effects would be substantially smaller. Program participation in the CPCs was significantly associated with eight different measures of social competence by age 15. Effects sizes were as high as .70 standard deviations, with improvements in performance of 50% or more over comparison groups. Thus, compared to many other social programs, the effects of the CPC program are relatively large. Based on this evidence, early childhood interventions like the CPCs appear to be good investments for promoting resilience among economically disadvantaged populations.

As further detailed in the chapter, early childhood interventions may be more effective than other interventions not just because they begin early in the life course or provide higher dosages. Early childhood interventions also encourage stability in school and home learning environments, and they occur at a very important time in children's development – the transition to formal schooling. Thus, these interventions support children's developmental continuity, a key factor in promoting resilience. As shown in Table 18.1 and Figure 18.1, at least three alterable factors appear that promote the likelihood of long-term intervention effects: (1) early cognitive development, as impacted by preschool intervention, (2) parental participation in children's education, and (3) the quality of elementary schools. The strong support for the cognitive advantage hypothesis found in this study indicates that programs may be more likely to have long-term effects if they directly impact cognitive and scholastic development during the early childhood years. Cognitively oriented and structured approaches like those in the CPCs as well as the Perry Preschool Program and the Abecedarian Project are illustrative of this focus.

A second but less powerful mechanism for longer-term program effects is that the intervention encourages parent involvement in school and in children's education such that when the intervention ends, parents are more likely to continue to provide the nurturance necessary to maintain learning gains. This is consistent with ecological systems theory. Because parent involvement in school appears to be a consistent mechanism for promoting long-term success from early intervention, program and schoolwide efforts to involve parents in their children's education may benefit not only early childhood interventions but, more generally, resilience. Based on the findings in this study, there are three ways to enhance parent participation to facilitate the development of protective processes: (1) require parents to participate in the program for a minimum amount of time, such as 2 days per month; (2) each early childhood center should staff a parent resource room; and (3) a diverse array of activities should be available in the centers, and they should accommodate family schedules.

That the quality of the schools in which children were enrolled mediated the effects of the duration of program participation on youth outcomes and was an independent predictor of achievement indicates that school quality can help reinforce and extend the effects of early intervention. Previous studies of the school support hypothesis (Currie & Thomas, 1998; Lee & Loeb, 1995; Reynolds et al., 1996) have provided suggestive but indirect evidence that school-related factors mediate the long-term effects of intervention. Both school mobility and school quality contributed to the transmission of effects.

Improvements in the quality of children's postprogram school environment may not only contribute independently to scholastic development but may also help maintain the effects of earlier intervention. Policies and practices to reduce the negative effects of school mobility, grade retention, and special education appear especially important in promoting healthy development because all three were associated with lower levels of performance. These and related school and family experiences deserve further attention in understanding the complex processes that link early childhood experiences to later adjustment and resilience.

References

Anderson, S., Auquier, A., Hauck, W. W., Oakes, D., Vandaele, W., & Weisberg, H. I. (1980). *Statistical methods for comparative studies: Techniques for bias reduction.* New York: Wiley.

Barnett, W. S., & Boocock, S. S. (Eds.). (1998). *Early care and education for children in poverty.* Albany: State University of New York Press.

Barnett, W. S., Young, J. W., & Schweinhart, L. J. (1998). How preschool education influences long-term cognitive development and school success: A causal model. In W. S. Barnett & S. S. Boocock (Eds.), *Early care and education for children in poverty* (pp. 167–184). Albany: State University of New York Press.

Berrueta-Clement, J. R., Schweinhart, L. J., Barnett, W. S., Epstein, A. S., & Weikart, D. P. (1984). *Changed lives: The effects of the Perry Preschool Program on youths through age 19.* Ypsilanti, MI: High/Scope.

Bronfenbrenner, U. (1975). Is early intervention effective? In M. Guttentag & E. Struening (Eds.), *Handbook of evaluation research* (Vol. 2, pp. 519–603). Beverly Hills: Sage.

Chen, H. T. (1990). *Theory-driven evaluations.* Newbury Park, CA: Sage.

Chicago Board of Education. (1988). *Chicago EARLY: Instructional activities for ages 3 to 6.* Vernon Hills, IL: ETA.

Coie, J. D., Watt, N. F., West, S. G., Harkins, J. D., Asarnow, J. R., Markman, H. J., Ramey, S. L., Shure, M. B. & Long, B. (1993). The science of prevention: A conceptual framework and some directions for a national research program. *American Psychologist, 48,* 1013–1022.

Consortium for Longitudinal Studies. (1983). *As the twig is bent . . . lasting effects of preschool programs.* Hillsdale, NJ: Erlbaum.

Cook, T. D., & Campbell, D. T. (1979). *Quasi-experimentation: Design and analysis issues for field settings.* Chicago: Rand McNally.

Cronbach, L. J. (1982). *Designing evaluations for educational and social programs.* San Francisco: Jossey-Bass.

Currie, J., & Thomas, D. (1998). *School quality and the longer-term effects of Head Start.* NBER *Working Paper* No. 6362. Cambridge, MA: National Bureau of Economic Research.

Durlak, J. A., & Wells, A. M. (1997). Primary prevention of mental health programs for children and adolescents: A meta-analytic review. *American Journal of Community Psychology, 25,* 115–152.

Guralnick, M. (Ed.). (1997). *The effectiveness of early intervention.* Baltimore: Paul H. Brookes.

Karoly, L. A., Greenwood, P. W., Everingham, S. S., Hoube, J., Kilburn, M. R., Rydell, C. P., Sanders, M., & Chiesa, J. (1998). *Investing in our children: What we know and don't know about the costs and benefits of early childhood interventions.* Santa Monica, CA: RAND.

Lally, J. R., Mangione, P. L., Honig, A. S., & Wittner, D. S. (1988, April 13–18). More pride, less delinquency: Findings from the ten-year follow-up study of the Syracuse University Family Development Research Program. *Zero to Three, 8*(4), 13–18.

Lazar, I., Darlington, R. B., Murray, H. W., & Snipper, A. S. (1982). Lasting effects of early education: A report from the consortium for longitudinal studies. *Monographs of the Society for Research in Child Development, 47* (2/3, Serial No. 195).

Lee, V. E., & Loeb, S. (1995). Where do Head Start attendees end up? One reason why preschool effects fade out. *Educational Evaluation and Policy Analysis, 17,* 62–82.

Lipsey, M. W. (1993). Theory as method: Small theories as treatments. In L. Sechrest & A. Scott (Eds.), *Understanding causes and generalizing about them. New directions for program evaluation* (No. 57, pp. 5–38). San Francisco: Jossey-Bass.

Lipsey, M. W., & Wilson, D. B. (1993). The efficacy of psychological, educational, and behavioral treatment: Confirmation from meta-analysis. *American Psychologist, 48,* 1181–1209.

Luthar, S. S., Cicchetti, D., & Becker, B. (2000). The construct of resilience: A critical evaluation and guidelines for future work *Child Development, 71,* 543–562.

Naisbitt, N. (1968). *Child–Parent Education Centers, ESEA Title I, Activity I.* Unpublished report, Chicago.

Powell, D. R. (1999). Early childhood development. In A. J. Reynolds, H. J. Walberg, & R. P. Weissberg (Eds.), *Promoting positive outcomes: Issues in children's and families' lives* (pp. 45–71). Washington, DC: Child Welfare League of America.

Ramey, S. L, & Ramey, C. T. (1992). Early educational intervention with disadvantaged children – To what effect? *Applied and Preventive Psychology, 1,* 131–140.

Ramey, C. T., & Ramey, S. L. (1998). Early intervention and early experience. *American Psychologist, 53,* 109–120.

Reynolds, A. J. (1998a). Confirmatory program evaluation: A method for strengthening causal inference. *American Journal of Evaluation, 17,* 21–35.

Reynolds, A. J. (1998b). Resilience among black urban youth: Prevalence, intervention effects and mechanisms of influence. *American Journal of Orthopsychiatry, 68,* 84–100.

Reynolds, A. J. (2000). *Success in early intervention: The Chicago Child–Parent Centers.* Lincoln: University of Nebraska Press.

Reynolds, A. J. (1999, April). *Pathways of long-term effects in the Title I Child–Parent Center Program.* Paper presented at the biennial meeting of the Society for Research in Child Development, Albuquerque, NM.

Reynolds, A. J., & Temple, J. A. (1995). Quasi-experimental estimates of the effects of a preschool intervention: Psychometric and econometric comparisons. *Evaluation Review, 19,* 347–373.

Reynolds, A. J., & Temple, J. A. (1998). Extended early childhood intervention and school achievement: Age 13 findings from the Chicago Longitudinal Study. *Child Development, 69,* 231–246.

Reynolds, A. J., Mavrogenes, N. A., Bezruczko, N., & Hagemann, M. (1996). Cognitive and family-support mediators of preschool effectiveness: A confirmatory analysis. *Child Development, 67,* 1119–1140.

Reynolds, A. J., Chang, H., & Temple, J. A. (1998). Early childhood intervention and juvenile delinquency: An exploratory analysis of the Child–Parent Centers. *Evaluation Review, 22,* 341–372.

Reynolds, A. J., Mann, E., Miedel, W., & Smokowski, P. (1997). The state of early childhood intervention: Effectiveness, myths and realities, new directions. *Focus, 19*(1), 3–11.

Reynolds, A. J., Temple, J. A., Robertson, D. L., & Mann, E. A. (2001). Long-term effects of an early childhood intervention on educational achievement and juvenile arrest: A 15-year follow-up of low-income children in public schools. *Journal of the American Medical Association, 285* (18), 2339–2346.

Rutter, M., Champion L., Quinton, D., Maughan, B., & Pickles, A. (1995). Understanding individual differences in environment-risk exposure. In P. Moen, G. H. Elder, Jr., & K. Lüscher (Eds.), *Examining lives in context: Perspectives on the ecology of human development.* Washington, DC: American Psychological Association.

Schweinhart, L. J., & Weikart, D. P. (1980). *Young children grow up: The effects of the Perry Preschool Program on youths through age 15.* Ypsilanti, MI: High/Scope Educational Research Foundation.

Schweinhart, L. J., Barnes, H. V., & Weikart, D. P. (1993). *Significant benefits: The High/Scope Perry Preschool study through age 27.* Ypsilanti, MI: High/Scope Educational Research Foundation.

Seitz, V. (1990). Intervention programs for impoverished children: A comparison of educational and family support models. *Annals of Child Development, 7,* 73–103.

Susser, M. (1973). *Causal thinking in the health sciences, concepts and strategies of epidemiology.* New York: Oxford University Press.

Tolan, P. H. (1996). How resilient is the concept of resilience? *Community Psychologist, 29,* 12–15.

U. S. General Accounting Office. (1997). *Head Start: Research provides little information on impact of current program.* Report no, HEHS-97-59. Washington, DC: GAO.

Yoshikawa, H. (1995). Long-term effects of early childhood programs on social outcomes and delinquency. *Future of Children, 5(3),* 51–75.

Wang, M. C., & Gordon, E. W. (Eds.). (1994). *Educational resilience in inner-city America: Challenges and prospects.* Hillsdale, NJ: Erlbaum.

Weissberg, R. P., & Greenberg, M. T. (1998). School and community competence-enhancement and prevention programs. In W. Damon (Ed.) *Handbook of child psychology: Child psychology in practice* (Vol. 4, pp. 877–954). New York: Wiley.

Werner, E. E., & Smith, R. S. (1992). *Overcoming the odds: High risk children from birth to adulthood.* Ithaca, NY: Cornell University Press.

Zigler, E., & Butterfield, E. C. (1968). Motivational aspects of change in IQ test performance of culturally deprived nursery school children. *Child Development, 39,* 1–14.

Zigler, E., & Styfco S. (1993). *Head Start and beyond: A national plan for extended childhood intervention.* New Haven, CT: Yale University Press.

Zigler, E., Abelson, W., Trickett, P. K., & Seitz, V. (1982). Is an intervention program necessary in order to improve economically disadvantaged children's IQ scores? *Child Development, 53,* 340–348.

Zimmerman, M. A., & Arunkumar, R. (1994). Resiliency research: Implications for schools and policy. *Social policy report* (Vol. VIII, No. 4, pp. 1–17). Ann Arbor, MI: Society for Research in Child Development.

PART III

COMMENTARIES

19

Toward Building a Better Brain

Neurobehavioral Outcomes, Mechanisms, and Processes of Environmental Enrichment

W. John Curtis and Charles A. Nelson

Research over the second half of the 20th century has painted a very consistent picture of the impact of differential environments on the brain and behavior of various nonhuman animal species. Beginning with the early pioneering work of Hebb in the 1940s (1947, 1949), scores of studies have demonstrated that rearing animals in enriched environments results in discernible differences in both brain morphology and observable behavior when compared to animals reared in standard laboratory conditions. Many different animal species have been utilized in many variations on this basic experimental design and, invariably, similar results emerge. Indeed, it has become nearly axiomatic that exposing experimental animals to enriched environments leads to positive outcomes in terms of brain development and their ability to learn.

During the early and mid-1960s, when many of the initial animal enrichment experiments were first underway, a social and political experiment, also based on the idea of environmental enrichment, was being formulated. The central idea was that enrichment of the environment of disadvantaged children would result in enhanced cognitive development and social competence beyond that which would be expected in these children given the disadvantage of poverty. The juxtaposition of these two endeavors, one occurring in the realm of biological

The writing of this chapter was made possible, in part, by a grant from the National Institutes of Health (NS34458) to the second author and, in part, by the John D. and Catherine T. MacArthur Foundation and J. S. McDonnell Foundation through their support of a research network on Early Experience and Brain Development, also to the second author.

Inquiries about this chapter should be directed to W. John Curtis, Mt. Hope Family Center, University of Rochester, 187 Edinburgh St. Rochester, NY 14608.

science and the other motivated by governmental social policy, was probably not coincidental. More likely, both were to some degree the result of a prevailing optimism in the culture during the 1960s about the potential for improving the human condition via modification of the environment.

Forty years later, at the beginning of the 21st century, substantial progress has been made in both lines of inquiry. Hundreds of studies examining the impact of enrichment on the biology and behavior of rats and other species have been published, and the results overwhelmingly appear to support the notion that being in an environment that is more complex and stimulating relative to an impoverished environment imparts great neurochemical, neuroanatomical, and behavioral advantages. Environmental enrichment studies with animals have further reinforced the idea that plasticity is a basic, and most likely inherent, property of the brain. On the other hand, over the past four decades, scores of enriched preschool intervention programs have been implemented and evaluated. The outcomes of these programs, for the most part, have been somewhat disappointing and puzzling. Immediate short-term cognitive gains were seen, but the hoped-for and expected enduring effects on IQ have largely not been obtained.

This chapter will attempt to derive a model of an effective human analogue to environmental enrichment. Given the relative lack of success of enrichment interventions with humans, considered together with the overwhelming effects seen in animal enrichment studies, it would appear that a reevaluation of human enrichment interventions from a developmental cognitive neuroscience perspective would elucidate the reasons underlying the successes and failures of human enrichment programs thus far. In addition, such a framework might provide theoretical guidance in the development of more effective human enrichment interventions. The model of human enrichment set forth will attempt to extrapolate from the extensive animal literature on enrichment the mechanisms and type of impact that enriched preschool programs may have on human brain development, cognitive abilities, and behavior.

A GENERAL DEFINITION OF ENRICHMENT

To avoid confusion over terminology, it is important to adopt a working definition of *enrichment* that could be applied to the general discussion of this subject area, and to provide a common framework on which to base comparisons between the human and animal enrichment literatures. In general, the concept of enrichment can be defined as the supplementation of naturally occurring experience (Horowitz & Paden, 1973). This early conceptualization, influential in subsequent treatments of the topic as it pertains to human development, provides a general grounding from which the term can be examined in more detail. In addition, these authors provide a useful distinction between enrichment as supplementation and enrichment as intervention. Enrichment as supplementation assumes that if the organism is left to the natural course of events adequate development will occur, whereas enrichment as intervention implies that the nonenriched environment is inadequate for ensuring normal development.

For the purposes of this chapter, enrichment will be defined as the provision of experience that supplements the environment that an organism would experience without the enrichment. Thus, using the terminology of Horowitz and Paden (1973), the types of enrichment considered here could be either supplementation or intervention. The terms *enrichment* and *environmental complexity* will be used interchangeably to some degree throughout the chapter in a way consistent with the usage employed by the particular investigator's work being reviewed.

EXPERIENCE AND THE BRAIN: A BRIEF HISTORY

In 1949 Donald Hebb published his seminal book, *The Organization of Behavior*, in which he outlined a comprehensive theory of behavior that attempted to integrate the physiology of the nervous system and behavioral psychology (Hebb, 1949). A central tenet of his theory was that experience modifies the brain. A few years before this book was published, Hebb (1947) reported on the first experiment that systematically compared the problem-solving ability of rats reared in different conditions. He reared two litters of rats in his home as pets. They were frequently out of their cages and had free run of Hebb's house (Hebb, 1949).[1] At maturity these home-raised rats scored better than laboratory-reared rats on the Hebb–Williams maze (Hebb & Williams, 1946). Hebb concluded that "*the richer experience of the pet group during development made them better able to profit by new experiences at maturity* – one of the characteristics of the 'intelligent' human being" (Hebb, 1949, p. 299; italics in the original). Subsequent replications of Hebb's research under more controlled experimental conditions resulted in similar findings (e.g., Hymovitch, 1952).

During the early 1960s, scientists at the University of California at Berkeley began to examine the relation between neurochemical changes in the brain and learning in rats. The results of a series of their early experiments confirmed their specific hypothesis of a linkage between increased cortical activity of the neurotransmitter acetylcholine (ACh), greater efficiency of synaptic transmission, and successful problem solving in rats (e.g., Krech, Rosenzweig, & Bennett, 1960). Indeed, rats that were better at learning mazes had higher ACh activity than those that were not, and it was later found that stimulation and training in fact increased the level of ACh (e.g., Bennett, Diamond, Krech, & Rosenzweig, 1964). This early work led to a now classic line of research comparing the brains of rats reared in complex environments to those reared in standard laboratory conditions.

THE ENRICHED ENVIRONMENT PARADIGM

The group of researchers at Berkeley developed an experimental paradigm that consisted of housing rats in one of three conditions, first detailed by Krech et al. (1960). The animals were placed in these conditions after they were weaned, at about 25 days of age, for approximately 80 days, and were all between 100 and 110 days of age when sacrificed for analysis of their brains.

The first of these conditions was called Environmental Complexity and Training (ECT). The animals in this condition were housed in groups of 10 to 12 in larger than standard cages, with a small maze and an assortment of toys inside. For 30 minutes each day, the rats were allowed to explore the Hebb–Williams maze, where the patterns of the barriers was changed daily, and from 60 days of age on they were given daily training on a variety of mazes.

The second condition was termed the Isolated Control (IC) condition. Littermates of the ECT rats were placed in small individual cages, could never see or come in physical contact with another rat, and were not handled by the experimenters. Finally, the third condition was termed the Social Condition (SC), which was designed to provide rats with an intermediate level of experience, representative of standard laboratory conditions, between those of the ECT and IC groups. Rats in this group, also littermates of rats in the ECT and IC conditions, were housed in ordinary laboratory conditions, with three rats in a regular laboratory colony cage. They were exposed to the ongoing activity in the room, could see other rats, and were handled once a week by the experimenters but received no special training.

Over the past four decades, this original experimental paradigm has been slightly modified, but the basic format of the ECT, IC, and SC manipulations is still employed. It is important to keep a caveat in mind when examining the animal enrichment literature utilizing this paradigm: The term enrichment must be considered in a relative sense. Standard laboratory conditions are most certainly an impoverished environment for the rat; any improvement in that circumstance by way of enrichment yields an environment more closely resembling rats' natural habitat. Thus, findings from enrichment studies primarily reflect the experiences of animals living in a relatively species-typical environment compared to those living in an impoverished environment. Greenough and his colleagues have been explicit in reiterating this point (e.g., Greenough et al., 1993), preferring to use the term environmental complexity (EC) rather than enrichment.

The following sections will provide a brief overview of environmental enrichment experiments with nonhuman species that have taken place over approximately the past 40 years. This extensive literature has indicated that being reared in enriched conditions results in changes in laboratory animals that take place within four general areas: (a) neurochemical, (b) physiological, (c) neuroanatomical, and (d) behavioral systems. Changes in each of these areas will be reviewed in turn.

NEUROCHEMICAL CHANGES

Early rat enrichment research examined neurochemical changes associated with intensive maze training, specifically changes in the cholinergic system, implicated in learning and memory. Results of these studies consistently demonstrated that the total activity of ACh was significantly greater in the cortex of the ECT rats than in the cortex of the IC rats, with the greatest increase occurring in the visual cortex (e.g., Bennett et al., 1964; Krech, Rosenzweig, & Bennett, 1962).

ECT-reared rats have been shown to have a 6% greater RNA/DNA ratio, suggesting higher metabolic activity in the brains of rats reared in enriched conditions (Bennett, 1976). There is also indirect evidence that rearing in complex environments enhances the efficiency of molecular transport through axons (Grouse, Schrier, Bennett, Rosenzweig, & Nelson, 1978).

PHYSIOLOGICAL CHANGES

Sleep patterns, often correlated with processes of learning and memory, have been examined in differentially reared rodents. EC rats spent a higher proportion of time in both slow-wave sleep and rapid eye movement sleep as early as the third week of enrichment, with the magnitude of the difference increasing with the length of time in the condition (e.g., Kiyono, Seo, & Shibagaki, 1981). Generally, electrophysiological studies have demonstrated that rats reared in enriched conditions modify their behavior more quickly in response to environmental feedback than do IC rats (e.g., Leah, Allardyce, & Cummins, 1985), and other evidence points to decreased nervous system excitability in EC rats (Juraska, Greenough, & Conlee, 1983).

NEUROANATOMICAL CHANGES

Numerous studies have demonstrated that the most obvious gross anatomical difference between EC- and IC-reared rats is in the total weight of the cortex. Replicated over 16 successive experiments, Rosenzweig, Bennett, and Diamond (1972) reported that the total cortical weight of ECT rats was on average 5% greater than that of IC rats, with an average 7.6% increase in the occipital (visual) cortex, 4% in the ventral cortex (which includes the hippocampus), and 3% in the somatosensory cortex. These changes were also found in rats blinded before being placed in the enriched condition or even when the differential rearing took place in total darkness (Rosenzweig et al., 1969). It thus appears that the brain effects seen in enriched rats are due to multisensory stimulation from the enriched environment and are not restricted to the visual modality. The observed increase in cortical weight has generally been attributed to, among other factors, a 20% to 30% increase in the number of glial cells in the brains of EC rats (Diamond, 1966). EC rats also exhibit thicker cortical regions, with an average increase in thickness of 5% overall (Diamond et al., 1964), as well as consistently larger neuronal cell bodies and nuclei than rats in the IC condition (Diamond, Linder, & Raymond, 1967).

Although a 5% increase in the weight of the cortex may not seem particularly large in an absolute sense, changes of this magnitude in such a central component of the central nervous system can, and do, result in large behavioral changes. For example, destruction of less than 5% of the tissue in the rat occipital cortex can result in a functionally blind animal (Renner & Rosenzweig, 1987), and small lesions in the cortex caused by stroke or injury in humans can result in behavioral changes of great magnitude, such as aphasia or other disorders.

During the 1970s, starting with work by William Greenough and his colleagues at the University of Illinois, enrichment research began to address how the organization of the brain is impacted by environmental complexity. Initial work from this laboratory demonstrated that rats reared in complex environments consistently had more higher-order dendritic branches and more dendritic synapses per neuron in several occipital cortical cell types and the temporal cortex, but not the frontal cortex (e.g., Greenough, Volkmar, & Juraska, 1973). Environmental enrichment also appears to actively induce synapse formation (Greenough, Hwang, & Gorman, 1985). In addition, rats reared in enriched environments have increased relative density of dendritic spines, more synapses per neuron, and more multiple synaptic boutons (Jones, Klintsova, Kilman, Sirevaag, & Greenough, 1997; Turner & Greenough, 1985). Other features indicative of greater synaptic efficiency, such as larger synaptic contacts, have also been found in EC rats (e.g., Turner & Greenough, 1985).

Neuroanatomical changes as a result of enriched rearing conditions have also been found in brain regions outside the cortex. For example, Floeter and Greenough (1979) have demonstrated structural plasticity of Purkinje cell bodies, critical in coordination of movement, in the cerebellum of the Japanese macaque as a function of rearing in differential environments. Somewhat more recently, EC rats have been shown to undergo structural modifications of the cerebellar cortex as a result of complex motor skill learning (e.g., Kleim et al., 1998).

Given the importance of the role the hippocampus plays in memory, the influence of differential rearing experiences on this brain structure would be of particular interest. Rats reared in enriched environments have been reported to have more granule cells in the dentate gyrus, a structure adjacent to the hippocampus and a key component of the hippocampal memory circuit, as well as increases in dendritic branching and overall size of the dendritic field (e.g., Susser & Wallace, 1982). Mice reared in enriched conditions showed an overall 15% increase in the depth and number of neurons in the hippocampus (Kempermann, Kuhn, & Gage, 1997).

BEHAVIORAL EFFECTS OF ENRICHMENT

At this juncture it is critical to ask, what impact does manipulation of the environment have on behavior? The most consistent finding across

studies is that of superior performance of EC animals in complex problem solving. For example, rats reared in complex environments show
advantages on tasks involving reversal of previously learned visual discrimination (Krech et al., 1962) and other tasks requiring response flexibility
(Morgan, 1973), and are superior at response inhibition in a bar pressing task (Ough, Beatty, & Khalili, 1972) and passive avoidance tasks (e.g.,
Lore, 1969).

Many studies of learning in rats reared in differential environments
have involved spatial problem-solving tasks with various types of mazes,
demonstrating improved learning in EC rats (e.g., Brown, 1968) and
mice (Kempermann et al., 1997). Also, EC rats are better able to utilize
extramaze cues in the solution of spatial problems, and they abandon a
previously forced indirect path through a maze more quickly (Luchins &
Forgus, 1955). This superior maze performance appears to be long-
lasting, even with a 300-day delay period between being taken out of
the complex environment and the beginning of the testing period
(Denenberg, Woodcock, & Rosenberg, 1968). Others have demonstrated
that pregnant rats housed in enriched conditions had offspring that
performed better on a Hebb–Williams maze than offspring of mothers
housed in isolated and control environments while pregnant (Kiyono,
Seo, Shibagaki, & Inouye, 1985). EC rats also demonstrated more organized and complex bouts of interactions with objects than IC rats, perhaps reflecting a higher level of exploratory behavior (Smith, 1972). In
addition, mice reared in enriched conditions were less fearful, and exhibited lower levels of both state and trait anxiety (Chapillon, Manneche,
Belzung, & Caston, 1999).

ALTERNATIVE EXPLANATIONS OF OBSERVED EFFECTS
OF ENRICHED ENVIRONMENTS

Several explanations have been proposed over the years to account for
the changes observed in animals reared in complex environments. These
have included the increased handling of the EC rats by human experimenters, the possibility that the deleterious effect of isolation on IC rats
may have been responsible for the observed brain differences between
the ECT and IC rats, and finally, the possibility that the complex environment and training that ECT rats were exposed to simply accelerated
the development of the normally rapidly growing brains of young rats.
A fairly extensive literature evolved that succeeded in countering these

arguments, and currently there is no credible evidence to indicate that the effects seen in these experimental animals are due to anything other than their exposure to complex environments.

ENVIRONMENTAL ENRICHMENT FOR HUMANS: EARLY CHILDHOOD EDUCATION AND ENRICHMENT

In the field of education there has historically been an interest in providing enriched preschool experiences to young children, much of it rooted in an empiricist view of the overriding importance of experience in human development. Early childhood enrichment programs such as Head Start were intended to help disadvantaged preschool-age children from poor families to literally get a head start in academics, with curricula focusing on language, cognition, and achievement motivation, so that they might begin school on an equal footing with more economically privileged children (Zigler & Valentine, 1979). A larger sociopolitical goal of such programs was to help break the cycle of poverty by increasing the probability that the targeted children would remain in school longer and thus in adulthood would be able to reap the economic benefits that are often correlated with more years of formal education. Generally, outcome studies of Head Start and other similar programs have shown initial IQ gains followed by subsequent declines, but with a positive impact on general school and social competence (Lazar, Darlington, Murray, Royce, & Snipper, 1982).

More recently, enriched preschool intervention programs developed and implemented in the 1980s by Craig Ramey and his colleagues have attempted to improve cognitive development and social competence in high-risk young children from birth to age 3 years (e.g., Ramey & Ramey, 1998). These programs were designed as research and intervention studies and thus were subject to systematic experimental control. The remainder of this section will focus on one of these programs, the Abecedarian Project, which was designed to test whether mental retardation correlated with inadequate environments could be prevented by providing intensive, high-quality preschool programs beginning shortly after birth and continuing at least until children entered kindergarten (Ramey & Ramey, 1992).

Children enrolled in this program were biologically healthy but came from very poor, high-risk families with a mean maternal education of 10 years and a mean maternal IQ of 85. Children were randomly assigned to intervention and control groups at birth. The intervention group received pediatric follow-up services (as did the controls) and were placed in an early childhood education program. The curriculum was targeted at multiple developmental domains and included work in cognitive, motor, language, and social skills as developmentally appropriate. Children started the program at 6 weeks of age, and attendance was full day, 5 days per week, 50 weeks per year through age 3 years (Ramey & Ramey, 1992).

At age 3, the mean IQ score of the intervention group was 101 and that of the control group was 84. Further, 95% of the children in the intervention group had IQ scores of at least 85 compared to only 49% of the children in the control group. Eighty-six percent of the control group children of mothers with the lowest IQs (below 70) had IQs below 85 at 4.5 years, whereas none of the intervention children with low-IQ mothers had IQ scores below 85 (Ramey & Ramey, 1992). At 12 years of age, the mean IQ of the intervention group was approximately 93 and that of the controls was 88, and at age 15 there was a 4.6 point IQ score difference in favor of the intervention group. At age 12 and at age 15, the intervention group scored significantly higher on a variety of achievement tests, and the intervention group had a 50% reduction in the rate of failing a grade during elementary school (Campbell & Ramey, 1995).

This project in particular has provided evidence that those children who began the program with greater risk benefited the most (Martin, Ramey, & Ramey, 1990). Children whose mothers had IQs less than 70 had IQs, on average, 21 points higher than the control children at $4^{1}/_{2}$ years of age. This is in contrast to the mean gain of approximately 8 IQ points for the intervention sample as a whole.

Several basic conclusions about the impact of enriched preschool programs developed since the 1960s, as discussed in comprehensive reviews by Farran (2000) and Barnett (1996), are as follows. (1) The programs all raise the IQ of children during their enrollment in the program, by as much as one standard deviation, with the largest IQ gains seen in children from programs that began in infancy (Farran, 2000). However, with the exception of the Abecedarian Project, IQ effects are nonexistent by or before age 12. In this context, it is important to remember that animal studies of enrichment, which generally employ enrichment that is all-encompassing for the organism and is not aimed at specific behaviors, show a pervasive, generalized impact on the brain and learning ability. Thus, specific narrow effects, such as an increase in IQ, may not be reasonably expected from preschool programs that provide broad-based enrichment. (2) Generally, improvement in achievement test scores is not maintained (Barnett, 1996). (3) There is fairly convincing evidence that these programs have had a long-term positive impact on school success by reducing grade retention and enrollment in special education classes and by increasing high school graduation rates.

It appears that early optimism at the inception of Head Start was perhaps unwarranted, with a decided underestimate of the depth and breadth of the intervention needed to produce long-term effects on IQ. However, the Abecedarian Project has demonstrated that more intensive efforts may have greater impact. The initial optimism of Hunt (1964) and others that IQ was easily changeable was unfounded, but at the same time the pessimistic view of Jensen (1969) that IQ could not be greatly impacted due to its largely genetic component was also overstated.

RATS 1, HUMANS 0: SOME FACTORS MEDIATING THE EFFECTIVENESS OF HUMAN ENRICHMENT

How does one make sense of the lack of overwhelming success of human enrichment programs in light of the huge impact that environmental complexity has on the brain and behavior of the rat, despite parallels between the experimental manipulations of rat environments and enriched preschool programs? For example, children from impoverished environments are placed in enriched preschool programs, where they are exposed to a variety of stimulating activities. In parallel fashion, typical animal enrichment experiments involve placing young animals, who would normally be reared in standard deprived laboratory conditions, in a so-called enriched environment. It could be hypothesized that the brain development of at-risk children placed in enriched preschools might proceed differently from that of at-risk children not exposed to an enriched preschool environment, realizing advantages similar to those found in the brains of rats reared in enriched laboratory conditions.

Of course, great caution must be employed when drawing analogies between findings from nonhuman animals and humans; rats and humans differ vastly on many key anatomical and cognitive variables. Generally, it is difficult to compare the complex human system, with multiple levels of higher cognition, emotion, language, and social relationships, with that of the rat. However, the relevance of knowledge gained from other species to human processes is fairly well established (Wahlsten & Gottlieb, 1997), and many nonhuman animals share cognitive processes that have characteristics in common with many conceptions of human intelligence (Griffin, 1982). In addition, mechanisms of memory formation at the molecular level are quite similar in humans and nonhuman animals (Kandel & Hawkins, 1992).

Are the Rat and Human Enrichment Paradigms Comparable?

Intensity and Quantity of Exposure

The first general observation when comparing human and rat enrichment is the all-encompassing nature of the modification of the rat environment compared to the modifications to the human environment by participation in an enriched preschool intervention. For example, in the Abecedarian Project, one of the most intensive programs to date, the intervention children were in the preschool setting for approximately 8 hours per day, 5 days a week, for the first 4 years of life, and home visits and other services were offered to their parents. However, these children were still spending most of their time living in the disadvantaged environment the program was attempting to supplement. Also, preschool enrichment programs are by definition time limited. After participation in these programs, children move on to standard public school classrooms, which, relative to the Abecedarian Project, are probably somewhat impoverished. Thus, it is perhaps not surprising that the long-term impact on the cognitive development of these children was minimal. In fact, early outcome studies of human enrichment programs suggested that the effects of these programs was directly proportional to their intensity (Horowitz & Paden, 1973).

In comparison, when rats are placed in their enriched environment, they experience a change that is extraordinarily complete and comprehensive, with every level of their system, from molecular to behavioral, impacted. The enriched environment is their only environment, 24 hours a day, 7 days a week. Recent work in the animal literature on the mechanisms of neuronal change resulting from enrichment has indicated that an important factor in such change is continuous exposure to the enriched environment (Torasdotter, Metsis, Henriksson, Winblad, & Mohammed, 1998).

Adoption, although not generally thought of as a form of environmental enrichment, is perhaps more comparable to the intensity of enrichment typically experienced by experimental animals. Adoption is a pervasive change in the environmental circumstances of the adoptee and can have significant influence on the development of the adopted child. Several major longitudinal studies of adoption have demonstrated that children adopted early in life had IQ scores later in life at least one standard deviation higher than those of children from comparable demographic backgrounds (e.g., Weinberg, Scarr, & Waldman, 1992).

Determining the amount of intervention necessary to shift IQ this much, in this case being reared in a different, ostensibly better environment than one ordinarily would have been in, is clearly well beyond the scope of any programmatic intervention that would be practical or ethical. However, it does provide an interesting parallel to the scope of enrichment provided in animal studies, and suggests that human enrichment programs do not provide a nearly intensive enough or sufficiently long-lasting intervention to significantly impact IQ.

The intensity or degree of enrichment of the enriched environment might also be examined. Could a so-called superenriched intervention produce greater results beyond those generated by a typically enriched environment? The impact of superenriched conditions (SEC), environments set up to be a close approximation to the natural environment of the animal, have been examined to see the effects beyond those resulting from typical laboratory-enriched environments (e.g., Kuenzle & Knusel, 1974). The consensus from these studies is that small but reliable gains in brain weight and behavioral outcomes in favor of the SEC rats over standard EC rats are seen.

It is also important to consider the possibility that the impoverished groups of rats are, relative to their enriched counterparts, so much more impoverished than disadvantaged children not enrolled in enriched preschools that the effects found are not directly comparable to those in humans. Thus, there may not be a simple linear relationship between level of enrichment and enhancement of functioning. Most likely, enhancement in functioning increases steadily at first, but then levels off at a point after which increased enrichment has little or no added effect.

Timing of Exposure

One early investigation in the animal literature examined the impact of environmental enrichment on newborn rat pups (Malkasian & Diamond, 1971). Rat pups 6 days of age and their mother were placed in enriched cages, and were compared to pups reared by their mother in standard laboratory cages. The brains of 14-day-old rat pups, after being housed in the enriched cage for only 8 days, had cortices that were 7% to 11% thicker than those of the control pups. This thickness difference reportedly was the largest encountered in rats by the group working in the Berkeley laboratories (Diamond, 1988). Rats examined at 19 days and

28 days also showed comparable cortical thickness differences in more areas of the cortex.

These results suggest that brain responses to environmental enrichment can occur very early in the life span of the rat, lending support to the notion of the importance of beginning human enrichment programs at a very early age. Also important to consider is the continued enrichment of rats beyond the human age equivalent of early childhood. Rats typically remain in an enriched environment for 30 to 60 days. Translating from the rat to the human life span, the rats experience enrichment from early childhood to early adolescence. Although measurable gains in neuroanatomical variables have been found in rats housed in enriched cages for as little as a week, continued enrichment may be critical for the maintenance of the effects accrued early in the life span. To provide a more comparable paradigm, studies examining the impact of removing rats from an enriched environment after brief exposure and returning them to standard laboratory conditions might be informative. It is important to consider that no enrichment maintenance program has been built into a human enrichment program, and the short-term cognitive gains made in infancy and early childhood may indeed be preserved if, as in animal experiments, children are exposed to an enriched environment for a longer period of time.

MECHANISMS OF ENRICHMENT: SO HOW DOES THE ENVIRONMENT GET INTO THE BRAIN?

Understanding the mechanisms by which adding toys and spatial complexity to the surroundings of a laboratory rat produces neuroanatomical and behavioral changes might allow some extrapolation to possible mechanisms of the impact of enrichment in humans, as well as provide insight into what types of enrichment might be effective in facilitating cognitive gains in humans. Such knowledge may assist policy makers in formulating realistic expectations concerning how much impact enrichment could possibly have in humans.

The mechanisms of impact of an enriched environment can be broken down into two vastly general phases: (1) Experience "gets into" the brain and results in changes in the nervous system, and (2) these resultant changes are subsequently manifested in the observed behavior of the organism. The first phase begins as soon as the rat is placed in the new environment. Immediately, its sensory systems detect the features of the environment, such as visually interesting stimuli and a variety of objects in varying locations available for tactile exploration. The perceptual systems act as a sort of experiential gate through which a physical representation of the environment enters the organism. The sensory systems have afferent connections to relevant brain areas, and hence at the beginning of this perceptual/sensory chain the environment interacts with the brain, with motor and sensory components acting in concert to allow navigation and exploration of the environment.

Greenough et al. (1993) have stressed that a necessary condition for the behavioral and brain effects of enrichment to be manifested in rats is direct physical interaction with the environment. Animals reared inside an enriched environment but kept in cages to prevent them from physically interacting with the environment do not show the brain or behavioral effects of their littermates that are allowed to interact physically with the enriched environment (Ferchmin, Bennett, & Rosenzweig, 1975). There is also evidence that direct physical interaction with the environment may be important for human development, as exemplified by the work of Bertenthal, Campos, and Barrett (1984), suggesting that interaction with the environment produced by self-locomotion may be an important component of cognitive and emotional development in early childhood.

Together, these motor and sensory processes facilitate learning. How learning-related neuronal activity is translated into changes in the structure of neurons, and the mechanisms by which environmental experience is translated into structural modifications of neuronal connections, are not yet completely understood (Torasdotter et al., 1998). It appears that the general mechanism responsible for this phenomenon is gene expression, which is one of the fundamental ways that cells adjust to changes and demands placed upon them (Greenough et al., 1993). This process involves the activation of genes in the nucleus of the cell, whereby messenger RNA (mRNA) is transcribed from the genes and codes for the proteins necessary for the formation of new synapses and dendrites. Several studies have begun to show a direct link between gene expression processes and the structural changes resulting from learning (e.g., Alcantra, Saks, & Greenough, 1991).

The second general phase in the process of the impact of enrichment on the brain is in the output, or how these neuronal changes are translated into the observed changes in behavior. If neurons have more synapses, then there is more opportunity for these synapses to form or participate in networks, leading to quicker and more efficient processing. This, in turn, would manifest itself in observable behavior. The behavioral attributes that would correlate with greater levels of neuronal connectivity are most likely the hallmark characteristics of increased flexibility in problem solving seen in rats exposed to complex environments. Finally, it is important to note that the cycle of modification of an organism in an enriched environment builds upon itself in the form of a feedback loop from the second phase to the first, with subsequent change building upon change resulting from previous experiences with the environment.

A MODEL OF HUMAN ENRICHMENT

In attempting to construct a model of effective human enrichment, it would be instructive to examine the specific components of an intervention in order to ascertain parallels in the animal literature that might inform the design of effective enrichment interventions for humans. Figure 19.1 presents a schematic of a general model of the impact of environmental enrichment on a human. The right side of the figure includes the behavioral outcomes that might presumably be the result of the selected modes of enrichment listed on the left side of the figure. The list of possible enrichment modes is not meant to be exhaustive; rather, it is limited to the modes of enrichment commonly employed in typical human enrichment programs similar to Head Start. Although there are many modes of enrichment (i.e., sensory, motor, cognitive, social, emotional) that could be addressed, the model to be developed here will use cognition as a model system.

The behavioral outcomes are mediated through two general pathways, illustrated in the center of Figure 19.1. The first, extensively studied in animals, involves changes that occur at the multiple levels within complex molecular, neurochemical, and neuroanatomical processes such as gene expression and alterations in neurotransmitter activity. The second pathway, although less exhaustively studied in animals, is highly salient for humans and involves the realm of social-emotional functioning. This includes factors such as the emotional well-being of the child or family, supportiveness of teachers, and other processes at the macro level of behavior, family, and community systems. Figure 19.1 also illustrates moderators, or processes that play a role in determining the degree to which the benefits of enrichment are actualized. These include factors such as genetics, the amount of time spent in the enriched environment, and the intensity of the enrichment.

In the ensuing discussion, it will generally be assumed that the major mechanisms and observable effects on the human brain as a result of

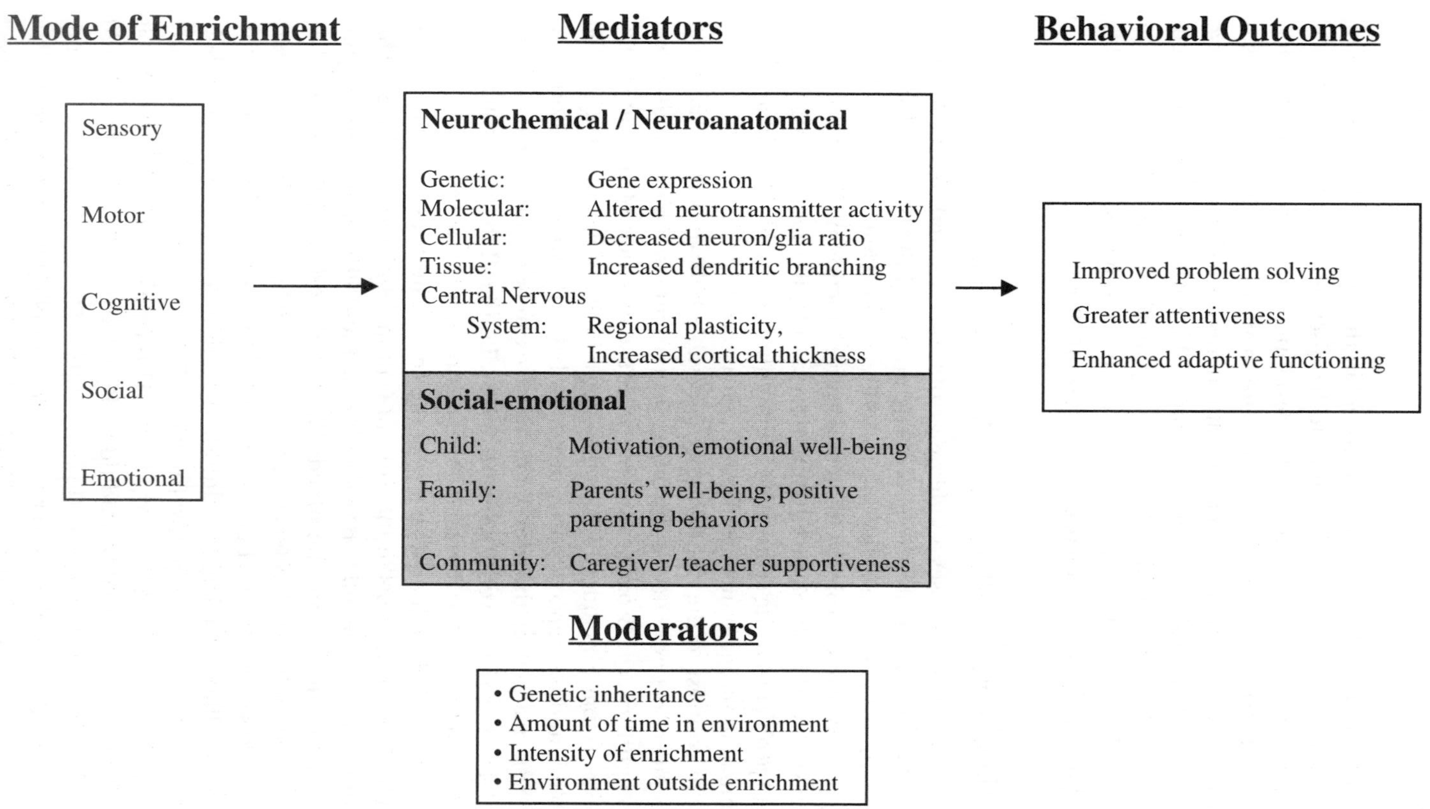

Mode of Enrichment

Sensory

Motor

Cognitive

Social

Emotional

Mediators

Neurochemical / Neuroanatomical

Genetic:	Gene expression
Molecular:	Altered neurotransmitter activity
Cellular:	Decreased neuron/glia ratio
Tissue:	Increased dendritic branching
Central Nervous System:	Regional plasticity, Increased cortical thickness

Social-emotional

Child:	Motivation, emotional well-being
Family:	Parents' well-being, positive parenting behaviors
Community:	Caregiver/teacher supportiveness

Moderators

- Genetic inheritance
- Amount of time in environment
- Intensity of enrichment
- Environment outside enrichment

Behavioral Outcomes

Improved problem solving

Greater attentiveness

Enhanced adaptive functioning

FIGURE 19.1 A general model of the impact of enrichment on a living organism.

enrichment would parallel those found in the rat. The characteristics of the human enrichment strategies to be discussed have primarily been adapted from descriptions of the developmental domains embedded in the Partners for Learning intervention utilized by the Abecedarian Project (Ramey & Ramey, 1998). Components from this intervention have been utilized because it is, to date, one of the most successful human enrichment projects. In addition, key components of enrichment environments designed for other animal species that may have some applicability to humans have been incorporated into the model.

A Model System: Cognition

Cognition encompasses a wide range of functions, and the relationship between the observable aspects of cognition and the brain is quite general, in that many brain regions, including cortical and subcortical areas, appear to play key roles in higher cognitive functioning. For a rat, cognitive skills can probably be circumscribed as adaptive motor, navigational, and problem-solving skills, most commonly measured by the ability of the animal to navigate successfully through a maze.

In contrast to the rat, defining observable behaviors in humans that might reflect evidence of the impact of enrichment on cognition is less straightforward. Broadly speaking, a consensus view of human intelligence is that it includes abstract thinking and reasoning, problem-solving ability, and the capacity to acquire knowledge (Snyderman & Rothman, 1988). In addition, theories of intelligence can be characterized as either low-level or high-level (Anderson, 1992). Low-level theories typically regard intelligence as a parameter of neurological functioning, a largely genetically determined attribute of the central nervous system that have their theoretical roots in the work of Galton (e.g., Eysenck, 1998). This would include cognitive processing speed and efficiency, memory, and other functions often subsumed under the general rubric of executive functioning. Eysenck refers to this type of intelligence as *biological intelligence* (Eysenck, 1998). High-level theories, on the other hand, conceptualize intelligence as largely culturally determined and as an experientially driven attribute of cognitive functions. Their tradition is rooted in the work of Binet (e.g., Sternberg, 1985). This type of intelligence is what is purportedly measured by traditional IQ tests and is sometimes referred to as *psychometric intelligence* (Eysenk, 1998). The importance of making these distinctions here is to reiterate that, depending on how an enrichment intervention is designed and evaluated, it may or may not impact intelligence and cognition, as defined and measured by these two major theoretical perspectives.

Enrichment could potentially impact both of these types of human intelligence. Successful enriched preschool programs have typically concentrated their efforts on enhancing cognitive functioning in areas that are believed to directly impact later school performance, which generally correspond to psychometric intelligence. For this cognitive realm, which generally encompasses problem-solving and language skills, the Partners for Learning curriculum specifically stresses training in cause-and-effect relationships, number concepts, and reasoning. In language, the curriculum emphasizes working with books, learning words, dialogue, and other activities that are designed to enhance language skills.

The level of enhancement of these types of cognitive skills has been assessed primarily by the traditional IQ test, as well as school achievement tests. The immediate gains seen in this realm suggest that this form of cognition is relatively plastic, at least for short periods of time. However, the lack of enduring change perhaps reflects that enrichment interventions for humans may not reach a critical intensity threshold, and thus do not produce long-lasting changes in the human brain. An alternative explanation is that the subsequent home and school experiences of these children, along with other potent negative environmental influences in the children's lives, do not support the maintenance of the gains made in an enriched program.

Also important to consider in this context is that brain development in humans is a very protracted process relative to that in the rat, with myelination and synaptic pruning continuing in some brain regions into puberty. Thus, in humans, the outcome of environmental events impacting brain development may be less stable and predictable than in the rat. It is also possible that by focusing enrichment on children in the first 3 years of life, we are not capitalizing on a protracted sensitive period in brain development for higher cognition and social competence that may extend into middle childhood and beyond.

Perhaps a more promising cognitive realm that might yield long-term effects from enrichment is the area of biological intelligence. Strategies for enriching these skills might include training in object permanence, memory skills, sorting and classifying, and novel problem solving. In addition, enhancing the skills involved in flexibility and creativity in problem solving would be important. The global brain changes that have been demonstrated in the rat, such as the reduced neuron/glia ratio and more complex dendritic branching, may manifest themselves behaviorally in these more basic cognitive operations. In addition, the brain areas that mediate these basic cognitive skills, including the frontal cortex and hippocampus, are still undergoing significant development during infancy and early childhood.

Unfortunately, in evaluating participants in enriched preschool programs, there have generally not been measures of general cognitive functioning utilizing specific neuropsychological tests that might be more sensitive to gains made in this sort of intelligence, such as specific assessments of memory or executive functioning, or nonverbal intelligence tests such as Raven's (1938) Progressive Matrices test, that tap into efficiency of processing. If there are brain changes in humans as a result of environmental enrichment parallel to those found in rats, it is likely that they would underlie performance on these types of measures, more so than performance on traditional psychometric measures of IQ that tend to measure crystallized intelligence.

Social and Emotional Functioning

Although enrichment geared to cognition provides an ideal framework for drawing an analogy between animal and human enrichment, taking into account social and emotional functioning is a necessity for a complete human enrichment model. There is some evidence from the animal literature that enrichment benefits emotional functioning: For example, mice exposed to environmental enrichment appear to be less emotionally reactive (Chapillon et al., 1999). However, comparing the emotional system of a mouse to that of a human is a somewhat tenuous proposition; thus, utilizing animal findings on emotion to inform human enrichment may not be as useful as comparisons from cognition.

Key components of the Abecedarian Project's curriculum do target social and emotional development, with emphasis on self-image, sharing, fostering creative play, and discussion of needs and feelings. It is not clear what specific brain areas might be involved in mediating social competence. However, the inhibitory and coordinating roles of executive functioning, mediated by the frontal cortex, may play a central role, as well as brain regions involved with attention.

IMPLICATIONS AND CONCLUSIONS

Many questions concerning enrichment of human potential remain unanswered. One obvious question is whether or not environmental enrichment of children from relatively deprived backgrounds has an impact on the neuroanatomy and/or neurochemistry of these children. This can be easily determined in other animal species by direct examination of their brains after exposure to a particular environment without the clear moral and ethical constraints that would prohibit such research methodology with humans.

One potential line of investigation that would allow some inferences to be made about the impact of enriched environments on the brain would be to perform neuroimaging studies of children who have participated in enriched preschool programs and compare them to matched control children who have not had the benefit of such a program. However, even with the great advances in spatial resolution of functional magnetic resonance imaging (fMRI), there is currently no neuroimaging tool that would allow a direct determination of dendritic branching or the creation of new synapses in the human brain. However, by examining the functioning of the brain with fMRI during tasks that require application of various cognitive skills, comparisons of utilization of brain areas could be made, and inferences drawn concerning the efficiency and architecture of cognitive processing. Also, magnetic resonance spectroscopy (MRS) could be employed to examine neurochemical changes as a result of exposure to enrichment. Finally, event-related potentials (ERPs) could be employed to examine the temporal aspects and efficiency of processing in children exposed to different environments.

Further investigations with rats, for example placing them in an enriched environment for only 8 hours per day (to mirror the human condition) and comparing the impact of this level of enrichment to that of continuous exposure to an enriched environment, might be informative. Placing rats in an enriched environment soon after birth and then removing them at an age equivalent in human terms to the age at which children begin regular schooling could provide a closer analogue to human enrichment. Carefully assessing the level of retention of improved problem solving across time might elucidate the process of retention of exposure to enrichment. Demonstrating loss of ability in such an experiment would serve as an analogue to the fadeout of gains seen in children after they finish their participation in human enrichment programs.

It would seem probable that the interventions provided to humans simply are not intensive enough to show substantial results. It is important to consider that one of the primary shortcomings of the human enrichment interventions in this regard is that they do not have a contextual focus (Farran, 2001). None of the programs to date have attempted to create an enrichment for the family, or for the broader social and economic context of the target child, that might include increasing economic resources, improvement of housing conditions, or providing a safe, violence-free living environment. Enrichment programs designed to impact the broad range of contexts and systems in which the disadvantaged child functions would be more likely to show effects than the more narrowly focused programs attempted thus far. Of course, the economic resources and political will necessary to implement such a far-reaching enrichment intervention may not be immediately available. Given the relative complexity of the human system, it is quite possible that the maximally effective enrichment intervention may not yet have been implemented.

Note

1. The second author, who was an undergraduate at McGill in the 1970s, was told that Hebb's wife actually did forbid the rats to have access to the bedroom, although this story may be apocryphal.

References

Alcantra, A. A., Saks, N. D., & Greenough, W. T. (1991). Fos is expressed in the rat during forelimb reaching task. *Society for Neuroscience Abstracts, 17,* 141.

Anderson, M. (1992). *Intelligence and development: A cognitive theory.* Oxford: Blackwell.

Barnett, W. S. (1996). Long-term effects of early childhood programs on cognitive and school outcomes. *Future Children, 5,* 25–50.

Bennett, E. L. (1976). Cerebral effects of differential experiences and training. In M. R. Rosenzweig & E. L. Bennett (Eds.), *Neural mechanisms of learning and memory* (pp. 279–289). Cambridge, MA: MIT Press.

Bennett, E. L., Diamond, M. C., Krech, D., & Rosenzweig, M. R. (1964). Chemical and anatomical plasticity of the brain, *Science, 46,* 610–619.

Bertenthal, B., Campos, J., & Barrett, K. (1984). Self-produced locomotion: An organizer of emotional, cognitive, and social development in infancy. In R. Emde & R. Harmon (Eds.), *Continuities and discontinuities in development* (pp. 175–210). New York: Plenum

Brown, R. T. (1968). Early experience and problem-solving ability. *Journal of Comparative and Physiological Psychology, 65,* 433–440.

Campbell, F. A., & Ramey, C. T. (1995). Cognitive and school outcomes for high-risk African-American students at middle adolescence: Positive effects of early intervention. *American Educational Research Journal, 32,* 743–772.

Chapillon, P., Manneche, C., Belzung, C., & Caston, J. (1999). Rearing environmental enrichment in two inbred strains of mice: 1. Effects on emotional reactivity. *Behavior Genetics, 29,* 41–46.

Denenberg, V. H., Woodcock, J. M., & Rosenberg, K. M. (1968). Long-term effects of preweaning and postweaning free-environment experience on rat problem-solving behavior. *Journal of Comparative and Physiological Psychology, 66,* 533–535.

Diamond, M. C. (1988). *Enriching heredity.* News York: Free Press.

Diamond, M. C., Law, F., Rhodes, H., Lindner, B., Rosenzweig, M. R., Krech, D., & Bennett, E. l. (1966). Increases in cortical depth and glia numbers in rats subjected to enriched environments. *Journal of Comparative Neurology, 128,* 117–126.

Diamond, M. C., Linder, B., & Raymond, A. (1967). Extensive cortical depth measurements and neuron size increases in the cortex of environmentally enriched rats. *Journal of Comparative Neurology, 131,* 357–364.

Eysenck, H. J. (1998). *Intelligence.* New Brunswick, NJ: Transaction.

Farran, D. C. (2000). Another decade of interventions for children who are low income or disabled: What do we know now? In J. P. Shonkoff & S. J. Meisels (Eds.), *Handbook of early childhood intervention* (2nd ed., pp. 510–548). New York: Cambridge University Press.

Farran, D. C. (2001). Critical periods and early intervention. In D. B. Bailey, F. Symons, J. Bruer, & J. Lichtman (Eds.), *Critical thinking about critical periods* (pp. 233–266). Baltimore: Paul Brookes.

Ferchmin, P. A., Bennett, E. L., & Rosenzweig, M. R. (1975). Direct contact with enriched environment is required to alter cerebral weights in rats. *Journal of Comparative and Physiological Psychology, 88,* 360–367.

Floeter, M. K. & Greenough, W. T. (1979). Cerebellar plasticity: Modification of Purkinje cell structure by differential rearing in monkeys. *Science, 206,* 227–229.

Greenough, W. T., Hwang, H. M. F., & Gorman, C. (1985). Evidence for active synapse formation, or altered post-synaptic metabolism, in visual cortex of rats reared in complex environments. *Proceedings of the National Academy of Sciences, 82,* 4549–4552.

Greenough, W. T., Volkmar, F. R., & Juraska, J. M. (1973). Effects of rearing complexity on dendritic branching in frontolateral and temporal cortex of the rat. *Experimental Neurology, 41,* 371–378.

Greenough, W. T., Wallace, C. S., Alcantra, A. A., Anderson, B. J., Hawrylak, N., Sirevaag, A. M., Weiler, I. J., & Withers, G. S. (1993). Development of the brain: Experience affects the structure of neurons, glia, and blood vessels. In N. J. Anastasiow & S. Harel (Eds.). *At-risk infants: Interventions, families, and research* (pp. 173–185). Baltimore: Paul H. Brookes.

Griffin, D. R. (Ed.). (1982). *Animal mind – human mind.* New York: Springer-Verlag.

Grouse, L. D., Schrier, B. K., Bennett, E. L., Rosenzweig, M. R., & Nelson, P. G. (1978). Sequence diversity studies of rat brain RNA: Effects of environmental complexity on rat brain RNA diversity. *Journal of Neurochemistry, 30,* 191–203.

Hebb, D. O. (1947). The effects of early experience on problem-solving at maturity. *American Psychologist, 2,* 306–307.

Hebb, D. O. (1949). *The organization of behavior: A neuropsychological theory.* New York: Wiley.

Hebb, D. O., & Williams, K. (1946). A method of rating animal intelligence. *Journal of General Psychology, 34,* 56–65.

Horowitz, F. D., & Paden, L. Y. (1973). The effectiveness of environmental intervention programs. In B. M. Caldwell & H. N. Ricciuti (Eds.), *Review of child development research* (Vol. 3, pp. 331–402). Chicago: University of Chicago Press.

Hunt, J. M. (1964). The psychological basis for using pre-school enrichment as an antidote for cultural deprivation. *Merrill-Palmer Quarterly, 10,* 209–248.

Hymovitch, B. (1952). The effects of experimental variations on problem solving in the rat. *Journal of Comparative and Physiological Psychology, 45,* 313–321.

Jensen, A. R. (1969). How much can we boost IQ and scholastic achievement? *Harvard Educational Review, 39,* 1–123.

Jones, T. A., & Greenough, W. T. (1996). Ultrastructural evidence for increased contact between astrocytes and synapses in rats reared in a complex environment. *Neurobiology of Learning and Memory, 65,* 48–56.

Jones, T. A., Klintsova, A. Y., Kilman, V. L., Sirevaag, A. M., & Greenough, W. T. (1997). Induction of multiple synapses by experience in the visual cortex of adult rats. *Neurobiology of Learning and Memory, 68,* 13–20.

Juraska, J. M., Greenough, W. T., & Conlee, J. W. (1983). Differential rearing affects responsiveness of rats to depressant and convulsant drugs. *Physiology and Behavior, 31,* 711–715.

Kandel, E. R., & Hawkins, R. D. (1992). The biological basis of learning and individuality. *Scientific American, 267,* 79–86.

Kempermann, G., Kuhn, H. G., & Gage, F. H. (1997). More hippocampal neurons in adult mice living in an enriched environment. *Nature, 386,* 493–495.

Kiyono, S., Seo, M. L., & Shibagahi, M. (1981). Effects of rearing environments upon sleep-waking parameters in rats. *Physiology and Behavior, 26,* 391–395.

Kiyono, S., Seo, M. L., Shibagaki, M., & Inouye, M. (1985). Facilitative effects of maternal environmental enrichment on maze learning in rat offspring. *Physiology and Behavior, 34,* 431–435.

Kleim, J. A., Swain, R. A., Armstrong, K. A., Napper, R. M. A., Jones, T. A., & Greenough, W. T. (1998). Selective synaptic plasticity within the cerebellar cortex following complex motor skill learning. *Neurobiology of Learning and Memory, 69,* 274–289.

Krech, D., Rosenzweig, M. R., & Bennett, E. L. (1960). Effects of environmental complexity and training on brain chemistry. *Journal of Comparative and Physiological Psychology, 53,* 509–519.

Krech, D., Rosenzweig, M. R., & Bennett, E. L. (1962). Relations between brain chemistry and problem-solving among rats raised in enriched and impoverished environments. *Journal of Comparative and Physiological Psychology, 55,* 801–807.

Kuenzle, C. C., & Knusel, A. (1974). Mass training of rats in a superenriched environment. *Physiology and Behavior, 13,* 205–210.

Lazar, I., Darlington, R., Murray, H., Royce, J., & Snipper, A. (1982). Lasting effects of early education: A report from the Consortium for Longitudinal Studies. *Monographs of the Society for Research in Child Development, 47* (Serial No. 195).

Leah, J., Allardyce, H., & Cummins, R. (1985). Evoked cortical potential correlates of rearing environment in rats. *Biological Psychology, 20,* 21–29.

Lore, R. K. (1969). Pain avoidance behavior of rats reared in restricted and enriched environments. *Developmental Psychology, 1,* 482–484.

Luchins, A. S., & Forgus, R. H. (1955). The effects of differential post-weaning environment on the rigidity of an animal's behavior. *The Journal of Genetic Psychology, 86,* 51–58.

Malkasian, D., & Diamond, M. C. (1971). The effect of environmental manipulation on the morphology of the neonatal rat brain. *International Journal of Neuroscience, 2,* 161–170.

Martin, S. L., Ramey, C. T., & Ramey, S. L. (1990). The prevention of intellectual impairment in children of impoverished families: Findings of a randomized trial of educational daycare. *American Journal of Public Health, 80,* 844–847.

Morgan, M. J. (1973). Effects of postweaning environment of learning in the rat. *Animal Behaviour, 21,* 429–442.

Ough, B. R., Beatty, W. W., & Khalili, J. (1972). Effects of isolated and enriched rearing on response inhibition. *Psychonomic Science, 27,* 293–294.

Ramey, C. T., & Ramey, S. L. (1992). Effective early intervention. *Mental Retardation, 30,* 337–345.

Ramey, C. T., & Ramey, S. L. (1998). Prevention of intellectual disabilities: Early interventions to improve cognitive development. *Preventive Medicine, 27,* 224–232.

Raven, J. C. (1938). *Progressive matrices.* London: Lewis.

Renner, M. J., & Rosenzweig, M. R. (1987). *Enriched and impoverished environments: Effects on brain and behavior.* New York: Springer-Verlag.

Rosenzweig, M. R., Bennett, E. L., & Diamond, M. C. (1972). Brain changes in response to experience. *Scientific American, 226,* 22–29.

Rosenzweig, M. R., Bennett, E. L., Diamond, M. C., Wu, S. Y., Slagle, R., & Saffran, E. (1969). Influence of environmental complexity and visual stimulation on development of occipital cortex in the rat. *Brain Research, 14,* 427–445.

Smith, H. V. (1972). Effects of environmental enrichment on open-field activity and Hebb–Williams problem solving in rats. *Journal of Comparative and Physiological Psychology, 80,* 163–168.

Snyderman, M., & Rothman, S. (1988). *The IQ controversy, the media, and public policy.* New Brunswick, NJ: Transaction.

Sternberg, R. J. (1985). *Beyond IQ: A triarchic theory of human intelligence.* Cambridge: Cambridge University Press.

Susser, E. R., & Wallace, R. B. (1982). The effects of environmental complexity on the hippocampal formation of the adult rat. *Acta Neurobiologica Experimentalis, 42,* 203–207.

Torasdotter, M., Metsis, M., Henriksson, B. G., Winblad, B., & Mohammed, A. H. (1998). Environmental enrichment results in higher levels of nerve growth factor mRNA in the rat visual cortex and hippocampus. *Behavioural Brain Research, 93,* 83–90.

Turner, A. M., & Greenough, W. T. (1985). Differential rearing effects on rat visual cortex synapses. I. Synaptic and neuronal density and synapses per neuron. *Brain Research, 329,* 195–203.

Wahlsten, D., & Gottlieb, G. (1997). The invalid separation of effects of nature and nurture: Lessons from animal experimentation. In R. J. Sternberg &

E. Grigorenko (Eds.), *Intelligence, heredity, and environment* (pp. 163–192). Cambridge: Cambridge University Press.

Weinberg, R. A., Scarr, S., & Waldman, I. D. (1992). The Minnesota Transracial Adoption Study: A follow-up of IQ test performance at adolescence. *Intelligence, 16,* 117–135.

Zigler, E., & Valentine, J. (Eds.). (1979). *Project head start: A legacy of the war on poverty.* New York: Free Press.

20

Genetic Influences on Risk and Protection

Implications for Understanding Resilience

Michael Rutter

CONCEPT OF RESILIENCE

Resilience has been conceptualized in several somewhat different ways (see Luthar, Cicchetti, & Becker, 2000; Masten, 2001; Rutter, 1999, 2000a) but, in essence, the starting point is a recognition that for all kinds of adverse experiences there is immense variation in how people respond. Some individuals appear to succumb to the most minor stresses, whereas others seem to cope successfully with the most terrible experiences. The latter phenomenon is what is generally viewed as resilience.

Particularly in recent years, there has been a growing acceptance of the need to take seriously the various methodological hazards that could create false impressions of resilience. The phenomenon is of little interest, and has no policy or practice implications, if the variation reflects no more than the fact that the adverse sequelae had not been covered by the measures used in a particular study, or that the supposed vulnerability factors did not truly mediate risk, or that the heterogeneity in outcome merely reflected variations in the severity of the stress experienced, or that the impression of resilience reflected only an artifact stemming from scaling considerations. In that connection, it has proved crucial to specify the environmental sequelae precisely. Thus, Jaffee et al. (in press) found that children suffered from fathers' involvement if the father was antisocial but benefited if he was not.

The reality of such conceptual and methodological problems should not, however, be construed as implying that resilience should be abandoned as a scientific construct; rather, these problems underscore the need for concerted attention to the specific processes or mechanisms

implicated in the transmission of risk, and in the exacerbation and miti-
gation of its effects (vulnerability and protection). However, it would be
unduly constraining to restrict resilience to the variation inherent in the
immediate response to the negative experience – the chemistry of the
moment, as it were. Clearly, there are important individual differences in
physiological and psychological reactivity, but the extent to which individuals succeed in overcoming adversity may derive as much from how they
approach (and conceptualize) the risk experience as from their intrinsic
reactivity. Similarly, resilience may derive from how people cope with the
emotional and practical challenges that follow the negative experience,
or from new experiences that either counteract the stress/adversity or
that counterbalance or compensate for the effects of the risk.

In this chapter, evidence on genetic factors is presented to highlight
the importance of considering the extensive array of possible mediating
and moderating mechanisms in resilience. Central to this chapter are two
notions: *gene–environment interaction* (G×E), which refers to genetically influenced differences in individuals' *sensitivity* to particular environmental
factors (Rutter & Silberg, 2002), and *gene–environment correlations* (rGE),
which refer to genetically influenced differences in individuals' liability
of *exposure* to particular environmental factors. The chapter begins with
a presentation of some relevant examples from biology, followed by a
consideration of G×E and rGE in relation to individuals' psychological
functioning. Discussions in the next section illustrate how particular risk
indices can have diverse roots and can operate through various mediating processes, using examples of passive, active, and evocative person–
environment correlations as well as evidence of sex and developmental
differences. The chapter concludes with an appraisal of critical directions
for future work, both for scientific inquiry and for interventions.

BIOLOGICAL PARALLELS

Before considering resilience in relation to psychopathology, it may be
helpful to turn to a broader body of biological evidence in order to check
whether there are good grounds for accepting the validity of this basic
concept. Four areas of research are pertinent. First, there are experimental studies in which there can be quantitative control of the dose of the
noxious agent administered. Studies of responses to infectious pathogens
constitute the most obvious example of this kind. They show immense
variation among individuals exposed to such pathogens in whether or
not they develop the clinical condition of the infectious disease (Petitto &
Evans 1999).

Second, there is the small, but growing, body of molecular genetic findings in which particular genetic variations have been found to be associated with marked differences in susceptibility to specific environmental risk factors. Examples are provided by the allelic variations that play a major moderating role in the response to head injury (Mayeux et al., 1995; Teasdale, Nicoll, Murray, & Fiddes, 1997), in the risk for coronary artery disease stemming from smoking (Talmud, Bujac, Hall, Miller, & Humphries, 2000), in the clinical severity of the response to the malaria parasite delivered by a mosquito bite (Knight et al., 1999), and in the vulnerability to other infectious agents (Hill, 1998). The extent to which the findings have been replicated varies across the examples, as does the understanding of how the genetic moderating effect operates. Nevertheless, already it is clear that there are true resilience effects and that molecular genetic advances are likely to shed important light on the basic biological processes underlying resilience (Rutter & Silberg, 2002).

Third, there are epidemiological findings. The best-known and best-documented example is the substantial protection against malaria afforded by sickle cell heterozygote status (Rotter & Diamond, 1987). The effect is sufficiently strong to carry an evolutionary advantage in malaria-endemic areas; conversely, the lack of advantage in other areas seems to have been followed by a decrease in the frequency of the sickle cell genes (Weatherall & Clegg, 2001).

The fourth area of relevant research is the field of pharmacogenetics (Evans & Relling, 1999; Wolf, Smith, & Smith, 2000). It has long been apparent that there is immense individual variation in people's beneficial response to therapeutic medication and in the likelihood that they will experience serious side effects. Evidence is beginning to accumulate that specific genes are involved in the regulation of these positive and negative features.

These several areas of research both set the agenda in the psychopathological arena and carry the promise that genetic factors are likely to play an important role in the phenomenon of psychological resilience.

G×E: PSYCHOLOGICAL RESILIENCE

The reality of genetically influenced individual differences in sensitivity to specific environmental features is evident in the range of studies of G×E in subhuman species (see Rutter & Silberg, 2002) and by the evidence from molecular genetic studies dealing with the effects of head injury in predisposing to cognitive impairment and to Alzheimer's disease (particularly as shown by cross-fostering experiments – see, e.g., Anisman,

Zaharia, Meaney, & Merali, 1998; Suomi 2000). Thus, individuals without the Apo-E-4 allele are much less likely to develop Alzheimer's disease following head injury (Mayeux et al., 1995), and older women without the same allele are more likely to be protected against cognitive decline by estrogen use (Yaffe, Haan, Byers, Tangen, & Kuller, 2000). A prospective study of patients suffering severe head injury has similarly shown that a very poor outcome is less likely in those without the Apo-E0-4 allele (Teasdale et al., 1997). As yet, there is only one comparable DNA example of genetic influences on resistance to psychosocial stressors. Caspi et al. (2002) found that children with a genotype associated with high levels of monoamine oxidase A (a neurotransmitter-metabolizing enzyme) were considerably less likely to develop antisocial behavior following maltreatment. Doubtless, other examples will emerge. Thus, animal studies have shown genes that influence emotional reactivity (Flint, 1997; Flint et al., 1995), a trait that is likely to be relevant to the role of neuroticism in vulnerability to anxiety and depression in humans (Kendler, 1996).

There are numerous methodological hazards that attend the use of twin and adoptee designs in quantitative genetic studies of G×E (see Rutter & Silberg, 2002), but there is evidence indicating the likely operation of G×E in relation to the risks of both emotional and behavioral disturbance. Thus, adoptee studies have shown that individuals without genetic risk, as indexed by antisocial disorders in the biological parents (who did not provide rearing), seem to be resistant to the environmental risks associated with either early institutional care (Crowe, 1974) or psychosocial adversities in the adoptive home in which the children were brought up (Cadoret, Cain, & Crowe, 1983; Cadoret, Yates, Troughton, Woodworth, & Stewart, 1995). Bohman's (1996) findings point to the same effect, although the number of individuals in the cell with both G risk and E risk was too small for the interaction to reach statistical significance. Substance abuse has shown somewhat similar G×E effects (Cadoret et al., 1996; Legrand, McGue, & Iacono, 1999). One study, too, has shown that nondisclosure of psychopathology in the biological parents seems to protect against the genetic risks associated with alcoholism and antisocial disorder in the biological parents (Riggins-Caspers et al., 1999).

Kendler et al. (1995), using a twin design, indirectly indexed genetic risk for major depressive disorder by attention to zygosity and disorder in the cotwin. Genetic risk was inferred to be highest in the case of monozygotic (MZ) twins with an affected cotwin, lowest in MZ twins without an affected cotwin, and intermediate for disygotic (DZ) twins with or without an affected cotwin. The risk of developing major depression following a major life event was found to be greatest in those with the highest genetic risk, suggesting that genetic factors operated in part through their influence on sensitivity to environmental stressors. Silberg, Rutter, Neale, and Eaves (2001) found a similar effect in adolescent girls, using the different twin design of examining differences in heritability according to the presence/absence of life events (confining attention to methodological reasons to those not showing rGE). There was little effect from the life events studied in the absence of genetic risk. Jaffee et al. (2002), using the same strategy as that employed by Kendler et al. (1995), showed an interaction between genetic vulnerability and child maltreatment in the genesis of antisocial behavior. Again, the inference is that genetic factors are involved in the moderation of environmentally mediated risks.

Heath and colleagues (1989, 1998) found that the heritability of both alcohol consumption and depression was lower in married women, implying that marriage provided a degree of protection against genetic risk. Similar effects have been reported with respect to a religious upbringing (Boomsma, de Geus, van Baal, & Koopmans, 1999; Koopmans, Slutske, van Baal, & Boomsma, 1999).

It has long been known that Japanese individuals who have the genotype that causes them to have an unpleasant flushing response to alcohol (because they are impaired in the metabolic conversion of acetaldehyde, the product of alcohol, to acetate) have a greatly reduced risk of alcoholism (Heath et al., 2001). This extremely negative response to alcohol does not have an equivalent in other ethnic groups, but variations in alcohol sensitivity (which are genetically influenced; Heath et al., 1999) are present in all populations and have been shown to be associated with variations in the risk for alcoholism. It is clear that they are likely to prove important in resilience to the risks of alcohol, but the evidence that their strength of effect seems to have varied over time, and differs between males and females, serves as a reminder of the complexities involved in nature–nurture interplay, with the role of genetic influences modified by sociocultural context (Heath et al., 2001).

The data are too sparse for firm conclusions to be drawn on the role of genetic factors in resistance to the psychopathological risks associated with psychosocial stressors, or on the role of psychosocial variables in resistance to genetic risk, but the points are consistent in indicating the likelihood of both types of mechanisms. Obviously, the study of G×E will be greatly facilitated once molecular genetic research succeeds in identifying individual genes associated with variations in psychopathological risk (see Plomin & Rutter, 1998), but the quantitative genetic findings suggest that important G×E effects will be found.

rGE: DIVERSITY IN MECHANISMS

The genetic mechanisms influencing variations in exposure to environmental risk factors, and engagement in the risk processes, involve rGE's of three main kinds: passive, active, and evocative (Plomin, DeFries, & Loehlin, 1977; Rutter et al 1997b; Rutter & Silberg, 2002). Passive correlations are usually conceptualized as purely genetic. That is, parents both pass on their genes to their offspring and provide the rearing environments that the children experience. On the whole, there is a tendency for parents who pass on genes carrying a susceptibility to psychopathology also to be more likely to provide suboptimal rearing environments (see Rutter et al., 1997a, 1997b). The process by which this occurs is reasonably straightforward; Parental mental disorders (especially those involving personality dysfunction) may make it more difficult for the parents to provide a cohesive, harmonious, well-functioning family environment (Rutter, 1989a). Almost all reports consider passive rGE in relation to the genetic factors (G) that provide the risk for the child's psychopathological phenotype (P) and the environment (E) in terms of the rearing environment that provides the risk for the same phenotype.

However, four points need to be added. First, the G that carries the risk for P may not be the same G that creates the susceptibility for E. For example, it could be that parental mental retardation or substance abuse (both of which are genetically influenced) may have predisposed to parenting breakdown, which, in turn, provided an E risk for, say, depression in the child, although the genes underlying the depression will not be the same genes as those responsible for mental retardation or substance abuse. That will not create rGE in relation to the child's phenotype, but it will involve a G effect on E that is relevant to that P. The point serves as a reminder that genes do not operate in just one way, and those that affect E may not be synonymous with those that provide a main effect on disorder (see Rutter & Silberg, 2002).

Second, the effect need not be only (or mainly) on the rearing environment. Thus, genetically influenced maternal alcoholism may damage the fetus through intrauterine alcohol exposure, damage that will create an increased psychopathological risk for the child. Mothers pass on genes and create rearing environments but, in addition, they provide the environment of the womb. In other words, the child's constitution may be influenced by genetically influenced parental characteristics that operate other than through the genes or the rearing environment. Recreational or therapeutic drugs (Altshuler et al., 1996; Weinberg, Harper,

& Brumberg, 2002), and stress experiences (Schneider & Moore, 2000) may also have effects of this kind.

Third, as animal studies show, there are some circumstances in which there can be intergenerational transmission of maternal adverse experiences, an effect that will serve to mimic genetic transmission (Denenberg & Rosenberg, 1967; Francis, Diorio, Liu, & Meaney, 1999). Thus, in rats, the amount of maternal licking, grooming, and nursing has been shown in cross-fostering studies to affect infant stress reactivity. This appears to be mediated by environmental effects on gene expression that are carried through to the next generation (Francis et al., 1999). As with the second issue, the point is that the unborn child's physical constitution can be affected by experiences in the womb. The difference is that the effects do not involve overt pathology such as is evident in the abnormalities of fetal development seen with the fetal alcohol syndrome. That constitution will be what the child carries forward in development, and it will interact with, and influence responses to, the postnatal environment.

Fourth, it tends to be assumed that passive rGE involves E risks that affect all children similarly. Obviously, that will not be the case. To begin with, the meaning of the same E will differ according to each child's age, sex, temperament, intelligence, and other genetically and environmentally influenced characteristics. In addition, of course, each child will receive a different mix of paternal and maternal genes that are relevant to risk and protective processes.

Active rGE concern G effects that are involved in the processes by which individuals shape and select their environments. It is obvious that environments are not randomly distributed. Academic, bookish children may tend to spend their time reading and going to libraries, and musically gifted children are likely to spend time at the piano or attending concerts. Similarly, a child with a predisposition to antisocial behavior may tend to seek out other antisocial youth with whom to affiliate. In each case, their genetically influenced attributes will affect their E. Two main points need to be made. First, genetic influences will be operative in shaping and selecting environments that will provide risk or protective features. The *experience* of the risk/protective E will have been genetically influenced, but the *mediation* will be environmental. The distinction is crucial because there is no necessary connection between the origin of a risk/protective experience and its mode of causal influence (Rutter, Silberg, & Simonoff, 1993). The presence of some antisocial tendencies may be strongly genetically influenced, but ultimate involvement in crime may be mediated by the environmental factor of participation in a delinquent peer group (Rutter et al., 1997a, Rutter, Giller, & Hagell, 1998).

The second point is a less obvious one: The presence of rGE may serve as a kind of multiplier for E effects. Dickens and Flynn (2001) discussed the point conceptually and mathematically in relation to the huge rise (about 20 points) in IQ that has occurred in industrialized countries over the past half century. They noted that this implied a difference in E of some three standard deviations, a clearly implausible difference. They suggested that the resolution of the paradox was likely to lie in the multiplier effect brought about by rGE. That is, initially small E effects are enhanced by the role of genetically influenced individual differences in leading people to shape and select among the environments to which they are exposed. Obviously, more data are required before there can be much confidence in this explanation, but what is clear is that rGE may be important, not only in terms of the origins of E effects but also as a multiplier of their influence.

It is not easy to identify, or isolate, specific E features that are both affected by rGE and are likely to play a role in resilience. What is clear, however, is that *all* aspects of the environment that might be relevant (coping styles, dyadic interaction, conflict, attachment, etc.) involve some genetic influence (Rutter & Silberg, 2002). It may be concluded that active rGE will play a role in both the origins of protective E operating in relation to resilience and in potentiating their effects.

However, the knowledge that there are genetic influences on environmental features that are likely to play a role in resilience is not very helpful on its own. It is necessary to go on to determine the particular traits through which genes have these effects (Rutter & Silberg, 2002). Evidence of the existence of rGE is important because it highlights the need to identify the causal mechanisms involved in the origins of risk and protective factors, and because it underlines the need to differentiate the genetic and environmental mediation of risk processes and of moderation or resistance to them. Thus, genetic influences on antisocial behavior may be mediated by risk factors such as hyperactivity, impulsivity, and sensation-seeking and by protective factors such as high intelligence, social qualities, and self-efficacy.

Evocative rGE differs only with respect to the fact that it concerns effects on the responses of other people, that is, social interactions, rather than the broader social or physical environment, as reflected in the peer group, social club, or school attended. The best example of such effects is provided by antisocial behavior in childhood, which has been shown to be associated with a greatly increased rate of broken friendships/love relationships, marriage to a behaviorally deviant partner, and lack of social support in adult life (Quinton, Pickles, Maughan, & Rutter, 1993; Robins, 1966; Rutter, Champion, Quinton, Maughan, & Pickles, 1995). In turn, the lack of marital support predisposes to the continuation of problems in adult life (Laub, Nagin, & Sampson, 1998; Quinton & Rutter, 1988; Sampson & Laub, 1993).

The genetic "message" that has received most publicity in recent years (see, e.g., Plomin, 1994; Plomin & Bergeman, 1991) has been that some supposedly environmental effects actually represent genetic, rather than environmental, risk or protective mediation. There is no doubt that that is the case. Resilience researchers need to be aware that unless they are using appropriate, genetically sensitive (or other quasi-experimental) designs, the supposedly protective effects of, say, effective coping may be artifactual because the true protection lies in the genetic factors that influence the coping style rather than in the emotional or practical strategies that constituted the supposedly effective, environmentally mediated response to the stress or adversity that gave rise to the psychopathological risk. The caution is necessary, and resilience researchers must make use of designs that can truly test environmental mediation. Such designs are available, and they extend well beyond twin and adoptee studies (see Rutter, Pickles, Murray, & Eaves, 2001); and the evidence from their use provides convincing support for environmentally mediated effects of risk factors (see Rutter, 2000b). In other words, the genetic influence on individual differences in environmental risk exposure is far from predominant; a substantial degree of environmental mediation is to be expected.

By the same token, it is important to recognize that genetic effects are also important in terms of their effects on personal characteristics that are involved in resilience. Thus, protective mechanisms are likely to involve low levels of personality features that carry psychopathological risk – such as neuroticism or sensation-seeking. Like all other behavioral features, each of these is influenced by genes to a significant extent (Loehlin, 1992; Plomin, DeFries, McClearn, & McGuffin, 2000). Less attention has been paid to positive features such as high self-esteem or good interpersonal relationships but, as would be expected, it seems that these, too, are genetically influenced to a modest extent (Kendler, Myers, & Neale, 2000). What has not been investigated so far, however, is the role of genes in the protective processes that involve such positive personality features.

In summary, it must be said that research that could differentiate genetic and environmental mediation in the operation of risk processes has scarcely begun; these issues constitute important research priorities for the years ahead. At the same time, existing findings in rGE clearly indicate substantial heterogeneity in the origins of particular risk and protective factors, as well as in their modes of causal mediation and moderation.

SEX DIFFERENCES

The possibility of sex differences in resilience raises the possibility of a rather different sort of genetic effect – namely, that through the genes determining whether an individual is male or female. Of course, the mere existence of a sex difference in response to stress or adversity is uninformative on whether or not the mechanism is genetically influenced (rather than socially mediated) or, if genetically influenced, which biological difference is relevant. Thus, it could be a consequence of prenatal or postnatal hormonal influences, or a difference in the threshold of genetic risk for the phenotype, or the operation of some X-linked protective gene.

Nevertheless, it has long been obvious that there are major sex differences in psychopathology. Several disorders manifest early in life that are associated with neurodevelopmental impairment and tend to be much more common in males. This is so, for example, with autism, attention deficit disorders with hyperactivity, developmental language disorders, and dyslexia. Interestingly, it also applies to life course persistent antisocial behavior, which is characterized by early onset and is usually accompanied by hyperactivity/inattention (Moffitt, Caspi, Rutter, & Silva, 2001). In this case, the evidence from the Dunedin longitudinal study showed that the risk and protective factors for males and females were closely comparable. There was no evidence that girls were less vulnerable; rather, they were less likely to have the key risk factor of inattention/hyperactivity, the reason for this sex difference being unknown.

By contrast, there are other forms of psychopathology, most obviously depressive conditions and eating disorders, that tend to arise during adolescence/early adult life and that are much more frequent in females after childhood. Surprisingly little is known about the reasons for any of these sex differences. There have been attempts to detect differences between males and females in their susceptibility to psychosocial stressors, with findings that are rather inconclusive (Zaslow, 1988, 1989). The possibility is certainly plausible in view of the known sex differences in vulnerability and physical stressors – males being more susceptible (Earls, 1987; Rutter, 1970). However, it has proved difficult to test sex differences in vulnerability satisfactorily because of problems in ensuring comparability of stressors and their meaning, and because of uncertainties over coverage of the range of relevant phenotypic outcomes.

Silberg et al. (1999), using the Virginia Twin Study of Adolescent Behavioral Development, found a significant genetic effect on the liability to life events; this was shared with the liability to depression and was associated with the increasing heritability of depression in girls that is evident during the adolescent period. There is some evidence that stressful life events may be more likely to lead to major depression in women than in men (Maciejewski, Prigerson, & Mazure, 2000); yet, the heritability of major depression seems to be greater in women than men (Kendler, Gardner, Neale, & Prescott, 2001). Together with the Silberg et al. (1999, 2001; Eaves, Silberg, & Erkanli, 2002) findings, there is the implication that a combination of rGE and G×E may bring about, during adolescence, both greater exposure to and greater sensitivity to life events in females than males. At present, the data are too sparse for this to be anything more than a suggestion, but the major rise of depression in females, but not males, during the teenage years points to the probability of something of this kind occurring. If it is confirmed, it would raise the further query of what it is in males that brings about this relative resilience.

DEVELOPMENTAL INFLUENCES

Up to this point, genetic influences have been considered in terms of the possible effects of segregating genes (i.e., those that vary among individuals), but it is necessary also to note the possible influence of biological development, as programmed by nonsegregating genes that have been present in all humans as a result of the process of evolution. There is surprisingly little systematic evidence of the importance of age differences in children's responses to stress and adversity (and, as with sex differences, insofar as they exist, there has to be the further question of whether age indexes biological maturity or variations in life experiences; Rutter, 1989b). However, such limited evidence as there is suggests that children in the age period between early infancy and the school-age years may be most vulnerable to the effects of stressful separation experiences (Rutter, 1979). Probably infants are less vulnerable because they have yet to develop selective attachments, whereas older children are resistant because they have the cognitive maturity to maintain relationships over the period of a separation. Conversely, the effects of institutional care on the development of selective social relationships are probably greatest on children under the age of 2 or 3 years because that is the age period during which these relationships are being established (Rutter, 1981). The evidence is fragmentary, but the point is that genetically influenced maturation features are likely to be important in shaping children's vulnerability or resistance to adverse psychosocial experiences.

FUTURE DIRECTIONS: ANALYTIC AND CONCEPTUAL CONSIDERATIONS IN STUDYING RESILIENCE

Several conceptual issues, each of which has analytic implications, require attention in considering the future investigation of resilience. First, some writers have deplored the apparently exclusive focus on negative influences and have urged that there should be more attention to the beneficial effects of good experiences – conceptualizing these as health-promotive or enhancing features rather than risk variables (Stouthamer-Loeber et al., 1993). Insofar as the relevant influences are dimensional, the issue is partly one of semantics. That is, it would be as reasonable to label a variable as reflecting degrees of family harmony as it would be to refer to degrees of family conflict. However, it would not seem sensible to talk about resilience in terms of a balance between risk and protective factors because they are the same thing – the terms referring to either the negative or positive end of the dimension. The analytic issues are twofold. First, there are likely to be some variables that exert their effect only at one end of the dimension – the test being whether the difference from the middle of the distribution applies only at one of the two extremes. Being born to a teenage mother might be an example of this kind; it is a well-established risk factor for antisocial behavior (Rutter et al., 1998) but, so far as is known, being born to a relatively elderly mother does not provide benefits compared with being born to a mother of intermediate age. The finding suggests that the risk probably does not derive from the biological age of the mother as such but, rather, from some other features that it happens to index.

The second possibility is that health enhancement involves curvilinear and not linear effects; that is, the enhancement stems from the middle of the distribution, with risks stemming from either extreme. Alcohol consumption possibly provides such an example in relation to coronary heart disease, with mortality and morbidity being greatest in heavy drinkers and total abstainers. The effects of parental control on children's disruptive behavior might conceivably provide a psychological parallel (because either excessive indulgence or undue restrictiveness may carry risks). The point of both of these analytic issues is that genetic influences may operate on a dimensional attribute, but the risk and protection may, nevertheless, derive not from the dimension as such but from the way it operates at some point on the continuum.

A rather different set of considerations arises from the detection of person–environment interactions (including G×E; see Rutter & Silberg, 2002). Four main points require emphasis. First, such interactions are not synonymous with the interaction term in statistical multivariate analyses (Rutter, 1983; Rutter & Pickles, 1991; Rutter & Silberg, 2002). Before deciding on the most appropriate statistical test, the concept to be tested needs to be specified accurately. Particular care is needed if the environmental risk factor does not show major variations in the population. Thus, a statistical interaction would not be apparent with phenylketonuria despite the fact that the genetic effect works entirely through susceptibility to phenylalanines in the diet, that is, because they are present in all ordinary diets. Statistical interaction requires variations in both variables. Second, a multiphase causal process will involve true interactions, but these will not be apparent in cross-sectional analyses (see Pickles, 1993). This is evident, for example, in some of the pathways involved in carcinogenesis. In the psychopathological arena, indirect causal chains are commonplace (Rutter, 1989c); consider, for example, the pathways to substance abuse (Rutter 2002a) or to delinquent acts (see Rutter et al., 1997b). Third, the statistical power to detect interactions is much weaker than that for main effects; accordingly, they are easily missed (McClelland & Judd, 1993; Wahlsten, 1990). However, the fourth point is that there is also the opposite danger of identifying interactions that are artifacts that derive from the way the variables have been scaled. With respect to G×E specifically, there is the additional concern that they may be artifacts of environment–environment or gene–gene interactions rather than true G×E (Rutter & Silberg, 2002). Some leverage on the these issues can be obtained through quantitative genetic modeling methods. However, the real way forward is provided by the use of molecular genetic methods to identify specific susceptibility and protection genes, by careful measurement of the relevant environmental risk factors, and by testing specific hypotheses about processes in general population epidemiological samples.

Another key issue in relation to resilience research concerns the immense variation in the likelihood that the risk variables impinge directly on a particular individual. Considered narrowly, this variation could be viewed as outside the resilience concept in that it does not concern differences in susceptibility to risk. However, that would serve to exclude one of the main processes by which people may avoid the ill effects of stress and adversity. Thus, in families characterized by conflict, discord, and disharmony, it is common for the negativity to focus much more on some children than on others; moreover, it is the focused negativity that causes the main psychopathological risk rather than the overall family atmosphere (Reiss et al., 1995). In such instances, an important research issue concerns the characteristics of children who are particularly likely to be scapegoated: What are the features of these children that provoke parental negativity (or set off vulnerability processes)? Similar individual variations apply to the likelihood that parental depression impinges on particular children (Rutter & Quinton, 1984; Rutter et al., 1997a). Again, the question is, what attributes might be implicated in this heightened risk of some siblings compared to others? The same considerations apply, perhaps even more strongly, to individual variations in exposure to the proximal risk mechanisms that derive from distal risk features (such as poverty or living in a high-risk neighborhood or attending a poorly functioning school). A child exposed to a distal risk such as poverty may manifest positive behavioral and psychological outcomes if he or she is buffered by consistent and firm parental monitoring, by supportive extended kin, or by an unusually close-knit neighborhood community.

FUTURE DIRECTIONS: IMPLICATIONS FOR INTERVENTIONS

From the standpoint of interventions, of most relevance are three inter-related conclusions that derive from this overview of G×E effects. First, it is clear that that some risks may be genetically determined but that they exert their effects through diverse environmental mediators. For those concerned with interventions, evidence of such mediated effects is critical in that it indicates the specific domains best targeted for change. Whether the associations reflect active or evocative G×E, there is often much potential to staunch the negative effects of global, genetically determined risks by targeting these environmental mediators – the proximal processes or "pipelines" through which they exerts their effects.

The second conclusion, analogously, is that some mediators or moderators may seem to be shaped by the environment, whereas in fact they are largely genetically influenced. As noted earlier, effective coping and sensation seeking are two child attributes often viewed as shaped by the environment, but they are also strongly influenced by genes. The third issue, finally, is an important caveat to the second; that is, that even attributes subject to strong genetic influences are not necessarily fixed or immutable to interventions. Even with diseases that are entirely due to a single gene (such as sickle cell disease; Weatherall, 1999), disease outcomes vary substantially according to the effects of other background genes. With multifactorial diseases, the effects of powerful susceptibility genes will be even more variable due to the impact of other genes, of developmental perturbations, and of environmental influences. Genetic effects are probabilistic, not deterministic, and the challenge is to identify the multiple factors that bring about that probabilistic variation. Such knowledge should lead to the better development of interventions that can foster outcomes closer to the well-functioning end of possibilities for children at genetic high risk.

CONCLUSIONS

Until relatively recently, much behavior genetic research was concerned with partitioning population variance into effects attributable to genes and those due to environmental influences, with the implicit assumptions that these effects summed to 100% and that no others could be involved. Both sets of assumptions are mistaken (Rutter, 2002b; Rutter & Silberg, 2002). Segregating genes (i.e., those that vary among individuals) and specific environments do not account for all variance. Biological maturation (genetically programmed by genes present in all people) may influence resilience; phenotypic outcomes are especially influenced by both rGE and G×E. In other words, both normal and abnormal psychological development will be influenced not only by G and E acting independently and additively, but also by a combination of G and E (interacting through both rGE and G×E). The implication for the study of resilience is that there needs to be a concern for the factors involved in individual variations to exposure to risk environments and in variations in susceptibility to them. This chapter has focused on the possible role of genetic factors in control of and sensitivity to the environment, but the issues apply equally to nongenetic influences. In both cases, the main questions do not concern how much is G and how much is E but, rather, how the interplay between the two occurs and through which proximal processes that interplay is mediated (Rutter & Silberg, 2002).

References

Altshuler, L. L., Cohen, L., Szuba, M. P., Burt, V. K., Gitlin, M., & Mintz, J. (1996). Pharmacologic management of psychiatric illness during pregnancy: Dilemmas and guidelines. *American Journal of Psychiatry, 153*, 592–606.

Anisman, H., Zaharia, M. D., Meaney, M. J., & Merali, Z. (1998). Do early-life events permanently alter behavioural and hormonal responses to stress? *International Journal of Developmental Neuroscience, 16,* 149–164.

Bohman, M. (1996). Predisposition to criminality: Swedish adoption studies in retrospect. In G. R. Bock & J. A. Goode (Eds.), *Genetics of criminal and antisocial behaviour. Ciba Foundation Symposium 194* (pp. 99–114). Chichester, U.K.: Wiley.

Boomsma, D. I., de Geus, E. J. C., van Baal, G. C. M., & Koopmans, J. R. (1999). A religious upbringing reduces the influence of genetic factors on disinhibition: Evidence for interaction between genotype and environment on personality. *Twin Research, 2,* 115–125.

Cadoret, R. J., Cain, C. A., & Crowe, R. R. (1983). Evidence for gene–environment interaction in the development of adolescent antisocial behavior. *Behavior Genetics, 13,* 301–310.

Cadoret, R. J., Winokur, G., Langbehn, D., Troughton, E., Yates, W. R., & Stewart, M. A. (1996). Depression spectrum disease, I: The role of gene–environment interaction. *American Journal of Psychiatry, 153,* 892–899.

Cadoret, R. J., Yates, W. R., Troughton, E., Woodworth, G., & Stewart, M. A. S. (1995). Genetic–environmental interaction in the genesis of aggressivity and conduct disorders. *Archives of General Psychiatry, 52,* 916–924.

Caspi, A., McClay, J., Moffitt, T. E., Mill, J., Martin, J., Craig, I. W., Taylor, A., & Poulton, R. (2002). Role of genotype in the cycle of violence in maltreated children. *Science, 297,* 851–854.

Crowe, R. R. (1974). An adoption study of antisocial personality. *Archives of General Psychiatry, 31,* 785–791.

Denenberg, V. H., & Rosenberg, K. M. (1967). Nongenetic transmission of information. *Nature, 216,* 549–550.

Dickens, W. T., & Flynn, J. R. (2001). Heritability estimates vs. large environmental effects: The IQ paradox resolved. *Psychological Review, 108,* 346–369.

Earls, F. (1987). Sex differences in psychiatric disorders: Origins and developmental influences. *Psychiatric Developments, 1,* 1–23.

Eaves, L., Silberg, J., & Erkanli, A. (2002). Interaction of genes and life events in the development of depression: A Markov Chain Monte Carlo approach. Manuscript submitted for publication.

Evans, W. E., & Relling, M. V. (1999). Pharmacogenomics: Translating functional genomics into rational therapeutics. *Science, 286,* 487–491.

Flint, J. (1997). Freeze! *Nature Genetics, 17,* 250–251.

Flint, J., Corley, R., DeFries, J. C., Fulker, D. W., Gray, J. A., Miller, S., & Collins, A. C. (1995). A simple genetic basis for a complex psychological trait in laboratory mice. *Science, 269,* 1432–1435.

Francis, D., Diorio, J., Liu, D., & Meaney, M. J. (1999). Nongenomic transmission across generations of maternal behavior and stress responses in the rat. *Science, 286,* 1155–1158.

Heath, A. C., Eaves, L. J., & Martin, N. G. (1998). Interaction of marital status and genetic risk for symptoms of depression. *Twin Research, 1,* 119–122.

Heath, A. C., Jardine, R., & Martin, N. G. (1989). Interactive effects of genotype and social environment on alcohol consumption in female twins. *Journal of Studies on Alcohol, 50,* 38–48.

Heath, A. C., Madden, P. A. F., Bucholz, K. K., Dinwiddie, S. H., Slutske, W. S., Bierut, L. J., Rohrbaugh, J. W., Statham, D. J., Dunne, M. P., & Martin, N. G. (1999). Genetic differences in alcohol sensitivity and the inheritance of alcoholism risk. *Psychological Medicine, 29,* 1069–1081.

Heath, A. C., Whitfield, J. B., Madden, P. A. F., Bucholz, K. K., Dinwiddie, S. H., Slutske, W. S., Bierut, L. J., Statham, D. B., & Martin, N. G. (2001). Towards a molecular epidemiology of alcohol dependence: Analysing the interplay of genetic and environmental risk factors. *British Journal of Psychiatry, 178* (Suppl 40), s33–s40.

Hill, A. V. S. (1998). Genetics and genomics of infectious disease susceptibility. *British Medical Bulletin, 55,* 401–413.

Jaffee, S. R., Moffitt, T. E., Caspi, A., & Taylor, A. (in press). Life with (and without) father: The benefits of living with two biological parents depends on the father's antisocial behavior. *Child Development.*

Jaffee, S. R., Caspi, A., Moffitt, T. E., Dodge, K. A., Rutter, M., Taylor, A., & Tully, L. A. (2002). *Nature × nurture: Genetic vulnerabilities interact with child maltreatment to promote behavior problems.* Manuscript submitted for publication.

Kendler, K. S. (1996). Major depression and generalised anxiety disorder. Same genes, (partly) different environments – revisited. *British Journal of Psychiatry, 168* (suppl 30), 68–75.

Kendler, K. S., Gardner, C. O., Neale, M. C., & Prescott, C. A. (2001). Genetic risk factors for major depression in men and women: Similar or different heritabilities and same or partly distinct genes? *Psychological Medicine, 31,* 605–616.

Kendler, K. S., Kessler, R. C., Walters, E. E., MacLean, C., Neale, M. C., Heath, A. C., & Eaves, L. J. (1995). Stressful life events, genetic liability, and onset of an episode of major depression in women. *American Journal of Psychiatry, 152,* 833–842.

Kendler, K. S., Myers, J. M., & Neale, M. C. (2000). A multidemensional twin study of mental health in women. *American Journal of Psychiatry, 157,* 506–513.

Knight, J. C., Udalova, I., Hill, A. V. S., Greenwood, B. M., Peshu, N., Marsh, K., & Kwiatkowksi, D. (1999). A polymorphism that affects OCT-1 binding to the TNF promoter region is associated with severe malaria. *Nature Genetics, 22,* 145–150.

Koopmans, J. R., Slutske, W. S., van Baal, G. C. M., & Boomsma, D. I. (1999). The influence of religion on alcohol use initiation: Evidence for genotype × environment interaction. *Behavior Genetics, 29,* 445–453.

Laub, J. H., Nagin, D. S., & Sampson, R. J. (1998). Trajectories of change in criminal offending: Good marriages and the desistance process. *American Sociological Review, 63,* 225–238.

Legrand, L. N., McGue, M., & Iacono, W. G. (1999). Searching for interactive effects in the etiology of early-onset substance use. *Behavior Genetics, 29,* 433–444.

Loehlin, J. C. (1992). *Genes and environment in personality development.* Newbury Park, CA: Sage.

Luthar, S. S., Cicchetti, D., & Becker, B. (2000). The construct of resilience: A critical evaluation and guidelines for future work. *Child Development, 71,* 543–562.

Maciejewski, P. K., Prigerson, H. G., & Mazure, C. M. (2000). Sex differences in event-related risk for major depression. *Psychological Medicine, 31,* 593–604.

Masten, A. S. (2001). Ordinary magic. *American Psychologist, 56,* 227–238.

Mayeux, R., Ottman, R., Maestre, G., Ngai, C., Tang, M.-X., Ginsberg, H., Chun, M., Tycko, B., & Shelanski, M. (1995). Synergistic effects of traumatic head injury and apolipoprotein-ε4 in patients with Alzheimer's disease. *Neurology, 45,* 555–557.

McClelland, G. H., & Judd, C. M. (1993). Statistical difficulties of detecting interactions and moderator effects. *Psychological Bulletin, 114,* 376–390.

Moffitt, T. E., Caspi, A., Rutter, M., & Silva, P. (2001). *Sex differences in antisocial behaviour: Conduct disorder, delinquency and violence in the Dunedin Longitudinal Study.* London and New York: Cambridge University Press.

Petitto, J. M., & Evans, D. L. (1999). Clinical neuroimmunology. In D. S. Charney, E. J. Nestler, & B. S. Bunney (Eds.), *Neurobiology of mental illness* (pp. 162–169). New York: Oxford University Press.

Pickles, A. (1993). Stages, precursors and causes in development. In D. F. Hay & A. Angold (Eds.), *Precursors and causes in development and psychopathology* (pp. 23–49). Chichester, U.K.: Wiley.

Plomin, R. (1994). *Genetics and experience: The interplay between nature and nurture.* Thousand Oaks, CA: Sage.

Plomin, R., & Bergeman, C. S. (1991). The nature of nurture: Genetic influence on "environmental" measures. *Behavioral and Brain Sciences, 14,* 373–427.

Plomin, R., DeFries, J. C., & Loehlin, J. C. (1977). Genotype–environment interaction and correlation in the analysis of human behavior. *Psychological Bulletin, 84,* 309–322.

Plomin, R., DeFries, J. C., McClearn, G. E., & McGuffin, P. (2000). *Behavioral genetics* (4th ed.). New York: Worth.

Plomin, R., & Rutter, M. (1998). Child development, molecular genetics and what to do with genes once they are found. *Child Development, 69,* 1223–1242.

Quinton, D., Pickles, A., Maughan, B., & Rutter, M. (1993). Partners, peers, and pathways: Assortative pairing and continuities in conduct disorder. *Development and Psychopathology, 5,* 763–783.

Quinton, D., & Rutter, M. (1988). *Parenting breakdown: The making and breaking of intergenerational links.* Aldershot, U.K.: Avebury.

Reiss, D., Hetherington, M., Plomin, R., Howe, G. W., Simmens, S. J., Henderson, S. H., O'Connor, T. J., Bussell, D. A., Anderson, E. R., & Law, T. (1995). Genetic questions for environmental studies: Differential parenting and psychopathology in adolescence. *Archives of General Psychiatry, 52,* 925–936.

Riggins-Caspers, K., Cadoret, R. J., Panak, W., Lempers, J. D., Troughton, E., & Stewart, M. A. (1999). Gene × environment interaction and the moderating effect of adoption agency disclosure on estimating genetic effects. *Personality and individual Differences, 27,* 357–380.

Robins, L. (1966). *Deviant children grown up: A sociological and psychiatric study of sociopathic personality.* Baltimore: Williams & Wilkins.

Rotter, J. I., & Diamond, J. M. (1987). What maintains the frequencies of human genetic diseases? *Nature, 329,* 289–290.

Rutter, M. (1970). Sex differences in children's responses to family stress. In E. J. Anthony & C. Koupernik (Eds.), *The child in his family* (pp. 165–196). New York: Wiley.

Rutter, M. (1979). Separation experiences: A new look at an old topic. *Journal of Pediatrics, 95,* 147–154.

Rutter, M. (1981). *Maternal deprivation reassessed* (2nd ed.). Harmondsworth, Middlesex, U.K.: Penguin Books.

Rutter, M. (1983). Statistical and personal interactions: Facets and perspectives. In D. M. Magnusson & V. Allen (Eds.), *Human development: An interactional perspective* (pp. 295–319). New York: Academic Press.

Rutter, M. (1989a). Psychiatric disorder in parents as a risk factor for children. In D. Shaffer, I. Philips, & N. B. Enzer (Eds.), *Prevention of mental disorders, alcohol and other drug use in children and adolescents. OSAP Prevention Monograph 2* (pp. 157–189). Rockville, MD: Office for Substance Abuse Prevention, U.S. Department of Health and Human Services.

Rutter, M. (1989b). Age as an ambiguous variable in developmental research: Some epidemiological considerations from developmental psychopathology. *International Journal of Behavioral Development, 12,* 1–34.

Rutter, M. (1989c). Pathways from childhood to adult life. *Journal of Child Psychology and Psychiatry, 30,* 23–51.

Rutter, M. (1999). Resilience concepts and findings: Implications for family therapy. *Journal of Family Therapy, 21,* 119–144.

Rutter, M. (2000a). Resilience reconsidered: Conceptual considerations, empirical findings, and policy implications. In J. P. Shonkoff & S. J. Meisels (Eds.), *Handbook of early childhood intervention* (2nd ed., pp. 651–682). New York: Cambridge University Press.

Rutter, M. (2000b). Psychosocial influences: Critiques, findings, and research needs. *Development and Psychopathology, 12,* 375–405.

Rutter, M. (2002a). Substance use and abuse: Causal pathways considerations. In M. Rutter & E. Taylor (Eds.), *Child and adolescent psychiatry* (4th ed., pp. 455–462). Oxford: Blackwell Scientific.

Rutter, M. (2002b). Nature, nurture and development: From evangelism through science towards policy and practice. *Child Development, 73,* 1–21.

Rutter, M., Champion, L., Quinton, D., Maughan, B., & Pickles, A. (1995). Understanding individual differences in environmental risk exposure. In P. Moen, G. H. Elder, Jr., & K. Lüscher (Eds.), *Examining lives in context: Perspectives on the ecology of human development* (pp. 61–93). Washington, DC: American Psychological Association.

Rutter, M., Dunn, J., Plomin, R., Simonoff, E., Pickles, A., Maughan, B., Ormel, J., Meyer, J., & Eaves, L. (1997a). Integrating nature and nurture: Implications of person–environment correlations and interactions for developmental psychology. *Development and Psychopathology, 9,* 335–364.

Rutter, M., Giller, H., & Hagell, A. (1998). *Antisocial behavior by young people.* New York: Cambridge University Press.

Rutter, M., Maughan, B., Meyer, J., Pickles, A., Silberg, J., Simonoff, E., & Taylor, E. (1997b). Heterogeneity of antisocial behavior: Causes, continuities, and consequences. In R. Dienstbier & D. W. Osgood (Eds.), *Nebraska symposium on motivation: Vol. 44. Motivation and delinquency* (pp. 45–118). Lincoln: University of Nebraska Press.

Rutter, M., & Pickles, A. (1991). Person–environment interactions: Concepts, mechanisms, and implications for data analysis. In T. D. Wachs & R. Plomin (Eds.), *Conceptualization and measurement of organism–environment interaction* (pp. 105–141). Washington, DC: American Psychological Association.

Rutter, M., Pickles, A., Murray, R., & Eaves, L. (2001). Testing hypotheses on specific environmental causal effects on behavior. *Psychological Bulletin, 127,* 291–324.

Rutter, M., & Quinton, D. (1984). Parental psychiatric disorder: Effects on children. *Psychological Medicine, 14,* 853–880.

Rutter, M., & Silberg, J. (2002). Gene–environment interplay in relation to emotional and behavioral disturbance. *Annual Review in Psychology, 53,* 463–490.

Rutter, M., Silberg, J., & Simonoff, E. (1993). Whither behavioral genetics? A developmental psychopathological perspective. In R. Plomin & G. E. McClearn (Eds.), *Nature, nurture, and psychology* (pp. 433–456). Washington, DC: APA Books.

Sampson, R. J., & Laub, J. H. (1993). *Crime in the making: Pathways and turning points through life.* Cambridge, MA: Harvard University Press.

Schneider, M. L., & Moore, C. F. (2000). Effect of prenatal stress on development: A nonhuman primate model. In C. Nelson (Ed.), *Minnesota symposium on child psychology* (pp. 201–243). Hillsdale, NJ: Erlbaum.

Silberg, J., Pickles, A., Rutter, M., Hewitt, J., Simonoff, E., Maes, H., Carbonneau, R., Murrelle, L., Foley, D., & Eaves, L. (1999). The influence of genetic factors and life stress on depression among adolescent girls. *Archives of General Psychiatry, 56,* 225–232.

Silberg, J., Rutter, M., Neale, M., & Eaves, L. (2001). Genetic moderation of environmental risk for depression and anxiety in adolescent girls. *British Journal of Psychiatry, 179,* 116–121.

Stouthamer-Loeber, M., Loeber, R., Farrington, D. P., Zhang, Q., van Kammen, W., & Maguin, E. (1993). The double edge of protective and risk factors for delinquency: Interrelations and development patterns. *Development and Psychopathology, 5,* 683–701.

Suomi, S. J. (2000). A biobehavioral perspective on developmental psychopathology: Excessive aggression and serotonergic dysfunction in monkeys. In A. J. Sameroff, M. Lewis, & S. Miller (Eds.), *Handbook of developmental psychopathology* (2nd ed., pp. 237–256). New York: Plenum.

Talmud, P. J., Bujac, S. R., Hall, S., Miller, G. J., & Humphries, S. E. (2000). Substitution of asparagine for aspartic acid at residue 9 (D9N) of lipoprotein lipase markedly augments risk of ischaemic heart disease in male smokers. *Atherosclerosis, 149,* 75–81.

Teasdale, G. M., Nicoll, J. A. R., Murray, G., & Fiddes, M. (1997). Association of apolipoprotein E polymorphism with outcome after head injury. *Lancet, 350,* 1069–1071.

Wahlsten, D. (1990). Insensitivity of the analysis of variance to heredity–environment interaction. *Behavioral and Brain Sciences, 13,* 109–161.

Weatherall, D. J. (1999). From genotype to phenotype: Genetics and medical practice in the new millennium. *Philosophical Transactions of the Royal Society of London – Series B: Biological Sciences, 354,* 1995–2010.

Weatherall, D. J., & Clegg, J. B. (2001). *The thalassaemia syndromes* (4th ed.). Oxford: Blackwell Scientific.

Weinberg, W. A., Harper, C., & Brumback, R. (2002). Substance use and abuse: Epidemiology, pharmacological considerations, identification, and suggestions towards management. In M. Rutter & E. Taylor (Eds.), *Child and adolescent psychiatry* (4th ed., pp. 437–454). Oxford: Blackwell Scientific.

Wolf, C. R., Smith, G., & Smith, R. L. (2000). Science, medicine, and the future: Pharmacogenetics. *British Medical Journal, 320,* 987–990.

Yaffe, K., Haan, M., Byers, A., Tangen, C., & Kuller, L. (2000). Estrogen use, APOE, and cognitive decline: Evidence of gene–environment interaction. *Neurology, 54,* 1949–1953.

Zaslow, M. J. (1988). Sex differences in children's responses to parental divorce: I. Research methodology and postdivorce family forms. *American Journal of Orthopsychiatry, 58,* 355–378.

Zaslow, M. J. (1989). Sex differences in children's responses to parental divorce: II. Samples, variables, ages and sources. *American Journal of Orthopsychiatry, 59,* 118–141.

21

Research on Resilience

An Integrative Review

Suniya S. Luthar and Laurel Bidwell Zelazo

The contributors to this volume have provided a wealth of information on children facing different life adversities, and in this concluding chapter we provide a distillation of two sets of themes. The first encompasses conceptual and methodological issues in studies of resilience – which, as defined in this book, is a process or phenomenon reflecting positive child adjustment despite conditions of risk. Since its inception a few decades ago, various commentaries have led to refinements in the research on resilience, yet several important issues have remained either unclear or controversial. The introductory chapter of this volume provides a succinct summary of this field at its initiation. In this chapter, we draw from the cutting-edge research presented throughout this book to clarify critical issues in studying resilience, with the ultimate goal of maximizing the contributions of future work on this construct. In turn, we consider (a) distinctions between the risk and resilience paradigms; (b) approaches to measuring adversity and competence; and (c) various concerns about protective and vulnerability factors, including the differences between them, issues about the specificity of effects, and the types of issues most usefully examined in future studies.

Contrasting with the focus on empirical research in the first half of this chapter, the second half is focused on applied issues. At the heart of

Preparation of the manuscript was supported in part by grants from the National Institutes of Health (RO1-DA10726 and RO1-DA11498), the William T. Grant Foundation, and the Spencer Foundation. The authors are grateful to Ann Masten, Dante Cicchetti, Sheree Toth, and Edward Zigler for their thoughtful critiques of an earlier version of this chapter. Comments from graduate students in our research laboratory are also acknowledged with thanks.

much resilience research is the desire to uncover salient protective and vulnerability processes that, if targeted in interventions, would substantially improve at-risk children's odds of doing well in life. Accordingly, we integrate findings on risk modifiers from all chapters in this book, discussing them in order of relative salience across different risk conditions and deriving associated directions for interventions. This is followed, in turn, by consideration of prevention efforts that are focused on mental health as well as behavioral resilience; directions for future applied research; and guidelines for future interventions designed within the resilience framework.

RESEARCH ON RESILIENCE: QUESTIONS AND CLARIFICATIONS

In integrating and clarifying the scientific approaches exemplified in this book, we begin at the broadest level, with consideration of the frameworks of risk versus resilience – the two approaches that have guided all chapters. The coexistence of these two paradigms within this volume begs the question of whether they are essentially similar heuristic perspectives or, if they are different, what are the potential advantages and limitations of each.

Risk Research versus Resilience Research

A perusal of the preceding chapters should make it clear that there are more similarities than differences between the risk and resilience paradigms: unsurprising, as the latter grew from the former (see Masten and Powell, Chapter 1[1]). At the most fundamental level, they share the same aims, with a focus on children facing substantial threats to well-being, and the goal of illuminating what shapes their adjustment. Working within the risk tradition, researchers have shown that good reading skills can reduce psychopathology (Zucker, Wong, Puttler, & Fitzgerald, Chapter 4), just as resilience researchers show that early achievement promotes later competence across multiple areas (Masten & Powell, Chapter 1).

Another area of similarity is the shared conceptual emphasis on the multidimensional nature of forces that affect children, as well as the transactional nature of child development. Major ecological theories, such as those of Bronfenbrenner (1977) or Sameroff and Chandler (1975), are commonly applied in studies conducted within the risk as well as the resilience perspectives (e.g., see Gorman-Smith & Tolan, Chapter 16; Masten & Powell, Chapter 1).

Coexisting with the recognition of multiple influences are shared constraints in studying them: Researchers in both traditions are forced to choose between breadth and depth of inquiry. The limits of social science research tools preclude the intensive study of all potentially important influences in any one investigation. Instead, our approach to knowledge accumulation is incremental, where studies involving relatively large numbers of discrete constructs, for example, complement those with fewer dimensions examined in depth. As illustrated by Sameroff, Gutman, and Peck (Chapter 15), the former can be critical in revealing the joint effects of ecological influences spanning both proximal and distal environments and ascertaining the unique contributions of each. Owens and Shaw (Chapter 11), on the other hand, demonstrate the value of the latter approach through in-depth consideration of different processes operating within the proximal environment of the family.

A methodological limitation common to both risk and resilience paradigms is lack of precision in measuring risk. Children with particular negative life circumstances are treated as homogeneous groups despite possible variations in the degree to which their lives are actually touched by the true risk processes (e.g., supportive grandparents may shield some children from maltreatment by alcoholic parents). Even as we acknowledge this limitation, however, it should be emphasized that it does not represent a fatal flaw for either risk or resilience research. Without question, there is value in continually refining our measurement approaches over time so that risks become more precisely quantified. In the interim, however, there is still much to be learned from studies in which the life adversity is treated as a global index connoting high statistical odds of maladjustment, and research is intensively focused on understanding the processes that substantially reduce those odds.

In terms of areas of divergence, at the broadest level, risk and resilience paradigms differ in the negative versus positive nature of focal constructs. In risk research, the outcomes examined usually have a negative valence (such as the presence of psychological disturbances), and influences of interest are also generally – though not always – negative in nature (such as parents' mental illness or low income; see Seifer, Chapter 2). Resilience research, by contrast, explicitly encompasses positive and negative dimensions of both outcomes and predictors. Studies are focused on functioning that is clearly adaptive, considering the risks experienced, and this can be defined in terms of the absence of disease as well as the presence of positive well-being or competence (see Luthar, Cicchetti, & Becker, 2000a; this issue is also further clarified later in this chapter in discussions of operational definitions). Predictors, similarly, include not only those that can lead to disease but also salutary influences that engender good health.

An advantage of this explicit focus on positives is that it can impel scientists to adopt fresh mind sets, leading them to consider strengths among groups usually thought of in terms of problems or failures. Notably, this attention to positives goes beyond focusing on the salutary end of double-edged constructs (Stouthamer-Loeber et al., 1993) such as intelligence – which can connote problems at one extreme and benefits at the other – to also consider variables that do not signify problems even at the lower extremes, such as altruism. Thus, urban poor teens might be appraised not only in terms of whether they avoid incarceration, but also in terms of their optimism or prosocial behaviors. Influences considered might include not just negative ones such as gang membership, but also positive constructs such as peer group loyalty or ego strength. As scientific mind sets on at-risk groups are thus expanded, there are related advantages for interventions. This more inclusive approach has the potential to engender more innovative intervention strategies, and disenfranchised groups tend to be more receptive when program goals reflect some acknowledgment of their strengths rather than simply seeking to circumvent abject failures (see Cicchetti, Toth, & Rogosch, 2000; Masten & Powell, Chapter 1).

Although the explicit focus on positive behaviors and processes may have some benefits, the resilience paradigm is by no means without pitfalls, and the greatest among these is the potential to foster perspectives that blame the victim (Luthar et al., 2000a). The very term *resilience* is construed by many to represent a personal trait that allows some at-risk youth to succeed in life, with the corollary, of course, that those who do poorly are personally responsible for their problems. Chapters in this volume amply illustrate the erroneousness of this inference: Resilient trajectories are enormously influenced by processes arising from the family and the wider environment.

To avert such damaging misimpressions, several precautions have been noted for future studies conducted in the resilience framework (Luthar & Cicchetti, 2000). Most important, all reports should include clear definitions of resilience, unequivocally stating that it refers to a process or phenomenon and *not* a trait. Additionally, it is best to avoid using the term *resiliency*, which carries the connotation of a personality characteristic even more so than does *resilience*. Finally, it is prudent to avoid using the term *resilient* as an adjective for individuals and apply it, instead, to profiles or trajectories, because phrases such as *resilient adaptation* carry no suggestion of who (the child or others) is responsible for manifest risk evasion.

In future research, scientists' decisions on whether to invoke the risk or resilience framework will depend partly on personal judgments about pros and cons such as those just noted but also, to some degree, on their ultimate research objectives. When the central goal is to maximize prediction of child outcomes, the risk paradigm may be the preferred one, as many risks considered together explain more variability in outcomes than do any considered individually (Masten & Powell, Chapter 1). For applied scientists focused on determining how best to maximize wellness (with attention to malleable strengths as well as problems), the resilience paradigm may often be the one of choice; but these researchers must be particularly careful in attending to various conceptual and methodological complexities in implementing their work.

The need for this extra vigilance in conducting resilience research stems from at least three factors. First, the very fact of the explicit focus on *modifiable modifiers* implies that findings from these studies can be used in delineating salient priorities in social policies and interventions. Second, the literature contains a growing number of investigations invoking the term resilience. Third, there are in fact many complexities surrounding major concepts in research on resilience, as a result of which misunderstandings or misinterpretations have occurred frequently. In the spirit of maximizing the clarity and scientific rigor of future investigations in this field, therefore, we address the more critical of these issues, illustrating them with examples gleaned from chapters in this book.

Defining Resilience: Approaches to Measuring Risk and Positive Adaptation

In designing empirical studies of resilience, the first task confronting all researchers is the operationalization of the term resilience itself. Investigators seeking to study this construct frequently ask how they might "measure resilience," and chapters in this volume converge in demonstrating that (a) resilience itself is never directly measured; (b) it is inferred based on direct measurement of the two component constructs, risk and positive adaptation.

Considering the two components in turn, a life condition might qualify as a *risk* indicator if it is significantly linked with children's subsequent maladjustment in important domains. For example, children from divorced and remarried families are two to three times more likely to show psychological and behavior problems than those in nondivorced families (Hetherington & Elmore, Chapter 8). Among children exposed to community violence, as many as 25% can meet diagnostic criteria for Posttraumatic Stress Disorder (Gorman-Smith & Tolan, Chapter 16). If the incidence of problems were no greater than those in normative populations, then the indicators in question could not be used to represent risk in studies of resilience.

Positive adaptation is that which is substantially better than what would be expected given exposure to the risk circumstance being studied. Constructs used to represent this dimension must be developmentally appropriate, as well as conceptually relevant to the risk examined in terms of both domains assessed and stringency of criteria used. Among at-risk toddlers, for example, competence might be assessed in terms of secure attachments to caregivers (Seifer, Chapter 2), whereas for school-age children, appropriate indicators might include success at school (Wyman, Chapter 12). When communities carry a high risk for antisocial problems, it would be particularly relevant to assess socially conforming behaviors (Seidman & Pedersen, Chapter 13), whereas among children of depressed parents, the absence of depressive diagnoses would be of special significance (Hammen, Chapter 3). With regard to stringency of criteria, decisions to define resilience in terms of excellence in functioning or absence of psychopathology must depend on the seriousness of the risks under consideration: For children facing serious traumas, it is entirely appropriate to define risk evasion simply in terms of the absence of psychiatric diagnoses rather than superiority in everyday adaptation (Masten & Powell, Chapter 1).

Competence must also be defined across multiple spheres, for overly narrow definitions can convey a misleading picture of success in the face of adversity (Gorman-Smith & Tolan, Chapter 16). When using variable-based strategies such as regressions, researchers can consider the multiple domains assessed within separate analyses (see Luthar, D'Avanzo, & Hites, Chapter 5) or, alternatively, integrate scores in composite indicators by adding standardized values (Bolger & Patterson, Chapter 7). When person-based analyses are used, cross-domain adjustment can be appraised by stipulating minimum cutoffs representing success in each of many domains and then identifying the children who meet the criteria across all of them (Owens & Shaw, Chapter 11). Whichever strategy is chosen, it is important that scientists explicitly note in their reports that success in the particular domains examined cannot be assumed to generalize to other important spheres; resilience is never an all-or-nothing phenomenon.

As various definitions of positive adaptation are considered in future research, it is important that we broaden our conceptions to go beyond facets of children's psychosocial adjustment. Particularly needed is more consideration of biological indicators. In the Foreword to this volume, Cicchetti has effectively explained the importance of biology, citing several empirical findings indicating that social and psychological experiences can engender changes in neuronal connections as well as gene expression, and that these, in turn, can be critical in maintaining behavioral anomalies provoked by life stressors. Also noted is the value of considering physiological indicators such as stress hormones in evaluating individuals' reactions to distressing experiences (see also Szalacha et al., Chapter 17).

In addition to using biological outcomes, it may be more appropriate, in some instances, to operationalize positive adaptation in terms of the family rather than the child. As Seifer (Chapter 2) has argued, infants and even toddlers are still too young to be judged reliably as manifesting resilience because their functioning is so integrally regulated by others. At these young ages, therefore, it may be more logical to operationalize positive adjustment in terms of the mother–child dyad or family unit.

Positive Adaptation: A Good Outcome or a Protective Factor?
Previous studies on resilience have reflected the interchangeable examination of some positive constructs (e.g., high self-esteem or ego strength) as outcomes in some instances but as predictors in others, engendering questions about what determines these choices (see Hammen, Chapter 3). As illustrated by chapters in this volume, research decisions in this regard must be based on a coherent conceptual rationale reflecting high relevance to the specific questions that are addressed. To illustrate, Bolger and Patterson (Chapter 7) considered good peer relationships as an outcome domain, as they sought to understand what helps maltreated school-age children achieve success in this critical age-salient task. By contrast, Seidman and Pedersen's (Chapter 13) goal was to explore ramifications of relationships for adolescents' personal psychopathology, and accordingly, they considered peer and family relations among the major predictors.

The preceding examples illustrate that the interchangeable examination of constructs as predictors and as outcomes should not be seen as reflecting confusion in the resilience literature; quite to the contrary, it is essential for advancing scientific knowledge. Human development involves reciprocal linkages over time across many overlapping sets of constructs, and there is value in understanding pathways (or predictors) that lead to each of the many critical nodes (or outcomes) within matrices of interrelated indices. Thus, it is as useful to identify major pathways to school readiness (Reynolds & Ou, Chapter 18) as it is to know that good early reading skills reduce the risk for later psychopathology (Zucker et al., Chapter 4). From the perspective of interventions, both findings are useful in suggesting how we might set into motion what Masten (2001) calls *cascading effects*, where changes in one subset of constructs have the potential to yield significant benefits in other overlapping spheres.

Protective and Vulnerability Factors

Although prior studies have engendered questions about defining risk and positive adaptation, there has been more controversy surrounding the two other pivotal constructs in resilience research: protective and vulnerability factors, which respectively mitigate or exacerbate effects of the adversity condition. In discussions that follow, we consider four of the more frequently debated issues: (a) whether protection and vulnerability are opposites on a single continuum or qualitatively distinct; (b) the degree to which processes in resilience are the same as those that predict positive adjustment in general; (c) the role of interaction effects in inferring protective processes; and (d) the appropriateness of different labels in describing particular patterns of findings. After discussing these four issues, we delineate specific themes that most warrant empirical attention in future studies of protective and vulnerability processes.

Protection and Vulnerability: The Same Continuum or Qualitatively Distinct?
As will be elucidated with examples in ensuing discussions, protective and vulnerability factors often do represent two extremes on a single continuum. On the other hand, some indices can only create disorder but not excellence, whereas others can do only the reverse. Still others can be involved in curvilinear effects, being most beneficial at medium levels rather than at either low or high extremes.

To elaborate on the first of these possibilities: Several constructs on continuous scales can engender maladjustment at one extreme as well as excellence at the other. Intelligence, for example, could hypothetically be spoken of in terms of protection or vulnerability because high levels can lead to scholastic excellence, just as a low IQ can result in academic failure. In deciding between these two terms within particular studies, it can be helpful to examine the distribution of scores on the outcome variable, as illustrated in the examples provided in Figure 21.1. In each graph, the vertical axis represents social competence outcomes (e.g., teacher ratings), with a sample mean of 0 and a standard deviation of 1. The left and right markers on the horizontal axes connote absence and presence of risk, respectively, and the solid and dotted lines represent high and low intelligence, respectively. Labels used for the different patterns indicate whether, in the presence of risk, (a) high IQ is *protective*, enabling unusually *high competence* or (b) low IQ confers *vulnerability*, implying *significant maladjustment*; (c) the terms protective and vulnerability could each be used (with neither involving exceptionally large deviations from the average). Stouthamer-Loeber and colleagues (1993) provide similar examples using data on psychopathology rather than competence as an outcome, elucidating protective factors that suppress serious nondeviance, and vulnerability factors that promote serious deviance (see also Luthar et al., 2000a).

In his overview commentary chapter in this volume, Rutter (Chapter 20) has explained ways in which risk modifiers can exert effects only at one but not the other extreme. Having a teenage mother, for example, is associated with various vulnerabilities, but being born to an older mother does not imply unusually positive adjustment. In parallel fashion, having musical or artistic talent can be beneficial in engendering many experiences of success over time, but being tone deaf does not imply that a child is more vulnerable than the average. Rutter has also noted the possibility of curvilinear effects where benefits are greatest at moderate levels of the risk modifier. To illustrate, a dearth of closeness with parents can be destructive, as can a surfeit of closeness or enmeshment (see Hammen, Chapter 3), and low self-esteem can cause maladjustment, just as excessively high levels can lead to conduct disturbances (Wyman, Chapter 12).

Protective Factors: Specificity versus Generality

Among the most hotly debated issues in resilience research (see Luthar Luthar, Cicchetti, & Becker, 2000b; Luthar et al., 2000a; Roosa, 2000) is whether predictors of resilience (or competence in the presence of risks) are synonymous with predictors of competence in general, and chapters in this book contain much evidence that is of relevance. The contextual specificity of developmental influences is most strongly underscored by Wyman (Chapter 12) via several examples from the Rochester Child

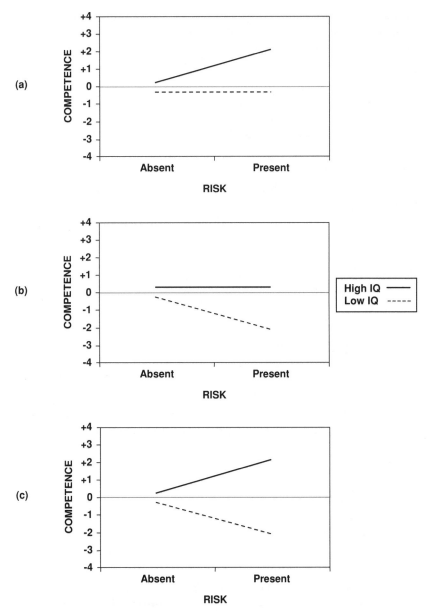

FIGURE 21.1 Labels for illustrative patterns of findings. In the presence of risk, (a) high IQ is protective and (b) low IQ confers vulnerability; (c) both terms, protective and vulnerability, can be appropriately used. *Note*: Competence here has a sample mean of 0 and a standard deviation of 1.

Resilience Project. Positive expectations for the future were salutary for many youth in this study but were linked to academic disengagement among those with conduct problems. For children to have low expectations of their parents was generally deleterious, but it was helpful for youngsters in highly dysfunctional families. Similarly, Szalacha and colleagues (Chapter 17) note that dismissing others' negative views of oneself may often reflect maladaptive denial, but it can be adaptive among groups commonly experiencing discrimination. Parental strictness, which is generally viewed as detrimental for children, has been found to benefit inner-city teens in more than one instance (Cauce, Stewart, Rodriguez, Cochran, & Ginzler, Chapter 14; Sameroff et al., Chapter 15).

Apart from such findings that discrete *constructs* are uniquely salient in specific risk conditions, conceptual considerations indicate, further, that the *pathways* collectively leading to child well-being must necessarily differ with and without major life adversities. Consider, for example, the role of parent–child relationships. Consistently supportive and responsive parenting is among the most robust predictors of children's well-being (Masten, 2001), and such parenting, is to a greater or lesser degree, threatened by all the risks considered in studies of resilience. At one extreme is child maltreatment, which by definition implies disturbed family relations. Diverse negative effects on parenting have been documented for risks ranging from chronic poverty (see Owens & Shaw, Chapter 11) to parental mental illness (Seifer, Chapter 2) and family disruptions such as divorce (Hetherington & Elmore, Chapter 8). Thus, for many at-risk children, everyday competence may *not* be predicated from consistently positive parent–child relationships (among the most potent predictors of well-being among youth in general); in many instances, something else must be invoked.

Of course, one might argue that many divorced or substance-abusing mothers are in fact satisfactory parents, and in such instances, it may well be their nurturance that underlies their children's success (again, implying similar predictors as for children in general). Without question, this is true. However, it is worthwhile to consider that even in these instances, it is often extraordinary for the *parents* to sustain positive functioning across critical domains. Maintaining optimal parenting is difficult enough under normal life circumstances; to do this in the face of stressors such as depression or homelessness is clearly noteworthy and must eventuate from additional positive influences (e.g., support from family or friends, high personal ego strength, or availability of mental health services).

As scientists continue to debate the specificity versus generality of health-promoting influences, therefore, it would be useful to consider that even on conceptual grounds, there cannot be congruence in the antecedents of success with and without major risks. Cicchetti and Rogosch's (1996) important notion of *equifinality*, which emphasizes that there can be heterogeneous pathways to particular disorders across different individuals, applies as much to competence as it does to psychopathology. If researchers consider the mosaic of paths leading up to children's well-being (rather than individual constructs or nodes on these), there will inevitably be variations, depending on the presence of major life adversities.

INTERACTION TERMS. Related to preceding discussions are recurring questions about whether statistical interaction effects are necessary to infer specificity of processes (e.g., Luthar et al., 2000b), and chapters in this volume indicate that these are important but by no means definitive. The presence of such effects can be critical in illuminating variations in socializing processes, establishing pronounced benefits in one group but not the other (Wyman, Chapter 12). On the other hand, the converse is not true. As Owens and Shaw (Chapter 11) indicate, the absence of interaction effects can simply be an artifact of the research design, deriving from close matching of the groups involved (often obligatory to rule out ethnic or social class differences as potential confounds in findings). It is more than likely that if comparisons were to involve minority children of single, substance-abusing, impoverished mothers with Caucasian sons of married, alcoholic fathers (see Luthar et al., Chapter 5, and Zucker et al., Chapter 4), some substantive differences would emerge in the salient predictors of competence in each.

Interaction effects are also usually small in magnitude and thus difficult to detect via variable-based analyses (Owens & Shaw, Chapter 11; Rutter, Chapter 20), and Seidman and Pedersen (Chapter 13) elucidate alternative strategies that may usefully be considered in future research. These authors conducted cluster analyses to determine whether benefits of adolescents' engagement in particular domains (such as athletics, religion, and employment) would depend on the number and type of other activities in which they were invested. Results showed in fact that the benefits of investment in any single domain depended on the diversity of other domains with which the youth was simultaneously involved. To examine such conditional links via variable-based regression analyses would necessitate several three-order interaction terms, which, again, are highly unstable and hard to find. In future studies, then, it would be useful for resilience researchers to employ person-based analyses not only to compare groups of manifestly resilient and nonresilient children on discrete attributes (e.g., via analyses of variance, see Bolger & Patterson, Chapter 7; Zucker et al., Chapter 4), but also to assess the implications of different combinations of risk, vulnerability, and protective influences in their lives (e.g., via cluster analyses).

LABELS AND TERMINOLOGY. These questions about interaction effects lead, in turn, to controversies about the types of associations that are appropriately described as reflecting protective processes, that is, those based only on interaction effects or those involving main effects as well. As originally used by pioneers in this field, Michael Rutter (1987) and Norman Garmezy (Garmezy, Masten, & Tellegen, 1984), the term *protective factors* referred to only the former, wherein benefits accrued in the presence of risk conditions but not in their absence. Subsequently, however, resilience researchers have tended to use this term to refer to all associations found among at-risk groups, regardless of whether there were benefits for others.

Recognizing these issues, Luthar and colleagues (2000a) suggested that the term protective be used in the broader, colloquial sense, referring to all links involving at-risk groups (with more elaborated terms for interaction effects, such as *protective-stabilizing*) – but Sameroff and colleagues' discussions (Chapter 15) suggest that even this can be problematic. Colloquially, the term protective implies some type of shielding from the effects of the risk, and this certainly may be true for many constructs so labeled, such as sensitive parenting or community cohesiveness. Many others, however, such as musical talent or emotional expressiveness, do not shield the child but rather independently yield benefits such as frequent success experiences. For such constructs, it may in fact be more appropriate to use terms such as *promotive*, as suggested by Sameroff et al. (Chapter 15), *compensatory*, as originally suggested by Garmezy and colleagues (1984), or other synonyms such as *salutary* or *beneficial*, none of which imply that the construct serves as a barrier that insulates the child from the risk.

Reaching consensus on such issues will undoubtedly be critical (as scientific classifications structure domains of inquiry; see Luthar et al., 2000a), but at the same time, it should not be viewed as an immutable road block precluding research that is of any value. Until we arrive at universally employed operational terminology, the resilience field can in fact be moved forward as long as scientists ensure precision and clarity in defining major terms. As exemplified by chapters in this volume, investigators must indicate what exactly they mean in using all pivotal terms in their own studies: resilience, risk, competence, vulnerability and protection (and whether the last two are inferred from main effects, interaction effects, or both). In addition, as Cauce and colleagues (Chapter 14) note, there must be greater precision in communicating findings, with specification of the contexts, conditions, and constructs underlying interpretations offered. Much as psychotherapy research progressively moved from questions of "Does therapy help?" to more differentiated ones such as "What type of therapy works for whom and under what circumstances?", resilience researchers would do well to present more differentiated conclusions, such as "Realistic control was linked with emotional resilience in the face of parental depression" or "Teacher support apparently facilitated academic resilience in high-crime communities."

Future Directions: Considerations in Studying Protective and Vulnerability Factors

In the past, resilience researchers have been criticized for examining largely unvarying lists of protective and vulnerability factors – with variables chosen simply because of correlations in prior studies rather than because of conceptual considerations. As Luthar et al. (2000a) have noted, it is critical that future studies be presented within cogent theoretical frameworks, with explicit conceptual consideration of the forces most *prominent in the specific risk condition and the developmental period* that is examined. Studies reported in this volume exemplify this practice. With a shared focus on low-income families, Owens and Shaw (Chapter 11) and Luthar and colleagues (Chapter 5) each examined aspects of mothers' well-being and parenting, based on the argument that these constitute major problems in the context of urban poverty. Other constructs were chosen based on prominence in the developmental stage studied, for example, quality of attachments in the former study involving young children and exposure to community violence in the latter investigation involving older youth.

Aside from ensuring conceptual salience of the indices chosen for study, resilience researchers would do well to broaden the types of protective and vulnerability factors examined in future studies. Prominent in this regard, again, are aspects of *biology and genetics*, as elucidated by Cicchetti (Foreword), by Curtis and Nelson (Chapter 19), and by Rutter (Chapter 20). Collectively, these authors provide several examples to show that not only do biological factors affect psychological processes, but in addition, psychological experiences can substantially modify the structure and functioning of the brain.[2]

Also warranting more attention are *risk modifiers operating during the adult years*. Although most resilience research has involved children, trajectories can be altered significantly later in life too, and there should be greater examination of protective and vulnerability processes unique to adulthood such as career changes, marriage, and having children (see Masten & Powell, Chapter 1; Rutter, Chapter 20).

Apart from exploring risk modifiers rarely considered so far, researchers must continue to examine the *precise mechanisms* underlying factors that are known to have beneficial or harmful effects. With evidence that teacher support is significantly related to children's competence, for example, it will be important to disentangle the various ingredients that might underlie those benefits, such as those based on the availability of a supportive confidante, a role model, or a mentor who encourages academic excellence. Such consideration of underlying processes will be particularly important for findings of paradoxical effects, wherein constructs usually positive in valence are deleterious or the reverse. To illustrate, closeness to parents is generally health-promoting, but emotional distance and firm boundaries from parents can sometimes be beneficial (see Hammen, Chapter 3; Seidman & Pedersen, Chapter 13; Wyman, Chapter 12). It is helpful for bereaved children to talk about their loss, but among bereaved adults, the suppression of negative emotion can be more adaptive (see Sandler, Wolchik, Davis, Haine, & Ayers, Chapter 9). Across all such instances, there is value in studies illuminating the precise conditions under which there is a reversal of effects that are commonly seen.

Apart from mechanisms underlying known protective and vulnerability factors, also needed is more attention to the *mediators of the major adversity conditions* (more often studied by risk than resilience researchers). To illustrate, maternal depression can affect children through various environmental processes including conflict between parents, stressful events in the family, children's modeling of ineffective coping styles, and negative parenting behaviors ranging from inattentiveness to enmeshment (Hammen, Chapter 3). As Rutter (Chapter 20) has underscored, knowledge of the relative salience of these mechanisms is invaluable for interventions in terms of identifying the specific conduits that should be targeted in most effectively inhibiting the transmission of risk.

In a related vein, also needed is more careful attention to disentangling *third variables that might be proxies for risk*, that is, constructs that may actually carry much of the adversity that is widely attributed to a co-occurring condition. To illustrate, parental psychopathology that predates marriage (and subsequent marital difficulties) may often be responsible for the child maladjustment that may otherwise be attributed to divorce (Hetherington & Elmore, Chapter 8). Depressive problems and life stressors co-occurring with maternal drug addiction may contribute as much or more to the child psychopathology that is typically attributed to mothers' substance abuse (Luthar et al., Chapter 5).

Finally, there is a need for greater consideration of *cross-cultural variations* in resilience processes. The literature in this field (as in developmental psychology more broadly) is markedly lacking in international perspectives, and it will be useful to illuminate the types of risk modifiers that tend to be highly robust across widely disparate cultural contexts and those more idiosyncratic to particular settings (e.g., Masten & Hubbard, 2002).

Summary: Conceptualizing and Designing Studies of Resilience

Chapters in this volume elucidate several complex issues involved in the relatively young field of resilience, clarifying various points of confusion and illustrating issues critical for future studies. To begin with the distinctions between the risk and resilience paradigms: The two are far more similar than different. Both are focused on understanding pathways in adjustment of at-risk children, and both have many of the same approaches to scientific inquiry as well as constraints in the methods used. Resilience research involves explicit attention to positive outcomes and influences (in addition to negative ones). This can enhance scientific attention to the strengths of groups usually perceived in terms of failures and, concomitantly, can enhance receptiveness to interventions. At the same time, however, the very use of the term resilience can inadvertently foster views involving blaming the victim. To avoid such misunderstandings, researchers must explicitly state in their reports that they are studying a process or phenomenon, and not a personal attribute of the child.

Studies in this volume show that the construct of resilience itself is never directly measured; it is inferred based on the presence of both risk and competence. Risk indices are constructs that have significant statistical links with child maladjustment, and competence indicators are those representing relatively good outcomes – the presence of health or the absence of disease, depending on the nature and severity of the risk under study. Competence should be assessed in terms of multiple theoretically important domains, and in future studies there is value in considering fresh approaches to operationalizing positive adaptations, including those based on biological indices and on the functioning of the family rather than the child.

Protective and vulnerability factors sometimes represent two extremes of the same continuum, and choosing between the two terms in presenting research findings can be facilitated by considering the actual distribution of scores. By their very nature, however, some indices can only create vulnerability and not unusual well-being (e.g., young age of mothers), whereas others can do only the reverse (e.g., high musical ability). Still others may have curvilinear effects, with maximal benefits at moderate levels rather than at either extreme (e.g., positive self-views).

Conceptually, there will always be some variations in the pathways that eventuate in children's psychological health in the presence versus the absence of major life adversities. At the very least, good parenting, among the most robust predictors of children's well-being, will necessitate additional resources in families that are contending with problems such as mental illness or chronic poverty, compared to those that are not. Empirically, statistical interaction effects are useful to establish specificity of processes. On the other hand, their absence does not necessarily establish universality of influences but instead can be an artifact of design and methods, due, for example, to the similarity of groups contrasted and the small effect sizes of interaction terms. In future studies, conditional effects of risk modifiers should be considered via person-based statistical analyses in addition to variable-based ones.

Many positive characteristics of children or families are usefully examined *both* as predictors *and* as outcomes in studies of resilience. Researchers must demonstrate the conceptual appropriateness of designating particular constructs as predictors versus outcomes in relation to the specific research questions that are being considered.

In selecting from among potential protective and vulnerability factors to be examined in future research, it is not helpful simply to seek to reestablish the salience of an often examined generic list of risk modifiers. To substantively advance knowledge, there is value in studies focusing on (a) forces of high conceptual salience in particular high-risk contexts; (b) little examined and likely important risk modifiers such as biological and genetic indices and those operating during adulthood; (c) constructs that explain the underlying mechanisms of known protective or vulnerability factors; (d) those implicated in the transmission of risk, including proxies for the focal adversity condition; and (e) processes salient across different cultures, such that there comes to be an enhanced international perspective in the literature on resilience.

INTERVENTIONS BASED ON RESILIENCE RESEARCH

Shifting the focus from basic research to applied science, in the second half of this chapter, we appraise evidence within this book to discern directions for interventions. Consonant with the broad goals of resilience research, the bulk of this section is focused on conclusions pertaining to protective and vulnerability influences that are salient across different risk conditions and the associated implications for conceptualizing interventions. It should be noted that our attempt here is not to catalog individual risk modifiers prominent in particular risk conditions (richly described in each chapter) but, rather, to distill the substantive overarching messages that derive across them considered collectively. Following these discussions of risk modifiers, we consider existing evidence on limits to resilience – in particular, the existence of emotional distress despite manifest competence – and discuss these findings in terms of current priorities in prevention, treatment, and health care. We then delineate issues profitably considered in future research that is of an applied nature, and conclude the chapter with a summary of guidelines for future resilience-based interventions.

Salient Risk Modifiers: Influences Involving the Family, the Community, and the Child

Reverberating throughout chapters in this book is a strong emphasis on the child's environment and, in particular, the *proximal environment of the family*. High levels of vulnerability are induced with disturbances in the parent–child relationship and in caregivers' personal adaptation.[3] Owens and Shaw (Chapter 11) report that impoverished infants with insecure attachment to their mothers were more than twice as likely to show later maladjustment as those with secure early attachments. Among maltreated children, positive adaptation is uncommon and, even when displayed, tends to be unstable over time (Bolger & Patterson, Chapter 7). Fergusson and Horwood (Chapter 6) report that youth exposed to multiple early family adversities showed almost twice as much serious psychopathology as did their low-risk counterparts. Children of mentally ill parents tend to manifest elevated problems through the life span and across multiple domains, including difficulties in school, problems with everyday social adjustment, and psychiatric disorders (Seifer, Chapter 2). Zucker and colleagues (Chapter 4) report that among young children with high parental psychopathology (one parent an antisocial alcoholic, two parents currently alcoholic, or both), the incidence of high adjustment problems was almost five times that of children in low-risk families, and Hammen (Chapter 3) indicates that among offspring of depressed mothers, as many as 8 out of 10 can show a psychiatric disorder by their adolescent years.

Whereas these authors elucidate the vulnerabilities induced by disturbances in families, other contributors, in parallel, highlight the substantive benefits that derive from *positive* family functioning. We summarize here excerpts from concluding statements. Based on their longitudinal studies of children in poverty, Yates, Egeland, and Sroufe (Chapter 10) strongly underscore the power of responsive, supportive early family environments: "It is within a framework of available care and positive self-regard that the child develops adaptive emotion regulation patterns, flexible problem-solving skills, and an expectation of success in the face of adversity." Data on two cohorts of school-age children in poverty led Wyman (Chapter 12) to conclude that "(a) functional family environments were strongly protective for children in buffering them from many chronic adversities, and (b) children's competence in adversity often reflected considerable resilience of parents and of family systems." Sandler and colleagues (Chapter 9) conclude that their programmatic studies "converge on identifying the critical role of parenting as a resilience resource for both bereaved children and children of divorce." Hetherington and Elmore (Chapter 8) state that "A close relationship with a supportive adult, most often an authoritative parent, plays a critical role in promoting the well-being of children in all families, but seems to be especially salient for children confronting the challenges of divorce and life in a single-parent family or stepfamily." Collectively, these statements indicate the strong protective effects of positive family forces across diverse at-risk groups and during various developmental phases.

Chapters in this volume also clearly establish that although there are generalities about what constitutes good parenting – for example, consistency in affection and limit-setting – specific dimensions are often required in addressing challenges that are unique to particular adversities. To illustrate, in inner-city neighborhoods, it is particularly beneficial when parents can restrict their children's exposure to antisocial peers or neighbors, for example by limiting the places they are allowed to go or by using adult chaperones (Cauce et al., Chapter 14). For children facing parental depression, it is important that they understand that they are not personally responsible for family problems (Hammen, Chapter 3), and for those experiencing parental divorce, consistency in everyday schedules (e.g., meal times) can be critical (Sandler et al., Chapter 9). Finally, minority youth can benefit substantially when parents provide socialization that fosters a strong ethnic identity and ethnic pride (Szalacha et al., Chapter 17).

Following the family, chapters in this volume elucidate the importance of influences in the *community*. This is most vividly evident in the context of urban poverty, where children are affected indirectly through their parents as well as more directly. As Cauce and colleagues (Chapter 14) note, the problems of inner-city children cannot be attributed simply to their families' pathologies, for prolonged exposure to poverty-ridden, violence-prone urban settings can debilitate the most competent parents. The dangers posed in such settings, along with the stresses of everyday family poverty, can sharply impair parents' well-being and efficacy, and also foster feelings of depression, frustration, and hopelessness (Gorman-Smith & Tolan, Chapter 16; Owens & Shaw, Chapter 11). In terms of direct vulnerability effects on children, diverse processes have been highlighted throughout this book including witnessing of and victimization by community violence, exposure to antisocial peers, experiences of racial discrimination, and attendance at poor-quality, underresourced schools (Cauce et al., Chapter 14; Gorman-Smith & Tolan, Chapter 16; Szalcha et al., Chapter 17).

By the same token, there is evidence of positive community forces that can compensate for the risks of urban poverty. Gorman-Smith and Tolan (Chapter 16) note that families can benefit substantially when there is high support and cohesion among neighbors, a sense of belonging to the community, and proactive supervision of youth by other adults. In terms of protective factors directly touching children, Reynolds and Ou (Chapter 18) underscore the benefits of integrative preschool interventions fostering school readiness. For older youth, involvement in structured afterschool activities can mitigate the risk for delinquency deriving from antisocial peers (Wyman, Chapter 12), as can engagement with peer groups that endorse prosocial behaviors (Seidman & Pedersen, Chapter 13).

Although families and communities can each exert powerful negative and positive influences on children, families assume some level of conceptual precedence because they are temporally prior and more proximal to the child. As Yates et al. argue (Chapter 10), early family relationships profoundly shape children's capacities to engage with psychosocial environments later in life and to utilize resources such as those inherent in good interpersonal relationships. Gorman-Smith and Tolan (Chapter 16) cite evidence dating back to World War II, where distress levels of children exposed to bombing raids depended largely on the degree to which their mothers remained calm. These authors also report more recent findings that the risks of violent inner-city neighborhoods affect children chiefly when they erode the stability of their homes; when families are able to provide a dependable structure and emotional support, children's problems tend to be lower. Similar inferences derive from empirical studies presented in this book. Among older children and adolescents in poverty, Luthar and colleagues (Chapter 5) found that effects of maternal stress remained significant even after considering various community and child attributes. Similarly, analyses reported by Sameroff et al. (Chapter 15) show that the three family variables considered (interactions, parents' mental health, parents' socioeconomic status) explained more unique variance than the five community variables combined in predicting both adolescents' mental health (.09 versus .04) and youth academic achievement (.07 versus .04).[4]

Following familial and community influences on resilience are *child attributes*. Studies have indicated the protective potential of various child characteristics such as high intelligence, internal locus of control, good coping skills, and easygoing temperament (e.g., Ferguson & Horwood, Chapter 6; Hammen, Chapter 3; Masten & Powell, Chapter 1; Zucker et al., Chapter 4). At the same time, several authors note that all things considered, children's own characteristics are likely to be less influential than aspects of the environment in promoting and sustaining resilience (e.g., Cauce et al., Chapter 14; Gorman-Smith & Tolan, Chapter 16). Reporting on their programmatic research, Sandler and colleagues (Chapter 9) state that they found powerful effects of families but that the evidence was "more limited or inconsistent concerning the effects of individual-level resilience resources." Based on several studies by their group, Sameroff and colleagues (Chapter 15) conclude that multirisk children with high personal resources can manifest more problems over time than economically advantaged children with *low* personal efficacy: "The negative effects of a disadvantaged environment seem to be more powerful contributors to child achievement at every age than the personality characteristics of the child."

Such evidence of the circumscribed power of positive children's attributes may sometimes reflect the susceptibility of these traits to environmental influences, and this is exemplified in findings on intelligence (among the most widely cited child protective factors). Yates and colleagues (Chapter 10) caution that in the absence of early environment data, researchers may often mistakenly infer that it is intelligence that is protective, whereas different conclusions may derive when such data are available. Using their own longitudinal data, these researchers established in fact that children's school competence was better predicted by the quality of their early environment than by their IQs. Corroborating these arguments is evidence from both natural experiments involving children and laboratory experiments with animals. In an article on children in Romanian orphanages, where caregiving conditions were described as poor to appalling, Rutter and colleagues (1998) reported that institutionalized infants had mean cognitive functioning scores in the mentally retarded range. However, longitudinal evaluations showed catchup effects with changed environments: Babies who were adopted by 2 years of age by families in the United Kingdom lost their profound early deficits and, by the age of 4, came to show near-average developmental status. Consonant with these findings are Curtis and Nelson's conclusions deriving from their rich exposition of laboratory studies (Chapter 19). Early enriched environments have been found to engender substantial gains in animals' neurochemical, physiological, and neuroanatomical functioning, with the last including increases in the weight of the brain and structural modifications of the cerebellar cortex. Viewed in tandem, these data provide powerful testimony to the deleterious effects of early deprivation on cognitive functioning, as well as the beneficial effects of salutary environmental conditions.

Chapters in this book contain other examples of instances where other child attributes commonly labeled as protective factors can be shaped substantially by the environment. For example, Sandler and colleagues (Chapter 9) showed that among children of divorce, child cognitions and dimensions of self-esteem both affect psychopathology, but these child attributes are themselves affected by parental warmth. Bolger and Patterson (Chapter 7) showed that early onset of maltreatment reduces the ability of children to maintain an internal locus of control. Other research has shown, similarly, that when teachers are perceived as cold and inconsistent, students tend to lose their convictions over time, that they produce their own academic successes and avoid failures (Skinner, Zimmer-Gembeck, & Connell, 1998).

Although admittedly alterable by external influences, child protective attributes must not by any means be considered inconsequential in themselves for a variety of reasons.[5] Most fundamentally, characteristics of children and their environments are inextricably linked in transactional developmental processes, so much so that it is sometimes difficult to label them categorically as one or the other (see Owen and Shaw's discussions on secure attachment status in Chapter 11). In addition, the relative influence of child and environment characteristics will inevitably shift over time: adolescents are far more able to shape what happens in their own lives than are preschoolers. Finally, if risk is "held constant," children's strengths can in fact be associated with competence outcomes. To illustrate, among a group of youth raised by parents with serious mental illness, those with high intelligence are likely to fare significantly better than those who are less intelligent (notwithstanding that neither group may fully realize what they are innately capable of achieving).

It should also be noted that the previously described malleability of child protective attributes does not necessarily extend to negative ones connoting high *vulnerability*. In fact, the latter can impose fixed limits to what can be accomplished, retaining ascendancy over environmental influences (at least until such time as we are able to alter genes). To illustrate, a child with severe mental retardation will not master all the skills necessary for self-sufficient living regardless of the best instruction offered, and children with high genetic loadings for antisocial personality disorder may struggle to maintain behavioral conformity throughout their lives (Rutter, Chapter 20). In sum, then, child vulnerability factors can impose ceiling effects on what children can accomplish on the disorder–normal continuum, even though positive attributes clearly do not impose parallel floor effects on the normal–excellent continuum (i.e., guaranteeing a certain minimum level of success irrespective of environmental toxins).

In concluding these discussions of the triad of risk modifiers, we must emphasize that our placement of child attributes last in the sequence does not, in any way, reflect perspectives that undermine what children themselves do to overcome adversities. Collectively, chapters in this volume reflect unambiguous respect for what children bring to their life successes; the overarching message is simply that they cannot make themselves enduringly resilient, remaining robust despite relentless onslaughts from the environment. As succinctly captured in the words of pioneer in this field, Emmy Werner, "When stressful life events outweigh the protective factors, even the most resilient child can develop problems" (Werner, 2000, p. 128). It is this sentiment, and not any views of children as being passive or ineffective, that underlies the organization of factors engendering resilience within this chapter.

Prioritizing Domains: Implications for Interventions

As with choices of predictors considered in basic research, resilience researchers have been criticized for producing lists of protective factors in which sundry variables are enumerated as correlates of resilience (see Gorman-Smith & Tolan, Chapter 16). Although possibly comprehensive, such lists are of limited practical use because all itemized indicators (ranging from parents' intelligence, to neighborhood cohesiveness, to children's social skills) can never be addressed in a given intervention. Without trivializing any of these forces (again, all of which have been shown to be beneficial in empirical research), what is needed is some type of prioritization of domains in terms of the overall likelihood of yielding robust benefits. Findings in this book yield useful guidelines in this regard.

A central message is that resilience-based interventions must address the *quality of parent–child relationships* and, more generally, the well-being of caregivers (see Healthy Families American, 2000). Although this message is implicit in prior discussions on family influences, several authors have made the connections explicit. Seifer (Chapter 2) notes the need for attention to specific dimensions of family functioning when parents have a mental illness: relationship qualities, emotion regulation of parents and children, and parents' attributions about themselves and their children. For children of depressed parents, Hammen (Chapter 3) recommends that preventive interventions preferentially focus on improvements in parent–child interaction patterns, as key elements of the risk transmission are likely to lie in the parent–child relationship. Based on their respective findings on families in poverty, Yates and colleagues (Chaper 10) argue strongly for programs promoting secure parent–child attachment relationships, whereas Luthar et al. (Chapter 5) underscore the need for attention to mothers' emotional well-being and their capacity to sustain effective parenting.

At a purely intuitive level, it makes sense to focus on family functioning in interventions, not just because this shapes the lens through which later relationships are viewed (Yates et al, Chapter 10), but also because of the relative endurance of benefits likely to be induced. For most children, parents represent not only the earliest but also the single most constant proximal socializing influences. Peer affiliations inevitably shift over time, as do teachers in schools and wider community influences. Thus, from the standpoint of promoting continuity of the protective factors that interventions bring into the lives of at-risk children, it is entirely logical to emphasize work with parents.

Exhortations for wellness promotion via the family are supported by intervention trials: Scientists have shown that children can benefit substantially from relationally based interventions with their mothers. Prominent in this regard is Olds's Prenatal/Early Infancy Project, a long-standing nurse home-visitation program in which poor, unmarried, pregnant women are provided support and developmentally based parenting guidance. Benefits have been found to include reduced child abuse and welfare dependency among mothers, and fewer behavioral difficulties and greater school completion among children by adolescence (see Olds et al., 1998). Similarly, Heinicke and colleagues (1999) demonstrated that when high-risk mothers are helped to cope effectively with stress and to develop supportive relationships, children's adjustment improves. In their work with depressed mothers and their children, Cicchetti, Toth, and Rogosch (1999) addressed their insecure attachment representations, and use of Toddler–Parent Psychotherapy (Lieberman, 1992) promoted secure attachments of children as well as benefits in cognitive development. Finally, relationally based psychotherapy with drug-abusing mothers has been linked with a decreased risk for child maltreatment, increased positive parenting behaviors, reduced drug use, and decreased maladjustment in children (Luthar & Suchman, 2000).

A recurrent theme across the parenting interventions cited here is an emphasis on promoting self-sufficiency, and this is done at various levels. Emotionally, there is attention to depression, life stressors, and coping difficulties, which, if left unalleviated, can continue to pose threats to effective parenting. Behaviorally, efforts to foster optimal parenting are not based simply on didactically teaching specific strategies, but rather on helping parents develop their own capacities to generate effective parenting solutions. Socially, mothers are helped to develop networks of informal supports that can be available to them once interventions are completed. Finally, many of the previously noted interventions provide opportunities to address issues pertaining to employment, housing, and child care as well.

Such parenting preventive interventions are best introduced as early as possible – prior to children's birth or in their infancy – but this does not imply that it is unnecessary to design programs for families with older children. It is unrealistic to expect that even with the best screening techniques, all at-risk new parents will be reached; some will inevitably slip through the cracks and may seek help as their children grow older. Furthermore, many problems can be specific to later developmental stages, and it will be difficult for new parents to engage fully in discussions of issues that will arise several years later (e.g., drug use or unprotected sex during the children's teen years). Finally, life crises such as divorce, death, or mental illness can afflict families at all stages, and there is value in developing interventions for different developmental stages, with consideration of children's varying levels of cognitive and emotional maturity (e.g. Forgatch & DeGarmo, 1999).

In weighing arguments for family-based interventions to promote resilience, some might question their potential effectiveness given the well-established role of heredity in the transmission of many psychological disorders. As several contributors to this volume have noted, parental psychopathology can engender problems in children not only via disturbed family processes (e.g., in particular parenting behaviors), but also because of genetic influences (Hammen, Chapter 3; Hetherington & Elmore, Chapter 8; Luthar et al., Chapter 5). Juxtaposed with these assertions, however, is Rutter's (Chapter 20) critically important conclusion that "genetic effects are probabilistic, not deterministic, and the challenge is to identify the multiple factors that bring about that probabilistic variation." For interventionists, therefore, knowledge of genetic mediation must not deter prevention efforts to move parents' functioning toward the upper reaches of the confidence limits that are conferred by genetics.

Having considered families, we turn next to *community-level interventions*, which also can play a substantial role in promoting resilient adaptation. In their studies of inner-city youth, Gorman-Smith and Tolan (Chapter 16) found that youngsters in dysfunctional families manifested serious delinquency when neighborhoods had low social organization, but when neighborhood organization was high, delinquency was not as pronounced. Based on these findings, the authors argue for additional prevention efforts that involve connecting youth to neighborhood supports. Particularly in situations where it is simply not feasible to change family environments, enhancing community supports can be invaluable in addressing children's emotional needs for belonging and support.

In developing future neighborhood interventions, two interrelated considerations are critical. The first is that they should involve constituent groups as far as possible, and the second is that (as with families) they should strive to promote benefits that can be sustained by recipients over time. This is well exemplified in Tolan and colleagues' intervention (see Gorman-Smith & Tolan, Chapter 16), which involves the organization of groups of families in poor urban neighborhoods. These groups are highly beneficial in forging social connections among caregivers in close proximity, and in promoting overall neighborhood cohesion and shared concern for the community. Gorman-Smith and Tolan also point to the promise of community efforts involving coalitions of local groups and agencies (such as police and faith-based organizations) to address risks associated with urban poverty (e.g., initiatives to inhibit the illegal gun trade).[6]

Moving from the neighborhood level to the more localized level of schools, Reynolds and Ou (Chapter 18) provide powerful testimony to the value of prevention that is crystallized around early childhood education (see also Zigler, Finn-Stevenson, & Stern, 1997). Children who participated in the Chicago Parent–Child Project as preschoolers showed significantly better adaptation than others on eight dimensions of social competence by age 15, with improvements in performance of 50% or more over comparison groups. Furthermore, results show that these benefits were mediated by the cognitive advantages linked with the early intervention, as well as the greater parent participation in school activities and improved quality of schools.

In Emory Cowen's groundbreaking Primary Mental Health Project (PMHP) (Cowen et al., 1996), the goals are to prevent mental health problems among elementary school children who show early signs of maladjustment. Following a systematic screening process, these students are referred to nonprofessional women called *child associates*, whose relationships with children, developed across approximately 20 sessions conducted at school, lie at the heart of the intervention. Child associates are selected based on personal qualities such as warmth and empathy, and they receive rigorous training and ongoing supervision by PMHP professional staff. Additionally, there is a regular exchange of information between them and both teachers and school mental health professionals (e.g., via clinical conferences) to determine the nature of interventions for individual children, to review the changes observed, and to chart further courses of action. Commenting on processes underlying its successes (in more than 1,500 schools over time), Cowen and colleagues (1996, p. 92) noted that "The existence of a warm, trusting associate–child relationship is the foundation on which significant attitudinal and behavioral change in children rests."

Considering that (a) supportive adults play a critical role in fostering resilience and (b) laws exist mandating education for all children, it is surprising that K-12 schools have not been considered more in promoting well-being.[7] Arguing for the use of relationships as resources for development, Pianta (1999) has described the benefits that can derive from close child–teacher relationships developed and then sustained for as long a period of time as feasible. In Felner and colleagues' School Transition Environment Program (STEP), similarly, the role of home room teachers was changed such that they accepted responsibility for counseling and administrative functions, and served as a consistent link between students, families, and the school (Felner et al., 1993; Felner, Ginter, & Primavera, 1982). It must be noted that programs such as these do not have to involve a large influx of new resources. Pianta (1999) has argued, for example, that in terms of sheer numbers, there are often enough adults in a given school building to provide some support to children who need it; to some degree, what is needed is creative reassigning of responsibilities and continuity in relationships forged.

In the spirit of optimally using existing relationship resources in schools, we note three additional issues that pertain to the diversity of personnel considered as supports or mentors: the use of student opinions in identifying mentors, the provision of training, and the provision of supervision. Traditionally, school-based adults designated for such informal supportive roles have been academic subject teachers, home room teachers, or counselors, but there are probably many others, such as sports coaches, music instructors, and/or administrative or support staff, who might do just as well or better. The value of soliciting students' opinions is evident in the fact that (like the rest of us) they are more likely to engage with, and disclose to, self-identified *preferred mentors* (Lindsey & Kalafat, 1998) rather than adults to whom they are compulsorily assigned. Finally, as Pianta (1999) has noted, several opportunities for in-service training and supervision already exist in schools. In addition, adult mentors could hold regular consultations not only with school psychologists (as in Cowen's PMHP), but also with advanced graduate students from local universities as part of supervised practice – a collaboration of potential value for all concerned (Denner, Cooper, Lopez, & Dunbar, 1999).

Such informal school-based support systems could be particularly helpful in maximizing the wellness of at-risk junior high and high school students. Paradoxically, with the onset of adolescence and the associated physical and emotional changes, youngsters tend to face schools that are increasingly impersonal, with diminishing supports infused into daily curricula (Doll & Lyon, 1998; Eccles et al., 1993). Furthermore, adolescents are often particularly reluctant to seek professional help for even the most serious adjustment problems (Forman & Kalafat, 1998). For many preteens and teenagers, therefore, ready access to informal school-based mentors could serve both secondary and tertiary prevention functions, helping to inhibit the escalation of minor problems and expediting referrals for those that are more serious. In the long term, resources devoted to such preventive efforts may well turn out to be a small fraction of what school districts have to expend on resolving well-entrenched problems, such as serious disciplinary problems among their older adolescent students.

Other community-based interventions warranting further exploration are those involving local groups such as afterschool clubs or religious communities. Based on their empirical findings, Seidman and Pedersen (Chapter 13) argue for the creation of multiple settings that can positively engage youth, such as athletic, religious, and academic organizations. Overviewing efforts that are currently in existence, Cauce and colleagues (Chapter 14) conclude that community youth organizations are often cited as *urban sanctuaries* for inner-city youth, although their benefits have yet to be rigorously evaluated (i.e., through randomized trials). Some preliminary evidence of the benefits of informal one-to-one community-based mentoring, via Big Brothers/Big Sisters, was cited by Werner (2000): The availability of a mentor for 1 year was found to reduce absenteeism in children by 52%, first-time drug use by 46%, and violent behavior by 33%. Clearly, there is a need for further consideration of such avenues to foster wellness among youth at risk.

At the broader *exosystemic level* – the macrocosm of the wider society – psychologists are admittedly constrained in their capacity to implement changes directly (Seidman & Pedersen, Chapter 13), but they can and should inform policies by disseminating their findings proactively, responsibly, and in easily understood terms (Luthar & Cicchetti, 2000).[8] Legislators, agency directors, and the public are all influenced by media reports (Zigler, 1998), so scientists must be clear about what is known about resilience and how it can come about. Particular care must be exercised in discussing attributes of the child versus the environment. As Cauce and colleagues (Chapter 14) have suggested, if scientists must choose between giving children "enough credit" for their own coping and running the risk that our conclusions will engender cutbacks in crucial benefits for vulnerable groups, it is probably most prudent to err on the side of caution and circumspection.

As suggested by preceding comments (and the previous section), *child attributes* follow aspects of the microcosmic and macrocosmic environments in weighing the most pressing priorities for future resilience-based interventions. Again, this by no means implies trivialization of children's strengths. Rather, it reflects the viewpoint that for applied scientists who seek to help at-risk youth, it is less productive to focus intensively on what children can do for themselves than it is to concentrate on what we as adults can do to bolster their innate capacities and efforts to overcome adversities.

Similarly, conclusions presented in this chapter are not intended to decry programs targeting discrete child protective factors (such as those promoting self-esteem or coping skills), but simply to underscore the limits of those that ignore ecological influences (Gorman-Smith & Tolan, Chapter 16). School psychologists, for example, have noted that the lives of many at-risk children routinely involve unpredictability and even chaos, such that they can become quite unsettled by multiple fragmented interventions reflecting little integration with salient aspects of their everyday ecologies (Doll & Lyon, 1998; Pianta & Walsh, 1998). A corollary to these assertions is that substantial benefits can derive from interventions that *do* carefully consider ecological forces. This is well exemplified by the programmatic efforts of Hawkins, Catalano, and their colleagues, such as their intervention to prevent high-risk behaviors among adolescents by increasing levels of school bonding and academic achievement (e.g., Hawkins, Catalano, Kosterman, Abbot, & Hill, 1999; Hawkins and Catalano, 1992).

Limits to Resilient Adaptation: Covert Distress Underlying Manifest Competence

For the most part, resilience research informs interventions by illuminating critical protective and vulnerability processes, but increasingly, studies have yielded evidence on another applied issue: the existence of overt behavioral competence along with covert psychological distress. There is a widespread tendency to assume that if youngsters are doing well in terms of their external behaviors – for example, they excel academically and are popular with peers – they have successfully eluded major adversities. This is not true, for many at-risk children with impressive behavioral profiles can experience considerable emotional distress, as has been demonstrated by several contributors to this volume. Hammen (Chapter 3), for example, reports that among children of depressed mothers, there is a distinct adaptation pattern involving adoption of the caretaker role: a kind of false maturity, which may initially appear to be healthy but is likely to have negative consequences over time. Similarly, Hetherington and Elmore (Chapter 8) indicate that in divorced, mother-headed families, a subgroup of daughters seem exceptionally well adjusted and socially responsible but, at the same time, experience elevated anxiety and depression as well as low self-esteem.

Empirical data presented in other chapters indicate, further, that the absence of externalizing disorders by no means implies the absence of serious internalizing problems. Fergusson and Horwood's (Chapter 6) results show that among adolescents exposed to more than six childhood adversities, 18% had one or more externalizing disorders, but more than twice this number (44%) had serious internalizing difficulties. Thus, for one-quarter of these at-risk youth at the very least, serious depression or anxiety must have existed in the absence of any flagrant behavioral disturbances. Similar conclusions derive from data presented by Luthar and colleagues (Chapter 5); among children of mentally ill mothers, between 17% and 26% of the sample had serious internalizing problems but no externalizing disorders.

Perhaps the most compelling evidence on this issue is that provided by Zucker and colleagues (Chapter 4). These authors report that among children of alcoholics, those who initially showed low externalizing problems generally continued to show low behavioral deviance several years later. This was not true for internalizing problems. By adolescence, children who were identified as resilient as preschoolers came to show levels of internalizing symptoms approximating those of the initially *most troubled* group. Thus, even when manifestly resilient children retain their outward behavioral advantages over time, they can develop as much depression or anxiety as those reflecting substantial maladjustment early in life.

We highlight these issues here to draw attention to a subset of intervention issues that often remain neglected in discussions of resilience – with potentially drastic consequences. In general, the behaviorally unruly child is more likely to receive the attention of teachers and parents than the well-behaved, responsible one, even when adults are well aware that the latter is quite depressed or anxious (Briggs-Gowan, Carter, Skuban, & Horwitz, 2001; Puura et al., 1998). This approach can be quite shortsighted, as high emotional distress, when left unattended, can lead to diverse negative outcomes ranging from academic failure, conduct problems, and substance abuse during childhood and adolescence to recurring psychiatric problems, problematic relationships, physical illnesses, and unemployment later in adulthood (Luthar & Cicchetti, 2000). In sheer economic costs, the ramifications of such accumulating problems can be enormous. To illustrate, it was estimated that in 1995, untreated and mistreated mental illness engendered a total cost of $113 billion to

American families, the government, and businesses (of the $113 billion, $105 billion was due to lost productivity alone; Rice & Miller, 1998).

A second reason for raising issues of emotional distress here is to point to the imbalance in domains that are emphasized in contemporary preventive interventions. Based on their findings with at-risk children, Zucker and colleagues (Chapter 4) argue that prevention must be conceptualized at two levels, one encompassing multilevel regimens for children who show early signs of vulnerability and the other for those who seem resilient early on but are likely to develop internalizing symptoms in adolescence (when such problems typically burgeon). There currently exists little or nothing of the latter type. Existing prevention programs are overwhelmingly focused on overt behavioral indices such as conduct problems, teenage pregnancy, or academic failure, with scant direct attention to the depression or anxiety that frequently underlie and engender these problem behaviors (Cowen, 1994, 1999; Knitzer, 2000). Such gaps in prevention clearly warrant reconsideration. Mental health can no longer be treated as the domain of clinical psychologists alone; it must be considered by applied developmental scientists too if they truly are to attend to the "whole child," as Edward Zigler (1970), leader in this field, has long exhorted.

In any future efforts to promote emotional resilience of children and families, several barriers to effective treatment will need explicit attention. Foremost is the inadequate insurance coverage for mental health problems, far lower than that for physical health problems (despite the fact that mental illness is the second leading cause of disability and premature mortality; Murray & Lopez, 1996). Another major problem to be addressed is the fragmented delivery of health care services (Seifer, Chapter 2). If the most needy families – that is, those who contend with emotional difficulties as well as other problems such as substance abuse, unemployment, housing problems, and poverty – are to access appropriate help, there must be accelerated integration of service delivery, providing diverse services under one roof and with shared fiscal and planning responsibilities across different agencies (Luthar & Cicchetti, 2000). Finally, it will be important to address public attitudes toward mental illness, including social stigmas and views of psychological disorders as not being critical or life-threatening. As Hammen (Chapter 3) has emphasized, there is an urgent need for policies that foster understanding of the serious problems that can result from untreated depression, as well as those that promote treatment-seeking, rather than denial or passive acceptance, for problems such as these.

Future Directions: Applied Research

In considering future research of an applied nature, of obvious value are studies harnessing scientific findings on salient risk modifiers in *designing preventive interventions* (Cicchetti et al., 2000; Cowen et al., 1996; Luthar & Suchman, 2000). To maximize contributions, such resilience-based interventions must be (a) grounded in collaborative consultation with stakeholders (to ensure appropriateness of goals and strategies), (b) clearly specified in manuals, and (c) subject to rigorous evaluations, for example, via randomized trials.

By the same token, there is a need for more intervention studies that inform basic science by *testing theories on mediators and moderators* in resilience (Lerner & Wertlieb, in press). Such work is exemplified in both chapters presented at the end of the two major parts of this book, addressing family- and poverty-related risks, respectively. Sandler and colleagues' work (Chapter 9) showed that experimentally induced maternal warmth did benefit children following parents' divorce, corroborating its salience as a protective influence. Using long-term follow-up data, Reynolds and Ou (Chapter 18) provide a detailed explication of confirmatory program evaluation, which involves testing an explicit theoretical model regarding how exactly (i.e., through which specific protective mechanisms) the intervention exerts its effects.

Also needed are more studies evaluating the long-term benefits of *interventions addressing the mental health of parents and the quality of their relationships with their children.* To date, most large-scale child interventions evaluated by stringent longitudinal research, like the Chicago Parent Child Study, have entailed a primary emphasis on school achievement, and accordingly, work with parents has revolved more around children's learning rather than aspects of mental health or family relationships (see Curtis & Nelson, Chapter 19; Reynolds & Ou, Chapter 18). What is needed now are studies explicitly testing postulates on the potential of strong early attachments to foster long-term resilience – as has been underscored by several contributors to this volume (e.g., Owens & Shaw, Chapter 11; Seifer, Chapter 2; and Yates et al., Chapter 10). The objective of these studies would be to ascertain whether interventions that foster good parent–child relationships early in life will, in fact, translate into healthy self-systems (adaptive patterns of emotion regulation, coping, and problem solving) that will enable children to effectively meet diverse challenges not only later in childhood, but also during adolescence and adulthood.

Finally, there is value in intervention studies involving therapeutic services for at-risk groups, which will inevitably be required for some youth, notwithstanding the potential of promising prevention programs (e.g., given varying individual susceptibilities; see Zucker et al., Chapter 4). In this regard, critical are Weisz's (2000) writings on ensuring the ecological validity of psychotherapies for children. Most child psychotherapy clinical trials are conducted in research laboratories, which inevitably allow for far more precision in implementing manual-driven approaches than is possible in community clinics. Thus, there is a need to further explore the degree to which treatments shown to be effective in laboratories can be transferred to community settings – with appropriate involvement of salient others in the environment – to help troubled at-risk children revert to more positive trajectories in their everyday lives.

Summary: Guidelines for Future Interventions

Foremost, contributors to this volume have emphasized the importance of the proximal environment of the family in resilience-based interventions for children. Optimally, these efforts should (a) address parents' mental health and optimize the parent–child relationship; (b) promote families' capacity to sustain benefits after the intervention is completed; (c) be instituted as early as possible and for as long a period as feasible; (d) consider developmental challenges of later childhood and adolescence as well as those of early childhood; and (e) explicitly attend to parenting issues unique to particular risks (e.g., protecting youth from antisocial influences in inner cities or explaining the causes of mental illness to children of depressed parents).

To maximize the benefits of community-based interventions, these should involve the recipient groups as far as possible and, again, should strive to bring about changes that can be self-sustaining even after the intervention is withdrawn (e.g., by forging neighborhood networks). For school-based interventions aiming to maximize resilience, there is value not only in preschool interventions involving parent participation, but also those for older students, involving supportive relationships with adults at school (preferably adults to whom students are naturally drawn and not just compulsorily assigned). Also warranting further exploration is the role of informal support provided by neighborhood afterschool organizations, by informal mentors, and by prosocial peer groups, especially for youth in later childhood. Although resilience researchers may not be able to directly effect changes in the macrocosmic context of the wider society, responsible communication of their findings can be not just useful, but critical, in informing social policies.

With regard to child attributes, there are certainly potential benefits to interventions targeting particular domains such as self-efficacy, coping skills, and control beliefs. However, if these interventions involve only the child and his or her ecological risks remain unaltered, the interventions are likely to have limited effectiveness. Whatever gains are accrued are likely to be lost over time.

In future preventive interventions, there must be attention not only to overt behavioral resilience but also to the covert aspects of emotional well-being. To dismiss problems such as depression and anxiety during childhood is ill advised not only from the standpoint of children's suffering, but also because they can engender various other problems such as delinquency, substance abuse, physical illnesses, disturbed relationships, and both academic and employment problems. If for no other reason than to promote a healthy, productive work force, therefore, it is vital that we pay more concerted attention not only to children's school achievement and work habits, but also to the more invisible forms of distress that can come to sharply impair their functioning across diverse domains of adjustment.

CONCLUDING THOUGHTS

In a day and age when societal risks are many and resources limited, many are invested in understanding what most effectively promotes resilient adaptation among children facing major life adversities. Clearly, resilience is a dynamic process involving shifting balances of protective and vulnerability forces in different risk contexts and at different developmental stages. At the same time, there are some fundamental components that extend across adversities and stages. The many decades of stellar empirical research encompassed in this book indicate that in large measure, *resilient adaptation rests on good relationships.* From the earliest pioneering studies of Norman Garmezy and Emmy Werner to more contemporaneous ones, investigators have consistently pointed to the critical importance of strong connections with at least one supportive adult: in many instances a primary caregiver, who is among the earliest, most proximal, and most enduring of socializing influences. Sound interpersonal relationships in the early years can engender the growth of effective coping skills and resources, which, in turn, can aid children in coping with sundry adversities subsequently in life.

Relationships outside the family can also be highly beneficial. For parents struggling with high-risk life circumstances, both informal and formal support systems (e.g., neighborhood networks or home-visit interventions) can be invaluable in helping them cope with their own stressors and in avoiding high personal distress (indispensable to sustain effective care of their children). Of equal value are support systems for the children, especially teachers at schools or informal mentors in communities. With enough contact and continuity over time, these relationships can compensate greatly for difficult family situations.

Although connections with others are highly significant, there are other factors that are indispensable: No child can live well, love well, or work well if his or her physical survival is in jeopardy. At a policy level, recognition of all of these issues is critical. If the next generation of youth is to manifest high resilience – to become psychological healthy adults and productive, responsible, contributing members of society – it is clear that they must receive emotional sustenance and support. At the same time, all such supports will come to naught as long as families must constantly struggle to meet the most basic needs of food, shelter, safety, and education, as do so many living in contemporary conditions of poverty. To maximize the potential of a new generation, concerted attention to all of these needs will be critical; let us invest wisely in the future of today's youth.

Notes

1. Consonant with its integrative intent, this chapter contains numerous references to the preceding chapters in this volume. In the interest of brevity, we refer simply to authors and chapter numbers for each of these citations (rather than to "Author, this volume," and the chapter number, as is the convention).
2. Biologically mediated protective mechanisms are also exemplified in recent research findings on social cooperation. Some resilience researchers have suggested that altruism can serve protective functions (e.g., Werner & Smith, 2001), and Rilling and colleagues (2002) showed that reciprocal altruism is associated with consistent activation in brain areas linked with reward processing (nucleus accumbens, caudate nucleus, ventromedial frontal/orbitofrontal cortex, and rostral anterior cingulate cortex). This positive reinforcement, in turn, can be instrumental in sustaining individuals' cooperative social behaviors over time (Rilling et al., 2002).
3. We use the terms *parent* and *parenting* to refer to the adult's primarily responsible for the child's care; obviously, the adult may be someone other than the biological parent
4. For youth problem behaviors, the reverse pattern was seen; however, if peer characteristics were excluded from the five community variables (because of some mutual redundancy; problem behaviors often occur with and thus

presuppose deviant peers), the percentage of variance explained was comparable, i.e., .04 versus .03.

5. Ann Masten's comments were particularly helpful in helping us think through this issue.

6. Exemplary among existing initiatives of this type is Fight Crime: Invest in Kids, a bipartisan anticrime coalition of police personnel, prosecutors, and victims of violence working together to prevent crime among urban risk youth (see http://www.fightcrime.org/top.php).

7. For examples of contemporary multifaceted school-based initiatives, see the 21st Century Community Learning Centers (2002) and the Beacon Schools initiative (Department for Education and Skills, 2002).

8. To illustrate, the Fight Crime: Invest in Kids organization has compiled extensive evidence that good early childhood programs and afterschool programs are significant in preventing crime among at-risk youth, and reports published by this group are widely disseminated to the lay public and policy makers (see Fight Crime: Invest in Kids, 2002). For additional examples of effective dissemination of research-based, policy-relevant evidence, see the Internet-based Child and Family Web Guide of Tufts University (http://www.cfw.tufts.edu) and the site of the Manpower Demonstration Research Corporation, a nonpartisan, nonprofit social policy research organization (http://www.mdrc.org).

References

Briggs-Gowan, M. J., Carter, A. S., Skuban, E. M., & Horwitz, S. M. (2001). Prevalence of social-emotional and behavioral problems in a community sample of 1- and 2-year-old children. *Journal of the American Academy of Child and Adolescent Psychiatry, 40*, 811–819.

Bronfenbrenner, U. (1977). Toward an experimental ecology of human development. *American Psychologist, 32*, 513–531.

Child and Family Web Guide of Tufts University. (http://www.cfw.tufts.edu)

Cicchetti, D., & Rogosch, F. A. (1996). Equifinality and multifinality in developmental psychopathology. *Development and Psychopathology, 8*, 597–600.

Cicchetti, D., Toth, S. L., & Rogosch, F. A. (1999). The efficacy of toddler–parent psychotherapy to increase attachment security in offspring of depressed mothers. *Attachment and Human Development, 1*, 34–66.

Cicchetti, D., Toth, S. L., & Rogosch, F. A. (2000). The development of psychological wellness in maltreated children. In D. Cicchetti, J. Rappaport, I. Sandler, & R. Weissberg (Eds.), *The promotion of wellness in children and adolescents* (pp. 395–426). Washington, DC: Child Welfare League of America Press.

Cowen, E. L. (1994). The enhancement of psychological wellness: Challenges and opportunities. *American Journal of Community Psychology, 22*, 149–179.

Cowen, E. L. (1999). In sickness and in health: Primary prevention's vows revisited. In D. Cicchetti & S. L. Toth (Eds.), *Rochester symposium on developmental psychopathology: Vol 9. Developmental approaches to prevention and intervention* (pp. 1–24). Rochester, NY: University of Rochester Press.

Cowen, E. L., Hightower, A. D., Pedro-Carroll, J. L., Work, W. C., Wyman, P. A., & Haffey, W. G. (1996). *School based prevention for children at risk: The Primary Mental Health Project.* Washington, DC: American Psychological Association.

Denner, J., Cooper, C. R., Lopez, E. M., & Dunbar, N. (1999). *Beyond "giving science away": How university–community partnerships inform youth programs, research, and policy.* Social Policy Report, Society for Research in Child Development, Vol. 13, No. 1.

Department for Education and Skills (2002). *Beacon Schools in the U.K.* Retrieved July 18, 2002, from http://www.standards.dfee.gov.uk/beacon.schools

Doll, B., & Lyon, M. A. (1998). Risk and resilience: Implications for the delivery of educational and mental health services in schools. *School Psychology Review, 27,* 348–363.

Eccles, J., Midgley, C., Wigfield, A., Buchanan, C. M., Reuman, D., Flanagan, C., & McIver, D. (1993). Development during adolescence: The impact of stage–environment fit on young adolescents' experiences in schools and in families. *American Psychologist, 48,* 90–101.

Felner, R. D., Brand, S., Adan, A. M., Mulhall, P. F., Flowers, N., Sartain, B., & DuBois, D. L. (1993). Restructuring the ecology of the school as an approach to prevention during school transitions: Longitudinal follow-ups and extensions of the School Transitional Environment Project (STEP). *Prevention in Human Services, 10,* 103–136.

Felner, R. D., Ginter, M., & Primavera, J. (1982). Primary prevention during school transitions: Social support and environmental structure. *American Journal of Community Psychology, 10,* 277–290.

Fight Crime: Invest in Kids (2002). *Fight Crime: Invest in Kids – Reports.* Retrieved July 28, 2002, from http://www.fightcrime.org/reports.php

Forgatch, M. S., & DeGarmo, D. S. (1999). Parenting through change: An effective prevention program for single mothers. *Journal of Consulting and Clinical Psychology, 67,* 711–724.

Forman, S. G., & Kalafat, J. (1998). *Substance abuse and suicide:* Promoting resilience against self-destructive behavior in youth. *School Psychology Review, 27,* 398–406.

Garmezy, N., Masten, A. S., & Tellegen, A. (1984). The study of stress and competence in children: A building block for developmental psychopathology. *Child Development, 55,* 97–111.

Hawkins, J. D., & Catalano, R. F. (1992). *Communities that care: Action for drug abuse prevention.* San Francisco: Jossey-Bass.

Hawkins, J. D., Catalano, R. F., Kosterman, R., Abbott, R., & Hill, K. G. (1999). Preventing adolescent health-risk behavior by strengthening protection during childhood. *Archives of Pediatrics and Adolescent Medicine, 153,* 226–234.

Healthy Families America (2002). *Why HFA is needed.* Retrieved July 23, 2002, from http://www.healthyfamiliesamerica.org/about_hfa/why_needed.html

Heinicke, C. M., Fineman, N. R., Ruth, G., Recchia, S. L., Guthrie, D., & Rodning, C. (1999). Relationship-based intervention with at-risk mothers: Outcome in the first year of life. *Infant Mental Health Journal, 20,* 349–374.

Knitzer, J. (2000). Early childhood mental health services: A policy and systems development perspective. In J. P. Shonkoff & S. J. Meisels (Eds.), *Handbook of early childhood intervention* (2nd ed., pp. 416–438). New York: Cambridge University Press.

Lieberman, A. F. (1992). Infant–parent psychotherapy with toddlers. *Development and Psychopathology, 4,* 559–574.

Lindsey, C. R., & Kalafat, J. (1998). Adolescents' views of preferred helper characteristics and barriers to seeking help from school-based adults. *Journal of Educational and Psychological Consultation, 9,* 171–193.

Luthar, S., & Cicchetti, D. (2000). The construct of resilience: Implications for interventions and social policies. *Development and Psychopathology, 12,* 857–885.

Luthar, S., Cicchetti, D., & Becker, B. (2000a). Research on resilience: Response to commentaries. *Child Development, 71,* 573–575.

Luthar, S., Cicchetti, D., & Becker, B. (2000b). The construct of resilience: A critical evaluation and guidelines for future work. *Child Development, 71,* 543–562.

Luthar, S. S., & Suchman, N. E. (2000). Relational psychotherapy mother's group: A developmentally informed intervention for at-risk mothers. *Development and Psychopathology, 12,* 235–253.

Manpower Demonstration Research Corporation, a nonpartisan, nonprofit social policy research organization (2002). Retrieved July 16, 2002, from http://www.mdrc.org

Masten, A. (2001). Ordinary magic: Resilience processes in development. *American Psychologist, 56,* 227–238.

Masten, A. S., & Hubbard, J. J. (2002). *Global threats to child development: A resilience framework for humanitarian intervention.* Unpublished manuscript.

Murray, C. J. L., & Lopez, A. D. (Eds.). (1996). *The global burden of disease: A comprehensive assessment of mortality and disability from diseases, injuries, and risk factors in 1990 and projected to 2020.* Boston: Harvard University Press.

Olds, D. L., Henderson, C., Kitzman, H., Eckenrode, J., Cole, R., & Tatelbaum, R. (1998). The promise of home visitation: Results of two randomized trials. *Journal of Community Psychology, 26,* 5–21.

Pianta, R. C. (1999). *Enhancing relationships between children and teachers.* Washington, DC: American Psychological Association.

Pianta, R. C., & Walsh, D. J. (1998). *High-risk children in schools: Constructing sustaining relationships.* New York: Routledge.

Puura, K., Almqvist, F., Tamminen, T., Piha, J., Kumpulainen, K., Rasanen, E., Moilanen, I., & Koivisto, A. (1998). Children with symptoms of depression – What do the adults see? *Journal of Child Psychology and Psychiatry, 39,* 577–585.

Rice, D. P. & Miller, L. S. (1998). Health economics and cast implications of anxiety and other mental disorders in the United States. *British Journal of Psychiatry, 173,* 4–9.

Rilling, J. K., Gutman, D. A., Zeh, T. R., Pagnoni, G., Berns, G. S., & Kitts, C. D. (2002). A neural basis for social cooperation. *Neuron, 35,* 395–405.

Roosa, M. (2000). Some thoughts about resilience versus positive development, main effects versus interactions, and the value of resilience. *Child Development, 71,* 567–569.

Rutter, M. (1987). Psychosocial resilience and protective mechanisms. *American Journal of Orthopsychiatry, 57,* 316–331.

Rutter, M., & The English and Romanian Adoptees (ERA) Study Team. (1998). Developmental catch-up, and deficit, following adoption after severe global early privation. *Journal of Child Psychology and Psychiatry, 39,* 465–476.

Sameroff, A. J., & Chandler, M. J. (1975). Reproductive risk and the continuum of caretaking casualty. In F. D. Horowitz, M. Hetherington, S. Scarr-Salapatek, & G. Siegel (Eds.), *Review of child development research* (pp.187–243). Chicago: University of Chicago Press.

Skinner, E. A., Zimmer-Gembeck, M. J., & Connell, J. P. (1998). Individual differences and the development of perceived control. *Monographs of the Society for Research in Child Development, 63,* v-220.

Stouthamer-Loeber, M., Loeber, R., Farrington, D. P., Zhang, Q., Van Kammen, W., & Maguin, E. (1993). The double edge of protective and risk factors for delinquency: Interrelations and developmental patterns. *Development and Psychopathology, 5,* 683–701.

21st Century Community Learning Centers. (2002). *Soaring beyond expectations.* Retrieved June 20, 2002, from http://www.ed.gov/21stcclc/index.html

Weisz, J. R. (2000). Agenda for child and adolescent psychotherapy research: On the need to put science into practice. *Archives of General Psychiatry, 57,* 837–838.

Werner, E. E. (2000). Protective factors and individual resilience. In R. Meisells & J. Shonkoff (Eds.), *Handbook of early intervention* (pp. 115–132). Cambridge: Cambridge University Press.

Werner, E. E., & Smith, R. S. (2001). *Journeys from childhood to midlife: Risk, resilience, and recovery.* Ithaca, NY: Cornell University Press.

Zigler, E. (1970). The environmental mystique: Training the intellect versus development of the child. *Childhood Education, 46,* 402–412.

Zigler, E. (1998). A place of value for applied and policy studies. *Child Development, 69,* 532–542.

Zigler, E. F., Finn-Stevenson, M., & Stern, B. M. (1997). Supporting children and families in the schools: The School of the 21st Century. *American Journal of Orthopsychiatry, 67,* 374–384.

Index

Abecedarian Project, and early childhood education, 455, 471, 472, 473, 474, 480, 482

Abelson, W., 444

academic achievement: and childhood maltreatment, 163–4; and childhood poverty, 109, 246, 268; and development of children of alcoholics, 91; and early childhood intervention, 442; and exposure to violence, 396; IQ tests as predictor of, 16; mental health and intelligence in high- and low-risk children, 384–5. *See also* schools

acetylcholine (Ach), and animal studies of brain development, 466, 467

Ackerman, B. P., 368

acquired immune deficiency syndrome (AIDS), 306

adaptation: and children of alcoholics, 78–84; children of depressed parents and limits of, 63–4; debate on criteria for adjustment and, 7; evaluation of in specific context, 307–14; interventions and limits to, 539–41; measurement of, 514–17; and organizational model of development, 247; perspectives on

context-specific, 294; and protective factors, 12–16; violence exposure and resilient, 402–403

additive model, of resilience, 13–14

adjustment: assessment of in maltreated children, 162–3; and childhood poverty, 269–75; and children of depressed parents, 69–70; of children in divorced and remarried families, 183–206; debate on criteria for adaptation and, 7; measures of parental, 137; prevalence of parental difficulties in, 140. *See also* social adjustment

adolescence and adolescents: and adjustment to divorced and remarried families, 185, 186, 190, 202–3; definition of, 344; and depression in parents, 52–3; and development of children of alcoholics, 85–91; and developmental perspective on competence, 5; holistic perspective and study of competence in low-income urban, 323–38; poverty and personal attitudes toward deviance, 109; and school-based interventions, 537–8; and violence exposure, 399; vulnerability and

551